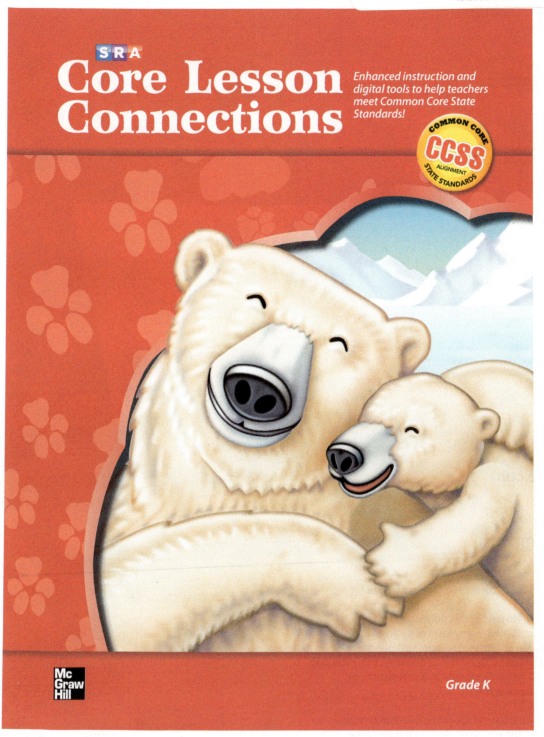

Nancy E. Marchand-Martella, Ph.D.
Ronald C. Martella, Ph.D.
Angela M. Przychodzin, M.Ed.
Susan Hornor, M.Ed.
Lisa Warner, M.Ed.

Bothell, WA • Chicago, IL • Columbus, OH • New York, NY

MHEonline.com

Copyright © 2013 The McGraw-Hill Companies, Inc.

All rights reserved. No part of this publication may be reproduced or distributed in any form or by any means, or stored in a database or retrieval system, without the prior written consent of The McGraw-Hill Companies, Inc., including, but not limited to, network storage or transmission, or broadcast for distance learning.

Permission is granted to reproduce the material contained on pages A3–A130 on the condition that such material be reproduced only for classroom use; be provided to students, teachers, or families without charge; and be used solely in conjunction with *SRA Reading Mastery Signature Edition*.

Send all inquiries to:
McGraw-Hill Education
8787 Orion Place
Columbus, OH 43240

ISBN: 978-0-02-128261-6
MHID: 0-02-128261-7

Printed in the United States of America.

6 7 LKV 20 19

Table of Contents

GRADE K

Overview of SRA *Core Lesson Connections*............................**cc1**

Summary of Skills **cc6**

Scope and Sequence of SRA *Core Lesson Connections* **cc8**

Lesson 1 1	Lesson 44.......................173
Lesson 2........................ 5	**Lesson 45** 176
Lesson 3 8	Lesson 46.......................180
Lesson 4........................11	**Lesson 47** 184
Lesson 5 14	Lesson 48.......................188
Lesson 6........................18	**Lesson 49** 191
Lesson 7 21	Lesson 50.......................195
Lesson 8........................24	**Lesson 51** 199
Lesson 9 28	Lesson 52.......................203
Lesson 10.......................32	**Lesson 53** 207
Lesson 11 37	Lesson 54.......................210
Lesson 12.......................41	**Lesson 55** 214
Lesson 13 45	Lesson 56.......................218
Lesson 14.......................49	**Lesson 57** 222
Lesson 15 53	Lesson 58.......................226
Lesson 16.......................57	**Lesson 59** 230
Lesson 17 61	Lesson 60.......................234
Lesson 18.......................65	**Lesson 61** 237
Lesson 19 69	Lesson 62.......................241
Lesson 20.......................73	**Lesson 63** 245
Lesson 21 77	Lesson 64.......................248
Lesson 22.......................81	**Lesson 65** 252
Lesson 23 85	Lesson 66.......................255
Lesson 24.......................89	**Lesson 67** 260
Lesson 25 93	Lesson 68.......................264
Lesson 26.......................97	**Lesson 69** 268
Lesson 27 101	Lesson 70.......................271
Lesson 28.......................105	**Lesson 71** 275
Lesson 29 109	Lesson 72.......................280
Lesson 30.......................113	**Lesson 73** 284
Lesson 31 117	Lesson 74.......................288
Lesson 32....................... 122	**Lesson 75** 292
Lesson 33 126	Lesson 76.......................296
Lesson 34.......................130	**Lesson 77** 301
Lesson 35 134	Lesson 78.......................305
Lesson 36.......................138	**Lesson 79** 309
Lesson 37 143	Lesson 80.......................313
Lesson 38.......................147	**Lesson 81** 317
Lesson 39 152	Lesson 82.......................322
Lesson 40.......................156	**Lesson 83** 326
Lesson 41 161	Lesson 84.......................330
Lesson 42.......................166	**Lesson 85** 334
Lesson 43 169	Lesson 86.......................338

Table of Contents (cont.)   GRADE K

Lesson 87	343	Lesson 124	503
Lesson 88	348	**Lesson 125**	507
Lesson 89	353	Lesson 126	510
Lesson 90	357	**Lesson 127**	515
Lesson 91	361	Lesson 128	519
Lesson 92	366	**Lesson 129**	523
Lesson 93	370	Lesson 130	527
Lesson 94	374	**Lesson 131**	531
Lesson 95	378	Lesson 132	535
Lesson 96	382	**Lesson 133**	539
Lesson 97	387	Lesson 134	542
Lesson 98	392	**Lesson 135**	546
Lesson 99	396	Lesson 136	549
Lesson 100	401	**Lesson 137**	553
Lesson 101	405	Lesson 138	557
Lesson 102	410	**Lesson 139**	561
Lesson 103	414	Lesson 140	564
Lesson 104	418	**Lesson 141**	568
Lesson 105	422	Lesson 142	572
Lesson 106	426	**Lesson 143**	577
Lesson 107	431	Lesson 144	581
Lesson 108	435	**Lesson 145**	586
Lesson 109	440	Lesson 146	590
Lesson 110	444	**Lesson 147**	594
Lesson 111	449	Lesson 148	597
Lesson 112	454	**Lesson 149**	600
Lesson 113	459	Lesson 150	603
Lesson 114	463	**Lesson 151**	607
Lesson 115	468	Lesson 152	611
Lesson 116	471	**Lesson 153**	614
Lesson 117	476	Lesson 154	617
Lesson 118	480	**Lesson 155**	620
Lesson 119	484	Lesson 156	623
Lesson 120	488	**Lesson 157**	627
Lesson 121	491	Lesson 158	631
Lesson 122	495	**Lesson 159**	635
Lesson 123	499	Lesson 160	638

Appendix A Blackline Masters, Phonemic Awareness Blackline Masters, Picture-Sound Cards

Appendix B: Differentiated Instruction

Appendix C: Levels of Support

Appendix D: Scope and Sequence of *Reading Mastery Signature Edition,* Grade K

Appendix E: Correlation to the Common Core State Standards

SRA Reading Mastery

Signature Edition

Your Master Plan for
Core Comprehensive Reading

The comprehensive program that helps at-risk students succeed

- Validated by extensive and exhaustive research
- Proven to work in a wide range of classrooms, schools, and districts
- Systematic, explicit instruction for heightened academic achievement

A Core Comprehension Solution

Welcome to **Reading Mastery Signature Edition**! It's a comprehensive solution that is flexible enough to serve as your intervention program, in addition to your core program, or combine all strands to work together as a complete program. **Reading Mastery Signature Edition** is research-based and field-tested, and it meets rigorous Common Core State Standards.

How Reading, Language Arts, and Literature work together

Three strands address Reading, Oral Language/Language Arts, and Literature

- Activities within each strand reflect clearly stated goals and objectives
- Skills and processes are clearly linked within, as well as across, each strand
- Each strand can be targeted for use as an intervention program, in addition to the core program, or combined for use as a comprehensive stand-alone reading program

Reading Strand

- Addresses all five essential components of reading as identified by Reading First: phonemic awareness, phonics and word analysis, fluency, vocabulary, and comprehension
- Provides spelling instruction to enable students to make the connection between decoding and spelling patterns
- Develops student decoding and word recognition skills that transfer to other subject areas

Oral Language/Language Arts Strand

- Teaches the oral language skills necessary to understand what is spoken, written, and read in the classroom
- Helps students to communicate ideas and information effectively
- Develops the ability to use writing strategies and writing processes successfully

Literature Strand

- Supports the reading strand with a wide variety of literary forms and text structures
- Provides multiple opportunities for students to work with useful and important words
- Gives ample opportunity for each student to read at his or her independent level

What makes *Reading Mastery Signature Edition* unique is how:

- Information is presented
- Assignments are structured
- Understanding is tested

Strategy-based instruction allows students to learn new information in a more efficient way:

- Complex tasks are analyzed and broken into component parts
- Each part is taught in a logical progression
- The amount of new information is controlled and connected to prior learning
- Ample practice opportunities ensure mastery

Intensive, explicit, systematic instruction helps students use skills and processes with a high rate of success, because:

- Whatever is presented is **taught**, clearly and directly
- Whatever is taught is actively **practiced**, multiple times
- Whatever is practiced is **linked and applied** to new learning

Fully aligned materials help you guide students through the learning cycle and promote independent learning through:

- Highly detailed lessons
- Consistent teacher-friendly instructional routines
- Frequent teacher-student interactions
- Deliberate and carefully scaffolded teaching
- Specific correction techniques
- Cumulative review and application of skills

Continuous informal tests and curriculum-based assessments help:

- Monitor and report student, class, and district progress.
- Determine areas that need attention
- Guide placement and movement through the program

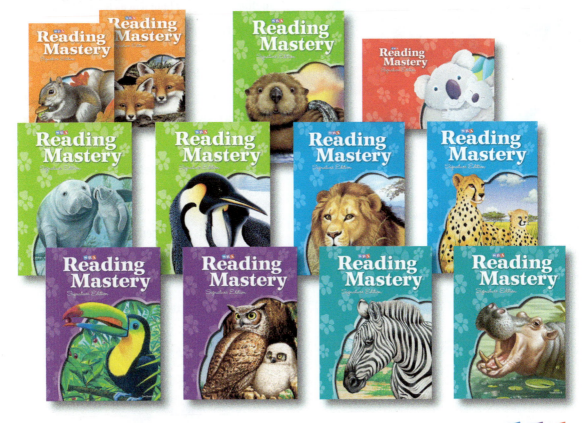

Reading Strand

Give students the keys to success

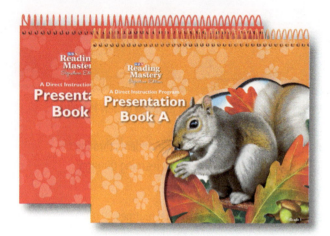

Grades K and 1

Designed to teach students skills needed to become **accurate and fluent readers**:

- Decoding is taught explicitly and systematically
- There are numerous opportunities for building fluency, allowing students to focus on the meaning of the text
- Comprehension instruction begins early to teach students how to infer, predict, and conclude

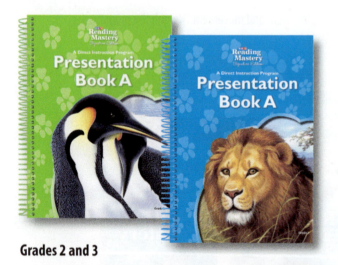

Grades 2 and 3

Continue to emphasize accurate and fluent decoding. The primary focus of these levels is to teach students how to **"read to learn."** Students are taught:

- The skills necessary to read, comprehend, and learn from informational text
- Background information needed for content area reading through information passages
- The background information that becomes the basis from which students make inferences as they read

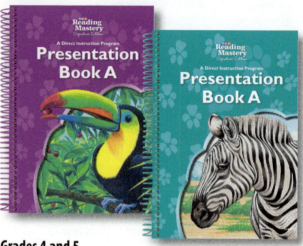

Grades 4 and 5

The focus is **literature**:

- Students are taught to analyze and interpret literature
- Students read classic and contemporary novels, short stories, poems, myths, folktales, biographies, and factual articles
- They learn new comprehension skills for interpreting all these different types of literature
- The reading selections are reinforced with literary analysis, reasoning strategies, and extended daily writing

Grades K–5

Spelling is explicitly taught at all levels to (Grades K–5):

- Engage beginning readers in activities at the phoneme and morphemic level
- Help older students identify known word parts
- Reduce confusion about words that are pronounced the same and provide a basis for using the appropriate word in context

A **Curriculum-Based Assessment and Fluency Handbook** combines with in-program mastery tests to provide a complete system for guiding student instruction. Use it to:

- Ensure students are properly placed in the program
- Measure student achievement within the program
- Identify skills students have mastered
- Present remedial exercises to students who are experiencing difficulty

Exactly the right components

Reading Mastery Signature Edition Core Components (Reading Strand)	K	1	2	3	4	5
Student Materials						
Storybook(s)	√	√				
Textbooks			√	√	√	√
Workbooks	√	√	√	√	√	√
Test Books	√	√	√	√	√	√
Teacher Materials						
Presentation Books	√	√	√	√	√	√
Teacher's Guide	√	√	√	√	√	√
Teacher's Takehome Book or Answer Key	√	√	√	√	√	√
Spelling Book	√	√	√	√	√	√
Curriculum-Based Assessment Handbook	√	√	√	√	√	
Skills Profile Folder	√	√				
Audio CD	√					

Reading Mastery Signature Edition Tools to Differentiate Instruction (Reading Strand)	K	1	2	3	4	5
Library of Independent Readers	√	√				
Seatwork	√	√				
Activities Across the Curriculum			√	√	√	√
Practice and Review Activities	√	√	√	√	√	√

Language Arts Strand

Oral language skills are an essential part of learning to read. The early grades of *Reading Mastery Signature Edition* teach oral language skills necessary to understand what is spoken, written, and read in the classroom.

Starting at **Grade K**, students learn the important background information, vocabulary, and thinking skills they need to achieve high levels of comprehension. Students:

- Learn vocabulary words commonly used in school
- Engage in talking and answering questions
- Use different sentence forms and structures
- Acquire important information and concepts

As they progress into **Grade 1**, specific activities are added to integrate language arts with other important reading skills including:

- Continued vocabulary development
- Instruction that focuses on elements of story grammar
- Sentence construction
- Cooperative story writing

Grades 2–5 provide the structure and challenging materials that allow students to communicate effectively in writing and critique the writing of others. Students learn to:

- Write stories with a clear beginning, middle, and end
- Maintain focus on a single idea and develop supporting details
- Edit for standard conventions of grammar, usage, and mechanics
- Analyze persuasive text for misleading claims, faulty or inadequate arguments, and contradictory statements
- Develop skills related to real-world tasks—recall and summarize information presented orally, write directions, and take notes

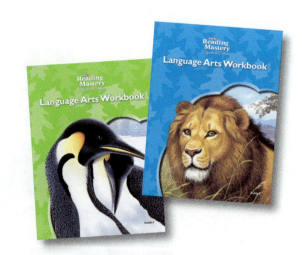

Core Components (Language Strand)	K	1	2	3	4	5
Student Materials						
Textbooks			√	√	√	√
Workbooks	√	√	√	√		
Teacher Materials						
Presentation Books	√	√	√	√	√	√
Teacher's Guide	√	√	√	√	√	√
Teacher's Take-Home Book or Answer Key	√	√	√	√	√	√
Skills Profile Folder	√					

Literature Strand

Learning to read opens new doors for students

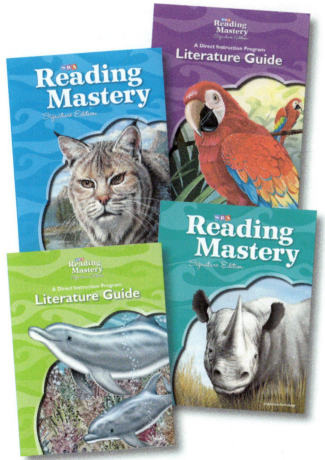

Literature Collection and Guide (Grades K and 1) expand on skills students are learning in **Reading Mastery Signature Edition**. The program:

- Develops their ability to listen attentively and demonstrate understanding
- Sharpens their understanding of story grammar and structure

Anthology and Guide (Grades 2–5) enrich students' experience with novels, poetry, and plays that complement the content and themes of the **Reading Mastery Signature Edition** Textbooks by featuring:

- Classics such as *The Bracelet; Thank You, Ma'am; The Velveteen Rabbit; Stone Soup;* and *The Story of Daedalus and Icarus*
- Insight into elements of story structure and literary strategies so students can discuss and write about the meanings of these selections

Literature Strand						
	K	1	2	3	4	5
Literature Guide	√	√	√	√	√	√
Collection	√	√				
Anthology			√	√	√	√

Literature

Robust vocabulary instruction tied closely to comprehension

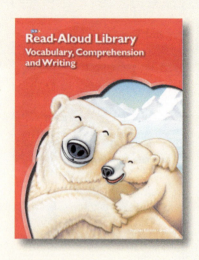

For **Grades K and 1**, daily reading with an emphasis on word meaning expands students' vocabulary into the world of mature speakers and provides:

- Lessons that offer direct teaching of Tier 2 words, enabling students to become more precise and descriptive with their language

- Numerous encounters with target words over time helps students to incorporate them into their speaking vocabulary
- Varied activities for students to interact with words in a variety of situations to deepen understanding
- Thirty high-quality books at each level including: folk tales, fairy tales, legends, poetry, as well as social studies and science expository works

From the introduction of new vocabulary to the informal assessment of understanding, the lesson plans expand oral language by encouraging conversation about the book.

Day 1: Students are introduced to the book and learn the key elements of a book such as title, author, and illustrator.
- They make predictions about what will happen in the story and share those predictions with their classmates.
- They formulate questions they may have about the story or the book.
- The story is read aloud to students with minimal interruptions.
- Target vocabulary words and their meanings are introduced within the context of how they are used in the story.

Day 2: The lesson begins with the story being read aloud by the teacher and discussed.
- Students become actively involved in responding to the story and constructing meaning.
- They are prompted to use target words throughout the discussion.
- Target vocabulary is reviewed.

Day 3: Students participate in varied activities using the new vocabulary words in and beyond the context of the story. Activities include:
- Retelling the story
- Playing word games
- Completing an activity sheet

8

Additional tools that teachers have used with Reading Mastery Signature Edition

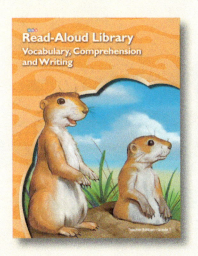
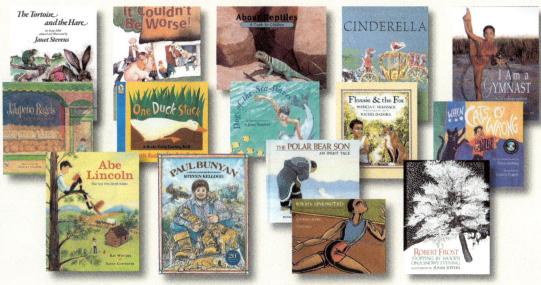

Day 4: Literary analysis and cumulative review are provided in the fourth day of instruction.

- Students play a verbal game that uses all of the new words in addition to words that have been taught in earlier lessons.
- Students also learn songs that help them recall the literary elements and patterns.

Day 5: On the last day students retell the story to a partner.

- An assessment is administered to measure students' mastery of the new vocabulary as well as review items.
- Students are allowed to choose a book they would like the teacher to read to them as a reward.
- Students are taught the routine for the learning center they will work in the following week.
  Students can practice new and previously learned vocabulary in the Super Words Center.

Reading Strand

Library of Independent Readers
Entertaining, trade-style books written in the special *Reading Mastery Signature Edition* alphabet, one library each for **Grades K and 1**.

Activities Across the Curriculum
Encourage students in **Grades 2–5** to use reading, reference, and writing skills through activities that support science, social studies, math, and language arts.

Seatwork
Provide fun and rewarding reinforcement for students in **Grades K and 1**, that is closely correlated with lessons in *Reading Mastery Signature Edition*.

Additional tools that teachers have used with Reading Mastery Signature Edition

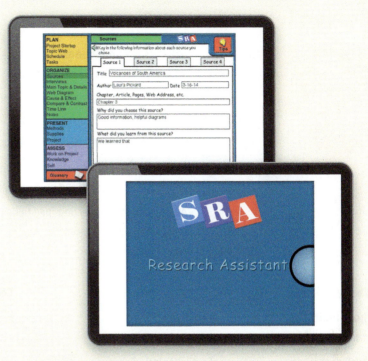

Practicing Standardized Test Formats help students understand test formats and learn test-taking skills by providing:

- Concepts to address important test content as well as instructional standards
- Short, daily activities familiarize students with questions and formats they will encounter on the most recent forms
- Help for students so they perform at their optimal levels and obtain scores that more accurately reflect the student's achievement

Research Assistant
Grades 2–5

Presents a systematic process for the collection, processing, and presentation of information. Helps students:

- Generate ideas for a search
- Use appropriate resources to obtain information
- Present informational reports that include main ideas and relevant details with visual supports

Interactive Student Review

Practice and Review Activities
Grades K–5

Practice Software offers engaging, interactive review to help students master key skills through:

- Brief, frequent practice activities and games
- Direct links to daily lessons
- Monitoring of student progress and performance

Practice Decodable Takehome Books
Grades K and 1

Offers short, decodable stories for students to read independently:

- Provides additional opportunities for students to apply the skills and vocabulary they've learned
- Are available as Blackline Masters or 4-color pages to fold and staple into books each student can keep and read
- Can be taken home and shared with families

11

Common Core Connection Kit

Proven lesson instruction

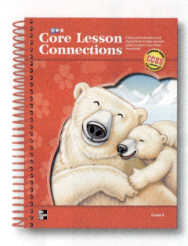

**Core Lesson Connections
Grades K–5**

Strategic, targeted instruction that supports and enhances the core reading program, including:

- Brief, 20-minute activities aligned to specific program lessons
- Explicit instruction with modeling, guided practice, and independent practice to develop word-learning and comprehension strategies
- An instructional model designed to be presented in conjunction with each program lesson

What you'll find:

**Phonological and phonemic awareness
Grades K and 1**

Develops through a wide variety of activities including:

- Word segmentation
- Rhyme recognition and production
- Syllable blending, segmentation, and deletion
- Onset-rime segmentation and blending
- Phoneme isolation (initial, medial, and final)
- Phoneme identification, segmentation, and blending

Vocabulary Instruction boosts the acquisition of word-learning strategies and contextual practice through:

- Daily instruction of specific words found in the core program
- Opportunities for students to develop, use, and apply word knowledge
- Word awareness through vocabulary journaling and practice activities
- Vocabulary notebook with word practice and study strategies

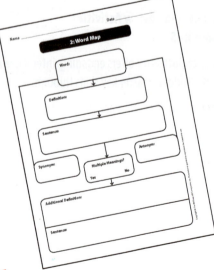

Comprehension Strategies are applied across lessons so students understand their usefulness while learning:

- Before-, during-, and after-reading strategies
- Bloom's Taxonomy level questions
- Narrative and expository text strategies
- Story grammar and story retell
- Graphic organizers
- Main idea and summarizing
- Comprehension monitoring
- Deep processing of text

Fluency Building through increased repetitions use core program stories and partner reading for:

- Emphasis on prosody and reading for meaning
- Effective partner reading
- Charting and decision making for maximum benefit

In addition, the following resources help you enhance learning for all students by providing:

- A **Scope and Sequence** chart to assist you in planning, conducting, and assessing instruction
- **Differentiated Instruction** with suggestions to boost the academic success for approaching mastery, at mastery, and ELL students
- **Professional Development** discusses how you can help students select appropriate material to read for personal pleasure and supplies tips/strategies to help students who struggle with reading fluency
- **Correlation** to the Common Core State Standards to help you keep students on target for meeting standards.

New tools help you promote student engagement and extend learning

Dynamic Digital Resources
Powered by **McGraw-Hill ConnectED**

Interactive Whiteboard Activities
Deliver key concepts and skills with academic vocabulary practice, graphic organizers, critical writing, and more

SRA 2 Inform
Online Progress Monitoring
Collect data, monitor performance, and administer reports to inform instruction

eInquiry
Helps students solve problems through writing, presenting, preparing reflection tasks, and completing assessments

Research Projects
Allow students to collaborate on common topics and systematically collect, process, and present information

Online Professional Development via the Teaching Tutor
Access on-demand routine formats for topics such as optimal pacing, classroom arrangement, daily lesson characteristics, error corrections, and achieving mastery

Professional Development Videos

eInquiry

SRA 2 Inform

SRA Reading Mastery
Signature Edition

Three strands
work together to form a
core comprehensive program

- Reading, Language Arts, and Literature integrated into a coherent instructional design
- Content focused on the five essential components of reading and aligned with Common Core State Standards
- Explicit instructional strategies for efficient, effective learning
- Student materials that support what you are teaching in daily lessons
- Frequent assessments that track student progress

SRA Core Lesson Connections

GRADE K

Introduction

What is SRA Core Lesson Connections?

SRA Core Lesson Connections provides targeted instruction that is related to the skills and information presented in the Reading Strand of the **Reading Mastery Signature Edition** program. Used in conjunction with **Reading Mastery Signature Edition,** *Core Lesson Connections* offers strategic support to master the Common Core State Standards for English Language Arts. Each lesson links with the core daily lesson. Explicit instruction through modeling, guided practice, and independent practice helps students meet the rigorous vocabulary, writing, and comprehension strands of the Common Core State Standards.

Core Lesson Connections uses the same teacher-script conventions that appear in **Reading Mastery Signature Edition.** These conventions include what the teacher says, what the teacher does, and what the correct students' responses should be. As with **Reading Mastery,** the teacher calls for group responses, uses clear signals, and employs specific correction procedures. Additionally, teachers deliver key concepts and skills with academic vocabulary practice, graphic organizers, critical writing, and more through interactive whiteboard activities.

How do you use Core Lesson Connections?

There are 160 lessons in Grade K Core *Lesson Connections,* aligned with Grade K of **Reading Mastery.** Each lesson requires approximately 20 minutes.

The **Reading Mastery Signature Edition** lesson should always take priority when scheduling instruction. The *Core Lesson Connections* activities are designed to enhance and extend the learning of the **Reading Mastery** lesson. Each lesson corresponds with the **Reading Mastery Signature Edition** lesson—for example, Lesson 11 of *Core Lesson Connections* corresponds with Lesson 11 of **Reading Mastery Signature Edition**—Reading Strand.

Some activities are important to conduct **before, during,** or **after** the **Reading Mastery Signature Edition** program lesson. These activities are specifically identified in the *Core Lesson Connections*. The following suggestions are noted:

- Set up a writing center with writing materials and correct models of letters learned for students to use in their free time.
- Provide a reading center to display books being read so that students can enjoy them again during free time.
- Choose narrative and informational texts that are appropriate for students in your class. You may want to refer to Appendix B of the Common Core State Standards for a list of exemplar texts for read-aloud selections for specific grade levels. Otherwise, you may choose from your own classroom or school library.

Core Lesson Connections lessons are divided into major parts or strands. For example, Comprehension Strategies is an important part of the *Core Lesson Connections* for Level K and appears as Part C. Each part includes:

- Suggested instructional minutes (top left-hand column),
- Instructional materials for the teacher and student (left-hand column),
- What the teacher does (black type, right-hand column),
- What the teacher says (blue type, right-hand column), and
- What the students say/do (black italic type, right-hand column).

Overview of SRA Lesson Connections **cc1**

Here's an example from Lesson 11.

9 minutes

Teacher Materials:
Reading *Teacher Presentation Book A*

Part C: Comprehension Strategies

Activity 1 Build Listening Comprehension

Elicit responses to questions. **Guide** as needed.
Today you'll hear a new story. What should you be doing when I'm reading the story? (Idea: *Thinking about the story.*)

During the story, I'll ask questions to see whether you understand what I'm reading. What will I ask as I read the story to you? *Questions.*

Later in today's lesson, you'll see a picture about the story. We'll talk more about the story when you see this picture. What will you see later in today's lesson? (Idea: *The picture from the story.*)

The title of the story is "The Walk to School." What's the title of the story? *The Walk to School.*

Lessons correspond to and enhance instruction found in the **Reading Mastery Signature Edition** program. The lesson example shown above and found in Lesson 11 of the *Core Lesson Connections* aligns with an illustration of three children walking to school located in Lesson 11 of the **Reading Mastery Signature Edition** Teacher Presentation Book for Level K. *Core Lesson Connections* enhances rather than supplants the **Reading Mastery** program.

What Major Parts Compose Core Lesson Connections?

There are three major parts of *Core Lesson Connections* for Level K. These include: **phonemic and phonological awareness, letter recognition and formation,** and **comprehension strategies.** Explicit instruction for each of these major parts is based on best practices in reading research (see recommendations provided by Armbruster, Lehr, & Osborn, 2003; Carnine, Silbert, Kame'enui, & Tarver, 2010; National Institute of Child Health & Human Development [NICHD], 2000; Snow, Burns, & Griffin, 1998; and Vaughn & Linan-Thompson, 2004). Skills taught and examples for each part follow.

Phonemic and Phonological Awareness
Overview
• Daily phonemic and phonological awareness instruction   • Explicit instruction with modeling, guided practice, and independent practice   • Phonemic segmentation and blending focus   • Phonemic and phonological awareness developed through a number of interesting activities
Skills Taught
• Word segmentation   • Rhyme recognition and production   • Syllable blending, segmentation, and deletion   • Onset-rime segmentation and blending   • Phoneme isolation (initial, final, and medial)   • Phoneme identification, segmentation, and blending

Letter Recognition and Formation

Overview

- Daily letter recognition and formation instruction
- Explicit instruction with modeling, guided practice, and independent practice
- Letter sounds linked to letter names
- Writing activities fit any type of writing program used in your school

Skills Taught

- Letter recognition
- Capital letter recognition
- Letter formation
- Capital letter formation
- Writing school, city, state, and country names

Comprehension Strategies

Overview

- Daily application of comprehension strategies with focus on listening comprehension
- Explicit instruction with modeling, guided practice, and independent practice
- Activities linked to stories from core lesson
- Reading for understanding and constructing meaning from text
- Story grammar vocabulary with cumulative review

Skills Taught

- Listening comprehension
- Narrative and informational text strategies
- Before-, during-, and after-reading strategies
- Bloom's Taxonomy level questions
- Making connections
- Story grammar
- Purpose for reading
- Predictions
- Story retell
- Graphic organizers
- Activating background knowledge
- Main idea
- KWL
- Summarizing
- Comprehension monitoring
- Connections through writing

Overview of SRA Lesson Connections **cc3**

What Other Components Compose Core Lesson Connections?

Core Lesson Connections includes six other important sections.

First, a **summary of skills** and **scope and sequence chart** are provided. These charts provide an overview of the skills taught in the program by major part. In a quick glance, teachers can see what skills are taught for each lesson of the program as well as the span of lessons that cover a specific skill.

Second, **graphic organizers** are used to carefully scaffold instruction for comprehension, writing, and phonemic awareness. These organizers also appear as interactive whiteboard activities online via McGraw-Hill's *ConnectED*. Teachers can write on, save, and print the organizers. Interactive whiteboard activities increase student engagement and improve understanding.

Third, **differentiated instruction** appears in *Core Lesson Connections* to help teachers enhance learning for **all** students. Instructional tips provide teachers and parents (called "home connection") with important suggestions to enhance academic success for approaching mastery, at mastery, and ELL students. Teacher and parent tips align with assessments found in the ***Reading Mastery*** program.

Here is an example from Mastery Test 1.

Test	Tips for Teachers	Home Connections
Mastery Test 1 (Lessons 1-8) **Approaching Mastery**	• See "What To Do" guidelines for "if the group is weak on Mastery Test 1" on page 52 in *Presentation Book A*. • Partner with "at mastery" student and review sounds. • Reteach difficult sounds using "good-bye" list.	• Provide sound flash cards for students to take home for additional practice. • Encourage students to share their take-home sheets with their families. • Encourage adult at home to conduct "see-say-write" activity for each sound.
At Mastery	• See "What To Do" guidelines for "if the group is firm on Mastery Test 1" on page 52 in *Presentation Book A*. • Have student "be the teacher": Partner with "approaching mastery" student and review sounds.	
ELL	• See "Tips for Teachers" for "approaching mastery" and "at mastery" students. • Describe and model mouth formations for sounds, then guide student while practicing with mirror.	• See "Home Connections" for "approaching mastery" and "at mastery" students. • Provide sounds audiotape to use with sound flash cards at home; encourage students to practice mouth formations with mirror at home.

Fourth, teachers can access tips to help ensure maximum access for students with intellectual disabilities. These suggestions are linked to the ***Reading Mastery*** content and provide guidance for three **levels of support** to allow all students the opportunity to access learning with the program materials.

Fifth, a **five-day lesson planning chart** is provided. This chart shows a "week at a glance," illustrating all major parts of the program and specific skills taught within these parts in groups of five lessons. This chart assists teachers in planning, conducting, and assessing instruction.

Finally, a **correlation to the Common Core State Standards** for English Language Arts is presented. The correlation notes the standards for the specified grade level with detailed notations of how the content of ***Reading Mastery Signature Edition*** supports the standard.

cc4   *Overview of SRA Lesson Connections*

References

Armbruster, B., Lehr, F., & Osborn, J. (2003). *Put reading first: The research building blocks of reading instruction: Grades K-3* (2nd ed.). Washington, DC: Center for the Improvement of Early Reading Achievement, National Institute for Literacy, U.S. Department of Education.

Carnine, D. W., Silbert, J., Kame'enui, E. J., & Tarver, S. G. (2010). *Direct Instruction reading* (5th ed.). Upper Saddle River, NJ: Pearson Education.

National Institute of Child Health and Human Development [NICHD]. (2000). *Report of the National Reading Panel. Teaching children to read: An evidence-based assessment of the scientific research literature on reading and its implications for reading instruction: Reports of the subgroups* (NIH Publication NO. 00-4754). Washington, DC: U.S. Government Printing Office.

Snow, C., Burns, M., & Griffin, P.(eds.). (1998). *Preventing reading difficulties in young children.* Washington, DC: National Academy Press.

Vaughn, S., & Linan-Thompson, S. (2004). *Research-based methods of reading instruction: Grades K-3.* Alexandria, VA: ASCD.

Summary of Skills

GRADE K

A. Phonological and Phonemic Awareness (1-160)

1. Word Segmentation (1–11, 13, 15, 17, 19)
2. Rhyme Recognition (1–11, 13, 16, 17, 19)
3. Rhyme Production (12, 14, 15, 18, 20, 21, 23, 25, 27, 29, 31, 33, 35, 37, 39)
4. Syllable Blending (6–10, 12, 14, 15, 17, 19, 21, 23, 26, 28, 29)
5. Syllable Segmentation (12, 14, 16, 18, 20–24, 26, 28, 30, 31, 33, 35, 37, 39)
6. Syllable Deletion (22, 24, 25, 27, 30, 32, 34, 36, 38, 40, 41, 43, 45, 47, 49)
7. Onset-Rime Blending (22, 24, 25, 27, 30, 32, 34, 36, 38, 40, 42, 44, 46, 48, 50)
8. Onset-Rime Segmentation (31, 33, 35, 37, 39, 41, 43, 45, 47, 49, 52, 54, 56, 58, 60)
9. Phoneme Isolation – Initial (32, 34, 36, 38, 40, 41, 43, 45, 47, 49, 51, 53, 55, 57, 59, 61–115, 117, 119)
10. Phoneme Isolation – Final (42, 44, 46, 48, 50, 52, 54, 56, 58, 60, 61, 63, 65, 67, 69, 71, 73, 75, 77, 79, 81, 83, 85, 87, 89, 91, 93, 95, 97, 99)
11. Phoneme Isolation – Medial (62, 64, 66, 68, 70, 72, 74, 76, 78, 80, 82, 84, 86, 88, 90, 92, 94, 96, 98, 100, 102, 104, 106, 108, 110)
12. Phoneme Identification – Initial (71, 73, 75, 77, 79, 81, 83, 85, 87, 89, 108, 110, 112, 114, 116, 117, 119)
13. Phoneme Identification – Final (91, 93, 95, 97, 99, 102, 104, 106, 121, 123, 125, 127, 129)
14. Phoneme Identification – Medial (131, 133, 135, 137, 139)
15. Phoneme Categorization – Initial (82, 84, 86, 88, 90, 92, 94, 96, 98, 100, 114, 116, 118, 120, 122, 124, 126, 128, 130)
16. Phoneme Categorization – Final (101, 103, 105, 107, 109, 112, 132, 134, 136, 138, 140)
17. Phoneme Categorization – Medial (141–145)
18. Phoneme Blending (92, 94, 96, 98, 100, 102, 104, 106, 108, 110, 111, 113, 116, 117, 119, 121, 123, 125, 127, 129, 131, 133, 135, 137, 139, 141–160)
19. Phoneme Segmentation (112, 114, 115, 118, 120, 122, 124, 126, 128, 130, 132, 134, 136, 138, 140–160)

B. Letter Recognition and Formation (11–160)

C. Comprehension Strategies

1. Explicit Instruction (1–160)
2. Listening Comprehension (1–125, 127–130, 132–135, 137–140, 142–145)
3. Narrative Text (1–125, 139, 146–160)
4. During-Reading Strategies (1–55, 57–65, 67–75, 77–85, 87–90, 92–95, 97–100, 102–105, 107–110, 112–115, 117–120, 122–125, 127–130, 132–135, 137–140, 142–158, 160).
5. After-Reading Strategies (1–30, 32, 37, 40–130, 132–135, 137–140, 142–160)

6. Bloom's Taxonomy Questions (1–30)
7. Make Connections (25–30, 61, 62, 66, 71, 76, 81, 86, 91, 93, 94, 96–98, 101, 103, 104, 106–108, 111, 113, 114, 116–118, 123, 124, 151–155)
8. Story Grammar (31–97, 99, 100–103, 105–107, 109-113, 115-123, 125, 126, 131, 141, 146-149, 151-155, 157-159)
9. Before-Reading Strategies (31–41, 46, 51, 56, 61, 62, 66, 71, 76, 81, 86, 91, 96, 101, 106, 111, 116, 121, 126, 131, 136, 141, 146–156, 158)
10. Predictions (31–41, 46, 56, 66, 76, 86, 91, 96, 101, 106, 111, 116, 121, 156–159)
11. Purpose for Reading (37, 121, 126, 131, 136, 141, 146–150)
12. Story Retell (40, 50, 60, 70, 77, 79, 80, 87, 90, 99, 100, 103, 105, 110, 115, 120, 125, 129, 134, 135, 139, 140, 144–155, 159, 160)
13. Graphic Organizers (45, 49, 50, 55, 59, 60, 63, 65, 69, 70, 73, 75, 79, 80, 83, 85, 89, 90, 95, 99, 100, 105, 109, 110, 119, 120, 126–128, 131–133, 136–138, 141–143, 146–155, 159, 160)
14. Activate background knowledge (61, 62, 66, 71, 76, 81, 86, 91, 96, 101, 106, 111, 116, 151–155)
15. Main Idea (107–109, 112, 113, 117, 118, 122, 123, 127, 132, 137, 142)
16. Expository Text (126–138, 140–145)
17. KWL (126–128, 131–133, 136–138, 141–143)
18. Summarizing (129, 130, 134, 135, 139–140, 144, 145, 156–158)
19. Comprehension monitoring (146–158, 160)
20. Connections through writing (25–30, 40, 45, 49, 50, 55, 59, 60, 62, 66, 70, 71, 76, 80, 81, 85, 86, 89, 90, 91, 95–100, 105–107, 110, 113, 116, 119, 120, 123, 130, 136, 137, 140–142, 150–155, 159, 160)

D. Vocabulary

1. Shades of Meaning (5, 10, 15, 20, 25, 30)

Scope and Sequence (1-80)

Skills	1 – 5	6-10	11-15	16-20	21-25	26-30
PHONEMIC AND PHONOLOGICAL AWARENESS	√	√	√	√	√	√
LETTER RECOGNITION AND FORMATION			√	√	√	√
COMPREHENSION STRATEGIES						
Explicit Instruction	√	√	√	√	√	√
Listening Comprehension	√	√	√	√	√	√
Narrative Text	√	√	√	√	√	√
During-Reading Strategies	√	√	√	√	√	√
After-Reading Strategies	√	√	√	√	√	√
Bloom's Taxonomy Questions	√	√	√	√	√	√
Make Connections						√
Story Grammar						
Before-Reading Strategies						
Predictions						
Purpose for Reading						
Story Retell						
Graphic Organizers						
Activate Background Knowledge						
Main Idea						
Expository Text						
KWL						
Summarizing						
Comprehension Monitoring						
Connections through writing					•	√
VOCABULARY						
Shades of Meaning	•	•	•	•	•	•

Key

√ = skill in every lesson

• = skill in some of the lessons

cc8   *Scope and Sequence*

GRADE K

31-35	36-40	41-45	46-50	51-55	56-60	61-65	66-70	71-75	76-80
√	√	√	√	√	√	√	√	√	√
√	√	√	√	√	√	√	√	√	√
√	√	√	√	√	√	√	√	√	√
√	√	√	√	√	√	√	√	√	√
√	√	√	√	√	√	√	√	√	√
√	√	√	√	√	•	√	•	√	•
•	•	√	√	√	√	√	√	√	√
						•	•	•	•
√	√	√	√	√	√	√	√	√	√
√	√	•	•	•	•	•	•	•	•
√	√	•	•		•		•		•
	•								
	•		•		•		•		•
		•	•	•	•	•	•	•	•
						•	•	•	•
	•	•	•	•	•	•	•	•	•

Scope and Sequence **cc9**

Scope and Sequence (81-160)

Skills	81 – 85	86-90	91-95	96-100	101-105	106-110
PHONEMIC AND PHONOLOGICAL AWARENESS	√	√	√	√	√	√
LETTER RECOGNITION AND FORMATION	√	√	√	√	√	√
COMPREHENSION STRATEGIES						
Explicit Instruction	√	√	√	√	√	√
Listening Comprehension	√	√	√	√	√	√
Narrative Text	√	√	√	√	√	√
During-Reading Strategies	√	•	•	•	•	•
After-Reading Strategies	√	√	√	√	√	√
Bloom's Taxonomy Questions						
Make Connections	•	•	•	•	•	•
Story Grammar	√	√	√	•	•	•
Before-Reading Strategies	•	•	•	•	•	•
Predictions		•	•	•	•	•
Purpose for Reading						
Story Retell		•		•	•	•
Graphic Organizers	•	•	•	•	•	•
Activate Background Knowledge	•	•	•	•	•	•
Main Idea						•
Expository Text						
KWL						
Summarizing						
Comprehension Monitoring						
Connections through writing	•	•	•	√	•	•
VOCABULARY						
Shades of Meaning						

Key

√ = skill in every lesson

• = skill in some of the lessons

GRADE K

111-115	116-120	121-125	126-130	131-135	136-140	141-145	146-150	151-155	156-160
√	√	√	√	√	√	√	√	√	√
√	√	√	√	√	√	√	√	√	√
√	√	√	√	√	√	√	√	√	√
√	√	√	•	•	•	√			
√	√	√			•		√	√	√
•	•	•	•	•	•	•	√	√	•
√	√	√	√	•	•	•	√	√	√
•	•	•						√	
•	√	•	•	•		•	•	√	•
•	•	•	•	•	•	•	√	√	•
•	•	•							•
		•	•	•	•	•	√		
•	•	•	•	•	•	•	√	√	•
	•	•	•	•	•	•	√	√	•
•	•							√	
•	•	•	•	•	•	•			
			√	√	•	√			
			•	•	•	•			
			•	•	•	•			•
							√	√	•
•	•	•	•		•	•	•	√	•

Lessons

Lesson 1

Materials
Teacher: Reading *Teacher Presentation Book A*
Student:

Part A: Phonemic and Phonological Awareness

Activity 1 Word Segmentation: One-Syllable Words and Two-, Three-, and Four-Word Sentences

Emphasize words in bold. **Elicit** responses. **Guide** as needed. **Model** distinguishing each word clearly.
Today we're going to learn about sentences and words. A sentence is a group of words that go together to tell or ask something. A sentence can have only a few words, or it can have many words. We're going to learn how to break a sentence into words. First, we're going to practice saying some sentences together.

Clap for words in bold. **Elicit** responses. **Guide** as needed.
Listen. I can say a sentence. **We run.** Say that sentence with me. *We run.* Now say that sentence by yourselves. *We run.*

Listen. I can say a sentence. **We walk.** Now say that sentence by yourselves. *We walk.*

Listen. I can say a sentence. **We eat.** Now say that sentence by yourselves. *We eat.*

Let's try that again, but this time we'll clap for each word in the sentence. Listen. I can say a sentence and clap for each word. **We run.** Say that sentence with me, and clap for each word. *We run.* Now say that sentence by yourselves, and clap for each word. *We run.*

Let's try a new one. Listen. I can say a sentence and clap for each word. **We walk.** Now say that sentence by yourselves, and clap for each word. *We walk.*

Here's another one. Listen. I can say a sentence and clap for each word. **We eat.** Now say that sentence by yourselves, and clap for each word. *We eat.*

Listen. **I like dogs.** Now say that sentence by yourselves, and clap for each word. *I like dogs.*

Listen. **I like toys.** Now say that sentence by yourselves, and clap for each word. *I like toys.*

Listen. **I like school.** Your turn. *I like school.*

Listen. **I see a dog.** Your turn. *I see a dog.*

Lesson 1   1

Listen. **I see a girl.** Your turn. *I see a girl.*

Listen. **I see a book.** Your turn. *I see a book.*

(Continue the activity with the following sentences.
That is my book.
That is my shirt.
That is a tree.
That is a flag.
My shirt is red.
My shoe is black.)

Activity 2 Rhyme Recognition

Emphasize italicized words. **Elicit** responses. **Guide** as needed.
I'm going to read a poem to you.

Rain, rain, go *away.*
Come again another *day!*

Now we're going to learn the poem together.
My turn. Rain, rain, go *away.*
Say it with me. *Rain, rain, go away.*
Your turn. *Rain, rain, go away.*

My turn. Rain, rain, go *away.* Come again another *day!*
Say it with me. *Rain, rain, go away. Come again another day!*
Your turn. *Rain, rain, go away. Come again another day!*

Part B: Letter Recognition and Formation

To be started in Lesson 11.

Part C: Comprehension Strategies

14 minutes

Teacher Materials:
Reading *Teacher Presentation Book A*

Activity 1 Build Listening Comprehension

Elicit responses to questions. **Guide** as needed.
Today you'll hear a story. You'll need to listen big as I read the story. As I read, I want you to think about what I'm reading. What should you be doing when I'm reading the story? (Idea: *Thinking about the story.*)

During the story, I'll ask questions to see whether you understand what I'm reading. What will I ask as I read the story to you? *Questions.*

Later in today's lesson, you'll see a picture about the story. We'll talk more about the story when you see this picture. What will you see later in today's lesson? (Idea: *The picture from the story.*) Are you ready to get started?

2   Lesson 1

The title of the story is "Joey Catches a Pass." What's the title of the story? *Joey Catches a Pass.*

Joey loved to play football. In fact, he loved football so much he played every day. Joey's best friend was Matt. Matt loved to play football too. Matt loved to throw the football. Joey loved to catch it. Matt could throw the ball far. He could also throw it hard. Joey was good at catching a **pass.** A **pass** is when you **throw the ball.** No matter how far or how hard Matt threw the football, Joey could almost always catch it.

1. What sport did Joey and Matt love to play? *Football.*

2. Who loved to throw the football? *Matt.*

3. What does it mean to **pass** the football? (Idea: *Throw the ball.*)

One day some older kids asked Joey to play football in the park. They asked him to bring a friend. Joey knew just who to ask—Matt! Matt and Joey played football against the older boys. They were not afraid because they had practiced so much together.

1. Where did the football game take place? *In the park.*

2. Why were Joey and Matt not afraid to play the older boys? (Idea: *They practiced so much.*)

The last play of the game, Matt threw a long **pass** to Joey. It went up and up. Joey had to run as fast as he could. The other boys chased him. The ball kept flying and Joey kept running. All at once, the football landed in Joey's hands and he scored a touchdown. Joey and Matt won the game! They were so happy.

1. Who won the game? (Idea: *Matt and Joey.*)

2. During the last play of the game, what did Matt throw? (Idea: *A long pass.*)

You learned a new word in the story today. **Pass. Pass** means **throw the ball.** What does **pass** mean? *Throw the ball.*

Activity 2 Review Vocabulary Word

Elicit responses to questions. **Guide** as needed.
Pass means **throw the ball.**
What does **pass** mean? *Throw the ball.*
What's another word for **throw the ball?** *Pass.*

Lesson 1 **3**

3 minutes

Activity 3, to be completed <u>after</u> the picture in Lesson 1 is shown to students.

Activity 3 Story Extension

 Show picture from Lesson 1, page 4, in *Teacher Presentation Book A*.

Elicit responses to questions. **Guide** as needed.

Listen as I ask you some questions about the story we read earlier and the picture you see now.

Which boy is Matt? (Student response.)

Which boy is Joey? (Student response.)

What are they playing? (Student response.)

Do they look like they're having fun? How do you know? (Student response.)

Do you like football? Does anyone you know play football? (Student response.)

Lesson 2

Materials
Teacher: Reading *Teacher Presentation Book A*
Student:

6 minutes

Part A: Phonemic and Phonological Awareness

Activity 1 Word Segmentation: One-Syllable Words and Three- and Four-Word Sentences

Remember, in our last lesson we learned that a sentence is a group of words that go together to tell or ask something. Today we're going to say more sentences and words. Let's clap for each word in the sentence.

Clap for words in bold. **Fade** clapping as students' responses become accurate. **Elicit** responses. **Guide** as needed. **Model** distinguishing each word clearly.
Listen. I can say a sentence and clap for each word. **I like eggs.** Say that sentence with me, and clap for each word. *I like eggs.* Now say that sentence by yourselves, and clap for each word. *I like eggs.*

Let's try a new one. Listen. I can say a sentence and clap for each word. **I like cats.** Now say that sentence by yourselves, and clap for each word. *I like cats.*

Here's another one. Listen. I can say a sentence and clap for each word. **I like rain.** Now say that sentence by yourselves, and clap for each word. *I like rain.*

Listen. **My sock is white.** Now say that sentence by yourselves, and clap for each word. *My sock is white.*

(Continue the activity with the following sentences.
My shoe is dirty; My cat is fluffy; That is a ball; That is a flower; That is a table; I see a cup; I see a bottle; I see a window.)

Activity 2 Rhyme Recognition

Emphasize italicized words. **Elicit** responses. **Guide** as needed.
Remember our poem from yesterday?

Rain, rain, go *away.*
Come again another *day!*

Let's say that poem together.
Rain, rain, go away.
Come again another day!

Your turn to say the poem by yourselves.
Rain, rain, go away.
Come again another day!

Lesson 2   5

Listen as I say the poem again. See whether you can hear which two words rhyme.
Rain, rain, go *away*.
Come again another *day!*
Discuss with children that rhyming words sound the same.

Part B: Letter Recognition and Formation

To be started in Lesson 11.

14 minutes

Teacher Materials:
Reading *Teacher Presentation Book A*

Part C: Comprehension Strategies

Activity 1 Build Listening Comprehension

Elicit responses to questions. **Guide** as needed.
Today you'll hear another story. You'll need to listen big as I read the story. As I read, I want you to think about what I'm reading. What should you be doing when I'm reading the story? (Idea: *Thinking about the story.*)

During the story, I'll ask questions to see whether you understand what I'm reading. What will I ask as I read the story to you? *Questions.*

Later in today's lesson, you'll see a picture about the story. We'll talk more about the story when you see this picture. What will you see later in today's lesson? (Idea: *The picture from the story.*) Are you ready to get started?

The title of the story is "Marietta's Experiment." What's the title of the story? *Marietta's Experiment.*

Marietta loved to cook. Her favorite food was peanuts. One day, Marietta wanted to fix herself a peanut butter and honey sandwich for lunch. She went to the cupboard and got the peanut butter jar. When she opened it, she saw that all the peanut butter was gone! What was she going to do? Marietta decided to do an **experiment. An experiment is when you try out a new idea.** Her idea was to make her own peanut butter. She really wanted that peanut butter and honey sandwich.

1. What is Marietta's favorite food? *Peanuts.*

2. What is it called when you try out a new idea? *Experiment.*

3. What experiment did Marietta decide to do? *Make peanut butter.*

Marietta found some plain peanuts, cracked them open, threw the shells into the garbage can, and put the peanuts into a big red bowl. Next, she took out a big wooden spoon and tried to mash the peanuts, but they just slid around in the bowl. She couldn't keep the peanuts still long enough to mash them! Marietta asked her mother for help. They put the peanuts into a blender. The blender only mashed the peanuts. So, Marietta and her mother added some oil and a little sugar. This time, the mashed peanuts stuck together. She had made peanut butter! Marietta proudly took her homemade peanut butter and put it into a jar.

6 Lesson 2

1. Marietta first tried to mash the peanuts with a big wooden spoon. What happened? (Idea: *They slid around in the bowl.*)

2. Who helped Marietta make peanut butter? *Her mother.*

Marietta was excited to taste her **experiment.** She took a spoon and dipped it into the jar to get a big scoop. Then she closed her eyes and tasted her homemade peanut butter. She couldn't believe how good it was! Marietta was so happy with her peanut butter that she wrote the recipe so she could make it again.

1. How did Marietta's peanut butter taste? *Good.*

2. Did Marietta want to make peanut butter again? *Yes.*

You learned a new word in the story today. **Experiment** means **when you try out a new idea.** What does **experiment** mean? *When you try out a new idea.*

Activity 2 Review Vocabulary Word

Elicit responses to questions. **Guide** as needed.
Experiment means **when you try out a new idea.**

What does **experiment** mean? *When you try out a new idea.*
What's another word for **when you try out a new idea?** *Experiment.*

Activity 3 Story Extension

 Show picture from Lesson 2, page 12, in *Teacher Presentation Book A*.

3 minutes

Activity 3, to be completed <u>after</u> the picture in Lesson 2 is shown to students.

Elicit responses to questions. **Guide** as needed.
Listen as I ask you some questions about the story we read earlier and the picture you see now.

What is Marietta doing? (Student response.)

What did she make? (Student response.)

What did she put her peanut butter in? (Student response.)

Does she look like she likes the peanut butter? How do you know? (Student response.)

Do you like peanut butter? What do you eat with peanut butter? (Student response.)

Marietta's experiment was making peanut butter. What experiment have you tried? (Student response.)

Lesson 2   7

Lesson 3

Materials
Teacher: Reading *Teacher Presentation Book A*
Student:

6 minutes

Part A: Phonemic and Phonological Awareness

Activity 1 Word Segmentation: Multi-syllabic Words; Three-, Four-, and Five-Word Sentences

Today we're going to clap for words in longer sentences. Listen carefully because some words might be tricky. Remember to clap only one time for each word.

Clap for words in bold. **Fade** clapping as students' responses become accurate. **Elicit** responses. **Guide** as needed.
Listen. I can say a sentence and clap for each word. **That cat is brown.** Now say that sentence by yourselves, and clap for each word. *That cat is brown.*

Direct students to clap one time for two-syllable words.
Let's try a new one. Listen. **That boy is jumping.** Now say that sentence by yourselves, and clap for each word. *That boy is jumping.*

Here's another one. Listen. **That dog is eating.** Your turn. *That dog is eating.*

(Continue the activity with the following sentences.
I see a rock; I see a window; I see a flag; The man went fishing; The girl was sleeping; The fish was swimming; The woman is pretty; My dog likes running; My friend is happy; Horses like to run; Children like to play; Teachers like to read; My wagon is red; My oven is on; My music is loud.)

Activity 2 Rhyme Recognition

Emphasize italicized words. **Elicit** responses. **Guide** as needed.
Here is a new poem.

One potato, two potato, three potato, *four*.
Five potato, six potato, seven potato, *more*.

Now we're going to learn the poem together.
My turn. One potato, two potato, three potato, *four*.
Say it with me. *One potato, two potato, three potato, four.*
Your turn. *One potato, two potato, three potato, four.*

My turn. Five potato, six potato, seven potato, *more*.
Say it with me. *Five potato, six potato, seven potato, more.*
Your turn. *Five potato, six potato, seven potato, more.*

Now let's try to say the whole poem.
My turn. One potato, two potato, three potato, *four.*
Five potato, six potato, seven potato, *more.*
Say it with me. *One potato, two potato, three potato, four.*
Five potato, six potato, seven potato, more.
Your turn. *One potato, two potato, three potato, four.*
Five potato, six potato, seven potato, more.

Part B: Letter Recognition and Formation

To be started in Lesson 11.

Part C: Comprehension Strategies

14 minutes

Teacher Materials:
Reading *Teacher Presentation Book A*

Activity 1 Build Listening Comprehension

Elicit responses to questions. **Guide** as needed.
Today you'll hear a story. You'll need to listen big as I read the story. As I read, I want you to think about what I'm reading. What should you be doing when I'm reading the story? (Idea: *Thinking about the story.*)

During the story, I'll ask questions to see whether you understand what I'm reading. What will I ask as I read the story to you? *Questions.*

Later in today's lesson, you'll see a picture about the story. We'll talk more about the story when you see this picture. What will you see later in today's lesson? (Idea: *The picture from the story.*) Are you ready to get started?

The title of the story is "A Day at the Lake." What's the title of the story? *A Day at the Lake.*

It was summer, and the Smith family wanted to take their boat out on the lake. Thursday would be the nicest day of the week, so Mr. Smith took the day off work. The family packed up their car and attached their boat. Then Mr. Smith made a **delicious** picnic lunch, and they drove to the lake for the day. **Delicious** is **when something tastes really good.**

1. What day of the week did the Smith family go on their picnic? *Thursday.*

2. What did the Smith family attach to their car and take to the lake? *Their boat.*

3. What kind of lunch did Mr. Smith make? *A delicious picnic lunch.*

When they reached the lake, the family put their boat in the water and unloaded their car. The family quickly got in the boat and went for a boat ride. The sun was warm, and the cool water splashed on their faces. The boat ride was really fun. After a long ride, the family was getting hungry, so they headed back for lunch.

Lesson 3   **9**

1. The Smith family took what kind of ride? *Boat ride.*

2. How was the boat ride? *Really fun.*

Mr. Smith had packed a **delicious** lunch of turkey sandwiches, grapes, and carrots. He also packed some chocolate chip cookies for dessert. After lunch, the children asked to go on one more boat ride before heading home. They all got back in the boat and took a quick spin around the lake. Then they took the boat out of the water, packed up, and drove home. They had a really nice day. The Smith family was excited for their next trip to the lake.

1. What did the family eat for lunch? (Idea: *Sandwiches, grapes, and carrots.*)

2. What did they have for dessert? *Chocolate chip cookies.*

3. What did the children ask to do after lunch? (Idea: *Go on one more boat ride.*)

You learned a new word in the story today. **Delicious** means **when something tastes really good.** What does **delicious** mean? *When something tastes really good.*

Activity 2 Review Vocabulary Word

Elicit responses to questions. **Guide** as needed.
Delicious means **when something tastes really good.**
What does **delicious** mean? *When something tastes really good.*
What's another word for **when something tastes really good?** *Delicious.*

Activity 3 Story Extension

3 minutes

Activity 3, to be completed <u>after</u> the picture in Lesson 3 is shown to students.

 Show picture from Lesson 3, page 19, in *Teacher Presentation Book A*.

Elicit responses to questions. **Guide** as needed.
Listen as I ask you some questions about the story we read earlier and the picture you see now.

What is the family doing? (Student response.)

Who do you think is driving the boat? (Student response.)

Do you think the family is having fun? Why do you think so? (Student response.)

Does the mom like riding in the boat? How do you know? (Student response.)

Do you know anyone who owns a boat? Have you ever gone on a boat ride? (Student response.)

Lesson 4

Materials
Teacher: Reading *Teacher Presentation Book A*
Student:

6 minutes

Part A: Phonemic and Phonological Awareness

Activity 1 Word Segmentation: Multi-syllabic Words in all positions; Three-, Four-, and Five-Word Sentences

Elicit responses. **Guide** as needed.
Today we're going to clap for each word in a sentence. Listen carefully because some sentences will be long and some sentences will be short. Remember to clap only one time for each word.
State sentence. **Have** students respond with the sentence and correct clapping.

(Continue the activity with the following sentences.
We went to the store; We went home; My friend is funny; We ran; He likes to fish; We like to watch movies; She is under the bed; She likes milk; Monkeys like to swing high; That is mine; That boy is very smart; Where are you?; Where did you go?; My sister likes to sing; My cat is sleeping.)

Activity 2 Rhyme Recognition

Emphasize italicized words. **Elicit** responses. **Guide** as needed.
Let's practice the poem we learned in the last lesson.

One potato, two potato, three potato, *four*.
Five potato, six potato, seven potato, *more*.

Listen as I say the poem again. See if you can hear which words rhyme.
One potato, two potato, three potato, *four*.
Five potato, six potato, seven potato, *more*.
Discuss the rhyming words and why they rhyme.

Part B: Letter Recognition and Formation

To be started in Lesson 11.

Lesson 4   11

14 minutes

Teacher Materials:
Reading *Teacher Presentation Book A*

Part C: Comprehension Strategies

Activity 1 Build Listening Comprehension

Elicit responses to questions. **Guide** as needed.

Today you'll hear a story. You'll need to listen big as I read the story. As I read, I want you to think about what I'm reading. What should you be doing when I'm reading the story? (Idea: *Thinking about the story.*)

During the story, I'll ask questions to see whether you understand what I'm reading. What will I ask as I read the story to you? *Questions.*

Later in today's lesson, you'll see a picture about the story. We'll talk more about the story when you see this picture. What will you see later in today's lesson? (Idea: *The picture from the story.*) Are you ready to get started?

The title of the story is "Hamburgers." What's the title of the story? *Hamburgers.*

Mario and Sasha are brother and sister. They spend a lot of time together, but they don't always like to do the same things. Mario likes to play basketball and write short stories. Sasha likes to swing and play with her kitten named Buttons. But when it comes to food, they have a lot of **similar** tastes. Things that are **similar** are **almost the same.**

1. Mario and Sasha love almost the same kinds of food. What's another word for **almost the same?** *Similar.*

2. What does Mario like to do? *Play basketball and write short stories.*

Mario and Sasha both love big juicy hamburgers with lots of ketchup. Mario even puts extra ketchup on his plate for dipping. They both love thick chocolate milkshakes as well. Whenever their parents take them out to dinner at a restaurant, they always order the same thing—a big juicy hamburger and a chocolate milkshake. Of course, Mario always gets extra ketchup for dipping. They always smile at each other as they enjoy their burgers. If their parents let them, they would eat hamburgers every day!

1. What is Mario and Sasha's favorite food? *Hamburgers.*

2. What do they like on their hamburgers? *Extra ketchup.*

3. What would they eat every day if they could? *Hamburgers.*

12   Lesson 4

Mario and Sasha's parents are glad they enjoy **similar** foods because it makes it easier to plan meals. Someday their tastes might change and hamburgers will not be their favorite food, but for now their favorite food is definitely a hamburger.

1. Why are Mario and Sasha's parents glad they like **similar** foods? (Idea: *It makes it easier to plan meals.*)

2. Do you have a favorite food? Would you like to eat it every day? (Student response.)

You learned a new word in the story today. **Similar** means **almost the same.** What does **similar** mean? *Almost the same.*

Activity 2 Review Vocabulary Word

Elicit responses to questions. **Guide** as needed.
What does **similar** mean? *Almost the same.*
What's another word for **almost the same?** *Similar.*

Activity 3 Story Extension

Activity 3, to be completed <u>after</u> the picture in Lesson 4 is shown to students.

 Show picture from Lesson 4, page 25, in *Teacher Presentation Book A.*

Elicit responses to questions. **Guide** as needed.
Listen as I ask you some questions about the story we read earlier and the picture you see now.

Which person is Mario? (Student response.)

Which is Sasha? (Student response.)

What are they doing? (Student response.)

How are Mario and Sasha almost alike in the picture? How are they different? (Student response.)

Do you like hamburgers? Do you like ketchup on your hamburger? (Student response.)

Lesson 5

Materials

Teacher: Reading *Teacher Presentation Book A;* 1-Phonemic Awareness; 5 manipulatives such as blocks, discs, chips, counters (if not using IWB)

Student: Copy of 1-Phonemic Awareness; 5 manipulatives such as blocks, discs, chips, counters

6 minutes

Teacher Materials:
Phonemic Awareness

5 manipulatives

Student Materials:
Phonemic Awareness

5 manipulatives

Part A: Phonemic and Phonological Awareness

Activity 1 Word Segmentation: Multi-syllabic Words; Three-, Four-, and Five-Word Sentences

Show Phonemic Awareness. **Elicit** responses. **Guide** as needed.
For each word in the sentence, we'll push one chip up to the arrow. I'll show you how to do the first one.

Model use of the chips by moving the chips to the arrow for each word and then back to the bottom when finished.
Listen. I can say a sentence and move a chip for each word. **We run.** Say that sentence with me, and move a chip for each word. *We run.*

Let's move our chips back to the bottom so that you can try it by yourselves. Say that sentence by yourselves, and move a chip for each word. *We run.*
Direct students to move one chip for each word in the sentence to the arrow. **Guide** chip placement as needed.

Move your chips back to the bottom, and try another one.
Remind students to move chips back to the bottom of page between sentences.

Continue the activity with the following sentences. **Fade** model of chip movement if students are performing well.
(We eat; We eat cake; They are happy; He likes ice cream; She likes apples; We found a cat; We are very tired; My teacher reads books; My dog is black.)

Let's count how many words are in that last sentence. Count the chips with me. *One, two, three, four.* Yes, there are four words in the sentence **My dog is black.** Let's go back and try a few of the sentences again. This time, let's count the number of words before we move our chips back to the bottom.
Direct students to leave a chip for the last sentence on the arrow. **Direct** students to count the chips moved for each word before moving the chips back to the bottom.

Activity 2 Rhyme Recognition

Emphasize italicized words. **Elicit** responses. **Guide** as needed.
Here is a new poem.

Baa, baa, black sheep, have you any *wool?*
Yes sir, yes sir, three bags *full.*

We're going to learn the poem together.
My turn. Baa, baa, black sheep, have you any *wool?*
Say it with me. *Baa, baa, black sheep, have you any wool?*
Your turn. *Baa, baa, black sheep, have you any wool?*

My turn. Yes sir, yes sir, three bags *full.*
Say it with me. *Yes sir, yes sir, three bags full.*
Your turn. *Yes sir, yes sir, three bags full.*

Let's try the whole poem.
My turn. Baa, baa, black sheep, have you any *wool?*
Yes sir, yes sir, three bags *full.*

Say it with me. *Baa, baa, black sheep, have you any wool?*
Yes sir, yes sir, three bags full.

Your turn. *Baa, baa, black sheep, have you any wool?*
Yes sir, yes sir, three bags full.

Let's try the poem again. See if you can tell me the words that rhyme.
Baa, baa, black sheep, have you any *wool?*
Yes sir, yes sir, three bags *full.*
Discuss rhyming words and why they rhyme.

Part B: Letter Recognition and Formation

To be started in Lesson 11.

14 minutes

Teacher Materials:
Reading *Teacher Presentation Book A*

Part C: Comprehension Strategies

Activity 1 Build Listening Comprehension

Elicit responses to questions. **Guide** as needed.
Today you'll hear a story. You'll need to listen big as I read the story. As I read, I want you to think about what I'm reading. What should you be doing when I'm reading the story? (Idea: *Thinking about the story.*)

During the story, I'll ask questions to see whether you understand what I'm reading. What will I ask as I read the story to you? *Questions.*

Later in today's lesson, you'll see a picture about the story. We'll talk more about the story when you see this picture. What will you see later in today's lesson? (Idea: *The picture from the story.*) Are you ready to get started?

The title of the story is "A Favorite Television Show." What's the title of the story? *A Favorite Television Show.*

We all watch television sometimes. There are many different kinds of shows on television. There are news programs, family shows, nature shows, and cartoons. Some shows you can watch while coloring in a coloring book or playing a board game. Some shows you need to **concentrate** on. When you **concentrate,** you **give all your attention to one thing.**

Lesson 5   **15**

1. What are some different kinds of shows on television? (Ideas: *News programs, family shows, nature shows, and cartoons.*)

2. What does it mean to **concentrate?** *Give all your attention to one thing.*

When you want to **concentrate** on something, it is best to have it quiet around you. For example, if you wanted to watch your favorite cowboy show, it wouldn't be a good idea to watch it with someone who doesn't like cowboy shows. They might want to talk or do other things during the show. But, if you had a friend who enjoyed cowboy shows as much as you, it would be fun to watch the show together. Your friend would probably want to **concentrate** on the cowboy show, too. When the show was over, you could both pretend to be cowboys and act out your favorite parts.

1. How should it sound around you when you **concentrate?** *Quiet.*

2. What kind of show did this story talk about in which you could pretend and act out your favorite parts? *A cowboy show.*

Sometimes it's hard to **concentrate,** but when you give your full attention to something, you'll learn a lot.

1. What happens when you **concentrate?** *You learn a lot.*

You learned a new word in the story today. **Concentrate** means **give all your attention to one thing.** What does **give all your attention to one thing** mean? *Concentrate.*

Activity 2 Review Vocabulary Word

Elicit responses to questions. **Guide** as needed.
Concentrate means **give all your attention to one thing.**
What does **concentrate** mean? *Give all your attention to one thing.*
What's another word for **give all your attention to one thing?** *Concentrate.*

Activity 3 Story Extension

 Show picture from Lesson 5, page 30, in *Teacher Presentation Book A*.

Elicit responses to questions. **Guide** as needed.
Listen as I ask you some questions about the story we read earlier and the picture you see now.

What are the children doing? (Student response.)

What kind of show are they watching? (Student response.)

What is your favorite television show? (Student response.)

Why isn't it good to have a lot of noise around you when you are trying to concentrate? (Idea: *Because it's hard to give all your attention to one thing.*)

3 minutes

Activity 3, to be completed <u>after</u> the picture in Lesson 5 is shown to students.

5 minutes

Part D: Vocabulary Strategies

Activity 1 Distinguish Shades of Meaning

Today we'll work with words and learn about how they are different. Tell me how these words are somewhat different. [**pass** and **throw**; **concentrate** and **think**]

Model acting out what a particular verb means. **Assign** student partners. **Have** students act out what the verb means with a partner. **Guide** students as needed. **Repeat** sequence for each word.

Lesson 5   **17**

Lesson 6

Materials

Teacher: Reading *Teacher Presentation Book A*; 1-Phonemic Awareness; 5 manipulatives such as blocks, discs, chips, counters (if not using IWB)

Student: Copy of 1-Phonemic Awareness; 5 manipulatives such as blocks, discs, chips, counters

6 minutes

Teacher Materials:
Phonemic Awareness

5 manipulatives

Student Materials:
Phonemic Awareness

5 manipulatives

Part A: Phonemic and Phonological Awareness

Activity 1 Word Segmentation: Multi-syllabic Words; Three-, Four-, and Five-Word Sentences

Show Phonemic Awareness. **Elicit** responses. **Guide** as needed.
In our last lesson, we used chips to show words in a sentence. Today we're going to try that again. We can also count our chips to find out how many words are in each sentence. Some of our sentences will be long, and some will be short. We have to listen carefully. Remember, for each word in the sentence, we'll push one chip up to the arrow on the page.

Model use of the chips by moving the chips to the arrow for each word. **Guide** chip placement and state how many chips were moved as needed.
Listen. I can say a sentence and move a chip for each word. **Ann likes to read.** Say that sentence with me, and move a chip for each word. *Ann likes to read.* Let's count our chips. *One, two, three, four.* How many words are in that sentence? *Four.*

Yes, four words. Let's move our chips back to the bottom so you can try it by yourselves. Say that sentence by yourselves, and move a chip for each word. *Ann likes to read.*

Let's move our chips back to the bottom and try another sentence.

Continue the activity with the following sentences. **Fade** model of chip placement when students are performing well.
(We like to eat fish; Do you like corn?; John eats fruit for lunch; That is a tall tree; I use a pencil; I have a green cup; Please close the door; Are you sick?; I am touching my nose; Flowers are pretty.)

Activity 2 Rhyme Recognition

Emphasize italicized words. **Have** students identify words that rhyme.
Here is a new poem.

Hickory, dickory, *dock.*
The mouse ran up the *clock.*
The clock struck one.
The mouse ran down.
Hickory, dickory, *dock.*

18   Lesson 6

Activity 3 | Syllable Blending

Elicit responses. **Guide** as needed.
Today we're going to try a new activity. I'm going to tell you two smaller words that make up a big word called a compound word. After I tell you the two words, tell me the big word.

Watch me try the first one.

Model making fists; turn your hands palm-side up in front of you; say the first word and then open your right hand; say the second word and then open your left hand; put both hands together and then say whole word.
Listen. My turn. Mail. Box. Mailbox. Let's try it together. Mail. Box. Put it together. *Mailbox.* Try it by yourselves. Mail. Box. Put it together. *Mailbox.*

Let's try making more big words. Listen. Butter. Fly. Put it together. Butterfly.

Your turn. Butter. Fly. Put it together. *Butterfly.*

(Continue the activity with the following words.
sidewalk, snowman, chalkboard, baseball.)

Part B: Letter Recognition and Formation

To be started in Lesson 11.

Part C: Comprehension Strategies

14 minutes

Teacher Materials:
Reading *Teacher Presentation Book A*

Activity 1 | Listening Comprehension—A During-Reading Strategy

Elicit responses to questions. **Guide** as needed.
Today, you'll hear a story. You'll need to listen big as I read the story. As I read, I want you to think about what I'm reading. What should you be doing when I'm reading the story? Idea: *Think about the story.*

During the story, I'll ask questions to see if you understand what I'm reading. What will I ask as I read the story to you? *Questions.*

Later in today's lesson, you'll see a picture about the story. We'll talk more about the story when you see this picture. What will you see later in today's lesson? Idea: *The picture from the story.*

The title of the story is, "Hungry Jerome." What's the title of the story? *Hungry Jerome.*

Read the story with prosody.
It was Saturday morning and Jerome's mother was going to make pancakes for breakfast. When she went to the refrigerator she discovered she was out of milk. Jerome's family lived across the street from the store, so Jerome's mother asked him if he would go to the store and buy some milk for her. She gave Jerome the exact amount of money he would need to buy the milk. Jerome was very hungry for those pancakes so he agreed to go.

Lesson 6   19

1. What was Jerome's mother going to make for breakfast? *Pancakes.*

2. Jerome's family lived across the street from what building? *The store.*

Jerome went to the store and got the milk. While he was waiting in line to pay for it, he saw some delicious candy bars next to the cash register. Jerome was so hungry that all he could think about was eating the candy bars, but he knew he didn't have the money to pay for them. Jerome decided to take a candy bar without paying for it and ran out of the store, leaving the milk on the floor next to the candy bars. He was a **thief**. A **thief** is **a person who takes something without paying for it.**

1. What did Jerome take from the store? *A candy bar.*

2. What is a thief? *A person who takes something without paying for it.*

As Jerome ran for the exit, the store clerk yelled out to the police officer who was standing in front of the store. The police officer chased Jerome and caught him. Jerome had to return the candy bar, and he agreed to sweep the floors in the store every Saturday for a month to make up for his mistake. Jerome promised his mother, the store clerk, and the police officer that he had learned his lesson and would never be a **thief** again.

1. Who chased Jerome? *A policeman.*

2. What did Jerome have to do to make up for his mistake? Idea: *Sweep the floors in the store every Saturday for a month.*

You learned a new word in the story today. **Thief. A thief** is **a person who takes something without paying for it.** What is a **thief?** *A person who takes something without paying for it.*

What's another word for **a person who takes something without paying for it?** *Thief.*

Activity 2 Story Recall—An After-Reading Strategy

3 minutes

Activity 2 to be completed <u>after</u> the picture in Lesson 6 is shown to students.

 Show picture from Lesson 6, page 36, in *Teacher Presentation Book A*.

Elicit responses to questions. **Guide** as needed.
Listen as I ask you some questions about the story we read earlier and the picture you see now.

Who's running? *Jerome.*

Why is the policeman running after Jerome? Idea: *He stole a candy bar from the store.*

Why shouldn't you take something from the store without paying for it? Idea: *You can get into trouble; it makes the store lose money.*

Lesson 6

Lesson 7

Materials

Teacher: Reading *Teacher Presentation Book A;* 1-Phonemic Awareness; 5 manipulatives such as blocks, discs, chips, counters (if not using IWB)

Student: Copy of 1-Phonemic Awareness; 5 manipulatives such as blocks, discs, chips, counters

6 minutes

Teacher Materials:
Phonemic Awareness

5 manipulatives

Student Materials:
Phonemic Awareness

5 manipulatives

Part A: Phonemic and Phonological Awareness

Activity 1 Word Segmentation: Multi-syllabic Words; Three-, Four-, and Five-Word Sentences

Show Phonemic Awareness. **Elicit** responses. **Guide** as needed.
You're getting very good at counting the words in a sentence. Don't let me fool you today. Listen carefully to each sentence. Remember, for each word in the sentence, we'll push one chip up to the arrow on the page.

Model use of the chips by moving the chips to the arrow for each word. **Guide** chip placement and state how many chips were moved as needed.
Listen. I can say a sentence and move a chip for each word. **We went to the movies.** Say that sentence by yourselves, and move a chip for each word. *We went to the movies.*

Move your chips back, and let's try some more sentences.

Continue the activity with the following sentences. **Fade** model of chip placement when students are performing well.
(Is it raining today?; My friend is very kind; He cooked dinner; How old are you?; I am mad; Where is the yellow pencil?; We listen to our teacher; My arm hurts; I am touching my toes; Trees have leaves.)

Activity 2 Rhyme Recognition

Emphasize italicized words. **Guide** as needed. **Have** students identify words that rhyme.
Here's a new poem.

Hey diddle *diddle,* the cat and the *fiddle,*
The cow jumped over the *moon.*
The little dog laughed to see such fun
And the dish ran away with the *spoon.*

Activity 3 Syllable Blending

Elicit responses. **Guide** as needed.
In our last lesson, we worked on putting two smaller words together to make a big word called a compound word. Let's try some more of those.

Watch me try the first one.

Lesson 7   21

Model making fists; turn your hands palm-side up in front of you; say the first word and then open your right hand; say the second word and then open your left hand; put both hands together and then say whole word.

Listen. My turn. Foot. Print. Footprint. Try it by yourselves. Foot. Print. Put it together. *Footprint.*

Let's try making more big words. Listen. Space. Ship. Put it together. *Spaceship.*

Your turn. Space. Ship. Put it together. *Spaceship.*

(Continue the activity with the following words.
raincoat, popcorn, cupcake, teapot, pancake, bubblegum.)

Part B: Letter Recognition and Formation

To be started in Lesson 11.

Part C: Comprehension Strategies

14 minutes

Teacher Materials:
Reading *Teacher Presentation Book A*

Activity 1 Build Listening Comprehension

Elicit responses to questions. **Guide** as needed.
Today you'll hear a story. You'll need to listen big as I read the story. As I read, I want you to think about what I'm reading. What should you be doing when I'm reading the story? (Idea: *Thinking about the story.*)

During the story, I'll ask questions to see whether you understand what I'm reading. What will I ask as I read the story to you? *Questions.*

Later in today's lesson, you'll see a picture about the story. We'll talk more about the story when you see this picture. What will you see later in today's lesson? (Idea: *The picture from the story.*) Are you ready to get started?

The title of the story is "Proud Jonathon." What's the title of the story? *Proud Jonathon.*

Jonathon was growing up and decided it was time to get rid of the training wheels on his bike. His older brother offered to let him try and ride his old two-wheeler, but Jonathon knew it was too big. Jonathon decided to earn some money so he could buy a two-wheeler bike of his own. Jonathon began by doing extra chores around the house. Jonathon would dust and clean up his room. He was very **proud** when he got paid for the work he had done. When you're **proud,** you **are pleased with yourself.**

1. What did Jonathon want to get rid of? (Idea: *The training wheels on his bike.*)

2. Why didn't Jonathon want his brother's bike? *It was too big.*

3. How did Jonathon feel when he got paid for cleaning his room? *Proud.*

22   Lesson 7

Jonathon still needed more money, so he set up a lemonade stand. He earned several dollars a day, but he was getting tired of sitting at the stand. Jonathan came up with a plan. He asked his older brother to take the training wheels off his old bike and raise the seat. The next thing you know, Jonathon was riding his own two-wheeler. Wow, did he feel **proud!**

1. Besides his chores, what did Jonathon do to earn money? *He set up a lemonade stand.*

2. Who took the training wheels off of Jonathon's bike? *His older brother.*

3. How did Jonathon feel riding his two-wheeler? *Proud.*

Jonathon continued to do his chores to earn money. Jonathon had a bike that worked for him now, but he knew that one day he would outgrow it. Jonathon was very **proud** of the work he was doing and the choices he had made.

1. What did Jonathon earn by doing his chores? *Money.*

2. Who was pleased with himself in this story? *Jonathon.*

You learned a new word in the story today. **Proud** means **pleased with yourself.** What does **pleased with yourself** mean? *Proud.*

Activity 2 Review Vocabulary Word

Elicit responses to questions. **Guide** as needed.
Proud means **pleased with yourself.**
What does **proud** mean? *Pleased with yourself.*
What's another word for **pleased with yourself?** *Proud.*

Activity 3 Story Extension

Show picture from Lesson 7, page 43, in *Teacher Presentation Book A.*

Elicit responses to questions. **Guide** as needed.
Listen as I ask you some questions about the story we read earlier and the picture you see now.

What is Jonathon putting in his pocket? (Student response.)

How did he get the money? (Student response.)

Why did Jonathon continue to do his chores to earn money? (Student response.)

Do you know someone who has a two-wheeler or a bike with training wheels? (Student response.)

What are you proud of doing or learning? (Student response.)

3 minutes

Activity 3, to be completed <u>after</u> the picture in Lesson 7 is shown to students.

Lesson 8

Materials
Teacher: Reading *Teacher Presentation Book A*; 1-Phonemic Awareness; 5 manipulatives such as blocks, discs, chips, counters (if not using the IWB)
Student: Copy of 1-Phonemic Awareness; 5 manipulatives such as blocks, discs, chips, counters

6 minutes

Teacher Materials:
Phonemic Awareness
5 manipulatives

Student Materials:
Phonemic Awareness
5 manipulatives

Part A: Phonemic and Phonological Awareness

Activity 1 Word Segmentation: Three-Word Sentences

Show Phonemic Awareness. **Elicit** responses. **Guide** as needed.
Today we're going to try something new. You have been working with words and sentences for several lessons. Now we're going to find the *first* and *last* words in a sentence. We'll start by finding the *first* word in a sentence.

Model use of the chips by moving the chips to the arrow for each word. **Guide** chip placement and state how many chips were moved as needed. **Speak** clearly so students hear each word as single unit.
Listen. My turn. I can say a sentence and tell you the *first* word in that sentence. **I like chips.** The *first* word is **I.** Your turn. Listen to the sentence. **I like chips.** Say that sentence. *I like chips.*

What is the *first* word in that sentence? *I.*

Yes, **I** is the *first* word in that sentence.

Let's try another one. **She likes apples.** Say that sentence. *She likes apples.*

What is the *first* word in that sentence? *She.*

Yes, **she** is the *first* word in that sentence.

Continue the activity with the following sentences. **Fade** model when students are performing well.
(He is funny; We are reading; They went home; Dogs like bones; I like to swim.)

Discuss with students that the chips on the arrow represent words; the first chip represents the first word; the last chip represents the last word.
Now we're going to find the *last* word in a sentence. Listen. My turn. I can say a sentence and tell you the *last* word in that sentence. **I like cats.** The last word is **cats.** Your turn. Listen to the sentence. **I like cats.** Say that sentence. *I like cats.*

What is the *last* word in that sentence? *Cats.*

Yes, **cats** is the *last* word in that sentence.

Let's try another one. **She likes apples.** Say that sentence. *She likes apples.*

What is the *last* word in that sentence? *Apples.*

Yes, **apples** is the *last* word in that sentence.

(Continue the activity with the following sentences:
He went swimming; We can write; They played ball; Cats chase mice; I like to dance.)

Activity 2 Rhyme Recognition

Emphasize words in bold. **Elicit** responses.

Today we're going to listen for words that rhyme. I'll tell you two words. If they rhyme, give me a thumbs-up. If they don't rhyme, don't do anything. Show me what you will do if the two words rhyme. Now show me what you will do if the two words *don't* rhyme. Let's try one for practice.

My turn. Ran. Fan. I put my thumbs up because **ran** and **fan** rhyme. My turn again. Can. Sick. I didn't do anything because **can** and **sick** *do not* rhyme.

Guide thumb movement as needed.
Your turn. Ran. Fan. You're right; **ran** and **fan** rhyme, so you put your thumbs up. Your turn again. Can. Sick. That's right; you don't do anything because **can** and **sick** *do not* rhyme.

(**Continue** the activity with the following pairs of words:

Cat, mat.	Bat, sat.
Hat, dog.	Sit, hit.
Pit, kit.	Fit, ham.
See, bee.	Me, up.
We, key.	Hot, not.
Pot, dot.	Got, feed.)

Activity 3 Syllable Blending

Elicit responses. **Guide** as needed.
You're showing smart thinking by putting two smaller words together to make a big word. Do you remember what that big word is called?
Compound word.

Yes, a compound word. Let's make some more compound words.

Model making fists; turn your hands palm-side up in front of you; say the first word and then open your right hand; say the second word and then open your left hand; put both hands together and then say whole word.
Listen. My turn. Grape. Fruit. Grapefruit. Your turn. Grape. Fruit. Put it together. *Grapefruit.*

Let's try making more big words or compound words. Listen. Sun. Flower. Put it together. *Sunflower.*

Your turn. Sun. Flower. Put it together. *Sunflower.*

(**Continue** the activity with the following words:
doughnut, basketball, peanut, triangle, sailboat, toothbrush, motorcycle.)

Lesson 8   **25**

Part B: Letter Recognition and Formation

To be started in Lesson 11.

Part C: Comprehension Strategies

14 minutes

Teacher Materials:
Reading *Teacher Presentation Book A*

Activity 1 Build Listening Comprehension

Elicit responses to questions. **Guide** as needed.

Today you'll hear a story. You'll need to listen big as I read the story. As I read, I want you to think about what I'm reading. What should you be doing when I'm reading the story? (Idea: *Thinking about the story.*)

During the story, I'll ask questions to see whether you understand what I'm reading. What will I ask as I read the story to you? *Questions.*

Later in today's lesson, you'll see a picture about the story. We'll talk more about the story when you see this picture. What will you see later in today's lesson? (Idea: *The picture from the story.*) Are you ready to get started?

The title of the story is "Our Kindergarten Teacher." What's the title of the story? *Our Kindergarten Teacher.*

We were all back at school after a long three-day weekend. Monday was a holiday, so we had the day off. Ms. Sanchez was having a hard time getting our class to **focus.** When you **focus, you give your attention to something.** She was reviewing letters and letter sounds. We started with the letter "A." Joey kept squirming and Katie kept yelling out answers without being called on. Oops!

1. What was Ms. Sanchez having a hard time getting the children to do? *Focus and pay attention.*

2. What letter was Ms. Sanchez reviewing? *A.*

3. Was everyone giving Ms. Sanchez their attention? *No.*

Then Ms. Sanchez told us she had a surprise. She told us that if we would **focus** on what she was teaching us by giving her all of our attention, she would give us an extra five minutes at recess. Wow! Well, this got our attention. Five extra minutes at recess would be great. After that, the entire class sat up straight and listened very carefully to what she was teaching. We all responded when she asked, and nobody talked unless they were called on.

1. Who had a surprise for the children? *Ms. Sanchez.*

2. What did the children need to do to get a longer recess? *Focus.*

3. How many extra minutes did she promise the children? *Five.*

26   Lesson 8

Ms. Sanchez was very happy with the class. She said, "I knew you all could **focus** on my lesson." She made sure to give us the extra five minutes at recess. When we came back in, we all gave her our complete attention. We wanted to earn another extra long recess. I'm sure you would do the same, wouldn't you?

1. What did Ms. Sanchez tell the children she knew they could do? *Focus.*

2. Why were the children so good when they came in from recess? (**Idea:** *They wanted another long recess.*)

You learned a new word in the story today. **Focus** means **give your attention to something.** What does **give your attention to something** mean? *Focus.*

Activity 2 Review Vocabulary Word

Elicit responses to questions. **Guide** as needed.
Focus means **give your attention to something.**
What does **focus** mean? *Give your attention to something.*
What's another word for **give your attention to something**? *Focus.*

Activity 3 Story Extension

Show picture from Lesson 8, page 49, in *Teacher Presentation Book A.*

Elicit responses to questions. **Guide** as needed.
Who do you see in the picture? (Student response.)

What letter did the students need to focus on? (Student response.)

Why is it important to focus during school? (Student response.)

What things do you focus your attention on? (Student response.)

3 minutes

Activity 3, to be completed <u>after</u> the picture in Lesson 8 is shown to students.

Lesson 8   27

Lesson 9

Materials

Teacher: Reading *Teacher Presentation Book A;* 1-Phonemic Awareness; 5 manipulatives such as blocks, discs, chips, counters (if not using the IWB)

Student: Copy of 1-Phonemic Awareness; 5 manipulatives such as blocks, discs, chips, counters

6 minutes

Teacher Materials:
Phonemic Awareness
5 manipulatives

Student Materials:
Phonemic Awareness
5 manipulatives

Part A: Phonemic and Phonological Awareness

Activity 1 Word Segmentation: Three-, Four-, and Five-Word Sentences

Show 1-Phonemic Awareness. **Elicit** responses. **Guide** as needed.
We're going to work on finding the *first* and *last* words of a sentence. We'll start with finding the *first* word in a sentence. Then you can tell me the *last* word in a sentence. Some sentences will be short, and others will be long.

Model use of the chips by moving the chips to the arrow for each word. **Guide** chip placement and state how many chips were moved as needed. **Speak** clearly so students hear each word as single unit.
Listen. My turn. I can say a sentence and tell you the *first* word in that sentence. **That cat is hungry.** The *first* word is **that.** Your turn. Listen to the sentence. **That cat is hungry.** Say that sentence. *That cat is hungry.*

What is the *first* word in that sentence? *That.*

Yes, **that** is the *first* word in that sentence.

Let's try another one. **He likes grapes and oranges.** Say that sentence. *He likes grapes and oranges.*

What is the *first* word in that sentence? *He.*

Yes, **he** is the *first* word in that sentence.

Continue the activity with the following sentences. **Fade** model when students are performing well.
(She can read big books; We ran; They went for a ride; Birds build nests; I went for a walk.)

Discuss with students that the chips on the arrow represent words; the first chip represents the first word; the last chip represents the last word.
Now we're going to find the *last* word in a sentence. Listen. My turn. I can say a sentence and tell you the *last* word in that sentence. **That cat is hungry.** The *last* word is **hungry.** Your turn. Listen to the sentence. **That cat is hungry.** Say that sentence. *That cat is hungry.*

What is the *last* word in that sentence? *Hungry.*

Yes, **hungry** is the *last* word in that sentence.

Let's try another one. **My aunt bakes cookies.** Say that sentence. *My aunt bakes cookies.*

What is the *last* word in that sentence? *Cookies.*

Yes, **cookies** is the *last* word in that sentence.

(Continue the activity with the following sentences:
It rained outside today; We went to art class; Turtles are slow; I like to skate; Where are you?)

Activity 2 **Rhyme Recognition**

Elicit responses. **Guide** thumb movement as needed.
Let's listen for words that rhyme. I'll say two words. If they rhyme, give me a thumbs-up. If they don't rhyme, don't do anything. Show me what you'll do if the two words rhyme. Now show me what you'll do if the two words *don't* rhyme. Let's try one for practice.

Your turn. Box. Fox. You're right; **box** and **fox** rhyme, so you put your thumbs up. Your turn again. Box. Fan. That's right; you don't do anything, because **box** and **fan** *do not* rhyme.

(Continue the activity with the following pairs of words:

Say, day.	May, pay.
Hay, hog.	By, my.
Pie, pot.	Lie, tie.
Fan, man.	Ran, rip.
Pan, van.	Bet, set.
Met, let.	Pet, pan.)

Activity 3 **Syllable Blending**

Elicit responses. **Guide** as needed.
Before we try something new, let's practice putting together two smaller words to make one big word. Do you remember what that big word is called? *Compound word.*

Yes, a compound word.

Model making fists; turn your hands palm-side up in front of you; say the first word and then open your right hand; say the second word and then open your left hand; put both hands together and then say whole word.
Let's make some more compound words. Your turn. Sun. Shine. Put it together. *Sunshine.*

(Continue the activity with the following words:
starfish, watermelon, peppermint, toothpaste, newspaper, football, neighborhood.)

Part B: Letter Recognition and Formation

To be started in Lesson 11.

Lesson 9

14 minutes

Teacher Materials:
Reading *Teacher Presentation Book A*

Part C: Comprehension Strategies

Activity 1 Build Listening Comprehension

Elicit responses to questions. **Guide** as needed.
Today you'll hear a story. You'll need to listen big as I read the story. As I read, I want you to think about what I'm reading. What should you be doing when I'm reading the story? (Idea: *Thinking about the story.*)

During the story, I'll ask questions to see whether you understand what I'm reading. What will I ask as I read the story to you? *Questions.*

Later in today's lesson, you'll see a picture about the story. We'll talk more about the story when you see this picture. What will you see later in today's lesson? (Idea: *The picture from the story.*) Are you ready to get started?

The title of the story is "Football." What's the title of the story? *Football.*

Mai-Ling is a young girl who enjoys drawing, swimming, and reading. But Mai-Ling also loves football. As far back as Mai-Ling can remember, she has watched football on television with her family. In the fall, her family will sometimes go to the local stadium on Friday nights to watch the high school football games.

1. What game does Mai-Ling love? *Football.*

2. What does Mai-Ling's family sometimes go to watch? *High school football games.*

Mai-Ling and her family often go to the park on Saturday afternoons to play football for **recreation.** When you do **something to fill your free time,** it's called **recreation.** Mai-Ling likes playing the position of quarterback. She throws the football as far as she can, and her family tries to catch it. Sometimes Mai-Ling will switch and try catching the ball instead of throwing it. This is how Mai-Ling's family likes to spend their Saturday afternoons. After playing for a while, they often end up at the ice cream shop.

1. What does Mai-Ling's family like to do for **recreation?** *Play football.*

2. What position does Mai-Ling like to play? *Quarterback.*

3. When does Mai-Ling's family like to go to the park? *Saturday afternoons.*

30   Lesson 9

Mai-Ling enjoys other types of **recreation,** but football is her favorite thing to do when she has free time. Maybe one day Mai-Ling will play on her high school football team.

1. What is Mai-Ling's favorite thing to do with her free time? *Play football.*

You learned a new word in the story today. **Recreation** means **something you do in your free time.** What does **something you do in your free time** mean? *Recreation.*

Activity 2 Review Vocabulary Word

Elicit responses to questions. **Guide** as needed.
Recreation means **something you do in your free time.**
What does **recreation** mean? *Something you do in your free time.*
What's another word for **something you do in your free time?** *Recreation.*

Activity 3 Story Extention

 Show picture from Lesson 9, page 55, in *Teacher Presentation Book A.*

Elicit responses to questions. **Guide** as needed.
Listen as I ask you some questions about the story we read earlier and the picture you see now.

What is Mai-Ling doing in the picture? (Student response.)

Do you like to play football? (Student response.)

Mai-Ling likes to play football in her free time. What do you like doing for recreation? (Student response.)

3 minutes

Activity 3, to be completed <u>after</u> the picture in Lesson 9 is shown to students.

Lesson 9   **31**

Lesson 10

Materials

Teacher: Reading *Teacher Presentation Book A;* 1-Phonemic Awareness; 5 manipulatives such as blocks, discs, chips, counters (if not using IWB)

Student: Copy of 1-Phonemic Awareness; 5 manipulatives such as blocks, discs, chips, counters

6 minutes

Part A: Phonemic and Phonological Awareness

Teacher Materials:
Phonemic Awareness

5 manipulatives

Student Materials:
Phonemic Awareness

5 manipulatives

Activity 1 Word Segmentation: Three-Word Sentences

Show Phonemic Awareness. **Elicit** responses. **Guide** as needed.
Let's practice finding the *first* and *last* words in a sentence. Some sentences will be short, and others will be long. Listen carefully.

Model use of the chips by moving the chips to the arrow for each word. **Guide** chip placement and state how many chips were moved as needed.
Your turn. Listen to the sentence. **The mouse ran away.** Say that sentence. *The mouse ran away.*

What is the *first* word in that sentence? *The.*

Yes, **the** is the *first* word in that sentence.

(Continue the activity with the following sentences:
Butterflies are very beautiful; Did you finish your lunch?; Snails crawl slowly.)

Now we're going to find the *last* word in a sentence. Your turn. Listen to the sentence. **Where are you going?** Say that sentence. *Where are you going?*

What is the *last* word in that sentence? *Going.*

Yes, **going** is the *last* word in that sentence.

Continue the activity with the following sentences. **Fade** model when students are performing well.
(My dog ran away; I can draw colorful pictures; Sharks swim quickly.)

Discuss with students that the chips on the arrow represent words; the first chip represents the first word; the last chip represents the last word.
You've done so well finding the *first* and *last* words in sentences. Now we're going to find the *middle* word in a sentence.

I'll say a sentence. **We can read.** Say that sentence. *We can read.*

What is the *first* word in that sentence? *We.*

Yes, **we** is the *first* word in that sentence. Say the sentence again. *We can read.*

What is the *last* word in that sentence? *Read.*

32   Lesson 10

Yes, **read** is the *last* word in that sentence. Listen. **We can read.** I'll tell you the *middle* word in that sentence. **Can.** Your turn. Tell me the *middle* word in the sentence **We can read.** *Can.*

Yes, **can** is the *middle* word in that sentence.

Let's try another one. **He likes oranges.** Say that sentence. *He likes oranges.*

What is the *first* word in that sentence? *He.*

Yes, **he** is the *first* word in that sentence. What is the *last* word in that sentence? *Oranges.*

Yes, **oranges** is the *last* word in that sentence. Listen. **He likes oranges.** What is the *middle* word in that sentence? *Likes.*

Yes, **likes** is the *middle* word in that sentence.

(Continue the activity with the following sentences:
She reads books; They ride bikes; Cows eat grass.)

Activity 2 Rhyme Recognition

Elicit responses. **Guide** thumb movement as needed.
Let's listen for words that rhyme. I'll tell you two words. Remember, if they rhyme, give me a thumbs-up. If they don't rhyme, don't do anything. Let's find some rhymes.

Beat. Seat. (Thumbs-up.)

Meat. Heat. (Thumbs-up.)

Neat. Not. (No Thumbs-up.)

Gate. Late. (Thumbs-up.)

Wait. Bait. (Thumbs-up.)

Hate. Hot. (No Thumbs-up.)

Fill. Bill. (Thumbs-up.)

Pill. Pole. (No thumbs-up.)

Chill. Will. (Thumbs-up.)

Sock. Clock. (Thumbs-up.)

Knock. Lock. (Thumbs-up.)

Rock. Rake. (No thumbs-up.)

Lesson 10   **33**

Activity 3 Syllable Blending

Elicit responses. **Guide** as needed.
Let's practice making compound words.

Model making fists; turn your hands palm-side up in front of you; say the first word and then open your right hand; say the second word and then open your left hand; put both hands together and then say whole word.
Your turn. Side. Ways. Put it together. *Sideways.*

(Continue the activity with the following words.
toothache, highway, birthday.)

Activity 4 Syllable Blending

Elicit responses. **Guide** as needed.
Let's try making more big words. I'm going to say two word parts, and you'll put them together to say the whole word. Listen to me try one.

Model making fists; turn your hands palm-side up in front of you; say the first word and then open your right hand; say the second word and then open your left hand; put both hands together and then say whole word.
My turn. Alli gator. I can put it together. Alligator. Your turn. Alli gator. Put it together. *Alligator.*

Your turn to try one by yourselves. Listen. Gi raffe. What word? *Giraffe.*

Yes, you made the word **giraffe.** Let's try some more. Toma to. What word? *Tomato.*

Multi ply. What word? *Multiply.*

Dyna mite. What word? *Dynamite.*

Apart ment. What word? *Apartment.*

Porcu pine. What word? *Porcupine.*

Part B: Letter Recognition and Formation

To be started in Lesson 11.

Part C: Comprehension Strategies

14 minutes

Teacher Materials:
Reading *Teacher Presentation Book A*

Activity 1 Build Listening Comprehension

Elicit responses to questions. **Guide** as needed.
Today you'll hear a story. You'll need to listen big as I read the story. As I read, I want you to think about what I'm reading. What should you be doing when I'm reading the story? (Idea: *Thinking about the story.*)

During the story, I'll ask questions to see whether you understand what I'm reading. What will I ask as I read the story to you? *Questions.*

Later in today's lesson, you'll see a picture about the story. We'll talk more about the story when you see this picture. What will you see later in today's lesson? (Idea: *The picture from the story.*) Are you ready to get started?

The title of the story is "Friends." What's the title of the story? *Friends.*

Crystal and Brian are sister and brother and best **friends. Friends** are **people you like.** Best **friends** are people you like the most. Crystal and Brian go to the same school, but they are a year apart. They live on "B" street. They play together every day after school, except for Fridays, when Brian has piano lessons. Because they are **friends,** Crystal and Brian know a lot about each other.

1. What are Crystal and Brian? *Best friends.*

2. What street do they live on? *"B" street.*

3. What kind of lessons does Brian have on Fridays? *Piano.*

Brian was born with an illness that prevents him from being able to walk on his own. Brian uses a wheelchair to get around. Since Crystal is his sister and his **friend,** she helps Brian whenever she can. Sometimes she just walks alongside him while they talk about things. Other times, she'll push Brian around. Sometimes when Brian is not using his wheelchair, he lets Crystal take it for a spin. That's a lot of fun! Just because Brian cannot walk, it does not stop them from playing and doing all the things that **friends** do together.

1. What are **friends?** *People you like.*

2. What does Crystal sometimes do when Brian is not using his wheelchair? *She takes it for a spin.*

Brian and Crystal think it's great to have **friends.** It's also good to be a **friend.** Good **friends** are always there when you need them. Isn't it great to have **friends?**

1. What do Brian and Crystal think about **friends?** (Idea: *It's great to have friends* or *It's good to be a friend.*)

You learned a new word in the story today. **Friends** are **people you like.** What are **people you like** called? *Friends.*

Activity 2 Review Vocabulary Word

Elicit responses to questions. **Guide** as needed.
Friends are **people you like.**
Who are **friends?** *People you like.*
What's another word for **people you like?** *Friends.*

Lesson 10 **35**

3 minutes

Activity 3, to be completed <u>after</u> the picture in Lesson 10 is shown to students.

Activity 3 Story Extension

 Show picture from Lesson 10, page 61, in *Teacher Presentation Book A*.

Elicit responses to questions. **Guide** as needed.
Listen as I ask you some questions about the story we read earlier and the picture you see now.

What are Brian and Crystal doing in the picture? How do you know? (Student response.)

Why is it important to have friends? (Student response.)

Brian and Crystal like to play together after school. What do you like to do with your friends? (Student response.)

5 minutes

Part D: Vocabulary Strategies

Activity 1 Distinguish Shades of Meaning

Today we'll work with words and learn about how they are different. Tell me how these words are somewhat different. [**focus** and **attend**; **concentrate** and **think**]

Model acting out what a particular verb means. **Assign** student partners. **Have** students act out what the verb means with a partner. **Guide** students as needed. **Repeat** sequence for each word.

36   Lesson 10

Lesson 11

Materials
Teacher: Reading *Teacher Presentation Book A*
Student: Lined paper

5 minutes

Part A: Phonemic and Phonological Awareness

Activity 1 Word Segmentation: Three-Word Sentences

Elicit responses. **Guide** as needed.
Let's work with some sentences and find the *first, last,* and *middle* words in the sentences.

Listen to the sentence. **Clowns are funny.** Say that sentence. *Clowns are funny.*

What is the *first* word in that sentence? *Clowns.*

Yes, **clowns** is the *first* word in that sentence. Say that sentence again. *Clowns are funny.*

What is the *last* word in that sentence? *Funny.*

Yes, **funny** is the *last* word in that sentence. *Listen.* **Clowns are funny.** I'll tell you the *middle* word in that sentence. **Are.** Your turn. Tell me the *middle* word in the sentence **Clowns are funny.** *Are.*

Yes, **are** is the *middle* word in that sentence. Let's try another one. **Dogs like bones.** Say that sentence. *Dogs like bones.*

What is the *first* word in the sentence? *Dogs.*

Yes, **dogs** is the *first* word in that sentence. What is the *last* word in that sentence? *Bones.*

Yes, **bones** is the *last* word in that sentence. Listen. **Dogs like bones.** What is the *middle* word in that sentence? *Like.*

Yes, **like** is the *middle* word in that sentence.

(Continue the activity with the following sentences:
Jimmy eats bananas; Horses run fast; Birds have feathers; Where are you?)

Activity 2 Rhyme Recognition

Elicit responses. **Guide** thumb movement as needed.
Let's listen for words that rhyme. I'll tell you two words. Remember, if they rhyme, give me a thumbs-up. If they don't rhyme, don't do anything. Let's find some rhymes.

Lesson 11   37

Row. Grow. (Thumbs-up.)

Crow. Know. (Thumbs-up.)

Toe. Tote. (No thumbs-up.)

Ray. May. (Thumbs-up.)

Gray. Tray. (Thumbs-up.)

Bay. Bake. (No thumbs-up.)

Cake. Make. (Thumbs-up.)

Take. Tame. (No thumbs-up.)

Flake. Wake. (Thumbs-up.)

Cheese. Please. (Thumbs-up.)

Tease. Team. (No thumbs-up.)

Peas. Keys. (Thumbs-up.)

Part B: Letter Recognition and Formation

6 minutes

Student Materials:
Lined paper

Activity 1 Letter Recognition—a

Elicit responses to questions. **Guide** as needed.
Besides learning the letter sounds, you'll also learn the letter names. Learning the letter names will make you smarter when it comes to spelling and writing words. It also helps when you learn to read.

Remember that every letter has a name. Did you know that every letter can be written in two ways? You'll learn both ways of writing each letter of the alphabet this year in kindergarten. Wow, will you be smart when you go to first grade!

Write a on the board. **Point** to a.
Every letter has a name.
The name of this letter is **a.** What letter name? *a.*
Again, what letter name? *a.*
Review as needed.

Activity 2 Letter Formation—a

Now we're going to practice writing **a.** When you practice writing, you'll learn not only where to start and stop the letter but also which way to move your hand when you're making the letter. It's tricky, but you're so smart you'll learn how to write **a** very quickly. Watch.

Here's how you write **a** in the air.
Model a formation in the air (with your back to students).

38   Lesson 11

Watch again.

Now let's practice writing **a** in the air. Hold up your writing hand, and make **a** in the air.
Guide students as they write a in the air.

Let's practice **a** again.

Here's how to write **a** with your writing hand pointer finger.
Model a formation on the board with your finger (with your back to students).

Watch again.

Now let's practice writing **a** on your table without using your pencil. Use your writing hand pointer finger, and make **a** on your table.
Guide students as they write a on their table or desktop.

Let's practice **a** again.

Remember that every letter has a name.

Model writing a on the board (with your back to students).
You learned the name of this letter is **a.**
What letter name? *a.*

Again, what letter name? *a.*

Provide lined paper to students.
Now let's practice writing **a** with your pencil.
Guide students as they write a on their paper. **Review** as needed.

 Link letter names to letter sounds as needed as they appear in the program.

Set up a writing center with writing materials and correct models of letters learned so far for students to use in their free time.

Part C: Comprehension Strategies

 9 minutes

Teacher Materials:
Reading *Teacher Presentation Book A*

Activity 1 Build Listening Comprehension

Elicit responses to questions. **Guide** as needed.
Today you'll hear a new story. What should you be doing when I'm reading the story? (Idea: *Thinking about the story.*)

During the story, I'll ask questions to see whether you understand what I'm reading. What will I ask as I read the story to you? *Questions.*

Later in today's lesson, you'll see a picture about the story. We'll talk more about the story when you see this picture. What will you see later in today's lesson? (Idea: *The picture from the story.*)

The title of the story is "The Walk to School." What's the title of the story? *The Walk to School.*

Lesson 11   **39**

Read story with prosody.
Phillip, Jane, and Sam do not live on the same street, and they aren't even in the same grade. But they all walk the same way to school. They don't really know one another very well. They have never played together, but they are still **friendly** to one another. When you are **friendly** to others, you're **kind** to them. Phillip, Jane, and Sam all meet up on their way to school so they have someone to walk with and talk to. Having someone to talk to while walking to school makes the walk go faster.

1. Do these children all live on the same street? *No.*

2. What do these children do together? *Walk to school.*

3. How do you act when you are **friendly** to others? *Kind.*

If one of the children acted mean, the others probably wouldn't want to walk with him or her. You don't need to know someone very well to be **friendly.** However, because they are **friendly,** these children are getting to know one another. Maybe one day they will become good friends.

1. How do you act to get to know other children? *Friendly.*

Remember that being **friendly** just means to be **kind.** Sometimes just by saying, "Hi" to someone, you can put a smile on his or her face. Sometimes you might even end up making a new friend!

1. If you are **friendly** to someone, what could happen? (Idea: *You might make a new friend.*)

You learned a new word in the story today. **Friendly. Friendly** means **kind.** What does **friendly** mean? *Kind.*

What's another word for **kind?** *Friendly.*

Activity 2 Story Recall—An After-Reading Strategy

 Show picture from Lesson 11, page 67, in *Teacher Presentation Book A.*

Elicit responses to questions. **Guide** as needed.
Listen as I ask you some questions about the story we read earlier and the picture you see now.

How many children are there? *Three.*

Where do you think the children are going? (Idea: *To school.*)

Why is it important to be friendly to others? (Student responses.)

Why do you think the children are being kind to one another? (Student responses.)

How do you act when you are friendly? (Student response.)

3 minutes

Activity 2, to be completed <u>after</u> the picture in Lesson 11 is shown to students.

40   Lesson 11

Lesson 12

Materials
Teacher: Reading *Teacher Presentation Book A*
Student: Lined paper

5 minutes

Part A: Phonemic and Phonological Awareness

Activity 1 Rhyme Production

Elicit responses. **Guide** as needed.
You have become very good at recognizing words that rhyme. Today you'll tell me words that rhyme with our *special* words. Let's pretend we have a truck. We're going to load the truck with *special* items.

Listen. **Our truck is loaded with dogs.** Can you tell me more things that rhyme with *dogs* that could go in the truck? (**Idea:** *logs, hogs, frogs.*)

Listen. **Our truck is loaded with cars.** Can you tell me more things that rhyme with *cars* that could go in the truck? (**Idea:** *stars, bars.*)

(Continue the activity with the following sentences:
Our truck is loaded with blocks; Our truck is loaded with hats.)

Activity 2 Syllable Blending

Elicit responses. **Guide** as needed.
Let's practice making compound words.

Model making fists; turn your hands palm-side up in front of you; say the first word and then open your right hand; say the second word and then open your left hand; put both hands together and then say whole word.
Your turn. Meat. Ball. Put it together. *Meatball.*

(Continue the activity with the following words:
rainbow, driveway, firefighter.)

Activity 3 Syllable Blending

Elicit responses. **Guide** as needed.
Let's make more big words. I'm going to say two word parts, and you'll put them together to say the whole word.

Model making fists; turn your hands palm-side up in front of you; say the first word and then open your right hand; say the second word and then open your left hand; put both hands together and then say whole word.
Listen to me try one. Din ner. I can put it together. Dinner. Your turn. Din ner. Put it together. *Dinner.*

Lesson 12   41

Now it's your turn to try one by yourselves. Listen. Flow er. What word? *Flower.*

Yes, you made the word flower. Let's try some more. Spi der. What word? *Spider.*

Broth er. What word? *Brother.*

Laun dry. What word? *Laundry.*

Sham poo. What word? *Shampoo.*

En ter. What word? *Enter.*

Activity 4 Syllable Segmentation

Elicit responses. **Guide** as needed.
Remember when we learned about compound words? A compound word is made up of two shorter words. Let's see if you can tell me the two shorter words when I tell you the compound word.

Model putting both hands together; pull apart for each word part.
My turn. Meatball. Meat. Ball. Your turn. Meatball. What is the first part? *Meat.*

What is the second part? *Ball.*

You're right. The two words are **meat** and **ball.**

(Continue the activity with the following words:
rainbow, mailbox, chalkboard, raincoat, cupcake, teapot.)

Part B: Letter Recognition and Formation

6 minutes

Student Materials:
Lined paper

Activity 1 Letter Recognition Review—a

Elicit responses to questions. **Guide** as needed. **Write** a on the board. **Point** to a.
We learned that this letter is **a.** What letter name? *a.*
Again, what letter name? *a.*
Review as needed.

Activity 2 Letter Formation Review—a

Now we're going to practice writing **a.** When you practice writing, you'll learn not only where to start and stop the letter, but also which way to move your hand when you're making the letter. It's tricky, but you're so smart you'll learn how to write **a** very quickly. Watch.

Here's how you write **a** in the air.
Model a formation in the air (with your back to students).

Watch again.

Now let's practice writing **a** in the air. Hold up your writing hand, and make **a** in the air.
Guide students as they write a in the air.

Lesson 12

Let's practice **a** again.

Here's how to write **a** with your writing hand pointer finger.
Model a formation on the board with your finger (with your back to students).

Watch again.

Now let's practice writing **a** on your table without using your pencil. Use your writing hand pointer finger, and make **a** on your table.
Guide students as they write a on their table or desktop.

Let's practice **a** again.

Model writing a on the board (with your back to students).
Remember that every letter has a name. You learned the name of this letter is **a.**
What letter name? *a.*

Again, what letter name? *a.*

Provide lined paper to students.
Now let's practice writing **a** with your pencil.
Guide students as they write a on their paper. **Review** as needed.

 Link letter names to letter sounds as needed as they appear in the program.

Part C: Comprehension Strategies

9 minutes

Teacher Materials:
Reading *Teacher Presentation Book A*

Activity 1 Listening Comprehension—A During-Reading Strategy

Elicit responses to questions. **Guide** as needed.
Today you'll hear a new story. What should you do while I read the story? (Idea: *Think about the story.*)

During the story, I'll ask questions to see whether you understand what I'm reading. What will I ask as I read the story to you? *Questions.*

Later in today's lesson, you'll see a picture about the story. We'll talk more about the story when you see this picture. What will you see later in today's lesson? (Idea: *The picture from the story.*)

The title of the story is "A Dog Named Spot." What's the title of the story? *A Dog Named Spot.*

Read story with prosody.
It had been a nice, warm, summer day, but that evening Walter noticed that dark clouds had rolled in. It was still pretty warm outside, but he could tell it was about to rain. Before long, the rain started coming down, and then came the thunder and lightning. Spot, Walter's dog, started acting funny. He began to **leap** all over the furniture. **Leap** means the same thing as **jump.**

1. What was the weather like? (Idea: *Dark clouds; thunder and lightning; rain.*)

Lesson 12   **43**

2. What was the name of Walter's dog? *Spot.*

3. How did Walter's dog start to act? (Idea: *Funny; leaping over furniture.*)

After a little while, Spot started scratching at the door. He really wanted out. Walter opened the door, and Spot ran out. Before Walter could stop him, Spot took a **leap** over the fence and ran down the street. Walter was afraid his dog was gone forever. When the storm ended, Walter ran outside and began looking for Spot. He yelled and yelled for him. Then he saw Spot off in the distance and called for him. Spot came running. Walter watched Spot **leap** right back over the fence and come to see him.

1. When Walter opened the door for Spot, what did Spot do? *He ran out.*

2. What is another way to say **jump?** *Leap.*

3. When did Walter go outside to look for Spot? *When the storm ended.*

Spot spent the rest of the night close to Walter. He kept licking Walter's face over and over again. Spot was happy to be home, and Walter was even happier to have his best friend back.

1. What did Spot do to Walter's face? *He licked it.*

2. How did Walter feel when Spot came back? *Happy.*

You learned a new word in the story today. **Leap** means **jump.** What does **leap** mean? *Jump.*

What's another word for **jump?** *Leap.*

Activity 2 Story Recall—An After-Reading Strategy

 Show picture from Lesson 12, page 74, in *Teacher Presentation Book A.*

Elicit responses to questions. **Guide** as needed.
Listen as I ask you some questions about the story we read earlier and the picture you see now.

What is Spot doing? *Jumping.*

Why did Spot leap over the fence? (Idea: *He was afraid of the storm.*)

What did Spot do after he came back to Walter? (Idea: *Spent the rest of the night close to Walter.*)

Have you ever seen a dog leap like Spot? (Student response.)

What other animals can leap? (Student response.)

3 minutes

Activity 2, to be completed <u>after</u> the picture in Lesson 12 is shown to students.

44   Lesson 12

Lesson 13

> **Materials**
> **Teacher:** Reading *Teacher Presentation Book A*
> **Student:** Lined paper

5 minutes

Part A: Phonemic and Phonological Awareness

Activity 1 Word Segmentation: Three-Word Sentences

Elicit responses. **Guide** as needed.
Let's work with some sentences and find the *first, last,* and *middle* words in the sentences.

Listen to the sentence. **Flags are flying.** Say that sentence. *Flags are flying.*

What is the *first* word in that sentence? *Flags.*

Yes, **flags** is the *first* word in that sentence. Say that sentence again. *Flags are flying.*

What is the last word in that sentence? *Flying.*

Yes, **flying** is the *last* word in that sentence. Say that sentence again. **Flags are flying.** What is the *middle* word in that sentence? *Are.*

Yes, **are** is the *middle* word in that sentence.

(Continue the activity with the following sentences:
I am smiling; She is standing; Monkeys like swinging; Boys are running.)

Activity 2 Word Segmentation

Elicit responses. **Guide** as needed.
Today we're going to change words in a poem. Let's see how well you can listen.

My turn. **Rain, rain,** go away. Come again another day. Now I'm going to change **rain** to **skunk.** Listen. **Skunk, skunk,** go away. Come again another day.

Your turn. Listen. **Rain, rain,** go away. Come again another day. Now change **rain** to **skunk.** *Skunk, skunk, go away. Come again another day.*

Great, now let's try another one. Listen. **Rain, rain,** go away. Come again another day. Now change **rain** to **bear.** Your turn. *Bear, bear, go away. Come again another day.*

(Continue the activity with the following changes:
snake, shark, lion.)

Lesson 13   45

Activity 3 Rhyme Recognition

Elicit responses. **Guide** thumb movement as needed.
Let's listen for words that rhyme. I'll tell you two words. Remember, if they rhyme, give me a thumbs-up. If they don't rhyme, don't do anything. Let's find some rhymes.

Toy. Joy. (Thumbs-up.)

Boy. Box. (No thumbs-up.)

Late. Date. (Thumbs-up.)

Skate. Rate. (Thumbs-up.)

Stars. Jars. (Thumbs-up.)

Bars. Barn. (No thumbs-up.)

Red. Head. (Thumbs-up.)

Bed. Bell. (No thumbs-up.)

Sell. Tell. (Thumbs-up.)

Well. Fell. (Thumbs-up.)

Grass. Pass. (Thumbs-up.)

Gas. Pan. (No thumbs-up.)

Part B: Letter Recognition and Formation

6 minutes

Student Materials:
Lined paper

Activity 1 Letter Recognition—Capital A

Elicit responses to questions. **Guide** as needed. Write capital A on the board. **Point** to capital A.
Today you'll learn another way to write **a.**
The name of this letter is **capital A.** What letter name? *Capital A.*
Again, what letter name? *Capital A.*
Review as needed.

Activity 2 Letter Formation—Capital A

Now we're going to practice writing **capital A.** When you practice writing, you'll learn not only where to start and stop the letter, but also which way to move your hand when you're making the letter. It's tricky, but you're so smart you'll learn how to write **capital A** very quickly. Watch.

Here's how you write **capital A** in the air.
Model capital A formation in the air (with your back to students).

Watch again.

Now let's practice writing **capital A** in the air. Hold up your writing hand, and make **capital A** in the air.
Guide students as they write capital A in the air.

Let's practice **capital A** again.

Here's how to write **capital A** with your writing hand pointer finger.
Model capital A formation on the board with your finger (with your back to students).

Watch again.

Now let's practice writing **capital A** on your table without using your pencil. Use your writing hand pointer finger, and make **capital A** on your table.
Guide students as they write capital A on their table or desktop.

Let's practice **capital A** again.

Remember, every letter has a name.
Model writing capital A on the board (with your back to students).
You learned the name of this letter is **capital A.** What letter name? *Capital A.*

Again, what letter name? *Capital A.*

Provide lined paper to students.
Now let's practice writing **capital A** with your pencil.
Guide students as they write capital A on their paper. **Review** as needed.

 Link letter names to letter sounds as needed as they appear in the program.

Part C: Comprehension Strategies

9 minutes

Teacher Materials:
Reading *Teacher Presentation Book A*

Activity 1 Build Listening Comprehension

Elicit responses to questions. **Guide** as needed.
What should you be doing when I'm reading the story? (Idea: *Thinking about the story.*)

During the story, I'll ask questions to see whether you understand what I'm reading. What will I ask as I read the story to you? *Questions.*

Later in today's lesson, you'll see a picture about the story. We'll talk more about the story when you see this picture. What will you see later in today's lesson? (Idea: *The picture from the story.*) Are you ready to get started?

The title of the story is "The Rocket Experiment." What's the title of the story? *The Rocket Experiment.*

Read story with prosody.
Malia's science teacher gave the class an **assignment. An assignment** is **work to do.** Students were asked to build something that would fly. Malia gave a lot of thought to what she should build. Malia had read about astronauts and the trips they had made to the moon, so she decided it would be interesting to try to build her own rocket.

Lesson 13   **47**

1. What's another word for work to do? *Assignment.*

2. What did Malia decide to do for her assignment? *Build a rocket.*

Malia got right to work on her **assignment.** First she gathered some cardboard. Next she got out the tape. She did her best to try to create a picture in her mind of what she thought a rocket looked like. Malia remembered that a rocket had a cone shape at the top. She also remembered that the body of it was shaped like an empty paper towel roll. She formed the cardboard into those shapes. She then added some small pieces of cardboard on the bottom for fins. Then Malia taped all the pieces of cardboard together. Before long, she had a rocket.

1. What did Malia do first? *Gathered cardboard.*

2. What other supply did she get? *Tape.*

Malia did not know whether her rocket would fly, but she was very happy with the way it looked. She was also proud that she had completed her **assignment** all by herself.

1. How did Malia feel about her assignment? (Idea: *Happy with how it looked.*)

2. Why was Malia proud? (Idea: *She completed her assignment all by herself.*)

You learned a new word in the story today. **Assignment** means **work to do.** What does **assignment** mean? *Work to do.*

What's another word for **work to do?** *Assignment.*

Activity 2 Story Recall—An After-Reading Strategy

Show picture from Lesson 13, page 82, in *Teacher Presentation Book A.*

Elicit responses to questions. **Guide** as needed.
Listen as I ask you some questions about the story we read earlier and the picture you see now.

What is Malia making? *A rocket.*

How did she know how to build a rocket? (Idea: *She thought hard about what a rocket looked like.*)

Why do you think it would be fun to build a rocket? (Student response.)

What kinds of things have you tried to build? (Student response.)

When you build things, what materials do you use? (Student response.)

3 minutes

Activity 2, to be completed <u>after</u> the picture in Lesson 13 is shown to students.

48   Lesson 13

Lesson 14

Materials
Teacher: Reading *Teacher Presentation Book A*
Student: Lined paper

5 minutes

Part A: Phonemic and Phonological Awareness

Activity 1 Rhyme Production

Elicit responses. **Guide** as needed.
For the next activity, think of words that will help make the poem rhyme. Listen closely to the poem, and see if you can tell me a word that will rhyme.

Listen. One potato, two potato, three potato, *four*. Five potato, six potato, seven potato, _____. Can you tell me a word that fits just right? *More*.

Listen to another poem. Rain, rain, go *away*. Come again another _____. Can you tell me a word that fits just right? *Day*.

Listen. Five little monkeys jumping on the *bed*. One fell off and bumped his _____. Can you tell me a word that fits just right? *Head*.

Activity 2 Syllable Blending

Elicit responses. **Guide** as needed.
Let's practice making compound words.

Model making fists; turn your hands palm-side up in front of you; say the first word and then open your right hand; say the second word and then open your left hand; put both hands together and then say whole word.
Your turn. Bath. Room. Put it together. *Bathroom*.

(Continue the activity with the following words: lunchtime, playtime, goldfish.)

Activity 3 Syllable Blending

Elicit responses. **Guide** as needed.
Let's make more big words. I'm going to say some word parts, and you'll put them together to say the whole word. Listen to me try one.

My turn. Tel e phone. I can put it together. Telephone. Your turn. Tel e phone. Put it together. *Telephone*.

Now it's your turn to try one by yourselves. Listen. Lem on ade. What word? *Lemonade*.

Lesson 14   49

Yes, you made the word **lemonade.** Let's try some more. Ba na na. What word? *Banana.*

Su per man. What word? *Superman.*

Bub ble gum. What word? *Bubblegum.*

Sun flow er. What word? *Sunflower.*

Sat ur day. What word? *Saturday.*

Activity 4 Syllable Segmentation

Elicit responses. **Guide** as needed.
What is the name of the long word that is made up of two shorter words? *Compound word.*

Yes, a compound word.

Model putting both hands together; pull apart for each word part.
Let's see if you can tell me the two shorter words when I tell you the compound word. My turn. Birdseed. Bird. Seed. Your turn. *Birdseed.* What is the first part? *Bird.*

What is the second part? *Seed.*

You're right. The two words are **bird** and **seed.**

(Continue the activity with the following words:
suitcase, spaceship, sweatshirt, someone.)

Part B: Letter Recognition and Formation

6 minutes

Student Materials:
Lined paper

Activity 1 Letter Recognition Review—Capital A

Elicit responses to questions. **Guide** as needed. **Write** capital A on the board. **Point** to capital A.
We learned that this letter is **capital A.** What letter name? *Capital A.*
Again, what letter name? *Capital A.*
Review as needed.

Activity 2 Letter Formation Review—Capital A

Now we're going to practice writing **capital A.** When you practice writing, you'll learn not only where to start and stop the letter, but also which way to move your hand when you're making the letter. It's tricky, but you're so smart you'll learn how to write **capital A** very quickly. Watch.

Here's how you write **capital A** in the air.
Model capital A formation in the air (with your back to students).

Watch again.

50 Lesson 14

Now let's practice writing **capital A** in the air. Hold up your writing hand, and make **capital A** in the air.
Guide students as they write capital A in the air.

Let's practice **capital A** again.

Here's how to write **capital A** with your writing hand pointer finger.
Model capital A formation on the board with your finger (with your back to students).

Watch again.

Now let's practice writing **capital A** on your table without using your pencil. Use your writing hand pointer finger, and make **capital A** on your table.
Guide students as they write capital A on their table or desktop.

Let's practice **capital A** again.

Remember that every letter has a name.
Model writing capital A on the board (with your back to students).
You learned the name of this letter is **capital A.** What letter name? *Capital A.* Again, what letter name? *Capital A.*

Provide lined paper to students.
Now let's practice writing **capital A** with your pencil.
Guide students as they write capital A on their paper. **Review** as needed.

 Link letter names to letter sounds as needed as they appear in the program.

Part C: Comprehension Strategies

9 minutes

Teacher Materials:
Reading *Teacher Presentation Book A*

Activity 1 Listening Comprehension—A During-Reading Strategy

Elicit responses to questions. **Guide** as needed.
Today you'll hear a new story. What should you do while I read the story? (Idea: *Think about the story.*)

During the story, I'll ask questions to see whether you understand what I'm reading. What will I ask as I read the story to you? *Questions.*

Later in today's lesson, you'll see a picture about the story. We'll talk more about the story when you see this picture. What will you see later in today's lesson? (Idea: *The picture from the story.*)

The title of the story is "Lenny the Snake." What's the title of the story? *Lenny the Snake.*

Lesson 14   **51**

Read story with prosody.
Francis was a boy who loved all kinds of animals. He talked his mother into getting him a hamster, a turtle, a kitten, and several fish. Now Francis wanted a snake, but his mother refused to buy him one. She didn't like snakes. So, Francis decided to make her a deal. He offered to set the table, clean his room, and dust every day for a month if she would buy him a snake. At the end of the month, Francis's mother decided to **reward** him by buying him a little snake. A **reward** is when you get a **prize** for something you've done.

1. What did Francis want his mother to get him? *A snake.*

2. What's another word for **prize?** *Reward.*

Francis loved his snake and decided to name him Lenny. He treated Lenny like a king. He fed him each day after breakfast or lunch. Lenny grew bigger and bigger. Soon Lenny got so big that Francis had to find him a new home. He thought a lot about whom he should give Lenny to. Finally Francis decided to give Lenny to the zoo.

1. What did Francis treat his snake like? *A king.*

2. Did Francis have to give his snake away? *Yes.*

Now Francis visits Lenny at the zoo every month. He reminds the zookeepers to feed Lenny after breakfast or lunch. Francis is now thinking of ways to get another **reward!**

1. Where does Lenny now live? *At the zoo.*

2. Francis is thinking of ways to get another what? *Reward.*

You learned a new word in the story today. **Reward** means **a prize.** What does **reward** mean? *A prize.*

What's another word for **prize?** *Reward.*

Activity 2 Story Recall—An After-Reading Strategy

 Show picture from Lesson 14, page 89, in *Teacher Presentation Book A*.

Elicit responses to questions. **Guide** as needed.
Listen as I ask you some questions about the story we read earlier and the picture you see now.

Who is in the picture? *Lenny the snake.*

What is Lenny eating? (Student response.)

Which meal do you think he is eating? Why? (Idea: *Dinner, because the food looks like dinner food.*)

Where else could Francis have taken his snake to live? (Idea: *A pet shop; a reptile zoo; an animal sanctuary.*)

Would you like to have a snake for a pet? Why or why not? (Student response.)

3 minutes

Activity 2, to be completed <u>after</u> the picture in Lesson 14 is shown to students.

Lesson 15

Materials
Teacher: Reading *Teacher Presentation Book A*, IWB-Letter Recognition
Student: Lined paper

5 minutes

Part A: Phonemic and Phonological Awareness

Activity 1 Word Segmentation

Elicit responses to questions. **Guide** as needed.
Today we're going to work on changing words in a sentence. Let's see how well you can listen and think.

My turn. One, two, buckle *my* shoe.
Say it with me. *One, two, buckle my shoe.*
Your turn. *One, two, buckle my shoe.*

Pick a student's name to use in the blank.
Let's change the word *my* to someone's name from our group. Listen. I can change the sentence by using *(name of child)'s* name. One, two, buckle *(name of child)'s* shoe.

Your turn. Change the word *my* to *(name of child)*. *One, two, buckle (name of child)'s shoe.*

(Continue the activity by substituting other children's names in the sentence.)

Activity 2 Rhyme Production

Emphasize italicized words. **Elicit** responses. **Guide** as needed.
For the next activity, I'll start the sentence, and you finish it by choosing a word that rhymes. Listen closely, and see if you can help me. I'll finish the first one.

Did you ever see a *pig* dancing a *jig*? Your turn. Did you ever see a *cat* wearing a _____? (Idea: *hat.*)

Did you ever see a *pig* wearing a _____? (Idea: *wig.*)

Did you ever see a *mouse* building a _____? (Idea: *house.*)

Did you ever see a *frog* kissing a _____? (Idea: *hog.*)

Did you ever see a *snake* eating a _____? (Idea: *cake.*)

Did you ever see a *goat* driving a _____? (Idea: *boat.*)

Did you ever see a *fish* eating from a _____? (Idea: *dish.*)

Did you ever see a *bear* combing his _____? (Idea: *hair.*)

Activity 3 Syllable Blending

Elicit responses to questions. **Guide** as needed.
Let's try making some big words. I'm going to say some word parts, and you'll put them together to say the whole word. Listen to me try one.

My turn. Drag on fly. I can put it together. Dragonfly. Your turn. Drag on fly. Put it together. *Dragonfly.*

Now it's your turn to try one by yourselves. Listen. Oc to pus. What word? *Octopus.*

Yes, you made the word **octopus.** Let's try some more. Val en tine. What word? *Valentine.*

Cir cus. What word? *Circus.*

Bi cy cle. What word? *Bicycle.*

Grand ma. What word? *Grandma.*

Pil low. What word? *Pillow.*

Dish wash er. What word? *Dishwasher.*

Mo tor cy cle. What word? *Motorcycle.*

Part B: Letter Recognition and Formation

6 minutes

Teacher Materials:

Student Materials:
Lined paper

Activity 1 Letter Recognition Cumulative Review—a/A

Display on IWB or **write** a and capital A on the board in the order shown (with your back to students). **Elicit** responses to questions. **Guide** as needed.
This week, you've learned one letter and one capital— **a** and **capital A.** Let's review them. Are you ready?

Letter	Question	Student Response
A	What letter?	Capital A.
a	What letter?	a.

Review as needed.

Activity 2 Letter Formation Cumulative Review—a/A

Write a and capital A on the board in the order shown (with your back to students).
Provide lined paper to students.
Show me how you can write this letter and capital.
Guide students as they write a and capital A on their paper. **Review** as needed.

  Link letter names to letter sounds as needed as they appear in the program.

54   Lesson 15

9 minutes

Teacher Materials:
Reading *Teacher Presentation Book A*

Part C: Comprehension Strategies

Activity 1 Listening Comprehension—A During-Reading Strategy

Elicit responses to questions. **Guide** as needed.
Today you'll hear a new story. What should you do while I read the story? (Idea: *Think about the story.*)

During the story, I'll ask questions to see whether you understand what I'm reading. What will I ask as I read the story to you? *Questions.*

Later in today's lesson, you'll see a picture about the story. We'll talk more about the story when you see this picture. What will you see later in today's lesson? (Idea: *The picture from the story.*)

The title of the story is "The Moping Sailor." What's the title of the story? *The Moping Sailor.*

Read story with prosody.
When George was little, he wanted to grow up and become a sailor. He dreamed of sailing around the world. He was excited about the places he would go and the people he would meet. When George grew up and became a sailor, he was disappointed to learn that being a sailor also meant that you had to do a lot of work. George's job was to clean the deck of the ship every morning. George didn't like to work, so he would **mope** while he cleaned the deck. When you **mope,** you **act sad.**

1. What did George want to be when he grew up? *A sailor.*

2. What was George's job as a sailor? *To clean the deck.*

3. What did George do while he cleaned the deck? *Mope.*

The other sailors began to notice that George was **moping** a lot, and they started calling him "the **moping** sailor." George didn't like being called that, so he decided to make a change. He started getting up every morning and putting a big smile on his face. He'd sing a happy song while going out to clean the deck. Before long, the other sailors started singing along. Everyone had a smile on their face by the time George was done.

1. When you **mope,** how do you act? *Sad.*

2. What kind of song did George sing? *A happy song.*

George is now known as "the happy sailor." He does not **mope.** George gets to see the world and meet new people, but first he gets his work done.

1. Now that George no longer *mopes,* what do the other sailors call him? *The "happy sailor."*

You learned a new word in the story today. **Mope** means **act sad.** What does **act sad** mean? *Mope.*

What's another word for **act sad**? *Mope.*

Lesson 15

3 minutes

Activity 2, to be completed <u>after</u> the picture in Lesson 15 is shown to students.

Activity 2 | Story Recall—An After-Reading Strategy

 Show picture from Lesson 15, page 96, in *Teacher Presentation Book A*.

Elicit responses to questions. **Guide** as needed.
Listen as I ask you some questions about the story we read earlier and the picture you see now.

Who is in the picture? (Idea: *George, the moping sailor.*)

Is this picture from the beginning when George is moping or at the end of the story when George is "the happy sailor"? (Idea: *The end of the story.*)

Why would you **mope**? (Student response.)

Would there ever be a good reason to **mope**? (Student response.)

5 minutes

Part D: Vocabulary Strategies

Activity 1 | Distinguish Shades of Meaning

Today we'll work with words and learn about how they are different. Tell me how these words are somewhat different. [**leap** and **hop**; **mope** and **pout**]

Model acting out what a particular verb means. **Assign** student partners. **Have** students act out what the verb means with a partner. **Guide** students as needed. **Repeat** sequence for each word.

56   Lesson 15

Lesson 16

Materials
Teacher: Reading *Teacher Presentation Book A*
Student: Lined paper

5 minutes

Part A: Phonemic and Phonological Awareness

Activity 1 Rhyme Recognition

Emphasize italicized words. **Elicit** responses. **Guide** as needed.
I'm going to tell you a poem. Listen closely. Raise your hand if you hear me make a mistake with the rhyming words.

One, *two,* buckle my *shoe.* (No hands raised.)

Three, *four,* open the *gate.* (Hands raised.)

Five, *six,* pick up *sticks.* (No hands raised.)

Seven, *eight,* close the *gate.* (No hands raised.)

Nine, *ten,* a big, fat *dog.* (Hands raised.)

Listen carefully while I say some words. All of the words will rhyme except for one word. I will read the words two times. The first time I read the words, listen carefully. The second time I read the words, give me a thumbs-up as soon as you hear the word that *does not* rhyme.

Let's try it.
Guide thumb movement as needed.

Red fed led green.
Red fed led green.

Correct. You should have given me a thumbs-up as soon as you word **green,** because **green** *does not* rhyme with **red, fed,**

(Continue the activity with the following rows of words, reading
Tell fell ran sell
Last past cast blue
My sky bean why
Seen green mean pot.)

Activity 2 | Syllable Segmentation

Elicit responses. **Guide** clapping as needed.
We're going to work with compound words in this activity. In the last lesson, you were able to tell me the two words that make up the compound word. We're going to try this again, but this time I want you to clap as you say each word in the compound word.

My turn. Milk shake. I can say the two parts and clap for each part. Milk. Shake. There are two parts, and I clapped two times.

Your turn. Milk shake. Say the two parts, and clap for each part. *Milk. Shake.*

You're right. The two words are **milk** and **shake.**

(Continue the activity with the following words: grandchild, cornfield, nightlight, haystack.)

6 minutes

Student Materials:
Lined paper

Part B: Letter Recognition and Formation

Activity 1 | Letter Recognition—m

Elicit responses to questions. **Guide** as needed. **Write** m on the board. **Point** to m.
Today you'll learn a new letter.
The name of this letter is **m.** What letter name? *m.*
Again, what letter name? *m.*
Review as needed.

Activity 2 | Letter Formation—m

Now we're going to practice writing **m.** When you practice writing, you'll learn not only where to start and stop the letter, but also which way to move your hand when you're making the letter. It's tricky, but you're so smart you'll learn how to write **m** very quickly. Watch.

Here's how you write **m** in the air.
Model m formation in the air (with your back to students).

Watch again.

Now let's practice writing **m** in the air. Hold up your writing hand, and make **m** in the air.
Guide students as they write m in the air.

Let's practice **m** again.

Here's how to write **m** with your writing hand pointer finger.
Model m formation on the board with your finger (with your back to students).

Watch again.

Now let's practice writing **m** on your table without using your pencil. Use your writing hand pointer finger, and make **m** on your table.
Guide students as they write m on their table or desktop.

Let's practice **m** again.

Model writing m on the board (with your back to students).
Remember that every letter has a name. You learned the name of this letter is **m.**
What letter name? *m.*

Again, what letter name? *m.*

Provide lined paper to students.
Now, let's practice writing **m** with your pencil.
Guide students as they write m on their paper. **Review** as needed.

 Link letter names to letter sounds as needed as they appear in the program.

Set up a writing center with writing materials and correct models of letters learned so far for students to use in their free time.

Part C: Comprehension Strategies

9 minutes

Teacher Materials:
Reading *Teacher Presentation Book A*

Activity 1 Listening Comprehension—A During-Reading Strategy

Elicit responses to questions. **Guide** as needed.
Today you'll hear a new story. What should you do while I read the story? (Idea: *Think about the story.*)

During the story, I'll ask questions to see whether you understand what I'm reading. What will I ask as I read the story to you? *Questions.*

Later in today's lesson, you'll see a picture about the story. We'll talk more about the story when you see this picture. What will you see later in today's lesson? (Idea: *The picture from the story.*)

The title of the story is "The Birthday Party." What's the title of the story? *The Birthday Party.*

Read story with prosody.
Isabelle is having a birthday. She is turning six. Her family has planned a surprise party. Isabelle's mother wants this to be the best party ever. All of Isabelle's classmates have been invited to the big day. Isabelle's family is keeping the party a secret. Isabelle's mother is making a chocolate cake with white frosting and sprinkles. Her father is blowing up fifty balloons for decorations. It should be a party everyone will **enjoy. Enjoy** means **have a good time.**

1. Who was turning six? *Isabelle.*

2. How many balloons did Isabelle's father blow up for her party? *Fifty.*

3. Who was invited to Isabelle's party? *Her classmates.*

Lesson 16

There will be many activities that are fun for the kids. Isabelle loves music, so they'll play lots of happy music. The children will dance around and be silly. They'll also sing Happy Birthday while Isabelle's sister plays the piano. Then the children will eat chocolate cake and vanilla ice cream. Later, Isabelle will open her presents. It will be a time to **enjoy.**

1. Name the song the children will sing to Isabelle. *Happy Birthday.*

2. What's another word for **have a good time?** *Enjoy.*

The day of the party arrived, and Isabelle was very surprised! She had a wonderful time with her friends and family. Isabelle felt very special. She remembered that great birthday for a very long time. It was truly a party to **enjoy!**

1. Who was surprised about the party? *Isabelle.*

2. Who did she have a wonderful time with? *Her friends and family.*

You learned a new word in the story today. **Enjoy** means **have a good time.** What does **enjoy** mean? *Have a good time.*

Activity 2 Story Recall—An After-Reading Strategy

 Show picture from Lesson 16, page 103, in *Teacher Presentation Book A.*

Elicit responses to questions. **Guide** as needed.
Listen as I ask you some questions about the story we read earlier and the picture you see now.

How can you tell the children are enjoying the party? (Idea: *The children are smiling, dancing, and putting their hands in the air.*)

What do you like to do for your birthday? (Student response.)

Have you ever been invited to a surprise party? (Student response.)

Why do people plan surprise parties? (Student response.)

3 minutes

Activity 2, to be completed <u>after</u> the picture in Lesson 16 is shown to students.

60 Lesson 16

Lesson 17

> **Materials**
> **Teacher:** Reading *Teacher Presentation Book A*
> **Student:** Lined paper

5 minutes

Part A: Phonemic and Phonological Awareness

Activity 1 Word Segmentation

Elicit responses. **Guide** as needed.
Today you're going to change words in a sentence. In another activity, we were looking for the *first, middle,* and *last* words in a sentence. This time you'll change a *first, middle,* or *last* word to another word I give you. Let me show you how.

Have students repeat the sentence. **Do** not go on until the sentence is fluent.
Use manipulatives to represent the words in the sentence if students have difficulty.
My turn. **The boy climbs.** Let's change the *last* word to **sleeps. The boy sleeps.** Your turn. **The boy climbs.** Change the *last* word to **sleeps.** *The boy sleeps.*

Let's try another one. **The girl runs.** Say that sentence. *The girl runs.*

Change the *last* word to **walks.** *The girl walks.*

(Continue the activity with the following examples:
The dog barks. Change the *last* word to digs.
The people sing. Change the *last* word to dance.)

Let's change the *first* word in a sentence. Say this sentence. **He walked quickly.** *He walked quickly.*

Change the *first* word to **she.** *She walked quickly.*

(Continue the activity with the following examples:
Mice like cheese. Change the *first* word to children.
Rabbits can hop. Change the *first* word to frogs.
Boys are running. Change the *first* word to girls.)

Activity 2 Rhyme Recognition

Elicit responses. **Guide** thumb movement as needed.
Listen carefully while I say some words. All of the words will rhyme except for one word. I will read the words two times. The first time I read the words, listen carefully. The second time I read the words, give me a thumbs-up as soon as you hear the word that *does not* rhyme.

Let's try it.

Day play my bay.
Day play my bay.

Correct. You should have given me a thumbs-up as soon as you heard the word **my,** because **my** *does not* rhyme with **day, play,** and **bay.**

(Continue the activity with the following rows of words, reading each row two times:
Fog duck log dog.
Go bow grow boat.
Pill chill line will.
Tent time went spent.)

Activity 3 Syllable Blending

Elicit responses. **Guide** as needed.
Let's try making some words. I'm going to say some word parts, and you'll put them together to say the whole word.

Your turn. Listen. Ac ci dent. What word? *Accident.*

Yes, you made the word **accident.** Let's try some more. Af ter. What word? *After.*

Sil ly. What word? *Silly.*

Sun flow er. What word? *Sunflower.*

Nap kin. What word? *Napkin.*

Pa per. What word? *Paper.*

Pop si cle. What word? *Popsicle.*

Cal en dar. What word? *Calendar.*

Part B: Letter Recognition and Formation

6 minutes

Student Materials:
Lined paper

Activity 1 Letter Recognition Review—m

Elicit responses. **Guide** as needed. **Write** m on the board. **Point** to m.
We learned that this letter is **m.** What letter name? *m.*
Again, what letter name? *m.*
Review as needed.

Activity 2 Letter Formation Review—m

Now we're going to practice writing **m.** When you practice writing, you'll learn not only where to start and stop the letter, but also which way to move your hand when you're making the letter. It's tricky, but you're so smart you'll learn how to write **m** very quickly. Watch.

Here's how you write **m** in the air.
Model m formation in the air (with your back to students).

62   Lesson 17

Watch again.

Now let's practice writing **m** in the air. Hold up your writing hand, and make **m** in the air.
Guide students as they write m in the air.

Let's practice **m** again.

Here's how to write **m** with your writing hand pointer finger.
Model m formation on the board with your finger (with your back to students).

Watch again.

Now let's practice writing **m** on your table without using your pencil. Use your writing hand pointer finger, and make **m** on your table.
Guide students as they write m on their table or desktop.
Let's practice **m** again.

Model writing m on the board (with your back to students).
Remember that every letter has a name. You learned the name of this letter is **m.**
What letter name? *m.*

Again, what letter name? *m.*

Provide lined paper to students.
Now let's practice writing **m** with your pencil.
Guide students as they write m on their paper. **Review** as needed.

 Link letter names to letter sounds as needed as they appear in the program.

Part C: Comprehension Strategies

9 minutes

Teacher Materials:
Reading *Teacher Presentation Book A*

Activity 1 Listening Comprehension—A During-Reading Strategy

Elicit responses to questions. **Guide** as needed.
Today you'll hear a new story. What should you do while I read the story? (Idea: *Think about the story.*)

During the story, I'll ask questions to see whether you understand what I'm reading. What will I ask as I read the story to you? *Questions.*

Later in today's lesson, you'll see a picture about the story. We'll talk more about the story when you see this picture. What will you see later in today's lesson? (Idea: *The picture from the story.*)

The title of the story is "The Mud Fight." What's the title of the story? *The Mud Fight.*

Lesson 17   **63**

Read story with prosody.

Margaret and her friends were **upset** when they had to stay inside one rainy day. When you're **upset,** you're **mad** about something. Since it was raining, Margaret and her friends stayed inside and played house. They took turns being the mother. They had fun, but they really just wanted to go outside and play.

1. Why did the friends have to stay inside? (Idea: *It was a rainy day.*)

2. What's another word for upset? *Mad.*

3. Where did the friends want to play? *Outside.*

The next day was sunny, so everyone went to Margaret's house. Margaret showed her friends the big mud puddle that had formed in the backyard. They could build a mud castle! Margaret and her friends got their shovels and pails and started building. Suddenly, Tessa moved her shovel too quickly and accidentally splashed mud all over Margaret! Margaret became very **upset.** She was wearing her brand new red overalls. Tessa did not like seeing her friend **upset.** She quickly said that she was sorry. Then Margaret smiled, and she threw mud back at Tessa. They had a huge mud fight. The girls laughed and laughed. The mud fight was more fun than building the castle.

1. What did Margaret show the girls in the backyard? *A mud puddle.*

2. Who became upset when mud got on her? *Margaret.*

3. Tessa said she was sorry. Why was that the right thing to do? (Student response.)

After that day, Margaret and her friends looked forward to rainy days. They had a new favorite thing to do. They always made sure to put on old clothes before going outside after it rained. Can you guess why?

1. What was more fun than building a mud castle? *A mud fight.*

2. What kind of clothes did the girls wear after rainy days? *Old clothes.*

You learned a new word in the story today. **Upset** means **mad.** What does **upset** mean? *Mad.*

Activity 2 Story Recall—An After-Reading Strategy

 Show picture from Lesson 17, page 110, in *Teacher Presentation Book A.*

Elicit responses to questions. **Guide** as needed.
Listen as I ask you some questions about the story we read earlier and the picture you see now.

How many girls are throwing mud? *Two.*

Who is upset? *Margaret.*

Have you ever played in the mud? (Student response.)

Do you think it's a good idea to throw mud at your friends? Why? (Student response.)

3 minutes

Activity 2, to be completed <u>after</u> the picture in Lesson 17 is shown to students.

Lesson 18

Materials
Teacher: Reading *Teacher Presentation Book A*
Student: Lined paper

5 minutes

Part A: Phonemic and Phonological Awareness

Activity 1 Rhyme Production

Emphasize italicized words. **Elicit** responses. **Guide** as needed.
For the next activity, I'll start the sentence, and you finish it by choosing a word that rhymes. Listen closely, and see if you can help me.
I'll finish the first one. Did you ever see a *cat* wearing a *hat*?

Your turn. Did you ever see a *pup* drinking from a _____? (Idea: *cup*.)

Did you ever see a *bug* under a _____? (Idea: *rug*.)

Did you ever see a *moose* playing with a _____? (Idea: *goose*.)

Did you ever see a *clown* wearing a _____? (Idea: *gown*.)

Did you ever see a *hook* reading a _____? (Idea: *book*.)

Did you ever see a *bear* sitting in a _____? (Idea: *chair*.)

Did you ever see a *fish* making a _____? (Idea: *dish*.)

Did you ever see a *kitten* wearing a _____? (Idea: *mitten*.)

Elicit responses to questions. **Guide** as needed.
Let's see how many words we can think of that rhyme with **cat**. (Idea: *hat, sat, mat*.)

Wow, you thought of _____ words.

Activity 2 Syllable Segmentation

Elicit responses to questions. **Guide** as needed.
I'll tell you the compound word. You tell me the two smaller words that make up the whole word. Be sure to clap as you say each smaller word.

Your turn. **Footprint.** Say the two parts, and clap for each part. *Foot. Print.*

You're right. The two parts are **foot** and **print.**

(Continue the activity with the following words:
seagull, doughnut, cupcake, football, highway, starfish.)

Lesson 18   **65**

Activity 3 — Syllable Segmentation

Elicit responses. **Guide** clapping as needed.
You've done so well finding the parts of a compound word. Now let's try to find the parts of other words. We're going to clap for each part of a word as we say it. I'll show you how to begin.

My turn. **Paper.** I can say each part and clap. Pa per. Your turn. **Paper.** Clap, and say each part. *Pa per.*

You're right. The parts of **paper** are **pa** and **per.** Let's try some more.
Dai sy. What word? *Daisy.*

Ta ble. What word? *Table.*

Re cess. What word? *Recess.*

Ti ger. What word? *Tiger.*

Si lent. What word? *Silent.*

Yel low. What word? *Yellow.*

Mid dle. What word? *Middle.*

Zip per. What word? *Zipper.*

But ter. What word? *Butter.*

Sun ny. What word? *Sunny.*

Part B: Letter Recognition and Formation

6 minutes

Student Materials:
Lined paper

Activity 1 — Letter Recognition—Capital M

Elicit responses to questions. **Guide** as needed. **Write** capital M on the board. **Point** to capital M.
Today you'll learn another way to write **m.**
The name of this letter is **capital M.** What letter name? *Capital M.*
Again, what letter name? *Capital M.*
Review as needed.

Activity 2 — Letter Formation—Capital M

Now we're going to practice writing **capital M.** When you practice writing, you'll learn not only where to start and stop the letter, but also which way to move your hand when you're making the letter. It's tricky, but you're so smart you'll learn how to write **capital M** very quickly. Watch.

Here's how you write **capital M** in the air.
Model capital M formation in the air (with your back to students).

Watch again.

66 Lesson 18

Now let's practice writing **capital M** in the air. Hold up your writing hand, and make **capital M** in the air.
Guide students as they write capital M in the air.

Let's practice **capital M** again.

Here's how to write **capital M** with your writing hand pointer finger.
Model capital M formation on the board with your finger (with your back to students).
Watch again.

Now let's practice writing **capital M** on your table without using your pencil. Use your writing hand pointer finger, and make **capital M** on your table.
Guide students as they write capital M on their table or desktop.
Let's practice **capital M** again.

Model writing capital M on the board (with your back to students).
Remember that every letter has a name.
You learned the name of this letter is **capital M.** What letter name? *Capital M.*
Again, what letter name? *Capital M.*

Provide lined paper to students.
Now let's practice writing **capital M** with your pencil.
Guide students as they write capital M on their paper. **Review** as needed.

 Link letter names to letter sounds as needed as they appear in the program.

Part C: Comprehension Strategies

9 minutes

Teacher Materials:
Reading *Teacher Presentation Book A*

Activity 1 Listening Comprehension—A During-Reading Strategy

Elicit responses to questions. **Guide** as needed.
Today, you'll hear a new story. What should you do while I read the story? (Idea: *Think about the story.*)

During the story, I'll ask questions to see whether you understand what I'm reading. What will I ask as I read the story to you? *Questions.*

Later in today's lesson, you'll see a picture about the story. We'll talk more about the story when you see this picture. What will you see later in today's lesson? (Idea: *The picture from the story.*)

The title of the story is "Hats." What's the title of the story? *Hats.*

Read story with prosody.
Carlos loves hats; he has **several** different kinds. If you have **several** of something, you have **more than two.** Carlos will buy a new hat only if it looks different from any other hat he owns. Sometimes, Carlos goes shopping with his mother just to look at hats. He has even been able to talk others into trading a hat for one of his hats. He does this only if the hat he wants to trade for is really special.

Lesson 18 **67**

1. How many hats does Carlos have? *Several.*

2. What does it mean to have **several** of something? *More than two.*

3. Who goes shopping with Carlos? *His mother.*

Carlos likes wearing his hats. Each day when Carlos wakes up, he makes a decision about what hat to wear. He makes this decision based on how he is feeling that day. If Carlos is feeling happy, then he wears his cowboy hat. If Carlos is feeling playful, then he wears his red hat with the long feather. Carlos's friends are always curious to see which hat he will be wearing. You never see Carlos without a hat!

1. What kind of hat does Carlos wear if he's happy? *A cowboy hat.*

2. What kind of hat does he wear when he's feeling playful? (Idea: *A red hat with a long feather.*)

3. What does Carlos always wear? *A hat.*

A lot of people have **several** of the same things. For example, some people have several TV sets. Some people have **several** dolls, but for Carlos it's hats. So, if you see someone walking down the street wearing a very special hat, it just might be Carlos.

1. How many hats does Carlos have? *Several.*

You learned a new word in the story today. **Several** means **more than two.** What does **several** mean? *More than two.*

What's another word for **more than two**? *Several.*

Activity 2 Story Recall—An After-Reading Strategy

 Show picture from Lesson 18, page 115, in *Teacher Presentation Book A.*

Elicit responses to questions. **Guide** as needed.
Listen as I ask you some questions about the story we read earlier and the picture you see now.

How many hats is Carlos wearing? *Three.*

How do you know that Carlos is wearing several hats? (Idea: *He is wearing more than two hats.*)

Which hat would you like to wear? (Student response.)

Carlos has several hats. Do you have **several** of any item? What do you have? (Student responses.)

---

3 minutes

Activity 2, to be completed <u>after</u> the picture in Lesson 18 is shown to students.

68   Lesson 18

Lesson 19

Materials
Teacher: Reading *Teacher Presentation Book A*
Student: Lined paper

5 minutes

Part A: Phonemic and Phonological Awareness

Activity 1 Word Segmentation

We're going to work on changing words in a sentence today. We can change the *first, middle,* or *last* words to a different word. Let's try one together.

Have students repeat the sentence. **Do** not go on until the sentence is fluent.
Use manipulatives to represent the words in the sentence if students have difficulty.
My turn. **He likes fishing.** I'll change the *last* word to **running. He likes running.** Your turn. **He likes fishing.** Change the *last* word to **running.** *He likes running.*

Let's try another one. **She likes oranges.** Say that sentence. *She likes oranges.*

Change the *last* word to **grapes.** *She likes grapes.*

(Continue the activity with the following examples. **Fade** model when students are performing well.
My brother runs. Change the *last* word to jumps.
Everyone likes cake. Change the *last* word to cookies.)

Let's change the *first* word in a sentence. Say this sentence. **We talked softly.** *We talked softly.*

Now change the *first* word to **she.** *She talked softly.*

(Continue the activity with the following examples:
Children like carrots. Change the *first* word to rabbits.
Snails are slow. Change the *first* word to turtles.
Learning is fun. Change the *first* word to reading.)

Activity 2 Rhyme Recognition

Elicit responses. **Guide** thumb movement as needed.
Listen carefully while I say some words. All of the words will rhyme except one. I will read the words two times. The first time I read the words, listen carefully. The second time I read the words, give me a thumbs-up as soon as you hear the word that does not rhyme.

Let's try it.

Cat mat bake sat.
Cat mat bake sat.

Yes, you should have given me a thumbs-up as soon as you heard the word **bake,** because **bake** *does not* rhyme with **cat, mat,** and **sat.**

(Continue the activity with the following rows of words, reading each row two times:
Make bake flake fan.
Meat seat wet wheat.
Line pine pick mine.
Boat got coat note.)

Activity 3 Syllable Blending

Elicit responses. **Guide** as needed.
Let's try making some words. I'm going to say some word parts, and you will put them together to say the whole word.

Your turn. Listen. Doc tor. What word? *Doctor.*

Yes, you made the word **doctor.** Let's try some more. Li brar y. What word? *Library.*

Sprink ler. What word? *Sprinkler.*

Pen cil. What word? *Pencil.*

E ras er. What word? *Eraser.*

Cray on. What word? *Crayon.*

Straw ber ry. What word? *Strawberry.*

Ta ble. What word? *Table.*

Part B: Letter Recognition and Formation

6 minutes

Student Materials:
Lined paper

Activity 1 Letter Recognition Review—Capital M

Elicit responses. **Guide** as needed. **Write** capital M on the board. **Point** to capital M.
We learned that this letter is **capital M.** What letter name? *Capital M.*
Again, what letter name? *Capital M.*
Review as needed.

Activity 2 Letter Formation Review—Capital M

Now we're going to practice writing **capital M.** When you practice writing, you'll learn not only where to start and stop the letter, but also which way to move your hand when you're making the letter. It's tricky, but you're so smart you'll learn how to write **capital M** very quickly. Watch.

Here's how you write **capital M** in the air.
Model capital M formation in the air (with your back to students).

70 Lesson 19

Watch again.

Now let's practice writing **capital M** in the air. Hold up your writing hand, and make **capital M** in the air.
Guide students as they write capital M in the air.

Let's practice **capital M** again.

Here's how to write **capital M** with your writing hand pointer finger.
Model capital M formation on the board with your finger (with your back to students).

Watch again.

Now let's practice writing **capital M** on your table without using your pencil. Use your writing hand pointer finger, and make **capital M** on your table.
Guide students as they write capital M on their table or desktop.

Let's practice **capital M** again.

Model writing capital M on the board (with your back to students).
Remember that every letter has a name.
You learned the name of this letter is **capital M.** What letter name? *Capital M.*
Again, what letter name? *Capital M.*

Provide lined paper to students.
Now let's practice writing **capital M** with your pencil.
Guide students as they write capital M on their paper. **Review** as needed.

 Link letter names to letter sounds as needed as they appear in the program.

Part C: Comprehension Strategies

 9 minutes

Teacher Materials:
Reading *Teacher Presentation Book A*

Activity 1 Listening Comprehension—A During-Reading Strategy

Elicit responses to questions. **Guide** as needed.
Today you'll hear a new story. What should you do while I read the story? (Idea: *Think about the story.*)

During the story, I'll ask questions to see whether you understand what I'm reading. What will I ask as I read the story to you? *Questions.*

Later in today's lesson, you'll see a picture about the story. We'll talk more about the story when you see this picture. What will you see later in today's lesson? (Idea: *The picture from the story.*)

The title of the story is "An Adventure." What's the title of the story? *An Adventure.*

Read story with prosody.
The Olson family likes a good adventure. Kathy and Lewis are always trying to come up with ideas of exciting things to do with their parents. They have gone on hikes, gone fishing, and even stayed up late at night watching for shooting stars in the sky.

Lesson 19   71

1. Who likes adventures? *The Olson family.*

2. What adventure did they have late at night? (Idea: *Watching for shooting stars in the sky.*)

Kathy and Lewis are **siblings.** A **sibling** is a **brother or sister.** Kathy and Lewis both have really good ideas for adventures. One afternoon, they were trying to come up with an adventure for the weekend. Kathy had an idea to visit the local carnival. Lewis had an idea to pack a picnic dinner and go to the park. The Olson family finally decided to go to the carnival, and then end their day with a picnic in the park. The weekend came, and Kathy and Lewis packed a picnic dinner. Then the Olsons left for the carnival. The whole family went on the roller coaster three times. Wow, the ride was scary, but it was fun! Then the **siblings** and their parents went to the park and ate their delicious picnic dinner.

1. What's another word for a **brother or sister?** *Sibling.*

2. How many times did the family go on the roller coaster? *Three.*

3. Where did they have a picnic? *In the park.*

Before they were even done eating, the **siblings,** Kathy and Lewis, began planning their next adventure. I think one of them said something about a trip to the moon!

1. Where did the family want to go next? *To the moon.*

You learned a new word in the story today. **Sibling** means **a brother or sister.** What does **sibling** mean? *A brother or sister.*

What's another word for **brother and sister?** *Sibling.*

Activity 2 Story Recall—An After-Reading Strategy

 Show picture from Lesson 19, page 122, in *Teacher Presentation Book A.*

Elicit responses to questions. **Guide** as needed.
Listen as I ask you some questions about the story we read earlier and the picture you see now.

What is the Olson family doing for their adventure in this picture? (Idea: *Having a picnic.*)

What did they bring the food in? (Idea: *A basket.*)

Where do you go for picnics? (Student response.)

Have you gone on an adventure with your family? (Student response.)

If you have a sibling, tell me about him or her. (Student response.)

3 minutes

Activity 2, to be completed <u>after</u> the picture in Lesson 19 is shown to students.

Lesson 20

Materials
Teacher: Reading *Teacher Presentation Book A*, IWB-Letter Recognition
Student: Lined paper

5 minutes

Part A: Phonemic and Phonological Awareness

Activity 1 Rhyme Production

Emphasize italicized words. **Elicit** responses. **Guide** as needed.
For the next activity, I'll start the sentence, and you finish the sentence by choosing a word that rhymes. Listen closely, and see if you can help me.

I'll finish the first one. Did you ever see a *goat* wearing a *coat*?

Your turn. Did you ever see a *fly* eating a _____? (Idea: *tie*.)

Did you ever see a *snail* with a big, long _____? (Idea: *tail*.)

Did you ever see a *bee* climbing a _____? (Idea: *tree*.)

Did you ever see a *rock* wearing a _____? (Idea: *sock*.)

Did you ever see a *cook* cutting with a _____? (Idea: *book*.)

Did you ever see a *dog* talking to a _____? (Idea: *frog*.)

Let's see how many words we can think of that rhyme with *pot*. (Idea: *cot, lot, dot, spot*.)

Wow, you thought of _____ words.

(Continue the activity with the following words: fly, ran.)

Activity 2 Syllable Segmentation

Elicit responses. **Guide** clapping as needed.
I'll tell you the compound word. You tell me the two smaller words that make up the whole word. Be sure to clap as you say each smaller word.

Your turn. **Hairbrush.** Say the two parts, and clap for each part. *Hair. Brush.*

You're right. The two words are **hair** and **brush.**

(Continue the activity with the following words: backpack, notebook, rosebush, hilltop.)

Lesson 20   73

Activity 3 Syllable Segmentation

Elicit responses. **Guide** clapping as needed.
You've done so well finding the parts of a compound word. Now let's try to find the parts of other words. We're going to clap for each part of a word as we say it. I'll show you how to begin.

My turn. **Lady.** I can say each part and clap. La dy. Your turn. **Lady.** Clap, and say each part. *La dy.*

Yes, you said the parts of **lady** were **la** and **dy.**

(Continue the activity with the following words:
pirate, tiger, needle, tummy, muddy, kitten, pepper, little.)

Part B: Letter Recognition and Formation

6 minutes

Teacher Materials:

IWB

Student Materials:
Lined paper

Activity 1 Letter Recognition Cumulative Review—a/A, m/M

Display on IWB or **write** letters and capitals on the board in the order shown.
Elicit responses to questions. **Guide** as needed.
This week, you've learned one letter and one capital—**m** and **capital M.** Let's review all the letters and capitals you've learned. Are you ready?

Letter	Question	Student Response
m	What letter?	*m.*
A	What letter?	*Capital A.*
M	What letter?	*Capital M.*
a	What letter?	*a.*

Review as needed.

Activity 2 Letter Formation Cumulative Review—a/A, m/M

Write a, capital A, m, and capital M on the board in the order shown (with your back to students). **Provide** lined paper to students.
Show me how you can write these letters and capitals.
Guide students as they write the letters and capitals on their paper. **Review** as needed.

 Link letter names to letter sounds as needed as they appear in the program.

9 minutes

Teacher Materials:
Reading *Teacher Presentation Book A*

Part C: Comprehension Strategies

Activity 1 Listening Comprehension—A During-Reading Strategy

Elicit responses to questions. **Guide** as needed.
Today you'll hear a new story. What should you do while I read the story? (Idea: *Think about the story*.)

During the story, I'll ask questions to see whether you understand what I'm reading. What will I ask as I read the story to you? *Questions.*

Later in today's lesson, you'll see a picture about the story. We'll talk more about the story when you see this picture. What will you see later in today's lesson? (Idea: *The picture from the story*.)

The title of the story is "Answering the Phone." What's the title of the story? *Answering the Phone.*

Read story with prosody.
Aziah was getting ready to enter first grade. She felt quite grown up, so she asked her father whether he thought she was old enough to answer the telephone. Aziah's father explained to her that there is a right way and a wrong way to answer the phone. He taught her that she should nicely say "Hello" when she answered the phone. He told her to never tell her own name to the caller and to take a message if someone the caller asks for cannot come to the phone.

1. What grade is Aziah going into? *First grade.*

2. What did Aziah want to start doing? *Answering the phone.*

That evening when the phone rang, Aziah answered it. She remembered to say "Hello." It was her grandmother, who was very surprised when Aziah answered the phone. Aziah's grandmother told her what a great job she had done. This made Aziah very proud. She knew she was growing up! Aziah and her grandmother had a nice conversation before hanging up. A **conversation** is when you **talk back and forth with another person.**

1. Who answered the phone that evening? *Aziah.*

2. Who called? *Her grandmother.*

3. Aziah and her grandmother had a nice talk. What word means to **talk back and forth with another person?** *Conversation.*

Aziah answers the phone all the time now. She is becoming very good at carrying on a **conversation** on the phone, but sometimes she still forgets to take messages.

1. What does Aziah like to do? *Answer the phone.*

2. What does Aziah sometimes forget to do? *Take a message.*

Lesson 20   75

You learned a new word in the story today. **Conversation. Conversation** means **talk back and forth with another person.** What does **conversation** mean? *Talk back and forth with another person.*
What's another word for **talk back and forth with another person?** *Conversation.*

Activity 2 Story Recall—An After-Reading Strategy

3 minutes

Activity 2, to be completed <u>after</u> the picture in Lesson 20 is shown to students.

 Show picture from Lesson 20, page 129, in *Teacher Presentation Book A.*

Elicit responses to questions. **Guide** as needed.
Listen as I ask you some questions about the story we read earlier and the picture you see now.

Who's answering the phone? *Aziah.*

Who answers the phone at your home? (Student response.)

What should you say when you answer the phone? (Idea: *Hello.*)

Who do you like to have a conversation with on the phone? (Student response.)

Part D: Vocabulary Strategies

5 minutes

Activity 1 Distinguish Shades of Meaning

Today we'll work with words and learn about how they are different. Tell me how these words are somewhat different. [**enjoy** and **appreciate; pass** and **throw; focus** and **attend**]

Model acting out what a particular verb means. **Assign** student partners. **Have** students act out what the verb means with a partner. **Guide** students as needed. **Repeat** sequence for each word.

76 Lesson 20

Lesson 21

Materials
Teacher: Reading *Teacher Presentation Book A*; 2-Phonemic Awareness
Student: Lined paper; copy of 2-Phonemic Awareness

Part A: Phonemic and Phonological Awareness

5 minutes

Teacher Materials:
Phonemic Awareness

Student Materials:
Phonemic Awareness

Activity 1 Rhyme Production

Show Phonemic Awareness. **Elicit** responses. **Guide** as needed.
Today we're going to try a new activity with pictures. We're going to look at the pictures and find pictures that rhyme.

Model use of Phonemic Awareness; point to each picture as word is said.
I'm going to name each picture in the top row. Touch each picture as you repeat the name to me. We're going to be listening for the words that rhyme. Let's try it.

This is a fish. What is this? *A fish.*

This is a dish. What is this? *A dish.*

This is a dog. What is this? *A dog.*

The words that rhyme are **fish** and **dish.** Which words rhyme? *Fish and dish.*

Yes, **fish** and **dish** rhyme. Let's try another one. Remember to touch each picture as you say what it is. This is a cat. What is this? *A cat.*

This is a mat. What is this? *A mat.*

This is a girl. What is this? *A girl.*

Which words rhyme? *Cat and mat.*

Yes, **cat** and **mat** rhyme.

(Continue the activity with the remaining rows of pictures:
Third row: car, man, can.
Fourth row: sock, sun, rock.)

Activity 2 Syllable Blending

Elicit responses. **Guide** as needed.
Let's make some words. I'm going to say some word parts, and you'll put them together to say the whole word.

Your turn. Listen. Va ca tion. What word? *Vacation.*

Lesson 21   77

Yes, you made the word **vacation.** Let's try some more. Win dow. What word? *Window.*

Wa ter fall. What word? *Waterfall.*

Jun gle. What word? *Jungle.*

To geth er. What word? *Together.*

Care ful. What word? *Careful.*

Pho to graph. What word? *Photograph.*

Num ber. What word? *Number.*

Activity 3 Syllable Segmentation

Elicit responses. **Guide** clapping as needed.
I'll tell you the compound word. You tell me the two smaller words that make up the whole word. Be sure to clap as you say each smaller word.

Your turn. **Flashlight.** Say the two parts, and clap for each part. *Flash. Light.*

You're right. The two words are **flash** and **light.**

(Continue the activity with the following words:
sailboat, homework, sunscreen, lighthouse.)

6 minutes

Student Materials:
Lined paper

Part B: Letter Recognition and Formation

Activity 1 Letter Recognition—s

Elicit responses to questions. **Guide** as needed. **Write** s on the board. **Point** to s.
Today you'll learn a new letter.
The name of this letter is **s.** What letter name? *s.*
Again, what letter name? *s.*
Review as needed.

Activity 2 Letter Formation—s

Now we're going to practice writing **s.** When you practice writing, you'll learn not only where to start and stop the letter, but also which way to move your hand when you're making the letter. It's tricky, but you're so smart you'll learn how to write **s** very quickly. Watch.

Here's how you write **s** in the air.
Model s formation in the air (with your back to students).

Watch again.

Now let's practice writing **s** in the air. Hold up your writing hand, and make **s** in the air.
Guide students as they write s in the air.

78   Lesson 21

Let's practice **s** again.

Here's how to write **s** with your writing hand pointer finger.
Model s̲ formation on the board with your finger (with your back to students).
Watch again.

Now let's practice writing **s** on your table without using your pencil. Use your writing hand pointer finger, and make **s** on your table.
Guide students as they write s̲ on their table or desktop.

Let's practice **s** again.

Model writing s on the board (with your back to students).
Remember that every letter has a name. You learned the name of this letter is **s.**
What letter name? *s.*

Again, what letter name? *s.*

Write s̲ on a piece of paper.

Provide lined paper to students.
Now let's practice writing **s** with your pencil.
Guide students as they write s̲ on their paper. **Review** as needed.

 Link letter names to letter sounds as needed as they appear in the program.

 Set up a writing center with writing materials and correct models of letters learned so far for students to use in their free time.

Part C: Comprehension Strategies

9 minutes

Teacher Materials:
Reading *Teacher Presentation Book A*

Activity 1 Listening Comprehension—A During-Reading Strategy

Elicit responses to questions. **Guide** as needed.
The title of today's story is "Hank's Apple Pie." What's the title of the story? *Hank's Apple Pie.*

Read story with prosody.
Hank likes spending time in the kitchen with his mother while she is cooking. Hank's mother is a very good cook. Now and then, Hank's mother will ask him to help her. Sometimes she asks him to stir the batter for a cake, and other times she asks him to roll out the crust for a pie. Hank wants to grow up and be a good cook like his mother. Whenever people come over for dinner, it makes Hank happy when he hears them tell his mother how **wonderful** her food is. Another way to say **wonderful** is **really good.**

1. Who does Hank think is a good cook? *His mother.*

2. What do people say about Hank's mother's cooking? (Idea: *It is wonderful; it is really good.*)

3. What does it mean when something is **wonderful?** *Really good.*

Lesson 21   **79**

Then one day Hank's mother asked him whether he would like to try to make his very first pie. Hank was so excited! His mother asked him what kind of pie he would like to make. Hank got a big grin on his face and blurted out, "Apple, of course!" Hank and his mother began cooking, and before long they had an apple pie that was ready for the oven. When that pie came out of the oven, Hank couldn't wait to try it.

1. What kind of pie did Hank want to make? *Apple.*

2. How many pies did Hank make? *One.*

Hank served the pie to his family for dessert that night. Everyone thought it was **wonderful.** Hank's mother had done a good job teaching him how to cook.

1. Who ate the pie Hank had made? *His family.*

2. Who taught Hank how to cook? *His mother.*

You learned a new word in the story today. **Wonderful. Wonderful** means **really good.** What does **wonderful** mean? *Really good.*

What's another word for **really good?** *Wonderful.*

3 minutes

Activity 2, to be completed <u>after</u> the picture in Lesson 21 is shown to students.

Activity 2 Story Recall—An After-Reading Strategy

 Show picture from Lesson 21, page 136, in *Teacher Presentation Book A.*

Elicit responses to questions. **Guide** as needed.
Listen as I ask you some questions about the story we read earlier and the picture you see now.

Who is holding the pie? *Hank.*

How do you know the pie is hot? (Idea: *Hank has mitts on his hands to protect his hands from the heat.*)

Do you like apple pie? (Student response.)

Does anyone in your family make pies? (Student response.)

Do you like to cook? (Student response.)

80   Lesson 21

Lesson 22

Materials
Teacher: Reading *Teacher Presentation Book A*
Student: Lined paper

5 minutes

Part A: Phonemic and Phonological Awareness

Activity 1 Syllable Segmentation

Elicit responses. **Guide** clapping as needed.

Let's try to find the parts of other words. We're going to clap for each part of a word as we say it. I'll show you how to begin.

My turn. **Jelly.** I can say each part and clap. Jel ly. Your turn. **Jelly.** Clap, and say each part. *Jel ly.*

Yes, you said the parts of **jelly** were **jel** and **ly.**

(Continue the activity with the following words:
ladder, giggle, running, swimming, walking, climbing, faster, slower.)

Let's try a tougher one. My turn. **Banana.** Ba na na. Your turn. **Banana.** Clap, and say each part. *Ba na na.*

Yes, you said the parts of **banana** were **ba na na.** Let's try some more. **Valentine.** *Va len tine.*

Alphabet. *Al pha bet.*

Dinosaur. *Di no saur.*

Vacation. *Va ca tion.*

Activity 2 Syllable Deletion

Elicit responses. **Guide** as needed.
I'm going to tell you a compound word, and you'll take off the *last* part of the word. This is how we do it.

Have students repeat the word. **Use** manipulatives to represent the syllables in the word if students have difficulty.
My turn. **Sunshine.** I can say **sunshine** without **shine. Sun.**
Your turn. Say **sunshine.** *Sunshine.*
Now, say **sunshine** without **shine.** *Sun.*
Yes, you took away the *last* part, **shine,** and all that is left is **sun.**

Your turn to try it by yourself. Say **sailboat.** *Sailboat.*
Now say **sailboat** without **boat.** *Sail.*

Lesson 22   81

Yes, **sailboat** without **boat** is **sail.**

(Continue the activity with the following examples.
Raincoat. Say it without coat.
Birdseed. Say it without seed.
Popcorn. Say it without corn.)

Activity 3   Onset-rime Blending

Elicit responses. **Guide** as needed.
Let's make some words. I'll give you two parts, and you put them together to make a whole word.

Model holding onset for two to three seconds; pause before saying rime; say rime quickly.
My turn. **/mmm/ . . . at.** I can put it together. **Mat.**
Your turn. **/mmm/ . . . at.** Put it together. *Mat.*
Great. You put the parts together to make the word **mat.**

Your turn. **/mmm/ . . . ake.** Put it together. *Make.*
Yes, you put the parts together to make the word **make.**

Let's try some more. **/mmm/ . . . itt.** *Mitt.*

/mmm/ . . . an. *Man.*

/mmm/ . . . y. *My.*

/mmm/ . . . eat. *Meat.*

/mmm/ . . . e. *Me.*

6 minutes

Student Materials:
Lined paper

Part B: Letter Recognition and Formation

Activity 1   Letter Recognition Review—s

Elicit responses to questions. **Guide** as needed. **Write** <u>s</u> on the board. **Point** to <u>s</u>.
We learned that this letter is **s.**
What letter name? *s.*
Again, what letter name? *s.*
Review as needed.

Activity 2   Letter Formation Review—s

Now we're going to practice writing **s.** When you practice writing, you'll learn not only where to start and stop the letter, but also which way to move your hand when you're making the letter. It's tricky, but you're so smart you'll learn how to write **s** very quickly. Watch.

Here's how you write **s** in the air.
Model <u>s</u> formation in the air (with your back to students).
Watch again.

82   Lesson 22

Now let's practice writing **s** in the air. Hold up your writing hand, and make **s** in the air.
Guide students as they write s̲ in the air.

Let's practice **s** again.

Here's how to write **s** with your writing hand pointer finger.
Model s̲ formation on the board with your finger (with your back to students).

Watch again.

Now let's practice writing **s** on your table without using your pencil. Use your writing hand pointer finger, and make **s** on your table.
Guide students as they write s̲ on their table or desktop.

Let's practice **s** again.

Model writing s̲ on the board (with your back to students).
Remember that every letter has a name. You learned the name of this letter is **s.**
What letter name? *s.*

Again, what letter name? *s.*

Provide lined paper to students.
Now let's practice writing **s** with your pencil.
Guide students as they write s̲ on their paper. **Review** as needed.

 Link letter names to letter sounds as needed as they appear in the program.

Part C: Comprehension Strategies

9 minutes

Teacher Materials:
Reading *Teacher Presentation Book A*

Activity 1 Listening Comprehension—An During-Reading Strategy

Elicit responses to questions. **Guide** as needed.
The title of today's story is "What's in the Box?" What's the title of the story? *What's in the Box?*

Read story with prosody.
Fernando's grandparents were coming to visit for the weekend. Fernando loved when they came because they always brought him a big chocolate candy bar. Fernando also enjoyed their visits because his grandfather would play catch with him, and his grandmother would always read to him. On this visit, they had a red and white striped box with them. Fernando couldn't help but **wonder** what was inside. When you **wonder,** you **want to know about something.**

1. Who was coming to visit Fernando for the weekend? *His grandparents.*

2. What's another word for **want to know about something?** *Wonder.*

3. What did his grandparents bring that made Fernando **wonder?** *A red and white striped box.*

Lesson 22   83

Fernando and his grandfather went outside to play catch. While they were playing, Fernando asked his grandfather what was in the box. His grandfather just laughed and said, "So you **wonder** what's in the box? Well, you're going to have to wait a bit to find out." Fernando did not like that answer, so when they went back inside he tried to peek in the box. When Fernando lifted the lid, he saw something squirm inside. His grandmother walked over to him and said, "Why don't you open it?" Fernando removed the lid and found a hamster inside.

1. Who did Fernando ask to tell him what was in the box? *His grandfather.*

2. What was in the box? *A hamster.*

Wow! Fernando was very excited. He had wanted a hamster for a long time. Fernando named his hamster Mr. **Wonder.** Can you guess why?

1. What did Fernando name his hamster? *Mr. Wonder.*

2. How did Fernando feel about getting a hamster? *Very excited.*

You learned a new word in the story today. **Wonder** means **want to know about something.** What does **wonder** mean? *Want to know about something.*

What's another word for **want to know about something?** *Wonder.*

Activity 2 Story Recall—An After-Reading Strategy

 Show picture from Lesson 22, page 142, in *Teacher Presentation Book A*.

Elicit responses to questions. **Guide** as needed.
What's in the box? *A hamster.*

What will Fernando name his hamster? *Mr. Wonder.*

Do you know anyone who owns a hamster? (Student response.)

What do you have to do to take care of a hamster or pet? (Student response.)

What would you like to have in the box if the box was for you? (Student response.)

3 minutes

Activity 2, to be completed <u>after</u> the picture in Lesson 22 is shown to students.

Lesson 23

Materials
Teacher: Reading *Teacher Presentation Book A*; 3-Phonemic Awareness
Student: Lined paper; copy of 3-Phonemic Awareness

5 minutes

Teacher Materials:
Phonemic Awareness

Student Materials:
Phonemic Awareness

Part A: Phonemic and Phonological Awareness

Activity 1 Rhyme Production

Elicit responses. **Guide** as needed.
I'm going to name each picture in the top row. Touch each picture as you repeat the name to me. We're going to be listening for the words that rhyme. Let's try it.

Model use of Phonemic Awareness; point to each picture as word is said.
This is a house. What is this? *A house.*

This is a man. What is this? *A man.*

This is a mouse. What is this? *A mouse.*

Which words rhyme? *House and mouse.*

Yes, **house** and **mouse** rhyme.

(Continue the activity with the remaining rows of pictures:
Second row: boat, goat, girl
Third row: hose, house, nose
Fourth row: glass, pan, man)

Activity 2 Syllable Blending

Elicit responses. **Guide** as needed.
Let's make some words. I'm going to say some word parts, and you'll put them together to say the whole word.

Your turn. Listen. Ta ble cloth. What word? *Tablecloth.*

Yes, you made the word **tablecloth.** Let's try some more. Blan ket. What word? *Blanket.*

Bub ble gum. What word? *Bubblegum.*

El e phant. What word? *Elephant.*

Pil low. What word? *Pillow.*

El e va tor. What word? *Elevator.*

Hel met. What word? *Helmet.*

Hap pi ness. What word? *Happiness.*

Activity 3 Syllable Segmentation

Elicit responses. **Guide** as needed.
We're going to clap for each part of a word as we say it. Be careful. Some words will have *two* parts, and some will have *three* parts. Listen carefully.

My turn. **Standing.** I can say each part and clap. Stand ing. Your turn. **Standing.** Clap, and say each part. *Stand ing.*

Yes, you said the parts of **standing** were **stand** and **ing.** Let's try some more. **Sleeping.** *Sleep ing.*

Eating. *Eat ing.*

Animal. *An i mal.*

Sitting. *Sit ting.*

Counting. *Count ing.*

Spaghetti. *Spa ghet ti.*

Porcupine. *Por cu pine.*

6 minutes

Student Materials:
Lined paper

Part B: Letter Recognition and Formation

Activity 1 Letter Recognition—Capital S

Elicit responses to questions. **Guide** as needed. **Write** capital S on the board. **Point** to capital S
Today you'll learn another way to write **s.**
The name of this letter is **capital S.** What letter name? *Capital S.*
Again, what letter name? *Capital S.*
Review as needed.

Activity 2 Letter Formation—Capital S

Now, we're going to practice writing **capital S.** When you practice writing, you'll learn not only where to start and stop the letter, but which way to move your hand when you're making the letter. It's tricky, but you're so smart you'll learn how to write **capital S** very quickly. Watch.

Here's how you write **capital S** in the air.
Model capital S formation in the air (with your back to students).

Watch again.

Now let's practice writing **capital S** in the air. Hold up your writing hand, and make **capital S** in the air.
Guide students as they write capital S in the air.
Let's practice **capital S** again.

86 Lesson 23

Here's how to write **capital S** with your writing hand pointer finger.
Model capital S formation on the board with your finger (with your back to students).

Watch again.

Now let's practice writing **capital S** on your table without using your pencil.
Use your writing hand pointer finger, and make **capital S** on your table.
Guide students as they write capital S on their table or desktop.

Let's practice **capital S** again.

Remember that every letter has a name.
Model writing capital S on the board (with your back to students).
You learned the name of this letter is **capital S.** What letter name? *Capital S.*

Again, what letter name? *Capital S.*

Provide lined paper to students.
Now let's practice writing **capital S** with your pencil.
Guide students as they write capital S on their paper. **Review** as needed.

 Link letter names to letter sounds as needed as they appear in the program.

Part C: Comprehension Strategies

9 minutes

Teacher Materials:
Reading *Teacher Presentation Book A*

Activity 1 Listening Comprehension—A During-Reading Strategy

Elicit responses to questions. **Guide** as needed.
The title of today's story is "A Walk in the Rain." What's the title of the story? *A Walk in the Rain.*

It was fall, and a new year of school had just started. Luisa and Johnny were friends who walked to school every day. The fall weather was unpredictable. One day it was hot and sunny, and everyone would wear their shorts to school. The next day it would be cold and rainy. So Luisa and Johnny had learned to be **prepared.** When you are **prepared,** you are **ready for anything.**

1. What did Luisa and Johnny do together? *They walked to school.*

2. What time of the year was it? *Fall.*

3. What's another word for **ready for anything?** *Prepared.*

It was Monday morning when Luisa stepped out her front door and saw that it was raining, and raining hard. She did not even think about asking her mother to drive her and Johnny to school because she already had rain boots and a raincoat to wear. Luisa called Johnny and told him to get **prepared** for a rainy walk to school. When they were both **prepared** for school, Johnny and Luisa met out in front of her house. Luisa had even brought her bright red umbrella along.

Lesson 23   **87**

1. What day of the week was it raining? *Monday.*

2. What did Luisa and Johnny wear to school? (Idea: *Raincoats; rain boots.*)

3. Why did Luisa tell Johnny when she called him? (Idea: *To get prepared for a rainy walk to school.*)

When Johnny and Luisa arrived at school and removed their rain gear, they were all dry. Many of the other kids had not been **prepared,** and they were very wet. Do you think it is good to be **prepared?**

1. When Johnny and Luisa arrived at school, were they wet or dry? *Dry.*

2. What about her classmates who were not **prepared** for the rain? Were they wet or dry? *Wet.*

You learned a new word in the story today. **Prepared** means **ready for anything.** What does **prepared** mean? *Ready for anything.*

What's another word for **ready for anything?** *Prepared.*

Activity 2 Story Recall—An After-Reading Strategy

 Show picture from Lesson 23, page 147, in *Teacher Presentation Book A.*

Elicit responses to questions. **Guide** as needed.
Listen as I ask you some questions about the story we read earlier and the picture you see now.

What is Luisa holding? *An umbrella.*

Why didn't Johnny need to walk under the umbrella? (Idea: *He has a rain hat.*)

Why do you think it would be fun to walk in the rain? (Student responses.)

What should you wear to be prepared to walk in the rain? (Ideas: *Umbrella, raincoat, rain hat, and rain boots.*)

3 minutes

Activity 2, to be completed <u>after</u> the picture in Lesson 23 is shown to students.

88   Lesson 23

Lesson 24

Materials
Teacher: Reading *Teacher Presentation Book A*
Student: Lined paper

5 minutes

Part A: Phonemic and Phonological Awareness

Activity 1 Syllable Segmentation

Elicit responses. **Guide** clapping as needed.
Let's go back and add a special step with our clapping. Listen. **Standing.** I can say each part and clap. Stand ing. I clapped twice, so that tells me there are *two* parts or *two* syllables.

Your turn. **Standing.** Clap, and say each part. *Stand ing.*

Yes. How many times did you clap? *Two.*

So how many parts or syllables are in that word? *Two.*

Yes, there are *two* parts or syllables.

(Continue the activity with the following words:
sleeping, eating, animal, sitting.)

Activity 2 Syllable Deletion

Show Phonemic Awareness. **Elicit** responses. **Guide** as needed.
We're going to work with compound words again. I'm going to tell you a compound word, and you'll take off the last part of the word. This is how we do it.

My turn. **Bunkbed.** I can say **bunkbed** without **bed. Bunk.**

Your turn. Say **bunkbed.** *Bunkbed.*
Now say **bunkbed** without **bed.** *Bunk.*
Yes, you took away the *last* part, **bed,** and all that is left is **bunk.**

Your turn to try one by yourself. Say **snowman.** *Snowman.*
Now say **snowman** without **man.** *Snow.*
Yes, **snowman** without **man** is **snow.**

(Continue the activity with the following examples.
Pancake. Say it without cake.
Starfish. Say it without fish.
Toothbrush. Say it without brush.)

Lesson 24   89

Activity 3 Onset-Rime Blending

Elicit responses. **Guide** as needed.
Let's make some words. I'll give you two parts, and you put them together to make a whole word.

Model holding onset for two to three seconds; pause before saying rime; say rime quickly.
My turn. **/sss/ . . . at.** I can put it together. **Sat.**
Your turn. **/sss/ . . . at.** Put it together. *Sat.*
Great. You put the parts together to make the word **sat.**

Your turn. **/sss/ . . . it.** Put it together. *Sit.*
Yes, you put the parts together to make the word **sit.**

Let's try some more. **/sss/ . . . eat.** *Seat.*

/sss/ . . . ick. *Sick.*

/sss/ . . . ee. *See.*

/sss/ . . . oap. *Soap.*

/sss/ . . . eed. *Seed.*

Part B: Letter Recognition and Formation

6 minutes

Student Materials:
Lined paper

Activity 1 Letter Recognition Review—Capital S

Elicit responses to questions. **Guide** as needed. **Write** capital S on the board. **Point** to capital S.
We learned that this letter is **capital S.**
What letter name? *Capital S.*
Again, what letter name? *Capital S.*
Review as needed.

Activity 2 Letter Formation Review—Capital S

Now we're going to practice writing **capital S.** When you practice writing, you'll learn not only where to start and stop the letter, but also which way to move your hand when you're making the letter. It's tricky, but you're so smart you'll learn how to write **capital S** very quickly. Watch.

Here's how you write **capital S** in the air.
Model capital S formation in the air (with your back to students).

Watch again.

Now let's practice writing **capital S** in the air. Hold up your writing hand, and make **capital S** in the air.
Guide students as they write capital S in the air.
Let's practice **capital S** again.

90   Lesson 24

Here's how to write **capital S** with your writing hand pointer finger.
Model capital S formation on the board with your finger (with your back to students).

Watch again.

Now let's practice writing **capital S** on your table without using your pencil.
Use your writing hand pointer finger, and make **capital S** on your table.
Guide students as they write capital S on their table or desktop.
Let's practice **capital S** again.

Remember that every letter has a name.
Model writing capital S on the board (with your back to students).
You learned the name of this letter is **capital S.** What letter name? *Capital S.*

Again, what letter name? *Capital S.*

Provide lined paper to students.
Now let's practice writing **capital S** with your pencil.
Guide students as they write capital S on their paper. **Review** as needed.

 Link letter names to letter sounds as needed as they appear in the program.

Part C: Comprehension Strategies

9 minutes

Teacher Materials:
Reading *Teacher Presentation Book A*

Activity 1 Listening Comprehension—A During-Reading Strategy

Elicit responses to questions. **Guide** as needed.
Do you like recess? (Student response.)

The title of today's story is "Recess." What's the title of the story? *Recess.*

Read story with prosody.
It was time for recess, and all the children rushed to line up at the door to go out. Ms. Vincent told the children to remember their manners and not push or shove while standing in line. She also told the children that the school had **purchased** new pieces of playground equipment including some new jump ropes and balls. When something is **purchased,** it has been **paid for.**

1. Why did the children rush to line up? (Idea: *It was time for recess.*)

2. What was **purchased** for the children? (Idea: *Jump ropes; balls.*)

3. What's another word for **paid for?** *Purchased.*

The children grabbed the new jump ropes and balls and went outside. They took turns holding the rope and jumping. At first, they had a hard time figuring out the best speed to twirl the rope. Sometimes the children made it go too fast, and other times they made it go too slow. Once they figured out the right speed, the children had fun. After each of them had one turn, recess was over and it was time to go back inside.

Lesson 24 **91**

1. What game did the children play outside? *Jump rope.*

2. How many turns did each child get? *One turn.*

Ms. Vincent asked the children to draw a picture of something they enjoyed doing. Most of them drew a picture of children jumping rope. The children were very happy with the new playground equipment that had been **purchased** for them.

1. What was the teacher's name? *Ms. Vincent.*

2. What did most of the children draw pictures of? *Children jumping rope.*

You learned a new word in the story today. **Purchased** means **paid for.** What does **purchased** mean? *Paid for.*

What's another word for **paid for?** *Purchased.*

Activity 2 Story Recall—An After-Reading Strategy

  Show picture from Lesson 24, page 152, in *Teacher Presentation Book A.*

Elicit responses to questions. **Guide** as needed.
Listen as I ask you some questions about the story we read earlier and the picture you see now.

How many students are in the picture? *Three.*

How can you tell the students are having fun while they jump rope? (Idea: *They are smiling; their faces look happy.*)

What do you like to do at recess? (Student response.)

What do you do when you purchase something? (Student response.)

What things do you like to purchase? (Student response.)

3 minutes

Activity 2, to be completed <u>after</u> the picture in Lesson 24 is shown to students.

Lesson 25

Materials
Teacher: Reading *Teacher Presentation Book A*; 4-Phonemic Awareness, IWB-Letter Recognition
Student: Lined and drawing paper; copy of 4-Phonemic Awareness

Part A: Phonemic and Phonological Awareness

5 minutes

Teacher Materials:
Phonemic Awareness

Student Materials:
Phonemic Awareness

Activity 1 Rhyme Production

Show Phonemic Awareness. **Elicit** responses. **Guide** as needed.
We're going to look at pictures and find pictures of words that rhyme. I'm going to name each picture in the top row. Touch each picture as you repeat the name to me. We're going to be listening for the words that rhyme.

Model use of Phonemic Awareness; point to each picture as word is said.
This is a nose. What is this? *A nose.*

These are toes. What are these? *Toes.*

This is a table. What is this? *A table.*

Which words rhyme? *Nose and toes.*

Yes, **nose** and **toes** rhyme.

(Continue the activity with the remaining rows of pictures:
Second row: book, ball, hook
Third row: clock, block, rake
Fourth row: tree, cup, bee.)

Activity 2 Syllable Deletion

Elicit responses. **Guide** as needed.
We're going to work with compound words again. I'm going to tell you a compound word, and you'll take off the *last* part of the word. This is how we do it.

Your turn. Say **French fry.** *French fry.*

Now, say **French fry** without **fry.** *French.*

Yes, you took away the *last* part, **fry,** and all that is left is **French.**

(Continue the activity with the following examples:
Baseball. Say it without ball.
Sidewalk. Say it without walk.
Meatball. Say it without ball.
Rainbow. Say it without bow.)

Lesson 25   93

Activity 3 — Onset-Rime Blending

Elicit responses. **Guide** as needed.
Let's make some words. I'll give you two parts, and you put them together to make a whole word.

My turn. **/fff/ . . . at.** I can put it together. **Fat.**
Your turn. **/fff/ . . . at.** Put it together. *Fat.*
Great. You put the parts together to make the word **fat.**
Your turn. **/fff/ . . . eet.** Put it together. *Feet.*
Yes, you put the parts together to make the word **feet.**

Let's try some more. **/fff/ . . . un.** *Fun.*

/fff/ . . . ill. *Fill.*

/fff/ . . . ox. *Fox.*

/fff/ . . . an. *Fan.*

/fff/ . . . all. *Fall.*

Part B: Letter Recognition and Formation

6 minutes

Activity 1 — Letter Recognition Cumulative Review—a/A, m/M, s/S

Teacher Materials:

Student Materials:
Lined paper

Display on IWB or **write** letters and capitals on the board in the order shown. **Elicit** responses to questions. **Guide** as needed.
This week you've learned one letter and one capital—**s** and **capital S**. Let's review all the letters and capitals you've learned. Are you ready?

Letter	Question	Student Response
s	What letter?	*s.*
M	What letter?	*Capital M.*
m	What letter?	*m.*
A	What letter?	*Capital A.*
S	What letter?	*Capital S.*
a	What letter?	*a.*

Review as needed.

94   Lesson 25

Activity 2 Letter Formation Cumulative Review—a/A, m/M, s/S

Write a, capital A, m, capital M, s, and capital S on the board in the order shown (with your back to students). **Provide** lined paper to students.
Show me how you can write these letters and capitals.
Guide students as they write the letters and capitals on their paper. **Review** as needed.

 Link letter names to letter sounds as they appear in the program as needed.

Part C: Comprehension Strategies

9 minutes

Teacher Materials:
Reading *Teacher Presentation Book A*

Student Materials:
Drawing paper

Activity 1 Listening Comprehension—A During-Reading Strategy

 Show students the picture in Lesson 2, page 12, in *Teacher Presentation Book A*.

Elicit responses to questions. **Guide** as needed.
Today we're going to listen to one of our favorite stories. Listen carefully, and see whether you remember this story. The title of the story is "Marietta's Experiment." What's the title of the story? *Marietta's Experiment.*

Read story with prosody.
Marietta loved to cook. Her favorite food was peanuts. One day, Marietta wanted to fix herself a peanut butter and honey sandwich for lunch. She went to the cupboard and got the peanut butter jar. When she opened it, she saw that all the peanut butter was gone! What was she going to do? Marietta decided to do an **experiment. An experiment is when you try out a new idea.** Her idea was to make her own peanut butter. She really wanted that peanut butter and honey sandwich.

1. What did Marietta see when she opened the peanut butter jar? (Idea: *The peanut butter was gone; the jar was empty.*)

2. What is it called when you try out a new idea? *Experiment.*

3. What **experiment** did Marietta decide to do? *Make peanut butter.*

Marietta found some plain peanuts, cracked them open, threw the shells into the garbage can, and put the peanuts into a big red bowl. Next, she took out a big wooden spoon and tried to mash the peanuts, but they just slid around in the bowl. She couldn't keep the peanuts still long enough to mash them! Marietta asked her mother for help. They put the peanuts into a blender. The blender only mashed the peanuts. So, Marietta and her mother added some oil and a little sugar. This time, the mashed peanuts stuck together. She had made peanut butter! Marietta proudly took her homemade peanut butter and put it into a jar.

1. What did she put the peanuts in? *A big red bowl.*

2. What did Marietta and her mother put the peanuts in to mash them? *The blender.*

Lesson 25   **95**

Marietta was excited to taste her **experiment.** She took a spoon and dipped it into the jar to get a big scoop. Then she closed her eyes and tasted her homemade peanut butter. She couldn't believe how good it was! Marietta was so happy with her peanut butter that she wrote the recipe so she could make it again.

1. What was Marietta excited to do? *Taste her experiment.*

2. Why did she write down the recipe? (**Idea:** *It was so good; so she could make it again.*)

You learned a new word in the story today. **Experiment** means **when you try out a new idea.** What does **experiment** mean? *When you try out a new idea.*

What's another word for **when you try out a new idea?** *Experiment.*

Activity 2 Make a Connection—An After-Reading Strategy

Provide drawing paper to students. **Elicit** responses to questions. **Guide** as needed.
Marietta loved to eat peanut butter. She loved it so much she figured out a way to make peanut butter. What's your favorite way to eat peanut butter? (Student response.)

Draw your favorite way to eat peanut butter. It might be in a sandwich. Or it could be on toast or pancakes. Maybe you have a different favorite way to eat peanut butter that you can draw.

Model writing a sentence based on a picture you drew about a connection you made. Write a sentence below your picture that describes what you drew from the connection you made. If you need help, ask me.
Monitor students. **Guide** as needed.

5 minutes

Part D: Vocabulary Strategies

Activity 1 Distinguish Shades of Meaning

Today we'll work with words and learn about how they are different. Tell me how these words are somewhat different. [**wonder** and **question; purchased** and **bought; enjoy** and **appreciate**]

Model acting out what a particular verb means. **Assign** student partners. **Have** students act out what the verb means with a partner. **Guide** students as needed. **Repeat** sequence for each word.

96   Lesson 25

Lesson 26

> **Materials**
> **Teacher:** Reading *Teacher Presentation Book A*
> **Student:** Lined and drawing paper

5 minutes

Part A: Phonemic and Phonological Awareness

Activity 1 Syllable Blending

Elicit responses. **Guide** as needed.
I'm going to say some word parts, and you'll put them together to say the whole word.

Your turn. Listen. Bi cy cle. What word? *Bicycle.*

Yes, you made the word **bicycle.** Let's try some more. Shad ow. What word? *Shadow.*

Wa ter mel on. What word? *Watermelon.*

Po lar bear. What word? *Polar bear.*

Qui et. What word? *Quiet.*

Yes ter day. What word? *Yesterday.*

El bow. What word? *Elbow.*

Sat ur day. What word? *Saturday.*

Activity 2 Syllable Segmentation

Elicit responses. **Guide** clapping as needed.
We're going to clap for each part of a word as we say it. Be careful. Some words will have *two* parts, and some will have *three* parts. Listen carefully.

Your turn. **Apple.** Clap, and say each part. *Ap ple.*

Yes, you said the parts of **apple** were **ap** and **ple.** Let's try some more. **Window.** *Win dow.*

Elbow. *El bow.*

Tomato. *To ma to.*

Video. *Vid e o.*

Lesson 26   97

Let's go back and add that special step with our clapping. First we will clap for each part of the word, and then you can tell me how many times you clapped. The number of times you clap will tell us how many parts or syllables are in the word.

Listen. **Apple.** I can say each part and clap. *Ap ple.* I clapped twice, so that tells me there are *two* parts or *two* syllables. Your turn. **Apple.** Clap, and say each part. *Ap ple.*

Yes. How many times did you clap? *Two.*

So how many parts or syllables are in that word? *Two.*

Yes, there are *two* parts or syllables in the word **apple.**

(Continue the activity with the following words: window, elbow, tomato, video, pencil, eraser.)

6 minutes

Student Materials:
Lined paper

Part B: Letter Recognition and Formation

Activity 1 Letter Recognition—e

Elicit responses to questions. **Guide** as needed. **Write** e on the board. Point to e.
Today you'll learn a new letter.
The name of this letter is **e.** What letter name? *e.*
Again, what letter name? *e.*
Review as needed.

Activity 2 Letter Formation—e

Now we're going to practice writing **e.** When you practice writing, you'll learn not only where to start and stop the letter, but also which way to move your hand when you're making the letter. It's tricky, but you're so smart you'll learn how to write **e** very quickly. Watch.

Here's how you write **e** in the air.
Model e formation in the air (with your back to students).

Watch again.

Now let's practice writing **e** in the air. Hold up your writing hand, and make **e** in the air.
Guide students as they write e in the air.

Let's practice **e** again.

Here's how to write **e** with your writing hand pointer finger.
Model e formation on the board with your finger (with your back to students).

Watch again.

Now let's practice writing **e** on your table without using your pencil. Use your writing hand pointer finger, and make **e** on your table.
Guide students as they write e on their table or desktop.

98   Lesson 26

Let's practice **e** again.

Remember that every letter has a name.
Model writing e on the board (with your back to students).
You learned the name of this letter is **e.** What letter name? *e.*

Again, what letter name? *e.*

Provide lined paper to students.
Now let's practice writing **e** with your pencil.
Guide students as they write e on their paper. **Review** as needed.

 Link letter names to letter sounds as needed as they appear in the program.

Set up a writing center with writing materials and correct models of letters learned so far for students to use in their free time.

Part C: Comprehension Strategies

 9 minutes

Teacher Materials:
Reading *Teacher Presentation Book A*

Student Materials:
Drawing paper

Activity 1 | Listening Comprehension—A During-Reading Strategy

 Show students the picture in Lesson 8, page 49, in *Teacher Presentation Book A*.

Elicit responses to questions. **Guide** as needed.
Today we're going to listen to one of our favorite stories. Listen carefully, and see whether you remember this story. The title of the story is "Our Kindergarten Teacher." What's the title of the story? *Our Kindergarten Teacher.*

Read story with prosody.
We were all back at school after a long three-day weekend. Monday was a holiday, so we had the day off. Ms. Sanchez was having a hard time getting our class to **focus.** When you **focus, you give your attention to something.** She was reviewing letters and letter sounds. We started with the letter "A." Joey kept squirming, and Katie kept yelling out answers without being called on. Oops!

1. What was Ms. Sanchez having a hard time getting the children to do? *Focus and pay attention.*

2. What was Katie doing? *Yelling out answers.*

Then Ms. Sanchez told us she had a surprise. She told us that if we would **focus** on what she was teaching us by giving her all of our attention, she would give us an extra five minutes at recess. Wow! Well, this got our attention. Five extra minutes at recess would be great. After that, the entire class sat up straight and listened very carefully to what she was teaching. We all responded when she asked, and nobody talked unless they were called on.

1. What was the surprise if the students would **focus?** *Extra recess.*

2. How many extra minutes did she promise the children? *Five.*

3. After Ms. Sanchez told the class the surprise, what did the entire class do? (Idea: *Sat up straight and listened very carefully to what she was teaching.*)

Ms. Sanchez was very happy with the class. She said, "I knew you all could **focus** on my lesson." She made sure to give us the extra five minutes at recess. When we came back in, we all gave her our complete attention. We wanted to earn another extra long recess. I'm sure you would do the same, wouldn't you?

1. What did Ms. Sanchez tell the children she knew they could do? *Focus.*

2. Why were the children so good when they came in from recess? (Idea: *They wanted another long recess.*)

You learned a new word in the story today. **Focus. Focus** means **give your attention to something.** What does **focus** mean? *Give your attention to something.*

What's another word for **give your attention to something?** *Focus.*

Activity 2 Make a Connection—An After-Reading Strategy

Provide drawing paper to students. **Guide** as needed.
The students in class were learning to focus. They were learning to sit up straight, look at the teacher, answer questions, and not talk out. What do you look like when you focus? (Ideas: *Sit up; look at the teacher; answer questions; do not talk out.*)

Draw yourself, and show how you focus on your work or on the teacher.

Model writing a sentence based on a picture you drew about a connection you made.
Write a sentence below your picture that describes what you drew from the connection you made. If you need help, ask me.
Monitor students. **Guide** as needed.

Lesson 27

Materials
Teacher: Reading *Teacher Presentation Book A*; 5-Phonemic Awareness
Student: Lined and drawing paper; copy of 5-Phonemic Awareness

Part A: Phonemic and Phonological Awareness

5 minutes

Teacher Materials:
Phonemic Awareness

Student Materials:
Phonemic Awareness

Activity 1 Rhyme Production

Show Phonemic Awareness. **Elicit** responses. **Guide** as needed.
We're going to look at pictures and find pictures of words that rhyme. I'm going to name each picture in the top row. Touch each picture as you repeat the name to me. We're going to be listening for the words that rhyme.

Model use of Phonemic Awareness; point to each picture as word is said.
This is a man. What is this? *A man.*

This is a mouse. What is this? *A mouse.*

This is a fan. What is this? *A fan.*

Which words rhyme? *Man and fan.*

Yes, **man** and **fan** rhyme.

(Continue the activity with the remaining rows of pictures:
Second row: hat, cat, flag
Third row: jar, car, jump
Fourth row: phone, ball, bone.)

Activity 2 Syllable Deletion

Elicit responses. **Guide** as needed.
We're going to work with compound words again. I'm going to tell you a compound word, and you'll take off the *last* part of the word. This is how we do it.

Your turn. Say **grapefruit**. *Grapefruit.*

Now say **grapefruit** without **fruit**. *Grape.*

Yes, you took away the *last* part, **fruit,** and all that is left is **grape.**

(Continue the activity with the following examples:
Spaceship. Say it without ship.
Teapot. Say it without pot.
Football. Say it without ball.
Rosebush. Say it without bush.)

Lesson 27   101

Activity 3 — Onset-Rime Blending

Elicit responses. **Guide** as needed.
Let's make some words. I'll give you two parts, and you put them together to make a whole word.

My turn. **/nnn/ . . . ap.** I can put it together. **Nap.**
Your turn. **/nnn/ . . . ap.** Put it together. *Nap.*
Great. You put the parts together to make the word **nap.**
Your turn. **/nnn/ . . . eat.** Put it together. *Neat.*
Yes, you put the parts together to make the word **neat.**

Let's try some more. **/nnn/ . . . ose.** *Nose.*

/nnn/ . . . ame. *Name.*

/nnn/ . . . ot. *Not.*

/nnn/ . . . o. *No.*

/nnn/ . . . et. *Net.*

/nnn/ . . . ote. *Note.*

Part B: Letter Recognition and Formation

6 minutes

Student Materials:
Lined paper

Activity 1 — Letter Recognition Review—e

Write e on the board. **Elicit** responses to questions. **Guide** as needed. **Point** to e.
We learned that this letter is **e.** What letter name? *e.*
Again, what letter name? *e.*
Review as needed.

Activity 2 — Letter Formation Review—e

Now we're going to practice writing **e.** When you practice writing, you'll learn not only where to start and stop the letter, but also which way to move your hand when you're making the letter. It's tricky, but you're so smart you'll learn how to write **e** very quickly. Watch.

Here's how you write **e** in the air.
Model e formation in the air (with your back to students).

Watch again.

Now let's practice writing **e** in the air. Hold up your writing hand, and make **e** in the air.
Guide students as they write e in the air.

Let's practice **e** again.

Here's how to write **e** with your writing hand pointer finger.
Model e formation on the board with your finger (with your back to students).

Lesson 27

Watch again.

Now let's practice writing **e** on your table without using your pencil. Use your writing hand pointer finger, and make **e** on your table.
Guide students as they write e on their table or desktop.

Let's practice **e** again.

Remember that every letter has a name.
Model writing e on the board (with your back to students).
You learned the name of this letter is **e.** What letter name? *e.*

Again, what letter name? *e.*

Provide lined paper to students.
Now let's practice writing **e** with your pencil.
Guide students as they write e on their paper. **Review** as needed.

 Link letter names to letter sounds as needed as they appear in the program.

Part C: Comprehension Strategies

9 minutes

Teacher Materials:
Reading *Teacher Presentation Book A*

Student Materials:
Drawing paper

Activity 1 Listening Comprehension—A During-Reading Strategy

 Show students the picture in Lesson 10, page 61, in *Teacher Presentation Book A*.

Elicit responses to questions. **Guide** as needed.
Today we're going to listen to one of our favorite stories. This story is about friends. Think about the friends you have made at school this year as you listen to today's story. Thinking about what the story is about helps you understand the story better. The title of today's story is "Friends." What's the title of the story? *Friends.*

Read story with prosody.
Crystal and Brian are sister and brother and best **friends. Friends** are **people you like.** Best **friends** are people you like the most. Crystal and Brian go to the same school, but they are a year apart. They live on "B" street. They play together every day after school, except for Fridays when Brian has piano lessons. Because they are **friends,** Crystal and Brian know a lot about each other.

1. Who are best friends? *Crystal and Brian.*

2. Why can't they play on Fridays? *Brian has piano lessons.*

Lesson 27

Brian was born with an illness that prevents him from being able to walk on his own. Brian uses a wheelchair to get around. Because Crystal is his sister and his **friend,** she helps Brian whenever she can. Sometimes she just walks alongside him while they talk about things. Other times, she'll push Brian around. Sometimes when Brian is not using his wheelchair, he lets Crystal take it for a spin. That's a lot of fun! Just because Brian cannot walk, it does not stop them from playing and doing all the things that **friends** do together.

1. What are **friends?** *People you like.*

2. How does Crystal help Brian? (Idea: *She pushes him around; walks with him.*)

Brian and Crystal think it's great to have **friends.** It's also good to be a **friend.** Good **friends** are always there when you need them. Isn't it great to have **friends?**

1. What are friends? *People you like.*

Today you reviewed a word we've read before. **Friends. Friends** means **people you like.** What does **friends** mean? *People you like.*

What's another word for **people you like?** *Friends.*

Activity 2 Make a Connection—An After-Reading Strategy

Provide drawing paper to students. **Elicit** responses to questions. **Guide** as needed. Crystal and Brian were brother and sister and friends who liked to do things together. What kinds of things do you like to do with your friends or brother or sister? (**Student response.**)

Draw a picture of you with your friends. You can draw a picture of you with your friends here at school, or you can draw a picture of you and your friends at home.

Model writing a sentence based on a picture you drew about a connection you made. Write a sentence below your picture that describes what you drew from the connection you made. If you need help, ask me.
Monitor students. **Guide** as needed.

104   *Lesson 27*

Lesson 28

Materials
Teacher: Reading *Teacher Presentation Book A*
Student: Lined and drawing paper

5 minutes

Part A: Phonemic and Phonological Awareness

Activity 1 Syllable Blending

Elicit responses. **Guide** as needed.
Let's make some words. I'm going to say some word parts, and you will put them together to say the whole word.

Your turn. Listen. Fri day. What word? *Friday.*

Yes, you made the word **Friday.** Let's try some more. Lo tion. What word? *Lotion.*

Pine ap ple. What word? *Pineapple.*

Rac coon. What word? *Raccoon.*

To mor row. What word? *Tomorrow.*

Mon day. What word? *Monday.*

Va nil la. What word? *Vanilla.*

Re mem ber. What word? *Remember.*

Activity 2 Syllable Segmentation

Elicit responses. **Guide** clapping as needed.
Let's work with some words and break them into parts. We're going to clap for each part of a word as we say it. Be careful. Some words will have *two* parts and some will have *three* parts. Listen carefully.

Your turn. **Sister.** Clap, and say each part. *Sis ter.*

Yes, you said the parts of **sister** were **sis** and **ter.** Let's try some more. **Mother.** *Moth er.*

Shoulder. *Shoul der.*

Family. *Fam i ly.*

Telephone. *Tel e phone.*

Lesson 28   105

Let's go back and add that special step with our clapping. First we'll clap for each part of the word, and then you can tell me how many times you clapped. The number of times you clap will tell us how many parts or syllables are in the word.

Your turn. **Sister.** Clap, and say each part. *Sis ter.*

Yes. How many times did you clap? *Two.*

So how many parts or syllables are in that word? *Two.*

Yes, there are *two* parts or syllables in the word **sister.**

(Continue the activity with the following words: mother, shoulder, family, telephone, ruler, marker.)

6 minutes

Student Materials:
Lined paper

Part B: Letter Recognition and Formation

Activity 1 Letter Recognition—Capital E

Elicit responses to questions. **Guide** as needed. **Write** capital E on the board. **Point** to capital E.
Today, you'll learn another way to write **e.**
The name of this letter is **capital E.** What letter name? *Capital E.*
Again, what letter name? *Capital E.*
Review as needed.

Activity 2 Letter Formation—Capital E

Now we're going to practice writing **capital E.** When you practice writing, you'll learn not only where to start and stop the letter, but also which way to move your hand when you're making the letter. It's tricky, but you're so smart you'll learn how to write **capital E** very quickly. Watch.

Here's how you write **capital E** in the air.
Model capital E formation in the air (with your back to students).

Watch again.

Now let's practice writing **capital E** in the air. Hold up your writing hand, and make **capital E** in the air.
Guide students as they write capital E in the air.

Let's practice **capital E** again.

Here's how to write **capital E** with your writing hand pointer finger.
Model capital E formation on the board with your finger (with your back to students).

Watch again.

Now let's practice writing **capital E** on your table without using your pencil. Use your writing hand pointer finger, and make **capital E** on your table.
Guide students as they write capital E on their table or desktop.

106   Lesson 28

Let's practice **capital E** again.

Remember that every letter has a name.
Model writing capital E on the board (with your back to students).
You learned the name of this letter is **capital E.** What letter name? *Capital E.*

Again, what letter name? *Capital E.*

Provide lined paper to students.
Now let's practice writing **capital E** with your pencil.
Guide students as they write capital E on their paper. **Review** as needed.

 Link letter names to letter sounds as needed as they appear in the program.

Part C: Comprehension Strategies

9 minutes

Teacher Materials:
Reading *Teacher Presentation Book A*

Student Materials:
Drawing paper

Activity 1 Listening Comprehension—A During-Reading Strategy

 Show students the picture in Lesson 12, page 74, in *Teacher Presentation Book A*.

Elicit responses to questions. **Guide** as needed.
Today we're going to listen to one of our favorite stories. This story is about a pet dog. Think about a dog you know and how it would act in a thunder and lightning storm. Thinking about what the story is about helps you understand the story better. The title of today's story is "A Dog Named Spot." What's the title of the story? *A Dog Named Spot.*

Read story with prosody.
It had been a nice warm summer day, but that evening Walter noticed that dark clouds had rolled in. It was still pretty warm outside, but he could tell it was about to rain. Before long, the rain started coming down, and then came the thunder and lightning. Spot, Walter's dog, started acting funny. He began to **leap** all over the furniture. **Leap** means the same thing as **jump.**

1. When did the weather change? *Evening.*

2. What happened after the rain started coming down? (Idea: *Thunder started; lightening started.*)

3. Why did Spot start leaping all over the furniture? (Idea: *He was afraid of the storm; the thunder and lightning frightened him.*)

After a little while, Spot started scratching at the door. He really wanted out. Walter opened the door, and Spot ran out. Before Walter could stop him, Spot took a **leap** over the fence and ran down the street. Walter was afraid his dog was gone forever. When the storm ended, Walter ran outside and began looking for Spot. He yelled and yelled for him. Then he saw Spot off in the distance and called for him. Spot came running. Walter watched Spot **leap** right back over the fence and come to see him.

Lesson 28   **107**

1. How did Spot tell Walter he wanted to go outside? *He scratched at the door.*

2. What is another way to say **jump?** *Leap.*

3. When did Walter go outside to look for Spot? *When the storm ended.*

Spot spent the rest of the night close to Walter. He kept licking Walter's face over and over again. Spot was happy to be home, and Walter was even happier to have his best friend back.

1. What did Spot do to Walter's face? *He licked it.*

2. How did Spot feel to be back home? *Happy.*

You learned a new word in the story today. **Leap** means **jump.** What does **leap** mean? *Jump.*

What's another word for **jump?** *Leap.*

Activity 2   Make a Connection—An After-Reading Strategy

Provide drawing paper to students. **Elicit** responses to questions. **Guide** as needed.
Spot was scared of the storm, so he leaped on the furniture, ran outside, and leaped over the fence. He even ran away. Then he came back and spent the rest of the night with Walter. What was your favorite part of the story? (Student response.)

Draw your favorite part of the story. Your favorite part might be the beginning, where Spot is leaping on the furniture. Your favorite part could be in the middle, where Spot leaped over the fence and ran away. Or your favorite part might be at the end, where Spot is back home licking Walter's face.

Model writing a sentence based on a picture you drew about a connection you made. Write a sentence below your picture that describes what you drew from the connection you made. If you need help, ask me.
Monitor students. **Guide** as needed.

Lesson 29

Materials
Teacher: Reading *Teacher Presentation Book A*
Student: Lined and drawing paper

5 minutes

Part A: Phonemic and Phonological Awareness

Activity 1 Rhyme Production

Elicit responses. **Guide** as needed.
You're doing so well with rhyming words that today we're going to try a new activity. I'm going to give you a word, and then I'll tell you the sound I want you to change in order to make a new rhyming word. You have to listen carefully. I'll do the first one for you.

My turn. The word is **man.** Now, I'm going to make a word that rhymes with **man** but starts with **/fff/.** The new rhyming word is **fan.** I rhymed with the word **man,** and made **fan.**

Allow students a few seconds to think about the answer.
Your turn. The word is **man.** Now, think of the word that rhymes with **man,** but starts with **/fff/.** *Fan.*
Yes, **fan** rhymes with **man.**

Let's try some more of these. Your turn. Say **rock.** *Rock.*
Now, think of a word that rhymes with **rock** but starts with **/sss/.** *Sock.*
Yes, **sock** rhymes with **rock.**

(Continue the activity with the following examples:
Mat. Say it with /sss/.
Seed. Say it with /fff/.)

Activity 2 Syllable Blending

Elicit responses. **Guide** as needed.
Let's try making some words. I'm going to say some word parts, and you'll put them together to say the whole word.

Your turn. Listen. Tues day. What word? *Tuesday.*

Yes, you made the word **Tuesday.** Let's try some more. Ap ril. What word? *April.*

Ap ple . . . sauce. What word? *Applesauce.*

Pan ther. What word? *Panther.*

As tro naut. What word? *Astronaut.*

De cem ber. What word? *December.*

Lesson 29   109

Pick le. What word? *Pickle.*

Prin ci pal. What word? *Principal.*

6 minutes

Student Materials:
Lined paper

Part B: Letter Recognition and Formation

Activity 1 Letter Recognition Review—Capital E

Elicit responses to questions. **Guide** as needed. **Write** capital E on the board. **Point** to capital E.
What letter name? *Capital E.*
Again, what letter name? *Capital E.*
Review as needed.

Activity 2 Letter Formation Review—Capital E

Now we're going to practice writing **capital E.** When you practice writing, you'll learn not only where to start and stop the letter, but also which way to move your hand when you're making the letter. It's tricky, but you're so smart you'll learn how to write **capital E** very quickly. Watch.

Here's how you write **capital E** in the air.
Model capital E formation in the air (with your back to students).

Watch again.

Now let's practice writing **capital E** in the air. Hold up your writing hand, and make **capital E** in the air.
Guide students as they write capital E in the air.

Let's practice **capital E** again.

Here's how to write **capital E** with your writing hand pointer finger.
Model capital E formation on the board with your finger (with your back to students).

Watch again.

Now let's practice writing **capital E** on your table without using your pencil. Use your writing hand pointer finger, and make **capital E** on your table.
Guide students as they write capital E on their table or desktop.

Let's practice **capital E** again.

Remember that every letter has a name.
Model writing capital E on the board (with your back to students).
You learned the name of this letter is **capital E.** What letter name? *Capital E.*

Again, what letter name? *Capital E.*

Provide lined paper to students.
Now let's practice writing **capital E** with your pencil.
Guide students as they write capital E on their paper. **Review** as needed.

 Link letter names to letter sounds as needed as they appear in the program.

110   Lesson 29

9 minutes

Teacher Materials:
Reading *Teacher Presentation Book A*

Student Materials:
Drawing paper

Part C: Comprehension Strategies

Activity 1 Listening Comprehension—A During-Reading Strategy

 Show students the picture in Lesson 13, page 82, in *Teacher Presentation Book A*.

Elicit responses to questions. **Guide** as needed.
Today we're going to listen to one of our favorite stories. Who remembers a story with a rocket in it? (Student response.)

The title of today's story is "The Rocket Experiment." What's the title of the story? *The Rocket Experiment.*

Read story with prosody.
Malia's science teacher gave the class an **assignment**. An **assignment** is **work to do.** Students were asked to build something that would fly. Malia gave a lot of thought to what she should build. Malia had read about astronauts and the trips they had made to the moon, so she decided it would be interesting to try and build her own rocket.

1. What was Malia supposed to build? *Something that could fly.*

2. What did Malia decide to do for her **assignment**? *Build a rocket.*

Malia got right to work on her **assignment.** First she gathered up some cardboard. Next she got out the tape. She did her best to try and create a picture in her mind of what she thought a rocket looked like. Malia remembered that a rocket had a cone shape at the top. She also remembered that the body of it was shaped like an empty paper towel roll. She formed the cardboard into those shapes. She then added some small pieces of cardboard on the bottom for fins. Then Malia taped all the pieces of cardboard together. Before long, she had a rocket.

1. Malia tried to make a picture of the rocket in her what? *Mind.*

2. She thought the body of the rocket was shaped like an empty what? *Paper towel roll.*

Malia did not know if her rocket would fly, but she was very happy with the way it looked. She was also proud that she had completed her **assignment** all by herself.

1. Do you think her rocket will fly? Why or why not? (Idea: *No, it's made of cardboard and tape; it has no engine, and so on.*)

You learned a new word in the story today. **Assignment** means **work to do.** What does **assignment** mean? *Work to do.*

What's another word for **work to do**? *Assignment.*

Lesson 29 **111**

Activity 2 Make a Connection—An After-Reading Strategy

Provide drawing paper to students. **Elicit** responses to questions. **Guide** as needed. Malia built a rocket by thinking hard about what a rocket looks like and then getting the materials with which to build. Then she figured out how to put her materials together into a rocket. What kinds of things have you tried to build? (Student response.)

Draw a picture of something that you have tried to build or something you would like to try to build.

Model writing a sentence based on a picture you drew about a connection you made. Write a sentence below your picture that describes what you drew from the connection you made. If you need help, ask me.
Monitor students. **Guide** as needed.

Lesson 30

> **Materials**
> **Teacher:** Reading *Teacher Presentation Book A*, IWB-Letter Recognition
> **Student:** Lined and drawing paper

5 minutes

Part A: Phonemic and Phonological Awareness

Activity 1 Syllable Segmentation

Elicit responses. **Guide** as needed.
Today we're going to clap for each part of a word, and count the number of parts in that word. Remember, the number of times you clap for each part tells us how many parts or syllables are in the word. Let's go.

Your turn. **Brother.** Clap, and say each part. *Broth er.*

Yes. How many times did you clap? *Two.*

So, how many parts or syllables are in that word? *Two.*

Yes, there are *two* parts or syllables in the word **brother.**

(Continue the activity with the following words:
winter, stomach, October, library, children, funny, December.)

Activity 2 Syllable Deletion

Elicit responses. **Guide** as needed.
We're going to work with compound words again. I'm going to tell you a compound word, and you'll take off the *first* part of the word. This is how we do it.

My turn. **Homework.** I can say **homework** without **home.** *Work.*

Your turn. Say **homework.** *Homework.*

Now, say **homework** without **home.** *Work.*
Yes, you took away the *first* part, **home,** and all that is left is **work.**

Your turn. Say **lunchroom.** *Lunchroom.*

Now, say **lunchroom** without **lunch.** *Room.*
Yes, you took away the *first* part, **lunch,** and all that is left is **room.**

(Continue the activity with the following examples:
Fireplace. Say it without fire.
Greenhouse. Say it without green.
Corndog. Say it without corn.
French fry. Say it without French.)

Lesson 30   113

Activity 3 **Onset-Rime Blending**

Elicit responses. **Guide** as needed.
Let's make some words. I'll say two parts, and you put them together to make a whole word.

Your turn. **/rrr/ . . . ead.** Put it together. *Read.*

Great, you put the parts together to make the word **read.** Let's try some more. **/rrr/ . . . ose.** *Rose.*

/rrr/ . . . un. *Run.*

/rrr/ . . . at. *Rat.*

/rrr/ . . . ide. *Ride.*

/rrr/ . . . ain. *Rain.*

/rrr/ . . . oad. *Road.*

Part B: Letter Recognition and Formation

6 minutes

Teacher Materials:

Student Materials:
Lined paper

Activity 1 **Letter Recognition Cumulative Review—a/A, m/M, s/S, e/E**

Display on IWB or **write** letters and capitals on the board in the order shown. **Elicit** responses to questions. **Guide** as needed.
This week you've learned one letter and one capital—**e** and **capital E.** Let's review all the letters and capitals you've learned. Are you ready?

Letter	Question	Student Response
A	What letter?	Capital A.
M	What letter?	Capital M.
e	What letter?	e.
S	What letter?	Capital S.
a	What letter?	a.
s	What letter?	s.
E	What letter?	Capital E.
m	What letter?	m.

Review as needed.

114   Lesson 30

Activity 2 | Letter Formation Cumulative Review—a/A, m/M, s/S, e/E

Write a, capital A, m, capital M, s, capital S, e, and capital E on the board in the order shown (with your back to students). **Provide** lined paper to students.

Show me how you can write these letters and capitals.
Guide students as they write the letters and capitals on their paper. **Review** as needed.

 Link letter names to letter sounds as needed as they appear in the program.

Part C: Comprehension Strategies

 9 minutes

 IWB

Teacher Materials:
Reading *Teacher Presentation Book A*

Student Materials:
Drawing paper

Activity 1 | Listening Comprehension—A During-Reading Strategy

 Show students the picture in Lesson 18, page 115, in *Teacher Presentation Book A*.

Elicit responses to questions. **Guide** as needed.
Today we're going to listen to one of our favorite stories. This story is about a boy who likes hats. Do you like hats? Did you wear a hat to school today? I bet you've already guessed that the title of today's story is "Hats." What's the title of today's story? *Hats.*

Read story with prosody.
Carlos loves hats; he has **several** different kinds. If you have **several** of something, you have **more than two.** Carlos will buy a new hat only if it looks different from any other hat he owns. Sometimes, Carlos goes shopping with his mother just to look at hats. He has even been able to talk others into trading their hat for one of his hats. He only does this if the hat he wants to trade for is really special.

1. Who loves hats? *Carlos.*

2. What does it mean to have **several** of something? *More than two.*

Carlos likes wearing his hats. Each day when Carlos wakes up, he makes a decision about what hat to wear. He makes this decision based on how he is feeling that day. If Carlos is feeling happy, then he wears his cowboy hat. If Carlos is feeling playful, then he wears his red hat with the long feather. Carlos's friends are always curious to see which hat he will be wearing. You never see Carlos without a hat!

1. What do you never see Carlos without? *A hat.*

2. Who takes him shopping for hats? *His mom.*

A lot of people have **several** of the same things. For example, some people have several TVs. Some people have **several** dolls, but for Carlos it's hats. So, if you see someone walking down the street wearing a very special hat, it just might be Carlos.

Lesson 30

1. If you have **several** of something, how many do you have? *More than two.*

You learned a new word in the story today. **Several** means **more than two.** What does **several** mean? *More than two.*

What's another word for **more than two?** *Several.*

Activity 2 Make a Connection—An After-Reading Strategy

Provide drawing paper to students. **Guide** as needed.
Carlos had several hats. That means he had more than two hats. What items do you have more than two of? (Student response.)

Draw a picture of something that you have several of. Maybe your picture will be of stuffed animals because you have several stuffed animals. Or maybe your picture will be of cars because you have several cars. Remember that **several** means **more than two.**

Model writing a sentence based on a picture you drew about a connection you made. Write a sentence below your picture that describes what you drew from the connection you made. If you need help, ask me.
Monitor students. **Guide** as needed.

Part D: Vocabulary Strategies

Activity 1 Distinguish Shades of Meaning

Today we'll work with words and learn about how they are different. Tell me how these words are somewhat different. [**wonder** and **question; leap** and **hop; mope** and **pout**]

Model acting out what a particular verb means. **Assign** student partners. **Have** students act out what the verb means with a partner. **Guide** students as needed. **Repeat** sequence for each word.

116   Lesson 30

Lesson 31

Materials
Teacher: Circle-pattern narrative trade book (same book for Lessons 31–35), 1-My Prediction Chart
Student: Lined paper

5 minutes

Part A: Phonemic and Phonological Awareness

Activity 1 Rhyme Production

Elicit responses. **Guide** as needed.
In our last lesson, you worked hard to think of rhyming words. We're going to try that again. I'm going to say a word, and then I'll tell you the sound I want you to change in order to make a new rhyming word. You have to listen carefully. I'll do the first one for you.

My turn. The word is **meat.** Now I'm going to make a word that rhymes with **meat** but starts with **/sss/.** The new rhyming word is **seat.** I rhymed with the word **meat** and made **seat.** Your turn. The word is **meat.** Now think of the word that rhymes with **meat** but starts with **/sss/.** *Seat.*

Yes, **seat** rhymes with **meat.** Let's try some more of these.

Allow students a few seconds to think about answer.
Your turn. Say **lake.** *Lake.*

Now think of a word that rhymes with **lake** but starts with **/mmm/.** *Make.*

Yes, **make** rhymes with **lake.**

(Continue the activity with the following examples:
More. Say it with /fff/.
Ran. Say it with /mmm/.
Mat. Say it with /b/.
Sit. Say it with /h/.)

Activity 2 Syllable Segmentation

Elicit responses. **Guide** clapping as needed.
Let's see if you can find out how many parts or syllables are in the words I tell you. Remember, the number of times you clap for each part tells us how many parts, or syllables, are in the word. Let's go.

Lesson 31   117

Listen carefully to the first one. **Spring.** Clap, and say each part. *Spring.*

Yes. How many times did you clap? *Once.*

So how many parts, or syllables, are in that word? *One.*

Yes, there is only *one* part, or *one* syllable, in the word **spring.**

(Continue the activity with the following words:
summer, fall, Tuesday, teacher, beautiful, sunny, calendar.)

Activity 3 Onset-Rime Segmentation

Elicit responses. **Guide** as needed.
Let's try something new with words. I'm going to say a word, and then I'll break the word into two parts. Sometimes I forget to say the *last* part of the word. You can help me by saying the *last* part after I say the *first* part.

Model holding onset for two to three seconds; if onset is a stop sound, say quickly.
My turn. The word is **cat.** I'll say the *first* part, /**c**/. Your turn. What is the *last* part? *at.*

Now what's the whole word? *Cat.*

My turn. **Hat.** Say **hat.** *Hat.*

Now I'll say the *first* part, /**h**/. What is the *last* part? *at.*

Whole word? *Hat.*

(Continue the activity with the following words:
Mat: /mmm/ at.
Sink: /sss/ ink.
Pink: /p/ ink.
Rink: /rrr/ ink.)

Part B: Letter Recognition and Formation

6 minutes

Student Materials:
Lined paper

Activity 1 Letter Recognition—r

Elicit responses to questions. **Guide** as needed. **Write** r on the board. **Point** to r.
Today you'll learn a new letter.
The name of this letter is **r.** What letter name? *r.*
Again, what letter name? *r.*
Review as needed.

118 Lesson 31

Activity 2 Letter Formation—r

Now we're going to practice writing r. When you practice writing, you'll learn not only where to start and stop the letter, but also which way to move your hand when you're making the letter. It's tricky, but you're so smart you'll learn how to write **r** very quickly. Watch.

Here's how you write **r** in the air.
Model r formation in the air (with your back to students).

Watch again.

Now let's practice writing **r** in the air. Hold up your writing hand, and make **r** in the air.
Guide students as they write r in the air.

Let's practice **r** again.

Here's how to write **r** with your writing hand pointer finger.
Model r formation on the board with your finger (with your back to students).

Watch again.

Now let's practice writing r on your table without using your pencil. Use your writing hand pointer finger, and make r on your table.
Guide students as they write r on their table or desktop.

Let's practice **r** again.

Remember that every letter has a name.
Model writing r on the board (with your back to students).
You learned the name of this letter is **r.** What letter name? r.

Again, what letter name? r.

Provide lined paper to students.
Now let's practice writing **r** with your pencil.
Guide students as they write r on their paper. **Review** as needed.

 Link letter names to letter sounds as needed as they appear in the program.

Set up a writing center with writing materials and correct models of letters learned so far for students to use in their free time.

Lesson 31 **119**

9 minutes

Teacher Materials:
Circle-pattern narrative trade book

My Prediction Chart

Part C: Comprehension Strategies

Activity 1 Title Identification—A Before-Reading Strategy

  Provide a reading center to display books being read so that students can enjoy them again during free time.

Direct students to narrative trade book of teacher choice. **Elicit** responses to questions. **Guide** as needed.
What do all books have? *A title.*

You'll find the title on the front cover of the book. Where do you find the title? *On the front cover of the book.*

The title tells what the book is about. What does the title tell? *What the book is about.*

If the title is *Little Bear*, I know the book will be about a little bear. If the title is *The Grouchy Ladybug*, I know there will be a ladybug in the story who feels grouchy. If the title of the book is *Spider on the Floor*, what do you think the story will be about? (Idea: *A spider that's on the floor.*)

Discuss other titles and what students think the books are about.

Show title on front cover of book.
Let's look on the front cover of today's book. The title is _____.

What's the title of today's book? (Student response.)

Activity 2 Make a Prediction—A Before-Reading Strategy

Elicit responses to questions. **Guide** as needed.
Now that we know the title of today's book, let's look at the cover and make some good guesses about what we think the story will be about. We call our good guesses **predictions**. What do we call our good guesses? *Predictions.*

What are **predictions**? *Good guesses.*

Show My Prediction Chart
Making good guesses, or predictions, helps us get interested in the story before we read it. Watch me make a good guess about the story I'll read to you today. I'll make a prediction.

Model think-aloud for making a correct prediction. **Show** title, front and back cover, and pictures inside the book.

120 Lesson 31

Sample Wording for Think-Aloud

When I make a prediction, I'll look at the title of the book. I see that the title is _____. I'll write the title in the box labeled "Book Title". Knowing the title helps me make a good guess, or prediction, about what the story will be about. I'll also look at the front and back covers of the book. I can see that there are pictures of _____ on the front and back covers. Seeing these pictures helps me make a good guess, or prediction, about what the story will be about. Finally, I'll open the book and flip through it. I'll look at the pictures. Looking at the pictures is another way to help me make a good guess, or prediction, about the book. Well, let's see. The title of the book is _____, the pictures on the front and back cover show _____, and the pictures inside the book show _____. I think this story will be about _____. I'll write _____ in the box labeled "I Predict That". I'll read the story and check to see whether my good guess, or prediction, was correct.

Activity 3 Listening Comprehension—A During-Reading Strategy

Today we're going to read _____. When a teacher reads to you, it's important to sit straight and tall, look at the book, and think about what the story tells you. It's also important to be very quiet while the teacher reads. If the teacher wants you to talk, the teacher will ask a question. Then it's your turn to talk. When you sit the right way and think hard about the story, you'll enjoy the story more, and so will your classmates.

Model a nonexample of appropriate sitting. **Point** out a student who is sitting appropriately. **Discuss** appropriate and inappropriate behavior for listening to a story.

Now we'll read our book as soon as I see all students sitting straight and tall with eyes on the teacher, mouths closed, and ears ready to listen.

Read trade book. **Model** prosody during read-aloud. **Ask** knowledge questions to engage students as you read (for example, who, what, when, where, why).
Guide as needed.

Lesson 31   **121**

Lesson 32

> **Materials**
> **Teacher:** Circle-pattern narrative trade book, 1-My Prediction Chart (from Lesson 31)
> **Student:** Lined paper

 **5 minutes**

Part A: Phonemic and Phonological Awareness

Activity 1 | Syllable Deletion

Elicit responses. **Guide** as needed.
We're going to work with compound words again. I'm going to tell you a compound word, and you'll take off the *first* part of the word. This is how we do it.

My turn. **Sunshine.** I can say **sunshine** without **sun.** Shine.

Your turn. Say **sunshine.** *Sunshine.*
Now say **sunshine** without **sun.** *Shine.*
Yes, you took away the *first* part, **sun,** and all that is left is **shine.**

Your turn. Say **bedroom.** *Bedroom.*
Now say **bedroom** without **bed.** *Room.*
Yes, you took away the *first* part, **bed,** and all that is left is **room.**

(Continue the activity with the following examples:
Pancake. Say it without pan.
Birdhouse. Say it without bird.
Starfish. Say it without star.
Subway. Say it without sub.)

Activity 2 | Onset-Rime Blending

Elicit responses. **Guide** as needed.
Let's make some words. I'll say two parts, and you put them together to make a whole word.

Model holding onset for two to three seconds; if onset is a stop sound, say quickly.

Your turn. /shshsh/ . . . ip. Put it together. *Ship.*
Great; you put the parts together to make the word **ship.**

Let's try some more. /shshsh/ . . . e. *She.*

/shshsh/ . . . op. *Shop.*

/shshsh/ . . . ake. *Shake.*

/shshsh/ . . . eep. *Sheep.*

/shshsh/ . . . ack. *Shack.*

/shshsh/ . . . ut. *Shut.*

Activity 3 Phoneme Isolation—Initial

Elicit responses. **Guide** thumb movements as needed.
You're working so well with words and parts of words. Let's work on *sounds* in words. I'm going to say a list of words. Some of the words will have the /**mmm**/ sound at the *beginning,* and some will not. I'll say the word first, and then you'll say the word. Give me a thumbs-up if you hear the /**mmm**/ sound. If you don't hear the /**mmm**/ sound at the *beginning* of the word, do nothing. Think about the *first* sound we hear in each word.

Remember, we are listening for the /**mmm**/ sound at the *beginning* of the word, as in the word **mat.** What sound are you listening for? /mmm/.

Listen. **Me.** Say **me.** *Me.*

Give me a thumbs-up if you hear /**mmm**/ at the *beginning* of **me.** (*Thumbs-up.*)

Yes, **me** *begins* with the sound /**mmm**/.

(Continue the activity with the following lists of words:
May. His. Milk. Mop. Run. Moon.
Hug. Mud. End. Make. Man. March.)

Part B: Letter Recognition and Formation

6 minutes

Student Materials:
Lined paper

Activity 1 Letter Recognition Review—r

Elicit responses to questions. **Guide** as needed. **Write** r on the board. **Point** to r.
We learned that this letter is **r.** What letter name? *r.*
Again, what letter name? *r.*
Review as needed.

Activity 2 Letter Formation Review—r

Now we're going to practice writing **r.** When you practice writing, you'll learn not only where to start and stop the letter, but also which way to move your hand when you're making the letter. It's tricky, but you're so smart you'll learn how to write **r** very quickly. Watch.

Lesson 32   **123**

Here's how you write **r** in the air.
Model r formation in the air (with your back to students).

Watch again.

Now let's practice writing **r** in the air. Hold up your writing hand, and make **r** in the air.
Guide students as they write r in the air.
Let's practice **r** again.

Here's how to write **r** with your writing hand pointer finger.
Model r formation on the board with your finger (with your back to students).

Watch again.

Now let's practice writing **r** on your table without using your pencil. Use your writing hand pointer finger, and make **r** on your table.
Guide students as they write r on their table or desktop.

Let's practice **r** again.

Remember that every letter has a name.
Model writing r on the board (with your back to students).
You learned the name of this letter is **r.** What letter name? *r.*
Again, what letter name? *r.*

Provide lined paper to students.
Now let's practice writing **r** with your pencil.
Guide students as they write r on their paper. **Review** as needed.

 Link letter names to letter sounds as needed as they appear in the program.

Part C: Comprehension Strategies

 9 minutes

Teacher Materials:
Circle-pattern narrative trade book

My Prediction Chart

Activity 1 Title and Author Identification—A Before-Reading Strategy

Elicit responses to questions. **Guide** as needed.
Remember that all books have a title. What do all books have? *A title.*

You'll find the title on the front cover of the book. Where do you find the title? *On the front cover of the book.*

The title tells what the book is about. What does the title tell? *What the book is about.*

Direct students to narrative trade book of teacher choice. **Show** title on front cover of book.
The title of today's story is _____. What's the title of today's story? (Student response.)

Other than the title, the front cover of the book also includes the author's name. The author is the person who wrote the book. What do you call the person who wrote the book? *The author.*

124 *Lesson 32*

What's an author? *The person who wrote the book.*

Show author's name on front cover of book.
The author of today's story is _____. Who's the author of today's story? (Student response.)

Activity 2 Check Prediction—An After-Reading Strategy

Elicit responses to questions. **Guide** as needed.
Remember that good guesses are called predictions. What do we call our good guesses? *Predictions.*

When we make a prediction, we need to check several parts of the book. Checking these parts of the book helps us find out what the story will be about. What parts of the book should we check? (Idea: *Title, front cover, back cover, pictures inside the book.*)

Show My Prediction Chart
Listen as I show you how I think to check if my prediction was correct.

Model think-aloud for making connections. **Guide** as needed.

Sample Wording for Think-Aloud

I thought this story would be about _____. I read the story to check to see whether my good guess, or prediction, was correct. I found out that the story was about _____. So my prediction was correct. I'll circle Yes in the box labeled "Was My Prediction Correct?".

Activity 3 Listening Comprehension—A During-Reading Strategy

Today we're going to read _____. When a teacher reads to you, it's important to sit straight and tall, look at the book, and think about what the story tells you. It's also important to be very quiet while the teacher reads. If the teacher wants you to talk, the teacher will ask a question. Then it's your turn to talk. When you sit the right way and think hard about the story, you'll enjoy the story more, and so will your classmates.

Model a nonexample of appropriate sitting. **Point** out a student who is sitting appropriately. **Discuss** appropriate and inappropriate behavior for listening to a story.

Now we'll read our book as soon as I see all students sitting straight and tall with eyes on the teacher, mouths closed, and ears ready to listen.

Read trade book. **Model** prosody during read-aloud. **Ask** knowledge questions to engage students as you read (for example, who, what, when, where, why). **Guide** as needed.

Lesson 32 **125**

Lesson 33

Materials
Teacher: Circle-pattern narrative trade book, 1-My Prediction Chart (from Lesson 32)
Student: Lined paper

5 minutes

Part A: Phonemic and Phonological Awareness

Activity 1 Rhyme Production

Elicit responses. **Guide** as needed.
In our last lesson, you worked hard to think of rhyming words. We're going to try that again. I'm going to say a word, and then I'll tell you the sound I want you to change in order to make a new rhyming word. You have to listen carefully. I'll do the first one for you.

My turn. The word is **seat.** I'm going to make a word that rhymes with seat but starts with **/fff/.** The new rhyming word is **feet.** I rhymed with the word **seat** and made **feet.** Your turn. The word is **seat.** Now think of the word that rhymes with **seat** but starts with **/fff/.** *Feet.*
Yes, **feet** rhymes with **seat.**

Let's try some more. Your turn. Say **wall.** *Wall.*
Now, think of a word that rhymes with **wall** but starts with **/fff/.** *Fall.*
Yes, **fall** rhymes with **wall.**

(Continue the activity with the following examples:
Sit. Say it with /h/.
Like. Say it with /b/.
Mouse. Say it with /h/.
Fox. Say it with /b/.)

Activity 2 Syllable Segmentation

Elicit responses. **Guide** clapping as needed.
Let's see if you can find out how many parts or syllables are in the words I tell you. Remember, the number of times you clap for each part tells us how many parts, or syllables, are in the word. Let's go.

Listen carefully. Your turn. **March.** Clap, and say each part. *March.*

Yes. How many times did you clap? *Once.*

So how many parts, or syllables, are in that word? *One.*

Yes, there is only *one* part, or *one* syllable, in the word **March.**

(Continue the activity with the following words:
weather, jump, seven, jacket, glass, computer, flower, January.)

126   Lesson 33

Activity 3 Onset-Rime Segmentation

Elicit responses. **Guide** as needed.
Let's work with some words. I'm going to say a word, and then I'll break the word into two parts. Sometimes I forget to say the *last* part of the word. You can help me by saying the *last* part after I say the *first* part.

Model holding onset for two to three seconds; if onset is a stop sound, say quickly.
My turn. The word is **seal.** I'll say the first part, **/sss/.** Your turn. What is the *last* part? *eal.*

Now, what's the whole word? *Seal.*

My turn. **Meal.** Say **meal.** *Meal.*

Now I'll say the *first* part, **/mmm/.** What is the *last* part? *eal.*

Whole word? *Meal.*

(Continue the activity with the following words:
How: /h/ ow.
Cow: /c/ ow.
Hoops: /h/ oops.
Loops: /lll/ oops.)

Part B: Letter Recognition and Formation

6 minutes

Student Materials:
Lined paper

Activity 1 Letter Recognition—Capital R

Elicit responses to questions. **Guide** as needed. **Write** capital R on the board. **Point** to capital R.
Today you'll learn another way to write **r.**
The name of this letter is **capital R.** What letter name? *Capital R.*
Again, what letter name? *Capital R.*
Review as needed.

Activity 2 Letter Formation—Capital R

Now we're going to practice writing **capital R.** When you practice writing, you'll learn not only where to start and stop the letter, but also which way to move your hand when you're making the letter. It's tricky, but you're so smart you'll learn how to write **capital R** very quickly. Watch.

Here's how you write **capital R** in the air.
Model capital R formation in the air (with your back to students).

Watch again.

Now let's practice writing **capital R** in the air. Hold up your writing hand, and make **capital R** in the air.
Guide students as they write capital R in the air.
Let's practice **capital R** again.

Here's how to write **capital R** with your writing hand pointer finger.
Model capital R formation on the board with your finger (with your back to students).
Watch again.

Lesson 33   **127**

Now let's practice writing **capital R** on your table without using your pencil. Use your writing hand pointer finger, and make **capital R** on your table.
Guide students as they write capital R on their table or desktop.

Let's practice **capital R** again.

Remember that every letter has a name.
Model writing capital R on the board (with your back to students).
You learned the name of this letter is **capital R.** What letter name? *Capital R.* Again, what letter name? *Capital R.*

Provide lined paper to students.
Now let's practice writing **capital R** with your pencil.
Guide students as they write capital R on their paper. **Review** as needed.

 Link letter names to letter sounds as needed as they appear in the program.

Part C: Comprehension Strategies

 9 minutes

IWB

Teacher Materials:
Circle-pattern narrative trade book

My Prediction Chart

Activity 1 Title and Author Identification—A Before-Reading Strategy

Direct students to narrative trade book of teacher choice. **Elicit** responses to questions. **Guide** as needed.
Where do you find the title? *On the front cover of the book.*

What does the title tell? *What the book is about.*

Other than the title, the front cover of the book also includes the author's name. The author is the person who wrote the book. What do you call the person who wrote the book? *The author.*

What's an author? *The person who wrote the book.*

Show author's name on front cover of book.
The author of today's story is _____. Who's the author of today's story? (Student response.)

Activity 2 Listening Comprehension—A During-Reading Strategy

Elicit responses to questions. **Guide** as needed.
Today we are going to read _____. When a teacher reads to you, it's important to sit straight and tall, look at the book, and think about what the story tells you.

Show me what you should look like when I read to you. (Students should sit straight and tall, look at the teacher, and pay attention.)

It's also important to be very quiet while the teacher reads. If the teacher wants you to talk, the teacher will ask you a question.

128   Lesson 33

When will it be your turn to talk? (**Idea:** *When the teacher asks a question.*)

When you sit the right way and think hard about the story, you'll enjoy the story more, and so will your classmates.

We'll begin as soon as I see all students sitting straight and tall with eyes on the teacher, mouths closed, and ears ready to listen.

Activity 3 Make and Confirm Predictions—A During-Reading Strategy

Show My Prediction Chart. **Elicit** responses to questions. **Guide** as needed.
Remember that good guesses are called predictions. What do we call our good guesses? *Predictions.*

In the last lesson, I predicted what the story was about. I said the story would be about _____. Was my prediction correct? *Yes.*

Besides making a prediction about what the story is about, we can also make a prediction as we read the story. In the last lesson, I noticed that this book was a pattern book. Pattern books are fun to read because they do something over and over again. A pattern is something that you see or hear again and again. When you figure out the pattern, you can make a good guess or prediction about what will happen next.

Listen carefully as I read _____ again, and then I'll show you the pattern. Finding a pattern helps us make a prediction about what will happen next in the story.

Read a few pages of trade book to show pattern of book. **Model** prosody during read-aloud.

Model think-aloud for finding story pattern.

Sample Wording for Think-Aloud

As I read the story, I look for a pattern. A pattern is something I see or hear again and again. Let me read a few pages and I'll see whether there is a pattern. Let's see. The pictures and words are the same or almost the same from one page to the next. When things are the same or almost the same from one page to the next, it means we are reading a pattern book.

I can predict what will happen on the next page from the pattern. The pattern works like this: _____. So I predict that _____ will happen on the next page.

Discuss prediction.
Was my prediction right? (**Student response.**)
Pattern books are fun to read.

Lesson 33 **129**

Lesson 34

Materials
Teacher: Circle-pattern narrative trade book
Student: Lined paper

5 minutes

Part A: Phonemic and Phonological Awareness

Activity 1 Syllable Deletion

Elicit responses. **Guide** as needed.
We're going to work with compound words again. I'm going to tell you a compound word, and you'll take off the *first* part of the word.

Your turn. Say **staircase.** *Staircase.*

Now, say **staircase** without **stair.** *Case.*

Yes, you took away the *first* part, **stair,** and all that is left is **case.**

(Continue the activity with the following examples:
Hot dog. Say it without hot.
Cell phone. Say it without cell.
Daytime. Say it without day.
High chair. Say it without high.)

Activity 2 Onset-Rime Blending

Elicit responses. **Guide** as needed.
Let's make some words. I'll say two parts, and you put them together to make a whole word.

Model holding onset for two to three seconds; if onset is a stop sound, say quickly.
Your turn. /lll/ . . . ike. Put it together. *Like.*
Great; you put the parts together to make the word **like.**

Let's try some more. /lll/ . . . ock. *Lock.*

/lll/ . . . ip. *Lip.*

/d/ . . . og. *Dog.*

/d/ . . . ig. *Dig.*

/d/ . . . eep. *Deep.*

/d/ . . . ate. *Date.*

130   Lesson 34

Activity 3 Phoneme Isolation—Initial

Elicit responses. **Guide** thumb movement as needed.
You're working so well with words and parts of words. Let's work on *sounds* in words. I'm going to say a list of words. Some of the words will have the **/sss/** sound at the *beginning,* and some will not. I'll say the word first, and then you'll say the word. Give me a thumbs-up if you hear the **/sss/** sound. If you don't hear the **/sss/** sound at the *beginning* of the word, do nothing. Think about the *first* sound we hear in each word.

Remember, we're listening for the **/sss/** sound at the *beginning* of the word like in the word **sat.** What sound are you listening for? */sss/.*

Listen. **See.** Say **see.** *See.*

Give me a thumbs-up if you hear **/sss/** at the *beginning* of **see.** (Thumbs-up.)

Yes, **see** *begins* with the sound **/sss/.**

(Continue the activity with the following lists of words.
Say. Tail. Mat. Salt. May. Sip.
Soap. Map. Sand. Hand. Sail. Sent.)

Part B: Letter Recognition and Formation

6 minutes

Student Materials:
Lined paper

Activity 1 Letter Recognition Review—Capital R

Elicit responses to questions. **Guide** as needed. **Write** capital R on the board. **Point** to capital R.
We learned that this letter is **capital R.** What letter name? *Capital R.*
Again, what letter name? *Capital R.*
Review as needed.

Activity 2 Letter Formation Review—Capital R

Now, we're going to practice writing **capital R.** When you practice writing, you'll learn not only where to start and stop the letter, but also which way to move your hand when you're making the letter. It's tricky, but you're so smart you'll learn how to write **capital R** very quickly. Watch.

Here's how you write **capital R** in the air.
Model capital R formation in the air (with your back to students).

Watch again.

Now let's practice writing **capital R** in the air. Hold up your writing hand, and make **capital R** in the air.
Guide students as they write capital R in the air.

Let's practice **capital R** again.

Here's how to write **capital R** with your writing hand pointer finger.
Model capital R formation on the board with your finger (with your back to students).

Lesson 34   131

Watch again.

Now let's practice writing **capital R** on your table without using your pencil. Use your writing hand pointer finger, and make **capital R** on your table.
Guide students as they write capital R on their table or desktop.

Let's practice **capital R** again.

Remember that every letter has a name.
Model writing capital R on the board (with your back to students).
You learned the name of this letter is **capital R.** What letter name? *Capital R.*
Again, what letter name? *Capital R.*

Provide lined paper to students.
Now let's practice writing **capital R** with your pencil.
Guide students as they write capital R on their paper. **Review** as needed.

 Link letter names to letter sounds as needed as they appear in the program.

Part C: Comprehension Strategies

9 minutes

Teacher Materials:
Circle-pattern narrative trade book

Activity 1 Title, Author, and Illustrator Identification—A Before-Reading Strategy

Direct students to narrative trade book of teacher choice. **Elicit** responses to questions. **Guide** as needed.
Where do you find the title? *On the front cover of the book.*

What does the title tell? *What the book is about.*

Show title on the front cover of the book.
The title of this book is _____.

Other than the title, the front cover of the book also includes the author's name. What's an author? *The person who wrote the book.*

The author of today's story is _____. Who's the author of today's story? (Student response.)

Besides the title and author, the front cover of the book also includes the illustrator's name. The illustrator is the person who drew the pictures in the book. What do you call the person who drew the pictures in the book? *The illustrator.*

What's an illustrator? *The person who drew the pictures in the book.*

We call the person who drew the pictures in the book the illustrator because he or she draws illustrations. Illustrations is a big word for pictures. What are illustrations? *Pictures.*

Show illustrator's name on the front cover of the book.
The illustrator of today's story is _____. Who's the illustrator of today's story? (Student response.)

132   Lesson 34

Activity 2 Listening Comprehension—A During-Reading Strategy

Elicit response to questions. **Guide** as needed.

Today we are going to read _____. When a teacher reads to you, it's important to sit straight and tall, look at the book, and think about what the story tells you.

Show me what you should look like when I read to you. (Students should sit straight and tall, look at the teacher, and pay attention.)

It's also important to be very quiet while the teacher reads. If the teacher wants you to talk, the teacher will ask you a question.

When will it be your turn to talk? (Idea: *When the teacher asks a question.*)

When you sit the right way and think hard about the story, you'll enjoy the story more, and so will your classmates.

We'll begin as soon as I see all students sitting straight and tall with eyes on the teacher, mouths closed, and ears ready to listen.

Activity 3 Make and Confirm Predictions—A During-Reading Strategy

Elicit response to questions. **Guide** as needed.

Besides making a prediction of what the story is about before we read, we can also make a prediction as we read the story. In the last lesson, I noticed that this book was a pattern book. Pattern books are fun to read because they do something over and over again. A pattern is something that you see or hear again and again. When you figure out the pattern, you can make a good guess, or prediction, about what will happen next.

Listen carefully as I read a few pages of _____ again, and then help me find the pattern.

Read a few more pages of the trade book not read in the last lesson. **Model** prosody during read-aloud.

Elicit pattern from students.

What's the pattern you notice in the book? (Student response.)

Elicit predictions from students.

From the pattern in the book, what do you predict will happen on the next page? (Student response.)

Read next page of trade book. **Elicit** responses about accuracy of prediction. **Assure** students that the prediction does not have to be accurate. **Guide** as needed.

Was your prediction right? (Student response.)

Finding a pattern helps us make a prediction about what will happen next in the story. Then we can read to check to see whether the prediction was correct. Pattern books are fun to read.

Lesson 34 **133**

Lesson 35

Materials
Teacher: Circle-pattern narrative trade book, IWB-Letter Recognition
Student: Lined paper

5 minutes

Part A: Phonemic and Phonological Awareness

Activity 1 Rhyme Production

Elicit responses. **Guide** as needed.
Let's work with some rhyming words. I'm going to say a word, and then I'll tell you the sound I want you to change in order to make a new rhyming word. You have to listen carefully.

Your turn. The word is **fall.** Now think of the word that rhymes with **fall** but starts with **/c/.** *Call.*

Yes, **call** rhymes with **fall.**

(Continue the activity with the following examples:
Road. Say it with /t/.
Make. Say it with /rrr/.
We. Say it with /mmm/.
Goat. Say it with /b/.
Car. Say it with /j/.)

Activity 2 Syllable Segmentation

Elicit responses. **Guide** clapping as needed.
Let's see if you can find out how many syllables or parts are in the words I tell you. Remember, the number of times you clap for each part tells us how many parts, or syllables, are in the word. Let's go.

Listen carefully. Your turn. **April.** Clap, and say each part. *April.*

Yes. How many times did you clap? *Two.*

So how many parts, or syllables, are in that word? *Two.*

Yes, there are two syllables in the word **April.**

(Continue the activity with the following words:
raining, school, fifteen, blueberry, milk, vehicle, dentist, wonderful.)

134 Lesson 35

Activity 3 | Onset-Rime Segmentation

Elicit responses. **Guide** as needed.
Let's work with words. I'm going to say a word, and then I'll break the word into two parts. Sometimes I forget to say the *last* part of the word. You can help me by saying the *last* part after I say the *first* part.

My turn. **Fair.** Say **fair.** *Fair.*

Now I'll say the *first* part, **/fff/.** What is the *last* part? *air.*

Whole word? *Fair.*

(Continue the activity with the following words:
Hair: /h/ air.
Hate: /h/ ate.
Late: /lll/ ate.
Tall: /t/ all.
Call: /c/ all.)

Part B: Letter Recognition and Formation

6 minutes

Teacher Materials:

Student Materials:
Lined paper

Activity 1 | Letter Recognition Cumulative Review—m/M, s/S, e/E, r/R

Display on IWB or **write** letters and capitals on the board in the order shown.
Elicit responses to questions. **Guide** as needed.
This week you've learned one letter and one capital—**s** and **capital S.** Let's review all the letters and capitals you've learned. Are you ready?

Letter	Question	Student Response
M	What letter?	Capital M.
e	What letter?	e.
R	What letter?	Capital R.
s	What letter?	s.
m	What letter?	m.
E	What letter?	Capital E.
S	What letter?	Capital S.
r	What letter?	r.

Review as needed.

Lesson 35 **135**

Activity 2 | Letter Formation Cumulative Review—m/M, s/S, e/E, r/R

Write m, capital M, s, capital S, e, capital E, r, and capital R on the board in the order shown (with your back to students). **Provide** lined paper to students.
Show me how you can write the letters and capitals you've learned.
Guide students as they write the letters and capitals on their paper. **Review** as needed.

 Link letter names to letter sounds as needed as they appear in the program.

Part C: Comprehension Strategies

9 minutes

Teacher Materials:
Circle-pattern narrative trade book

Activity 1 | Title, Author, and Illustrator Identification—A Before-Reading Strategy

Direct students to narrative trade book of teacher choice. **Elicit** responses to questions. **Guide** as needed.
What does the title tell? *What the book is about.*

Show title on front cover of book.
The title of the book is _____. What do you call the person who wrote the book? *The author.*

Show author's name on front cover of book.
The author of today's story is _____. Who is the author of today's story? (Student response.)

Other than the title and author, the front cover of the book also includes the illustrator's name. The illustrator is the person who drew the pictures in the book. What do you call the person who drew the pictures in the book? *The illustrator.*

What's an illustrator? *The person who drew the pictures in the book.*

We call the person who drew the pictures in the book the illustrator because he or she drew the illustrations. **Illustrations** is another word for **pictures.** What are **illustrations**? *Pictures.*

Show illustrator's name on front cover of book.
The illustrator of today's story is _____. Who's the illustrator of today's story? (Student response.)

Activity 2 | Listening Comprehension—A During-Reading Strategy

Elicit responses to questions. **Guide** as needed.
Today we are going to read _____. When a teacher reads to you, it's important to sit straight and tall, look at the book, and think about what the story tells you.

Show me what you should look like when I read to you. (Students should sit straight and tall, look at the teacher, and pay attention.)

136   Lesson 35

It's also important to be very quiet while the teacher reads. If the teacher wants you to talk, the teacher will ask you a question.

When will it be your turn to talk? (Idea: *When the teacher asks a question.*)

When you sit the right way and think hard about the story, you'll enjoy the story more, and so will your classmates.

We'll begin as soon as I see all students sitting straight and tall with eyes on the teacher, mouths closed, and ears ready to listen.

Activity 3 Make and Confirm Predictions—A During-Reading Strategy

Elicit responses to questions. **Guide** as needed.
Besides making a prediction of what the story is about before we read, we can also make a prediction as we read the story. In the last lesson, I noticed that this book was a pattern book. Pattern books are fun to read because they do something over and over again. A pattern is something that you see or hear again and again. When you figure out the pattern, you can make a good guess, or prediction, about what will happen next.

What do you call something you see again and again in a book? *A pattern.*

Listen carefully as I read a few pages of _____ again, and then help me find the pattern.
Read a few more pages of the trade book not read in the last lesson. **Model** prosody during read-aloud.

Elicit pattern from students.
What's the pattern you notice in the book? (Student response.)

Elicit predictions from students. **Elicit** responses about accuracy of prediction. **Assure** students that the prediction does not have to be accurate. **Guide** as needed.
From the pattern in the book, what do you predict will happen on the next page? (Student response.)

Read next page of trade book.
Was your prediction right? (Student response.)

Finding a pattern helps us make a prediction about what will happen next in the story. Then we can read to check to see whether the prediction was correct. Pattern books are fun to read.

Lesson 35 **137**

Lesson 36

> **Materials**
> **Teacher:** Linear-pattern narrative trade book (same book for Lessons 36–40), 1-My Prediction Chart
> **Student:** Lined paper

5 minutes

Part A: Phonemic and Phonological Awareness

Activity 1 Syllable Deletion

Elicit responses. **Guide** as needed.
We're going to work with compound words again. I'm going to tell you a compound word, and you'll take off the *first* part of the word.

Your turn. Say **bluebird.** *Bluebird.*

Now say **bluebird** without **blue.** *Bird.*

Yes, you took away the *first* part, **blue,** and all that is left is **bird.**

(Continue the activity with the following examples:
Catfish. Say it without cat.
Doghouse. Say it without dog.
Highway. Say it without high.
Flip flop. Say it without flip.)

Activity 2 Onset-Rime Blending

Elicit responses. **Guide** as needed.
Let's make some words. I'll say two parts, and you put them together to make a whole word.

Your turn. /www/ . . . e. Put it together. *We.*
Great you put the parts together to make the word **we.**

Let's try some more. /www / . . . ent. *Went.*

/www/ . . . in. *Win.*

/b/ . . . ig. *Big.*

/b/ . . . ox. *Box.*

/b/ . . . ake. *Bake.*

/b/ . . . ed. *Bed*

138 Lesson 36

Activity 3 Phoneme Isolation—Initial

Elicit responses. **Guide** thumb movement as needed.
Let's work on *sounds* in words. I'm going to say a list of words. Some of the words will have the **/aaa/** sound at the *beginning,* and some will not. I'll say the word first, and then you'll say the word.

When I say a word that *begins* with **/aaa/,** what are you going to do? *Thumbs-up.*

What will you do if you don't hear **/aaa/** at the *beginning* of the word? *Nothing.*

Remember, we're listening for the **/aaa/** sound at the *beginning* of the word. What sound are you listening for? */aaa/.*

Listen. **At.** Say **at.** *At.*

Give me a thumbs-up if you hear **/aaa/** at the *beginning* of **at.** (Thumbs-up.)

Yes, **at** *begins* with the sound **/aaa/.**

(Continue the activity with the following lists of words:
Sit. Ax. Miss. Top. Add. Apple.
Bed. As. Bus. Meat. After. Act.)

6 minutes

Student Materials:
Lined paper

Part B: Letter Recognition and Formation

Activity 1 Letter Recognition—d

Elicit responses to questions. **Guide** as needed. **Write** d on the board. **Point** to d.
Today you'll learn a new letter.
The name of this letter is **d.** What letter name? *d.*
Again, what letter name? *d.*
Review as needed.

Activity 2 Letter Formation—d

Now we're going to practice writing **d.** When you practice writing, you'll learn not only where to start and stop the letter, but also which way to move your hand when you're making the letter. It's tricky, but you're so smart you'll learn how to write **d** very quickly. Watch.

Here's how you write **d** in the air.
Model d formation in the air (with your back to students).

Watch again.

Now let's practice writing **d** in the air. Hold up your writing hand, and make **d** in the air.
Guide students as they write d in the air.

Let's practice **d** again.

Lesson 36 **139**

Here's how to write **d** with your writing hand pointer finger.
Model d formation on the board with your finger (with your back to students).
Watch again.

Now let's practice writing **d** on your table without using your pencil. Use your writing hand pointer finger, and make **d** on your table.
Guide students as they write d on their table or desktop.

Let's practice **d** again.

Remember that every letter has a name.
Model writing d on the board (with your back to students).
You learned the name of this letter is **d.** What letter name? *d.*

Again, what letter name? *d.*

Provide lined paper to students.
Now let's practice writing **d** with your pencil.
Guide students as they write d on their paper. **Review** as needed.

 Link letter names to letter sounds as needed as they appear in the program.

Set up a writing center with writing materials and correct models of letters learned so far for students to use in their free time.

Part C: Comprehension Strategies

9 minutes

Teacher Materials:
Linear-pattern narrative trade book

My Prediction Chart

Activity 1 Title, Author, and Illustrator Identification—A Before-Reading Strategy

Provide a reading center to display books being read so that students can enjoy them again during free time.

Direct students to narrative trade book of teacher choice. **Elicit** responses to questions. **Guide** as needed.
What do all books have? *A title.*

What does the title tell? *What the book is about.*

Show title on front cover of book.
The title of today's story is _____. What's the title of today's story?
(Student response.)

What do you call the person who wrote the book? *The author.*

Show author's name on front cover of book.
The author of today's story is _____. Who is the author of today's story?
(Student response.)

Other than the title and author, the front cover of the book also includes the illustrator's name. The illustrator is the person who drew the pictures in the book. What do you call the person who drew the pictures in the book? *The illustrator.*

140   Lesson 36

What's an illustrator? *The person who drew the pictures in the book.*

Remember that we call the person who drew the pictures in the book the illustrator because he or she drew the illustrations. **Illustrations** is another word for **pictures.** What are **illustrations**? *Pictures.*

Show illustrator's name on front cover of book.
The illustrator of today's story is _____. Who's the illustrator of today's story? (Student response.)

Activity 2   Make Predictions—A Before-Reading Strategy

Show My Prediction Chart. **Elicit** responses to questions. **Guide** as needed.
The title of today's book is _____. Now that we know the title of today's book, let's look at the cover and make some good guesses about what we think the story will be about. We call our good guesses **predictions.** What do we call our good guesses? *Predictions.*

What are predictions? *Good guesses.*

Making good guesses, or predictions, helps us get interested in the story before we read it. Let's make a prediction about the story I'll read to you today.

Show title, front and back cover, and pictures inside the book.
When you make predictions, you look at the title of the book. The title of today's book is _____. I'll write the title in the box labeled "Book Title".

Then you look at the front and back covers. What pictures do you see? (Student response.)

Then you flip through the book and look at the pictures. What pictures do you see? (Student response.)

Elicit predictions from students. **Guide** as needed.
What do you think this story will be about? (Student response.)

I'll write your predictions in the box labeled "I Predict That".
Write predictions from students on chart.

Now, let's read the story and see whether your good guess, or prediction, was correct.

Activity 3   Listening Comprehension—A During-Reading Strategy

Elicit responses to questions. **Guide** as needed.
Today we are going to read _____.

When a teacher reads to you, what should you do? (Idea: *Sit straight and tall, look at the book, and think about what the story tells you.*)

Show me what you should look like when I read to you. (Students should sit straight and tall, look at the teacher, and pay attention.)

Lesson 36   **141**

When will it be your turn to talk? (Idea: *When the teacher asks a question.*)

When you sit the right way and think hard about the story, you'll enjoy the story more, and so will your classmates.

We'll begin as soon as I see all students sitting straight and tall with eyes on the teacher, mouths closed, and ears ready to listen.

Read trade book. **Model** prosody during read-aloud. **Ask** knowledge questions to engage students as you read (for example, who, what, when, where, why). **Guide** as needed.

Were our predictions correct?

Check next to the predictions that were correct. **Circle** Yes or No as appropriate.

Lesson 37

Materials
Teacher: Linear-pattern narrative trade book, 1-My Prediction Chart (from Lesson 36)
Student: Lined paper

5 minutes

Part A: Phonemic and Phonological Awareness

Activity 1 Rhyme Production

Elicit responses. **Guide** as needed.
Let's work with rhyming words. I'm going to say a word, and then I'll tell you the sound I want you to change in order to make a new rhyming word. You have to listen carefully.

Your turn. The word is **map.** Now think of the word that rhymes with **map** but starts with **/c/.** *Cap.*

Yes, **cap** rhymes with **map.**

(Continue the activity with the following examples:
Rat. Say it with /h/.
Gold. Say it with /c/.
Cake. Say it with /t/.
Cup. Say it with /p/.
Boat. Say it with /g/.)

Activity 2 Syllable Segmentation

Elicit responses. **Guide** clapping as needed.
Let's see if you can find out how many syllables are in the words I tell you. Remember, the number of times you clap for each part tells us how many syllables are in the word. Let's go.

Listen carefully. Your turn. **Garden.** Clap, and say each part. *Garden.*

Yes. How many times did you clap? *Two.*

So how many syllables are in that word? *Two.*

Yes, there are *two* syllables in the word **garden.**

(Continue the activity with the following words:
monkey, chair, nineteen, container, bread, magazine, bottle, sunglasses.)

Activity 3 Onset-Rime Segmentation

Elicit responses. **Guide** as needed.
Let's work with words. I'm going to say a word, and then I'll break the word into two parts. Sometimes I forget to say the *last* part of the word. You can help me by saying the *last* part after I say the *first* part.

Lesson 37   **143**

My turn. **Seed.** Say **seed.** *Seed.*

Now I'll say the *first* part, **/sss/.** What is the *last* part? *eed.*

Whole word? *Seed.*

(Continue the activity with the following words:
Need: /nnn/ eed.
Room: /rrr/ oom.
Boom: /b/ oom.
Beep: /b/ eep.
Deep: /d/ deep.)

Part B: Letter Recognition and Formation

6 minutes

Student Materials:
Lined paper

Activity 1 Letter Recognition Review—d

Elicit responses to questions. **Guide** as needed. **Write** d on the board. **Point** to d.
We learned that this letter is **d.** What letter name? *d.*
Again, what letter name? *d.*
Review as needed.

Activity 2 Letter Formation Review—d

Now we're going to practice writing **d.** When you practice writing, you'll learn not only where to start and stop the letter, but also which way to move your hand when you're making the letter. It's tricky, but you're so smart you'll learn how to write **d** very quickly. Watch.

Here's how you write **d.**
Model d formation in the air (with your back to students).
Watch again.

Now let's practice writing **d** in the air. Hold up your writing hand, and make **d** in the air.
Guide students as they write d in the air.

Let's practice **d** again.

Here's how to write **d** with your writing hand pointer finger.
Model d formation on the board with your finger (with your back to students).

Watch again.

Now let's practice writing **d** on your table without using your pencil. Use your writing hand pointer finger, and make **d** on your table.
Guide students as they write d on their table or desktop.

Let's practice **d** again.

Remember that every letter has a name.

144   Lesson 37

Model writing d on the board (with your back to students)

You learned the name of this letter is **d.** What letter name? *d.*

Again, what letter name? *d.*

Provide lined paper to students.
Now let's practice writing **d** with your pencil.
Guide students as they write d on their paper. **Review** as needed.

 Link letter names to letter sounds as needed as they appear in the program.

Part C: Comprehension Strategies

9 minutes

Teacher Materials:
Linear-pattern narrative trade book

My Prediction Chart

Activity 1 — Title, Author, and Illustrator Identification—A Before-Reading Strategy

Direct students to narrative trade book of teacher choice. **Elicit** responses to questions. **Guide** as needed.

What do all books have? *A title.*

Where do you find the title? *On the front cover of the book.*

What does the title tell? *What the book is about.*

Show title on front cover of book.
The title of today's story is _____. What's the title of today's story? (**Student response.**)

What do you call the person who wrote the book? *The author.*

What's an author? *The person who wrote the book.*

Show author's name on front cover of book.
The author of today's story is _____. Who's the author of today's story? (**Student response.**)

What do you call the person who drew the pictures in the book? *The illustrator.*

What's an illustrator? *The person who drew the pictures in the book.*

What are illustrations? *Pictures.*

Show illustrator's name on front cover of book.
The illustrator of today's story is _____. Who's the illustrator of today's story? (**Student response.**)

Lesson 37   145

Activity 2 Listening Comprehension—A During-Reading Strategy

Show My Prediction Chart. **Elicit** responses to questions. **Guide** as needed.
Today we are going to read _____.

When a teacher reads to you, what should you do? (Idea: *Sit straight and tall, look at the book, and think about what the story tells you.*)

Show me what you should look like when I read to you. (Students should sit straight and tall, look at the teacher, and pay attention.)

When will it be your turn to talk? (Idea: *When the teacher asks a question.*)

When you sit the right way and think hard about the story, you'll enjoy the story more, and so will your classmates.

Why do you sit the right way and think hard about the story? (Idea: *So you can enjoy the story.*)

We'll begin as soon as I see all students sitting straight and tall with eyes on the teacher, mouths closed, and ears ready to listen.

What do we call our good guesses? *Predictions.*

When we make a prediction, what parts of the book should we look over? (Idea: *Title, front cover, back cover, pictures inside the book.*)

In the last lesson, the class predicted what the story was about. The class said the story would be about _____. Was the class's prediction correct? *Yes.*

How do you know? (Student response.)

Activity 3 Establish a Purpose for Reading—A Before-Reading Strategy

Today as I read, I want you to think about the predictions you made yesterday. You predicted that the book would be about _____. Listen carefully to see whether your prediction was correct.
Read trade book. **Model** prosody during read-aloud.

Activity 4 Confirm Predictions—An After-Reading Strategy

Elicit responses to questions. **Guide** as needed.
Remind students that a prediction does not have to be completely accurate to be useful.
In the last lesson, the class predicted what the story was about. The class said the story would be about _____. Was the class's prediction correct? (Student response.)

When we check our predictions after we read to see whether they're correct, it helps make us smart at reading.

146 *Lesson 37*

Lesson 38

Materials
Teacher: Linear-pattern narrative trade book
Student: Lined paper

5 minutes

Part A: Phonemic and Phonological Awareness

Activity 1 Syllable Deletion

Elicit responses. **Guide** as needed.
We're going to work with compound words again. I'm going to say a compound word, and you'll take off the *first* part of the word.

Your turn. Say **placemat.** *Placemat.*

Now say **placemat** without **place.** *Mat.*

Yes, you took away the *first* part, **place,** and all that is left is **mat.**

(Continue the activity with the following examples:
Boardwalk. Say it without board.
School bus. Say it without school.
Sunscreen. Say it without sun.
Sidewalk. Say it without side.)

Activity 2 Onset-Rime Blending

Elicit responses. **Guide** as needed.
Let's make some words. I'll say two parts, and you put them together to make a whole word.

Your turn. /vvv/ . . . an. Put it together. *Van.*
Great, you put the parts together to make the word **van.**

Let's try some more. /vvv/ . . . ase. *Vase.*

/vvv/ . . . ote. *Vote.*

/t/ . . . op. *Top.*

/t/ . . . ape. *Tape.*

/t/ . . . ake. *Take.*

/t/ . . . oad. *Toad.*

Lesson 38   **147**

Activity 3 Phoneme Isolation—Initial

Elicit responses. **Guide** as needed.
Let's work on *sounds* in words. I'm going to say a list of words. Some of the words will have the **/ēēē/** sound at the *beginning,* and some will not. I'll say the word first, and then you'll say the word.

When I say a word that *begins* with **/ēēē/,** what are you going to do? *Thumbs-up.*

What will you do if you don't hear **/ēēē/** at the *beginning* of the word? *Nothing.*

Remember, we are listening for the **/ēēē/** sound at the *beginning* of the word. What sound are we listening for? /ēēē/.

Listen. **Eat.** Say **eat.** *Eat.*

Give me a thumbs-up if you hear **/ēēē/** at the *beginning* of **eat.** (Thumbs-up.)

Yes, **eat** *begins* with the sound **/ēēē/.**

(Continue the activity with the following lists of words.
Make. Ear. Sun. Tape. Eel. Bun.
Cup. Easy. Ball. Mix. Each. Eagle.)

Part B: Letter Recognition and Formation

6 minutes

Student Materials:
Lined paper

Activity 1 Letter Recognition—Capital D

Elicit responses to questions. **Guide** as needed. **Write** capital D on the board. **Point** to capital D.
Today you'll learn another way to write **d.**
The name of this letter is **capital D.** What letter name? *Capital D.*
Again, what letter name? *Capital D.*
Review as needed.

Activity 2 Letter Formation—Capital D

Now we're going to practice writing **capital D.** When you practice writing, you'll learn not only where to start and stop the letter, but also which way to move your hand when you're making the letter. It's tricky, but you're so smart you'll learn how to write **capital D** very quickly. Watch.

Here's how you write **capital D** in the air.
Model capital D formation in the air (with your back to students).

Watch again.

Now let's practice writing **capital D** in the air. Hold up your writing hand and make **capital D** in the air.
Guide students as they write capital D in the air.

148   Lesson 38

Let's practice **capital D** again.

Here's how to write **capital D** with your writing hand pointer finger.
Model capital D formation on the board with your finger (with your back to students).

Watch again.

Now let's practice writing **capital D** on your table without using your pencil.
Use your writing hand pointer finger, and make **capital D** on your table.
Guide students as they write capital D on their table or desktop.

Let's practice **capital D** again.

Remember that every letter has a name.
Model writing capital D on the board (with your back to students).
You learned the name of this letter is **capital D.** What letter name? *Capital D.*
Again, what letter name? *Capital D.*

Provide lined paper to students.
Now let's practice writing **capital D** with your pencil.
Guide students as they write capital D on their paper. **Review** as needed.

 Link letter names to letter sounds as needed as they appear in the program.

Part C: Comprehension Strategies

9 minutes

Teacher Materials:
Linear-pattern narrative trade book

Activity 1 Title, Author, and Illustrator Identification—A Before-Reading Strategy

Direct students to narrative trade book of teacher choice. **Elicit** responses to questions.
Guide as needed.
Where do you find the title? *On the front cover of the book.*

What does the title tell? *What the book is about.*

Show title on cover of trade book.
The title of today's story is _____. What's the title of today's story?
(Student response.)

What do you call the person who wrote the book? *The author.*

What's an author? *The person who wrote the book.*

The author of today's story is _____. Who's the author of today's story?
(Student response.)

What do you call the person who drew the pictures in the book? *The illustrator.*

What's an illustrator? *The person who drew the pictures in the book.*

What are illustrations? *Pictures.*

Lesson 38   **149**

Show illustrator's name on cover of trade book.
The illustrator of today's story is _____. Who's the illustrator of today's story? (Student response.)

Activity 2 Listening Comprehension—A During-Reading Strategy

Elicit responses to questions. **Guide** as needed.
Today we are going to read _____.

When a teacher reads to you, what should you do? (Idea: *Sit straight and tall, look at the book, and think about what the story tells you.*)

Show me what you should look like when I read to you. (Students should sit straight and tall, look at the teacher, and pay attention.)

When will it be your turn to talk? (Idea: *When the teacher asks a question.*)

Why do you sit the right way and think hard about the story? (Idea: *So you can enjoy the story.*)

We'll begin as soon as I see all students sitting straight and tall with eyes on the teacher, mouths closed, and ears ready to listen.

Activity 3 Make and Confirm Predictions—A During-Reading Strategy

Elicit responses to questions. **Guide** as needed.
What do we call our good guesses? *Predictions.*

Besides making a prediction of what the story is about before we read, we can also make a prediction as we read the story. In the last lesson, I noticed that this book was a pattern book.

What do you call something you see again and again in a book? *A pattern.*

What is a pattern? (Idea: *Something that you see or hear again and again.*)

When you figure out the pattern, you can make a good guess, or prediction, about what will happen next.

Listen carefully as I read a few pages of _____ again, and then we'll figure out the pattern. Finding a pattern helps us make a prediction about what will happen next in the story.
Read a few pages of trade book. **Model** prosody during read-aloud. **Elicit** pattern from students.

What's the pattern that you notice in the book? (Student response.)

Elicit predictions from students.
From the pattern in the book, what do you predict will happen on the next page? (Student response.)

150 *Lesson 38*

Read next page of trade book. **Elicit** response about accuracy of prediction. **Remind** students that a prediction does not have to be completely accurate to be useful. **Guide** as needed.

Was your prediction right? (Student response.)

Finding a pattern helps us make a prediction about what will happen next in the story. Then we can read to check to see whether the prediction was correct. Pattern books are fun to read.

Lesson 38 **151**

Lesson 39

Materials
Teacher: Linear-pattern narrative trade book
Student: Lined paper

5 minutes

Part A: Phonemic and Phonological Awareness

Activity 1 Rhyme Production

Elicit responses. **Guide** as needed.
Let's work with rhyming words. I'm going to say a word, and then I'll tell you the sound I want you to change in order to make a new rhyming word. You have to listen carefully.

Your turn. The word is **last.** Now think of the word that rhymes with **last** but starts with **/p/.** *Past.*

Yes, **past** rhymes with **last.**

(Continue the activity with the following examples:
Turn. Say it with /b/.
Sink. Say it with /p/.
Wheat. Say it with /fff/.
Shop. Say it with /mmm/.
Win. Say it with /p/.)

Activity 2 Syllable Segmentation

Elicit responses. **Guide** clapping as needed.
Let's see if you can find out how many syllables are in the words I tell you. Remember, the number of times you clap for each part tells us how many syllables are in the word. Let's go.

Listen carefully. Your turn. **Hammer.** Clap, and say each part. *Hammer.*

Yes. How many times did you clap? *Two.*

So, how many syllables are in that word? *Two.*

Yes, there are *two* syllables in the word **hammer.**

(Continue the activity with the following words:
zebra, light, fourteen, lemonade, zip, hamburger, pizza, watermelon.)

Activity 3 — Onset-Rime Segmentation

Elicit responses. **Guide** as needed.
Let's work with words. I'm going to say a word, and then I'll break the word into two parts. Sometimes I forget to say the *last* part of the word You can help me by saying the *last* part after I say the *first* part.

My turn. **Dump.** Say **dump.** *Dump.*

Now I'll say the *first* part, **/d/.** What is the *last* part? *ump.*

Whole word? *Dump.*

(Continue the activity with the following words:
Jump: /j/ ump.
Nice: /nnn/ ice.
Dice: /d/ ice.
Mist: /mmm/ ist.
List: /lll/ ist.)

Part B: Letter Recognition and Formation

6 minutes

Student Materials:
Lined paper

Activity 1 — Letter Recognition Review—Capital D

Elicit responses to questions. **Guide** as needed. **Write** capital <u>D</u> on the board. **Point** to capital <u>D</u>.
We learned that this letter is **capital D.** What letter name? *Capital D.*
Again, what letter name? *Capital D.*
Review as needed

Activity 2 — Letter Formation Review—Capital D

Now we're going to practice writing **capital D.** When you practice writing, you'll learn not only where to start and stop the letter, but also which way to move your hand when you're making the letter. It's tricky, but you're so smart you'll learn how to write **capital D** very quickly. Watch.

Here's how you write **capital D** in the air.
Model capital <u>D</u> formation in the air (with your back to students).

Watch again.

Now let's practice writing **capital D** in the air. Hold up your writing hand and make **capital D** in the air.
Guide students as they write capital <u>D</u> in the air.

Let's practice **capital D** again.

Here's how to write **capital D** with your writing hand pointer finger.
Model capital <u>D</u> formation on the board with your finger (with your back to students).

Watch again.

Lesson 39   153

Now let's practice writing **capital D** on your table without using your pencil. Use your writing hand pointer finger, and make **capital D** on your table.
Guide students as they write capital D̲ on their table or desktop.

Let's practice **capital D** again.

Remember that every letter has a name.
Model writing capital D̲ on the board (with your back to students).
You learned the name of this letter is **capital D.** What letter name? *Capital D.*
Again, what letter name? *Capital D.*

Provide lined paper to students.
Now let's practice writing **capital D** with your pencil.
Guide students as they write capital D̲ on their paper. **Review** as needed.

 Link letter names to letter sounds as needed as they appear in the program.

Part C: Comprehension Strategies

 9 minutes

Teacher Materials:
Linear-pattern narrative trade book

Activity 1 Title, Author, and Illustrator Identification—A Before-Reading Strategy

Direct students to narrative trade book of teacher choice. **Elicit** responses to questions. **Guide** as needed.

The title of today's story is _____. What's the title of today's story? (Student response.)

The author of today's story is _____. Who's the author of today's story? (Student response.)

The illustrator of today's story is _____. Who's the illustrator of today's story? (Student response.)

Activity 2 Listening Comprehension—A During-Reading Strategy

Elicit responses to questions. **Guide** as needed.

Today we are going to read _____.

Show me what you should look like when I read to you. (Students should sit straight and tall, look at the teacher, and pay attention.)

When will it be your turn to talk? (Idea: *When the teacher asks a question.*)

Why do you sit the right way and think hard about the story? (Idea: *So you can enjoy the story.*)

We'll begin as soon as I see all students sitting straight and tall with eyes on the teacher, mouths closed, and ears ready to listen.

Activity 3   Make and Confirm Predictions—A During-Reading Strategy

Elicit responses to questions. **Guide** as needed.
What do we call our good guesses? *Predictions.*

Besides making a prediction of what the story is about before we read, we can also make a prediction as we read the story. In the last lesson, I noticed that this book was a pattern book.

What's a pattern? (Idea: *Something that you see or hear again and again.*)

When you figure out the pattern, you can make a good guess, or prediction, about what will happen next.

Listen carefully as I read a few pages of _____ again, and then we'll figure out the pattern. Finding a pattern helps us make a prediction about what will happen next in the story.
Read a few pages of trade book. **Model** prosody during read-aloud. **Elicit** pattern from students.

What's the pattern you notice in the book? (Student response.)

Elicit predictions from students.
From the pattern in the book, what do you predict will happen on the next page? (Student response.)

Read next page of trade book. **Elicit** response about accuracy of prediction. **Remind** students that a prediction does not have to be completely accurate to be useful. **Guide** as needed.
Was your prediction right? (Student response.)

Finding a pattern helps us make a prediction about what will happen next in the story. Then we can read to check to see whether the prediction was correct.

Lesson 39   **155**

Lesson 40

Materials
Teacher: Linear-pattern narrative trade book, IWB-Letter Recognition, 8-My Book Review
Student: Lined paper, copy of 8-My Book Review

5 minutes

Part A: Phonemic and Phonological Awareness

Activity 1 Syllable Deletion

Elicit responses. **Guide** as needed.
We're going to work with compound words again. I'm going to tell you a compound word, and you'll take off either the *first* or *last* part of the word.

Your turn. Say **notebook.** *Notebook.*

Now say **notebook** without **note.** *Book.*

Yes, you took away the *first* part, **note,** and all that is left is **book.**

(Continue the activity with the following examples:
Bathtub. Say it without bath.
Bathroom. Say it without room.
Teapot. Say it without pot.
Stop sign. Say it without stop.)

Activity 2 Onset-Rime Blending

Elicit responses. **Guide** as needed.
Let's make some words. I'll say two parts, and you put them together to make a whole word.

Your turn. /zzz/ . . . ip. Put it together. *Zip.*
Great; you put the parts together to make the word **zip.**

Let's try some more. /zzz/ . . . oo. *Zoo.*

/c/ . . . an. *Can.*

/c/ . . . ake. *Cake.*

/c/ . . . oat. *Coat.*

/k/ . . . iss. *Kiss.*

/c/ . . . omb. *Comb.*

Activity 3 Phoneme Isolation—Initial

Elicit responses. **Guide** thumb movement as needed.
Let's work on *sounds* in words. I'm going to say a list of words. Some of the words will have the **/rrr/** sound at the *beginning,* and some will not. I'll say the word first, and then you'll say the word.

When I say a word that *begins* with **/rrr/,** what are you going to do? *Thumbs-up.*

What will you do if you don't hear **/rrr/** at the *beginning* of the word? *Nothing.*

Remember, we're listening for the **/rrr/** sound at the *beginning* of the word. What sound are we listening for? */rrr/.*

Listen. **Rat.** Say **rat.** *Rat.*

Give me a thumbs-up if you hear **/rrr/** at the *beginning* of **rat.** *(Thumbs-up.)*

Yes, **rat** *begins* with the sound **/rrr/.**

(Continue the activity with the following lists of words:
Rake. Pain. Rain. Pool. Roof. Run.
Cake. Read. Bend. Red. Rock. Eat.)

Part B: Letter Recognition and Formation

6 minutes

Teacher Materials:

Student Materials:
Lined paper

Activity 1 Letter Recognition Cumulative Review—s/S, e/E, r/R, d/D

Disply on IWB or **write** letters and capitals on the board in the order shown.
Elicit responses to questions. **Guide** as needed.
This week you've learned one letter and one capital—**d** and **capital D.** Let's review all the letters and capitals you've learned. Are you ready?

Lesson 40

Letter	Question	Student Response
R	What letter?	Capital R.
e	What letter?	e.
d	What letter?	d.
s	What letter?	s.
E	What letter?	Capital E.
r	What letter?	r.
D	What letter?	Capital D.
S	What letter?	Capital S.

Review as needed.

Activity 2 Letter Formation Cumulative Review—s/S, e/E, r/R, d/D

Write s, capital S, e, capital E, r, capital R, d, and capital D on the board in the order shown (with your back to students). **Provide** lined paper to students.
Show me how you can write the letters and capitals you've learned.

Guide students as they write the letters and capitals on their paper. **Review** as needed.

 Link letter names to letter sounds as needed as they appear in the program.

Part C: Comprehension Strategies

9 minutes

Teacher Materials:
Linear-pattern narrative trade book

My Book Review

Student Materials:
My Book Review

Activity 1 Title, Author, and Illustrator Identification—A Before-Reading Strategy

Direct students to narrative trade book of teacher choice. **Elicit** responses to questions. **Guide** as needed.

The title of today's story is _____. What's the title of today's story? (Student response.)

The author of today's story is _____. Who's the author of today's story? (Student response.)

The illustrator of today's story is _____. Who's the illustrator of today's story? (Student response.)

Activity 2 Make and Confirm Predictions—A During-Reading Strategy

Elicit responses to questions. **Guide** as needed.

Besides making a prediction of what the story is about before we read, we can also make a prediction as we read the story. In the last lesson, you noticed that this book was a pattern book. Pattern books are fun to read because they do something over and over again. When you figure out the pattern, you can make a good guess, or prediction, about what will happen next.

What do you call something you see again and again in a book? *A pattern.*

Elicit correct listening behavior from students.

Listen carefully as I read _____ again, and then you'll tell me the pattern. Finding a pattern helps us make a prediction about what will happen next in the story.

Read a few pages of trade book. **Model** prosody during read-aloud. **Elicit** pattern from students.

What's the pattern you notice in the book? (Student response.)

Elicit predictions from students.

From the pattern in the book, what do you predict will happen on the next page? (Student response.)

Read next page of trade book. **Elicit** response about accuracy of prediction. **Remind** students that a prediction does not have to be completely accurate to be useful.

Was your prediction right? (Student response.)

Finding a pattern helps us make a prediction about what will happen next in the story. Then we can read to check to see whether the prediction was correct.

Lesson 40 **159**

Activity 3 Retell the Story—An After-Reading Strategy

Elicit responses to questions. **Guide** as needed.
You've heard me read the story several times this week. I want you to think of your favorite part of the story and think of the pattern in the story. Listen to me retell my favorite part.

Model think-aloud for retelling page of story.

Sample Wording for Think-Aloud

My favorite part of the story is when _____. I like the pattern because it goes _____. This part says _____.

Assign student partners. **Monitor** students as they retell story.
Now it's your turn to tell your favorite part to your partner. Then have your partner tell you his or her favorite part of the story. Retelling stories helps you remember what you read.

Activity 4 Connections Through Shared Writing— Express Opinions

Show My Book Review. **Elicit** responses to questions. **Guide** as needed.
Think about the two books we read, _____ and _____. Let's talk about the two books. Which one did you like best and why?

Provide copies of My Book Review to students. **Guide** students through completion of My Book Review. **Share** with class as time permits.

160 *Lesson 40*

Lesson 41

> **Materials**
> **Teacher:** Narrative trade book with animals as characters (same book for Lessons 41–45), 1-My Prediction Chart
> **Student:** Lined paper

5 minutes

Part A: Phonemic and Phonological Awareness

Activity 1 Syllable Deletion

Elicit responses. **Guide** as needed.
We're going to work with compound words again. I'm going to say a compound word, and you'll take off either the *first* or *last* part of the word.

Your turn. Say **homework**. *Homework.*

Now say **homework** without **work**. *Home.*

Yes, you took away the last part, **work,** and all that is left is **home.**

(Continue the activity with the following examples:
Bathtub. Say it without tub.
Field trip. Say it without field.
Birthday. Say it without birth.
Sidewalk. Say it without walk.)

Activity 2 Onset-Rime Segmentation

Elicit responses. **Guide** as needed.
In the lessons we did before, we broke a word into two parts. I said the *first* part, and you said the *last* part. Now, we're going to change parts. This time, I'm going to forget to say the *first* part. You'll say the *first* part, and I'll say the *last* part. Let's get started.

Model rime quickly in normal speaking voice.
My turn. The word is **fox**. I'll say the *last* part, **ox**. Your turn. What is the *first* part? */f/.*

What is the whole word? *Fox.*

My turn. **Feel.** Say **feel.** *Feel.*

I'll say the *last* part, **eel.** What is the *first* part? */f/.*

Whole word? *Feel.*

(Continue the activity with the following words:
Fat: /f/ at.
Fold: /f/ old.
Farm: /f/ arm.

Lesson 41 **161**

Activity 3 Phoneme Isolation—Initial

Elicit responses. **Guide** as needed.
Let's work on *sounds* in words. I'm going to say a list of words. Some of the words will have the **/d/** sound at the *beginning,* and some will not. I'll say the word first, and then you'll say the word.

When I say a word that *begins* with **/d/,** what are you going to do? *Thumbs-up.*

What will you do if you don't hear **/d/** at the *beginning* of the word? *Nothing.*

Remember, we're listening for the **/d/** sound at the *beginning* of the word. What sound are we listening for? */d/.*

Listen. **Dig.** Say **dig.** *Dig.*

Give me a thumbs-up if you hear **/d/** at the *beginning* of **dig.** (Thumbs-up.)

Yes, **dig** *begins* with the sound **/d/.**

(Continue the activity with the following lists of words:
Deep. Pig. Rake. Day. Deer. Soap.
Dime. Met. Dip. Deal. Face. Don't.)

Part B: Letter Recognition and Formation

6 minutes

Student Materials:
Lined paper

Activity 1 Letter Recognition—f

Elicit responses to questions. **Guide** as needed. **Write** f on the board. **Point** to f.
Today you'll learn a new letter. The name of this letter is **f.** What letter name? *f.*
Point to f.
Again, what letter name? *f.*
Review as needed.

Activity 2 Letter Formation—f

Now we're going to practice writing **f.** When you practice writing, you'll learn not only where to start and stop the letter, but also which way to move your hand when you're making the letter. It's tricky, but you're so smart you'll learn how to write **f** very quickly. Watch.

Here's how you write **f** in the air.
Model f formation in the air (with your back to students).

Watch again.

162   Lesson 41

Now let's practice writing **f** in the air. Hold up your writing hand, and make **f** in the air.
Guide students as they write f in the air.

Let's practice **f** again.

Here's how to write **f** with your writing hand pointer finger.
Model f formation on the board with your finger (with your back to students).

Watch again.

Now let's practice writing **f** on your table without using your pencil. Use your writing hand pointer finger, and make **f** on your table.
Guide students as they write f on their table or desktop.

Let's practice **f** again.

Model writing f on the board (with your back to students).
Remember that every letter has a name.
You learned the name of this letter is **f**. What letter name? *f.*
Again, what letter name? *f.*

Provide lined paper to students.
Now let's practice writing **f** with your pencil.
Guide students as they write f on their paper. **Review** as needed.

 Link letter names to letter sounds as needed as they appear in the program.

Set up a writing center with writing materials and correct models of letters learned so far for students to use in their free time.

Part C: Comprehension Strategies

9 minutes

Activity 1 Title, Author, and Illustrator Identification—A Before-Reading Strategy

Teacher Materials:
Narrative trade book with animals as characters (same book for Lessons 41–45)

My Prediction Chart

 Provide a reading center to display books being read so that students can enjoy them again during free time.

Direct students to narrative trade book of teacher choice. **Show** front cover of book and point to name of title, author and illustrator as you discuss them. **Elicit** responses to questions. **Guide** as needed.
The title of today's story is _____. What's the title of today's story? (Student response.)

What does the title tell about the book? (Idea: *What the book is about.*)

Lesson 41 **163**

The author of today's story is _____. Who's the author of today's story? (Student response.)

What does the author do? (Idea: *Write the book.*)

The illustrator of today's story is _____. Who's the illustrator? (Student response.)

What does the illustrator do? (Idea: *Make the pictures in the book.*)

Activity 2 Make and Confirm Predictions—A Before- and After-Reading Strategy

Show title, front and back cover, and pictures inside book. **Elicit** responses to questions. **Guide** as needed.

Show My Prediction Chart and fill in the book title.

I'll write the title of today's book in the box labeled "Book Title".

Now that we know the title of today's book, let's look at the front and back cover and pictures in the book and make some good guesses about what you think the story is about. We call our good guesses predictions.

What do you think the story is about? (Student response.)

Fill in the prediction.

I'll write your prediction in the box labeled "I Predict That". When we read the story we'll check to see whether your predictions are right.

Activity 3 Listening Comprehension: Characters—A During-Reading Strategy

Elicit correct listening behavior from students. **Elicit** responses to questions. **Guide** as needed.

Today you're going to listen carefully as I read the story to figure out who the characters are in the story. Characters are animals or people in the story. What are characters? (Idea: *Animals or people in the story.*)

Characters say things or do things in the story. Sometimes characters are animals. Sometimes they are people. But all stories have characters. What do all stories have? *Characters.*

Read trade book. **Model** prosody during read-aloud. **Ask** questions to elicit character identification as you read story. **Guide** as needed.

Activity 4 Story Elements: Identify Characters—An After Reading Strategy

Now that we've read the book, let's talk about the characters in the book. Remember that the characters are the people or animals that do things or say things in the book. Watch me as I think about who the characters were in this story.

Model think-aloud for identifying characters.

164   *Lesson 41*

Sample Wording for Think-Aloud

I'm thinking about the book and thinking about who is in the story. I remember _____. That is a character because that is an animal that did _____ and said "_____." (Continue identifying characters with above pattern.)

Remember that characters are people or animals that do things and say things in stories.

Activity 5 Confirm Predictions—An After-Reading Strategy

Show My Prediction Chart. **Confirm** prediction made in Activity 2. **Elicit** responses to questions. **Guide** as needed.

You predicted that the story would be about _____. Was your prediction correct? (Student response.)

Circle Yes or No in the box labeled "Was My Prediction Correct?".

Remember that it doesn't matter whether your prediction is correct. Making a prediction and then checking to see whether it is correct makes you think about the story while you are reading it.

Lesson 41   **165**

Lesson 42

Materials
Teacher: Narrative trade book with animals as characters (from Lesson 41), 2-Character Sheet
Student: Lined paper

5 minutes

Part A: Phonemic and Phonological Awareness

Activity 1 Onset-Rime Blending

Elicit responses. **Guide** as needed.
I'll say two parts, and you put them together to make a whole word.

Your turn. /yyy/ . . . ou. Put it together. *You.*
Great you put the parts together to make the word **you.**

Let's try some more. /yyy/ . . . es. *Yes.*

/h/ . . . am. *Ham.*

/h/ . . . ill. *Hill.*

/h/ . . . ome. *Home.*

/h/ . . . eat. *Heat.*

/h/ . . . ut. *Hut.*

Activity 2 Phoneme Isolation—Final

Elicit responses. **Guide** as needed.
You've been doing so well finding the sound at the *beginning* of a word. Now let's work on the sound at the *end* of a word. I'm going to say a list of words. Some of the words will have the **/mmm/** sound at the *end,* and some will not. I'll say the word first, and then you'll say the word. Give me a thumbs-up if you hear the **/mmm/** sound at the *end* of the word. If you don't hear the **/mmm/** sound at the *end* of the word, do nothing. Think about the *last* sound we hear in each word.

Remember, we're listening for the **/mmm/** sound at the *end* of the word, as in **ram.** What sound are you listening for at the end? /mmm/.

Listen. **Sam.** Say **Sam.** *Sam.*

Give me a thumbs-up if you hear **/mmm/** at the *end* of **Sam.** (Thumbs-up.)

Yes, **Sam** *ends* with the sound **/mmm/.**

166 Lesson 42

(Continue the activity with the following lists of words:
Trim. Hit. Game. Cut. Slim. Ram.
Lime. Off. Came. Take. Man. Dime.)

6 minutes

Student Materials:
Lined paper

Part B: Letter Recognition and Formation

Activity 1 Letter Recognition Review—f

Elicit responses to questions. **Guide** as needed. **Write** f on the board. **Point** to f.
We learned that this letter is **f.** What letter name? *f.*
Again, what letter name? *f.*
Review as needed.

Activity 2 Letter Formation Review—f

Now we're going to practice writing **f.** When you practice writing, you'll learn not only where to start and stop the letter, but which way to move your hand when you're making the letter. It's tricky, but you're so smart you'll learn how to write **f** very quickly. Watch.

Here's how you write **f** in the air.
Model f formation in the air (with your back to students).

Watch again.

Now let's practice writing **f** in the air. Hold up your writing hand, and make **f** in the air.
Guide students as they write f in the air.

Let's practice **f** again.

Here's how to write **f** with your writing hand pointer finger.
Model f formation on the board with your finger (with your back to students).

Watch again.

Now let's practice writing **f** on your table without using your pencil. Use your writing hand pointer finger, and make **f** on your table.
Guide students as they write f on their table or desktop.

Let's practice **f** again.

Model writing f on the board (with your back to students).
Remember that every letter has a name.
You learned the name of this letter is **f.** What letter name? *f.*
Again, what letter name? *f.*

Provide lined paper to students.
Now let's practice writing **f** with your pencil.
Guide students as they write f on their paper. **Review** as needed.

 Link letter names to letter sounds as needed as they appear in the program.

Lesson 42   **167**

Part C: Comprehension Strategies

9 minutes

Teacher Materials:
Narrative trade book with animals as characters (from Lesson 41)

Character Sheet

Activity 1 Listening Comprehension: Characters—A During-Reading Strategy

Direct students to narrative trade book of teacher choice. **Elicit** response to question. **Guide** as needed.

In the last lesson, you learned about characters in a story. Characters are the people or animals in the story. What are characters? (Idea: *The people or animals in the story.*)

Elicit correct listening behavior from students.
Today we'll read the story again. As I read, listen and look to see whether you can figure out the name of a character in the book. Think about what the character does and says. When I'm finished reading, we'll figure out who the characters were and what they did or said.

Reread trade book. **Model** prosody during read-aloud. **Ask** questions to elicit character identification as you read story. **Guide** as needed.

Activity 2 Story Elements: Identify Characters—An After-Reading Strategy

Show Character Sheet. **Elicit** responses to questions. **Guide** as needed.
You did a great job of listening to the story. Now let's think about who the characters were in the story. Remember that characters are the people or animals that do or say things in a story. As we think of the characters, I will write the names on the board.

Elicit names of characters as you read. **Write** names of characters on Character Sheet.
What was the name of a character? (Student response.)

What did that character do? (Student response.)

What did that character say? (Student response.)
Repeat questions for each character as necessary.
Save list of characters for Lesson 43.

168 *Lesson 42*

Lesson 43

> **Materials**
> **Teacher:** Narrative trade book with animals as characters (from Lesson 41); 2-Character Sheet (from Lesson 42)
> **Student:** Lined paper

5 minutes

Part A: Phonemic and Phonological Awareness

Activity 1 Syllable Deletion

Elicit responses. **Guide** as needed.
We're going to work with compound words again. I'm going to say a compound word, and you will take off either the *first* or *last* part of the word.

Your turn. Say **basketball.** *Basketball.*

Now, say **basketball** without **basket.** *Ball.*

Yes, you took away the *first* part, **basket,** and all that is left is **ball.**

(Continue the activity with the following examples:
Mailbox. Say it without box.
Tinfoil. Say it without foil.
Rooftop. Say it without top.
Babysit. Say it without baby.)

Activity 2 Onset-Rime Segmentation

Elicit responses. **Guide** as needed.
Let's work on breaking a word into parts. Remember, this time I'm going to forget to say the *first* part. You say the *first* part, and I'll say the *last* part. Let's get started.

My turn. The word is **sand.** I'll say the *last* part, **and.** Your turn. What is the *first* part? */s/.*

What is the whole word? *Sand.*

My turn. **Seal.** Say **seal.** *Seal.*

Now I'll say the *last* part, **eal.** What is the *first* part? */s/.*

Whole word? *Seal.*

(Continue the activity with the following words:
Sink: /s/ ink.
Heart: /h/ eart.
Hop: /h/ op.
Hand: /h/ and.)

Lesson 43   **169**

Activity 3 Phoneme Isolation—Initial

Elicit responses. **Guide** as needed.
Let's work on a sound at the *beginning* of a word. I'm going to say a list of words. Some of the words will have the **/fff/** sound at the *beginning*, and some will not. I'll say the word first, and then you'll say the word.

When I say a word that *begins* with **/fff/**, what are you going to do? *Thumbs-up.*

What will you do if you don't hear **/fff/** at the beginning of the word? *Nothing.*

Remember, we're listening for the **/fff/** sound at the *beginning* of the word. What sound are we listening for? */fff/.*

Listen. **Fast.** Say **fast**. *Fast.*

Give me a thumbs-up if you hear **/fff/** at the *beginning* of **fast**. (Thumbs-up.)

Yes, **fast** *begins* with the sound **/fff/.**

(Continue the activity with the following lists of words:
Fish. Pick. Man. Feet. Fox. Sit.
Feel. Fin. Deep. Box. Face. Fist.)

6 minutes

Student Materials:
Lined paper

Part B: Letter Recognition and Formation

Activity 1 Letter Recognition—Capital F

Elicit responses to questions. **Guide** as needed. **Write** capital F on the board. **Point** to capital F.
Today you'll learn another way to write **f**.
The name of this letter is **capital F.** What letter name? *Capital F.*
Again, what letter name? *Capital F.*
Review as needed.

Activity 2 Letter Formation—Capital F

Now we're going to practice writing **capital F.** When you practice writing, you'll learn not only where to start and stop the letter, but also which way to move your hand when you're making the letter. It's tricky, but you're so smart you'll learn how to write **capital F** very quickly. Watch.

Here's how you write **capital F** in the air.
Model capital F formation in the air (with your back to students).

Watch again.

Now let's practice writing **capital F** in the air. Hold up your writing hand, and make **capital F** in the air.
Guide students as they write capital F in the air.

170   Lesson 43

Let's practice **capital F** again.

Here's how to write **capital F** with your writing hand pointer finger.
Model capital F formation on the board with your finger (with your back to students).

Watch again.

Now let's practice writing **capital F** on your table without using your pencil.
Use your writing hand pointer finger, and make **capital F** on your table.
Guide students as they write capital F on their table or desktop.

Let's practice **capital F** again.

Model writing capital F on the board (with your back to students).
Remember that every letter has a name.
You learned the name of this letter is **capital F.** What letter name? *Capital F.*
Again, what letter name? *Capital F.*

Provide lined paper to students.
Now let's practice writing **capital F** with your pencil.
Guide students as they write capital F on their paper. **Review** as needed.

 Link letter names to letter sounds as needed as they appear in the program.

Part C: Comprehension Strategies

9 minutes

Activity 1 Listening Comprehension: Characters—A During-Reading Strategy

Teacher Materials:
Narrative trade book with animals as characters (from Lesson 41)

Character Sheet from Lesson 42

Show Character Sheet. **Direct** students to narrative trade book of teacher choice.
Elicit responses to questions. **Guide** as needed.
You're learning how to identify characters in stories. Characters are the people or animals that do or say things in stories.

What are characters? (Idea: *The people or animals that do or say things in the story.*)

Elicit correct listening behavior from students.
Listen carefully as I read the story to you again. Every time you hear the name of a character, put up your hand so we can put a check by that character's name. We are checking to make sure we have the name of every character in the book.
Reread trade book. **Model** prosody during read-aloud.

Guide students to raise hand when they identify a character. **Assist** students to make check marks next to character's name as you find them in the story. If character is not on list from Lesson 42, add the name to the list. **Guide** as needed.

Lesson 43   **171**

Activity 2 Story Elements: Identify Characters—An After Reading Strategy

Show Character Sheet. **Guide** students to look at list of characters on board. **Elicit** responses to questions. **Guide** as needed.

Touch name of character on board as you ask question about each character.
Let's go over the characters in the story. What are characters? (Idea: *People or animals that do or say things in the story.*)

Did we get all the characters in the book listed on the board? (**Student responses.**)

If not, what character did we miss? (**Student responses.**)

Tell me what _____ did or said? (**Student response.**)
Repeat question for each character as time permits.
Save list of characters for Lesson 45.

172 *Lesson 43*

Lesson 44

> **Materials**
> **Teacher:** Narrative trade book with animals as characters (from Lesson 41)
> **Student:** Lined paper

5 minutes

Part A: Phonemic and Phonological Awareness

Activity 1 Onset-Rime Blending

Elicit responses. **Guide** as needed.
Let's make some words. I'll say two parts, and you put them together to make a whole word.

Your turn. /thththl/ . . . ink. Put it together. *Think.*

Great; you put the parts together to make the word **think.**

Let's try some more. /d/ . . . esk. *Desk.*

/ch/ . . . alk. *Chalk.*

/shshsh/ . . . ape. *Shape.*

/b/ . . . ead. *Bead.*

/gr/ . . . een. *Green.*

/bl/ . . . ue. *Blue.*

Activity 2 Phoneme Isolation—Final

Elicit responses. **Guide** as needed.
Now let's work on the sound at the *end* of a word. I'm going to say a list of words. Some of the words will have the **/sss/** sound at the *end,* and some will not. I'll say the word first, and then you'll say the word. Give me a thumbs-up if you hear the **/sss/** sound at the *end* of the word. If you don't hear the **/sss/** sound at the *end* of the word, do nothing. Think about the *last* sound we hear in each word.

Remember, we're listening for the **/sss/** sound at the *end* of the word, as in **bus.** What sound are you listening for at the end? */sss/.*

Listen. **Gas.** Say **gas.** *Gas.*

Give me a thumbs-up if you hear **/sss/** at the *end* of **gas.** (Thumbs-up.)

Yes, **gas ends** with the sound **/sss/.**

Lesson 44   173

(Continue the activity with the following lists of words:
Kiss. Hat. Face. Call. Mess. Dress.
Time. Case. Ring. Grass. Fuss. Train.)

6 minutes

Student Materials:
Lined paper

Part B: Letter Recognition and Formation

Activity 1 Letter Recognition Review—Capital F

Elicit responses to questions. Guide as needed. **Write** capital F on the board. **Point** to capital F.
We learned that this letter is **capital F.** What letter name? *Capital F.*
Again, what letter name? *Capital F.*
Guide as needed.

Activity 2 Letter Formation Review—Capital F

Now we're going to practice writing **capital F.** When you practice writing, you'll learn not only where to start and stop the letter, but also which way to move your hand when you're making the letter. It's tricky, but you're so smart you'll learn how to write **capital F** very quickly. Watch.

Here's how you write **capital F** in the air.
Model capital F formation in the air (with your back to students).

Watch again.

Now let's practice writing **capital F** in the air. Hold up your writing hand, and make **capital F** in the air.
Guide students as they write capital F in the air.

Let's practice **capital F** again.

Here's how to write **capital F** with your writing hand pointer finger.

Model capital F formation on the board with your finger (with your back to students).
Watch again.

Now let's practice writing **capital F** on your table without using your pencil. Use your writing hand pointer finger, and make **capital F** on your table.

Guide students as they write capital F on their table or desktop.

Let's practice **capital F** again.

Model writing capital F on the board (with your back to students).
Remember that every letter has a name.
You learned the name of this letter is **capital F.** What letter name? *Capital F.*
Again, what letter name? *Capital F.*

Provide lined paper to students.
Now, let's practice writing **capital F** with your pencil.
Guide students as they write capital F on their paper. **Review** as needed.

 Link letter names to letter sounds as needed as they appear in the program.

174 Lesson 44

Part C: Comprehension Strategies

9 minutes

Teacher Materials:
Narrative trade book with animals as characters (from Lesson 41)

Activity 1 Listening Comprehension: Characters—A During-Reading Strategy

Direct students to narrative trade book of teacher choice. **Elicit** responses to questions. **Guide** as needed.

Today as I read the story, I want you to think about a character in the story. What are characters? (Idea: *The people or animals that say and do things in a story.*)

I want you to remember what a character does and says in the story so we can play what that character does and says. We will play what _____ does and says after I read the story. Listen carefully.

Elicit correct listening behavior from students. **Reread** trade book. **Model** prosody during read-aloud.

Guide students to focus on teacher-selected character. **Elicit** answers to questions about what character said and did. **Guide** as needed.

Activity 2 Story Elements: Play the Character—An After-Reading Strategy

I'm going to play what I think _____ would do and say in one part of the story. Watch me as I play the character.

Model playing a brief episode for one character in the story by saying and doing what the character said and did in the story. **Show** students how the character might have said the words or done the actions.

Let's all play the character together. Do the actions, and say the words as I do them.

Guide students to play the character with you. **Prompt** everyone to bow as you applaud them.

Wow, that was fun!

Lesson 44 175

Lesson 45

Materials
Teacher: Narrative trade book with animals as characters (from Lesson 41); 2-Character Sheet (from Lesson 42 and 43); 2-Character Sheet, IWB-Letter Recognition
Student: Lined paper; copy of 2-Character Sheet with writing lines

5 minutes

Part A: Phonemic and Phonological Awareness

Activity 1 Syllable Deletion

Elicit responses. **Guide** as needed.
We're going to work with compound words again. I'm going to say a compound word, and you'll take off either the *first* or *last* part of the word.

Your turn. Say **dragonfly.** D*ragonfly.*

Now, say **dragonfly** without **dragon.** *Fly.*

Yes, you took away the *first* part, **dragon,** and all that is left is **fly.**

(Continue the activity with the following examples:
Tablecloth. Say it without cloth.
Jungle gym. Say it without jungle.
Swing set. Say it without set.
Seesaw. Say it without see.
Hourglass. Say it without hour.)

Activity 2 Onset-Rime Segmentation

Elicit responses. **Guide** as needed.
Let's work on breaking a word into parts. Remember, this time I'm going to forget to say the *first* part. You'll say the *first* part, and I'll say the *last* part. Let's get started.

My turn. The word is **toe.** I'll say the *last* part, **oe.** Your turn. What is the *first* part? */t/.*

What is the whole word? *Toe.*

My turn. **Ten.** Say **ten.** *Ten.*

I'll say the *last* part, **en.** What is the *first* part? */t/.*

Whole word? *Ten.*

(Continue the activity with the following words:
Bed: /b/ ed.
Back: /b/ ack.
Hall: /h/ all.
Hat: /h/ at.)

Activity 3 Phoneme Isolation—Initial

Elicit responses. **Guide** as needed.
Let's work on a sound at the *beginning* of a word. I'm going to say a list of words. Some of the words will have the **/iii/** sound at the *beginning,* and some will not. I'll say the word first, and then you'll say the word.

Remember, we are listening for the **/iii/** sound at the *beginning* of the word. What sound are we listening for? /iii/.

Listen. **It.** Say **it.** *It.*

Give me a thumbs-up if you hear **/iii/** at the *beginning* of **it.** (Thumbs-up.)

Yes, **it** *begins* with the sound **/iii/.**

(Continue the activity with the following lists of words:
Itch. Pan. Dog. Is. Fall. If.
In. Soap. I'll. Bed. Ham. It.

Part B: Letter Recognition and Formation

6 minutes

Teacher Materials:

Student Materials:
Lined paper

Activity 1 Letter Recognition Cumulative Review—e/E, r/R, d/D, f/F

Display on IWB or **write** letters and capitals on the board in the order shown.
Elicit responses to questions. **Guide** as needed.
This week you've learned one letter and one capital— **f** and **capital F.** Let's review all the letters and capitals you've learned. Are you ready?

Letter	Question	Student Response
e	What letter?	e.
F	What letter?	Capital F.
R	What letter?	Capital R.
d	What letter?	d.
E	What letter?	Capital E.
f	What letter?	f.
r	What letter?	r.
D	What letter?	Capital D.

Review as needed.

Lesson 45

Activity 2 | Letter Formation Cumulative Review—e/E, r/R, d/D, f/F

Write e, capital E, r, capital R, d, capital D, f, and capital F on the board in the order shown (with your back to students). **Provide** lined paper to students.
Show me how you can write the letters and capitals you've learned.
Guide students as they write the letters and capitals on their paper. **Review** as needed.

 Link letter names to letter sounds as needed as they appear in the program.

Part C: Comprehension Strategies

9 minutes

Teacher Materials:
Narrative trade book with animals as characters (from Lesson 41)

Character Sheet (from 42–43)

Character Sheet

Student Materials:
Character Sheet

Activity 1 | Listening Comprehension: Illustrations—A During-Reading Strategy

Direct students to narrative trade book of teacher choice. **Elicit** responses to questions. **Guide** as needed.
The job of a book illustrator is to make pictures for books. What does an illustrator do? *Make pictures for books.*

The illustrator of our book is _____. Who's the illustrator of this book? (Student response.)

Today as I read the story, I want you to look carefully at the pictures of the characters in the book. The illustrator made the pictures for you so that the book would be fun to read. Look for how the illustrator drew pictures of what characters are doing. After I read the story, you'll become an illustrator and draw a picture of a character in the book.
Elicit correct listening behavior from students. **Reread** trade book. **Model** prosody during read-aloud.
Guide students to focus on illustrations of characters. **Elicit** answers to questions about how the illustrator shows the character's actions in the pictures. **Guide** as needed.

Activity 2 | Story Elements: Illustrate Character—An After-Reading Strategy

Elicit responses to questions. **Guide** as needed.
Now you'll become an illustrator. Remember that an illustrator is the person who draws the pictures in a story. What does an illustrator do? (Idea: *Draw pictures for the book.*)

Show Character Sheet.
I'll show you what I do when I work as an illustrator.
Model drawing a character in the story by drawing a sketch that shows a character and fills the space provided.

As an illustrator, your job today is to draw a picture of a character from the story. Let's review all the characters on our list to help you pick which character to draw.

Review list of characters from Lessons 42 and 43.
Tell your neighbor the name of the character you'll draw. (Student responses.)

Provide Character Sheet to each student.
Now it's your turn to draw a character from the book. Try not to make a tiny drawing in the middle of the page. Make your drawing big enough so that we can all see it when you show us your picture.
Share illustrations with class as time permits or make a class book of characters.

Activity 3 Collaborate to Strengthen Writing

Show Character Sheet.
Now let's write one sentence that describes the character. Watch as I write mine.
Model writing a sentence that describes a character from the story.

Write one sentence that describes the character you drew. If you need help, ask me.
Monitor students. **Guide** as needed.

Assign student partners.
Share your picture and your sentence with your neighbor. Make suggestions to make your neighbor's sentence better if you think it needs it.

Model how to share a picture and a sentence with a neighbor and how to give feedback on the sentence if it needs it. **Monitor** students. **Guide** as needed.

Lesson 45 **179**

Lesson 46

Materials
Teacher: Narrative trade book with people as characters (same book for Lessons 46–50), 1-My Prediction Sheet, 2-Character Sheet
Student: Lined paper

5 minutes

Part A: Phonemic and Phonological Awareness

Activity 1 Onset-Rime Blending

Elicit responses. **Guide** as needed.
Let's make some words. I'll say two parts, and you put them together to make a whole word.

Your turn. /b/ . . . each. Put it together. *Beach.*

Great; you put the parts together to make the word **beach.**

Let's try some more. /sw/ . . . ing. *Swing.*

/whwhwh/ . . . ere. *Where.*

/d/ . . . ime. *Dime.*

/cl/ . . . ip. *Clip.*

/yyy/ . . . ell. *Yell.*

/br/ . . . own. *Brown.*

Activity 2 Phoneme Isolation—Final

Elicit responses. **Guide** as needed.
Now let's work on the sound at the *end* of a word. I'm going to say a list of words. Some of the words will have the **/ēēē/** sound at the *end,* and some will not. I'll say the word first, and then you'll say the word. Give me a thumbs-up if you hear the **/ēēē/** sound at the *end* of the word. If you don't hear the **/ēēē/** sound at the *end* of the word, do nothing. Think about the *last* sound we hear in each word.

Remember, we're listening for the **/ēēē/** sound at the *end* of the word, as in **me.** What sound are you listening for at the end? */ēēē/.*

Listen. **See.** Say **see.** *See.*

Give me a thumbs-up if you hear **/ēēē/** at the *end* of **see.** (Thumbs-up.)

Yes, **see** ends with the sound **/ēēē/.**

180   Lesson 46

6 minutes

Student Materials:
Lined paper

Part B: Letter Recognition and Formation

Activity 1 — Letter Recognition—i

Elicit responses to questions. **Guide** as needed. **Write** i on the board. **Point** to i.
Today you'll learn a new letter.
The name of this letter is **i.** What letter name? *i.*
Again, what letter name? *i.*
Review as needed.

Activity 2 — Letter Formation—i

Now we're going to practice writing **i.** When you practice writing, you'll learn not only where to start and stop the letter, but also which way to move your hand when you're making the letter. It's tricky, but you're so smart you'll learn how to write **i** very quickly. Watch.

Here's how you write **i** in the air.
Model i formation in the air (with your back to students).

Watch again.

Now, let's practice writing **i** in the air. Hold up your writing hand, and make **i** in the air.
Guide students as they write i in the air.

Let's practice **i** again.

Here's how to write **i** with your writing hand pointer finger.
Model i formation on the board with your finger (with your back to students).

Watch again.

Now let's practice writing **i** on your table without using your pencil. Use your writing hand pointer finger, and make **i** on your table.
Guide students as they write i on their table or desktop.

Let's practice **i** again.

Model writing i on the board (with your back to students).
Remember that every letter has a name.
You learned the name of this letter is **i.** What letter name? *i.*
Again, what letter name? *i.*

Provide lined paper to students.
Now let's practice writing **i** with your pencil.
Guide students as they write i on their paper. **Review** as needed.

 Link letter names to letter sounds as needed as they appear in the program.

Set up a writing center with writing materials and correct models of letters learned so far for students to use in their free time.

Lesson 46   181

9 minutes

Teacher Materials:
Narrative trade book with people as characters (same book for Lessons 46–50)

My Prediction Sheet

Character Sheet

Part C: Comprehension Strategies

Activity 1 Title, Author, and Illustrator Identification—A Before-Reading Strategy

Provide a reading center to display books being read so that students can enjoy them again during free time.

Direct students to narrative trade book of teacher choice. **Show** front cover of book and point to name of title, author, and illustrator as you discuss them. **Elicit** responses to questions. **Guide** as needed.
The title of today's story is _____. What's the title of today's story? (Student response.)

What does the title tell about the book? (Idea: *What the book is about*.)

The author of today's story is _____. Who's the author of today's story? (Student response.)

What does the author do? (Idea: *Write the book*.)

The illustrator of today's story is _____. Who's the illustrator? (Student response.)

What does the illustrator do? (Idea: *Make the pictures in the book*.)

Activity 2 Make Predictions—A Before-Reading Strategy

Elicit responses to questions. **Guide** as needed.
Show My Prediction Chart and fill in the book title.
I'll write the title of today's book in the box labeled "Book Title". Now that we know the title of today's book, let's look at the front and back cover and pictures in the book and make some good guesses about what you think the story is about. We call our good guesses predictions.

Show title, front and back cover, and pictures inside the book to make predictions.

What do you think the story is about? (Student responses.)

You can also make a prediction for what character will be in the story. What character do you think will be in the story? (Student response.)

Fill in the prediction.
I'll write your prediction in the box labeled "I Predict That". When we read the story we'll check to see whether your predictions are right.

Activity 3 Listening Comprehension—A During-Reading Strategy

Elicit responses to questions. **Guide** as needed.
Today you're going to listen carefully as I read the story to figure out who the characters are in the story. Characters are the people or animals in the story.

What are characters? (Idea: *People or animals in the story.*)

Characters say and do things in the story. Sometimes characters are people. Sometimes they are animals. But all stories have characters.

What do all stories have? *Characters.*

Stories have characters that do and say things in the story. Why do stories have characters? (Idea: *To do things and say things in the story.*)

Today we'll read the story again. As I read, listen and look to see whether you can figure out the name of a character in the book. Think about what the character does and says. When I'm finished reading, we will write the names of the characters on the board, and we'll talk about what they did and said. **Elicit** correct listening behavior from students. **Read** trade book. **Model** prosody during read-aloud.

Ask questions to elicit character identification, actions, and words as you read story. **Guide** as needed.

Activity 4 Story Elements: Identify Characters—An After-Reading Strategy

Show Character Sheet. **Elicit** responses to questions. **Guide** as needed.
You did a great job of listening to the story. Now let's think about who the characters were in the story. Remember that characters are the people or animals that do or say things in a story. As we think of the characters, I'll write the names on the board.
Elicit names of characters as you read. **Write** names of characters on the Character Sheet.

What was the name of a character? (Student response.)

What did that character do? (Student response.)

What did that character say? (Student responses.)
Repeat questions for each character as time permits. **Save** list of characters on the board for Lesson 47.

Activity 5 Confirm Predictions—An After-Reading Strategy

Show My Prediction Sheet. **Elicit** responses to questions. **Guide** as needed.
You predicted that the story would be about _____. Was your prediction correct? (Student response.)
Confirm predictions made in Activity 2. **Circle** Yes or No in the box labeled "Was My Prediction Correct?".

You predicted that _____ was a character in the story. Was your prediction correct? (Student responses.)

Remember that it doesn't matter whether your prediction is exactly correct. Making a prediction and then checking to see whether it is correct makes you think about the story while you're reading it.

Lesson 46 **183**

Lesson 47

Materials
Teacher: Narrative trade book with people as characters (from Lesson 46); 2-Character Sheet (from Lesson 46)
Student: Lined paper

Part A: Phonemic and Phonological Awareness

Activity 1 Syllable Deletion

Elicit responses. **Guide** as needed.
We're going to work with compound words again. I'm going to tell you a compound word, and you'll take off either the *first* or *last* part of the word.

Your turn. Say **grasshopper.** *Grasshopper.*

Now, say **grasshopper** without **hopper.** *Grass.*

Yes, you took away the *last* part, **hopper,** and all that is left is **grass.**

(Continue the activity with the following examples.
Lawnmower. Say it without mower.
Treetop. Say it without tree.
Snowball. Say it without ball.
Snowflake. Say it without snow.
Earring. Say it without ring.
Necklace. Say it without lace.
Clockwise. Say it without clock.)

Activity 2 Onset-Rime Segmentation

Elicit responses. **Guide** as needed.
Let's work on breaking a word into parts. Remember, this time I'm going to forget to say the *first* part. You'll say the *first* part, and I'll say the *last* part. Let's get started.

My turn. **Call.** Say **call.** *Call.*

Now I'll say the *last* part, **all.** What is the *first* part? */c/.*

Whole word? *Call.*

(Continue the activity with the following words:
Coat: /c/ oat.
Dig: /d/ ig.
Deep: /d/ eep.
Ship: /sh/ ip.
Sheep: /sh/ eep.)

184 Lesson 47

Activity 3 Phoneme Isolation—Initial

Elicit responses. **Guide** as needed.
Let's work on a sound at the *beginning* of a word. I'm going to say a list of words. Some of the words will have the **/t/** sound at the *beginning*, and some will not. I'll say the word first, and then you'll say the word.

Remember, we're listening for the **/t/** sound at the *beginning* of the word. What sound are we listening for? /t/.

Listen. **Toe.** Say **toe.** *Toe.*

Give me a thumbs-up if you hear **/t/** at the *beginning* of **toe.** (Thumbs-up.)

Yes, **toe** *begins* with the sound **/t/.**

(Continue the activity with the following lists of words.
Ten. Made. Tap. Tea. Fill. Tack.
Ask. Read. Town. Team. Soak. Time.)

6 minutes

Student Materials:
Lined paper

Part B: Letter Recognition and Formation

Activity 1 Letter Recognition Review—i

Elicit responses to questions. **Guide** as needed. **Write** i on the board. **Point** to i.
We learned that this letter is **i.** What letter name? *i.*
Again, what letter name? *i.*
Review as needed.

Activity 2 Letter Formation Review—i

Now, we're going to practice writing **i.** When you practice writing, you'll learn not only where to start and stop the letter, but also which way to move your hand when you're making the letter. It's tricky, but you're so smart you'll learn how to write **i** very quickly. Watch.

Here's how you write **i.**
Model i formation in the air (with your back to students).
Watch again.

Now, let's practice writing **i** in the air. Hold up your writing hand and make **i** in the air.
Guide students as they write i in the air.

Lesson 47   **185**

Let's practice **i** again.

Here's how to write **i** with your writing hand pointer finger.
Model i formation on the board with your finger (with your back to students).

Watch again.

Now, let's practice writing **i** on your table without using your pencil. Use your writing hand pointer finger and make **i** on your table.
Guide students as they write i on their table or desktop.

Let's practice **i** again.

Model writing i on the board (with your back to students).
Remember, every letter has a name.
You learned the name of this letter is **i.** What letter name? *i.*
Again, what letter name? *i.*

Provide lined paper to students.
Now let's practice writing **i** with your pencil.
Guide students as they write i on their paper. **Review** as needed.

Link letter names to letter sounds as needed as they appear in the program.

Part C: Comprehension Strategies

9 minutes

Activity 1 Listening Comprehension: Characters—A During-Reading Strategy

Teacher Materials:
Narrative trade book with people as characters (from Lesson 46)

Character Sheet (from Lesson 46)

Direct students to narrative trade book of teacher choice. **Elicit** responses to questions. **Guide** as needed.
You are learning how to identify characters in stories. What are characters?
(Idea: *The people or animals that do or say things in the story.*)

Listen carefully as I read the story to you again. Every time you hear the name of a character, put up your hand so we can put a check by that character's name. We are checking to make sure we have the name of every character in the book.
Elicit correct listening behavior from students. **Reread** trade book. **Model** prosody during read-aloud.

Guide students to raise hand when they identify a character. **Assist** students to make check marks next to character's name on Character Sheet every time the character appears in the story; if a character isn't on list, add name to the list. **Guide** as needed.

186 Lesson 47

Activity 2 Story Elements: Identify Characters and Main Character—An After-Reading Strategy

Elicit responses to questions. **Guide** as needed.
Let's go over the names of the characters in the story.
Guide students to look at list of characters.

Did we get all the characters in the book listed on the board? (Student response.)

If not, what character did we miss? (Student response.)

Which character has the most checkmarks by his or her name? (Student response.)

That character with the most check marks is called the main character. The main character does or says the most things in the story.

What do we call the character that does or says the most things in a story?
The main character.

Now let's talk about all the characters and what they said and did.
Touch name of character as you ask questions about each character.

Tell me what _____ did or said. (Student response.)
Repeat question for each character as time permits. **Save** list of characters for Lesson 49.

Lesson 47 **187**

Lesson 48

Materials
Teacher: Narrative trade book with people as characters (from Lesson 46)
Student: Lined paper

Part A: Phonemic and Phonological Awareness

Activity 1 Onset-Rime Blending

Elicit responses. **Guide** as needed.
Let's make some words. I'll say two parts, and you put them together to make a whole word.

Your turn. /p/ . . . ink. Put it together. *Pink.*
Great; you put the parts together to make the word **pink.**

Let's try some more. /bl/ . . . ack. *Black.*

/tr/ . . . ack. *Track.*

/pl/ . . . um. *Plum.*

/st/ . . . amp. *Stamp.*

/ch/ . . . ill. *Chill.*

Activity 2 Phoneme Isolation—Final

Elicit responses. **Guide** as needed.
Now let's work on the sound at the *end* of a word. I'm going to say a list of words. Some of the words will have the **/rrr/** sound at the *end,* and some will not. I'll say the word first, and then you'll say the word. Think about the *last* sound we hear in each word.

Remember, we're listening for the **/rrr/** sound at the *end* of the word, as in **stir.** What sound are you listening for at the end? */rrr/.*

Listen. **Fair.** Say **fair.** *Fair.*

Give me a thumbs-up if you hear **/rrr/** at the *end* of **fair.** (Thumbs-up.)
Yes, **fair** ends with the sound **/rrr/.**

(Continue the activity with the following lists of words.
Sent. Poor. Tip. Hear. Hit. Tan.
Tear. Nail. Rag. Bear. More. Fast.)

6 minutes

Student Materials:
Lined paper

Part B: Letter Recognition and Formation

Activity 1 — Letter Recognition—Capital I

Elicit responses to questions. **Guide** as needed. **Write** capital I on the board. **Point** to capital I.
Today, you'll learn another way to write **i**.
The name of this letter is **capital I**. What letter name? *Capital I.*
Again, what letter name? *Capital I.*
Review as needed.

Activity 2 — Letter Formation—Capital I

Now we're going to practice writing **capital I**. When you practice writing, you'll learn not only where to start and stop the letter, but also which way to move your hand when you're making the letter. It's tricky, but you're so smart you'll learn how to write **capital** I very quickly. Watch.

Here's how you write **capital** I in the air.
Model capital I formation in the air (with your back to students).

Watch again.

Now let's practice writing **capital** I in the air. Hold up your writing hand, and make **capital** I in the air.
Guide students as they write capital I in the air.

Let's practice **capital** I again.

Here's how to write **capital** I with your writing hand pointer finger.
Model capital I formation on the board with your finger (with your back to students).

Watch again.

Now let's practice writing **capital** I on your table without using your pencil. Use your writing hand pointer finger and make **capital** I on your table.
Guide students as they write capital I on their table or desktop.

Let's practice **capital** I again.

Model writing capital I on the board (with your back to students).
Remember that every letter has a name.
You learned the name of this letter is **capital I**. What letter name? *Capital I.*
Again, what letter name? *Capital I.*

Provide lined paper to students.
Now let's practice writing **capital** I with your pencil.
Guide students as they write capital I on their paper. **Review** as needed.

 Link letter names to letter sounds as they appear in the program as needed.

Lesson 48 **189**

Part C: Comprehension Strategies

9 minutes

Teacher Materials:
Narrative trade book with people as characters (from Lesson 46)

Activity 1 Listening Comprehension: Characters—A During-Reading Strategy

Direct students to narrative trade book of teacher choice. **Elicit** responses to questions. **Guide** as needed.

Today as I read the story, I want you to think about a character in the story. What are characters? (Idea: *The people or animals that say and do things in a story.*)

I want you to really remember what the main character does and says in the story so we can play what that character does and says. The main character is the character that says and does the most in the story.

Who's the main character in this story? (Student response.)

We'll play what _____ does and says after I read the story. Listen carefully.
Elicit correct listening behavior from students. **Reread** trade book. **Model** prosody during read-aloud.

Guide students to focus on main character. **Elicit** answers to questions about what character says and does. **Guide** as needed.

Activity 2 Story Elements: Play the Character—An After-Reading Strategy

I'm going to play what I think _____ would do and say in one part of the story. Watch me as I play the character for you.
Model playing a very brief episode for main character in the story by saying and doing what the character said and did. **Show** the students how the character might have said the words or done the actions.

Let's all play the character together. Do the actions and say the words with me.
Guide students to play the character with you. **Prompt** everyone to bow as you applaud them.

Wow, that was fun!

190 Lesson 48

Lesson 49

> **Materials**
> **Teacher:** Narrative trade book with people as characters (from Lesson 46); 2-Character Sheet (from Lesson 46–47)
> **Student:** Lined paper; copy of 2-Character Sheet with writing lines

5 minutes

Part A: Phonemic and Phonological Awareness

Activity 1 Syllable Deletion

Elicit responses. **Guide** as needed.
We're going to work with compound words again. I'm going to say a compound word, and you'll take off either the *first* or *last* part of the word.

Your turn. Say **rowboat.** *Rowboat.*

Now say **rowboat** without **row.** *Boat.*

Yes, you took away the *first* part, **row,** and all that is left is **boat.**

(Continue the activity with the following examples:
Steamboat. Say it without boat.
Suntan. Say it without tan.
Sunset. Say it without sun.
Sunrise. Say it without sun.
Shoelace. Say it without lace.
Buttonhole. Say it without button.)

Activity 2 Onset-Rime Segmentation

Elicit responses. **Guide** as needed.
Let's work on breaking a word into parts. Remember, this time I'm going to forget to say the *first* part. You'll say the *first* part, and I'll say the *last* part. Let's get started.

My turn. **Mop.** Say **mop.** *Mop.*

Now I'll say the *last* part, **op.** What is the *first* part? */m/.*

Whole word? *Mop.*

(Continue the activity with the following words:
Make: /m/ ake.
Jar: /j/ ar.
Jump: /j/ ump.
Lamp: /l/ amp.
Load: /l/ oad.)

Lesson 49   **191**

Activity 3 Phoneme Isolation—Initial

Elicit responses. **Guide** as needed.
Let's work on a sound at the *beginning* of a word. I'm going to say a list of words. Some of the words will have the **/nnn/** sound at the *beginning,* and some will not. I'll say the word first, and then you'll say the word.

Remember, we're listening for the **/nnn/** sound at the *beginning* of the word. What sound are we listening for? */nnn/.*

Listen. **Net.** Say **net.** *Net.*

Give me a thumbs-up if you hear **/nnn/** at the *beginning* of **net.** (Thumbs-up.)

Yes, **net** *begins* with the sound **/nnn/.**
(Continue the activity with the following lists of words.
Need. Fire. Nut. Toad. Note. Nice.
Eat. Nine. Now. Dip. Fall. Nap.)

Part B: Letter Recognition and Formation

6 minutes

Student Materials:
Lined paper

Activity 1 Letter Recognition Review—Capital I

Elicit responses to questions. **Guide** as needed. **Write** capital I on the board. **Point** to capital I.
We learned that this letter is **capital I.** What letter name? *Capital I.*
Again, what letter name? *Capital I.*
Review as needed.

Activity 2 Letter Formation Review—Capital I

Now we're going to practice writing **capital I.** When you practice writing, you'll learn not only where to start and stop the letter, but also which way to move your hand when you're making the letter. It's tricky, but you're so smart you'll learn how to write **capital** I very quickly. Watch.

Here's how you write **capital** I in the air.
Model capital I formation in the air (with your back to students).

Watch again.

Now let's practice writing **capital** I in the air. Hold up your writing hand, and make **capital** I in the air.
Guide students as they write capital I in the air.

Let's practice **capital** I again.

Here's how to write **capital** I with your writing hand pointer finger.
Model capital I formation on the board with your finger (with your back to students).

Watch again.

Now let's practice writing **capital** I on your table without using your pencil.

192   Lesson 49

Use your writing hand pointer finger, and make **capital** I on your table.
Guide students as they write capital I on their table or desktop.

Let's practice **capital** I again.

Model writing capital I on the board (with your back to students).
Remember that every letter has a name.
You learned the name of this letter is **capital I.** What letter name? *Capital I.*
Again, what letter name? *Capital I.*

Provide lined paper to students.
Now let's practice writing **capital** I with your pencil.
Guide students as they write capital I on their paper. **Review** as needed.

 Link letter names to letter sounds as needed as they appear in the program.

Part C: Comprehension Strategies

9 minutes

Teacher Materials:
Narrative trade book with people as characters (from Lesson 46)

Character Sheet (from Lesson 46–47)

Character Sheet

Student Materials:
Character Sheet

Activity 1 Listening Comprehension: Illustrations—A During-Reading Strategy

Direct students to narrative trade book of teacher choice. **Elicit** responses to questions. **Guide** as needed.
The job of a book illustrator is to make pictures for books. What does an illustrator do? *Make pictures for books.*

The illustrator of our book is _____. Who's the illustrator of this book? (Student response.)

Today as I read the story, I want you to look carefully at the pictures of the characters in the book. The illustrator made the pictures for you so that the book would be fun to read. Look for what the illustrator drew to show what the characters are doing. After I read the story, you'll become an illustrator and draw a picture of a character in the book.
Elicit correct listening behavior from students. **Reread** trade book. **Model** prosody during read-aloud.

Guide students to focus on illustrations of characters. **Elicit** answers to questions about how the illustrator shows the character's actions in the pictures. **Guide** as needed.

Activity 2 Story Elements: Illustrate Character—An After Reading Strategy

Show Character Sheet. **Elicit** responses to questions. **Guide** as needed.
Now you'll become an illustrator. Remember that an illustrator is the person who draws the pictures in a story. What does an illustrator do? (Idea: *Draw pictures for the book.*)

I'll show you what I do when I work as an illustrator.
Model drawing a character in the story by drawing a sketch that shows a character doing an action from the story and fills the space provided.

Lesson 49 **193**

As an illustrator, your job today is to draw a picture of a character doing something from the story. Let's review all the characters on our list to help you pick which character to draw.

Review list of characters from Lessons 46 and 47.

Tell your neighbor the name of the character you'll draw and what action your character will do in the picture. **(Student response.)**

Provide copy of Character Sheet to each student.

Now it's your turn to draw a character from the book. Remember to show an action that the character did in the story. Try to fill the space on your page. Make your drawing big enough so that we can all see it when you show us your picture.

In the next lesson, you'll share your picture of the character and tell what action the character's doing.

Save teacher and student illustrations for Lesson 50.

Activity 3 Collaborate to Strengthen Writing

Show Character Sheet.

Now let's write one sentence that describes the character. Watch as I write mine.

Model writing a sentence that describes a character from the story.

Write one sentence that describes the character you drew. If you need help, ask me.

Monitor students. **Guide** as needed.

Assign student partners.

Share your picture and your sentence with your neighbor. Make suggestions to make your neighbor's sentence better if you think it needs it.

Model how to share a picture and a sentence with a neighbor and how to give feedback on the sentence if it needs it. **Monitor** students. **Guide** as needed.

194 *Lesson 49*

Lesson 50

Materials

Teacher: Narrative trade book with people as characters (from Lesson 46); 2-Character Sheet (from Lesson 49), IWB-Letter Recognition; 8-My Book Review

Student: Lined paper; 2-Character Sheet completed in Lesson 49; copy of 8-My Book Review

5 minutes

Part A: Phonemic and Phonological Awareness

Activity 1 Onset-Rime Blending

Elicit responses. **Guide** as needed.
Let's make some words. I'll say two parts, and you put them together to make a whole word.

Your turn. /gl/ . . . ass. Put it together. *Glass.*
Great; you put the parts together to make the word **glass.**

Let's try some more. /cl/ . . . ock. *Clock.*

/br/ . . . ush. *Brush.*

/sw/ . . . im. *Swim.*

/st/ . . . ick. *Stick.*

/gl/ . . . ove. *Glove.*

Activity 2 Phoneme Isolation—Final

Elicit responses. **Guide** as needed.
Now, let's work on the sound at the *end* of a word. I'm going to say a list of words. Some of the words will have the **/d/** sound at the *end,* and some will not. I'll say the word first, and then you'll say the word. Think about the *last* sound we hear in each word.

Remember, we're listening for the **/d/** sound at the *end* of the word, as in **add.** What sound are you listening for at the end? /d/.

Listen. **Odd.** Say **odd.** *Odd.*

Give me a thumbs-up if you hear **/d/** at the *end* of **odd.** (Thumbs-up.)

Lesson 50   195

Yes, **odd** *ends* with the sound **/d/.**

(Continue the activity with the following lists of words.
Hide. Sip. Food. Him. Bead Nod.
Pan. Trip Led. Face. Some. Feed.)

Part B: Letter Recognition and Formation

6 minutes

Activity 1 Letter Recognition Cumulative Review—r/R, d/D, f/F, i/I

Teacher Materials:

Student Materials:
Lined paper

Display on IWB or **write** letters and capitals on the board in the order shown. **Elicit** responses to questions. **Guide** as needed.
This week you've learned one letter and one capital— **i** and **capital** I. Let's review all the letters and capitals you've learned. Are you ready?

Letter	Question	Student Response
i	What letter?	i.
d	What letter?	d.
I	What letter?	Capital I.
R	What letter?	Capital R.
D	What letter?	Capital D.
f	What letter?	f.
F	What letter?	Capital F.
r	What letter?	r.

Review as needed.

196 Lesson 50

Activity 2 | Letter Formation Cumulative Review—r/R, d/D, f/F, i/I

Write r, capital R, d, capital D, f, capital F, i, and capital I on the board in the order shown (with your back to students). **Provide** lined paper to students.
Show me how you can write the letters and capitals you've learned.
Guide students as they write the letters and capitals on their paper. **Review** as needed.

 Link letter names to letter sounds as needed as they appear in the program.

Part C: Comprehension Strategies

9 minutes

Teacher Materials:
Narrative trade book with people as characters (from Lesson 46)

Character Sheet (from Lesson 49)

My Book Review

Student Materials:
Character Sheet (from Lesson 49)

My Book Review

Activity 1 | Listening Comprehension: Characters—A During-Reading Strategy

Direct students to narrative trade book of teacher choice. **Elicit** responses to questions. **Guide** as needed.
Today I'll read the story one last time. Listen to the story to find the character you drew in the last lesson. Listen for what that character does and says. After you listen to the story, you'll get to tell about the character you drew and the action that character is doing.

Elicit correct listening behavior from students. **Reread** trade book. **Model** prosody during read-aloud.

Guide students to focus on the character they chose to draw. **Elicit** answers to questions about characters' actions and words as you read. **Guide** as needed.

Activity 2 | Retell the Story: Characters—An After-Reading Strategy

Show Character Sheet. **Elicit** responses to questions. **Guide** as needed.
I made a picture of a character in the story doing an action. My picture shows _____ doing _____. Watch me as I tell you about my picture.
Listen the right way so you'll know how to tell about your picture.
Elicit correct listening behavior from students.

Model think-aloud for retelling about the character from Character Sheet.

Sample Wording for Think-Aloud
This is my picture of _____. I like this character because _____. He/She is doing _____. He/She is saying _____.

Lesson 50   197

Provide students their copy of Character Sheet completed in Lesson 49.

Now it's your turn. You are going to tell a partner all about the character in your picture. Your partner will listen to you the right way. Then you will listen politely, as your partner tells you about his or her picture.

Assign student partners.

When you're done, if there is time, you can tell the class who your character is and what the character is doing in your picture.

Share illustrations with class as time permits or make a class book of characters.

Activity 3 Connections Through Shared Writing— Express Opinions

Show My Book Review. **Elicit** responses to questions. **Guide** as needed.

Think about the two books we read, _____ and _____. Let's talk about the two books. Which one did you like best and why?

Provide copies of My Book Review to students. **Guide** students through completion of My Book Review. **Share** with class as time permits.

Lesson 51

Materials
Teacher: Narrative trade book with a clear setting (same book for Lessons 51–55); Picture-Sound Cards for /m/, /s/, /a/, and /ē/
Student: Lined paper

Part A: Phonemic and Phonological Awareness

5 minutes

Teacher Materials:
Picture-Sound Cards for /m/, /s/, /a/, and /ē/

Activity 1 Phoneme Isolation—Initial

Elicit responses. **Guide** as needed.
Let's work on a sound at the *beginning* of a word. I'm going to say a list of words. Some of the words will have the **/k/** sound at the *beginning,* and some will not. I'll say the word first, and then you'll say the word.

Remember, we're listening for the **/k/** sound at the *beginning* of the word. What sound are we listening for? /k/.

Listen. **Cat.** Say **cat.** *Cat.*

Give me a thumbs-up if you hear **/k/** at the *beginning* of **cat.** (Thumbs-up.)

Yes, **cat** *begins* with the sound **/k/.**

(Continue the activity with the following lists of words.
Cold. Fire. Cut. Cow. Note. Cash.
Eat. Nine. Care. Dip. Coin. Cup.)

Activity 2 Phoneme Isolation—Initial

Use IWB interactive cards or picture-sound cards. **Elicit** responses. **Guide** as needed.
You have worked hard on listening for the *first* sound in a word. We're going to try something new today. We're going to look at Picture-Sound Cards and find pictures that match the sounds.

I'm going to show you two cards and name the object on each card. Then I'll tell you a sound. Think about which word starts with that sound. Let's try it. Today we'll be listening for the **/mmm/** sound at the *beginning* of the words.

Show /m/ card; use any of four Picture-Sound Cards per phoneme for activity.
This is a _____. What is this? (Student response.)

Show /s/ card; use any of four Picture-Sound Cards per phoneme for activity.
This is a _____. What is this? (Student response.)

Which picture *begins* with **/mmm/?** (Student response.)

Lesson 51   199

Show /e/ card; use any of four Picture-Sound Cards per phoneme for activity.
This is a _____. What is this? (Student response.)

Show /m/ card; use any of four Picture-Sound Cards per phoneme for activity.
This is a _____. What is this? (Student response.)

Which picture *begins* with **/mmm/?** (Student response.)

(Continue the activity with the following examples:
/m/ and /a/.
/s/ and /m/.
/a/ and /m/.
/m/ and /ē/.)

6 minutes

Student Materials:
Lined paper

Part B: Letter Recognition and Formation

Activity 1 Letter Recognition—t

Elicit responses to questions. **Guide** as needed. **Write** t on the board. **Point** to t.
Today, you'll learn a new letter.
The name of this letter is **t.** What letter name? *t.*
Again, what letter name? *t.*
Review as needed.

Activity 2 Letter Formation—t

Now we're going to practice writing **t.** When you practice writing, you'll learn not only where to start and stop the letter, but also which way to move your hand when you're making the letter. It's tricky, but you're so smart you'll learn how to write **t** very quickly. Watch.

Here's how you write **t** in the air.
Model t formation in the air (with your back to students).

Watch again.

Now let's practice writing **t** in the air. Hold up your writing hand, and make **t** in the air.
Guide students as they write t in the air.

Let's practice **t** again.

Here's how to write **t** with your writing hand pointer finger.
Model t formation on the board with your finger (with your back to students).

Watch again.

Now let's practice writing **t** on your table without using your pencil. Use your writing hand pointer finger, and make **t** on your table.
Guide students as they write t on their table or desktop.

Let's practice **t** again.

Model writing t on the board (with your back to students).

200   Lesson 51

Remember that every letter has a name.
You learned the name of this letter is **t.** What letter name? *t.*
Again, what letter name? *t.*

Provide lined paper to students.
Now let's practice writing **t** with your pencil.
Guide students as they write t on their paper. **Review** as needed.

 Link letter names to letter sounds as they appear in the program as needed.

Set up a writing center with writing materials and correct models of letters learned so far for students to use in their free time.

Part C: Comprehension Strategies

9 minutes

Teacher Materials:
Narrative trade book

Activity 1   Title, Author, and Illustrator Identification—A Before-Reading Strategy

Provide a reading center to display books being read so that students can enjoy them again during free time.

Direct students to narrative trade book of teacher choice. **Elicit** responses to questions. **Guide** as needed.

Show front cover of book and point to name of title, author, and illustrator as you discuss them.
The title of today's story is _____. What's the title of today's story?
(Student response.)

What does the title tell about the book? (Idea: *What the book is about.*)

The author of today's story is _____. Who's the author of today's story?
(Student response.)

What does the author do? (Idea: *Write the book.*)

The illustrator of today's story is _____. Who's the illustrator?
(Student response.)

What does the illustrator do? (Idea: *Make the pictures in the book.*)

Activity 2   Listening Comprehension: Setting—A During-Reading Strategy

Elicit responses to questions. **Guide** as needed.
Another part of a story is the setting. Today you're going to help me figure out where the story happens. The setting is where the story happens. What's the setting? *Where the story happens.*

What do you call the place where the story happens? *The setting.*

Lesson 51   **201**

When you want to find out where a story happens, you figure out the place the story happens. If the story happens on a farm, the setting is a farm. If the story happens at a boy's house, the setting is a house.

If the story happens at a park, what's the setting? *A park.*

If the story happens at our school, what's the setting? *Our school.*

Discuss the settings in other familiar stories.
Note: The setting is often found in a picture, rather than in the words of the text in picture books.

Today as I read the story, I want you to look carefully at the pictures and think hard about the place where the story happens. You'll look for the setting.

Elicit correct listening behavior from students. **Read** trade book. **Model** prosody during read-aloud.

Ask questions to elicit identification of setting as you read story. **Guide** as needed.

Activity 3 Story Elements: Identify Setting—An After-Reading Strategy

Elicit responses to questions. **Guide** as needed.
The setting is where the story happens. What's the setting? *Where the story happens.*

Listen as I show you how I think about the place where the story happens. I'll think about the setting.

Model think-aloud for finding setting.

Sample Wording for Think-Aloud

I'm thinking about this book and thinking about the place this story happened. I remember that on the first page there was a picture of a place that looked like _____. So I think that _____ is the setting.

Remember that the setting is the place where the story happens. What do you call the place where the story happens? *The setting.*

202   *Lesson 51*

Lesson 52

Materials
Teacher: Narrative trade book with a clear setting (from Lesson 51)
Student: Lined paper

5 minutes

Part A: Phonemic and Phonological Awareness

Activity 1 Onset-Rime Segmentation

Elicit responses. **Guide** as needed.
Let's work on breaking a word into parts. You have helped me remember the *first* part and the *last* part of our words. Let's do some of these together.

Remember, this time I'm going to forget to say the *last* part. I'll say the *first* part, and you'll say the *last* part. Let's get started.

Listen. **Score.** Say **score.** *Score.*

Now I'll say the *first* part, **/sc/.** What is the *last* part? *ore.*

Whole word? *Score.*

(Continue the activity with the following words:
Stone: /st/ one.
Price: /pr/ ice.)

Remember, this time I'm going to forget to say the *first* part. I'll say the *last* part, and you'll say the *first* part. Let's get started.

Listen. **More.** Say **more.** *More.*

Now I'll say the *last* part, **ore.** What is the *first* part? */m/.*

Whole word? *More.*

(Continue the activity with the following words:
Bone: /b/ one.
Rice: /r/ ice.)

Lesson 52   203

Activity 2 Phoneme Isolation—Final

Elicit responses. **Guide** as needed.
Now let's work on the sound at the *end* of a word. I'm going to say a list of words. Some of the words will have the **/fff/** sound at the *end,* and some will not. I'll say the word first, and then you'll say the word. Think about the *last* sound we hear in each word.

Remember, we're listening for the **/fff/** sound at the *end* of the word, as in **puff.** What sound are you listening for at the *end?* */fff/.*

Listen. **If.** Say **if.** *If.*

Give me a thumbs-up if you hear **/fff/** at the *end* of **if.** (Thumbs-up.)

Yes, **if** *ends* with the sound **/fff/.**

(Continue the activity with the following lists of words.
Huff. Hat. Laugh. Way. Same. Rough.
Pet. Huff. Game. Gas. Reef. Leaf.)

Part B: Letter Recognition and Formation

6 minutes

Student Materials:
Lined paper

Activity 1 Letter Recognition Review—t

Elicit responses to questions. **Guide** as needed. **Write** t on the board. **Point** to t.
We learned that this letter is **t.** What letter name? *t.*
Again, what letter name? *t.*
Review as needed.

Activity 2 Letter Formation Review—t

Now we're going to practice writing **t.** When you practice writing, you'll learn not only where to start and stop the letter, but also which way to move your hand when you're making the letter. It's tricky, but you're so smart you'll learn how to write **t** very quickly. Watch.

Here's how you write **t** in the air.
Model t formation in the air (with your back to students).

Watch again.

Now let's practice writing **t** in the air. Hold up your writing hand, and make **t** in the air.
Guide students as they write t in the air.

Let's practice **t** again.

Here's how to write **t** with your writing hand pointer finger.
Model t formation on the board with your finger (with your back to students).

204 Lesson 52

Watch again.

Now let's practice writing **t** on your table without using your pencil. Use your writing hand pointer finger, and make **t** on your table.
Guide students as they write t on their table or desktop.

Let's practice **t** again.

Model writing t on the board (with your back to students).
Remember that every letter has a name.
You learned the name of this letter is **t.** What letter name? *t.*
Again, what letter name? *t.*

Provide lined paper to students.
Now, let's practice writing **t** with your pencil.
Guide students as they write t on their paper. **Review** as needed.

 Link letter names to letter sounds as they appear in the program as needed.

Part C: Comprehension Strategies

9 minutes

Teacher Materials:
Narrative trade book

Activity 1 Listening Comprehension: Setting—A During-Reading Strategy

Direct students to narrative trade book of teacher choice. **Elicit** responses to questions. **Guide** as needed.
In the last lesson, you learned about the setting in a story. The setting is the place the story happens.

What is the setting? (Idea: *The place the story happens.*)

Today we'll read the story again. As I read, listen and look to see whether you can think about the setting in the book. See whether you can tell me where the setting is and what things are found in the setting.

You also know how to figure out who the characters are. See whether you can tell me some characters after I finish reading.

Elicit correct listening behavior from students. **Reread** trade book. **Model** prosody during read-aloud.

Ask questions to elicit identification of setting and characters as you read story. **Guide** as needed.

Lesson 52   **205**

Activity 2 **Story Elements: Identify Setting and Characters—An After-Reading Strategy**

Elicit responses to questions. **Guide** as needed.
In the last lesson, you learned about the setting in a story. The setting is where the story takes place. What's the setting? *Where the story takes place.*

Different settings have different things in them. If the setting is a forest, the book will have lots of trees in the picture. If the setting is a house, the book will have rooms and furniture in the picture. If the setting is a pond, there will be water and plants in the picture. If the setting is a farm, what items will you see in the picture? (**Ideas:** *A barn, pastures, fences, and farm animals.*)

Discuss items found in different settings.
What things did you see in the picture in our book? (Student response.)

So where did the story take place? (Student response.)

Yes, the setting is _____ .

You also know how to tell who the characters are in the story. Tell me who some of the characters were in our story. (Student response.)

Lesson 53

Materials

Teacher: Narrative trade book with a clear setting (from Lesson 51); Picture-Sound Cards for /m/, /s/, /a/, and /ē/, 3-Setting Sheet
Student: Lined paper

5 minutes

Part A: Phonemic and Phonological Awareness

Teacher Materials:
Picture-Sound Cards for /m/, /s/, /a/, and /ē/.

Activity 1 Phoneme Isolation—Initial

Elicit responses. **Guide** as needed.
Let's work on a sound at the *beginning* of a word. I'm going to say a list of words. Some of the words will have the **/ooo/** sound at the *beginning*, and some will not. I'll say the word first, and then you'll say the word.

Remember, we're listening for the **/ooo/** sound at the *beginning* of the word. What sound are we listening for? */ooo/*.

Listen. **Off.** Say **off.** *Off.*

Give me a thumbs-up if you hear **/ooo/** at the *beginning* of **off.** (Thumbs-up.)

Yes, **off** *begins* with the sound **/ooo/.**

(Continue the activity with the following lists of words.
Ox. Rain. Great. Otter. Next. On.
Egg. Two. Odd. Deep. Off. Nine.)

Activity 2 Phoneme Isolation—Initial

Use IWB interactive cards or picture-sound cards. **Elicit** responses. **Guide** as needed.
I'm going to show you two cards and name the object on each card. Then I'll tell you a sound. Think about which word starts with that sound. Let's try it. Today we'll be listening for the **/sss/** sound at the *beginning* of the words.

Show /s/ card; use any of four Picture-Sound Cards per phoneme for activity.
This is a _____. What is this? (Student response.)

Show /a/ card; use any of four Picture-Sound Cards per phoneme for activity.
This is a _____. What is this? (Student response.)

Which word *begins* with **/sss/**? (Student response.)

Show /ē/ card; use any of four Picture-Sound Cards per phoneme for activity.
This is a _____. What is this? (Student response.)

Lesson 53   **207**

Show /s/ card; use any of four Picture-Sound Cards per phoneme for activity.
This is a _____. What is this? (Student response.)

Which word *begins* with **/sss/**? (Student response.)

(Continue the activity with the following examples:
/m/ and /s/.
/s/ and /a/.
/s/ and /m/.
/s/ and /ē/.)

6 minutes

Student Materials:
Lined paper

Part B: Letter Recognition and Formation

Activity 1 Letter Recognition—Capital T

Elicit responses to questions. **Guide** as needed. **Write** capital T on the board.
Point to capital T.
Today you'll learn another way to write **t.**
The name of this letter is **capital T.** What letter name? *Capital T.*
Again, what letter name? *Capital T.*
Review as needed.

Activity 2 Letter Formation—Capital T

Now we're going to practice writing **capital T.** When you practice writing, you'll learn not only where to start and stop the letter, but also which way to move your hand when you're making the letter. It's tricky, but you're so smart you'll learn how to write **capital T** very quickly. Watch.

Here's how you write **capital T** in the air.
Model capital T formation in the air (with your back to students).

Watch again.

Now let's practice writing **capital T** in the air. Hold up your writing hand, and make **capital T** in the air.
Guide students as they write capital T in the air.

Let's practice **capital T** again.

Here's how to write **capital T** with your writing hand pointer finger.
Model capital T formation on the board with your finger (with your back to students).

Watch again.

Now let's practice writing **capital T** on your table without using your pencil. Use your writing hand pointer finger, and make **capital T** on your table.
Guide students as they write capital T on their table or desktop.

Let's practice **capital T** again.

Model writing capital T on the board (with your back to students).

208   Lesson 53

Remember that every letter has a name.
You learned the name of this letter is **capital T.** What letter name? *Capital T.*
Again, what letter name? *Capital T.*

Provide lined paper to students.
Now let's practice writing **capital T** with your pencil.
Guide students as they write capital T on their paper. **Review** as needed.

 Link letter names to letter sounds as they appear in the program as needed.

Part C: Comprehension Strategies

9 minutes

Teacher Materials:
Narrative trade book
3-Setting Sheet

Activity 1 Listening Comprehension: Setting—A During-Reading Strategy

Direct students to narrative trade book of teacher choice. **Show** 3-Setting Sheet.
Elicit response to question. **Guide** as needed.
You're learning how to identify the setting in stories. The setting is where the story takes place. What's the setting? *Where the story takes place.*

Listen carefully as I read the story to you again. Today as I read our story I want to write the setting on the board. We'll see whether the setting stays the same for the whole story or whether the setting changes from the beginning to the end of the story. Remember that the setting is where the story takes place.

Elicit correct listening behavior from students. **Reread** trade book. **Model** prosody during read-aloud.

Elicit setting at the beginning and end of the story from students. **Record** the setting or settings. **Guide** as needed.

Activity 2 Story Elements: Identify Setting—An After-Reading Strategy

Elicit responses to questions. **Guide** as needed.
We're learning about setting in stories. The setting is the place where a story happens. What was the setting at the beginning of the story? (Student response.)

What clues in the story or pictures made you think that? (Student response.)

What was the setting at the end of the story? (Student response.)

What clues in the story or pictures made you think that? (Student response.)

Did the setting stay the same from the beginning to end of the story or did it change? (Student response.)

Lesson 53 **209**

Lesson 54

Materials
Teacher: Narrative trade book with a clear setting (from Lesson 51)
Student: Lined paper

Part A: Phonemic and Phonological Awareness

Activity 1 Onset-Rime Segmentation

Elicit responses. **Guide** as needed.
Let's work on breaking a word into parts. You have helped me remember the *first* part and the *last* part of our words. Let's do some of these together.

Remember, this time I'm going to forget to say the *last* part. I'll say the *first* part, and you'll say the *last* part. Let's get started.

Listen. **Crust.** Say **crust.** *Crust.*

Now I'll say the *first* part, **/cr/.** What is the *last* part? *ust.*

Whole word? *Crust.*

(Continue the activity with the following words:
Fled: /fl/ ed.
Snow: /sn/ ow.)

Remember, this time I'm going to forget to say the *first* part. I'll say the *last* part, and you'll say the *first* part. Let's get started.

Listen. **Must.** Say **must.** *Must.*

Now, I'll say the *last* part, **ust.** What is the *first* part? */m/.*

Whole word? *Must.*

(Continue the activity with the following words:
Red: /r/ ed.
Mow: /m/ ow.)

210 Lesson 54

Activity 2 — Phoneme Isolation—Final

Elicit responses. **Guide** as needed.
Now let's work on the sound at the *end* of a word. I'm going to say a list of words. Some of the words will have the **/t/** sound at the *end,* and some will not. I'll say the word first, and then you'll say the word. Think about the *last* sound we hear in each word.

Remember, we're listening for the **/t/** sound at the *end* of the word, as in **at.** What sound are you listening for at the *end?* /t/.

Listen. **It.** Say **it.** *It.*

Give me a thumbs-up if you hear **/t/** at the *end* of **it.** (Thumbs-up.)

Yes, **it** *ends* with the sound **/t/.**

(Continue the activity with the following lists of words.
Pit. Hat. Hit. We. For. Hot.
Pet. Home. Sat. Go. Hut. Pet.)

Part B: Letter Recognition and Formation

6 minutes

Student Materials:
Lined paper

Activity 1 — Letter Recognition Review—Capital T

Elicit responses to questions. **Guide** as needed. **Write** capital T on the board.
Point to capital T.
We learned that this letter is **capital T.** What letter name? *Capital T.*
Again, what letter name? *Capital T.*
Review as needed.

Activity 2 — Letter Formation Review—Capital T

Now we're going to practice writing **capital T.** When you practice writing, you'll learn not only where to start and stop the letter, but also which way to move your hand when you're making the letter. It's tricky, but you're so smart you'll learn how to write **capital T** very quickly. Watch.

Here's how you write **capital T** in the air.
Model capital T formation in the air (with your back to students).

Lesson 54

Watch again.

Now let's practice writing **capital T** in the air. Hold up your writing hand, and make **capital T** in the air.
Guide students as they write capital T in the air.

Let's practice **capital T** again.

Here's how to write **capital T** with your writing hand pointer finger.
Model capital T formation on the board with your finger (with your back to students).

Watch again.

Now let's practice writing **capital T** on your table without using your pencil. Use your writing hand pointer finger, and make **capital T** on your table.
Guide students as they write capital T on their table or desktop.

Let's practice **capital T** again.

Model writing capital T on the board (with your back to students).
Remember that every letter has a name.
You learned the name of this letter is **capital T.** What letter name? *Capital T.*
Again, what letter name? *Capital T.*

Provide lined paper to students.
Now let's practice writing **capital T** with your pencil.
Guide students as they write capital T on their paper. **Review** as needed.

 Link letter names to letter sounds as they appear in the program as needed.

Part C: Comprehension Strategies

9 minutes

Teacher Materials:
Narrative trade book

Activity 1 Listening Comprehension: Setting—A During-Reading Strategy

Direct students to narrative trade book of teacher choice. **Elicit** responses to questions. **Guide** as needed.
Today as I read the story, I want you to think about the setting in the story. What's the setting? (Idea: *The place where the story happens.*)

I want you to watch the pictures and listen to the words of the story very carefully. When I'm finished with the story, we'll play the setting. We'll play the things that you find in the setting. I'll need your ideas for what items are in the setting.
Elicit correct listening behavior from students. **Reread** trade book. **Model** prosody during read-aloud.

Guide students to focus on items in the setting. **Elicit** answers to questions about items in the setting. **Guide** as needed.

Activity 2 Story Elements: Play the Setting—An After-Reading Strategy

Elicit responses to questions. **Guide** as needed.

Now we're going to play the setting. What's the setting of this story? (Student response.)

If there was a rock in the story, this is how I would "be a rock."
Model how to be a rock.

If there was a tree in the setting, how could you "be a tree"? (Students pose as a tree.)

If there was a sun in the setting, how could you "be the sun"? (Students pose as the sun.)
Elicit poses from students. **Praise** creativity in posing.

Each of you can play a part of the setting. But first we have to tell what items we found in the setting.
Elicit a list of items found in the setting from students.

Now I want you to think about which item you'll play in the setting. Tell your neighbor which item you'll be. (Student response.)

Think about what pose you'll take to be part of the setting. Now put your body into that position.
Guide students to **play** the setting. **Allow** students to pose as a different part of the setting as time permits. **Prompt** everyone to bow as you applaud them.

Wow, that was fun!

Lesson 54 **213**

Lesson 55

Materials
Teacher: Narrative trade book with a clear setting (from Lesson 51); 3-Setting Sheet; Picture-Sound Cards for /m/, /s/, /a/, and /ē/, IWB-Letter Recogntion
Student: Lined paper; copy of 3-Setting Sheet with writing lines

5 minutes

Part A: Phonemic and Phonological Awareness

Teacher Materials:
Picture-Sound Cards for /m/, /s/, /a/, and /ē/

Activity 1 Phoneme Isolation—Initial

Elicit responses. **Guide** as needed.
Let's work on a sound at the *beginning* of a word. I'm going to say a list of words. Some of the words will have the **/h/** sound at the *beginning,* and some will not. I'll say the word first, and then you'll say the word.

Remember, we're listening for the **/h/** sound at the *beginning* of the word. What sound are we listening for? /h/.

Listen. **Hat.** Say **hat.** *Hat.*

Give me a thumbs-up if you hear **/h/** at the *beginning* of **hat.** (Thumbs-up.)

Yes, **hat** *begins* with the sound **/h/.**

(Continue the activity with the following lists of words.
Hat. Rain. Hip. Otter. Next. Hen.
Hop. Two. Hand. Deep. Hum. Hole.)

Activity 2 Phoneme Isolation—Initial

Use IWB interactive cards or picture-sound cards. **Elicit** responses. **Guide** as needed.
I'm going to show you two cards and name the object on each card. Then I'll tell you a sound. Think about which word starts with that sound. Let's try it. Today we'll be listening for the **/aaa/** sound at the *beginning* of the words.

Show /a/ card; use any of four Picture-Sound Cards per phoneme for activity.
This is a _____ . What is this? (Student response.)

Show /m/ card; use any of four Picture-Sound Cards per phoneme for activity.
This is a _____ . What is this? (Student response.)

Which word *begins* with **/aaa/?** (Student response.)

Show /ē/ card; use any of four Picture-Sound Cards per phoneme for activity.
This is a _____ . What is this? (Student response.)

214   Lesson 55

Show /m/ card; use any of four Picture-Sound Cards per phoneme for activity.
This is a _____. What is this? (Student response.)

Which word *begins* with **/aaa/**? (Student response.)

(Continue the activity with the following examples:
/a/ and /s/.
/s/ and /a/.
/a/ and /m/.
/a/ and /ē/.)

Part B: Letter Recognition and Formation

6 minutes

Student Materials:
Lined paper

Activity 1 Letter Recognition Cumulative Review—d/D, f/F, i/I, t/T

Display on IWB or **write** letters and capitals on the board in the order shown.
Elicit responses to questions. **Guide** as needed.
This week you've learned one letter and one capital— **t** and **capital T.**
Let's review all the letters and capitals you've learned. Are you ready?

Letter	Question	Student Response
d	What letter?	d.
f	What letter?	f.
I	What letter?	Capital I.
D	What letter?	Capital D.
F	What letter?	Capital F.
t	What letter?	t.
i	What letter?	i.
T	What letter?	Capital T.

Review as needed.

Lesson 55

Activity 2 — Letter Formation Cumulative Review—d/D, f/F, i/I, t/T

Write d, capital D, f, capital F, i, capital I, t, and capital T on the board in the order shown (with your back to students). **Provide** lined paper to students.
Show me how you can write these letters and capitals.
Guide students as they write the letters and capitals on their paper. **Review** as needed.

 Link letter names to letter sounds as they appear in the program as needed.

Part C: Comprehensive Strategies

9 minutes

Teacher Materials:
Narrative trade book
Setting Sheet

Student Materials:
Setting Sheet

Activity 1 — Listening Comprehension: Illustrations—A During-Reading Strategy

Direct students to narrative trade book of teacher choice. **Elicit** responses to questions. **Guide** as needed.
The job of a book illustrator is to make pictures for books. What does an illustrator do? *Make pictures for books.*

The illustrator of our book is _____. Who's the illustrator of this book? (Student response.)

Today as I read the story, I want you to look carefully at the pictures of the setting in the book. The illustrator made the pictures for you so that the book would be fun to read. Look for what the illustrator did to show the setting. After I read the story, you'll become an illustrator and draw a picture of the setting. While I read, think about whether the setting stays the same or changes in the story.

Elicit correct listening behavior from students. **Reread** trade book. **Model** prosody during read-aloud.

Guide students to focus on illustrations of the setting. **Elicit** answers to questions about how the illustrator shows the items in the setting and whether the setting changes or stays the same. **Guide** as needed.

Activity 2 — Story Elements: Illustrate Setting—An After-Reading Strategy

Show Setting Sheet. **Elicit** responses. **Guide** as needed.
Now you'll become an illustrator. Remember that an illustrator is the person who draws the pictures in a story.

What does an illustrator do? (Idea: *Draw pictures for the book.*)

Before you draw the setting, we have to decide whether we will use the top part of our paper or the bottom. If the setting stays the same, we'll use the top. There is room for only one picture. If the setting changes from the beginning to end of the story, we'll use the bottom. That has two places to show the setting at the beginning and the end.

Did the setting change or stay the same? (Student response.)

So will you draw in the top or the bottom of your sheet? (Student response.)

I'll show you what I do when I work as an illustrator to draw the setting.
Model drawing the setting in the story by drawing a sketch that fills the space provided. [Draw at the top if the setting stays the same. Draw two sketches in the two boxes at the bottom if the setting changes.]

Provide Setting Sheet to each student.
As an illustrator, your job today is to draw the setting from the story. Be sure to draw the setting in the right box/boxes.
Share illustrations with class as time permits, or make a class book of settings.

Activity 3 Collaborate to Strengthen Writing

Show Setting Sheet.
Now let's write one sentence that describes the setting. Watch as I write mine.
Model writing a sentence that describes the setting from the story.

Write one sentence that describes the setting you drew. If you need help, ask me.
Monitor students. **Guide** as needed.

Assign student partners.
Share your picture and your sentence with your neighbor. Make suggestions to make your neighbor's sentence better if you think it needs it.
Model how to share a picture and a sentence with a neighbor and how to give feedback on the sentence if it needs it. **Monitor** students. **Guide** as needed.

Lesson 55

Lesson 56

Materials
Teacher: Narrative trade book with a clear setting (same book for Lessons 56–60), 1-My Prediction Chart
Student: Lined paper, 1-My Prediction Chart

5 minutes

Part A: Phonemic and Phonological Awareness

Activity 1 Onset-Rime Segmentation

Elicit responses. **Guide** as needed.
Let's work on breaking a word into parts. You have helped me remember the *first* part and the *last* part of our words. Let's do some of these together.

Remember, this time I'm going to forget to say the *last* part. I'll say the *first* part, and you'll say the *last* part. Let's get started.

Listen. **Store.** Say **store.** *Store.*

Now I'll say the *first* part, **/st/.** What is the *last* part? *ore.*

Whole word? *Store.*

(Continue the activity with the following words:
Broom: /br/ oom.
Gray: /gr/ ay.)

Remember, this time I'm going to forget to say the *first* part. I'll say the *last* part, and you'll say the *first* part. Let's get started.

Listen. **Core.** Say **core.** *Core.*

Now I'll say the *last* part, **ore.** What is the *first* part? */c/.*

Whole word? *Core.*

(Continue the activity with the following words:
Room: /r/ oom.
Say: /s/ ay.)

Activity 2 Phoneme Isolation—Final

Elicit responses. **Guide** as needed.
Now let's work on the sound at the *end* of a word. I'm going to say a list of words. Some of the words will have the **/nnn/** sound at the *end,* and some will not. I'll say the word first, and then you'll say the word. Think about the *last* sound we hear in each word.

218 Lesson 56

Remember, we're listening for the **/nnn/** sound at the *end* of the word, as in **in.** What sound are you listening for at the *end*? */nnn/*.

Listen. **In.** Say **in.** *In.*

Give me a thumbs-up if you hear **/nnn/** at the *end* of **in.** (Thumbs-up.)

Yes, **in** *ends* with the sound **/nnn/.**

(Continue the activity with the following lists of words.
Seen. Hope. Sit. Rain. Green. Head.
Spoon. Oak. Beat. Bean. Train. Pill.)

Part B: Letter Recognition and Formation

6 minutes

Student Materials:
Lined paper

Activity 1 Letter Recognition—n

Elicit responses to questions. **Guide** as needed. **Write** n on the board. **Point** to n.
Today you'll learn a new letter.
The name of this letter is **n.** What letter name? *n.*
Again, what letter name? *n.*
Review as needed.

Activity 2 Letter Formation—n

Now we're going to practice writing **n.** When you practice writing, you'll learn not only where to start and stop the letter, but also which way to move your hand when you're making the letter. It's tricky, but you're so smart you'll learn how to write **n** very quickly. Watch.

Here's how you write **n** in the air.
Model n formation in the air (with your back to students).

Watch again.

Now let's practice writing **n** in the air. Hold up your writing hand, and make **n** in the air.
Guide students as they write n in the air.

Let's practice **n** again.

Here's how to write **n** with your writing hand pointer finger.
Model n formation on the board with your finger (with your back to students).

Watch again.

Now let's practice writing **n** on your table without using your pencil. Use your writing hand pointer finger, and make **n** on your table.
Guide students as they write n on their table or desktop.

Let's practice **n** again.

Lesson 56   219

Model writing n on the board (with your back to students).
Remember that every letter has a name.
You learned the name of this letter is **n.** What letter name? *n.*
Again, what letter name? *n.*

Provide lined paper to students.
Now let's practice writing **n** with your pencil.
Guide students as they write n on their paper. **Review** as needed.

 Link letter names to letter sounds as they appear in the program as needed.

Set up a writing center with writing materials and correct models of letters learned so far for students to use in their free time.

Part C: Comprehension Strategies

9 minutes

Teacher Materials:
Narrative trade book
My Prediction Chart

Student Materials:
My Prediction Chart

Activity 1 — Title, Author, and Illustrator Identification—A Before-Reading Strategy

 Provide a reading center to display books being read so that students can enjoy them again during free time.

Direct students to narrative trade book of teacher choice. **Elicit** responses to questions. **Guide** as needed.

Show front cover of book and allow student to point to name of title, author, and illustrator as you discuss them.
The title of today's story is _____. What's the title of today's story? (Student response.)

What does the title tell about the book? (Idea: *What the book is about.*)

The author of today's story is _____. Who's the author of today's story? (Student response.)

What does the author do? (Idea: *Write the book.*)

The illustrator of today's story is _____. Who's the illustrator? (Student response.)

What does the illustrator do? (Idea: *Make the pictures in the book.*)

Activity 2 — Make Predictions—A Before-Reading Strategy

Show Prediction Chart and provide copy to students. **Show** title, front and back cover, and pictures inside the book. **Elicit** responses to questions. **Guide** as needed.
The title of today's book is _____. Write the book title in the box labeled "Book Title".

Now that we know the title of today's book, let's look at the cover and pictures inside the book for clues to make some good guesses about what we think the story will be about. We call our good guesses predictions.

Making good guesses, or predictions, helps us get interested in the story before we read it. Let's make some predictions about the story before I read to you.

What do you predict this story will be about? (Student responses.)

What characters do you predict will be in the story? (Student responses.)

What do you predict the setting will be? (Student responses.)

Write your prediction in the box labeled "I Predict That".
Guide as needed.
When we read the book, we will check your predictions and see whether they are correct.

Elicit correct listening behavior from students. **Read** trade book. **Model** prosody during read-aloud. **Ask** questions to confirm predictions for what the story is about, the characters, and the setting as you read story. **Guide** as needed.

Activity 3 Confirm Predictions—An After-Reading Strategy

Elicit responses to questions. **Guide** as needed.
Now let's check your predictions to see whether they were correct. You predicted that the story was about _____.

Was your prediction correct? (Student responses.)
Circle whether or not your prediction was correct in the box labeled "Was My Prediction Correct?".
Guide as needed.

You predicted that _____ were characters in the story. Was your prediction correct? (Student responses.)

You predicted that the setting was _____. Was your prediction correct? (Student responses.)

Remember that your predictions don't have to be correct. Just making a prediction and listening to see whether your prediction is correct helps you understand what you read.

Lesson 56   **221**

Lesson 57

Materials

Teacher: Narrative trade book with a clear setting (from Lesson 56); Picture-Sound Cards for /m/, /s/, /a/, and /ē/, 2-Character Sheet, 3-Setting Sheet
Student: Lined paper

Part A: Phonemic and Phonological Awareness

5 minutes

Teacher Materials:
Picture-Sound Cards for /m/, /s/, /a/, and /ē/

Activity 1 Phoneme Isolation—Initial

Elicit responses. **Guide** as needed.
Let's work on a sound at the *beginning* of a word. I'm going to say a list of words. Some of the words will have the **/āāā/** sound at the *beginning,* and some will not. I'll say the word first, and then you'll say the word.

Remember, we're listening for the **/āāā/** sound at the *beginning* of the word. What sound are we listening for? /āāā/.

Listen. **Ate.** Say **ate.** *Ate.*

Give me a thumbs-up if you hear **/āāā/** at the *beginning* of **ate.** (Thumbs-up.)

Yes, **ate** *begins* with the sound **/āāā/.**

(Continue the activity with the following lists of words.
April. Rip. Ache. Over. Nut. Ace.
Help. Aim. Feed. Dust. Age. Aid.)

Activity 2 Phoneme Isolation—Initial

Use IWB interactive cards or picture-sound cards. **Elicit** responses. **Guide** as needed.
I'm going to show you two cards and name the object on each card. Then I'll tell you a sound. Think about which word starts with that sound. Let's try it. Today we'll be listening for the **/ēēē/** sound at the *beginning* of the words.

Show /ē/ card; use any of four Picture-Sound Cards per phoneme for activity.
This is a _____. What is this? (Student response.)

Show /m/ card; use any of four Picture-Sound Cards per phoneme for activity.
This is a _____. What is this? (Student response.)

Which picture *begins* with **/ēēē/?** (Student response.)

Show /ē/ card; use any of four Picture-Sound Cards per phoneme for activity.
This is a _____. What is this? (Student response.)

Show /a/ card; use any of four Picture-Sound Cards per phoneme for activity.
This is a _____. What is this? (Student response.)

Which picture *begins* with /ēēē/? (Student response.)

(Continue the activity with the following examples:
/s/ and /ē/.
/ē/ and /a/.
/ē/ and /m/.
/s/ and /ē/.)

6 minutes

Student Materials:
Lined paper

Part B: Letter Recognition and Formation

Activity 1 Letter Recognition Review—n

Elicit responses to questions. **Guide** as needed. **Write** n on the board. **Point** to n.
We learned that this letter is **n.** What letter name? *n.*
Again, what letter name? *n.*
Review as needed.

Activity 2 Letter Formation Review—n

Now we're going to practice writing **n.** When you practice writing, you'll learn not only where to start and stop the letter, but also which way to move your hand when you're making the letter. It's tricky, but you're so smart you'll learn how to write **n** very quickly. Watch.

Here's how you write **n** in the air.
Model n formation in the air (with your back to students).

Watch again.

Now let's practice writing **n** in the air. Hold up your writing hand, and make **n** in the air.
Guide students as they write n in the air.

Let's practice **n** again.

Here's how to write **n** with your writing hand pointer finger.
Model n formation on the board with your finger (with your back to students).

Lesson 57   223

Watch again.

Now let's practice writing **n** on your table without using your pencil. Use your writing hand pointer finger, and make **n** on your table.
Guide students as they write n on their table or desktop.

Let's practice **n** again.

Model writing n on the board (with your back to students).
Remember that every letter has a name.
You learned the name of this letter is **n.** What letter name? *n.*
Again, what letter name? *n.*

Provide lined paper to students.
Now let's practice writing n with your pencil.
Guide students as they write n on their paper. **Review** as needed.

 Link letter names to letter sounds as they appear in the program as needed.

Part C: Comprehension Strategies

 9 minutes

Activity 1 Listening Comprehension: Setting—A During-Reading Strategy

Teacher Materials:
Narrative trade book

Character Sheet

Setting Sheet

Direct students to narrative trade book of teacher choice. **Show** Setting Sheet and Character Sheet. **Elicit** responses to questions. **Guide** as needed.
You're learning how to identify the setting in stories. The setting is where the story takes place. What's the setting? *Where the story takes place.*

Listen carefully as I read the story to you again. Today as I read our story I want to write the setting on the board. We'll see whether the setting stays the same for the whole story or whether the setting changes from the beginning to the end of the story. Remember that the setting is where the story takes place. I also want you to listen for the characters in the story. When you hear a setting or a character, raise your hand and we'll write them on the board.

Elicit correct listening behavior from students. **Reread** trade book. **Model** prosody during read-aloud.

Elicit settings and characters from students as you read. **Record** setting(s) and characters. **Guide** as needed.

224   Lesson 57

Activity 2 Story Elements: Identify Characters and Setting—An After-Reading Strategy

Elicit responses to questions. **Guide** as needed.
We're learning about settings in stories. The setting is the place where a story happens. What was the setting at the beginning of the story? (Student response.)

Touch name(s) of setting(s) as you discuss them.
What clues in the story or pictures made you think that? (Student response.)

What was the setting at the end of the story? (Student response.)

What clues in the story or pictures made you think that? (Student response.)

Did the setting stay the same from the beginning to end of the story or did it change? (Student response.)

Touch name of character as you ask questions about each character.
Now let's talk about all the characters and what they said and did. Tell me what _____ did or said. (Student response.)
Repeat question for each character as time permits.

The character that the story is mostly about is called the main character.

What do you call the character that the story is mostly about? *The main character.*

What character is the story mostly about? (Student response.)

So, _____ is the main character.

Who's the main character? (Student response.)

Lesson 57   **225**

Lesson 58

Materials
Teacher: Narrative trade book with a clear setting
Student: Lined paper

Part A: Phonemic and Phonological Awareness

Activity 1 Onset-Rime Segmentation

Elicit responses to questions. **Guide** as needed.
Let's work on breaking a word into parts. You have helped me remember the *first* part and the *last* part of our words. Let's do some of these together.

Remember, this time I'm going to forget to say the *last* part. I'll say the *first* part, and you'll say the *last* part. Let's get started.

Listen. **Smart.** Say **smart.** *Smart.*

Now I'll say the *first* part, **/sm/.** What is the *last* part? *art.*

Whole word? *Smart.*

(Continue the activity with the following words:
Scare: /sc/ are.
Stop: /st/ op.)

Remember, this time I'm going to forget to say the *first* part. I'll say the *last* part, and you'll say the *first* part. Let's get started.

Listen. **Cart.** Say **cart.** *Cart.*

Now I'll say the *last* part, **art.** What is the *first* part? */c/.*

Whole word? *Cart.*

(Continue the activity with the following words:
Hair: /h/ air.
Hop: /h/ op.)

Activity 2 Phoneme Isolation—Final

Elicit responses to questions. **Guide** as needed.
Now let's work on the sound at the *end* of a word. I'm going to say a list of words. Some of the words will have the **/k/** sound at the *end,* and some will not. I'll say the word first, and then you say the word. Think about the *last* sound we hear in each word.

Remember, we're listening for the **/k/** sound at the *end* of the word, as in **tack.** What sound are you listening for at the *end*? */k/.*

Listen. **Bike.** Say **bike.** *Bike.*

Give me a thumbs-up if you hear **/k/** at the *end* of **bike.** (Thumbs-up.)

Yes, **bike** *ends* with the sound **/k/.**

(Continue the activity with the following lists of words.
Poke. Here. Sack. Race. Glass. Rack.
Will. Oak. Sack. Jet. Fix. Pick.)

Part B: Letter Recognition and Formation

6 minutes

Student Materials:
Lined paper

Activity 1 Letter Recognition—Capital N

Elicit responses to questions. **Guide** as needed. **Write** capital N on the board.
Point to capital N.
Today you'll learn another way to write **n.**
The name of this letter is **capital N.** What letter name? *Capital N.*
Again, what letter name? *Capital N.*
Review as needed.

Activity 2 Letter Formation—Capital N

Now we're going to practice writing **capital N.** When you practice writing, you'll learn not only where to start and stop the letter, but also which way to move your hand when you're making the letter. It's tricky, but you're so smart you'll learn how to write **capital N** very quickly. Watch.

Here's how you write **capital N** in the air.
Model capital N formation in the air (with your back to students).

Watch again.

Now let's practice writing **capital N** in the air. Hold up your writing hand, and make **capital N** in the air.
Guide students as they write capital N in the air.

Let's practice **capital N** again.

Here's how to write **capital N** with your writing hand pointer finger.
Model capital N formation on the board with your finger (with your back to students).

Watch again.

Lesson 58   **227**

Now let's practice writing **capital N** on your table without using your pencil. Use your writing hand pointer finger, and make **capital N** on your table.
Guide students as they write capital N on their table or desktop.

Let's practice **capital N** again.

Model writing capital N on the board (with your back to students).
Remember that every letter has a name.
You learned the name of this letter is **capital N.** What letter name? *Capital N.*
Again, what letter name? *Capital N.*

Provide lined paper to students.
Now let's practice writing **capital N** with your pencil.
Guide students as they write capital N on their paper. **Review** as needed.

 Link letter names to letter sounds as they appear in the program as needed.

Part C: Comprehension Strategies

9 minutes

Teacher Materials:
Narrative trade book

Activity 1 Listening Comprehension: Setting—A During-Reading Strategy

Direct students to narrative trade book of teacher choice. **Elicit** responses to questions. **Guide** as needed.
Today as I read the story, I want you to think about the setting and the main character in the story. What's the setting? (**Idea:** *The place where the story happens.*)

The character that the story is mostly about is the main character.

Who's the main character in the story? (**Idea:** *The character that the story is mostly about.*)

I want you to watch the pictures and listen to the words of the story very carefully. When I am finished with the story, we will play the setting. We'll play the things that you find in the setting. I'll need your ideas for what items are in the setting. We'll also play the main character. So listen carefully to hear something the main character did or said that we can play.

Elicit correct listening behavior from students. **Reread** trade book. **Model** prosody during read-aloud.

Guide students to focus on items in the setting and an action that the main character does. **Elicit** answers to questions about items in the setting and words or an action by the main character that you can play. **Guide** as needed.

Activity 2 Story Elements: Play the Main Character and Setting—An After-Reading Strategy

Elicit responses to questions. **Guide** as needed.
Now we're going to play the setting.

What's the setting of this story? (Student response.)

Each of you can play a part of the setting. But first we have to tell what items we found in the setting.
Elicit a list from the students of items found in the setting.

Watch _____ and _____ as they pose together to make one item in the setting.

You'll work with a partner to play an item in the setting. Decide with your partner what item in the setting you will be. Work together to play that item.

Assign student partners. **Ask** two students to model how to work together to pose as one item for the setting (for example, two students hold hands to form an arch to show a door to a house).

Now we're going to play the main character.
Guide students to play the main character for each other.

What event in the story shall we play? (Student response.)

What did the character do? (Student response.)

What did the character say? (Student response.)

Play the character for your partner. Do what the character did and say what the character said for your partner. Then let your partner play the character for you.
Elicit poses from students. **Praise** creativity in posing. **Allow** students to perform for the class as time permits.

Lesson 58   **229**

Lesson 59

Materials

Teacher: Narrative trade book with a clear setting (from Lesson 56); 3-Setting Sheet; Picture-Sound Cards for /m/, /s/, /a/, and /ē/, and /r/

Student: Lined paper; copy of 3-Setting Sheet with writing lines

5 minutes

Teacher Materials:
Picture-Sound Cards for /m/, /s/, /a/, and /ē/, and /r/

Part A: Phonemic and Phonological Awareness

Activity 1 Phoneme Isolation—Initial

Elicit responses. **Guide** as needed.
Let's work on a sound at the *beginning* of a word. I'm going to say a list of words. Some of the words will have the **/thththth/** sound at the *beginning*, and some will not. I'll say the word first, and then you'll say the word.

Remember, we're listening for the **/thththth/** sound at the *beginning* of the word. What sound are we listening for? /thththth/.

Listen. **This.** Say **this.** *This.*

Give me a thumbs-up if you hear **/thththth/** at the *beginning* of **this.** (Thumbs-up.)

Yes, **this** *begins* with the sound **/thththth/.**

(Continue the activity with the following lists of words.
Ask. There. Over. Way. Then. They.
His. The. Stop. Ship. That. Any.)

Activity 2 Phoneme Isolation—Initial

Use IWB interactive cards or picture-sound cards. **Elicit** responses. **Guide** as needed.
I'm going to show you two cards and name the object on each card. Then I'll tell you a sound. Think about which word starts with that sound. Let's try it. Today we'll be listening for the **/rrr/** sound at the *beginning* of the words.

Show /r/ card; use any of four Picture-Sound Cards per phoneme for activity.
This is a _____. What is this? (Student response.)

Show /a/ card; use any of four Picture-Sound Cards per phoneme for activity.
This is a _____. What is this? (Student response.)

Which word *begins* with **/rrr/?** (Student response.)

Show /ē/ card; use any of four Picture-Sound Cards per phoneme for activity.
This is a _____. What is this? (Student response.)

230 Lesson 59

Show /r/ card; use any of four Picture-Sound Cards per phoneme for activity.
This is a _____. What is this? (Student response.)

Which word *begins* with **/rrr/?** (Student response.)

(Continue the activity with the following examples:
/r/ and /s/.
/r/ and /a/.
/ē/ and /r/.
/m/ and /r/.)

Part B: Letter Recognition and Formation

6 minutes

Student Materials:
Lined paper

Activity 1 Letter Recognition Review—Capital N

Elicit responses to questions. **Guide** as needed. **Write** capital N on the board.
Point to capital N.
We learned that this letter is **capital N.** What letter name? *Capital N.*
Again, what letter name? *Capital N.*
Review as needed.

Activity 2 Letter Formation Review—Capital N

Now we're going to practice writing **capital N.** When you practice writing, you'll learn not only where to start and stop the letter, but also which way to move your hand when you're making the letter. It's tricky, but you're so smart you'll learn how to write **capital N** very quickly. Watch.

Here's how you write **capital N** in the air.
Model capital N formation in the air (with your back to students).

Watch again.

Now let's practice writing **capital N** in the air. Hold up your writing hand, and make **capital N** in the air.
Guide students as they write capital N in the air.

Let's practice **capital N** again.

Here's how to write **capital N** with your writing hand pointer finger.
Model capital N formation on the board with your finger (with your back to students).

Watch again.

Now let's practice writing **capital N** on your table without using your pencil. Use your writing hand pointer finger, and make **capital N** on your table.
Guide students as they write capital N on their table or desktop.

Let's practice **capital N** again.

Lesson 59 **231**

Model writing capital N on the board (with your back to students).
Remember that every letter has a name.
You learned the name of this letter is **capital N.** What letter name? *Capital N.*
Again, what letter name? *Capital N.*

Provide lined paper to students.
Now let's practice writing **capital N** with your pencil.
Guide students as they write capital N on their paper. **Review** as needed.

 Link letter names to letter sounds as they appear in the program as needed.

Part C: Comprehension Strategies

9 minutes

Teacher Materials:
Narrative trade book
Setting Sheet

Student Materials:
Setting Sheet

Activity 1 Listening Comprehension: Illustrations—A During-Reading Strategy

Direct students to narrative trade book of teacher choice. **Elicit** responses to questions. **Guide** as needed.
The job of a book illustrator is to make pictures for books.

What does an illustrator do? *Make pictures for books.*

The illustrator of this book is _____. Who's the illustrator of this book? (Student response.)

Today as I read the story, I want you to look carefully at the pictures of the setting in the book. The illustrator made the pictures for you so that the book would be fun to read. Look for what the illustrator did to show the setting. After I read the story, you'll become an illustrator and draw a picture of the setting. You'll also draw a picture of the main character in the picture. While I read, think about whether the setting stays the same or changes in the story. Also think about who the main character is.

Elicit correct listening behavior from students. **Reread** trade book. **Model** prosody during read-aloud.

Guide students to focus on illustrations of the setting and main character. **Elicit** answers to questions about how the illustrator shows the items in the setting and whether the setting changes or stays the same. **Elicit** answer to identify main character. **Guide** as needed.

Activity 2 Story Elements: Illustrate Main Character and Setting—An After-Reading Strategy

Show Setting Sheet. **Elicit** responses to questions. **Guide** as needed.
Now you'll become an illustrator. Remember that an illustrator is the person who draws the pictures in a story.

What does an illustrator do? (Idea: *Draw pictures for the book.*)

Before you draw the setting, we have to decide whether we'll use the top part of our paper or the bottom. If the setting stays the same, we'll use the top. There is room for only one picture. If the setting changes from the beginning to end of the story, we'll use the bottom. That has two places to show the setting at the beginning and the end.

Guide students to correct place on sheet to draw picture of setting.
Did the setting change or stay the same? (**Student response.**)

So will you draw in the top or the bottom of your sheet? (**Student response.**)

Provide copy of Setting Sheet to each student.
Let's work as illustrators to draw the setting. Remember that you'll also draw the main character in your setting boxes.
Draw illustrations for setting and main character on Setting Sheet while students draw.

In the next lesson, you'll tell about your illustration.
Save teacher and student illustrations for Lesson 60.

Activity 3 Collaborate to Strengthen Writing

Show Setting Sheet.
Now let's write one sentence that describes the setting. Watch as I write mine.
Model writing a sentence that describes the setting from the story.

Write one sentence that describes the setting you drew. If you need help, ask me.
Monitor students. **Guide** as needed.

Assign student partners.
Share your picture and your sentence with your neighbor. Make suggestions to make your neighbor's sentence better if you think it needs it.
Model how to share a picture and a sentence with a neighbor and how to give feedback on the sentence if it needs it. **Monitor** students. **Guide** as needed.

Lesson 59   **233**

Lesson 60

Materials

Teacher: Narrative trade book with a clear setting (from Lesson 56); 3-Setting Sheet (from Lesson 59), IWB-Letter Recognition; 8-My Book Review

Student: Lined paper; copy of 3-Setting Sheet (from Lesson 59); copy of 8-My Book Review

5 minutes

Part A: Phonemic and Phonological Awareness

Activity 1 Onset-Rime Segmentation

Elicit responses. **Guide** as needed.
Let's work on breaking a word into parts. You have helped me remember the *first* part and the *last* part of our words. Let's do some of these together.

Remember, this time I'm going to forget to say the *last* part. I'll say the *first* part, and you'll say the *last* part. Let's get started.

Listen. **Stub.** Say **stub.** *Stub.*

Now I'll say the *first* part, **/st/.** What is the *last* part? *ub.*

Whole word? *Stub.*

(Continue the activity with the following words:
Bride: /br/ ide.
Bread: /br/ ead.)

Remember, this time I'm going to forget to say the *first* part. I'll say the *last* part, and you'll say the *first* part. Let's get started.

Listen. **Tub.** Say **tub.** *Tub.*

Now I'll say the *last* part, **ub.** What is the *first* part? */t/.*

Whole word? *Tub.*

(Continue the activity with the following words:
Hide: /h/ ide.
Head: /h/ ead.)

Activity 2 Phoneme Isolation—Final

Elicit responses. **Guide** as needed.
Now let's work on the sound at the *end* of a word. I'm going to say a list of words. Some of the words will have the **/āāā/** sound at the *end,* and some will not. I'll say the word first, and then you'll say the word. Think about the *last* sound we hear in each word.

Remember, we're listening for the /āāā/ sound at the *end* of the word, as in **may.** What sound are you listening for at the *end? /āāā/.*

234   Lesson 60

Listen. **Play.** Say **play.** *Play.*

Give me a thumbs-up if you hear **/āāā/** at the *end* of **play.** (Thumbs-up.)

Yes, **play** *ends* with the sound **/āāā/.**

(Continue the activity with the following lists of words.
Day. Goat. Fix. Ray. Say. Ride.
Fall. Jay. So. Gray. Glass. Sway.)

Part B: Letter Recognition and Formation

6 minutes

Student Materials:
Lined paper

Activity 1 Letter Recognition Cumulative Review—f/F, i/I, t/T, n/N

Display on IWB or **write** letters and capitals on the board in the order shown.
Elicit responses to questions. **Guide** as needed.
This week you've learned one letter and one capital—**n** and **capital N.**
Let's review all the letters and capitals you've learned. Are you ready?

Letter	Question	Student Response
f	What letter?	f.
T	What letter?	Capital T.
i	What letter?	i.
N	What letter?	Capital N.
t	What letter?	t.
F	What letter?	Capital F.
n	What letter?	n.
I	What letter?	Capital I.

Review as needed.

Activity 2 Letter Formation Cumulative Review—f/F, i/I, t/T, n/N

Write f, capital F, i, capital I, t, capital T, n, and capital N on the board in the order shown (with your back to students). **Provide** lined paper to students.
Show me how you can write these letters and capitals.
Guide students as they write the letters and capitals on their paper. **Review** as needed.

 Link letter names to letter sounds as they appear in the program as needed.

Lesson 60   **235**

Part C: Comprehension Strategies

9 minutes

Teacher Materials:
Narrative trade book

Setting Sheet

My Book Review

Student Materials:
Setting Sheet

My Book Review

Activity 1 Listening Comprehension: Characters and Setting—A During-Reading Strategy

Direct students to narrative trade book. **Elicit** responses. **Guide** as needed.
Today I will read the story one last time. Listen to the story to find the character and setting or settings you drew in the last lesson. Listen for what that character did and what that character said, and look at the pictures of the setting. After you listen to the story, you'll get to tell about the character you drew in the last lesson and the setting that character was in.

Elicit correct listening behavior from students. **Reread** trade book. **Model** prosody.

Guide students to focus on the setting and the main character they drew. **Elicit** answers to questions about the main character and the setting as you read. **Guide** as needed.

Activity 2 Retell the Story: Characters and Setting—An After-Reading Strategy

Show Setting Sheet. **Elicit** responses to questions. **Guide** as needed.
I made a picture of the main character from the story in the setting. My picture shows _____ in the setting of _____. Watch as I show how I tell you about my picture. Listen the right way as I tell you about my picture.

Elicit correct listening behavior from students. **Model** think-aloud for retelling the character and setting from Setting Sheet.

Sample Wording for Think-Aloud
This is my picture of _____ who is found in the setting of _____. I like this character because _____. I like the setting because _____.

Assign student partners. **Provide** copy of Setting Sheet completed in Lesson 59.
Now it's your turn. You're going to tell a partner all about the character and setting in your picture. Your partner will listen to you the right way. Then you'll listen politely as your partner tells you about his or her picture.

When you are done, if there is time, you can show us your illustration and tell the class about your character and setting.
Share illustrations with class or make a class book of characters and settings.

Activity 3 Connections Through Shared Writing—Express Opinions

Show My Book Review. **Elicit** responses to questions. **Guide** as needed.
Think about the two books we read, _____ and _____. Let's talk about the two books. Which one did you like best and why?

Provide copies of My Book Review to students. **Guide** students through completion of My Book Review. **Share** with class as time permits.

Lesson 61

Materials
Teacher: Narrative trade book (same book for Lessons 61–65); 6-Phonemic Awareness
Student: Lined paper; copy of 6-Phonemic Awareness

Part A: Phonemic and Phonological Awareness

5 minutes

IWB

Teacher Materials: Phonemic Awareness

Student Materials: Phonemic Awareness

Activity 1 Phoneme Isolation—Initial

Elicit responses. **Guide** as needed.
Let's work on a sound at the *beginning* of a word. I'm going to say a list of words. Some of the words will have the **/uuu/** sound at the *beginning*, and some will not. I'll say the word first, and then you'll say the word.

Remember, we're listening for the **/uuu/** sound at the *beginning* of the word. What sound are we listening for? */uuu/*.

Listen. **Up.** Say **up.** *Up.*

Give me a thumbs-up if you hear **/uuu/** at the *beginning* of **up.** (Thumbs-up.)

Yes, **up** *begins* with the sound **/uuu/.**

(Continue the activity with the following lists of words.
Under. My. Have. Uncle. Think. This.
Uncut. Over. Sink. Us. First. Underwear.)

Activity 2 Phoneme Isolation—Final

Show Phonemic Awareness. **Distribute** copy of Phonemic Awareness. **Elicit** responses. **Guide** as needed.
You have worked hard on listening for the *last* sound in a word. We're going to try something new today.

We're going to look at pictures on this page and find pictures to match our sounds. I'm going to name each picture in the top row. Touch each picture after I name it, and repeat the name. We're going to be listening for the *last* sound in each picture. Let's try it.

Model use of Phonemic Awareness; point to each picture as word is said.

This is a cup. What is this? (Student response.)

This is a lamb. What is this? (Student response.)

This is a tree. What is this? (Student response.)

Which word has the *last* sound **/mmm/**? (Student response.)

(Continue the activity with the remaining rows:
Second row: bus, cat, fan. Which word has the last sound /sss/?
Third row: nail, bee, table. Which word has the last sound /ēēē/?
Fourth row: tree, fork, ham. Which word has the last sound /mmm/?)

Part B: Letter Recognition and Formation

6 minutes

Student Materials:
Lined paper

Activity 1 Letter Recognition—c

Elicit responses to questions. **Guide** as needed. **Write** c on the board. **Point** to c.
Today you'll learn a new letter. The name of this letter is **c.** What letter name? *c.*
Again, what letter name? *c.*
Review as needed.

Activity 2 Letter Formation—c

Now we're going to practice writing **c.** When you practice writing, you'll learn not only where to start and stop the letter, but also which way to move your hand when you're making the letter. It's tricky, but you're so smart you'll learn how to write **c** very quickly. Watch.

Here's how you write **c** in the air.
Model c formation in the air (with your back to students).

Watch again.

Now let's practice writing **c** in the air. Hold up your writing hand, and make **c** in the air.
Guide students as they write c in the air.

Let's practice **c** again.

Here's how to write **c** with your writing hand pointer finger.
Model c formation on the board with your finger (with your back to students).

Watch again.

Now let's practice writing **c** on your table without using your pencil. Use your writing hand pointer finger, and make **c** on your table.
Guide students as they write c on their table or desktop.

Let's practice **c** again.

Model writing c on the board (with your back to students).
Remember that every letter has a name.
You learned the name of this letter is **c.** What letter name? *c.*
Again, what letter name? *c.*

238   Lesson 61

Provide lined paper to students.
Now let's practice writing **c** with your pencil.
Guide students as they write c on their paper. **Review** as needed.

 Link letter names to letter sounds as they appear in the program as needed.

Set up a writing center with writing materials and correct models of letters learned so far for students to use in their free time.

Part C: Comprehension Strategies

9 minutes

Teacher Materials:
Narrative trade book

Activity 1 Title, Author, and Illustrator Identification—A Before-Reading Strategy

Provide a reading center to display books being read so that students can enjoy them again during free time.

Direct students to narrative trade book of teacher choice. **Elicit** responses.
Guide as needed.

Show front cover of book and allow student to point to name of title, author, and illustrator as you discuss them.
We will read a new book today. The title of today's story is _____. What's the title of today's story? (**Student response.**)

The author of today's story is _____. Who's the author of today's story? (**Student response.**)

The illustrator of today's story is _____. Who's the illustrator? (**Student response.**)

Activity 2 Activate Background Knowledge—A Before-Reading Strategy

Your brain has all kinds of information in it. You've already learned lots of things. Today I'll show you how I look in my brain to see what I know about _____.
Choose a topic to activate background knowledge from story you will read.
Model think-aloud for activating background knowledge.

Sample Wording for Think-Aloud
When I think of _____ I remember when I did _____.
It was a fun experience because _____. (or) I know about _____ because _____. (or) I learned about _____ when _____.

When you think about what you know before you read, it helps you better understand the story. You can connect what you know to the story.

Lesson 61 239

Activity 3 Listening Comprehension—A During-Reading Strategy

Elicit responses to questions. **Guide** as needed.

You've learned about characters and setting. Stories also have events that happen. Events are things that happen in the story. Events happen at the beginning, in the middle, and at the end of a story. So stories have a beginning, a middle, and an end. What do stories have? *A beginning, a middle, and an end.*

In the story *The Little Red Hen,* the beginning of the story is when the little red hen found the wheat and decided to plant it. That's the first thing that happened in the story.

Today as I read the story, I want you to listen carefully and think hard about the things that happened first in the story. We will talk about the beginning of the story after I read the story.

Elicit correct listening behavior from students. **Read** trade book. **Model** prosody during read-aloud.

Ask questions to elicit identification of beginning events in the story as well as connecting background knowledge to story as you read. **Guide** as needed.

Activity 4 Story Elements: Identify Beginning—An After-Reading Strategy

Elicit responses to questions. **Guide** as needed.

You're learning all about stories. You know about characters and setting. Now you're learning about the beginning, the middle, and the end of the story. Things happen in stories. We call those things events. What do we call things that happen in stories? *Events.*

Listen as I show you how I think about the events that happened at the beginning of the story.

Model think-aloud for finding beginning.

Sample Wording for Think-Aloud

I'm thinking about this book and thinking about the beginning of this story. I want to think about the things, or events, that happened at the beginning of the story. At first, the story tells me about the characters and the setting. Then it tells the beginning of the story. I remember that _____ happened first, so that's the beginning of the story.

Remember that the beginning of the story is the events that happened first in the story.

What do you call the events that happened first in a story? *The beginning.*

240   *Lesson 61*

Lesson 62

Materials

Teacher: Narrative trade book (from Lesson 61); Picture-Sound Cards for /m/, /s/, /a/, /ē/, /r/, and /d/

Student: Lined paper

5 minutes

Teacher Materials: Picture-Sound Cards for /m/, /s/, /a/, /ē/, /r/, and /d/

Part A: Phonemic and Phonological Awareness

Activity 1 Phoneme Isolation—Initial

Use IWB interactive cards or picture-sound cards. **Elicit** responses. **Guide** as needed. I'm going to show you two cards and name the object on each card. Then I'll tell you a sound. Think about which word starts with that sound. Let's try it. Today we'll be listening for the **/d/** sound at the *beginning* of the words.

Show /d/ card; use any of four Picture-Sound Cards per phoneme for activity. This is a _____. What is this? (Student response.)

Show /m/ card; use any of four Picture-Sound Cards per phoneme for activity. This is a _____. What is this? (Student response.)

Which word *begins* with **/d/?** (Student response.)

Show /a/ card; use any of four Picture-Sound Cards per phoneme for activity. This is a _____. What is this? (Student response.)

Show /d/ card; use any of four Picture-Sound Cards per phoneme for activity. This is a _____. What is this? (Student response.)

Which word *begins* with **/d/?** (Student response.)

(Continue the activity with the following examples:
/d/ and /s/.
/r/ and /d/.
/ē/ and /d/.
/d/ and /r/.)

Activity 2 Phoneme Isolation—Medial

Model holding sound for two to three seconds. **Elicit** responses. **Guide** as needed. You've been doing so well finding the sound at the *beginning* and the *end* of a word. Now let's work on the sound in the *middle* of a word. I'm going to say a list of words. Some of the words will have the **/aaa/** sound in the *middle*, and some will not. I'll say the word first, and then you'll say the word. Give me a thumbs-up sign if you hear the **/aaa/** sound in the *middle* of the word. If you don't hear the **/aaa/** sound in the *middle* of the word, do nothing. Think about the *middle* sound we hear in each word.

Remember, we're listening for the **/aaa/** sound in the *middle* of the word, as in **ram.** What sound are you listening for in the *middle*? /aaa/.

Listen. **Sam.** Say **Sam.** *Sam.*

Give me a thumbs-up if you hear **/aaa/** in the *middle* of **Sam.** (Thumbs-up.)

Yes, **Sam** has the *middle* sound **/aaa/.**

(Continue the activity with the following lists of words.
Rack. Heat. Go. Cat. Slip. Tap.
Line. Open. Tack. Teeth. Pat. Sat.)

Part B: Letter Recognition and Formation

6 minutes

Student Materials:
Lined paper

Activity 1 Letter Recognition Review—c

Elicit responses to questions. **Guide** as needed. **Write** c on the board. **Point** to c.
We learned that this letter is **c.** What letter name? *c.*
Again, what letter name? *c.*
Review as needed.

Activity 2 Letter Formation Review—c

Now we're going to practice writing **c.** When you practice writing, you'll learn not only where to start and stop the letter, but also which way to move your hand when you're making the letter. It's tricky, but you're so smart you'll learn how to write **c** very quickly. Watch.

Here's how you write **c** in the air.
Model c formation in the air (with your back to students).

Watch again.

Now let's practice writing **c** in the air. Hold up your writing hand, and make **c** in the air.
Guide students as they write c in the air.

Let's practice **c** again.

Here's how to write **c** with your writing hand pointer finger.
Model c formation on the board with your finger (with your back to students).

Watch again.

Now let's practice writing **c** on your table without using your pencil. Use your writing hand pointer finger, and make **c** on your table.
Guide students as they write c on their table or desktop.

Let's practice **c** again.

242 Lesson 62

Model writing c on the board (with your back to students).
Remember that every letter has a name.
You learned the name of this letter is **c.** What letter name? c.
Again, what letter name? c.

Provide lined paper to students.
Now let's practice writing **c** with your pencil.
Guide students as they write c on their paper. **Review** as needed.

 Link letter names to letter sounds as they appear in the program as needed.

Part C: Comprehension Strategies

9 minutes

Teacher Materials:
Narrative trade book

Student Materials:
Lined paper

Activity 1 Activate Background Knowledge—A Before-Reading Strategy

Direct students to narrative trade book of teacher choice. **Elicit** responses to questions. **Guide** as needed.

Choose the same topic as in last lesson to activate background knowledge from story you will read.
Your brain has all kinds of information in it. You've already learned lots of things. Look in your brain and think about what you know about _____.

Now tell me what you know about _____.
Discuss students' background knowledge briefly.

Provide lined paper. **Model** writing a sentence about what you know.
Write a sentence that tells me what you know about _____. If you need help, ask me.
Monitor students. **Guide** students as needed.

When you think about what you know before you read, it helps you better understand the story. You can connect what you know to the story.

Activity 2 Listening Comprehension—A During-Reading Strategy

Elicit responses to questions. **Guide** as needed.
In the last lesson, you learned about the beginning of a story. The beginning is the first things or events that happened in the story. What's the beginning of a story? (Idea: *The things that happened first in the story.*)

Stories also have events that happen in the middle and at the end, but we'll talk about those later.

Lesson 62   **243**

Today we'll read the story again. As I read, listen and think about the events at the beginning of the book. See whether you can tell me what the beginning is by telling what things happened first in the story.

Elicit correct listening behavior from students. **Reread** trade book. **Model** prosody during read-aloud.

Ask questions to elicit identification of events at the beginning of the story. **Guide** as needed.

Activity 3 Story Elements: Identify Beginning—An After-Reading Strategy

Elicit responses. **Guide** as needed.
In the last lesson, you learned about the beginning of a story. The beginning is the events that happened first in the story. What's the beginning? (Idea: *The events that happened first in the story.*)

Different stories have different things that happen at the beginning of the story. In *Goldilocks and the Three Bears,* the event that happened first is that the three bears went on a walk while their porridge cooled. In *Little Red Riding Hood,* the event that happened first is that Little Red Riding Hood walked on a path in the forest to her grandmother's house.

Discuss the beginning events of the story. **Guide** as needed.
In our story, what events happened at the beginning of the story? (Student responses.)

Activity 4 Story Elements: Identify Characters and Setting—An After-Reading Strategy

Elicit responses to questions. **Guide** as needed.
You know how to tell who the characters are in the story. Tell me who some of the characters were in our story. (Student response.)

You know how to tell what the setting is in the story. What's the setting in this story? (Student response.)

244 *Lesson 62*

Lesson 63

Materials
Teacher: Narrative trade book (from Lesson 61); 4-Story Map; 7-Phonemic Awareness
Student: Lined paper; copy of 7-Phonemic Awareness

5 minutes

Teacher Materials:
Phonemic Awareness

Student Materials:
Phonemic Awareness

Part A: Phonemic and Phonological Awareness

Activity 1 Phoneme Isolation—Initial

Elicit responses. **Guide** as needed.
Let's work on a sound at the *beginning* of a word. I'm going to say a list of words. Some of the words will have the **/g/** sound at the *beginning*, and some will not. I'll say the word first, and then you'll say the word.

Remember, we're listening for the **/g/** sound at the *beginning* of the word. What sound are we listening for? /g/.

Listen. **Go.** Say **go.** *Go.*

Give me a thumbs-up if you hear **/g/** at the *beginning* of **go**. (Thumbs-up.)

Yes, **go** *begins* with the sound **/g/.**

(Continue the activity with the following lists of words.
Get. Fit. Gone. Game. Like. Gift.
Bed. Goat. Sink. Us. Give. Got.)

Activity 2 Phoneme Isolation—Final

Show Phonemic Awareness. **Distribute** copy of Phonemic Awareness. **Elicit** responses. **Guide** as needed.
We're going to look at pictures on this page and find pictures to match our sounds. I'm going to name each picture in the top row. Touch each picture after I name it, and repeat the name. We're going to be listening for the *last* sound in each picture. Let's try it.

Model use of Phonemic Awareness; point to each picture as word is said.
This is a chair. What is this? (Student response.)

This is a piano. What is this? (Student response.)

This is a vase. What is this? (Student response.)

Which word has the *last* sound **/sss/**? (Student response.)

Lesson 63   **245**

(Continue the activity with the remaining rows:
Second row: log, ear, sock. Which word has the last sound /rrr/?
Third row: tree, star, hammer. Which word has the last sound /ēēē/?
Fourth row: glass, dog, lamp. Which word has the last sound /sss/?)

Part B: Letter Recognition and Formation

6 minutes

Student Materials:
Lined paper

Activity 1 Letter Recognition—Capital C

Elicit responses to questions. **Guide** as needed. **Write** capital C on the board. **Point** to capital C.
Today you'll learn another way to write **c.**

The name of this letter is **capital C.** What letter name? *Capital C.*
Again, what letter name? *Capital C.*
Review as needed.

Activity 2 Letter Formation—Capital C

Now we're going to practice writing **capital C.** When you practice writing, you'll learn not only where to start and stop the letter, but also which way to move your hand when you're making the letter. It's tricky, but you're so smart you'll learn how to write **capital C** very quickly. Watch.

Here's how you write **capital C** in the air.
Model capital C formation in the air (with your back to students).

Watch again.

Now let's practice writing **capital C** in the air. Hold up your writing hand, and make **capital C** in the air.
Guide students as they write capital C in the air.

Let's practice **capital C** again.

Here's how to write **capital C** with your writing hand pointer finger.
Model capital C formation on the board with your finger (with your back to students).

Watch again.

Now let's practice writing **capital C** on your table without using your pencil. Use your writing hand pointer finger, and make **capital C** on your table.
Guide students as they write capital C on their table or desktop.

Let's practice **capital C** again.

Model writing capital C on the board (with your back to students).
Remember that every letter has a name.
You learned the name of this letter is **capital C.** What letter name? *Capital C.*
Again, what letter name? *Capital C.*

246   Lesson 63

Provide lined paper to students.
Now let's practice writing **capital C** with your pencil.
Guide students as they write capital <u>C</u> on their paper. **Review** as needed.

 Link letter names to letter sounds as they appear in the program as needed.

Part C: Comprehension Strategies

 9 minutes

Teacher Materials:
Narrative trade book
Story Map

Activity 1 — Listening Comprehension—A During-Reading Strategy

Direct students to narrative trade book of teacher choice. **Elicit** response to question. **Guide** as needed.
You're learning about the beginning of a story. The beginning is the first things or events that happened in the story. What's the beginning of a story? (Idea: *The events that happened first in the story.*)

Stories also have events that happen in the middle and at the end, but we'll talk about those later.

Today we'll read the story again. As I read, listen and think about the events at the beginning of the book. See whether you can tell me what the beginning is by telling what things happened first in the story. I'll draw a little picture on the board to help me remember the beginning.

Elicit correct listening behavior from students. **Reread** trade book. **Model** prosody during read-aloud.

Elicit beginning events in story. **Draw** a quick sketch of beginning events on board. **Guide** as needed.

Activity 2 — Story Elements: Identify Beginning—An After-Reading Strategy

Elicit responses to questions. **Guide** as needed.
In the last lesson you learned about the beginning of a story. The beginning is the events that happened first in the story.

What's the beginning? (Idea: *The events that happened first in the story.*)

Show Story Map.
In our story, what events happened at the beginning of the story?
(Student response.)

I drew a picture on the board to help me remember the beginning of the story. Now I'll show you how I use a Story Map to draw the beginning of the story. This Story Map has a place to draw the beginning, the middle, and the end of the story. But today I'm only going to fill in the box for the beginning.
Model drawing a quick sketch of beginning on Story Map.

Now I'll be able to remember how to tell about the beginning of the story because my Story Map has a picture to remind me about the beginning.
Save Story Map for Lesson 65.

Lesson 63

Lesson 64

Materials

Teacher: Narrative trade book (from Lesson 61); Picture-Sound Cards for /m/, /s/, /a/, /ē/, /r/, /d/, and /f/

Student: Lined paper

5 minutes

Teacher Materials:
Picture-Sound Cards for /m/, /s/, /a/, /ē/, /r/, /d/, and /f/

Part A: Phonemic and Phonological Awareness

Activity 1 Phoneme Isolation—Initial

Use IWB interactive cards or picture-sound cards. **Elicit** responses. **Guide** as needed. I'm going to show you two cards and name the object on each card. Then I'll tell you a sound. Think about which word starts with that sound. Let's try it. Today we'll be listening for the **/fff/** sound at the *beginning* of the words.

Show /f/ card; use any of four Picture-Sound Cards per phoneme for activity.
This is a _____ . What is this? (Student response.)

Show /a/ card; use any of four Picture-Sound Cards per phoneme for activity.
This is a _____ . What is this? (Student response.)

Which word *begins* with **/fff/?** (Student response.)

Show /s/ card; use any of four Picture-Sound Cards per phoneme for activity.
This is a _____ . What is this? (Student response.)

Show /f/ card; use any of four Picture-Sound Cards per phoneme for activity.
This is a _____ . What is this? (Student response.)

Which word *begins* with **/fff/?** (Student response.)

(Continue the activity with the following examples:
/m/ and /f/.
/f/ and /r/.
/ē/ and /f/.
/d/ and /f/.)

248   Lesson 64

Activity 2 Phoneme Isolation—Medial

Model holding sounds for two to three seconds. **Elicit** responses. **Guide** as needed.
You've been doing so well finding the sound at the *beginning* and the *end* of a word. Now let's work on the sound in the *middle* of a word. I'm going to say a list of words. Some of the words will have the **/ēēē/** sound in the *middle*, and some will not. I'll say the word first, and then you'll say the word. Give me a thumbs-up if you hear the **/ēēē/** sound in the *middle* of the word. If you don't hear the **/ēēē/** sound in the *middle* of the word, do nothing. Think about the *middle* sound we hear in each word.

Remember, we're listening for the **/ēēē/** sound in the *middle* of the word, as in **feet**. What sound are you listening for in the *middle*? /ēēē/.

Listen. **Seed.** Say **seed.** *Seed.*

Give me a thumbs-up if you hear **/ēēē/** in the *middle* of **seed.** (Thumbs-up.)

Yes, **seed** has the *middle* sound **/ēēē/.**

(Continue the activity with the following lists of words.
Feed. Heat. My. Meat. Slop. Seat.
Lime. Teeth. Beat. Toe. Pain. Leaf.)

Part B: Letter Recognition and Formation

6 minutes

Student Materials:
Lined paper

Activity 1 Letter Recognition Review—Capital C

Elicit responses to questions. **Guide** as needed. **Write** capital C on the board. **Point** to capital C.
We learned that this letter is **capital C.** What letter name? *Capital C.*
Again, what letter name? *Capital C.*
Review as needed.

Activity 2 Letter Formation Review—Capital C

Now we're going to practice writing **capital C.** When you practice writing, you'll learn not only where to start and stop the letter, but also which way to move your hand when you're making the letter. It's tricky, but you're so smart you'll learn how to write **capital C** very quickly. Watch.

Here's how you write **capital C** in the air.
Model capital C formation in the air (with your back to students).

Watch again.

Now let's practice writing **capital C** in the air. Hold up your writing hand, and make **capital C** in the air.
Guide students as they write capital C in the air.

Lesson 64   **249**

Let's practice **capital C** again.

Here's how to write **capital C** with your writing hand pointer finger.
Model capital C formation on the board with your finger (with your back to students).

Watch again.

Now let's practice writing **capital C** on your table without using your pencil.
Use your writing hand pointer finger, and make **capital C** on your table.
Guide students as they write capital C on their table or desktop.

Let's practice **capital C** again.

Model writing capital C on the board (with your back to students).
Remember that every letter has a name.
You learned the name of this letter is **capital C.** What letter name? *Capital C.*
Again, what letter name? *Capital C.*

Provide lined paper to students.
Now let's practice writing **capital C** with your pencil.
Guide students as they write capital C on their paper. **Review** as needed.

 Link letter names to letter sounds as they appear in the program as needed.

Part C: Comprehension Strategies

9 minutes

Teacher Materials:
Narrative trade book

Activity 1 Listening Comprehension—A During-Reading Strategy

Direct students to narrative trade book of teacher choice. **Elicit** responses to questions. **Guide** as needed.
Today as I read the story, I want you to think about the beginning in the story. What's the beginning of a story? (**Idea:** *The things that happened first in the story.*)

Stories also have events that happen in the middle and at the end, but we'll talk about those later.

I want you to watch the pictures and listen to the words of the story very carefully. When I'm finished with the story, we'll play the things that happened first in the story. I will need your ideas for what events happened first.

Elicit correct listening behavior from students. **Reread** trade book. **Model** prosody during read-aloud.

Guide students to focus on beginning events. **Elicit** answers to questions about the beginning events in the story. **Guide** as needed.

250 Lesson 64

Activity 2 Story Elements: Play the Beginning—An After-Reading Strategy

Elicit responses to questions. **Guide** as needed.

Now we're going to play the beginning. What events happened at the beginning of the story? (Student responses.)

How would I play those events? (Student responses.)

Coach all students to play the story by telling the events that happened and guiding students to play or mime the actions. If there is dialogue, say the words and then have students repeat the words.

I'll tell the beginning of the story. As I tell the beginning, each of you can do the actions I'm telling about. If there are words to say, I'll help you say them.

Praise creativity in playing the beginning of the story. **Prompt** everyone to bow as you applaud them.

Wow, that was fun!

Lesson 64   **251**

Lesson 65

Materials
Teacher: Narrative trade book (from Lesson 61); 4-Story Map completed in Lesson 63; 8-Phonemic Awareness; Letter Recognition
Student: Lined paper; copy of 4-Story Map; copy of 8-Phonemic Awareness

Part A: Phonemic and Phonological Awareness

5 minutes

Teacher Materials:
Phonemic Awareness

Student Materials:
Phonemic Awareness

Activity 1 Phoneme Isolation—Initial

Elicit responses. **Guide** as needed.
Let's work on a sound at the *beginning* of a word. I'm going to say a list of words. Some of the words will have the /lll/ sound at the *beginning,* and some will not. I'll say the word first, and then you'll say the word.

Remember, we're listening for the /lll/ sound at the *beginning* of the word. What sound are we listening for? /lll/.

Listen. **Long.** Say **long.** *Long.*

Give me a thumbs-up if you hear /lll/ at the *beginning* of **long.** (Thumbs-up.)

Yes, **long** *begins* with the sound /lll/.

(Continue the activity with the following lists of words.
List. Bay. Fist. Like. Lick. Gave.
Three. Let. Same. Love. Boy. Laugh.)

Activity 2 Phoneme Isolation—Final

Show Phonemic Awareness. **Distribute** copy of Phonemic Awareness. **Elicit** responses. **Guide** as needed.
We're going to look at pictures on this page and find pictures to match our sounds. I'm going to name each picture in the top row. Touch each picture after I name it, and repeat the name. We're going to be listening for the *last* sound in each picture. Let's try it.

Model use of Phonemic Awareness; point to each picture as word is said.
This is three. What is this? (Student response.)

This is a horse. What is this? (Student response.)

This is a pan. What is this? (Student response.)

Which word has the *last* sound /ēēē/? (Student response.)

252 *Lesson 65*

(Continue the activity with the remaining rows:
Second row: dish, pear, cow. Which word has the last sound /rrr/?
Third row: sad, flower, lock. Which word has the last sound /ddd/?
Fourth row: arm, fox, key. Which word has the last sound /ēēē/?)

Part B: Letter Recognition and Formation

6 minutes

Teacher Materials:
Letter Recognition

Student Materials:
Lined paper

Activity 1 — Letter Recognition Cumulative Review—i/I, t/T, n/N, c/C

Display on IWB or **write** letters and capitals on the board in the order shown. **Elicit** responses to questions. **Guide** as needed.

This week you've learned one letter and one capital—**c** and **capital C**. Let's review all the letters and capitals you've learned. Are you ready?

Letter	Question	Student Response
C	What letter?	Capital C.
i	What letter?	i.
t	What letter?	t.
N	What letter?	Capital N.
I	What letter?	Capital I.
n	What letter?	n.
c	What letter?	c.
T	What letter?	Capital T.

Review as needed.

Activity 2 — Letter Formation Cumulative Review—i/I, t/T, n/N, c/C

Write i, capital I, t, capital T, n, capital N, c, and capital C on the board in the order shown (with your back to students). **Provide** lined paper to students.

Show me how you can write these letters and capitals.
Guide students as they write the letters and capitals on their paper. **Review** as needed.

 Link letter names to letter sounds as they appear in the program as needed.

Lesson 65 253

Part C: Comprehension Strategies

9 minutes

Teacher Materials:
Narrative trade book
Story Map

Student Materials:
Story Map

Activity 1 Listening Comprehension—A During-Reading Strategy

Direct students to narrative trade book of teacher choice. **Elicit** responses to questions. **Guide** as needed.
The job of a book illustrator is to make pictures for books. What does an illustrator do? *Make pictures for books.*

The illustrator of our book is _____. Who's the illustrator of this book? (Student response.)

Today as I read the story, I want you to look carefully at the pictures of the beginning events in the story. The illustrator made the pictures for you so that the book would be fun to read. Look for what the illustrator did to show the events at the beginning. After I read the story, you'll become an illustrator and draw a picture of the beginning. While I read, think about what you want to draw for the beginning.

Elicit correct listening behavior from students. **Reread** trade book. **Model** prosody during read-aloud.

Guide students to focus on illustrations of the beginning. **Elicit** answers to questions about how illustrator shows events in the beginning of the story. **Guide** as needed.

Activity 2 Story Elements: Illustrate Beginning—An After-Reading Strategy

Elicit responses to questions. **Guide** as needed.
Now you'll become an illustrator. Remember that an illustrator is the person who draws the pictures in a story. What does an illustrator do? (Idea: *Draws the pictures in a story.*)

Show Story Map completed in Lesson 63.
I'll show you the picture I made in the box for the beginning events. I drew my picture in the box for the beginning.

Provide copy of Story Map to each student.
As an illustrator, your job today is to draw the beginning of the story in the box for Beginning. When you're finished, you can share your illustration with your neighbor.
Share illustrations with class if time permits, or make a class book of beginnings from the story.

254 *Lesson 65*

Lesson 66

Materials

Teacher: Narrative trade book (same book for Lessons 56–60); Picture-Sound Cards for /m/, /s/, /ē/, /r/, /d/, /f/, and /i/, 1-My Prediction Chart

Student: Lined paper, Copy of 1-My Prediction Chart

5 minutes

Part A: Phonemic and Phonological Awareness

Teacher Materials:
Picture-Sound Cards for /m/, /s/, /ē/, /r/, /d/, /f/, and /i/

Activity 1 Phoneme Isolation—Initial

Use IWB interactive cards or picture-sound cards. **Elicit** responses. **Guide** as needed. I'm going to show you two cards and name the object on each card. Then I'll tell you a sound. Think about which word starts with that sound. Let's try it. Today we'll be listening for the sound at the *beginning* of a word.

Show /i/ card; use any of four Picture-Sound Cards per phoneme for activity.
This is a _____ . What is this? (Student response.)

Show /d/ card; use any of four Picture-Sound Cards per phoneme for activity.
This is a _____ . What is this? (Student response.)

Which word *begins* with **/iii/?** (Student response.)

Show /s/ card; use any of four Picture-Sound Cards per phoneme for activity.
This is a _____ . What is this? (Student response.)

Show /i/ card; use any of four Picture-Sound Cards per phoneme for activity.
This is a _____ . What is this? (Student response.)

Which word *begins* with **/iii/?** (Student response.)

(Continue the activity with the following examples:
/m/ and /i/: Which word begins with /iii/?
/i/ and /f/: Which word begins with /iii/?
/ē/ and /r/: Which word begins with /rrr/?
/d/ and /f/: Which word begins with /fff/?)

Lesson 66   **255**

Activity 2 Phoneme Isolation—Medial

Elicit responses. **Guide** as needed.
You've been doing so well finding the sound at the *beginning* and the *end* of a word. Now let's work on the sound in the *middle* of a word. I'm going to say a list of words. Some of the words will have the **/iii/** sound in the *middle,* and some will not. I'll say the word first, and then you'll say the word. Give me a thumbs-up if you hear the **/iii/** sound in the *middle* of the word. If you don't hear the **/iii/** sound in the *middle* of the word, do nothing. Think about the *middle* sound we hear in each word.

Remember, we're listening for the **/iii/** sound in the *middle* of the word, as in **sit**. What sound are you listening for in the *middle*? /iii/.

Listen. **Mitt.** Say **mitt.** *Mitt.*

Give me a thumbs-up if you hear **/iii/** in the *middle* of **mitt.** (Thumbs-up.)

Yes, **mitt** has the *middle* sound **/iii/.**

(Continue the activity with the following lists of words.
Pit. Cake. Low. Rib. Bit. Seat.
Leak. Lip. Boat. Sip. Pail. Bib.)

Part B: Letter Recognition and Formation

6 minutes

Student Materials:
Lined paper

Activity 1 Letter Recognition—o

Elicit responses to questions. **Guide** as needed. **Write** o on the board. **Point** to o.
Today you'll learn a new letter.
The name of this letter is **o.** What letter name? *o.*
Again, what letter name? *o.*
Review as needed.

Activity 2 Letter Formation—o

Now we're going to practice writing **o.** When you practice writing, you'll learn not only where to start and stop the letter, but also which way to move your hand when you're making the letter. It's tricky, but you're so smart you'll learn how to write **o** very quickly. Watch.

Here's how you write **o** in the air.
Model o formation in the air (with your back to students).

Watch again.

Now let's practice writing **o** in the air. Hold up your writing hand, and make **o** in the air.
Guide students as they write o in the air.

Let's practice **o** again.

256   Lesson 66

Here's how to write **o** with your writing hand pointer finger.
Model o formation on the board with your finger (with your back to students).

Watch again.

Now let's practice writing **o** on your table without using your pencil. Use your writing hand pointer finger, and make **o** on your table.
Guide students as they write o on their table or desktop.

Let's practice **o** again.

Model writing o on the board (with your back to students).
Remember that every letter has a name.
You learned the name of this letter is **o.** What letter name? *o.*
Again, what letter name? *o.*

Provide lined paper to students.
Now let's practice writing **o** with your pencil.
Guide students as they write o on their paper. **Review** as needed.

 Link letter names to letter sounds as they appear in the program as needed.

Set up a writing center with writing materials and correct models of letters learned so far for students to use in their free time.

Part C: Comprehension Strategies

9 minutes

IWB

Teacher Materials:
Narrative trade book

My Prediction Chart

Student Materials:
Lined paper

My Prediction Chart

Activity 1 Title, Author, and Illustrator Identification—A Before-Reading Strategy

Provide a reading center to display books being read so that students can enjoy them again during free time.

Direct students to narrative trade book of teacher choice. **Elicit** responses to questions. **Guide** as needed.

Show front cover of book and allow students to point to name of title, author, and illustrator as you discuss them.
The title of today's story is _____. What's the title of today's story?
(Student response.)

The author of today's story is _____. Who's the author of today's story?
(Student response.)

The illustrator of today's story is _____. Who's the illustrator?
(Student response.)

Lesson 66   **257**

Activity 2 Activate Background Knowledge—A Before-Reading Strategy

Choose a topic to activate background knowledge from story you will read. **Elicit** responses. **Guide** as needed.

Your brain has all kinds of information in it. You've already learned lots of things. Today we're going to look in your brain to see what you know about _____ .

Discuss background knowledge for topic chosen.

Tell me what you know about _____ .

Provide lined paper. **Model** writing a sentence about what you know.

Write a sentence that tells me what you know about _____ . If you need help, ask me.

Monitor students. **Guide** students as needed.

When you think about what you know before you read, it helps you better understand the story. You can connect what you know to what happens in the story.

Activity 3 Make Predictions—A Before-Reading Strategy

Show My Prediction Chart. **Elicit** responses to questions. **Guide** as needed.

The title of today's book is _____ . Write the book title in the box labeled "Book Title".

Now that we know the title of today's book, let's look at the cover and pictures inside the book for clues to make some good guesses for what we think the story will be about. We call our good guesses predictions.

Making good guesses, or predictions, helps us get interested in the story before we read it. Let's make some predictions about the story before I read to it you.

Show title, front and back cover, and pictures inside book.

What do you predict this story will be about? (Student response.)

Write your prediction in the box labeled "I Predict That".
Guide as needed.

What characters do you predict will be in the story? (Student response.)

What do you predict the setting will be? (Student response.)

What do you predict might happen in the story? (Student response.)

When we read the book, we'll check your predictions to see whether they're correct.

Elicit correct listening behavior from students. **Read** trade book. **Model** prosody during read-aloud.

258 *Lesson 66*

Guide students to confirm predictions and connect background knowledge as you read story. **Ask** questions to confirm predictions or connect background knowledge. **Guide** as needed.

Activity 4 Confirm Predictions—An After-Reading Strategy

Show My Prediction Chart. **Elicit** responses to questions. **Guide** as needed.
Now let's check your predictions to see whether they were correct. You predicted that the story was about _____. Was your prediction correct? (Student response.)

You predicted that _____ were characters in the story. Was your prediction correct? (Student response.)

You predicted that the setting was _____. Was your prediction correct? (Student response.)

You predicted that some events would be _____. Was your prediction correct? (Student response.)

Circle whether or not your prediction was correct in the box labeled "Was My Prediction Correct?".

Remember that your predictions don't have to be correct. Just making a prediction and listening to see whether your prediction is correct helps you stay interested in the story.

Lesson 66 **259**

Lesson 67

Materials
Teacher: Narrative trade book (from Lesson 66); 9-Phonemic Awareness, 2-Character Sheet, 3-Setting Sheet
Student: Lined paper; copy of 9-Phonemic Awareness

5 minutes

Teacher Materials:
Phonemic Awareness

Student Materials:
Phonemic Awareness

Part A: Phonemic and Phonological Awareness

Activity 1 Phoneme Isolation—Initial

Elicit responses. **Guide** as needed.
Let's work on a sound at the *beginning* of a word. I'm going to say a list of words. Some of the words will have the **/www/** sound at the *beginning*, and some will not. I'll say the word first, and then you'll say the word.

Remember, we're listening for the **/www/** sound at the *beginning* of the word. What sound are we listening for? /www/.

Listen. **We.** Say **we.** *We.*

Give me a thumbs-up if you hear **/www/** at the *beginning* of **we** (Thumbs-up.)

Yes, **we** *begins* with the sound **/www/.**

(Continue the activity with the following lists of words.
Wish. Boy. Fish. Want. Water. Many.
Six. Wave. Will. Lend. Went. Window.)

Activity 2 Phoneme Isolation—Final

Show Phonemic Awareness. **Distribute** copy of Phonemic Awareness. **Elicit** responses. **Guide** as needed.
We're going to look at pictures on this page and find pictures to match our sounds. I'm going to name each picture in the top row. Touch each picture after I name it, and repeat the name. We're going to be listening for the *last* sound in each picture. Let's try it.

Model use of Phonemic Awareness; point to each picture as word is said.
This is a man. What is this? (Student response.)

This is a window. What is this? (Student response.)

This is a fire. What is this? (Student response.)

Which word has the *last* sound **/rrr/**? (Student response.)

260 Lesson 67

(Continue the activity with the remaining rows:
Second row: wood, spoon, cat. Which word has the last sound /d/?
Third row: shirt, knife, clock. Which word has the last sound /fff/?
Fourth row: scarf, girl, door. Which word has the last sound /fff/?

Part B: Letter Recognition and Formation

6 minutes

Student Materials:
Lined paper

Activity 1 Letter Recognition Review—o

Elicit responses to questions. **Guide** as needed. **Write** o on the board. **Point** to o.
We learned that this letter is **o**. What letter name? *o*.
Again, what letter name? *o*.
Review as needed.

Activity 2 Letter Formation Review—o

Now we're going to practice writing **o**. When you practice writing, you'll learn not only where to start and stop the letter, but also which way to move your hand when you're making the letter. It's tricky, but you're so smart you'll learn how to write **o** very quickly. Watch.

Here's how you write **o** in the air.
Model o formation in the air (with your back to students).

Watch again.

Now let's practice writing **o** in the air. Hold up your writing hand, and make **o** in the air.
Guide students as they write o in the air.

Let's practice **o** again.

Here's how to write **o** with your writing hand pointer finger.
Model o formation on the board with your finger (with your back to students).

Watch again.

Now let's practice writing **o** on your table without using your pencil. Use your writing hand pointer finger, and make **o** on your table.
Guide students as they write o on their table or desktop.

Let's practice **o** again.

Model writing o on the board (with your back to students).
Remember that every letter has a name.
You learned the name of this letter is **o**. What letter name? *o*.
Again, what letter name? *o*.

Provide lined paper to students.
Now let's practice writing **o** with your pencil.
Guide students as they write o on their paper. **Review** as needed.

 Link letter names to letter sounds as they appear in the program as needed.

Lesson 67   **261**

Part C: Comprehension Strategies

9 minutes

Teacher Materials:
Narrative trade book
Character Sheet
Setting Sheet

Activity 1 Listening Comprehension—A During-Reading Strategy

Direct students to narrative trade book of teacher choice. **Elicit** response to question. **Guide** as needed.
You're learning about the beginning of a story. The beginning is the thing or event that happened first in the story. What's the beginning of a story? (Idea: *The events that happened first in the story.*)

Stories also have events that happen in the middle and at the end, but we'll talk about those later.

Today we'll read the story again. As I read, listen and think about the events at the beginning of the book. After I read, I want to see whether you can tell a partner what the beginning is by telling what things happened first in the story. I'll draw a little picture on the board to help you remember the beginning.

Show Character Sheet and Setting Sheet.
Help me find the characters and setting(s) in this book as I read by putting up your hand when you see a setting or hear about a character. Then I'll write the names of the characters and setting(s) on the board as I read.

Elicit correct listening behavior from students. **Reread** trade book. **Model** prosody during read-aloud.

Elicit settings and characters from students as you read. **Write** the setting(s), characters, and beginning on charts. **Guide** as needed.

Activity 2 Story Elements: Identify and Retell the Beginning—An After-Reading Strategy

Elicit responses to questions. **Guide** as needed.
You're learning about the beginning of the story. What do you call the events that happened at the beginning of the story? *The beginning.*

I made a picture of the beginning of the story on the board. Listen as I retell the beginning of the story.
Model retelling beginning of story from picture.

Assign student partners.
Now it's your turn to retell the beginning of the story to your partner. Just retell the things that happened at the beginning of the story.

How should you listen to your partner when it's his or her turn to talk? (Idea: *Look at partner and listen politely.*)

Take turns with your partner retelling the beginning of the story.
Monitor students as they retell the beginning of the story.

262   Lesson 67

Activity 3 Story Elements: Identify Characters and Setting—An After-Reading Strategy

Touch the setting(s) as you discuss them. **Elicit** responses to questions. **Guide** as needed.
What was the setting at the beginning of the story? (Student response.)

Ask next two questions if setting changes.
What clues in the story or pictures made you think that? (Student response.)

What was the setting at the end of the story? (Student response.)

What clues in the story or pictures made you think that? (Student response.)

Did the setting stay the same from the beginning to the end of the story or did it change? (Student response.)

Now let's talk about all the characters and what they said and did.

Touch name of characters as you ask questions about each character.
Tell me what _____ did or said. (Student response.)

The character that the story is mostly about is called the main character. What do you call the character that the story is mostly about? *The main character.*

What character is the story mostly about? (Student response.)

So _____ is the main character. Who's the main character? (Student response.)

Repeat question for each character as time permits.

Lesson 67 **263**

Lesson 68

Materials
Teacher: Narrative trade book (from Lesson 66); Picture-Sound Cards for /m/, /s/, /a/, /ē/, /r/, /d/, /i/, and /t/
Student: Lined paper

5 minutes

Teacher Materials:
Picture-Sound Cards for /m/, /s/, /a/, /ē/, /r/, /d/, /i/, and /t/

Part A: Phonemic and Phonological Awareness

Activity 1 Phoneme Isolation—Initial

Use IWB interactive cards or picture-sound cards. **Elicit** responses. **Guide** as needed.
I'm going to show you two cards and name the object on each card. Then I'll tell you a sound. Think about which word starts with that sound. Let's try it. Today we'll be listening for the sound at the *beginning* of a word.

Show /t/ card; use any of four Picture-Sound Cards per phoneme for activity.
This is a _____. What is this? (Student response.)

Show /r/ card; use any of four Picture-Sound Cards per phoneme for activity.
This is a _____. What is this? (Student response.)

Which word *begins* with **/t/?** (Student response.)

Show /m/ card; use any of four Picture-Sound Cards per phoneme for activity.
This is a _____. What is this? (Student response.)

Show /t/ card; use any of four Picture-Sound Cards per phoneme for activity.
This is a _____. What is this? (Student response.)

Which word *begins* with **/t/?** (Student response.)

(Continue the activity with the following examples:
/t/ and /i/: Which word begins with /t/?
/s/ and /t/: Which word begins with /t/?
/ē/ and /d/: Which word begins with /d/?
/r/ and /a/: Which word begins with /aaa/?)

Activity 2 Phoneme Isolation—Medial

Elicit responses. **Guide** as needed.
You've been doing so well finding the *middle* sound in a word. Let's practice finding **/aaa/, /ēēē/, and /iii/.**

264   Lesson 68

First, let's listen for the /aaa/ sound in the *middle* of the word. What sound are you listening for in the *middle*? /aaa/.

Listen. **Mat.** Say **mat.** *Mat.*

Give me a thumbs-up if you hear /aaa/ in the *middle* of **mat.** (Thumbs-up.)

Yes, **mat** has the *middle* sound /aaa/.

(Continue the activity with the following list of words.
Cap. Hope. Move. Lap. Mad.)

First, let's listen for the /ēēē/ sound in the *middle* of the word. What sound are you listening for in the *middle*? /ēēē/.

Listen. **Beat.** Say **beat.** *Beat.*

Give me a thumbs-up if you hear /ēēē/ in the *middle* of **beat.** (Thumbs-up.)

Yes, **beat** has the *middle* sound /ēēē/.

(Continue the activity with the following list of words.
Leap. Home. Seed. Wet. Feed.)

First, let's listen for the /iii/ sound in the *middle* of the word. What sound are you listening for in the *middle*? /iii/.

Listen. **Fit.** Say **fit.** *Fit.*

Give me a thumbs-up if you hear /iii/ in the *middle* of **fit.** (Thumbs-up.)

Yes, **fit** has the *middle* sound /iii/.

(Continue the activity with the following list of words.
Clip. Turn. Hip. Miss. Make.)

Part B: Letter Recognition and Formation

6 minutes

Student Materials:
Lined paper

Activity 1 Letter Recognition—Capital O

Elicit responses to questions. **Guide** as needed. **Write** capital O on the board. **Point** to capital O.
Today you'll learn another way to write **o.**
The name of this letter is **capital O.** What letter name? *Capital O.*
Again, what letter name? *Capital O.*
Review as needed.

Lesson 68 **265**

Activity 2 Letter Formation—Capital O

Now we're going to practice writing **capital O.** When you practice writing, you'll learn not only where to start and stop the letter, but also which way to move your hand when you're making the letter. It's tricky, but you're so smart you'll learn how to write **capital O** very quickly. Watch.

Here's how you write **capital O** in the air.
Model capital O formation in the air (with your back to students).

Watch again.

Now let's practice writing **capital O** in the air. Hold up your writing hand, and make **capital O** in the air.
Guide students as they write capital O in the air.

Let's practice **capital O** again.

Here's how to write **capital O** with your writing hand pointer finger.
Model capital O formation on the board with your finger (with your back to students).

Watch again.

Now let's practice writing **capital O** on your table without using your pencil. Use your writing hand pointer finger, and make **capital O** on your table.
Guide students as they write capital O on their table or desktop.

Let's practice **capital O** again.

Model writing capital O on the board (with your back to students).
Remember that every letter has a name.
You learned the name of this letter is **capital O.** What letter name? *Capital O.*
Again, what letter name? *Capital O.*

Provide lined paper to students.
Now let's practice writing **capital O** with your pencil.
Guide students as they write capital O on their paper. **Review** as needed.

 Link letter names to letter sounds as they appear in the program as needed.

9 minutes

Teacher Materials:
Narrative trade book

Part C: Comprehension Strategies

Activity 1 Listening Comprehension—A During-Reading Strategy

Direct students to narrative trade book of teacher choice. **Elicit** responses to questions. **Guide** as needed.
Today as I read the story, I want you to think about the beginning of the story, the setting, and the main character.

What's the beginning of the story? (Idea: *The events that happen first in the story.*)

What's a setting? (Idea: *The place the story happens.*)

The character that the story is mostly about is the main character. Who's the main character in the story? (Student response.)

Listen for the main character and setting. Then listen for the beginning. I want you to watch the pictures and listen to the words of the story very carefully. When I'm finished with the story, you'll play the beginning. You'll play the events that you find at the beginning. I'll need your ideas for what events you should play.

Elicit correct listening behavior from students. **Reread** trade book. **Model** prosody during read-aloud.

Guide students to focus on characters, setting and events in the beginning of story. **Elicit** answers to questions about events that students could play to show the beginning. **Guide** as needed.

Activity 2 Story Elements: Play the Beginning—An After-Reading Strategy

Elicit responses to questions. **Guide** as needed.
Now we're going to play the beginning. What are some events at the beginning of this story? (Student response.)

I'll tell the beginning of the story. As I tell the beginning, each of you can do the actions I'm telling about. If there are words to say, I'll help you say them.
Coach all students to play the story by telling the events that happened and guiding students to play or mime the actions. If there is dialogue, say the words and then have students repeat the words.

Praise creativity in playing the beginning of the story. **Prompt** everyone to bow as you applaud them.

Wow, that was fun!

Lesson 68

Lesson 69

Materials
Teacher: Narrative trade book (from Lesson 66); 4-Story Map; 10-Phonemic Awareness
Student: Lined paper; copy of 3-Story Map; copy of 10-Phonemic Awareness

5 minutes

Teacher Materials:
Phonemic Awareness

Student Materials:
Phonemic Awareness

Part A: Phonemic and Phonological Awareness

Activity 1 Phoneme Isolation—Initial

Elicit responses. **Guide** as needed.
Let's work on a sound at the *beginning* of a word. I'm going to say a list of words. Some of the words will have the **/shshsh/** sound at the *beginning,* and some will not. I'll say the word first, and then you'll say the word.

Remember, we're listening for the **/shshsh/** sound at the *beginning* of the word. What sound are we listening for? */shshsh/*.

Listen. **She.** Say **she**. *She.*

Give me a thumbs-up if you hear **/shshsh/** at the *beginning* of **she**. (Thumbs-up.)

Yes, **she** *begins* with the sound **/shshsh/.**

(Continue the activity with the following lists of words.
Ship. Box. Shore. Wake. Shake. Mind. Seven. Shed. Tea. Like. Sheep. Show.)

Activity 2 Phoneme Isolation—Final

Show Phonemic Awareness. **Distribute** copy of Phonemic Awareness. **Elicit** responses.
We're going to find pictures to match our sounds. I'm going to name each picture in the top row. Touch each picture after I name it, and repeat the name. Listen for the *last* sound in each picture. Let's try it.

Model use of Phonemic Awareness; point to each picture as word is said.
This is milk. What is this? (Student response.)

This is a seed. What is this? (Student response.)

This is a pillow. What is this? (Student response.)

Which word has the *last* sound **/d/?** (Student response.)

(Continue the activity with the remaining rows:
Second row: leaf, bike, box. Which word has the last sound /fff/?
Third row: book, car, coat. Which word has the last sound /t/?
Fourth row: bowl, shoe, mat. Which word has the last sound /t/?)

6 minutes

Student Materials:
Lined paper

Part B: Letter Recognition and Formation

Activity 1 Letter Recognition Review—Capital O

Elicit responses to questions. **Guide** as needed. **Write** capital O on the board.
Point to capital O.

We learned that this letter is **capital O.** What letter name? *Capital O.*
Again, what letter name? *Capital O.*
Review as needed.

Activity 2 Letter Formation Review—Capital O

Now we're going to practice writing **capital O.** When you practice writing, you'll learn not only where to start and stop the letter but which way to move your hand when you're making the letter. It's tricky, but you're so smart you'll learn how to write **capital O** very quickly. Watch.

Here's how you write **capital O** in the air.
Model capital O formation in the air (with your back to students).

Watch again.

Now let's practice writing **capital O** in the air. Hold up your writing hand, and make **capital O** in the air.
Guide students as they write capital O in the air.

Let's practice **capital O** again.

Here's how to write **capital O** with your writing hand pointer finger.
Model capital O formation on the board with your finger (with your back to students).

Watch again.

Now let's practice writing **capital O** on your table without using your pencil. Use your writing hand pointer finger, and make **capital O** on your table.
Guide students as they write capital O on their table or desktop.

Let's practice **capital O** again.

Model writing capital O on the board (with your back to students).
Remember that every letter has a name.
You learned the name of this letter is **capital O.** What letter name? *Capital O.*
Again, what letter name? *Capital O.*

Provide lined paper to students.
Now let's practice writing **capital O** with your pencil.
Guide students as they write capital O on their paper. **Review** as needed.

 Link letter names to letter sounds as they appear in the program as needed.

Lesson 69   **269**

9 minutes

Teacher Materials:
Narrative trade book
Story Map

Student Materials:
Story Map

Part C: Comprehension Strategies

Activity 1 Listening Comprehension—A During-Reading Strategy

Direct students to narrative trade book of teacher choice. **Elicit** responses to questions. **Guide** as needed.
What does an illustrator do? (Idea: *Make pictures for books.*)

The illustrator of this book is _____. Who's the illustrator of this book? (Student response.)

Today as I read the story, I want you to look carefully at the pictures of the events at the beginning in the story. The illustrator made the pictures for you so that the book would be fun to read. Look for what the illustrator did to show the events at the beginning. After I read the story, you'll become an illustrator and draw a picture of the beginning. You'll also draw a picture of the main character in the picture, so think about the main character in the story.

Elicit correct listening behavior from students. **Reread** trade book. **Model** prosody during read-aloud.

Guide students to focus on illustrations of events at the beginning and main character. **Elicit** answers to questions about how illustrator shows events at the beginning. **Elicit** answer for identifying main character. **Guide** as needed.

Activity 2 Story Elements: Illustrate Main Character and Setting—An After-Reading Strategy

Elicit responses to questions. **Guide** as needed.
Remember that an illustrator is the person who draws the pictures in a story. What does an illustrator do? (Idea: *Draws the pictures in a story.*)

Show Story Map. **Provide** Story Map to each student.
We'll draw quick pictures to show the events that happened at the beginning of the story.

Guide students to the correct place on sheet to draw picture of main character and beginning.
What events could we draw in our Beginning box? (Student response.)

You can also put the main character in the Beginning box. Who's the main character in the story? (Student response.)

Let's work as illustrators to draw the main character and an event that happened at the beginning of the story.
Draw illustrations for main character and beginning on Story Map while students draw.

In the next lesson, you'll tell about your illustration.
Save teacher and student illustrations for Lesson 70.

270 Lesson 69

Lesson 70

Materials

Teacher: Narrative trade book (from Lesson 66); 3-Story Map (from Lesson 69); Picture-Sound Cards for /m/, /a/, /ē/, /r/, /f/, /t/, and /n/; Letter Recognition; 8-My Book Review

Student: Lined paper; copy of 3-Story Map (from Lesson 69); copy of 8-My Book Review

5 minutes

Teacher Materials:
Picture-Sound Cards for /m/, /a/, /ē/, /r/, /f/, /t/, and /n/

Part A: Phonemic and Phonological Awareness

Activity 1 Phoneme Isolation—Initial

Use IWB interactive cards or picture-sound cards. **Elicit** responses. **Guide** as needed.
I'm going to show you two cards and name the object on each card. Then I'll tell you a sound. Think about which word starts with that sound. Let's try it. Today we'll be listening for the sound at the *beginning* of a word.

Show /n/ card; use any of four Picture-Sound Cards per phoneme for activity.
This is a _____. What is this? (Student response.)

Show /t/ card; use any of four Picture-Sound Cards per phoneme for activity.
This is a _____. What is this? (Student response.)

Which word *begins* with **/nnn/?** (Student response.)

Show /a/ card; use any of four Picture-Sound Cards per phoneme for activity.
This is a _____. What is this? (Student response.)

Show /n/ card; use any of four Picture-Sound Cards per phoneme for activity.
This is a _____. What is this? (Student response.)

Which word *begins* with **/nnn/?** (Student response.)

(Continue the activity with the following examples:
/r/ and /n/: Which word begins with /nnn/?
/n/ and /f/: Which word begins with /nnn/?
/ē/ and /t/: Which word begins with /t/?
/r/ and /m/: Which word begins with /mmm/?)

Activity 2 Phoneme Isolation—Medial

Elicit responses. **Guide** as needed.
You've been doing so well finding the *middle* sound in a word. Let's practice finding **/aaa/, /ēēē/,** and **/iii/.**

First let's listen for the **/aaa/** sound in the *middle* of the word. What sound are you listening for in the *middle*? /aaa/.

Listen. **Mat.** Say **mat.** *Mat.*

Give me a thumbs-up if you hear **/aaa/** in the *middle* of **mat.** (Thumbs-up.)

Lesson 70   271

Yes, **mat** has the *middle* sound */aaa/*.

(Continue the activity with the following lists of words.
Tap. Load. Mind. Fat. Sad.)

First let's listen for the */ēēē/* sound in the *middle* of the word. What sound are you listening for in the middle? */ēēē/*.

Listen. **Beat.** Say **beat.** *Beat.*

Give me a thumbs-up if you hear */ēēē/* in the *middle* of **beat.** (Thumbs-up.)

Yes, **beat** has the *middle* sound */ēēē/*.

(Continue the activity with the following list of words.
Keep. Pair. Read. Woke. Tear.)

First let's listen for the */iii/* sound in the *middle* of the word. What sound are you listening for in the middle? */iii/*.

Listen. **Fit.** Say **fit.** *Fit.*

Give me a thumbs-up if you hear */iii/* in the *middle* of **fit.** (Thumbs-up.)

Yes, **fit** has the *middle* sound */iii/*.

(Continue the activity with the following list of words.
Sip. Bird. Pit. Kiss. More.)

Part B: Letter Recognition and Formation

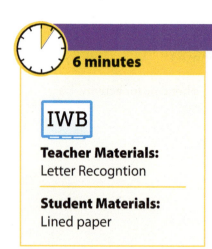

6 minutes

Teacher Materials:
Letter Recogntion

Student Materials:
Lined paper

Activity 1 — Letter Recognition Cumulative Review—t/T, n/N, c/C, o/O

Display on IWB or **write** letters and capitals on the board in the order shown.
Elicit responses to questions. **Guide** as needed.
This week you've learned one letter and one capital—**o** and **capital O.**
Let's review all the letters and capitals you've learned. Are you ready?

Letter	Question	Student Response
o	What letter?	o.
T	What letter?	Capital T.
c	What letter?	c.
O	What letter?	Capital O.
N	What letter?	Capital N.
t	What letter?	t.
n	What letter?	n.
C	What letter?	Capital C.

Review as needed.

272   Lesson 70

Activity 2 | Letter Formation Cumulative Review—t/T, n/N, c/C, o/O

Write t, capital T, n, capital N, c, capital C, o, and capital O on the board in the order shown (with your back to students). **Provide** lined paper to students.

Show me how you can write these letters and capitals.

 Link letter names to letter sounds as they appear in the program as needed.

Part C: Comprehension Strategies

 9 minutes

 IWB

Teacher Materials:
Narrative trade book
Story Map
My Book Review

Student Materials:
Story Map
My Book Review

Activity 1 | Listening Comprehension—A During-Reading Strategy

Direct students to narrative trade book of teacher choice. **Elicit** responses to questions. **Guide** as needed.

Today I'll read the story one last time. Listen to the story to find the character and events at the beginning of the story. Listen for what that character did and what that character said, and look at pictures of the events at the beginning. After you listen to the story, you'll get to tell about your illustration of the main character and the event from the beginning.

Elicit correct listening behavior from students. **Reread** trade book. **Model** prosody during read-aloud.

Guide students to focus on main character and event from the beginning that they illustrated. **Elicit** answers to questions about main character and events at beginning as you read. **Guide** as needed.

Lesson 70

Activity 2 — Retell the Story: Main Character and Beginning—An After-Reading Strategy

Show Story Map. **Elicit** correct listening behavior from students. **Elicit** responses to questions. **Guide** as needed.

I'll tell you about my illustration. I'll tell about the main character and the event I drew from the beginning of the story.

Model retelling the main character and beginning event from your illustration.

Assign student partners. **Provide** copy of Story Map completed in Lesson 69.

Now it's your turn. You're going to tell a partner all about the character and event at the beginning from your picture. Your partner will listen to you the right way. Then you'll listen politely as your partner tells you about his or her picture.

When you're done, if there is time, you can show us your illustration and tell the class about your illustration.

Share illustrations with class as time permits, or make a class book of beginnings.

Activity 3 — Connections Through Shared Writing—Express Opinions

Show My Book Review. **Elicit** responses to questions. **Guide** as needed.

Think about the two books we read, _____ and _____. Let's talk about the two books. Which one did you like best and why?

Provide copies of My Book Review to students. **Guide** students through completion of My Book Review. **Share** with class as time permits.

274   *Lesson 70*

Lesson 71

Materials
Teacher: Narrative trade book (same book for Lessons 71–75)
Student: Lined paper

Part A: Phonemic and Phonological Awareness

Activity 1 Phoneme Isolation—Initial

Elicit responses. **Guide** as needed.
Let's work on a sound at the *beginning* of a word. I'm going to say a list of words. Some of the words will have the **/ōōō/** sound at the *beginning,* and some will not. I'll say the word first, and then you'll say the word.

Remember, we're listening for the **/ōōō/** sound at the *beginning* of the word. What sound are we listening for? /ōōō/.

Listen. **Oak.** Say **oak.** *Oak.*

Give me a thumbs-up if you hear **/ōōō/** at the *beginning* of **oak.** (Thumbs-up.)

Yes, **oak** *begins* with the sound **/ōōō/.**

(Continue the activity with the following lists of words.
Over. Beat. Mist. Oats. Check. Vase.
Five. Own. Plate. Feed. Oboe. Run.)

Activity 2 Phoneme Isolation—Final

Elicit responses. **Guide** as needed.
Now let's work on the sound at the *end* of a word. I'm going to say a list of words. Some of the words will have the **/ththth/** sound at the *end,* and some will not. I'll say the word first, and then you'll say the word. Think about the *last* sound we hear in each word.

Remember, we're listening for the **/ththth/** sound at the *end* of the word, as in **bath.** What sound are you listening for at the *end?* /ththth/.

Listen. **Tooth.** Say **tooth.** *Tooth.*

Give me a thumbs-up if you hear **/ththth/** at the *end* of **tooth.** (Thumbs-up.)

Yes, **tooth** *ends* with the sound **/ththth/.**

(Continue the activity with the following lists of words.
Dig. Both. Find. Path. With. Bowl.
Teeth. Day. Sink. Moth. Hair. Cloth.)

Lesson 71   275

Activity 3 Phoneme Identity—Initial

Elicit responses. **Guide** as needed.
We're going to try a new game today. I'm going to say three words. Listen closely and see if you can tell which sound is the same. I'll show you how to do the first one.

My turn. What sound is the same in **milk, man,** and **mind?** **/mmm/.** That is because **milk, man,** and **mind** all *begin* with the first sound **/mmm/.** Your turn. What sound is the same in **mouse, make,** and **many?** /mmm/.

Yes, **mouse, make,** and **many** all *begin* with the first sound **/mmm/.** Let's try some more. What sound is the same in **sand, soak,** and **sip?** /sss/.

What sound is the same in **at, apple,** and **add?** /aaa/.

What sound is the same in **sick, seat,** and **so?** /sss/.

What sound is the same in **ax, act,** and **as?** /aaa/.

What sound is the same in **mold, meat,** and **mule?** /mmm/.

Part B: Letter Recognition and Formation

6 minutes

Student Materials:
Lined paper

Activity 1 Letter Recognition—h

Elicit responses to questions. **Guide** as needed. **Write** <u>h</u> on the board. **Point** to <u>h</u>.
Today you'll learn a new letter.
The name of this letter is **h.** What letter name? h.
Again, what letter name? h.
Review as needed.

Activity 2 Letter Formation—h

Now we're going to practice writing **h.** When you practice writing, you'll learn not only where to start and stop the letter, but also which way to move your hand when you're making the letter. It's tricky, but you're so smart you'll learn how to write **h** very quickly. Watch.

Here's how you write **h** in the air.
Model <u>h</u> formation in the air (with your back to students).

Watch again.

Now let's practice writing **h** in the air. Hold up your writing hand, and make **h** in the air.
Guide students as they write <u>h</u> in the air.

Let's practice **h** again.

Here's how to write **h** with your writing hand pointer finger.
Model h formation on the board with your finger (with your back to students).

Watch again.

Now let's practice writing **h** on your table without using your pencil. Use your writing hand pointer finger, and make **h** on your table.
Guide students as they write h on their table or desktop.

Let's practice **h** again.

Model writing h on the board (with your back to students).
Remember that every letter has a name.
You learned the name of this letter is **h**. What letter name? *h*.
Again, what letter name? *h*.

Provide lined paper to students.
Now let's practice writing **h** with your pencil.
Guide students as they write h on their paper. **Review** as needed.

 Link letter names to letter sounds as they appear in the program as needed.

Set up a writing center with writing materials and correct models of letters learned so far for students to use in their free time.

Part C: Comprehension Strategies

9 minutes

Teacher Materials:
Narrative trade book

Student Materials:
Lined paper

Activity 1 Title, Author, and Illustrator Identification—A Before-Reading Strategy

Provide a reading center to display books being read so that students can enjoy them again during free time.

Direct students to narrative trade book of teacher choice. **Elicit** responses to questions. **Guide** as needed.

Show front cover of book and allow student to point to name of title, author, and illustrator as you discuss them.
We'll read a new book today. The title of today's story is _____.
What's the title of today's story? (**Student response.**)

The author of today's story is _____. Who's the author of today's story? (**Student response.**)

The illustrator of today's story is _____. Who's the illustrator? (**Student response.**)

Lesson 71   **277**

Activity 2 Activate Background Knowledge—A Before-Reading Strategy

Choose a topic to activate background knowledge from story you will read.
Elicit responses to questions. **Guide** as needed.

Your brain has all kinds of information in it. You've already learned lots of things. Today, you'll look in your brains to see what you know about _____. Tell me what you know or experiences you have had that help you know about this topic. (**Student response.**)

Discuss background knowledge of students as it relates to topic chosen.

Provide lined paper. **Model** writing a sentence about what you know.

Write a sentence that tells me what you know about _____. If you need help, ask me.

Monitor students. **Guide** students as needed.

When you think about what you know before you read, it helps you better understand the story. You can connect what you know to the story.

Activity 3 Listening Comprehension—A During-Reading Strategy

Elicit responses to questions. **Guide** as needed.

You've learned about characters and setting. Another thing that you find in stories is events that happened. Events are things that happened in the story. Events happen at the beginning, in the middle, and at the end of a story. So stories have a beginning, a middle, and an end.

What do stories have? *A beginning, a middle, and an end.*

Today you're going to think about events that happened at the beginning and the middle of the story.

In the story *The Little Red Hen,* the beginning of the story was when the little red hen found the wheat and decided to plant it. That's the first thing that happened in the story. The next thing that happened is that she tried to get help with all the jobs it takes to make wheat into bread. She couldn't get any help. Those were the middle events of story.

Today as I read the story, I want you to listen carefully and think hard about the things that happened first and next in the story. We will talk about the beginning and the middle of the story after I read the story.

Elicit correct listening behavior from students. **Read** trade book. **Model** prosody during read-aloud.

Ask questions to elicit identification of beginning and middle events in story as well as connecting background knowledge to story as you read. **Guide** as needed.

278 *Lesson 71*

Activity 4 **Story Elements: Identify Beginning and Middle—An After-Reading Strategy**

Elicit responses to questions. **Guide** as needed.
You're learning all about stories. You know about characters and setting. Now you're learning about the beginning, the middle, and the end of the story. Things happen in stories. We call those things events. What do we call the things that happened in stories? *Events.*

Listen as I show you how I think about the events that happened at the beginning and the middle of the story.
Model identifying beginning and middle events of story.

Remember that the beginning of the story is the events that happened first in the story. The middle of the story is the events that happened next.

what do you call the events that happened first in a story? *The beginning.*

What do you call the events that happened next in a story? *The middle.*

Lesson 71 **279**

Lesson 72

Materials

Teacher: Narrative trade book (from Lesson 71); Picture-Sound Cards for /a/, /ē/, /r/, /d/, /f/, /t/, /n/, and /c/

Student: Lined paper

5 minutes

Teacher Materials:
Picture-Sound Cards for /a/, /ē/, /r/, /d/, /f/, /t/, /n/, and /c/

Part A: Phonemic and Phonological Awareness

Activity 1 Phoneme Isolation—Initial

Use IWB interactive cards or picture-sound cards. **Elicit** responses. **Guide** as needed. I'm going to show you two cards and name the object on each card. Then I'll tell you a sound. Think about which word starts with that sound. Let's try it. Today we'll be listening for the sound at the *beginning* of a word.

Show /n/ card; use any of four Picture-Sound Cards per phoneme for activity.
This is a _____. What is this? (Student response.)

Show /t/ card; use any of four Picture-Sound Cards per phoneme for activity.
This is a _____. What is this? (Student response.)

Which word begins with /nnn/? (Student response.)

Show /c/ card; use any of four Picture-Sound Cards per phoneme for activity.
This is a _____. What is this? (Student response.)

Show /a/ card; use any of four Picture-Sound Cards per phoneme for activity.
This is a _____. What is this? (Student response.)

Which word begins with /c/? (Student response.)

(Continue the activity with the following examples:
/r/ and /n/: Which word begins with /n/?
/c/ and /f/: Which word begins with /c/?
/ē/ and /c/: Which word begins with /c/?
/d/ and /n/: Which word begins with /n/?)

280 Lesson 72

Activity 2 Phoneme Isolation—Medial

Elicit responses. **Guide** as needed.
You did so well finding the *beginning sound* and the *ending sound* of a word. Now let's work on the sound in the *middle* of a word. I'm going to say a list of words. Some of the words will have the **/ooo/** sound in the *middle,* and some will not. I'll say the word first, and then you'll say the word. Give me a thumbs-up if you hear the **/ooo/** sound in the *middle* of the word. If you don't hear the **/ooo/** sound in the *middle* of the word, do nothing. Think about the *middle* sound we hear in each word.

Remember, we're listening for the **/ooo/** sound in the *middle* of the word, as in **not.** What sound are you listening for in the *middle?/ooo/.*

Listen. **Lot.** Say **lot.** *Lot.*

Give me a thumbs-up if you hear **/ooo/** in the *middle* of **lot.** (Thumbs-up.)

Yes, **lot** has the *middle* sound **/ooo/.**

(Continue the activity with the following lists of words.
Tot. Pain. Pot. Ride. Bean. Rock.
Got. Clip. Sock. Ready. Paint. Top.)

Part B: Letter Recognition and Formation

6 minutes

Student Materials:
Lined paper

Activity 1 Letter Recognition Review—h

Elicit responses to questions. **Guide** as needed. **Write** h on the board. **Point** to h.
We learned that this letter is **h.** What letter name? *h.*
Again, what letter name? *h.*
Review as needed.

Activity 2 Letter Formation Review—h

Now we're going to practice writing **h.** When you practice writing, you'll learn not only where to start and stop the letter, but also which way to move your hand when you're making the letter. It's tricky, but you're so smart you'll learn how to write **h** very quickly. Watch.

Here's how you write **h** in the air.
Model h formation in the air (with your back to students).

Watch again.

Now let's practice writing **h** in the air. Hold up your writing hand, and make **h** in the air.
Guide students as they write h in the air.

Let's practice **h** again.

Lesson 72   **281**

Here's how to write **h** with your writing hand pointer finger.
Model h formation on the board with your finger (with your back to students).

Watch again.

Now let's practice writing **h** on your table without using your pencil. Use your writing hand pointer finger, and make **h** on your table.
Guide students as they write h on their table or desktop.

Let's practice **h** again.

Model writing h on the board (with your back to students).
Remember that every letter has a name.
You learned the name of this letter is **h.** What letter name? *h.*
Again, what letter name? *h.*

Provide lined paper to students.
Now let's practice writing **h** with your pencil.
Guide students as they write h on their paper. **Review** as needed.

 Link letter names to letter sounds as they appear in the program as needed.

Part C: Comprehension Strategies

9 minutes

Teacher Materials:
Narrative trade book

Activity 1 Listening Comprehension—A During-Reading Strategy

Direct students to narrative trade book of teacher choice. **Elicit** responses to questions. **Guide** as needed.
In the last lesson you learned about the beginning of a story. The beginning is the first things or events that happened in the story. What's the beginning of a story? (Idea: *The events that happened first in the story.*)

Stories also have events that happened in the middle. What's the middle of a story? (Idea: *Events that happened next or in the middle of the story.*)

Stories also have things that happened at the end, but we'll talk about those later.

Today we'll read the story again. As I read, listen and think about the events at the beginning and the middle of the story. See whether you can tell me what the beginning is by telling what events happened first in the story. Then tell me about the middle by telling the events that happened next.

Elicit correct listening behavior from students. **Reread** trade book. **Model** prosody during read-aloud.

Ask questions to elicit identification of events at beginning and middle of story. **Guide** as needed.

282 Lesson 72

Activity 2 **Story Elements: Identify Beginning and Middle—An After-Reading Strategy**

Elicit responses. **Guide** as needed.

You're learning about the beginning and the middle of a story. The beginning is the events that happened first in the story. What's the beginning? (Idea: *The events that happened first in the story.*)

The middle is the events that happened next or in the middle of the story. What's the middle? (Idea: *Events that happened next or in the middle of the story.*)

Different stories have different events that happened at the beginning of the story. In *Goldilocks and the Three Bears,* the event that happened first was that the three bears went on a walk while their porridge cooled. In the middle of the story, Goldilocks ate the porridge, broke the chair, and slept in the baby bear's bed. That was the middle of the story.

Discuss beginning and middle events of story. **Guide** as needed.

In our story, what events happened at the beginning of the story? (Student response.)

In our story, what events happened in the middle of the story? (Student response.)

Lesson 72   **283**

Lesson 73

Materials
Teacher: Narrative trade book (from Lesson 71); 4-Story Map
Student: Lined paper

Part A: Phonemic and Phonological Awareness

Activity 1 Phoneme Isolation—Initial

Elicit responses. **Guide** as needed.
Let's work on a sound at the *beginning* of a word. I'm going to say a list of words. Some of the words will have the **/vvv/** sound at the *beginning,* and some will not. I'll say the word first, and then you'll say the word.

Remember, we're listening for the **/vvv/** sound at the *beginning* of the word. What sound are we listening for? */vvv/.*

Listen. **Vase.** Say **vase.** *Vase.*

Give me a thumbs-up if you hear **/vvv/** at the *beginning* of **vase.** (Thumbs-up.)

Yes, **vase** *begins* with the sound **/vvv/.**

(Continue the activity with the following lists of words.
Veil. Beat. Mist. Visit. Check. Van.
Five. Violin. Plate. Vine. Oboe. Volcano.)

Activity 2 Phoneme Isolation—Final

Elicit responses. **Guide** as needed.
Now let's work on the sound at the *end* of a word. I'm going to say a list of words. Some of the words will have the **/g/** sound at the *end,* and some will not. I'll say the word first, and then you'll say the word. Think about the *last* sound we hear in each word.

Remember, we're listening for the **/g/** sound at the *end* of the word, as in **tag.** What sound are you listening for at the *end?* */g/.*

Listen. **Rag.** Say **rag.** *Rag.*

Give me a thumbs-up if you hear **/g/** at the *end* of **rag.** (Thumbs-up.)

Yes, **rag** *ends* with the sound **/g/.**

284 Lesson 73

(Continue the activity with the following lists of words.
My. Dig. Fox. Dog. Pot. Fog.
Leg. Pet. Log. Hog. Green. Pig.)

Activity 3 Phoneme Identity—Initial

Elicit responses. **Guide** as needed.
We're going to play a game and find something the same. I'm going to say three words. Listen closely and see if you can tell which sound is the same. I'll show you how to do the first one.

My turn. What sound is the same in **dog, dig,** and **dime?** /d/. That is because **dog, dig,** and **dime** all *begin* with the first sound /d/. Your turn. What sound is the same in **dish, deep,** and **day?** /d./

Yes, **dish, deep,** and **day** all *begin* with the first sound /d/.

Let's try some more. What sound is the same in **ear, each,** and **eagle?** /ēēē/.

What sound is the same in **rat, race,** and **red?** /rrr/.

What sound is the same in **eat, even,** and **eel?** /ēēē/.

What sound is the same in **ride, rose,** and **ran?** /rrr/.

What sound is the same in **deal, donut,** and **does?** /d/.

Part B: Letter Recognition and Formation

6 minutes

Student Materials:
Lined paper

Activity 1 Letter Recognition—Capital H

Elicit responses to questions. **Guide** as needed. **Write** capital H on the board.
Point to capital H.
Today you'll learn another way to write **h.**
The name of this letter is **capital H.** What letter name? *Capital H.*
Again, what letter name? *Capital H.*
Review as needed.

Activity 2 Letter Formation—Capital H

Now we're going to practice writing **capital H.** When you practice writing, you'll learn not only where to start and stop the letter, but also which way to move your hand when you're making the letter. It's tricky, but you're so smart you'll learn how to write **capital H** very quickly. Watch.

Here's how you write **capital H** in the air.
Model capital H formation in the air (with your back to students).

Watch again.

Now let's practice writing **capital H** in the air. Hold up your writing hand, and make **capital H** in the air.

Lesson 73   **285**

Guide students as they write capital H in the air.

Let's practice **capital H** again.

Here's how to write **capital H** with your writing hand pointer finger.
Model capital H formation on the board with your finger (with your back to students).

Watch again.

Now let's practice writing **capital H** on your table without using your pencil.
Use your writing hand pointer finger, and make **capital H** on your table.
Guide students as they write capital H on their table or desktop.

Let's practice **capital H** again.

Model writing capital H on the board (with your back to students).
Remember that every letter has a name.
You learned the name of this letter is **capital H.** What letter name? *Capital H.*
Again, what letter name? *Capital H.*

Provide lined paper to students.
Now let's practice writing **capital H** with your pencil.
Guide students as they write capital H on their paper. **Review** as needed.

 Link letter names to letter sounds as they appear in the program as needed.

Part C: Comprehension Strategies

9 minutes

Teacher Materials:
Narrative trade book

Story Map

Activity 1 Listening Comprehension—A During-Reading Strategy

Direct students to narrative trade book of teacher choice. **Elicit** responses to questions. **Guide** as needed.
You're learning about the beginning and the middle of a story. The beginning is the first things or events that happened in the story.

What's the beginning of a story? (**Idea:** *The events that happened first in the story.*)

The middle is the events that happened next in the story. What's the middle of the story? (**Idea:** *Events that happened next in the story.*)

Today we'll read the story again. As I read, listen and think about the events at the beginning and the middle of the story. See whether you can tell me what the beginning is by telling what things happened first in the story. I'll draw a little picture on the board to help me remember the beginning. Then think about what happened next. I'll draw a little picture to help me remember the middle.

Elicit correct listening behavior from students. **Reread** trade book. **Model** prosody during read-aloud.

Elicit beginning and middle events in story. **Draw** a quick sketch of beginning and middle events on board. **Guide** as needed.

286 Lesson 73

Activity 2 Story Elements: Identify Beginning and Middle—An After-Reading Strategy

Elicit responses to questions. **Guide** as needed.
In the last lesson, you learned about the beginning of a story. The beginning is the events that happened first in the story. What's the beginning? (Idea: *The events that happened first in the story.*)

Show Story Map.
In our story, what events happened at the beginning of the story? (Student response.)

Model drawing quick sketches of the beginning and the middle on Story Map.
I drew a picture on the board to help me remember the beginning of the story. Now I'll use a Story Map and draw a picture in the box for the beginning to help me remember what happened first.

What's the middle? (Idea: *The events that happened next in the story.*)

In our story, what events happened at the middle of the story? (Student response.)

I drew a picture on the board to help me remember the middle of the story. Now I'll use a Story Map and draw a picture in the box for the middle to help me remember what happened next.

Now I'll be able to remember how to tell about the beginning and the middle of the story because my Story Map has pictures to remind me.
Save Story Map for Lesson 75.

Lesson 73 **287**

Lesson 74

Materials

Teacher: Narrative trade book (from Lesson 71); Picture-Sound Cards for /a/, /r/, /d/, /t/, /n/, /o/, and /h/

Student: Lined paper

5 minutes

Teacher Materials:
Picture-Sound Cards for /a/, /r/, /d/, /t/, /n/, /o/, and /h/

Part A: Phonemic and Phonological Awareness

Activity 1 Phoneme Isolation—Initial

Use IWB interactive cards or picture-sound cards. **Elicit** responses. **Guide** as needed. I'm going to show you two cards and name the object on each card. Then I'll tell you a sound. Think about which word starts with that sound. Let's try it. Today we'll be listening for the sound at the *beginning* of a word.

Show /h/ card; use any of four Picture-Sound Cards per phoneme for activity.
This is a _____. What is this? (Student response.)

Show /t/ card; use any of four Picture-Sound Cards per phoneme for activity.
This is a _____. What is this? (Student response.)

Which word begins with /h/? (Student response.)

Show /o/ card; use any of four Picture-Sound Cards per phoneme for activity.
This is a _____. What is this? (Student response.)

Show /n/ card; use any of four Picture-Sound Cards per phoneme for activity.
This is a _____. What is this? (Student response.)

Which word begins with /ooo/? (Student response.)

(Continue the activity with the following examples:
/r/ and /o/: Which word begins with /ooo/?
/h/ and /d/: Which word begins with /h/?
/o/ and /a/: Which word begins with /ooo/?
/r/ and /h/: Which word begins with /h/?)

288   Lesson 74

Activity 2 Phoneme Isolation—Medial

Elicit responses. **Guide** as needed.
You did so well finding the *beginning sound* and the *ending sound* of a word. Now let's work on the sound in the *middle* of a word. I'm going to say a list of words. Some of the words will have the /ăăă/ sound in the *middle,* and some will not. I'll say the word first, and then you'll say the word. Give me a thumbs-up if you hear the /ăăă/ sound in the *middle* of the word. If you don't hear the /ăăă/ sound in the *middle* of the word, do nothing. Think about the *middle* sound we hear in each word.

Remember, we're listening for the /ăăă/ sound in the *middle* of the word, as in **cat.** What sound are you listening for in the *middle?* /ăăă/.

Listen. **Mat.** Say **mat.** *Mat.*

Give me a thumbs-up if you hear /ăăă/ in the *middle* of **mat.** (Thumbs-up.)

Yes, **mat** has the *middle* sound /ăăă/.

(Continue the activity with the following lists of words.
Bad. Pole. Sat. Cold. Best. Sack.
Rat. Fox. Mad. Hat. Peel. Pad.)

Part B: Letter Recognition and Formation

6 minutes

Student Materials:
Lined paper

Activity 1 Letter Recognition Review—Capital H

Elicit responses to questions. **Guide** as needed. **Write** capital H on the board.
Point to capital H.
We learned that this letter is **capital H.** What letter name? *Capital H.*
Again, what letter name? *Capital H.*
Review as needed.

Activity 2 Letter Formation Review—Capital H

Now we're going to practice writing **capital H.** When you practice writing, you'll learn not only where to start and stop the letter, but also which way to move your hand when you're making the letter. It's tricky, but you're so smart you'll learn how to write **capital H** very quickly. Watch.

Here's how you write **capital H** in the air.
Model capital H formation in the air (with your back to students).

Watch again.

Now let's practice writing **capital H** in the air. Hold up your writing hand, and make **capital H** in the air.
Guide students as they write capital H in the air.

Let's practice **capital H** again.

Lesson 74   **289**

Here's how to write **capital H** with your writing hand pointer finger.
Model capital H̲ formation on the board with your finger (with your back to students).

Watch again.

Now let's practice writing **capital H** on your table without using your pencil. Use your writing hand pointer finger, and make **capital H** on your table.
Guide students as they write capital H̲ on their table or desktop.

Let's practice **capital H** again.

Model writing capital H̲ on the board (with your back to students).
Remember that every letter has a name.
You learned the name of this letter is **capital H.** What letter name? *Capital H.*
Again, what letter name? *Capital H.*

Provide lined paper to students.
Now let's practice writing **capital H** with your pencil.
Guide students as they write capital H̲ on their paper. **Review** as needed.

 Link letter names to letter sounds as they appear in the program as needed.

Part C: Comprehension Strategies

9 minutes

Teacher Materials:
Narrative trade book

Activity 1 Listening Comprehension—A During-Reading Strategy

Direct students to narrative trade book of teacher choice. **Elicit** responses to questions. **Guide** as needed.
What's the beginning of a story? (Idea: *The events that happened first in the story.*)

What's the middle of the story? (Idea: *The events that happened next in the story.*)

I want you to look at the pictures and listen to the words of the story very carefully. When I'm finished with the story, we'll play the things that happened at the beginning and in the middle of the story. I'll need your ideas for what events happened first and what happens next.

Elicit correct listening behavior from students. **Reread** trade book. **Model** prosody during read-aloud.

Guide students to focus on beginning and middle events. **Elicit** answers to questions about beginning and middle events in story. **Guide** as needed.

Activity 2 **Story Elements: Play the Beginning and Middle—An After-Reading Strategy**

Coach all students to play the story by telling events that happened and guiding students to play or mime the actions. If there is dialogue, say the words and then have students repeat the words. **Elicit** responses to questions. **Guide** as needed.

Now you're going to play the beginning and the middle. What events happened at the beginning of the story? (Student response.)

How would you play those events? (Student response.)

What events happened in the middle of the story? (Student response.)

How would you play those events? (Student response.)

I'll tell the beginning and the middle of the story. As I tell the events, each of you can to do the actions I'm telling about. If there are words to say, I'll help you say them.

Praise creativity in playing beginning and middle of story. **Prompt** everyone to bow as you applaud them.

Wow, that was fun!

Lesson 74   **291**

Lesson 75

Materials
Teacher: Narrative trade book (from Lesson 71); 4-Story Map (from Lesson 73); Letter Recognition
Student: Lined paper; copy of 4-Story Map

Part A: Phonemic and Phonological Awareness

Activity 1 Phoneme Isolation— Initial

Elicit responses. **Guide** as needed.
Let's work on a sound at the *beginning* of a word. I'm going to say a list of words. Some of the words will have the **/p/** sound at the *beginning* and some will not. I'll say the word first, and then you'll say the word.

Remember, we're listening for the **/p/** sound at the *beginning* of the word. What sound are we listening for? */p/*.

Listen. **Pig.** Say **pig.** *Pig.*

Give me a thumbs-up if you hear **/p/** at the *beginning* of **pig.** (Thumbs-up.)

Yes, **pig** *begins* with the sound **/p/.**

(Continue the activity with the following lists of words.
Pet. Bee. Pink. Paste. She. Own.
Paint. Wish. Purple. Vine. Pine. Pill.)

Activity 2 Phoneme Isolation—Final

Elicit responses. **Guide** as needed.
Now let's work on the sound at the *end* of a word. I'm going to say a list of words. Some of the words will have the **/lll/** sound at the *end,* and some will not. I'll say the word first, and then you'll say the word. Think about the *last* sound we hear in each word.

Remember, we're listening for the **/lll/** sound at the *end* of the word, as in **pill.** What sound are you listening for at the *end?* */lll/*.

Listen. **Pill.** Say **pill.** *Pill.*

Give me a thumbs-up if you hear **/lll/** at the *end* of **pill.** (Thumbs-up.)

Yes, **pill** *ends* with the sound **/lll/.**

(Continue the activity with the following lists of words.
Whale. Seen. Spoon. Tall. Oak. Pal.
Tail. Gate. Twist. Cool. Name. Mail.)

292 Lesson 75

Activity 3 Phoneme Identity— Initial

Elicit responses. **Guide** as needed.
We're going to play a game and find something the same. I'm going to say three words. Listen closely and see if you can tell which sound is the same.

Your turn. What sound is the same in **fish, feet,** and **fig**? /fff/.

Yes, **fish, feet,** and **fig** all *begin* with the first sound **/fff/.** Let's try some more. What sound is the same in **inch, it,** and **in**? /iii/.

What sound is the same in **tap, taste,** and **tank**? /t/.

What sound is the same in **ill, if,** and **is**? /iii/.

What sound is the same in **feel, far,** and **fin**? /fff/.

What sound is the same in **tea, tip,** and **toe**? /t/.

Part B: Letter Recognition and Formation

6 minutes

Teacher Materials:
Letter Recognition

Student Materials:
Lined paper

Activity 1 Letter Recognition Cumulative Review—n/N, c/C, o/O, h/H

Display on IWB or **write** letters and capitals on the board in the order shown.
Elicit responses to questions. **Guide** as needed.
This week you've learned one letter and one capital—**h** and **capital H.**
Let's review all the letters and capitals you've learned. Are you ready?

Letter	Question	Student Response
N	What letter?	Capital N.
C	What letter?	Capital C.
o	What letter?	o.
H	What letter?	Capital H.
n	What letter?	n.
O	What letter?	Capital O.
h	What letter?	h.
c	What letter?	c.

Review as needed.

Lesson 75

Activity 2 | Letter Formation Cumulative Review—n/N, c/C, o/O, h/H

Write n, capital N, c, capital C, o, capital O, h, and capital H on the board in the order shown (with your back to students). **Provide** lined paper to students.
Show me how you can write these letters and capitals.
Guide students as they write the letters and capitals on their paper. **Review** as needed.

 Link letter names to letter sounds as they appear in the program as needed.

Part C: Comprehension Strategies

9 minutes

Teacher Materials:
Narrative trade book

Story Map

Student Materials:
Story Map

Activity 1 | Listening Comprehension—A During-Reading Strategy

Direct students to narrative trade book of teacher choice. **Elicit** responses to questions. **Guide** as needed.
The job of a book illustrator is to make pictures for books. What does an illustrator do? *Make pictures for books.*

The illustrator of our book is _____. Who's the illustrator of this book? (Student response.)

Today as I read the story, I want you to look carefully at the pictures of the beginning and middle events in the story. The illustrator made the pictures for you so that the book would be fun to read. Look for what the illustrator did to show the events at the beginning and in the middle. After I read the story, you'll become an illustrator and draw pictures of the beginning and the middle of the story. While I read, think about what you want to draw.

Elicit correct listening behavior from students. **Reread** trade book. **Model** prosody during read-aloud.

Guide students to focus on illustrations of events for the beginning and middle of story. **Elicit** answers to questions about how illustrator shows events in beginning and middle of story. **Guide** as needed.

Activity 2 Story Elements: Illustrate Beginning and Middle—An After-Reading Strategy

Elicit responses to questions. **Guide** as needed.
Now you'll become an illustrator. Remember that an illustrator is the person who draws the pictures in a story. What does an illustrator do? (**Idea:** *Draw pictures for the book.*)

Show Story Map completed in Lesson 73.
I'll show you the pictures I made in the boxes for the beginning and middle events.

Provide copy of Story Map to each student.
As an illustrator, your job today is to draw the beginning and the middle of the story in the Beginning and Middle boxes. When you're finished, you can share your illustrations with your neighbor.
Guide students to draw illustrations in the correct boxes and to work quickly.

Share illustrations with class if time permits, or make a class book of beginnings and middles.

Lesson 75   **295**

Lesson 76

Materials

Teacher: Narrative trade book (same book for Lessons 76–80); Picture-Sound Cards for /r/, /t/, /n/, /h/, /ā/, and /th/, 1-My Prediction Chart

Student: Lined paper, Copy of 1-My Prediction Chart

5 minutes

Teacher Materials:
Picture-Sound Cards for /r/, /t/, /n/, /h/, /ā/, and /th/

Part A: Phonemic and Phonological Awareness

Activity 1 Phoneme Isolation— Initial

Use IWB interactive cards or picture-sound cards. **Elicit** responses. **Guide** as needed. I'm going to show you two cards and name the object on each card. Then I'll tell you a sound. Think about which word starts with that sound. Let's try it. Today we'll be listening for the sound at the *beginning* of a word.

Show /h/ card; use any of four Picture-Sound Cards per phoneme for activity. This is a _____. What is this? (Student response.)

Show /th/ card; use any of four Picture-Sound Cards per phoneme for activity. This is a _____. What is this? (Student response.)

Which word *begins* with **/ththth/?** (Student response.)

Show /ā/ card; use any of four Picture-Sound Cards per phoneme for activity. This is a _____. What is this? (Student response.)

Show /n/ card; use any of four Picture-Sound Cards per phoneme for activity. This is a _____. What is this? (Student response.)

Which word *begins* with **/āāā/?** (Student response.)

(Continue the activity with the following examples:
/m/ and /ā/: Which word begins with /āāā/?
/th/ and /n/: Which word begins with /ththth/?
/ā/ and /r/: Which word begins with /āāā/?
/t/ and /th/: Which word begins with /ththth/?)

Activity 2 Phoneme Isolation—Medial

Elicit responses. **Guide** as needed.
You did so well finding the *beginning sound* and the *ending sound* of a word. Now let's work on the sound in the *middle* of a word. I'm going to say a list of words. Some of the words will have the **/uuu/** sound in the *middle,* and some will not.

Remember, we're listening for the **/uuu/** sound in the *middle* of the word, as in **cup.** What sound are you listening for in the *middle?* /uuu/.

Listen. **Nut.** Say **nut.** *Nut.*

Give me thumbs-up if you hear **/uuu/** in the *middle* of **nut.** (Thumbs-up.)

Yes, **nut** has the *middle* sound **/uuu/.**

(Continue the activity with the following lists of words.
Mud. Pet. Tug. Cast. Mug. Dud.
Black. Sun. Hand. Run. Rug. Tooth.)

Part B: Letter Recognition and Formation

6 minutes

Student Materials:
Lined paper

Activity 1 Letter Recognition—u

Elicit responses to questions. **Guide** as needed. **Write** u on the board. **Point** to u.
Today you'll learn a new letter.
The name of this letter is **u.** What letter name? *u.*
Again, what letter name? *u.*
Review as needed.

Activity 2 Letter Formation—u

Now we're going to practice writing **u.** When you practice writing, you'll learn not only where to start and stop the letter, but also which way to move your hand when you're making the letter. It's tricky, but you're so smart you'll learn how to write **u** very quickly. Watch.

Here's how you write **u** in the air.
Model u formation in the air (with your back to students).

Watch again.

Now let's practice writing **u** in the air. Hold up your writing hand, and make **u** in the air.
Guide students as they write u in the air.

Let's practice **u** again.

Here's how to write **u** with your writing hand pointer finger.
Model u formation on the board with your finger (with your back to students).

Watch again.

Lesson 76   **297**

Now let's practice writing **u** on your table without using your pencil.
Use your writing hand pointer finger, and make **u** on your table.
Guide students as they write u on their table or desktop.

Let's practice **u** again.

Model writing u on the board (with your back to students).
Remember that every letter has a name.
You learned the name of this letter is **u.** What letter name? *u.*
Again, what letter name? *u.*

Provide lined paper to students.
Now let's practice writing **u** with your pencil.
Guide students as they write u on their paper. **Review** as needed.

 Link letter names to letter sounds as they appear in the program as needed.

Set up a writing center with writing materials and correct models of letters learned so far for students to use in their free time.

Part C: Comprehension Strategies

9 minutes

Teacher Materials:
Narrative trade book

My Prediction Chart

Student Materials:
Lined paper

My Prediction Chart

Activity 1 Title, Author, and Illustrator Identification—A Before-Reading Strategy

 Provide a reading center to display books being read so that students can enjoy them again during free time.

Direct students to narrative trade book of teacher choice. **Elicit** responses to questions. **Guide** as needed.

Show front cover of book and allow student to point to name of title, author, and illustrator as you discuss them.

The title of today's story is _____. What's the title of today's story?
(Student response.)

The author of today's story is _____. Who's the author of today's story?
(Student response.)

The illustrator of today's story is _____. Who's the illustrator?
(Student response.)

298   Lesson 76

Activity 2   Activate Background Knowledge—A Before-Reading Strategy

Choose a topic to activate background knowledge from story you will read. **Elicit** responses to questions. **Guide** as needed.

Your brain has all kinds of information in it. You've already learned lots of things. Today, we're going to look in your brain to see what you know about _____.

Discuss background knowledge for topic chosen.

Tell me what you know about _____.

Provide lined paper. **Model** writing a sentence about what you know.

Write a sentence that tells me what you know about _____.
If you need help, ask me.

Monitor students. **Guide** students as needed.

When you think about what you know before you read, it helps you better understand the story. You can connect what you know to what happens in the story.

Activity 3   Make Predictions—A Before-Reading Strategy

Show My Prediction Chart. **Show** title, front and back cover, and pictures inside the book. **Elicit** responses to questions. **Guide** as needed.

The title of today's book is _____. Write the book title in the box labeled "Book Title".

Now that we know the title of today's book, let's look at the cover and pictures inside the book for clues to make some good guesses for what we think the story will be about. We call our good guesses predictions.

Making good guesses, or predictions, helps us get interested in the story before we read it. Let's make some predictions about the story before I read to you.

What do you predict this story will be about? (Student response.)
Write your prediction in the box labeled "I Predict That".
Guide as needed.

What characters do you predict will be in the story? (Student response.)

What do you predict the setting will be? (Student response.)

What do you predict might happen in the story? (Student response.)

When we read the book we'll check your predictions to see whether they're correct.

Elicit correct listening behavior from students. **Read** trade book. **Model** prosody during read-aloud.

Guide students to confirm predictions and/or connect background knowledge as you read story. **Ask** questions to confirm predictions and/or connect background knowledge. **Guide** as needed.

Lesson 76   **299**

Activity 4 Confirm Predictions—An After-Reading Strategy

Show My Prediction Chart. **Elicit** responses to questions. **Guide** as needed.
Now let's check your predictions to see whether they were correct.
You predicted that the story was about _____.

Was your prediction correct? (Student response.)
Circle whether or not your prediction was correct in the box labeled "Was My Prediction Correct?".
Guide as needed

You predicted that _____ were characters in the story. Was your prediction correct? (Student response.)

You predicted that the setting was _____. Was your prediction correct? (Student response.)

You predicted that some events would be _____. Was your prediction correct? (Student response.)

Remember that your predictions don't have to be correct. Just making a prediction and listening to see whether your prediction is correct helps you stay interested in the story.

300 *Lesson 76*

Lesson 77

Materials
Teacher: Narrative trade book (from Lesson 76), 2-Character Sheet, 3-Setting Sheet
Student: Lined paper

5 minutes

Part A: Phonemic and Phonological Awareness

Activity 1 Phoneme Isolation— Initial

Elicit responses. **Guide** as needed.
Let's work on a sound at the *beginning* of a word. I'm going to say a list of words. Some of the words will have the **/ch/** sound at the *beginning,* and some will not. I'll say the word first, and then you'll say the word.

Remember, we're listening for the **/ch/** sound at the *beginning* of the word. What sound are we listening for? */ch/.*

Listen. **Chip.** Say **chip.** *Chip.*

Give me a thumbs-up if you hear **/ch/** at the *beginning* of **chip.** (Thumbs-up.)

Yes, **chip** *begins* with the sound **/ch/.**

(**Continue** the activity with the following lists of words.
Chop. Bend. Plane. Chalk. Milk. Cheese.
Fall. Water. Church. Go. Hill. Chance.)

Activity 2 Phoneme Isolation—Final

Elicit responses. **Guide** as needed.
Now let's work on the sound at the *end* of a word. I'm going to say a list of words. Some of the words will have the **/shshsh/** sound at the *end,* and some will not. I'll say the word first, and then you'll say the word. Think about the *last* sound we hear in each word.

Remember, we're listening for the **/shshsh/** sound at the *end* of the word, as in **dish.** What sound are you listening for at the *end?* */shshsh/.*

Listen. **Fish.** Say **fish.** *Fish.*

Give me a thumbs-up if you hear **/shshsh/** at the *end* of **fish.** (Thumbs-up.)

Yes, **fish** *ends* with the sound **/shshsh/.**

(Continue the activity with the following lists of words.
Dial. Push. Letter. Mush. Fine. Hold.
Wish. Like. Turn. Wash. Splash. May.)

Lesson 77   **301**

Activity 3 Phoneme Identity—Initial

Elicit responses. **Guide** as needed.
We're going to play a game and find something the same. I'm going to say three words. Listen closely and see if you can tell which sound is the same.

Your turn. What sound is the same in **net, nice,** and **not?** /nnn/.
Yes, **net, nice,** and **not** all *begin* with the first sound **/nnn/.**

Let's try some more. What sound is the same in **cat, cool,** and **came?** /k/.

What sound is the same in **off, ox,** and **on?** /ooo/.

What sound is the same in **care, calf,** and **call?** /k/.

What sound is the same in **neat, new,** and **no?** /nnn/.

What sound is the same in **odd, olive,** and **octopus?** /ooo/.

Part B: Letter Recognition and Formation

6 minutes

Student Materials:
Lined paper

Activity 1 Letter Recognition Review—u

Elicit responses to questions. **Guide** as needed. **Write** u on the board. **Point** to u.
We learned that this letter is **u.** What letter name? *u.*
Again, what letter name? *u.*
Review as needed.

Activity 2 Letter Formation Review—u

Now, we're going to practice writing **u.** When you practice writing, you'll learn not only where to start and stop the letter, but also which way to move your hand when you're making the letter. It's tricky, but you're so smart you'll learn how to write **u** very quickly. Watch.

Here's how you write **u** in the air.
Model u formation in the air (with your back to students).

Watch again.

Now let's practice writing **u** in the air. Hold up your writing hand, and make **u** in the air.
Guide students as they write u in the air.

Let's practice **u** again.

Here's how to write **u** with your writing hand pointer finger.
Model u formation on the board with your finger (with your back to students).

Watch again.

302   Lesson 77

Now let's practice writing **u** on your table without using your pencil. Use your writing hand pointer finger, and make **u** on your table.
Guide students as they write u on their table or desktop.

Let's practice **u** again.

Model writing u on the board (with your back to students).
Remember that every letter has a name.
You learned the name of this letter is **u.** What letter name? *u.*
Again, what letter name? *u.*

Provide lined paper to students.
Now let's practice writing **u** with your pencil.
Guide students as they write u on their paper. **Review** as needed.

 Link letter names to letter sounds as they appear in the program as needed.

Part C: Comprehension Strategies

 9 minutes

Activity 1 Listening Comprehension—A During-Reading Strategy

Teacher Materials:
Narrative trade book
Character Sheet
Setting Sheet

Show Character Sheet and Setting Sheet. **Direct** students to narrative trade book of teacher choice. **Elicit** responses to questions. **Guide** as needed.
You're learning about the beginning and the middle of a story. What's the beginning of a story? (Idea: *The events that happened first in the story.*)

What's the middle of a story? (Idea: *The events that happened next in the story.*)

Today we'll read the story again. As I read, listen and look so you can think about the events at the beginning and middle of the book.

After I read, I want to see whether you can tell a partner about the beginning and the middle by telling what events happened first and what events happened next. I'll draw little pictures on the board to help you remember the beginning and the middle.

Help me find the characters and setting(s) in this book as I read by putting up your hand when you see a setting or hear about a character.

Then I'll write the names of the characters and setting(s) on the charts as I read.

Elicit correct listening behavior from students. **Reread** trade book. **Model** prosody during read-aloud.

Elicit settings and characters from students as you read. **Write** the setting(s) and characters, and draw beginning and middle. **Guide** as needed.

Lesson 77 **303**

Activity 2 Story Elements: Identify and Retell the Beginning and Middle—An After-Reading Strategy

Elicit responses to questions. **Guide** as needed.
You're learning about the beginning and the middle of the story. What do you call the events that happened first in a story? *The beginning.*

What do you call the events that happened next in a story? *The middle.*

Model retelling beginning and middle of story from pictures on board.
I made pictures of the beginning and the middle of the story on the board. Listen as I retell the beginning and the middle of the story.

Assign student partners.
Just retell the things that happened at the beginning and the middle. Use the pictures on the board to help you remember what to tell.

How should you listen to your partner when it's his or her turn to talk? (Idea: *Look at partner and listen politely.*)

Take turns with your partner, retelling the beginning and the middle of the story.
Monitor students as they retell beginning and middle of story.

Activity 3 Story Elements: Identify Characters and Setting—An After-Reading Strategy

Touch the setting(s) as you discuss them. **Elicit** responses to questions. **Guide** as needed.
What was the setting at the beginning of the story? (Student response.)

What clues in the story or pictures made you think that? (Student response.)

What was the setting at the end of the story? (Student response.)

What clues in the story or pictures made you think that? (Student response.)

Ask next two questions if setting changes.
Did the setting stay the same from the beginning to the end of the story or did it change? (Student response.)

Now let's talk about all the characters and what they said and did.

Touch name of character as you ask questions about each character.
Tell me what _____ did or said. (Student response.)
Repeat question for each character as time permits.

The character that the story is mostly about is called the main character. What do you call the character that the story is mostly about? *The main character.*

What character is the story mostly about? (Student response.)

So _____ is the main character.

Who's the main character? (Student response.)

304 *Lesson 77*

Lesson 78

Materials
Teacher: Narrative trade book (from Lesson 76); Picture-Sound Cards for /s/, /r/, /d/, /t/, /n/, /k/, /u/, and /g/
Student: Lined paper

Part A: Phonemic and Phonological Awareness

5 minutes

Teacher Materials:
Picture-Sound Cards for /s/, /r/, /d/, /t/, /n/, /k/, /u/, and /g/

Activity 1 Phoneme Isolation—Initial

Use IWB interactive cards or picture-sound cards. **Elicit** responses. **Guide** as needed.
I'm going to show you two cards and name the object on each card. Then I'll tell you a sound. Think about which word starts with that sound. Let's try it. Today we'll be listening for the sound at the *beginning* of a word.

Show /n/ card; use any of four Picture-Sound Cards per phoneme for activity.
This is a _____. What is this? (Student response.)

Show /u/ card; use any of four Picture-Sound Cards per phoneme for activity.
This is a _____. What is this? (Student response.)

Which word *begins* with **/uuu/**? (Student response.)

Show /g/ card; use any of four Picture-Sound Cards per phoneme for activity.
This is a _____. What is this? (Student response.)

Show /t/ card; use any of four Picture-Sound Cards per phoneme for activity.
This is a _____. What is this? (Student response.)

Which word *begins* with **/g/?** (Student response.)

(Continue the activity with the following examples:
/d/ and /u/: Which word begins with /uuu/?
/u/ and /c/: Which word begins with /uuu/?
/g/ and /r/: Which word begins with /g/?
/s/ and /g/: Which word begins with /g/?)

Activity 2 Phoneme Isolation— Medial

Elicit responses. **Guide** as needed.
You've been doing so well finding the *middle* sound in a word. Let's practice finding **/ooo/, /āāā/,** and **/uuu/.**

First, let's listen for the **/ooo/** sound in the *middle* of the word. What sound are you listening for in the *middle*? /ooo/.

Listen. **Dog.** Say **dog.** *Dog.*

Give me a thumbs-up if you hear **/ooo/** in the *middle* of **dog.** (Thumbs-up.)

Yes, **dog** has the *middle* sound **/ooo/.**

(Continue the activity with the following list of words.
Fog. Fade. Smog. Mine. Sod.)

Now let's listen for the **/āāā/** sound in the *middle* of the word. What sound are you listening for in the middle? /āāā/.

Listen. **Cake.** Say **cake.** *Cake.*

Give me a thumbs-up if you hear **/āāā/** in the *middle* of **cake.** (Thumbs-up.)

Yes, **cake** has the *middle* sound **/āāā/.**

(Continue the activity with the following list of words.
Lake. Pine. Paid. Wait. Bean.)

Now, let's listen for the **/uuu/** sound in the *middle* of the word. What sound are you listening for in the middle? /uuu/.

Listen. **Fun.** Say **fun.** *Fun.*

Give me a thumbs-up if you hear **/uuu/** in the *middle* of **fun.** (Thumbs-up.)

Yes, **fun** has the *middle* sound **/uuu/.**

(Continue the activity with the following list of words.
Soap. Mud. Paint. Pup. Cut.)

Part B: Letter Recognition and Formation

6 minutes

Student Materials:
Lined paper

Activity 1 Letter Recognition—Capital U

Elicit responses to questions. **Guide** as needed. **Write** capital U on the board.
Point to capital U.
Today you'll learn another way to write **u.**
The name of this letter is **capital U.** What letter name? *Capital U.*
Again, what letter name? *Capital U.*
Review as needed.

Activity 2 Letter Formation—Capital U

Now we're going to practice writing **capital U.** When you practice writing, you'll learn not only where to start and stop the letter, but also which way to move your hand when you're making the letter. It's tricky, but you're so smart you'll learn how to write **capital U** very quickly. Watch.

Here's how you write **capital U** in the air.
Model capital U formation in the air (with your back to students).

Watch again.

Now let's practice writing **capital U** in the air. Hold up your writing hand, and make **capital U** in the air.
Guide students as they write capital U in the air.

Let's practice **capital U** again.

Here's how to write **capital U** with your writing hand pointer finger.
Model capital U formation on the board with your finger (with your back to students).

Watch again.

Now let's practice writing **capital U** on your table without using your pencil.
Use your writing hand pointer finger, and make **capital U** on your table.
Guide students as they write capital U on their table or desktop.

Let's practice **capital U** again.

Model writing capital U on the board (with your back to students).
Remember that every letter has a name.
You learned the name of this letter is **capital U.** What letter name? *Capital U.*
Again, what letter name? *Capital U.*

Provide lined paper to students.
Now let's practice writing **capital U** with your pencil.
Guide students as they write capital U on their paper. **Review** as needed.

 Link letter names to letter sounds as they appear in the program as needed.

Part C: Comprehension Strategies

9 minutes

Teacher Materials:
Narrative trade book

Activity 1 Listening Comprehension—A During-Reading Strategy

Direct students to narrative trade book of teacher choice. **Elicit** responses to questions.
Guide as needed.
Today as I read the story, I want you to think about the beginning and the middle of the story

What's the beginning of the story? (Idea: *The events that happened first in the story.*)

What's the middle of the story? (Idea: *The events that happen next in the story.*)

I want you to look at the pictures and listen to the words of the story very carefully. When I'm finished with the story, you'll play the beginning and the middle of the story. You'll play events from the beginning and events from the middle. I'll need your ideas for what events you should play.

Elicit correct listening behavior from students. **Reread** trade book. **Model** prosody during read-aloud.

Guide students to focus on events in beginning and middle of story. **Elicit** answers to questions about events that students could play to show beginning and middle.
Guide as needed.

Lesson 78   **307**

Activity 2 Story Elements: Play the Beginning and Middle—An After-Reading Strategy

Elicit responses to questions. **Guide** as needed.

Now you're going to play the beginning and the middle. What events happened at the beginning of the story? (Student response.)

How would you play those events? (Student response.)

What events happened in the middle of the story? (Student response.)

How would you play those events? (Student response.)

I'll tell the beginning and the middle of the story. As I tell the events, each of you can do the actions I'm telling about. If there are words to say, I'll help you say them.

Coach all students to play story by telling events that happened and guiding students to play or mime the actions. If there is dialogue, say the words and then have students repeat the words.

Praise creativity in playing the beginning of the story. **Prompt** everyone to bow as you applaud them.

Wow, that was fun!

Lesson 79

Materials
Teacher: Narrative trade book (from Lesson 76); 4-Story Map
Student: Lined paper; copy of 4-Story Map

5 minutes

Part A: Phonemic and Phonological Awareness

Activity 1 Phoneme Isolation—Initial

Elicit responses. **Guide** as needed.
Let's work on a sound at the *beginning* of a word. I'm going to say a list of words. Some of the words will have the **/eee/** sound at the *beginning,* and some will not. I'll say the word first, and then you'll say the word.

Remember, we're listening for the **/eee/** sound at the *beginning* of the word. What sound are we listening for? */eee/*.

Listen. **Egg.** Say **egg.** *Egg.*

Give me a thumbs-up if you hear **/eee/** at the *beginning* of **egg.** (Thumbs-up.)

Yes, **egg** *begins* with the sound **/eee/.**

(Continue the activity with the following lists of words.
End. Boat. Elf. Cheese Snow. Enter.
Face. Edge. Pink. Goes. Echo. Shake.)

Activity 2 Phoneme Isolation—Final

Elicit responses. **Guide** as needed.
Now let's work on the sound at the *end* of a word. I'm going to say a list of words. Some of the words will have the **/ōōō/** sound at the *end,* and some will not. I'll say the word first, and then you'll say the word. Think about the *last* sound we hear in each word.

Remember, we're listening for the **/ōōō/** sound at the *end* of the word, as in **snow.** What sound are you listening for at the *end*? */ōō/*.

Listen. **Go.** Say **go**. *Go.*

Give me a thumbs-up if you hear **/ōōō/** at the *end* of **go.** (Thumbs-up.)

Yes, **go** *ends* with the sound **/ōōō/.**

(Continue the activity with the following lists of words.
Mow. Put. Low. Finger. Spoon. So.
No. Guess. Blow. When. Grow. Slow.)

Lesson 79   309

Activity 3 Phoneme Identity—Initial

Elicit responses. **Guide** as needed.
We're going to play a game and find something the same. I'm going to say three words. Listen closely and see if you can tell which sound is the same.

Your turn. What sound is the same in **hit, hi,** and **hope?** /h/.

Yes, **hit, hi,** and **hope** all *begin* with the first sound **/h/.** Let's try some more. What sound is the same in **this, there,** and **then?** /ththth/.

What sound is the same in **ate, age,** and **ape?** /āāā/.

What sound is the same in **that, the,** and **then?** /ththth/.

What sound is the same in **hole, how,** and **home?** /h/.

What sound is the same in **acorn, aim,** and **able?** /āāā/.

Part B: Letter Recognition and Formation

6 minutes

Student Materials:
Lined paper

Activity 1 Letter Recognition Review—Capital U

Elicit responses to questions. **Guide** as needed. **Write** capital U on the board.
Point to capital U.
We learned that this letter is **capital U.** What letter name? *Capital U.*
Again, what letter name? *Capital U.*
Review as needed.

Activity 2 Letter Formation Review—Capital U

Now we're going to practice writing **capital U.** When you practice writing, you'll learn not only where to start and stop the letter, but also which way to move your hand when you're making the letter. It's tricky, but you're so smart you'll learn how to write **capital U** very quickly. Watch.

Here's how you write **capital U** in the air.
Model capital U formation in the air (with your back to students).

Watch again.

Now let's practice writing **capital U** in the air. Hold up your writing hand, and make **capital U** in the air.
Guide students as they write capital U in the air.

Let's practice **capital U** again.

Here's how to write **capital U** with your writing hand pointer finger.
Model capital U formation on the board with your finger (with your back to students).

Watch again.

310   Lesson 79

Now let's practice writing **capital U** on your table without using your pencil.
Use your writing hand pointer finger, and make **capital U** on your table.
Guide students as they write capital U on their table or desktop.

Let's practice **capital U** again.

Model writing capital U on the board (with your back to students).
Remember that every letter has a name.
You learned the name of this letter is **capital U.**
What letter name? *Capital U.*
Again, what letter name? *Capital U.*

Provide lined paper to students.
Now let's practice writing **capital U** with your pencil.
Guide students as they write capital U on their paper. **Review** as needed.

 Link letter names to letter sounds as they appear in the program as needed.

Part C: Comprehension Strategies

 9 minutes

Activity 1 Listening Comprehension—A During-Reading Strategy

Teacher Materials:
Narrative trade book
Story Map

Student Materials:
Story Map

Direct students to narrative trade book of teacher choice. **Elicit** responses to questions.
Guide as needed.
What does an illustrator do? *Draws pictures for books.*

The illustrator of our book is _____. Who's the illustrator of this book?
(Student response.)

Today as I read the story, I want you to look carefully at the pictures of the events at the beginning and the middle of the story. The illustrator made the pictures for you so that the book would be fun to read. Look for what the illustrator did to show the events at the beginning and in the middle. After I read the story, you'll become an illustrator and draw pictures of the beginning and the middle.

Elicit correct listening behavior from students. **Reread** trade book. **Model** prosody during read-aloud.

Guide students to focus on illustrations of events at beginning and middle of story.
Elicit answers to questions about how illustrator shows events at beginning and in middle. **Guide** as needed.

Lesson 79   **311**

Activity 2 Story Elements: Illustrate Main Character and Setting—An After-Reading Strategy

Elicit responses to questions. **Guide** as needed.

Now you'll become an illustrator. What does an illustrator do? (Idea: *Draws pictures for the book.*)

Show Story Map. **Provide** Story Map to each student. **Guide** students to the correct place on sheet to draw pictures of beginning and middle of story.

We'll draw quick pictures to show the events that happened at the beginning and in the middle of the story. What events could we draw in our beginning box? (Student response.)

What events could we draw in our middle box? (Student response.)

Let's work as illustrators to draw an event that happens at the beginning and middle of the story.

Draw illustrations for beginning and middle on Story Map while students draw.

In the next lesson, you'll tell about your illustration.

Save teacher and student illustrations for Lesson 80.

312 Lesson 79

Lesson 80

Materials

Teacher: Narrative trade book (from Lesson 76); 4-Story Map (from Lesson 79); Picture-Sound Cards for /m/, /s/, /r/, /d/, /f/, /t/, /n/, /c/, /o/, /h/, and /g/; Letter Recognition; 8-My Book Review

Student: Lined paper; copy of 4-Story Map (from Lesson 79); copy of 8-My Book Review

Part A: Phonemic and Phonological Awareness

5 minutes

Activity 1 — Phoneme Isolation—Initial

Teacher Materials:
Picture-Sound Cards for /m/, /s/, /r/, /d/, /f/, /t/, /n/, /c/, /o/, /h/, and /g/

Use IWB interactive cards or picture-sound cards. **Elicit** responses. **Guide** as needed.
I'm going to show you two cards and name the object on each card. Then I'll tell you a sound. Think about which word starts with that sound. Let's try it. Today we'll be listening for the sound at the *beginning* of a word.

Show /n/ card; use any of four Picture-Sound Cards per phoneme for activity.
This is a _____. What is this? (Student response.)

Show /h/ card; use any of four Picture-Sound Cards per phoneme for activity.
This is a _____. What is this? (Student response.)

Which word begins with **/nnn/?** (Student response.)

Show /t/ card; use any of four Picture-Sound Cards per phoneme for activity.
This is a _____. What is this? (Student response.)

Show /c/ card; use any of four Picture-Sound Cards per phoneme for activity.
This is a _____. What is this? (Student response.)

Which word begins with **/c/?** (Student response.)

(Continue the activity with the following examples:
/d/ and /ooo/: Which word begins with /ooo/?
/h/ and /r/: Which word begins with /h/?
/u/ and /m/: Which word begins with /uuu/?
/f/ and /g/: Which word begins with /g/?
/s/ and /n/: Which word begins with /nnn/?)

Activity 2 — Phoneme Isolation—Medial

Elicit responses. **Guide** as needed.
You've been doing so well finding the *middle* sound in a word. Now let's practice finding **/ooo/, /āāā/,** and **/uuu/.**

First, let's listen for the **/ooo/** sound in the *middle* of the word. What sound are you listening for in the *middle*? **/ooo/.**

Listen. **Log.** Say **log.** *Log.*

Lesson 80   313

Give me a thumbs-up if you hear **/ooo/** in the *middle* of **log.** (Thumbs-up.)

Yes, **log** has the *middle* sound **/ooo/.**

(Continue the activity with the following list of words.
Pop. Fix. Lot. Mop. Sail.)

Now let's listen for the **/āāā/** sound in the *middle* of the word. What sound are you listening for in the *middle*? /āāā/.

Listen. **Fade.** Say **fade.** *Fade.*

Give me a thumbs-up if you hear **/āāā/** in the *middle* of **fade.** (Thumbs-up.)

Yes, **fade** has the *middle* sound **/āāā/.**

(Continue the activity with the following list of words.
Lot. Maid. Vase. Cut. Bake.)

Now let's listen for the **/uuu/** sound in the *middle* of the word. What sound are you listening for in the *middle*? /uuu/.

Listen. **Bun.** Say **bun**. *Bun.*

Give me a thumbs-up if you hear **/uuu/** in the *middle* of **bun.** (Thumbs-up.)

Yes, **bun** has the *middle* sound **/uuu/.**

(Continue the activity with the following list of words.
Run. Made. Spun. Plum. Box.)

Part B: Letter Recognition and Formation

6 minutes

Activity 1 Letter Recognition Cumulative Review—c/C, o/O, h/H, u/U

Teacher Materials:
Letter Recognition

Student Materials:
Lined paper

Display on IWB or **write** letters and capitals on the board in the order shown.
Elicit responses to questions. **Guide** as needed.
This week you've learned one letter and one capital—**u** and **capital U.**
Let's review all the letters and capitals you've learned. Are you ready?

314   Lesson 80

Letter	Question	Student Response
h	What letter?	h.
C	What letter?	Capital C.
o	What letter?	o.
U	What letter?	Capital U.
O	What letter?	Capital O.
c	What letter?	c.
H	What letter?	Capital H.
u	What letter?	u.

Review as needed.

Activity 2 Letter Formation Cumulative Review—c/C, o/O, h/H, u/U

Write c, capital C, o, capital O, h, capital H, u, and capital U on the board in the order shown (with your back to students). **Provide** lined paper to students.
Show me how you can write these letters and capitals.
Guide students as they write the letters and capitals on their paper. **Review** as needed.

 Link letter names to letter sounds as they appear in the program as needed.

Part C: Comprehension Strategies

9 minutes

Teacher Materials:
Narrative trade book
Story Map
My Book Review

Student Materials:
Story Map
My Book Review

Activity 1 Listening Comprehension—A During-Reading Strategy

Direct students to narrative trade book of teacher choice.
Today I'll read the story one last time. Listen to the story to find the events that happen at the beginning and in the middle of the story. After you listen to the story, you'll get to tell about the illustrations of the beginning and middle of the story that you made in the last lesson.

Elicit correct listening behavior from students. **Reread** trade book. **Model** prosody during read-aloud.

Guide students to focus on events from beginning and middle that they illustrated.
Elicit answers to questions about events in beginning and middle as you read.
Guide as needed.

Lesson 80   315

Activity 2 Retell the Story: Beginning and Middle—An After-Reading Strategy

Show Story Map. **Elicit** correct listening behavior from students.
I'll tell you about my illustration. I'll tell about events I drew for the beginning and the middle of the story.

Model retelling beginning and middle events from your illustrations.

Assign student partners. **Provide** copy of Story Map completed in Lesson 79.
Now it's your turn. You're going to tell a partner all about the events at the beginning and middle of the story from your pictures. Your partner will listen to you the right way. Then you'll listen politely, as your partner tells you about his or her pictures.

When you're done, if there is time, you can show us your illustration and tell the class about your illustration.
Share illustrations with class as time permits, or make a class book of beginnings.

Activity 3 Connections Through Shared Writing— Express Opinions

Show My Book Review. **Elicit** responses to questions. **Guide** as needed.
Think about the two books we read, _____ and _____. Let's talk about the two books. Which one did you like best and why?

Provide copies of My Book Review to students. **Guide** students through completion of My Book Review. **Share** with class as time permits.

316 *Lesson 80*

Lesson 81

Materials
Teacher: Narrative trade book (same book for Lessons 81–85)
Student: Lined paper

Part A: Phonemic and Phonological Awareness

Activity 1 Phoneme Isolation—Initial

Elicit responses. **Guide** as needed.
Let's work on a sound at the *beginning* of a word. I'm going to say a list of words. Some of the words will have the **/b/** sound at the *beginning,* and some will not. I'll say the word first, and then you'll say the word.

Remember, we're listening for the **/b/** sound at the *beginning* of the word. What sound are we listening for? */b/.*

Listen. **Box.** Say **box.** *Box.*

Give me a thumbs-up if you hear */b/* at the *beginning* of **box.** (Thumbs-up.)

Yes, **box** *begins* with the sound **/b/.**

(Continue the activity with the following lists of words.
Bee. Boat. Elf. Cheese. Bone. Enter.
Bang. Edge. Bar. Goes. Bake. Beat.)

Activity 2 Phoneme Isolation—Final

Elicit responses. **Guide** as needed.
Now let's work on the sound at the *end* of a word. I'm going to say a list of words. Some of the words will have the **/vvv/** sound at the *end,* and some will not. I'll say the word first, and then you'll say the word. Think about the *last* sound we hear in each word.

Remember, we're listening for the **/vvv/** sound at the *end* of the word; like in the word **love.** What sound are you listening for at the *end?* */vvv/.*

Listen. **Love.** Say **love.** *Love.*

Give me a thumbs-up if you hear **/vvv/** at the *end* of **love.** (Thumbs-up.)

Yes, **love** *ends* with the sound **/vvv/.**

(Continue the activity with the following lists of words.
Mix. Dove. Low. Cove. Gave. So.
No. Give. Have. When. Save. Shave.)

Lesson 81   **317**

Activity 3 Phoneme Identity—Initial

Elicit responses. **Guide** as needed.
We're going to play a game and find something the same. I'm going to say three words. Listen closely and see if you can tell which sound is the same.

Your turn. What sound is the same in **up, us,** and **under?** /uuu/.

Yes, **up, us,** and **under** all *begin* with the first sound **/uuu/.**

Let's try some more. What sound is the same in **get, goes,** and **game?** /g/.

What sound is the same in **love, lane,** and **let?** /lll/.

What sound is the same in **give, gas,** and **goose?** /g/.

What sound is the same in **like, lean,** and **loose?** /lll/.

What sound is the same in **umbrella, utter,** and **uncut?** /uuu/.

Part B: Letter Recognition and Formation

6 minutes

Student Materials:
Lined paper

Activity 1 Letter Recognition—g

Elicit responses to questions. **Guide** as needed. **Write** g on the board. **Point** to g.
Today you'll learn a new letter.
The name of this letter is **g.** What letter name? *g.*
Again, what letter name? *g.*
Review as needed.

Activity 2 Letter Formation—g

Now we're going to practice writing **g.** When you practice writing, you'll learn not only where to start and stop the letter, but also which way to move your hand when you're making the letter. It's tricky, but you're so smart you'll learn how to write **g** very quickly. Watch.

Here's how you write **g** in the air.
Model g formation in the air (with your back to students).

Watch again.

Now let's practice writing **g** in the air. Hold up your writing hand, and make **g** in the air.
Guide students as they write g in the air.

Let's practice **g** again.

Here's how to write **g** with your writing hand pointer finger.
Model g formation on the board with your finger (with your back to students).

318   Lesson 81

Watch again.

Now let's practice writing **g** on your table without using your pencil. Use your writing hand pointer finger, and make **g** on your table.
Guide students as they write g on their table or desktop.

Let's practice **g** again.

Model writing g on the board (with your back to students).
Remember that every letter has a name.
You learned the name of this letter is **g.** What letter name? *g.*
Again, what letter name? *g.*

Provide lined paper to students.
Now let's practice writing **g** with your pencil.
Guide students as they write g on their paper. **Review** as needed.

 Link letter names to letter sounds as they appear in the program as needed.

Set up a writing center with writing materials and correct models of letters learned so far for students to use in their free time.

Part C: Comprehension Strategies

9 minutes

Teacher Materials:
Narrative trade book

Student Materials:
Lined paper

Activity 1 Title, Author, and Illustrator Identification—A Before-Reading Strategy

Provide a reading center to display books being read so that students can enjoy them again during free time.

Direct students to narrative trade book of teacher choice. **Elicit** responses to questions. **Guide** as needed.

Show front cover of book and allow a student to point to name of title, author, and illustrator as you discuss them.
We'll read a new book today. The title of today's story is _____. What's the title of today's story? (Student response.)

The author of today's story is _____. Who's the author of today's story? (Student response.)

The illustrator of today's story is _____. Who's the illustrator? (Student response.)

Lesson 81 319

Activity 2 Activate Background Knowledge—A Before-Reading Strategy

Choose a topic to activate background knowledge from story you'll read.
Elicit responses to questions. **Guide** as needed.

Your brain has all kinds of information in it. You've already learned lots of things. Today you'll look in your brains to see what you know about _____.

Tell me what you know or experiences you have had that help you know about _____. (Student response.)

Discuss background knowledge of students as it relates to topic chosen.

Provide lined paper. **Model** writing a sentence about what you know.

Write a sentence that tells me what you know about _____. If you need help, ask me.

Monitor students. **Guide** students as needed.

When you think about what you know before you read, it helps you better understand the story. You can connect what you know to the story.

Activity 3 Listening Comprehension—A During-Reading Strategy

Elicit responses to questions. **Guide** as needed.

You've learned about characters and setting. Another thing that you find in stories is events that happen. Events are things that happen in the story. Events happen at the beginning, in the middle, and at the end of a story. So stories have a beginning, a middle, and an end. What do stories have? *A beginning, a middle, and an end.*

Today you're going to think about events that happened at the beginning, the middle, and the end of the story.

In the story of *The Little Red Hen,* the beginning of the story is when the little red hen found the wheat and decided to plant it. That was the first thing that happened in the story. The next thing that happened is that she tried to get help with all the jobs it takes to make wheat into bread. She couldn't get any help. Those were the middle events of story. At the end, because no one would help her, she ate the bread herself. That was the end of the story.

Today as I read the story, I want you to listen carefully and think hard about the events that happened first, next, and last in the story. We will talk about the beginning, the middle, and the end of the story after I read it.

Elicit correct listening behavior from students. **Read** trade book. **Model** prosody during read-aloud.

Ask questions to elicit identification of beginning, middle, and end events in story as well as connecting background knowledge to story as you read. **Guide** as needed.

320 *Lesson 81*

Activity 4 Story Elements: Identify Beginning, Middle, and End—An After-Reading Strategy

Elicit responses to questions. **Guide** as needed.
You're learning all about stories. You know about characters and setting. Now you are learning about the beginning, the middle, and the end of the story. Things happen in stories. We call those things events. What do we call the things that happen in stories? *Events.*

Model identifying beginning, middle, and end events of story.
Listen as I show you how I think about the events that happen at the beginning, the middle, and the end of the story.

Remember that the event that happened first is called the beginning. The events that happened next are called the middle. The events that happened last are called the end.

What do you call the events that happened first in a story? *The beginning.*

What do you call the events that happened next in a story? *The middle.*

What do you call the events that happened last in a story? *The end.*

Lesson 81 **321**

Lesson 82

> **Materials**
> **Teacher:** Narrative trade book (from Lesson 81); Picture-Sound Cards for /a/, /r/, /d/, /k/, /h/, /g/, /l/, and /w/
> **Student:** Lined paper

5 minutes

Teacher Materials:
Picture-Sound Cards for /a/, /r/, /d/, /k/, /h/, /g/, /l/, and /w/

Part A: Phonemic and Phonological Awareness

Activity 1 Phoneme Isolation—Initial

Use IWB interactive cards or picture-sound cards. **Elicit** responses. **Guide** as needed.
I'm going to show you two cards and name the object on each card. Then I'll tell you a sound. Think about which word starts with that sound. Let's try it. Today we'll be listening for the sound at the *beginning* of a word.

Show /l/ card; use any of four Picture-Sound Cards per phoneme for activity.
This is a _____. What is this? (Student response.)

Show /h/ card; use any of four Picture-Sound Cards per phoneme for activity.
This is a _____. What is this? (Student response.)

Which word *begins* with **/lll/?** (Student response.)

Show /r/ card; use any of four Picture-Sound Cards per phoneme for activity.
This is a _____. What is this? (Student response.)

Show /w/ card; use any of four Picture-Sound Cards per phoneme for activity.
This is a _____. What is this? (Student response.)

Which word *begins* with **/www/?** (Student response.)

(Continue the activity with the following examples.
/a/ and /w/: Which word begins with /www/?
/d/ and /l/: Which word begins with /lll/?
/l/ and /g/: Which word begins with /lll/?
/w/ and /c/: Which word begins with /www/?)

Activity 2 Phoneme Isolation—Medial

Elicit responses. **Guide** as needed.
You did so well finding the *beginning* sound and the *ending* sound of a word. Now let's work on the sound in the *middle* of a word. I'm going to say a list of words. Some of the words will have the **/ōōō/** sound in the *middle,* and some will not.

Remember, we're listening for the **/ōōō/** sound in the *middle* of the word, as in **soap.** What sound are you listening for in the *middle?* /ōōō/.

322 Lesson 82

Listen. **Boat.** Say **boat.** *Boat.*

Give me a thumbs-up if you hear **/ōōō/** in the *middle* of **boat.** (Thumbs-up.)

Yes, **boat** has the *middle* sound **/ōōō/.**

(Continue the activity with the following lists of words.
Goat. Pet. Tug. Rope. Coat. Dud.
Black. Load. Hand. Road. Home. Phone.)

Activity 3 Phoneme Categorization—Initial

Elicit responses. **Guide** as needed.
We're going to try a new game today that is like another game we play. I'm going to say three words. Listen closely and see if you can tell which word *does not* belong. I'll show you how to do the first one.

My turn. Listen. **Man, milk, toe.** Which word *doesn't* belong? **Toe.** That is because **man** and **milk** both start with the first sound **/mmm/,** and **toe** starts with the first sound **/t/.** The word **toe** *doesn't* belong. Your turn. Listen. **Mouse, make, sing.** Which word *doesn't* belong? *Sing.*

Right. **Sing** *doesn't* belong because it starts with **/s/,** and **mouse** and **make** start with **/m/.**

(Continue the activity with the following examples:
Side, bath, seed.
Apple, add, fish.
Sick, my, seat.
Act, as, bone.
Sister, mix, milk.)

Part B: Letter Recognition and Formation

6 minutes

Student Materials:
Lined paper

Activity 1 Letter Recognition Review—g

Elicit responses to questions. **Guide** as needed. **Write** g on the board. **Point** to g.
We learned that this letter is **g.** What letter name? *g.*
Again, what letter name? *g.*
Review as needed.

Activity 2 Letter Formation Review—g

Now we're going to practice writing **g.** When you practice writing, you'll learn not only where to start and stop the letter, but also which way to move your hand when you're making the letter. It's tricky, but you're so smart you'll learn how to write **g** very quickly. Watch.

Here's how you write **g** in the air.
Model g formation in the air (with your back to students).

Lesson 82

Watch again.

Now let's practice writing **g** in the air. Hold up your writing hand, and make **g** in the air.
Guide students as they write g in the air.

Let's practice **g** again.

Here's how to write **g** with your writing hand pointer finger.
Model g formation on the board with your finger (with your back to students).

Watch again.

Now let's practice writing **g** on your table without using your pencil. Use your writing hand pointer finger, and make **g** on your table.
Guide students as they write g on their table or desktop.

Let's practice **g** again.

Model writing g on the board (with your back to students).
Remember that every letter has a name.
You learned the name of this letter is **g.** What letter name? *g*.
Again, what letter name? *g*.

Provide lined paper to students.
Now let's practice writing **g** with your pencil.
Guide students as they write g on their paper. **Review** as needed.

 Link letter names to letter sounds as they appear in the program as needed.

Part C: Comprehension Strategies

 9 minutes

Teacher Materials:
Narrative trade book

Activity 1 Listening Comprehension—A During-Reading Strategy

Direct students to narrative trade book of teacher choice.
Stories have things that happen at the beginning, in the middle and at the end. Today we'll read the story again. As I read, listen and look to see whether you can think about the events at the beginning, the middle, and the end of the story. See whether you can tell me what the beginning is by telling what events happened first in the story. Then tell me about the middle by telling the events that happened next. Last tell me about the end by telling what events happened at the end.

Elicit correct listening behavior from students. **Reread** trade book. **Model** prosody during read-aloud.

Ask questions to elicit identification of events at beginning, middle, and end of story. **Guide** as needed.

324 Lesson 82

Activity 2 Story Elements: Identify Beginning, Middle, and End—An After-Reading Strategy

Elicit responses to questions. **Guide** as needed.
You're learning about the beginning, the middle, and the end of a story. The beginning is the events that happened first in the story. What's the beginning? (Idea: *The events that happened first in the story.*)

The middle is the events that happened next in the story. What's the middle? (Idea: *Events that happened next in the story.*)

The end is the events that happen last in the story. What's the end? (Idea: *Events that happened last in the story.*)

Different stories have different events that happened at the beginning, in the middle and at the end of the story. In *Goldilocks and the Three Bears,* the event that happened first is that the three bears went on a walk while their porridge cooled. In the middle of the story, Goldilocks ate the porridge, broke the chair, and slept in the baby bear's bed. At the end of the story, the bears found Goldilocks and chased her away.

Discuss beginning, middle, and end events of story. **Guide** as needed.
In our story, what events happened at the beginning of the story? (Student responses.)

In our story, what events happened in the middle of the story? (Student response.)

In our story, what events happened at the end of the story? (Student response.)

Lesson 82   **325**

Lesson 83

> **Materials**
> **Teacher:** Narrative trade book (from Lesson 81); 4-Story Map
> **Student:** Lined paper

Part A: Phonemic and Phonological Awareness

Activity 1 Phoneme Isolation—Initial

Elicit responses. **Guide** as needed.
Let's work on a sound at the *beginning* of a word. I'm going to say a list of words. Some of the words will have the /iii/ sound at the *beginning*, and some will not. I'll say the word first, and then you'll say the word.

Remember, we're listening for the /iii/ sound at the *beginning* of the word. What sound are we listening for? /iii/.

Listen. **Ice.** Say **ice.** *Ice.*

Give me a thumbs-up if you hear /iii/ at the *beginning* of **ice.** (Thumbs-up.)

Yes, **ice** *begins* with the sound /iii/.

(Continue the activity with the following lists of words.
Island. Hill. End. Iron. Wing. Iceberg.
Whale. Idle. Cup. Stay. Idaho. Drum.)

Activity 2 Phoneme Isolation—Final

Elicit responses. **Guide** as needed.
Now let's work on the sound at the *end* of a word. I'm going to say a list of words. Some of the words will have the /p/ sound at the *end,* and some will not. I'll say the word first, and then you'll say the word. Think about the *last* sound we hear in each word.

Remember, we're listening for the /p/ sound at the *end* of the word, as in **cup.** What sound are you listening for at the *end?* /p/.

Listen. **Top.** Say **top.** *Top.*

Give me a thumbs-up if you hear /p/ at the *end* of **top.** (Thumbs-up.)

Yes, **top** *ends* with the sound /p/.

(Continue the activity with the following lists of words.
Cap. Bird. High. Sleep. Trap. Wash.
Deep. Hold. Stop. Where. Shape. Tape.)

326 Lesson 83

Activity 3 Phoneme Identity—Initial

Elicit responses. **Guide** as needed.
We're going to play a game and find something the same. I'm going to say three words. Listen closely and see if you can tell which sound is the same.

Your turn. What sound is the same in **wind, wet,** and **wake**? /www/.

Yes, **wind, wet,** and **wake** all begin with the first sound **/www/.**

Let's try some more. What sound is the same in **she, shape,** and **shed**? /shshsh/.

What sound is the same in **over, own,** and **oak**? /ōōō/.

What sound is the same in **we, wish,** and **water**? /www/.

What sound is the same in **ship, shy,** and **shin**? /shshsh/.

What sound is the same in **oats, oboe,** and **oasis**? /ōōō/.

Part B: Letter Recognition and Formation

6 minutes

Student Materials:
Lined paper

Activity 1 Letter Recognition—Capital G

Elicit responses to questions. **Guide** as needed. **Write** capital G on the board. **Point** to capital G.
Today you'll learn another way to write **g.**
The name of this letter is **capital G.** What letter name? *Capital G.*
Again, what letter name? *Capital G.*
Review as needed.

Activity 2 Letter Formation—Capital G

Now we're going to practice writing **capital G.** When you practice writing, you'll learn not only where to start and stop the letter, but also which way to move your hand when you're making the letter. It's tricky, but you're so smart you'll learn how to write **capital G** very quickly. Watch.

Here's how you write **capital G** in the air.
Model capital G formation in the air (with your back to students).

Watch again.

Now, let's practice writing **capital G** in the air. Hold up your writing hand, and make **capital G** in the air.
Guide students as they write capital G in the air.

Let's practice **capital G** again.

Here's how to write **capital G** with your writing hand pointer finger.
Model capital G formation on the board with your finger (with your back to students).

Watch again.

Lesson 83   327

Now let's practice writing **capital G** on your table without using your pencil. Use your writing hand pointer finger, and make **capital G** on your table.
Guide students as they write capital G on their table or desktop.

Let's practice **capital G** again.

Model writing capital G on the board (with your back to students).
Remember that every letter has a name.
You learned the name of this letter is **capital G.** What letter name? *Capital G.*
Again, what letter name? *Capital G.*

Provide lined paper to students.
Now let's practice writing **capital G** with your pencil.
Guide students as they write capital G on their paper. **Review** as needed.

 Link letter names to letter sounds as they appear in the program as needed.

Part C: Comprehension Strategies

 9 minutes

Teacher Materials:
Narrative trade book

Story Map

Activity 1 Listening Comprehension—A During-Reading Strategy

Direct students to narrative trade book of teacher choice. **Elicit** responses to questions. **Guide** as needed
You're learning about the beginning, the middle, and the end of a story. The beginning is the first things or events that happened in the story. What's the beginning of a story? *The events that happened first in the story.*

The middle is the events that happened next in the story. What's the middle of the story? *Events that happened next in the story.*

The end is the events that happened last in the story. What's the end of the story? *Events that happened last in the story.*

Today we'll read the story again. As I read, listen and look to see whether you can think about the events at the beginning, the middle, and the end of the book. See whether you can tell me what the beginning is by telling what things happened first in the story. I'll draw a little picture on the board to help me remember the beginning. Then think about what happens next. I'll draw a little picture to help me remember the middle. Then think about what happens last. I'll draw a little picture to help me remember the end.

Elicit correct listening behavior from students. **Reread** trade book. **Model** prosody during read-aloud.

Elicit beginning, middle, and end events in story. **Draw** a quick sketch of the beginning, middle, and end events on board. **Guide** as needed.

328 Lesson 83

Activity 2 **Story Elements: Identify Beginning, Middle, and End—An After-Reading Strategy**

Elicit responses to questions. **Guide** as needed.
You learned about the beginning, the middle, and the end of stories.
What's the beginning? (Idea: *The events that happened first in the story.*)

Show Story Map.
In our story, what events happened at the beginning of the story?
(Student response.)

Model drawing quick sketches of the beginning, middle, and end on Story Map.
I drew a picture on the board to help me remember the beginning of the story. Now I'll use a Story Map and draw a picture in the box for the beginning to help me remember what happens first.

What's the middle? (Idea: *The events that happened next in the story.*)

In our story, what events happened in the middle of the story? (Student response.)

I drew a picture on the board to help me remember the middle of the story. Now I'll use a Story Map and draw a picture in the box for the middle to help me remember what happens next.

What's the end? (Idea: *The events that happen last in the story.*)

In our story, what events happened at the end of the story? (Student response.)

I drew a picture on the board to help me remember the end of the story. Now I'll use a Story Map and draw a picture in the box for the end to help me remember what happens last.

Now I'll be able to remember how to tell about the beginning, the middle, and the end of the story because my Story Map has pictures to remind me.
Save Story Map for Lesson 85.

Lesson 83   **329**

Lesson 84

Materials

Teacher: Narrative trade book (from Lesson 81); Picture-Sound Cards for /ā/, /th/, /u/, /g/, /l/, /w/, /sh/, and /ō/

Student: Lined paper

5 minutes

Teacher Materials:
Picture-Sound Cards for /ā/, /th/, /u/, /g/, /l/, /w/, /sh/, and /ō/

Part A: Phonemic and Phonological Awareness

Activity 1 Phoneme Isolation - Initial

Use IWB interactive cards or picture-sound cards. **Elicit** responses. **Guide** as needed.
I'm going to hold up two cards and name the object on each card. Then I'll tell you a sound. Think about which word starts with that sound. Let's try it. Today, we'll be listening for the sound at the *beginning* of a word.

Show /sh/ card; use any of four Picture-Sound Cards per phoneme for activity.
This is a _____. What is this? (Student response.)

Show /w/ card; use any of four Picture-Sound Cards per phoneme for activity.
This is a _____. What is this? (Student response.)

Which word *begins* with **/shshsh/?** (Student response.)

Show /l/ card; use any of four Picture-Sound Cards per phoneme for activity.
This is a _____. What is this? (Student response.)

Show /ō/ card; use any of four Picture-Sound Cards per phoneme for activity.
This is a _____. What is this? (Student response.)

Which word *begins* with **/ōōō/?** (Student response.)

(Continue the activity with the following examples.
/u/ and /sh/: Which word begins with /shshsh/?
/g/ and /ō/: Which word begins with /ōōō/?
/ō/ and /th/: Which word begins with /ōōō/?
/sh/ and /ā/: Which word begins with /shshsh/?)

Activity 2 Phoneme Isolation—Medial

Elicit responses. **Guide** as needed.
You did so well finding the *beginning* sound and the *ending* sound of a word. Now let's work on the sound in the *middle* of a word. I'm going to say a list of words. Some of the words will have the **/eee/** sound in the *middle,* and some will not.

Remember, we're listening for the **/eee/** sound in the *middle* of the word, as in **met.** What sound are you listening for in the *middle*? */eee/*.

Listen. **Wet.** Say **wet.** *Wet.*

Give me a thumbs-up if you hear **/eee/** in the *middle* of **wet**. (Thumbs-up.)

Yes, **wet** has the *middle* sound **/eee/**.

(Continue the activity with the following lists of words.
Neck. Pet. Pull. Net. Shirt. Corn.
Bed. Truck. Red. Street. Peck. Lamp.)

Activity 3   Phoneme Categorization—Initial

Elicit responses. **Guide** as needed.
We're going to find words that *don't* belong. I'm going to say three words. Listen closely and see if you can tell which word *does not* belong. I'll show you how to do the first one.

My turn. Listen. **Even, eat, miss.** Which word *doesn't* belong? *Miss.* That is because **even** and **eat** both start with the first sound **/ēēē/,** and **miss** starts with the first sound **/mmm/.** The word **miss** *doesn't* belong.

Your turn. Listen. **Read, run, apple.** Which word *doesn't* belong? *Apple.*

Right. **Apple** *doesn't* belong because it starts with **/aaa/,** and **read** and **run** start with **/rrr/.**

(Continue the activity with the following examples:
Dog, sing, deep.
Eagle, snake, eel.
Dance, date, mix.
Red, ask, road.
Milk, deal, dig.)

Part B: Letter Recognition and Formation

6 minutes

Student Materials:
Lined paper

Activity 1   Letter Recognition Review—Capital G

Elicit responses to questions. **Guide** as needed. **Write** capital G on the board.
Point to capital G.
We learned that this letter is **capital G.** What letter name? *Capital G.*
Again, what letter name? *Capital G.*
Review as needed.

Activity 2   Letter Formation Review—Capital G

Now we're going to practice writing **capital G.** When you practice writing, you'll learn not only where to start and stop the letter, but also which way to move your hand when you're making the letter. It's tricky, but you're so smart you'll learn how to write **capital G** very quickly. Watch.

Here's how you write **capital G** in the air.
Model capital G formation in the air (with your back to students).

Watch again.

Lesson 84

Now let's practice writing **capital G** in the air. Hold up your writing hand, and make **capital G** in the air.
Guide students as they write capital G in the air.

Let's practice **capital G** again.

Here's how to write **capital G** with your writing hand pointer finger.
Model capital G formation on the board with your finger (with your back to students).

Watch again.

Now let's practice writing **capital G** on your table without using your pencil. Use your writing hand pointer finger, and make **capital G** on your table.
Guide students as they write capital G on their table or desktop.

Let's practice **capital G** again.

Model writing capital G on the board (with your back to students).
Remember that every letter has a name.

You learned the name of this letter is **capital G**. What letter name? *Capital G.* Again, what letter name? *Capital G.*

Provide lined paper to students.
Now let's practice writing **capital G** with your pencil.
Guide students as they write capital G on their paper. **Review** as needed.

 Link letter names to letter sounds as they appear in the program as needed.

Part C: Comprehension Strategies

9 minutes

Teacher Materials:
Narrative trade book

Activity 1 Listening Comprehension—A During-Reading Strategy

Direct students to narrative trade book of teacher choice. **Elicit** responses to questions. **Guide** as needed.
Today as I read the story, I want you to think about the events that happened in the beginning, the middle, and the end in the story. What's the beginning of a story? (Idea: *The events that happened first in the story.*)

What's the middle of the story? (Idea: *The events that happened next in the story.*)

What's the end of the story? (Idea: *The events that happened last in the story.*)

I want you to look at the pictures and listen to the words of the story very carefully. When I'm finished with the story, we'll play the things that happened at the beginning, the middle, and the end of the story. I'll need your ideas for what events happened first, what happened next, and what happened last.

Elicit correct listening behavior from students. **Reread** trade book. **Model** prosody during read-aloud.

Guide students to focus on beginning, middle, and end events. **Elicit** answers to questions about beginning, middle, and end events in story. **Guide** as needed.

Activity 2 Story Elements: Play the Beginning, Middle, and End—An After-Reading Strategy

Coach all students to play the story by telling the events that happened and guiding students to play or mime the actions. If there is dialogue, say the words and then have students repeat the words. **Elicit** responses to questions. **Guide** as needed.
Now you're going to play the beginning, the middle, and the end of the story. What events happened at the beginning of the story? (Student response.)

How would you play those events? (Student response.)

What events happened in the middle of the story? (Student response.)

How would you play those events? (Student response.)

What events happened at the end of the story? (Student response.)

How would you play those events? (Student response.)

I'll tell the beginning, the middle, and the end of the story. As I tell the events, each of you can do the actions I'm telling about. If there are words to say, I'll help you say them.

Praise creativity in playing the beginning and middle of the story. **Prompt** everyone to bow as you applaud them.

Wow, that was fun!

Lesson 84 **333**

Lesson 85

Materials
Teacher: Narrative trade book (from Lesson 81); 4-Story Map (from Lesson 83); Letter Recognition
Student: Lined paper; copy of 4-Story Map with writing lines

5 minutes

Part A: Phonemic and Phonological Awareness

Activity 1 Phoneme Isolation—Initial

Elicit responses. **Guide** as needed.
Let's work on a sound at the *beginning* of a word. I'm going to say a list of words. Some of the words will have the **/yyy/** sound at the *beginning,* and some will not. I'll say the word first, and then you'll say the word.

Remember, we're listening for the **/yyy/** sound at the *beginning* of the word. What sound are we listening for? */yyy/.*

Listen. **Yes.** Say **yes.** *Yes.*

Give me a thumbs-up if you hear **/yyy/** at the *beginning* of **yes.** (Thumbs-up.)

Right, **yes** *begins* with the sound **/yyy/.**

(Continue the activity with the following lists of words.
Yell. Relax. Year. Stove. Feather. Young.
Shark. You. Mug. Come. Yawn. Yucky.)

Activity 2 Phoneme Isolation—Final

Elicit responses. **Guide** as needed.
Now let's work on the sound at the *end* of a word. I'm going to say a list of words. Some of the words will have the **/ch/** sound at the *end,* and some will not. I'll say the word first, and then you'll say the word. Think about the *last* sound we hear in each word.

Remember, we're listening for the **/ch/** sound at the *end* of the word, as in **much.** What sound are you listening for at the *end?* */ch/.*

Listen. **Such.** Say **such.** *Such.*

Give me a thumbs-up if you hear **/ch/** at the *end* of **such.** (Thumbs-up.)

Yes, **such** *ends* with the sound **/ch/.**

(Continue the activity with the following lists of words.
Scarf. Touch. West. Each. Peach. Dry.
Pool. Witch. Skip. Beach. Round. Pitch.)

334 Lesson 85

Activity 3 Phoneme Identity—Initial

Elicit responses. **Guide** as needed.
We're going to play a game and find something the same. I'm going to say three words. Listen closely and see if you can tell which sound is the same.

Your turn. What sound is the same in **vase, vet,** and **vine?** /vvv/.
Yes, **vase, vet,** and **vine** all begin with the first sound **/vvv/.**

Let's try some more. What sound is the same in **pet, pitch,** and **pond?** /p/.

What sound is the same in **chin, cheek,** and **chance?** /ch/.

What sound is the same in **voice, van,** and **volume?** /vvv/.

What sound is the same in **chill, change,** and **chop?** /ch/.

What sound is the same in **pick, package,** and **pail?** /p/.

Part B: Letter Recognition and Formation

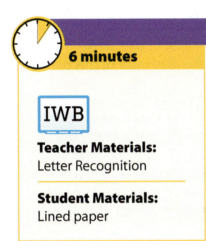

6 minutes

Teacher Materials:
Letter Recognition

Student Materials:
Lined paper

Activity 1 Letter Recognition Cumulative Review—o/O, h/H, u/U, g/G

Display on IWB or **write** letters and capitals on the board in the order shown. **Elicit** responses to questions. **Guide** as needed.
This week you've learned one letter and one capital—**g** and **capital G.** Let's review all the letters and capitals you've learned. Are you ready?

Letter	Question	Student Response
H	What letter?	Capital H.
g	What letter?	g.
u	What letter?	u.
G	What letter?	Capital G.
O	What letter?	Capital O.
h	What letter?	h.
U	What letter?	Capital U.
o	What letter?	o.

Lesson 85   **335**

Activity 2 Letter Formation Cumulative Review—o/O, h/H, u/U, g/G

Write o, capital O, h, capital H, u, capital U, g, and capital G on the board in the order shown (with your back to students). **Provide** lined paper to students.
Show me how you can write these letters and capitals.
Guide students as they write the letters and capitals on their paper. **Review** as needed.

 Link letter names to letter sounds as they appear in the program as needed.

Part C: Comprehension Strategies

 9 minutes

Teacher Materials:
Narrative trade book
Story Map

Student Materials:
Story Map

Activity 1 Listening Comprehension—A During-Reading Strategy

Direct students to narrative trade book of teacher choice. **Elicit** responses to questions. **Guide** as needed.
What does an illustrator do? (Idea: *Make pictures for books.*)

The illustrator of our book is _____. Who's the illustrator of this book? (Student response.)

Today as I read the story, I want you to look carefully at the pictures of the beginning, middle, and end events in the story. The illustrator made the pictures for you so that the book would be fun to read. Look for what the illustrator did to show the events in the beginning, the middle, and the end. After I read the story, you'll become an illustrator and draw pictures of events for the beginning, the middle, and the end of the story. While I read, think about what you want to draw.

Elicit correct listening behavior from students. **Reread** trade book. **Model** prosody during read-aloud.

Guide students to focus on illustrations of events for beginning, middle, and end. **Elicit** answers to questions about how illustrator shows events in beginning, middle, and end of story. **Guide** as needed.

Activity 2 Story Elements: Illustrate Beginning, Middle and End—An After-Reading Strategy

Elicit responses to questions. **Guide** as needed.
Now you'll become an illustrator. Remember that an illustrator is the person who draws the pictures in a story. What does an illustrator do? (Idea: *Draws the pictures for a story.*)

Show Story Map completed in Lesson 83.
I'll show you the pictures I made in the boxes for the beginning, the middle, and the end events.

336 Lesson 85

Provide copy of Story Map to each student.

As an illustrator, your job today is to draw the beginning, the middle, and the end of the story in the Beginning, Middle, and End boxes. When you're finished, you can share your illustrations with your neighbor.

Guide students to draw illustrations in the correct boxes and to work quickly.

Share illustrations with class if time permits, or make a class book of Story Maps.

Activity 3 Collaborate to Strengthen Writing

Show Story Map.

Now let's write about what happened in our story. Watch as I write about the beginning, the middle, and the end of the story.

Model writing 3 separate sentences that tell about the beginning, the middle, and the end of the story.

Now it is your turn to write about what happens **first** at the beginning of the story, **then** what happens in the middle of the story, and **finally** what happens at the end of the story. If you need help, ask me.

Monitor students. **Guide** as needed.

Assign student partners.

Share your writing with your neighbor. Add suggestions to make your neighbor's writing better if you think it needs it.

Model how to give feedback on what was written if it needs it. **Monitor** students. **Guide** as needed.

Lesson 85 **337**

Lesson 86

> **Materials**
> **Teacher:** Narrative trade book (same book for Lessons 86–90), Picture-Sound Cards for /u/, /g/, /l/, /w/, /sh/, /ō/, /v/, and /p/, 1-My Prediction Chart
> **Student:** Lined paper, copy of 1-My Prediction Chart

5 minutes

Teacher Materials:
Picture-Sound Cards for /u/, /g/, /l/, /w/, /sh/, /ō/, /v/, and /p/

Part A: Phonemic and Phonological Awareness

Activity 1 Phoneme Isolation—Initial

Use IWB interactive cards or picture-sound cards. **Elicit** responses. **Guide** as needed.
I'm going to show you two cards and name the object on each card. Then I'll tell you a sound. Think about which word starts with that sound. Let's try it. Today we'll be listening for the sound at the *beginning* of a word.

Show /v/ card; use any of four Picture-Sound Cards per phoneme for activity.
This is a _____. What is this? (Student response.)

Show /sh/ card; use any of four Picture-Sound Cards per phoneme for activity.
This is a _____. What is this? (Student response.)

Which word *begins* with **/vvv/?** (Student response.)

Show /ō/ card; use any of four Picture-Sound Cards per phoneme for activity.
This is a _____. What is this? (Student response.)

Show /p/ card; use any of four Picture-Sound Cards per phoneme for activity.
This is a _____. What is this? (Student response.)

Which word *begins* with **/p/?** (Student response.)

(Continue the activity with the following examples:
/l/ and /v/: Which word begins with /vvv/?
/w/ and /p/: Which word begins with /p/?
/p/ and /u/: Which word begins with /p/?
/v/ and /g/: Which word begins with /vvv/?)

Activity 2 Phoneme Isolation—Medial

Elicit responses. **Guide** as needed.
You did so well finding the *beginning* sound and the *ending* sound of a word. Now let's work on the sound in the *middle* of a word. I'm going to say a list of words. Some of the words will have the **/īīī/** sound in the *middle*, and some will not.

Remember, we're listening for the **/īīī/** sound in the *middle* of the word, as in **bite.** What sound are you listening for in the *middle*? /ī/.

Listen. **Kite.** Say **kite.** *Kite.*

338   Lesson 86

Give me a thumbs-up if you hear /īīī/ in the *middle* of **kite**. (Thumbs-up.)

Yes, **kite** has the *middle* sound /īīī/.

(Continue the activity with the following lists of words.
Light. Duck. Purse. White. Hide. Peas.
Crib. Time. Yellow. Night. Kind. Watch.)

Activity 3 Phoneme Categorization—Initial

Elicit responses. **Guide** as needed.
We're going to find words that *don't* belong. I'm going to say three words. Listen closely and see if you can tell which word *does not* belong.

Your turn. Listen. **Fun, farm, eat.** Which word *doesn't* belong? *Eat.*

Right, **eat** *doesn't* belong because it starts with **/ēēē/**, and **fun** and **farm** start with **/fff/.**

(Continue the activity with the following examples:
It, run, in.
Toss, tank, dip.
Far, fence, eagle.
Table, tell, read.
Igloo, is, even.)

Part B: Letter Recognition and Formation

6 minutes

Student Materials:
Lined paper

Activity 1 Letter Recognition—I

Elicit responses to questions. **Guide** as needed. **Write** l on the board. **Point** to l.
Today you'll learn a new letter.
The name of this letter is **I**. What letter name? *I.*
Again, what letter name? *I.*
Review as needed.

Activity 2 Letter Formation—I

Now we're going to practice writing **I**. When you practice writing, you'll learn not only where to start and stop the letter, but also which way to move your hand when you're making the letter. It's tricky, but you're so smart you'll learn how to write **I** very quickly. Watch.

Here's how you write **I** in the air.
Model l formation in the air (with your back to students).

Watch again.

Now let's practice writing **I** in the air. Hold up your writing hand, and make **I** in the air.
Guide students as they write l in the air.

Lesson 86   **339**

Let's practice **l** again.

Here's how to write **l** with your writing hand pointer finger.
Model l formation on the board with your finger (with your back to students).

Watch again.

Now let's practice writing **l** on your table without using your pencil. Use your writing hand pointer finger, and make **l** on your table.
Guide students as they write l on their table or desktop.

Let's practice **l** again.

Model writing l on the board (with your back to students).
Remember that every letter has a name.
You learned the name of this letter is **l**. What letter name? *l*.
Again, what letter name? *l*.

Provide lined paper to students.
Now let's practice writing **l** with your pencil.
Guide students as they write l on their paper. **Review** as needed.

  Link letter names to letter sounds as they appear in the program as needed.

  Set up a writing center with writing materials and correct models of letters learned so far for students to use in their free time.

Part C: Comprehension Strategies

9 minutes

IWB

Teacher Materials:
Narrative trade book
My Prediction Chart

Student Materials:
Lined paper
My Prediction Chart

Activity 1 Title, Author, and Illustrator Identification—A Before-Reading Strategy

  Provide a reading center to display books being read so that students can enjoy them again during free time.

Direct students to narrative trade book of teacher choice. **Elicit** responses to questions. **Guide** as needed.

Show front cover of book and allow student to point to name of title, author, and illustrator as you discuss them.
We'll read a new story today. The title of today's story is _____. What's the title of today's story? (Student response.)

The author of today's story is _____. Who's the author of today's story? (Student response.)

The illustrator of today's story is _____. Who's the illustrator? (Student response.)

Activity 2 Activate Background Knowledge—A Before-Reading Strategy

Choose a topic to activate background knowledge from story you'll read.
Elicit responses to questions. **Guide** as needed.
Your brain has all kinds of information in it. You've already learned lots of things. Today we're going to look in your brain to see what you know about _____ .

Discuss background knowledge for topic chosen.
Tell me what you know about _____ .

Provide lined paper. **Model** writing a sentence about what you know.
Write a sentence that tells me what you know about _____ . If you need help, ask me.
Monitor students. **Guide** students as needed.

When you think about what you know before you read, it helps you better understand the story. You can connect what you know to what happens in the story.

Activity 3 Make Predictions—A Before-Reading Strategy

Show My Prediction Chart. **Show** title, front and back cover, and pictures inside the book. **Elicit** responses to questions. **Guide** as needed.
The title of today's book is _____ . Write the book title in the box labeled "Book Title".

Now that we know the title of today's book, let's look at the cover and pictures inside the book for clues to make some good guesses for what we think the story will be about. We call our good guesses predictions.

Making good guesses, or predictions, helps us get interested in the story before we read it. Let's make some predictions about the story before I read to you. What do you predict this story will be about? (Student response.)

Write your prediction in the box labeled "I Predict That".
Guide as needed.

What characters do you predict will be in the story? (Student response.)

What do you predict the setting will be? (Student response.)

What do you predict might happen in the story? (Student response.)

When we read the book, we'll check your predictions to see whether they're correct.

Elicit correct listening behavior from students. **Read** trade book. **Model** prosody during read-aloud.

Guide students to confirm predictions and/or connect background knowledge as you read story. **Ask** questions to confirm predictions and/or connect background knowledge. **Guide** as needed.

Lesson 86 **341**

Activity 4 Confirm Predictions—An After-Reading Strategy

Elicit responses to questions. **Guide** as needed.

Now let's check your predictions to see whether they were correct. You predicted that the story was about _____ . Was your prediction correct? (Student response.)

Circle whether or not your prediction was correct in the box labeled "Was My Prediction Correct?".

Guide as needed.

You predicted that _____ were characters in the story. Was your prediction correct? (Student response.)

You predicted that the setting was _____ . Was your prediction correct? (Student response.)

You predicted that some events would be _____ . Was your prediction correct? (Student response.)

Remember that your predictions don't have to be correct. Just making a prediction and listening to see whether your prediction is correct helps you stay interested in the story.

342   *Lesson 86*

Lesson 87

Materials
Teacher: Narrative trade book (from Lesson 86), 4-Story Map
Student: Lined paper

 5 minutes

Part A: Phonemic and Phonological Awareness

Activity 1 Phoneme Isolation—Initial

Elicit responses. **Guide** as needed.
Let's work on a sound at the *beginning* of a word. I'm going to say a list of words. Some of the words will have the **/ūūū/** sound at the *beginning*, and some will not. I'll say the word first, and then you'll say the word.

Remember, we're listening for the **/ūūū/** sound at the *beginning* of the word. What sound are we listening for? /ūūū/.

Listen. **United.** Say **united.** *United.*

Give me a thumbs-up if you hear **/ūūū/** at the *beginning* of **united.** (Thumbs-up.)

Right, **united** *begins* with the sound **/ūūū/.**

(Continue the activity with the following lists of words.
Unit. Tough. Twist. Union. Wing. Uniform.
Cloud. Dust. Ukelele. Fin. Said. Unicorn.)

Activity 2 Phoneme Isolation—Final

Elicit responses. **Guide** as needed.
Now let's work on the sound at the *end* of a word. I'm going to say a list of words. Some of the words will have the **/b/** sound at the *end*, and some will not. I'll say the word first, and then you'll say the word. Think about the *last* sound we hear in each word.

Remember, we're listening for the **/b/** sound at the *end* of the word, as in **tub.** What sound are you listening for at the *end*? /b/.

Listen. **Cab.** Say **cab.** *Cab.*

Give me a thumbs-up if you hear **/b/** at the *end* of **cab.** (Thumbs-up.)

Yes, **cab** *ends* with the sound **/b/.**

(Continue the activity with the following lists of words.
Web. Cub. Vet. Crib. Beef. Jelly.
Knob. Crab. Idea. Sub. Hunts. Globe.)

Lesson 87   343

Activity 3 Phoneme Identity—Initial

Elicit responses. **Guide** as needed.
We're going to play a game and find something the same. I'm going to say three words. Listen closely and see if you can tell which sound is the same.

Your turn. What sound is the same in **egg, edge,** and **echo?** /eee/.

Yes, **egg, edge,** and **echo** all *begin* with the first sound **/eee/.**

Let's try some more. What sound is the same in **bath, bean,** and **bike?** /b/.

What sound is the same in **ice, ivory,** and **idea?** /īī/.

What sound is the same in **enter, elbow,** and **ever?** /eee/.

What sound is the same in **island, iceberg,** and **Idaho?** /īī/.

What sound is the same in **bottle, bush,** and **bacon?** /b/.

Part B: Letter Recognition and Formation

6 minutes

Student Materials:
Lined paper

Activity 1 Letter Recognition Review—l

Elicit responses to questions. **Guide** as needed. **Write** l on the board. **Point** to l.
We learned that this letter is **l.** What letter name? *l.*
Again, what letter name? *l.*
Review as needed.

Activity 2 Letter Formation Review—l

Now we're going to practice writing **l.** When you practice writing, you'll learn not only where to start and stop the letter, but also which way to move your hand when you're making the letter. It's tricky, but you're so smart you'll learn how to write **l** very quickly. Watch.

Here's how you write **l** in the air.
Model l formation in the air (with your back to students).

Watch again.

Now let's practice writing **l** in the air. Hold up your writing hand, and make **l** in the air.
Guide students as they write l in the air.

Let's practice **l** again.

Here's how to write **l** with your writing hand pointer finger.
Model l formation on the board with your finger (with your back to students).

344 Lesson 87

Watch again.

Now let's practice writing **l** on your table without using your pencil. Use your writing hand pointer finger, and make **l** on your table.
Guide students as they write l on their table or desktop.

Let's practice **l** again.

Model writing l on the board (with your back to students).
Remember that every letter has a name.
You learned the name of this letter is **l.** What letter name? *l.*
Again, what letter name? *l.*

Provide lined paper to students.
Now let's practice writing **l** with your pencil.
Guide students as they write l on their paper. **Review** as needed.

 Link letter names to letter sounds as they appear in the program as needed.

Part C: Comprehension Strategies

 9 minutes

Teacher Materials:
Narrative trade book
Story Map

Activity 1 Listening Comprehension—A During-Reading Strategy

Direct students to narrative trade book of teacher choice. **Elicit** responses to questions. **Guide** as needed.
You're learning about the beginning, the middle, and the end of a story.
What's the beginning of a story? (Idea: *The events that happen first in the story.*)

What's the middle of a story? (Idea: *The events that happen next in the story.*)

What's the end of a story? (Idea: *The events that happen last in the story.*)

Show Story Map.
Today we'll read the story again. As I read, listen and think about the events at the beginning, the middle, and the end of the story. After I read, I want to see whether you can tell a partner about the beginning, the middle, and the end by telling what events happened first, what events happened next, and what events happened last. I'll draw little pictures on the board to help you remember the beginning, the middle, and the end.

Help me find the characters and setting(s) in this book as I read by putting up your hand when you see a setting or hear about a character.

Then I'll write the names of the characters and setting(s) on the board as I read.

Elicit correct listening behavior from students. **Reread** trade book. **Model** prosody during read-aloud.

Elicit settings and characters from students as you read. **Write** the setting(s) and characters. **Draw** beginning, middle, and end on Story Map. **Guide** as needed.

Lesson 87 **345**

Activity 2 Story Elements: Identify and Retell the Beginning, Middle, and End—An After-Reading Strategy

Elicit responses to questions. **Guide** as needed.
You're learning about the beginning, the middle, and the end of the story.
What do you call the events that happen first in a story? *The beginning.*

What do you call the events that happen next in a story? *The middle.*

What do you call the events that happen last in a story? *The end.*

Model retelling beginning, middle, and end of story from pictures on Story Map.
I made pictures of the beginning, the middle, and the end of the story on the board. Listen as I retell the beginning, the middle, and the end of the story.

Assign student partners.
Now it's your turn to retell the beginning, the middle, and the end of the story to your partner. You'll retell the whole story. Use the pictures on the Story Map to help you remember what to tell.

How should you listen to your partner when it's his or her turn to talk? (Idea: *Look at partner and listen politely.*)

Take turns with your partner retelling the beginning, the middle, and the end of the story.
Monitor students as they retell beginning, middle, and end of story.

346 *Lesson 87*

Activity 3 **Story Elements: Identify Characters and Setting—An After-Reading Strategy**

What was the setting at the beginning of the story? (Student response.)

Touch the setting(s) on board as you discuss them.
What clues in the story or pictures made you think that? (Student response.)

What was the setting at the end of the story? (Student response.)

Ask next two questions if setting changes.
What clues in the story or pictures made you think that? (Student response.)

Did the setting stay the same from the beginning to the end of the story or did it change? (Student response.)

Now let's talk about all the characters and what they said and did.

Touch name of character on board as you ask questions about each character.
Tell me what _____ did or said. (Student response.)
Repeat question for each character as time permits.

The character that the story is mostly about is called the main character.

What do you call the character that the story is mostly about? *The main character.*

What character is the story mostly about? (Student response.)

So _____ is the main character. Who's the main character? (Student response.)

Lesson 87   **347**

Lesson 88

Materials
Teacher: Narrative trade book (from Lesson 86); Picture-Sound Cards for /l/, /w/, /sh/, /ō/, /v/, /p/, /ch/, and /e/
Student: Lined paper

5 minutes

Teacher Materials: Picture-Sound Cards for /l/, /w/, /sh/, /ō/, /v/, /p/, /ch/, and /e/

Part A: Phonemic and Phonological Awareness

Activity 1   Phoneme Isolation—Initial

Use IWB interactive cards or picture-sound cards. **Elicit** responses. **Guide** as needed.
I'm going to show you two cards and name the object on each card. Then I'll tell you a sound. Think about which word starts with that sound. Let's try it. Today we'll be listening for the sound at the *beginning* of a word.

Show /ch/ card; use any of four Picture-Sound Cards per phoneme for activity.
This is a _____. What is this? (Student response.)

Show /p/ card; use any of four Picture-Sound Cards per phoneme for activity.
This is a _____. What is this? (Student response.)

Which word *begins* with **/ch/?** (Student response.)

Show /v/ card; use any of four Picture-Sound Cards per phoneme for activity.
This is a _____. What is this? (Student response.)

Show /e/ card; use any of four Picture-Sound Cards per phoneme for activity.
This is a _____. What is this? (Student response.)

Which word *begins* with **/eee/?** (Student response.)

(Continue the activity with the following examples:
/sh/ and /ch/: Which word begins with /ch/?
/ō/ and /e/: Which word begins with /eee/?
/e/ and /l/: Which word begins with /eee/?
/ch/ and /w/: Which word begins with /ch/?)

Activity 2   Phoneme Isolation—Medial

Elicit responses. **Guide** as needed.
You've been doing so well finding the *middle* sound in a word. Let's practice finding **/ōōō/, /eee/,** and **/īīī/.**

First let's listen for the **/ōōō/** sound in the *middle* of the word. What sound are you listening for in the *middle*? /ōōō/.

Listen. **Toad.** Say **toad.** *Toad.*

Give me a thumbs-up if you hear **/ōōō/** in the *middle* of **toad.** (Thumbs-up.)

348   Lesson 88

Yes, **toad** has the *middle* sound **/ōōō/.**

(Continue the activity with the following list of words.
Soap. Fox. Bone. Wrote. Read.)

Now let's listen for the /eee/ sound in the *middle* of the word. What sound are you listening for in the *middle*? /eee/.

Listen. **Net.** Say **net.** *Net.*

Give me a thumbs-up if you hear **/eee/** in the *middle* of **net.** (Thumbs-up.)

Yes, **net** has the *middle* sound **/eee/.**

(Continue the activity with the following list of words.
Loan. Fed. Deck. We. Led.)

Now let's listen for the /īī/ sound in the *middle* of the word. What sound are you listening for in the *middle*? /īī/.

Listen. **Bite.** Say **bite.** *Bite.*

Give me a thumbs-up if you hear **/īīī/** in the *middle* of **bite.** (Thumbs-up.)

Yes, **bite** has the *middle* sound **/īīī/.**

(Continue the activity with the following list of words.
Fight. Dime. Pick. Right. Cute.)

Activity 3 Phoneme Categorization—Initial

Elicit responses. **Guide** as needed.
We're going to find words that *don't* belong. I'm going to say three words. Listen closely and see if you can tell which word *does not* belong.

Your turn. Listen. **New, next, fan.** Which word *doesn't* belong? *Fan.*

Right, **fan** *doesn't* belong because it starts with **/fff/,** and **new** and **next** start with **/nnn/.**

(Continue the activity with the following examples:
Call, if, cone.
Off, odd, ten.
No, name, igloo.
Cub, town, cave.
On, otter, feet.)

Lesson 88   **349**

6 minutes

Student Materials:
Lined paper

Part B: Letter Recognition and Formation

Activity 1 Letter Recognition—Capital L

Elicit responses to questions. **Guide** as needed. **Write** capital L on the board. **Point** to capital L.
Today you'll learn another way to write **l.**
The name of this letter is **capital L.** What letter name? *Capital L.*
Again, what letter name? *Capital L.*
Review as needed.

Activity 2 Letter Formation—Capital L

Now we're going to practice writing **capital L.** When you practice writing, you'll learn not only where to start and stop the letter, but also which way to move your hand when you're making the letter. It's tricky, but you're so smart you'll learn how to write **capital L** very quickly. Watch.

Here's how you write **capital L** in the air.
Model capital L formation in the air (with your back to students).

Watch again.

Now let's practice writing **capital L** in the air. Hold up your writing hand, and make **capital L** in the air.
Guide students as they write capital L in the air.

Let's practice **capital L** again.

Here's how to write **capital L** with your writing hand pointer finger.
Model capital L formation on the board with your finger (with your back to students).

Watch again.

Now let's practice writing **capital L** on your table without using your pencil. Use your writing hand pointer finger, and make **capital L** on your table.
Guide students as they write capital L on their table or desktop.

Let's practice **capital L** again.

350 Lesson 88

Model writing capital L on the board (with your back to students).
Remember that every letter has a name.
You learned the name of this letter is **capital L.** What letter name? *Capital L.*
Again, what letter name? *Capital L.*

Provide lined paper to students.
Now let's practice writing **capital L** with your pencil.
Guide students as they write capital L on their paper. **Review** as needed.

 Link letter names to letter sounds as they appear in the program as needed.

Part C: Comprehension Strategies

9 minutes

Teacher Materials:
Narrative trade book

Activity 1 Listening Comprehension—A During-Reading Strategy

Direct students to narrative trade book of teacher choice. **Elicit** responses to questions. **Guide** as needed.
Today as I read the story, I want you to think about the beginning, the middle, and the end of the story. What's the beginning of the story? (Idea: *The events that happen first in the story.*)

What's the middle of the story? (Idea: *The events that happen next in the story.*)

What's the end of the story? (Idea: *The events that happen last in the story.*)

I want you to look at the pictures and listen to the words of the story very carefully. When I'm finished with the story, you'll play the beginning, the middle, and the end of the story. You'll play the events that you find at the beginning, the middle, and the end. I'll need your ideas for what events you should play.

Elicit correct listening behavior from students. **Reread** trade book. **Model** prosody during read-aloud.

Guide students to focus on events in beginning, middle, and end of story. **Elicit** answers to questions about events that students could play to show beginning, middle, and end. **Guide** as needed.

Lesson 88   **351**

Activity 2 Story Elements: Play the Beginning, Middle, and End—An After-Reading Strategy

Coach all students to play story by telling events that happened and guiding students to play or mime the actions. If there is dialogue, say the words and then have students repeat the words. **Elicit** responses to questions. **Guide** as needed.

Now you're going to play the beginning, the middle, and the end of the story. What events happened at the beginning of the story? (Student response.)

How would you play those events? (Student response.)

What events happened in the middle of the story? (Student response.)

How would you play those events? (Student response.)

What events happened at the end of the story? (Student response.)

How would you play those events? (Student response.)

I'll tell the beginning, the middle, and the end of the story. As I tell the events, each of you can do the actions I'm telling about. If there are words to say, I'll help you say them.

Praise creativity in playing beginning of story. **Prompt** everyone to bow as you applaud them.

Wow, that was fun!

352   *Lesson 88*

Lesson 89

Materials
Teacher: Narrative trade book (from Lesson 86); 4-Story Map
Student: Lined paper; of 4-Story Map with writing lines

5 minutes

Part A: Phonemic and Phonological Awareness

Activity 1 Phoneme Isolation—Initial

Elicit responses. **Guide** as needed.
Let's work on a sound at the *beginning* of a word. I'm going to say a list of words. Some of the words will have the **/j/** sound at the *beginning,* and some will not. I'll say the word first, and then you'll say the word.

Remember, we are listening for the **/j/** sound at the *beginning* of the word. What sound are we listening for? /j/.

Listen. **Jet.** Say **jet.** *Jet.*

Give me a thumbs-up if you hear **/j/** at the *beginning* of **jet.** (Thumbs-up.)

Right, **jet** *begins* with the sound **/j/.**

(Continue the activity with the following lists of words.
Jam. Jog. Belt. Joke. Please. Jump.
Plant. Jeans. Chain. Gate. Jaguar. Juicy.)

Activity 2 Phoneme Isolation—Final

Elicit responses. **Guide** as needed.
Now let's work on the sound at the *end* of a word. I'm going to say a list of words. Some of the words will have the **/īī/** sound at the *end,* and some will not. I'll say the word first, and then you'll say the word. Think about the *last* sound we hear in each word.

Remember, we are listening for the **/īī/** sound at the *end* of the word, as in **my.** What sound are you listening for at the *end?* /īī/.

Listen. **Fly.** Say **fly.** *Fly.*

Give me a thumbs-up if you hear **/īī/** at the *end* of **fly.** (Thumbs-up.)

Yes, **fly** *ends* with the sound **/īī/.**

(Continue the activity with the following lists of words.
High. Grape. Tie. Sky. Sting. Crib.
Cry. Shy. Thumb. Sigh. Crutch. Fry.)

Lesson 89   353

Activity 3 Phoneme Identity—Initial

Elicit responses. **Guide** as needed.
We're going to play a game and find something the same. I'm going to say three words. Listen closely and see if you can tell which sound is the same.

Your turn. What sound is the same in **yell, yawn,** and **yolk?** /yyy/.
Yes, **yell, yawn,** and **yolk** all *begin* with the first sound **/yyy/.**

Let's try some more. What sound is the same in **jazz, job,** and **July?** /j/.

What sound is the same in **unicorn, union,** and **unit?** /ūūū/.

What sound is the same in **yes, yellow,** and **young?** /yyy/.

What sound is the same in **universe, use,** and **united?** /ūūū/.

What sound is the same in **jeep, juice,** and **journal?** /j/.

Part B: Letter Recognition and Formation

6 minutes

Student Materials:
Lined paper

Activity 1 Letter Recognition Review—Capital L

Elicit responses to questions. **Guide** as needed. **Write** capital L on the board.
Point to capital L.
We learned that this letter is **capital L.** What letter name? *Capital L.*
Again, what letter name? *Capital L.*
Review as needed.

Activity 2 Letter Formation Review—Capital L

Now we're going to practice writing **capital L.** When you practice writing, you'll learn not only where to start and stop the letter, but also which way to move your hand when you're making the letter. It's tricky, but you're so smart you'll learn how to write **capital L** very quickly. Watch.

Here's how you write **capital L** in the air.
Model capital L formation in the air (with your back to students).

Watch again.

Now let's practice writing **capital L** in the air. Hold up your writing hand, and make **capital L** in the air.
Guide students as they write capital L in the air.

Let's practice **capital L** again.

Here's how to write **capital L** with your writing hand pointer finger.
Model capital L formation on the board with your finger (with your back to students).

Watch again.

354 Lesson 89

Now let's practice writing **capital L** on your table without using your pencil.
Use your writing hand pointer finger, and make **capital L** on your table.
Guide students as they write capital L on their table or desktop.

Let's practice **capital L** again.

Model writing capital L on the board (with your back to students).
Remember that every letter has a name.
You learned the name of this letter is **capital L.** What letter name? *Capital L.*
Again, what letter name? *Capital L.*

Provide lined paper to students.
Now let's practice writing **capital L** with your pencil.
Guide students as they write capital L on their paper. **Review** as needed.

 Link letter names to letter sounds as they appear in the program as needed.

Part C: Comprehension Strategies

 9 minutes

 IWB

Teacher Materials:
Narrative trade book

Story Map

Student Materials:
Story Map

Activity 1 Listening Comprehension—A During-Reading Strategy

Direct students to narrative trade book of teacher choice. **Elicit** responses to questions. **Guide** as needed.
What does an illustrator do? (Idea: *Draws pictures for books.*)

The illustrator of our book is _____. Who's the illustrator of this book? (Student response.)

Today as I read the story, I want you to look carefully at the pictures of the events for the beginning, the middle, and the end of the story. The illustrator made the pictures for you so that the book would be fun to read. Look for what the illustrator did to show the events at the beginning, the middle, and the end. After I read the story, you'll become an illustrator and draw pictures of the beginning, the middle, and the end.

Elicit correct listening behavior from students. **Reread** trade book. **Model** prosody during read-aloud.

Guide students to focus on illustrations of events for beginning, middle, and end of story. **Elicit** answers to questions about how illustrator shows events for beginning, middle, and end. **Guide** as needed.

Lesson 89

Activity 2 Story Grammar: Illustrate Main Character and Setting—An After-Reading Strategy

Show Story Map. **Elicit** responses to questions. **Guide** as needed.
Now you'll become an illustrator. What does an illustrator do? (Idea: *Draw pictures for the book.*)

Guide students to the correct place on sheet to draw pictures of beginning, middle, and≈end of story.

We'll draw quick pictures to show the events that happened at the beginning, the middle, and the end of the story. What events could we draw in our Beginning box? (Student response.)

What events could we draw in our Middle box? (Student response.)

What events could we draw in our End box? (Student response.)

Let's work as illustrators to draw events that happen at the beginning, the middle, and the end of the story.
Draw illustrations for beginning, middle, and end on Story Map while students draw.

In the next lesson, you'll tell about your illustration.
Save teacher and student illustrations for Lesson 90.

Activity 3 Collaborate to Strengthen Writing

Show Story Map.
Now let's write about what happened in our story. Watch as I write about the beginning, the middle, and the end of the story.
Model writing 3 separate sentences that tell about the beginning, the middle, and the end of the story.

Now it is your turn to write about what happens **first** at the beginning of the story, **then** what happens in the middle of the story, and **finally** what happens at the end of the story. If you need help, ask me.
Monitor students. **Guide** as needed.

Assign student partners.
Share your writing with your neighbor. Add suggestions to make your neighbor's writing better if you think it needs it.
Model how to give feedback on what was written if it needs it. **Monitor** students.
Guide as needed.

356 *Lesson 89*

Lesson 90

> **Materials**
>
> **Teacher:** Narrative trade book (from Lesson 86); Story Map (from Lesson 89); Picture-Sound Cards for /n/, /c/, /o/, /h/, /ā/, /th/, /u/, /g/, /l/, /w/, /sh/, /ō/, /v/, /p/, /ch/, and /e/; Letter Recognition; 8-My Book Review
>
> **Student:** Lined paper; copy of Story Map completed in Lesson 89; copy of 8-My Book Review

Part A: Phonemic and Phonological Awareness

5 minutes

Teacher Materials:
Picture-Sound Cards for /n/, /c/, /o/, /h/, /ā/, /th/, /u/, /g/, /l/, /w/, /sh/, /ō/, /v/, /p/, /ch/, and /e/

Activity 1 Phoneme Isolation—Initial

Use IWB interactive cards or picture-sound cards. **Elicit** responses. **Guide** as needed. I'm going to show you two cards and name the object on each card. Then I'll tell you a sound. Think about which word starts with that sound. Let's try it. Today we'll be listening for the sound at the *beginning* of a word.

Show /l/ card; use any of four Picture-Sound Cards per phoneme for activity.
This is a _____. What is this? (Student response.)

Show /n/ card; use any of four Picture-Sound Cards per phoneme for activity.
This is a _____. What is this? (Student response.)

Which word *begins* with **/lll/?** (Student response.)

Show /c/ card; use any of four Picture-Sound Cards per phoneme for activity.
This is a _____. What is this? (Student response.)

Show /w/ card; use any of four Picture-Sound Cards per phoneme for activity.
This is a _____. What is this? (Student response.)

Which word *begins* with **/www/?** (Student response.)

Continue the activity with the following examples:
/h/ and /sh/: Which word begins with /shshsh/?
/ō/ and /o/: Which word begins with /ōōō/?
/v/ and /ā/: Which word begins with /vvv/?
/th/ and /p/: Which word begins with /p/?
/ch/ and /u/: Which word begins with /ch/?
/g/ and /e/: Which word begins with /eee/?)

Lesson 90   357

Activity 2 Phoneme Isolation—Medial

Elicit responses. **Guide** as needed.

You've been doing so well finding the *middle* sound in a word. Let's practice finding **/ōōō/, /eee/,** and **/īīī/.**

First let's listen for the **/ōōō/** sound in the *middle* of the word. What sound are you listening for in the *middle?* /ōōō/.

Listen. **Joke.** Say **joke.** *Joke.*

Give me a thumbs-up if you hear **/ōōō/** in the *middle* of **joke.** (Thumbs-up.)

Yes, **joke** has the *middle* sound **/ōōō/.**

(Continue the activity with the following list of words.
Foam. Chin. Coke. Rope. Hot.)

First let's listen for the **/eee/** sound in the *middle* of the word. What sound are you listening for in the middle? /eee/.

Listen. **Guess.** Say **guess.** *Guess.*

Give me a thumbs-up if you hear **/eee/** in the *middle* of **guess.** (Thumbs-up.)

Yes, **guess** has the *middle* sound **/eee/.**

(Continue the activity with the following list of words.
Lock. Yes. Mesh. Feet. Wreck.)

First let's listen for the **/īīī/** sound in the *middle* of the word. What sound are you listening for in the middle? /īīī/.

Listen. **Ride.** Say **ride.** *Ride.*

Give me a thumbs-up if you hear **/īīī/** in the *middle* of **ride.** (Thumbs-up.)

Yes, **ride** has the *middle* sound **/īīī/.**

(Continue the activity with the following list of words.
Tight. Mice. Drip. Side. Bump.)

Activity 3 Phoneme Categorization—Initial

Elicit responses. **Guide** as needed.
We're going to find words that *don't* belong. I'm going to say three words. Listen closely and see if you can tell which word *does not* belong.

Your turn. Listen. **Hat, hope, next.** Which word *doesn't* belong? *Next.*

Right. **Next** *doesn't* belong because it starts with **/nnn/,** and **hat** and **hope** start with **/h/.**

(Continue the activity with the following examples:
Aim, corn, ache.
This, then, olive.
Heat, have, candle.
Able, off, acorn.
There, those, nice.)

Part B: Letter Recognition and Formation

6 minutes

IWB

Teacher Materials:
Letter Recognition

Student Materials:
Lined paper

Activity 1 Letter Recognition Cumulative Review—h/H, u/U, g/G, l/L

Display on IWB or **write** letters and capitals on the board in the order shown.
Elicit responses to questions. **Guide** as needed.
This week you've learned one letter and one capital—**l** and **capital L.**
Let's review all the letters and capitals you've learned. Are you ready?

Letter	Question	Student Response
H	What letter?	Capital H.
I	What letter?	l.
U	What letter?	Capital U.
g	What letter?	g.
L	What letter?	Capital L.
h	What letter?	h.
u	What letter?	u.
G	What letter?	Capital G.

Review as needed.

Lesson 90 **359**

Activity 2 | Letter Formation Cumulative Review—h/H, u/U, g/G, l/L

Write h, capital H, u, capital U, g, capital G, l, and capital L on the board in the order shown (with your back to students). **Provide** lined paper to students.
Show me how you can write these letters and capitals.
Guide students as they write the letters and capitals on their paper. **Review** as needed.

 Link letter names to letter sounds as they appear in the program as needed.

Part C: Comprehension Strategies

9 minutes

Teacher Materials:
Narrative trade book
Story Map
My Book Review

Student Materials:
Story Map
My Book Review

Activity 1 | Listening Comprehension—A During-Reading Strategy

Direct students to narrative trade book of teacher choice.
Today I'll read the story one last time. Listen to the story to remember the events that happen at the beginning, the middle, and the end of the story. After you listen to the story, you'll get to tell about the illustrations that you made in the last lesson.

Elicit correct listening behavior from students. **Reread** trade book. **Model** prosody.
Guide students to focus on events from beginning, middle, and end that they illustrated.
Elicit answers to questions about events in beginning, middle, and end as you read.

Activity 2 | Retell the Story: Beginning, Middle, and End—An After-Reading Strategy

Assign student partners. **Provide** copy of Story Map completed in Lesson 89.
You're going to tell a partner all about the events at the beginning, the middle, and the end of the story from your pictures. Your partner will listen to you the right way. Then you'll listen politely as your partner tells you about his or her pictures.

When you're done, if there is time, you can show the class your illustrations and tell the events from the beginning, the middle, and the end.
Share illustrations with class as time permits, or make a class book of beginnings.

Activity 3 | Connections Through Shared Writing—Express Opinions

Show My Book Review. **Elicit** responses to questions. **Guide** as needed.

Think about the two books we read, _____ and _____. Let's talk about the two books. Which one did you like best and why?

Provide copies of My Book Review to students. **Guide** students through completion of My Book Review. **Share** with class as time permits.

Lesson 91

Materials
Teacher: Narrative trade book (same book for Lessons 91–95), 1-My Prediction Chart
Student: Lined paper, Copy of 1-My Prediction Chart

5 minutes

Part A: Phonemic and Phonological Awareness

Activity 1 Phoneme Isolation—Initial

Elicit responses. **Guide** as needed.
Let's work on a sound at the *beginning* of a word. I'm going to say a list of words. Some of the words will have the **/kw/** sound at the *beginning*, and some will not. I'll say the word first, and then you'll say the word.

Remember, we're listening for the **/kw/** sound at the *beginning* of the word. What sound are we listening for? /kw/.

Listen. **Quit.** Say **quit.** *Quit.*

Give me a thumbs-up if you hear **/kw/** at the *beginning* of **quit.** Student response.

Right, **quit** *begins* with the sound **/kw/.**

(Continue the activity with the following lists of words.
Queen. Raft. Quiet. Quote. Lick. Proud.
Quite. Wrote. Chick. Quick. Paint. Question.)

Activity 2 Phoneme Isolation—Final

Elicit responses. **Guide** as needed.
Now let's work on the sound at the *end* of a word. I'm going to say a list of words. Some of the words will have the **/ûr/** sound at the *end,* and some will not. I'll say the word first, and then you'll say the word. Think about the *last* sound we hear in each word.

Remember, we're listening for the **/ûr/** sound at the *end* of the word, as in **stir.** What sound are you listening for at the *end*? /ûr/.

Lesson 91   **361**

Listen. **Her.** Say **her.** *Her.*

Give me a thumbs-up if you hear **/ûr/** at the *end* of **her.** Student response.

Yes, **her** ends with the sound **/ûr/.**

(Continue the activity with the following lists of words.
Purr. Grape. Tie. Sure. Sure. Fur.
Were. Shy. Blur. Sigh. Crutch. Sir.)

Activity 3 Phoneme Identity—Final

Elicit responses. **Guide** as needed.
We're going to play a game and find something the same. I'm going to say three words. Listen closely and see if you can tell which sound is the same. I'll show you how to do the first one.

My turn. What sound is the same in **team, home,** and **rim? /mmm/.** That is because **team, home,** and **rim** all *end* with the last sound **/mmm/.**

Your turn. What sound is the same in **team, home,** and **rim?** */mmm/.*

Yes, **team, home,** and **rim** all *end* with the last sound **/mmm/.** Let's try some more.

What sound is the same in **gas, miss,** and **toss?** */sss/.*

What sound is the same in **me, we,** and **see?** */ēēē/.*

What sound is the same in **time, comb,** and **foam?** */mmm/.*

What sound is the same in **key, she,** and **free?** */ēēē/.*

What sound is the same in **juice, loss,** and **race?** */sss/.*

Part B: Letter Recognition and Formation

6 minutes

Student Materials:
Lined paper

Activity 1 Letter Recognition—w

Elicit responses to questions. **Guide** as needed. **Write** w on the board. **Point** to w.
Today you'll learn a new letter. The name of this letter is **w.** What letter name? *w.*
Again, what letter name? *w.*
Review as needed.

Activity 2 **Letter Formation—w**

Now we're going to practice writing **w.** When you practice writing, you'll learn not only where to start and stop the letter, but also which way to move your hand when you're making the letter. It's tricky, but you're so smart you'll learn how to write **w** very quickly. Watch.

Here's how you write **w** in the air.
Model w formation in the air (with your back to students).

Watch again.

Now let's practice writing **w** in the air. Hold up your writing hand, and make **w** in the air.
Guide students as they write w in the air.

Let's practice **w** again.

Here's how to write **w** with your writing hand pointer finger.
Model w formation on the board with your finger (with your back to students).

Watch again.

Now let's practice writing **w** on your table without using your pencil. Use your writing hand pointer finger, and make **w** on your table.

Guide students as they write w on their table or desktop.

Let's practice **w** again.

Model writing w on the board (with your back to students).
Remember that every letter has a name.
You learned the name of this letter is **w.** What letter name? *w.*
Again, what letter name? *w.*

Provide lined paper to students.
Now let's practice writing **w** with your pencil.
Guide students as they write w on their paper. **Review** as needed.

Link letter names to letter sounds as they appear in the program as needed.

Set up a writing center with writing materials and correct models of letters learned so far for students to use in their free time.

Lesson 91   **363**

Part C: Comprehension Strategies

9 minutes

Teacher Materials:
Narrative trade book

My Prediction Chart

Student Materials:
Lined paper

My Prediction Chart

Activity 1 Title, Author, and Illustrator Identification—A Before- Reading Strategy

Provide a reading center to display books being read so that students can enjoy them again during free time.

Direct students to narrative trade book of teacher choice. **Elicit** responses to questions. **Guide** as needed.

Show front cover of book and allow student to point to name of title, author, and illustrator as you discuss them.
We'll read a new book today. The title of today's story is _____ . What's the title of today's story? (Student response.)

The author of today's story is _____ . Who's the author of today's story? (Student response.)

The illustrator of today's story is _____ . Who's the illustrator? (Student response.)

Activity 2 Activate Background Knowledge—A Before-Reading Strategy

Choose a topic to activate background knowledge from story you'll read. **Elicit** responses to questions. **Guide** as needed.
Your brain has all kinds of information in it. You have already learned lots of things. So now you'll look in your brains to see what you know about _____ .

Tell me what you know or experiences you have had that help you know about this topic. (Student response.)
Discuss background knowledge of students as it relates to topic chosen.

Provide lined paper. **Model** writing a sentence about what you know.
Write a sentence that tells me what you know about _____ . If you need help, ask me.
Monitor students. **Guide** students as needed.

When you think about what you know before you read, it helps you better understand the story. You can connect what you know to the story.

Activity 3 Make Predictions—A Before-Reading Strategy

Show title, front and back cover, and pictures inside book. **Elicit** responses to questions. **Guide** as needed.
The title of today's book is _____ . Write the book title in the box labeled "Book Title".

364 Lesson 91

Now that you know the title of today's book, let's look at the cover and pictures inside the book for clues to make some good guesses of what you think the story will be about. We call our good guesses predictions. What do you call your good guesses? *Predictions.*

Making predictions helps you get interested in the story before you read it. Let's make some predictions about the story before I read it to you. What do you predict this story will be about? (Student response.)

Write your prediction in the box labeled "I Predict That".
Guide as needed.

What characters do you predict will be in the story? (Student response.)

What do you predict the setting will be? (Student response.)

What do you predict might happen in the story? (Student response.)

When we read the book you'll check your predictions to see whether they're correct.

Elicit correct listening behavior from student. **Read** trade book. **Model** prosody during read-aloud.
Guide students to confirm predictions and/or connect background knowledge as you read story. **Ask** questions to confirm predictions and/or connect background knowledge. **Guide** as needed.

Activity 4 Confirm Predictions—An After-Reading Strategy

Elicit responses to questions. **Guide** as needed.
Now let's check your predictions to see whether they were correct. You predicted that the story was about _____. Was your prediction correct? (Student response.)

You predicted that _____ were characters in the story. Was your prediction correct? (Student response.)

Circle whether or not your prediction was correct in the box labeled "Was My Prediction Correct?"
Guide as needed.

You predicted that the setting was _____. Was your prediction correct? (Student response.)

You predicted that some events would be _____. Was your prediction correct? (Student response.)

Remember that your predictions don't have to be correct. Just making a prediction and listening to see whether your prediction is correct helps you stay interested in the story.

Lesson 91 **365**

Lesson 92

Materials
Teacher: Narrative trade book (from Lesson 91); Picture-Sound Cards for /sh/, /ō/, /v/, /p/, /ch/, /e/, /b/, and /ī/
Student: Lined paper

5 minutes

Teacher Materials:
Picture-Sound Cards for /sh/, /ō/, /v/, /p/, /ch/, /e/, /b/, and /ī/

Part A: Phonemic and Phonological Awareness

Activity 1 Phoneme Isolation—Initial

Use IWB interactive cards or picture-sound cards. **Elicit** responses. **Guide** as needed.
I'm going to show you two cards and name the object on each card. Then I'll tell you a sound. Think about which word starts with that sound. Let's try it. Today we'll be listening for the sound at the *beginning* of a word.

Show /b/ card; use any of four Picture-Sound Cards per phoneme for activity.
This is a _____. What is this? (Student response.)

Show /ch/ card; use any of four Picture-Sound Cards per phoneme for activity.
This is a _____. What is this? (Student response.)

Which word *begins* with **/b/?** (Student response.)

Show /e/ card; use any of four Picture-Sound Cards per phoneme for activity.
This is a _____. What is this? (Student response.)

Show /ī/ card; use any of four Picture-Sound Cards per phoneme for activity.
This is a _____. What is this? (Student response.)

Which word *begins* with **/īīī/?** (Student response.)

(Continue the activity with the following examples:
/v/ and /ī/: Which word begins with /īīī/?
/b/ and /p/: Which word begins with /b/?
/ī/ and /sh/: Which word begins with /īīī/?
/ō/ and /b/: Which word begins with /b/?)

Activity 2 Phoneme Isolation—Medial

Elicit responses. **Guide** as needed.
You did so well finding the *beginning* sound and the *ending* sound of a word. Now let's work on the sound in the *middle* of a word. I'm going to say a list of words. Some of the words will have the **/oo/** sound in the *middle,* and some will not.

Remember, we're listening for the **/oo/** sound in the *middle* of the word, as in **soup.** What sound are you listening for in the *middle?* /oo/.

Listen. **Hoop.** Say **hoop.** *Hoop.*

366   Lesson 92

Give me a thumbs-up if you hear **/oo/** in the *middle* of **hoop.** Student response.

Yes, **hoop** has the *middle* sound **/oo/.**

(Continue the activity with the following lists of words.
Tube. Paid. Tide. Moon. Boot. Bus.
Green. Hoot. Food. Hose. Pretty. Soon.)

Activity 3 Phoneme Categorization—Initial

Elicit responses. **Guide** as needed.
We're going to find words that *don't* belong. I'm going to say three words. Listen closely and see if you can tell which word *does not* belong.

Your turn. Listen. **Up, under, hit.** Which word *doesn't* belong? *Hit.*

Right, **hit** *doesn't* belong because it starts with **/h/,** and **up** and **under** start with **/uuu/.**

(Continue the activity with the following examples:
Girl, angel, guess.
Lucky, live, thing.
Utter, uncle, April.
Give, thumb, goose.
Lip, last, happy.)

Activity 4 Phoneme Blending

Elicit responses. **Guide** as needed.
We have a new activity today that is going help you to become very good readers. I'm going to say a word very slowly so you can hear each sound. You need to listen carefully so you can put the sounds together and say the word. Let me show you how it works.

Model holding each continuous sound for 2 to 3 seconds without stopping between sounds.
My turn. Listen. **/mmm/ /ēēē/.** Listen again. **/mmm/ /ēēē/.** I can put it together. **Me.**
Your turn. Listen. **/mmm/ /ēēē/.** Listen again. **/mmm/ /ēēē/.** Put it together. *Me.*

(Continue the activity with the following examples:
knee [nnn-ēēē], see [sss-ēēē], we [www-ēēē].)

Lesson 92   **367**

6 minutes

Student Materials:
Lined paper

Part B: Letter Recognition and Formation

Activity 1 Letter Recognition Review—w

Elicit responses to questions. **Guide** as needed. **Write** w on the board. **Point** to w.
We learned that this letter is **w.** What letter name? *w.*
Again, what letter name? *w.*
Review as needed.

Activity 2 Letter Formation Review—w

Now we're going to practice writing **w.** When you practice writing, you'll learn not only where to start and stop the letter, but also which way to move your hand when you're making the letter. It's tricky, but you're so smart you'll learn how to write **w** very quickly. Watch.

Here's how you write **w** in the air.
Model w formation in the air (with your back to students).

Watch again.

Now let's practice writing **w** in the air. Hold up your writing hand, and make **w** in the air.
Guide students as they write w in the air.

Let's practice **w** again.

Here's how to write **w** with your writing hand pointer finger.
Model w formation on the board with your finger (with your back to students).

Watch again.

Now let's practice writing **w** on your table without using your pencil. Use your writing hand pointer finger, and make **w** on your table.
Guide students as they write w on their table or desktop.

Let's practice **w** again.

Model writing w on the board (with your back to students).
Remember that every letter has a name.
You learned the name of this letter is **w.** What letter name? *w.*
Again, what letter name? *w.*

Provide lined paper to students.
Now let's practice writing **w** with your pencil.
Guide students as they write w on their paper. **Review** as needed.

 Link letter names to letter sounds as they appear in the program as needed.

368 Lesson 92

Part C: Comprehension Strategies

9 minutes

Teacher Materials:
Narrative trade book

Activity 1 Listening Comprehension—A During-Reading Strategy

Direct students to narrative trade book of teacher choice. **Elicit** responses to questions. **Guide** as needed.

You've learned all about stories. Stories have characters, a setting, a beginning, a middle, and an end. Listen to the story again and see whether you can tell me all the parts of the story after I read it.

Elicit correct listening behavior from students. **Reread** trade book. **Model** prosody during read-aloud.

Ask questions to elicit identification of characters, setting, and events. **Guide** as needed.

Activity 2 Story Elements: Identify Characters, Setting, Beginning, Middle, and End—An After-Reading Strategy

Elicit responses to questions. **Guide** as needed.

You listened to the story. Now you can tell me all the parts of the story that you heard as you listened. What characters are in the story? (Student response.)

Who do you think is the main character? (Student response.)

What's the setting of the story? (Student response.)

Does the setting change or stay the same? (Student response.)

What events happened at the beginning? (Student response.)

What events happened in the middle? (Student response.)

What events happened at the end? (Student response.)

You told all the parts of the story. Excellent job listening to the story and remembering all the parts.

Lesson 92

Lesson 93

Materials
Teacher: Narrative trade book (from Lesson 91)
Student: Lined paper

5 minutes

Part A: Phonemic and Phonological Awareness

Activity 1 Phoneme Isolation—Initial

Elicit responses. **Guide** as needed.
Let's work on a sound at the *beginning* of a word. I'm going to say a list of words. Some of the words will have the **/zzz/** sound at the *beginning,* and some will not. I'll say the word first, and then you'll say the word.

Remember, we're listening for the **/zzz/** sound at the *beginning* of the word. What sound are we listening for? /zzz/.

Listen. **Zoo.** Say **zoo.** *Zoo.*

Give me a thumbs-up if you hear **/zzz/** at the *beginning* of **zoo.** Student response.

Right, **zoo** *begins* with the sound **/zzz/.**

(Continue the activity with the following lists of words.
Zip. Soap. Zoom. Zero. Tan. Weed.
Zebra. Book. Rope. Zone. Candle. Zigzag.)

Activity 2 Phoneme Isolation—Final

Elicit responses. **Guide** as needed.
Now let's work on the sound at the *end* of a word. I'm going to say a list of words. Some of the words will have the **/ks/** sound at the *end,* and some will not. I'll say the word first, and then you'll say the word. Think about the *last* sound we hear in each word.

Remember, we're listening for the **/ks/** sound at the *end* of the word, as in **sticks.** What sound are you listening for at the *end*? /ks/.

Listen. **Fox.** Say **fox.** *Fox.*

Give me a thumbs-up if you hear **/ks/** at the *end* of **fox.** Student response.

Yes, **fox** *ends* with the sound **/ks/.**

370 Lesson 93

(Continue the activity with the following lists of words.
Box. Apple. Socks. Tricks. Match. Thumb.
Rocks. Fur. Why. Blocks. Picks. Much.)

Activity 3 Phoneme Identity—Final

Elicit responses. **Guide** as needed.
We're going to play a game and find something the same. I'm going to say three words. Listen closely and see if you can tell which sound is the same. I'll show you how to do the first one.

My turn. What sound is the same in **fair, hear,** and **bear?** **/rrr/.** That is because **fair, hear,** and **bear** all *end* with the last sound **/rrr/.**

Your turn. What sound is the same in **fair, hear,** and **bear?** /rrr/.

Yes, **fair, hear,** and **bear** all *end* with the last sound **/rrr/.** Let's try some more.

What sound is the same in **had, toad,** and **red?** /d/.

What sound is the same in **off, rough,** and **puff?** /fff/.

What sound is the same in **tear, poor,** and **more?** /rrr/.

What sound is the same in **feed, side,** and **glad?** /d/.

What sound is the same in **cough, reef,** and **deaf?** /fff/.

Part B: Letter Recognition and Formation

6 minutes

Student Materials:
Lined paper

Activity 1 Letter Recognition—Capital W

Elicit responses to questions. **Guide** as needed. **Write** capital W on the board. **Point** to capital W.
Today you'll learn another way to write **w.**
The name of this letter is **capital W.** What letter name? *Capital W.*
Again, what letter name? *Capital W.*
Review as needed.

Activity 2 Letter Formation—Capital W

Now we're going to practice writing **capital W.** When you practice writing, you'll learn not only where to start and stop the letter, but also which way to move your hand when you're making the letter. It's tricky, but you're so smart you'll learn how to write **capital W** very quickly. Watch.

Here's how you write **capital W** in the air.
Model capital W formation in the air (with your back to students).

Watch again.

Lesson 93 **371**

Now let's practice writing **capital W** in the air. Hold up your writing hand, and make **capital W** in the air.
Guide students as they write capital W in the air.

Let's practice **capital W** again.

Here's how to write **capital W** with your writing hand pointer finger.
Model capital W formation on the board with your finger (with your back to students).

Watch again.

Now let's practice writing **capital W** on your table without using your pencil. Use your writing hand pointer finger, and make **capital W** on your table.
Guide students as they write capital W on their table or desktop.

Let's practice **capital W** again.

Model writing capital W on the board (with your back to students).
Remember that every letter has a name.
You learned the name of this letter is **capital W.** What letter name? *Capital W.*
Again, what letter name? *Capital W.*

Provide lined paper to students.
Now let's practice writing **capital W** with your pencil.
Guide students as they write capital W on their paper. **Review** as needed.

 Link letter names to letter sounds as they appear in the program as needed.

Part C: Comprehension Strategies

9 minutes

Activity 1 Listening Comprehension—A During-Reading Strategy

Teacher Materials:
Narrative trade book

Student Materials:
Lined paper

Direct students to narrative trade book of teacher choice. **Elicit** responses to questions. **Guide** as needed.
We'll read the story again today. When we read the story today, I want you to think about anything in the story that reminds you of something that you know or something that has happened to you. We'll connect the story to your life after we read the story.

Elicit correct listening behavior from students. **Reread** trade book. **Model** prosody during read-aloud.

Elicit text-to-self connections. **Guide** as needed.

372 Lesson 93

Activity 2 **Make Connections: Text-to-Self—An After-Reading Strategy**

Elicit responses to questions. **Guide** as needed.
Making connections helps me to understand what I read. It helps make reading more fun and interesting. Let's talk about this story and see how it matches or connects to my own life.

Listen as I make some connections.

Model think-aloud for making text-to-self connections.

Sample Wording for Think-Aloud

When _____ happened in the story, it reminded me of . . .

This story makes me think about myself because . . .

The character named _____ reminds me of . . .

I know about _____ because one time . . .

Discuss how characters, events, or items in story relate to things in students' lives.
What connections from the story can you make to your life? (Student response.)

Provide lined paper. **Model** writing a sentence about a connection you made.
Write a sentence that describes the connection you made to your life. If you need help, ask me.
Monitor students. **Guide** students as needed.

Remember that when you read, making connections to your life helps you better understand and remember the story.

Lesson 93   **373**

Lesson 94

> **Materials**
> **Teacher:** Narrative trade book (from Lesson 91); additional trade book that has similar story elements for text-to-text connection; Picture-Sound Cards for /v/, /p/, /ch/, /e/, /b/, /ī/, /y/, and /j/
> **Student:** Lined paper

5 minutes

Teacher Materials:
Picture-Sound Cards for /v/, /p/, /ch/, /e/, /b/, /ī/, /y/, and /j/

Part A: Phonemic and Phonological Awareness

Activity 1 Phoneme Isolation—Initial

Use IWB interactive cards or picture-sound cards. **Elicit** responses. **Guide** as needed. I'm going to show you two cards and name the object on each card. Then I'll tell you a sound. Think about which word starts with that sound. Let's try it. Today we'll be listening for the sound at the *beginning* of a word.

Show /y/ card; use any of four Picture-Sound Cards per phoneme for activity.
This is a _____. What is this? (Student response.)

Show /b/ card; use any of four Picture-Sound Cards per phoneme for activity.
This is a _____. What is this? (Student response.)

Which word *begins* with **/yyy/**? (Student response.)

Show /ī/ card; use any of four Picture-Sound Cards per phoneme for activity.
This is a _____. What is this? (Student response.)

Show /j/ card; use any of four Picture-Sound Cards per phoneme for activity.
This is a _____. What is this? (Student response.)

Which word *begins* with **/j/?** (Student response.)

Continue the activity with the following examples:
/ch/ and /j/: Which word begins with /j/?
/y/ and /e/: Which word begins with /yyy/?
/j/ and /v/: Which word begins with /j/?
/p/ and /y/: Which word begins with /yyy/?

Activity 2 Phoneme Isolation—Medial

Elicit responses. **Guide** as needed.
We're going to work on the *middle* sound in some words. I'm going to say two words. Listen carefully to find out which word has the special sound in the *middle*. One word will have the **/aaa/** sound in the *middle,* and the other word will not. Tell me the word that has the **/aaa/** sound in the *middle*. Let's try it. What sound are we listening for in the *middle* of the word? */aaa/*.

374   Lesson 94

Listen. My turn. **Cat. Kite.** Listen again. **Cat. Kite.** I'll tell you which word has the *middle* sound **/aaa/. Cat.**

Your turn. Listen. **Cat. Kite.** Listen again. **Cat. Kite.** Which word has the *middle* sound **/aaa/?** *Cat.*

Yes, **cat** has the *middle* sound **/aaa/.** Let's try another one. Remember to listen for our special sound **/aaa/.**

Your turn. Listen. **Mat. Meat.** Listen again. **Mat. Meat.** Which word has the *middle* sound **/aaa/?** *Mat.*

Yes, **mat** has the *middle* sound **/aaa/.**

(Continue the activity with the following list of words.
Take, tack
Sap, soap.
Rake, rack.)

Activity 3 Phoneme Categorization—Initial

Elicit responses. **Guide** as needed.
We're going to find words that *don't* belong. I'm going to say three words. Listen closely and see if you can tell which word *does not* belong.

Your turn. Listen. **Wish, wet, up.** Which word *doesn't* belong? *Up.*

Right, **up** *doesn't* belong because it starts with **/uuu/,** and **wish** and **wet** start with **/www/.**

(Continue the activity with the following list of words.
Ship, gas, shake.
Own, ocean, lucky.
Web, won, lake.
Sheep, under, shin.
Oak, oval, girl.)

Activity 4 Phoneme Blending

Elicit responses. **Guide** as needed.
Let's put some sounds together to make words. I'm going to say a word very slowly so you can hear each sound. You need to listen carefully so you can put the sounds together and say the word. Let me show you how it works.

Model holding each continuous sound for two to three seconds; say sounds for each word without stopping.
My turn. Listen. **/nnn/ /ōōō/.** Listen again. **/nnn/ /ōōō/.** I can put it together. **No.**

Your turn. Listen. **/nnn/ /ōōō/.** Listen again. **/nnn/ /ōōō/.** Put it together. *No.*

(Continue the activity with the following list of words.
So (sss-ōōō). Row (rrr-ōōō). Mow (mmm-ōōō).)

Lesson 94   **375**

6 minutes

Student Materials:
Lined paper

Part B: Letter Recognition and Formation

Activity 1 Letter Recognition Review—Capital W

Elicit responses to questions. **Guide** as needed. **Write** capital W on the board. **Point** to capital W.
We learned that this letter is **capital W.** What letter name? *Capital W.*
Again, what letter name? *Capital W.*
Review as needed.

Activity 2 Letter Formation Review—Capital W

Now we're going to practice writing **capital W.** When you practice writing, you'll learn not only where to start and stop the letter, but also which way to move your hand when you're making the letter. It's tricky, but you're so smart you'll learn how to write **capital W** very quickly. Watch.

Here's how you write **capital W** in the air.
Model capital W formation in the air (with your back to students).

Watch again.

Now let's practice writing **capital W** in the air. Hold up your writing hand, and make **capital W** in the air.
Guide students as they write capital W in the air.

Let's practice **capital W** again.

Here's how to write **capital W** with your writing hand pointer finger.
Model capital W formation on the board with your finger (with your back to students).

Watch again.

Now let's practice writing **capital W** on your table without using your pencil. Use your writing hand pointer finger, and make **capital W** on your table.
Guide students as they write capital W on their table or desktop.

Let's practice **capital W** again.

Model writing capital W on the board (with your back to students).
Remember that every letter has a name.
You learned the name of this letter is **capital W.** What letter name? *Capital W.*
Again, what letter name? *Capital W.*

Provide lined paper to students.
Now let's practice writing **capital W** with your pencil.
Guide students as they write capital W on their paper. **Review** as needed.

 Link letter names to letter sounds as they appear in the program as needed.

376 Lesson 94

Part C: Comprehension Strategies

9 minutes

Teacher Materials:
Narrative trade book
Additional trade book

Activity 1 Listening Comprehension—A During-Reading Strategy

Direct students to narrative trade book of teacher choice. **Elicit** responses to questions. **Guide** as needed.

We'll read the story again today. When we read the story today, I want you to think about all the stories you have heard. I want you to think of which story you have heard that reminds you of this one.

Elicit correct listening behavior from students. **Reread** trade book. **Model** prosody during read-aloud.

Guide students to focus on thinking of another story like this one for a text-to-text connection. **Elicit** responses to questions about text-to-text connections. **Guide** as needed.

You have heard lots of stories this year.

What story have you heard that reminds you of this story? (Student responses.)

Elicit names of stories that are like today's story. **Guide** as needed.

Activity 2 Make Connections: Text-to-Text—An After-Reading Strategy

Elicit responses to questions. **Guide** as needed.
When I read this story, it reminded me right away of the time I read _____. Listen as I show you what I mean.

Elicit correct listening behavior from students. **Reread** other story for text-to-text connection. **Model** prosody during read-aloud.

Guide students to think of similarities for text-to-text connection.

Model think-aloud for making text-to-text connections by telling all the things between the two stories that are similar.

Sample Wording for Think-Aloud
This story reminds me of _____ because the characters both _____. The settings are similar because _____. The events that happened were similar because _____. The end of the story reminded me of the end of this story because _____.

When I can connect a story that I'm reading to another story that I know, it helps me to understand the story better. Making a connection to another story I have heard is a smart thing to do.

Lesson 94 377

Lesson 95

Materials

Teacher: Narrative trade book (from Lesson 91); 5-Story Map; 11-Phonemic Awareness; Letter Recognition

Student: Lined paper; copy of 5-Story Map with writing lines; copy of 11-Phonemic Awareness

5 minutes

Teacher Materials:
Phonemic Awareness

Student Materials:
Phonemic Awareness

Part A: Phonemic and Phonological Awareness

Activity 1 Phoneme Isolation—Initial

Elicit responses. **Guide** as needed.

Let's work on a sound at the *beginning* of a word. I'm going to say a list of words. Some of the words will have the **/bl/** sound at the *beginning*, and some will not. I'll say the word first, and then you'll say the word.

Remember, we're listening for the **/bl/** sound at the *beginning* of the word. What sound are we listening for? */bl/*.

Listen. **Black.** Say **black.** *Black.*

Give me a thumbs-up if you hear **/bl/** at the *beginning* of **black.** (Student response.)

Right, **black** *begins* with the sound **/bl/.**

(Continue the activity with the following list of words.
Blink. Union. Blue. Blank. Queen. Young.
Blood. Snap. Blend. Zoo. Block. Blister.)

Let's work on a sound at the *beginning* of a word. I'm going to say a list of words. Some of the words will have the **/br/** sound at the *beginning*, and some will not. I'll say the word first, and then you'll say the word. Remember, we are listening for the **/br/** sound at the *beginning* of the word. What sound are we listening for? */br/*.

Listen. **Brick.** Say **brick.** *Brick.*

Give me a thumbs-up if you hear **/br/** at the *beginning* of **brick.** Student response.

Right, **brick** *begins* with the sound **/br/.**

(Continue the activity with the following list of words.
Five. Breeze. Bread. Green. Brain. Use.
Zone. Break. Beef. Broad. Broke. Coach.)

Activity 2 Phoneme Isolation—Final

Show Phonemic Awareness. **Distribute** copy of Phonemic Awareness. **Elicit** responses. **Guide** as needed.

You have worked so hard to listen for many different sounds at the *end* of a word. Let's go back and review some of those sounds.

We're going to look at pictures on this page and find pictures to match our sounds. I'm going to name each picture in the top row. Touch each picture after I name it, and repeat the name. Remember, I want you to think about the *last* sound in each word. Let's try it.

Model use of Phonemic Awareness; point to each picture as word is said.
Touch the picture in the first row.

This is a toe. What is this? *Toe.*

This is a knife. What is this? *Knife.*

This is a bone. What is this? *Bone.*

Which word has the *last* sound **/fff/?** *Knife.*

Yes, the last sound in **knife** is **/fff/.** Now circle the picture of the knife with your pencil. When we are finished with our lesson, you can color the pictures that end with our special sounds.

(Continue the activity with the following list of words.
Second row: ant, moon, sad. Which word has the last sound /t/?
Third row: hand, phone, boat. Which word has the last sound /nnn/?
Fourth row: kite, mop, duck. Which word has the last sound /k/?

Activity 3 Phoneme Identity—Final

Elicit responses. **Guide** as needed.
We're going to play a game and find something the same. I'm going to say three words. Listen closely and see if you can tell which sound is the same.

Your turn. What sound is the same in **kite, bat,** and **pot?** */t/.*

Yes, **kite, bat,** and **pot** all *end* with the last sound **/t/.** Let's try some more.

What sound is the same in **pack, check,** and **sick?** */k/.*

What sound is the same in **fun, spin,** and **won?** */nnn/.*

What sound is the same in **meat, flute,** and **wait?** */t/.*

What sound is the same in **woke, hike,** and **trick?** */k/.*

What sound is the same in **moon, run,** and **brown?** */nnn/.*

Lesson 95 **379**

Part B: Letter Recognition and Formation

6 minutes

Teacher Materials:
Letter Recognition

Student Materials:
Lined paper

Activity 1 — Letter Recognition Cumulative Review—u/U, g/G, l/L, w/W

Display on IWB or **write** letters and capitals on the board in the order shown. **Elicit** responses to questions. **Guide** as needed.

*This week you've learned one letter and one capital—***w** *and* **capital W.**
Let's review all the letters and capitals you've learned. Are you ready?

Letter	Question	Student Response
G	What letter?	Capital G.
u	What letter?	u.
L	What letter?	Capital L.
w	What letter?	w.
g	What letter?	g.
W	What letter?	Capital W.
l	What letter?	l.
U	What letter?	Capital U.

Review as needed.

Activity 2 — Letter Formation Cumulative Review—u/U, g/G, l/L, w/W

Write u, capital U, g, capital G, l, capital L, w, and capital W on the board in the order shown (with your back to students). **Provide** lined paper to students.

Show me how you can write these letters and capitals.

Guide students as they write the letters and capitals on their paper. **Review** as needed.

 Link letter names to letter sounds as they appear in the program as needed.

Part C: Comprehension Strategies

9 minutes

Teacher Materials:
Narrative trade book
Story Map

Student Materials:
Story Map

Activity 1 — Listening Comprehension—A During-Reading Strategy

Direct students to narrative trade book of teacher choice. **Elicit** responses to questions. **Guide** as needed.

Today as I read the story, I want you to think carefully about all the parts of the story. The illustrator made the pictures for you so that the book would be fun to read. Look for what the illustrator did to show the characters, setting, and events in the beginning, the middle, and the end. After I read the story, you'll become an illustrator and draw pictures of the characters, setting, and

380   Lesson 95

events in the beginning, the middle, and the end of the story. While I read, think about what you want to draw.

Elicit correct listening behavior from students. **Reread** trade book. **Model** prosody during read-aloud.

Guide students to focus on illustrations for all story elements. **Elicit** responses to questions about how illustrator shows all story elements. **Guide** as needed.

Activity 2 Story Elements: Illustrate Character, Setting, Beginning, Middle, and End—An After-Reading Strategy

Show Story Map. **Provide** copy of Story Map to each student. **Elicit** responses to questions. **Guide** as needed.

This is a new Story Map. It has places for you to make pictures for the characters, setting, and the beginning, the middle, and the end.

Touch the box for characters. Just put a picture of the most important character(s) in that box.

Touch the box for setting. Put a picture of the main setting for the story in that box.

Touch the Beginning, Middle, and End boxes. Those are just like the Story Map you had before, so put the pictures of the events of the story in those boxes.

Guide students to draw illustrations in the correct boxes and to work quickly.

When you're finished, you can share your illustrations with your neighbor.

Share illustrations with class if time permits or make a class book of Story Maps.

Activity 3 Collaborate to Strengthen Writing

Show Story Map.

Now let's write about what happened in our story. Watch as I write about the beginning, the middle, and the end of the story.

Model writing 3 separate sentences that tell about the beginning, the middle, and the end of the story.

Now it is your turn to write about what happens **first** at the beginning of the story, **then** what happens in the middle of the story, and **finally** what happens at the end of the story. If you need help, ask me.

Monitor students. **Guide** as needed.

Assign student partners.

Share your writing with your neighbor. Add suggestions to make your neighbor's writing better if you think it needs it.

Model how to give feedback on what was written if it needs it. **Monitor** students. **Guide** as needed.

Lesson 95   **381**

Lesson 96

Materials

Teacher: Narrative trade book (same book for Lessons 96–100); Picture-Sound Cards for /ch/, /e/, /b/, /ī/, /j/, /kw/, and /z/, 1-My Prediction Chart

Student: Lined paper, Copy of 1-My Prediction Chart

Part A: Phonemic and Phonological Awareness

5 minutes

Teacher Materials:
Picture-Sound Cards for /ch/, /e/, /b/, /ī/, /j/, /kw/, and /z/

Activity 1 Phoneme Isolation—Initial

Elicit responses. **Guide** as needed.
I'm going to show you two cards and name the object on each card. Then I'll tell you a sound. Think about which word starts with that sound. Let's try it. Today we'll be listening for the sound at the *beginning* of a word.

Show /kw/ card; use any of four Picture-Sound Cards per phoneme for activity.
This is a _____. What is this? (**Student response.**)

Show /j/ card; use any of four Picture-Sound Cards per phoneme for activity.
This is a _____. What is this? (**Student response.**)

Which word *begins* with **/kwww/?** (**Student response.**)

Show /j/ card; use any of four Picture-Sound Cards per phoneme for activity.
This is a _____. What is this? (**Student response.**)

Show /z/ card; use any of four Picture-Sound Cards per phoneme for activity.
This is a _____. What is this? (**Student response.**)

Which word *begins* with **/zzz/?** (**Student response.**)

(Continue the activity with the following examples:
/ī/ and /z/: Which word begins with /zzz/?
/kw/ and /b/: Which word begins with /kwww/?
/z/ and /ch/: Which word begins with /zzz/?
/e/ and /kw/: Which word begins with /kwww/?)

Activity 2 Phoneme Isolation—Medial

Elicit responses. **Guide** as needed.
We're going to keep working on the *middle* sound of a word. I'm going to say two words. Listen carefully to find out which word has the special sound in the *middle*. One word will have **/ēēē/** in the *middle*, and the other word will not. Tell me the word that has **/ēēē/** in the *middle* of the word. What sound are we listening for in the *middle* of the word? **/ēēē/.**

Let's try it. Listen. My turn. Meat. Mat. Listen again. Meat. Mat. I'll tell you which word has the *middle* sound **/ēēē/.** Meat.

382 Lesson 96

Your turn. Listen. Meat. Mat. Listen again. Meat. Mat. Which word has the *middle* sound **/ēēē/?** *Meat.*

Yes, **meat** has the *middle* sound **/ēēē/.** Let's try another one. Remember to listen for our special sound **/ēēē/.**

Your turn. Listen. Sheep. Ship. Listen again. Sheep. Ship. Which word has the *middle* sound **/ēēē/?** *Sheep.*

Yes, **sheep** has the *middle* sound **/ēēē/.**

(Continue the activity with the following list of words.
Rod, read.
Luck, leak.
Bean, bone.)

Activity 3 Phoneme Categorization—Initial

Elicit responses. **Guide** as needed.
We're going to find words that *don't* belong. I'm going to say three words. Listen closely and see if you can tell which word *does not* belong.

Your turn. Listen. **Van, vase, wet.** Which word *doesn't* belong? *Wet.*

Right. **Wet** *doesn't* belong because it starts with **/www/,** and **van** and **vase** start with **/vvv/.**

(Continue the activity with the following list of words
Party, shed, pig.
Chance, change, ocean.
Vine, violet, ship.
Peek, over, pool.
Cheese, chill, winter.)

Activity 4 Phoneme Blending

Elicit responses. **Guide** as needed.
Let's put some sounds together to make words. I'm going to say a word very slowly so you can hear each sound. You need to listen carefully and put the sounds together and say the word. Let me show you how it works.

My turn. Listen. **/mmm/ /īīī/.** Listen again. **/mmm/ /īīī/.** I can put it together. **My.**

Your turn. Listen. **/mmm/ /īīī/.** Listen again. **/mmm/ /īīī/.** Put it together. *My.*

(Continue the activity with the following list of words.
Why (hwww-īīī). Lie (lll-īīī). Shy (shshsh-īīī).)

Lesson 96 **383**

6 minutes

Student Materials:
Lined paper

Part B: Letter Recognition and Formation

Activity 1 Letter Recognition—k

Elicit responses to questions. **Guide** as needed. **Write** k on the board. **Point** to k.
Today you'll learn a new letter. The name of this letter is **k.** What letter name? *k.*
Again, what letter name? *k.*
Review as needed.

Activity 2 Letter Formation—k

Now we're going to practice writing **k.** When you practice writing, you'll learn not only where to start and stop the letter, but also which way to move your hand when you're making the letter. It's tricky, but you're so smart you'll learn how to write **k** very quickly. Watch.

Here's how you write **k** in the air.
Model k formation in the air (with your back to students).

Watch again.

Now let's practice writing **k** in the air. Hold up your writing hand, and make **k** in the air.
Guide students as they write k in the air.

Let's practice **k** again.

Here's how to write **k** with your writing hand pointer finger.
Model k formation on the board with your finger (with your back to students).

Watch again.

Now let's practice writing **k** on your table without using your pencil. Use your writing hand pointer finger, and make **k** on your table.
Guide students as they write k on their table or desktop.

Let's practice **k** again.

Model writing k on the board (with your back to students).
Remember that every letter has a name.
You learned the name of this letter is **k.** What letter name? *k.*
Again, what letter name? *k.*

Provide lined paper to students.
Now let's practice writing **k** with your pencil.
Guide students as they write k on their paper. **Review** as needed.

📕 **Link** letter names to letter sounds as they appear in the program as needed.

📕 **Set up** a writing center with writing materials and correct models of letters learned so far for students to use in their free time.

384 Lesson 96

Part C: Comprehension Strategies

9 minutes

Teacher Materials:
Narrative trade book
My Prediction Chart

Student Materials:
Lined paper
My Prediction Chart

Activity 1 Title, Author, and Illustrator Identification—A Before-Reading Strategy

Provide a reading center to display books being read so that students can enjoy them again during free time.

Direct students to narrative trade book of teacher choice. **Elicit** responses to questions. **Guide** as needed.

Show front cover of book and allow student to point to name of title, author, and illustrator as you discuss them.

We'll read a new story today. The title of today's story is _____. What's the title of today's story? (Student response.)

The author of today's story is _____. Who's the author of today's story? (Student response.)

The illustrator of today's story is _____. Who's the illustrator? (Student response.)

Activity 2 Activate Background Knowledge—A Before-Reading Strategy

Elicit responses to questions. **Guide** as needed.
The information that you already have in your brain is called background knowledge.

What's the information you have in your brain called? *Background knowledge.*

Choose a topic to activate background knowledge from story you'll read.
Tell me your background knowledge for _____.
Discuss background knowledge for topic chosen.

Provide lined paper. **Model** writing a sentence about what you know.
Write a sentence that tells me what you know about _____. If you need help, ask me.
Monitor students. **Guide** students as needed.

When you think about your background knowledge before you read, it helps you better understand the story. You can connect what you know to what happens in the story.

Activity 3 Make Predictions—A Before-Reading Strategy

Show title, front and back cover, and pictures inside the book. **Elicit** responses to questions. **Guide** as needed.

The title of today's book is _____. Write the book title in the box labeled "Book Title".

Lesson 96 **385**

Now that you know the title of today's book, let's look at the cover and pictures inside the book for clues to make some good guesses of what you think the story will be about.

What do you call your good guesses? *Predictions.*

Making predictions helps us get interested in the story before we read it. Let's make some predictions about the story before I read it to you. What do you predict this story will be about? (Student response.)

Write your prediction in the box labeled "I Predict That".
Guide as needed

What characters do you predict will be in the story? (Student response.)

What do you predict the setting will be? (Student response.)

What do you predict might happen in the story? (Student response.)

When we read the book, we'll check your predictions to see whether they're correct.

Elicit correct listening behavior from students. **Read** trade book. **Model** prosody during read-aloud.

Guide students to confirm predictions and/or connect background knowledge as you read story. **Ask** questions to confirm predictions and/or connect background knowledge. **Guide** as needed.

Activity 4 Confirm Predictions—An After-Reading Strategy

Elicit responses to questions. **Guide** as needed.
Now let's check your predictions to see whether they were correct. You predicted that the story was about _____.

Was your prediction correct? (Student response.)

Circle whether or not your prediction was correct in the box labeled "Was My Prediction Correct?"

You predicted that _____ were characters in the story. Was your prediction correct? (Student response.)

You predicted that the setting was _____. Was your prediction correct? (Student response.)

You predicted that some events would be _____. Was your prediction correct? (Student response.)

Remember that your predictions don't have to be correct. Just making a prediction and listening to see whether your prediction is correct helps you stay interested in the story.

386   *Lesson 96*

Lesson 97

Materials
Teacher: Narrative trade book (from Lesson 96); 12-Phonemic Awareness
Student: Lined paper; copy of 12-Phonemic Awareness

Part A: Phonemic and Phonological Awareness

5 minutes

Teacher Materials:
Phonemic Awareness

Student Materials:
Phonemic Awareness

Activity 1 Phoneme Isolation—Initial

Elicit responses. **Guide** as needed.
Let's work on a sound at the *beginning* of a word. I'm going to say a list of words. Some of the words will have the **/cl/** sound at the *beginning,* and some will not. I'll say the word first, and then you'll say the word.

Remember, we're listening for the **/cl/** sound at the *beginning* of the word. What sound are we listening for? /cl/.

Listen. **Clock.** Say **clock.** *Clock.*

Give me a thumbs-up if you hear **/cl/** at the *beginning* of **clock.** (Student response.)

Right, **clock** *begins* with the sound **/cl/.**

(Continue the activity with the following list of words:
Click. Bread. Clean. Blink. Zebra. Close.
Car. Clam. Under. Closet. Cloud. Blue.)

Let's work on another sound at the *beginning* of a word. I'm going to say a list of words. Some of the words will have the **/cr/** sound at the *beginning,* and some will not. I'll say the word first, and then you'll say the word.

Remember, we are listening for the **/cr/** sound at the *beginning* of the word. What sound are we listening for? /cr/.

Listen. **Cream.** Say **cream.** *Cream.*

Give me a thumbs-up if you hear **/cr/** at the *beginning* of **cream.** Student response.

Right, **cream** *begins* with the sound **/cr/.**

(Continue the activity with the following list of words:
Fifty. Crib. Crust. Black. Crazy. Cane.
Dizzy. Crab. Crayon. Bead. Crime. Crow.)

Lesson 97   387

Activity 2 Phoneme Isolation—Final

Show Phonemic Awareness. **Distribute** copy of Phonemic Awareness. **Elicit** responses. **Guide** as needed.

You have worked so hard to listen for many different sounds at the end of a word. Let's go back and review some of those sounds.

We're going to look at pictures on this page and find pictures to match our sounds. I'm going to name each picture in the top row. Touch each picture after I name it, and repeat the name. Remember, I want you to think about the *last* sound in each word. Let's try it.

Model use of Phonemic Awareness; point to each picture as word is said.
Touch the picture in the first row.

This is a tooth. What is this? *Tooth.*

This is a bike. What is this? *Bike.*

This is a flag. What is this? *Flag.*

Which word has the *last* sound **/th/?** *Tooth.*

Yes, the last sound in tooth is **/th/.** Now circle the picture of the tooth with your pencil. When we're finished with our lesson, you'll color the pictures that end with our special sounds.

(Continue the activity with the following
Second row: bath, desk, frog. Which word has the last sound /g/?
Third row: thumb, doll, pig. Which word has the last sound /lll/?
Fourth row: fish, bell, egg. Which word has the last sound /shshsh/?)

Activity 3 Phoneme Identity—Final

Elicit responses. **Guide** as needed.
We're going to play a game and find something the same. I'm going to tell you three words. Listen closely and see if you can tell which sound is the same. I'll show you how to do the first one.

Your turn. What sound is the same in **may, day,** and **say?** */āāā/.*

Yes, **may, day,** and **say** all *end* with the last sound **/āāā/.**

(Continue the activity with the following words:
Leg, rug, and chug.
Bath, tooth, and wreath.
Gray, play, and pay.
Dog, wig, and beg.
Math, north, and earth.)

6 minutes

Student Materials:
Lined paper

Part B: Letter Recognition and Formation

Activity 1 Letter Recognition Review—k

Elicit responses to questions. **Guide** as needed. **Write** k on the board. **Point** to k.
We learned that this letter is **k.** What letter name? *k.*
Again, what letter name? *k.*
Review as needed.

Activity 2 Letter Formation Review—k

Now we're going to practice writing **k.** When you practice writing, you'll learn not only where to start and stop the letter, but also which way to move your hand when you're making the letter. It's tricky, but you're so smart you'll learn how to write **k** very quickly. Watch.

Here's how you write **k** in the air.
Model k formation in the air (with your back to students).

Watch again.

Now let's practice writing **k** in the air. Hold up your writing hand, and make **k** in the air.
Guide students as they write k in the air.

Let's practice **k** again.

Here's how to write **k** with your writing hand pointer finger.
Model k formation on the board with your finger (with your back to students).

Watch again.

Now let's practice writing **k** on your table without using your pencil. Use your writing hand pointer finger, and make **k** on your table.
Guide students as they write k on their table or desktop.

Let's practice **k** again.

Model writing k on the board (with your back to students).
Remember that every letter has a name.
You learned the name of this letter is **k.** What letter name? *k.*
Again, what letter name? *k.*

Provide lined paper to students.
Now let's practice writing **k** with your pencil.
Guide students as they write k on their paper. **Review** as needed.

 Link letter names to letter sounds as they appear in the program as needed.

Lesson 97   389

Part C: Comprehension Strategies

9 minutes

Teacher Materials:
Narrative trade book

Student Materials:
Lined paper

Activity 1 Listening Comprehension—A During-Reading Strategy

Direct students to narrative trade book of teacher choice. **Elicit** responses to questions. **Guide** as needed.
We'll read the story again today. When we read the story today, I want you to think about anything in the story that reminds you of something that you know or something that has happened to you. We will connect the story to your life after we read the story.

Elicit correct listening behavior from students. **Reread** trade book. **Model** prosody during read-aloud.

Elicit text-to-self connections. **Guide** as needed.

Activity 2 Make Connections: Text-to-Self—An After-Reading Strategy

Elicit responses to questions. **Guide** as needed.
Making connections helps me to understand what I read. It helps make reading more fun and interesting. Let's talk about this story and see how it matches or connects to my own life. Listen as I make some connections.
Model making text-to-self connections.

Discuss how characters, events, or items in the story relate to things in students' lives.
What connections from the story can you make to your life? (Student response.)

Provide lined paper. **Model** writing a sentence about a connection you made.
Write a sentence that describes the connection you made to your life. If you need help, ask me.
Monitor students. **Guide** students as needed.

Remember that making connections to your life helps you better understand and remember the story.

Activity 3 **Story Elements: Identify Characters and Setting—An After-Reading Strategy**

Elicit responses to questions. **Guide** as needed.

Let's see whether you can tell me about some of the parts of the story we just read. What was the setting at the beginning of the story? (Student response.)

What clues in the story or pictures made you think that? (Student response.)

Did the setting stay the same from the beginning to end of the story or did it change? (Student response.)

Tell me some of the characters in the story? (Student response.)

Who's the main character? (Student response.)

Why is _____ the main character? (Idea: *The story is mostly about* _____.)

Lesson 97   **391**

Lesson 98

Materials

Teacher: Narrative trade book (from Lesson 96); additional trade book that has similar story elements for text-to-text connection; Picture-Sound Cards for /y/, /j/, /kw/, /z/, and /ū/

Student: Lined paper

5 minutes

Teacher Materials:
Picture-Sound Cards for /y/, /j/, /kw/, /z/, and /ū/

Part A: Phonemic and Phonological Awareness

Activity 1 Phoneme Isolation—Initial

Use IWB interactive cards or picture-sound cards. **Elicit** responses. **Guide** as needed.
I'm going to show you two cards, and name the object on each card. Then I'll tell you a sound. Think about which word starts with that sound. Let's try it. Today we'll be listening for the sound at the *beginning* of a word.

Show /ū/ card; use any of four Picture-Sound Cards per phoneme for activity.
This is a _____. What is this? (Student response.)

Show /kw/ card; use any of four Picture-Sound Cards per phoneme for activity.
This is a _____. What is this? (Student response.)

Which word *begins* with **/ūūū/?** (Student response.)

Show /z/ card; use any of four Picture-Sound Cards per phoneme for activity.
This is a _____. What is this? (Student response.)

Show /ū/ card; use any of four Picture-Sound Cards per phoneme for activity.
This is a _____. What is this? (Student response.)

Which word *begins* with **/ūūū/?** (Student response.)

Continue the activity with the following examples:
/y/ and /ū/: Which word begins with /ūūū/?
/ū/ and /j/: Which word begins with /ūūū/?)

Activity 2 Phoneme Isolation—Medial

Elicit responses. **Guide** as needed.
We're going to keep working on the *middle* sound of a word. I'm going to say two words. Listen carefully to find out which word has the special sound in the *middle*. One word will have **/iii/** in the *middle,* and the other word will not. Tell me the word that has **/iii/** in the *middle* of the word. What sound are we listening for in the *middle* of the word? **/iii/**.

Let's try it. Listen. My turn. Pit. Pot. Listen again. Pit Pot. I'll tell you which word has the *middle* sound **/iii/**. Pit.

392   Lesson 98

Your turn. Listen. Pit. Pot. Listen again. Pit. Pot. Which word has the *middle* sound **/iii/?** *Pit*

Yes, **pit** has the *middle* sound **/iii/.**

Let's try another one. Remember to listen for our special sound **/iii/**

Your turn. Listen. Chip. Chop. Listen again. Chip. Chop. Which word has the *middle* sound **/iii/?** *Chip.*

Yes, **chip** has the *middle* sound **/iii/.**

(Continue the activity with the following words.
Fine, fin.
Sick, sack.
Peek, pick.)

Activity 3 Phoneme Categorization—Initial

Elicit responses. **Guide** as needed.
We're going to find words that *don't* belong. I'm going to say three words. Listen closely and see if you can tell which word *does not* belong.

Your turn. Listen. **Egg, else, voice.** Which word *doesn't* belong? *Voice.*

Right. **Voice** *doesn't* belong because it starts with **/vvv/,** and **egg** and **else** start with **/eee/.**

(Continue the activity with the following words.
Bone, park, bag.
Ice, island, chip.
Elbow, edge, pond.
Bank, chain, basket.
Ivy, idea, vote.)

Activity 4 Phoneme Blending

Elicit responses. **Guide** as needed.
Let's put some sounds together to make words. I'm going to say a word very slowly so you can hear each sound. Listen carefully and put the sounds together and say the word. Let me show you how it works.

My turn. Listen. **/sss/ /āāā/.** Listen again. **/sss/ /āāā/.** I can put it together. **Say**

Your turn. Listen. **/sss/ /āāā/.** Listen again. **/sss/ /āāā/.** Put it together. *Say.*

(Continue the activity with the following words.
May (mmm-āāā). Way (www-āāā). Ray (rrr-āāā).)

Lesson 98 **393**

6 minutes

Student Materials:
Lined paper

Part B: Letter Recognition and Formation

Activity 1 Letter Recognition—Capital K

Elicit responses to questions. **Guide** as needed. **Write** capital K on the board. **Point** to capital K.
Today you'll learn another way to write **k.**
The name of this letter is **capital K.** What letter name? *Capital K.*
Again, what letter name? *Capital K.*
Review as needed.

Activity 2 Letter Formation—Capital K

Now we're going to practice writing **capital K.** When you practice writing, you'll learn not only where to start and stop the letter, but also which way to move your hand when you're making the letter. It's tricky, but you're so smart you'll learn how to write **capital K** very quickly. Watch.

Here's how you write **capital K** in the air.
Model capital K formation in the air (with your back to students).

Watch again.

Now let's practice writing **capital K** in the air. Hold up your writing hand, and make **capital K** in the air.
Guide students as they write capital K in the air.

Let's practice **capital K** again.

Here's how to write **capital K** with your writing hand pointer finger.
Model capital K formation on the board with your finger (with your back to students).

Watch again.

Now let's practice writing **capital K** on your table without using your pencil. Use your writing hand pointer finger, and make **capital K** on your table.
Guide students as they write capital K on their table or desktop.

Let's practice **capital K** again.

Model writing capital K on the board (with your back to students).
Remember that every letter has a name.
You learned the name of this letter is **capital K.** What letter name? *Capital K.*
Again, what letter name? *Capital K.*

Provide lined paper to students.
Now let's practice writing **capital K** with your pencil.
Guide students as they write capital K on their paper. **Review** as needed.

 Link letter names to letter sounds as they appear in the program as needed.

394 Lesson 98

Part C: Comprehension Strategies

9 minutes

Teacher Materials:
Narrative trade book
Additional trade book

Activity 1 Listening Comprehension—A During-Reading Strategy

Direct students to narrative trade book of teacher choice. **Elicit** responses to questions. **Guide** as needed.
We'll read the story again today. When we read the story today, I want you to think about all the stories you have heard. I want you to think of which story reminds you of this one.

Elicit correct listening behavior from students. **Reread** trade book. **Model** prosody during read-aloud.

Guide students to focus on thinking of another story like this one for a text-to-text connection. **Elicit** responses to questions about text-to-text connections. **Guide** as needed.

You have heard lots of stories this year.

Elicit names of stories that are like today's story. **Guide** as needed.
What story have you heard that reminds you of this story? (Student response.)

Activity 2 Make Connections: Text-to-Text—An After-Reading Strategy

Elicit responses to questions. **Guide** as needed.
When I read this story, it reminded me right away of the time I read _____. Listen as I show you what I mean.

When I can connect a story that I'm reading to another story that I know, it helps me to understand the story better. Making a connection to another story I have heard is a smart thing to do.
Elicit correct listening behavior from students. **Reread** other story for text-to-text connection. **Model** prosody during read-aloud.

Guide students to think of similarities for text-to-text connection.

Model making text-to-text connections by telling all the story elements between the two stories that are similar.

Lesson 98   395

Lesson 99

Materials
Teacher: Narrative trade book (from Lesson 96); 5-Story Map; 13-Phonemic Awareness
Student: Lined paper; copy of 5-Story Map with writing lines; copy of 13-Phonemic Awareness

5 minutes

Teacher Materials:
Phonemic Awareness

Student Materials:
Phonemic Awareness

Part A: Phonemic and Phonological Awareness

Activity 1 Phoneme Isolation—Initial

Elicit responses. **Guide** as needed.
Let's work on a sound at the *beginning* of a word. I'm going to say a list of words. Some of the words will have the **/dr/** sound at the *beginning,* and some will not. I'll say the word first, and then you'll say the word.

Remember, we're listening for the **/dr/** sound at the *beginning* of the word. What sound are we listening for?/dr/.

Listen. **Drop.** Say **drop.** *Drop.*

Give me a thumbs-up if you hear **/dr/** at the *beginning* of **drop.** Student response.

Yes, **drop** *begins* with the sound **/dr/.**

(Continue the activity with the following words:
Drink. Dream. Clean. Blind. Dress. Cream.
Drum. Drill. Dip. Coast. Drizzle. Green.)

Let's work on another sound at the *beginning* of a word. I'm going to say a list of words. Some of the words will have the **/fl/** sound at the *beginning,* and some will not. I'll say the word first, and then you'll say the word.

Remember, we're listening for the **/fl/** sound at the *beginning* of the word. What sound are we listening for? /fl/.

Listen. **Flag.** Say **flag.** *Flag.*

Give me a thumbs-up if you hear **/fl/** at the *beginning* of **flag.** Student response.

Yes, **flag** *begins* with the sound **/fl/.**

(Continue the activity with the following words:
Dress. Flame. Fleet. Brown. Swim. Flower.
Float. Flip. Just. Leaf. Flute. Five.)

396   Lesson 99

Activity 2 Phoneme Isolation—Final

Show Phonemic Awareness. **Distribute** copy of Phonemic Awareness. **Elicit** responses. **Guide** as needed.

You have worked so hard to listen for many different sounds at the end of a word. Let's go back and review some of those sounds.

We're going to look at pictures on this page and find pictures to match our sounds. I'm going to name each picture in the top row. Touch each picture after I name it, and repeat the name. Remember, I want you to think about the *last* sound in each word. Let's try it.

Model use of Phonemic Awareness; point to each picture as word is said.

Touch the picture in the first row.

This is a rake. What is this? *Rake.*

This is a drum. What is this? *Drum.*

This is a stove. What is this? *Stove.*

Which word has the *last* sound **/vvv/?** *Stove.*

Yes, the last sound in **stove** is **/vvv/.** Now circle the picture of the stove with your pencil. When we are finished with our lesson, you'll color the pictures that end with our special sounds.

(Continue the activity with the following words:
Second row: sheep, dog, bed. Which word has the last sound /p/?
Third row: sock, bench, comb. Which word has the last sound /ch/?
Fourth row: crab, leaf, cup. Which word has the last sound /b/?)

Activity 3 Phoneme Identity—Final

Elicit responses. **Guide** as needed.

We're going to play a game and find something the same. I'm going to say three words. Listen closely and see if you can tell which sound is the same.

Your turn. What sound is the same in **wish, push,** and **cash?** */shshsh/.*

Yes, **wish, push,** and **cash** all end with the last sound **/shshsh/.**

(Continue the activity with the following words:
Doll, call, and pull.
Show, mow, and grow.
Bush, dish, and brush.
Fall, bull, and tell.
Blow, snow, and bow.)

Lesson 99 **397**

6 minutes

Student Materials:
Lined paper

Part B: Letter Recognition and Formation

Activity 1 Letter Recognition Review—Capital K

Elicit responses to questions. **Guide** as needed. **Write** capital K on the board. **Point** to capital K.
We learned that this letter is **capital K.** What letter name? *Capital K.*
Again, what letter name? *Capital K.*
Review as needed.

Activity 2 Letter Formation Review—Capital K

Now we're going to practice writing **capital K.** When you practice writing, you'll learn not only where to start and stop the letter, but also which way to move your hand when you're making the letter. It's tricky, but you're so smart you'll learn how to write **capital K** very quickly. Watch.

Here's how you write **capital K** in the air.
Model capital K formation in the air (with your back to students).

Watch again.

Now let's practice writing **capital K** in the air. Hold up your writing hand, and make **capital K** in the air.
Guide students as they write capital K in the air.

Let's practice **capital K** again.

Here's how to write **capital K** with your writing hand pointer finger.
Model capital K formation on the board with your finger (with your back to students).

Watch again.

Now let's practice writing **capital K** on your table without using your pencil. Use your writing hand pointer finger, and make **capital K** on your table.
Guide students as they write capital K on their table or desktop.

Let's practice **capital K** again.

Model writing capital K on the board (with your back to students).
Remember that every letter has a name.
You learned the name of this letter is **capital K.** What letter name? *Capital K.*
Again, what letter name? *Capital K.*

Provide lined paper to students.
Now let's practice writing **capital K** with your pencil.
Guide students as they write capital K on their paper. **Review** as needed.

 Link letter names to letter sounds as they appear in the program as needed.

398 Lesson 99

Part C: Comprehension Strategies

9 minutes

Teacher Materials:
Narrative trade book
Story Map

Student Materials:
Story Map

Activity 1 Listening Comprehension—A During-Reading Strategy

Direct students to narrative trade book of teacher choice. **Elicit** responses to questions. **Guide** as needed.

Today as I read the story, I want you to look carefully at the pictures of all the parts of the story. The illustrator made the pictures for you so that the book would be fun to read. Look for what the illustrator did to show the parts of the story. After I read the story, you'll become an illustrator and draw pictures of all the parts.

Elicit correct listening behavior from students. **Reread** trade book. **Model** prosody during read-aloud.

Guide students to focus on illustrations for all the story elements. **Elicit** answers to questions about how the illustrator shows all the story elements. **Guide** as needed.

Activity 2 Story Grammar: Illustrate Main Character and Setting—An After-Reading Strategy

Show Story Map. **Provide** Story Map to each student. **Guide** students to correct place on sheet to draw pictures for story elements. **Elicit** responses to questions. **Guide** as needed.

Now you'll become an illustrator. Make pictures to show all the parts of the story. What can you draw for the main character? (Student response.)

What can you draw for the setting? (Student response.)

What events could you draw in your beginning box? (Student response.)

What events could you draw in your middle box? (Student response.)

What events could you draw in your end box? (Student response.)
Draw illustrations for story elements on Story Map while students draw.

In the next lesson, you'll get to tell about your illustration.
Save student illustrations for Lesson 100.

Lesson 99 **399**

Activity 3 Collaborate to Strengthen Writing

Show Story Map.

Now let's write about what happened in our story. Watch as I write about the beginning, the middle, and the end of the story.

Model writing 3 separate sentences that tell about the beginning, the middle, and the end of the story.

Now it is your turn to write about what happens **first** at the beginning of the story, **then** what happens in the middle of the story, and **finally** what happens at the end of the story. If you need help, ask me.

Monitor students. **Guide** as needed.

Assign student partners.

Share your writing with your neighbor. Add suggestions to make your neighbor's writing better if you think it needs it.

Model how to give feedback on what was written if it needs it. **Monitor** students. **Guide** as needed.

Lesson 100

Materials

Teacher: Narrative trade book (from Lesson 96); 5-Story Map (from Lesson 99), Picture-Sound Cards for /m/, /n/, /d/, /b/, /k/, /g/, /ā/, /ē/, /t/, /r/, /p/, and /h/; Letter Recognition; 8-My Book Review

Student: Lined paper; copy of 5-Story Map (from Lesson 99); copy of 8-My Book Review

Part A: Phonemic and Phonological Awareness

5 minutes

Teacher Materials:
Picture-Sound Cards for /m/, /n/, /d/, /b/, /k/, /g/, /ā/, /ē/, /t/, /r/, /p/, and /h/

Activity 1 Phoneme Isolation—Initial

Use IWB interactive cards or picture-sound cards. **Elicit** responses. **Guide** as needed. Let's review some of the Picture Sound Cards that you learned so well. I'm going to show you two cards and name the object on each card. Then I'll tell you a sound. Think about which word starts with that sound. Let's try it. Today we'll be listening for the sound at the *beginning* of a word.

Show /m/ card; use any of four Picture-Sound Cards per phoneme for activity.
This is a _____. What is this? (Student response.)

Show /n/ card; use any of four Picture-Sound Cards per phoneme for activity.
This is a _____. What is this? (Student response.)

Which word *begins* with **/mmm/?** (Student response.)

Show /d/ card; use any of four Picture-Sound Cards per phoneme for activity.
This is a _____. What is this? (Student response.)

Show /b/ card; use any of four Picture-Sound Cards per phoneme for activity.
This is a _____. What is this? (Student response.)

Which word *begins* with **/b/?** (Student response.)

(Continue the activity with the following examples.
/k/ and /g/: Which word begins with /k/?
/ā/ and /ē/: Which word begins with /ēēē/?
/t/ and /r/: Which word begins with /rrr/?
/p/ and /h/: Which word begins with /h/?)

Lesson 100   401

Activity 2 **Phoneme Isolation—Medial**

Elicit responses. **Guide** as needed.
We're going to keep working on the *middle* sound of a word. I'm going to say two words. Listen carefully to find out which word has the special sound in the *middle*. One word will have **/ooo/** in the *middle,* and the other word will not. Tell me the word that has **/ooo/** in the *middle* of the word. What sound are we listening for in the *middle* of the word? */ooo/.*

Let's try it. Remember to listen for our special sound **/ooo/.**

Your turn. Listen. Hop. Hope. Listen again. Hop. Hope. Which word has the *middle* sound **/ooo/?** *Hop.*

Yes, **hop** has the *middle* sound **/ooo/.**

(Continue the activity with the following list of words.
Sheep, shop.
Luck, lock.
Log, leg.
Duck, dock.)

Activity 3 **Phoneme Categorization—Initial**

Elicit responses. **Guide** as needed.
We're going to find words that *don't* belong. I'm going to say three words. Listen closely and see if you can tell which word *does not* belong.

Your turn. Listen. **Young, yes, edge.** Which word *doesn't* belong? *Edge.*

Right, **edge** *doesn't* belong because it starts with **/eee/,** and **young** and **yes** start with **/yyy/.**

(Continue the activity with the following list of words.
Unicorn, bend, use.
Jump, jolly, island.
Yellow, yummy, balloon.
United, icicle, unicycle.
Jaguar, junk, every.)

402   *Lesson 100*

Activity 4 Phoneme Blending

Elicit responses. **Guide** as needed.
Let's put some sounds together to make words. I'm going to say a word very slowly so you can hear each sound. Listen carefully and put the sounds together and say the word.

Your turn. Listen. **/ēēē/ /t/.** Listen again. **/ēēē/ /t/.** Put it together. *Eat.*

(Continue the activity with the following list of words.
At (aaa-t). Off (ooo-fff). If (iii-fff).)

Part B: Letter Recognition and Formation

6 minutes

Teacher Materials:
Letter Recognition

Student Materials:
Lined paper

Activity 1 Letter Recognition Cumulative Review—g/G, l/L, w/W, k/K

Display on IWB or **write** letters and capitals on the board in the order shown. **Elicit** responses to questions. **Guide** as needed.
This week you've learned one letter and one capital—**k** and **capital K.** Let's review all the letters and capitals you've learned. Are you ready?

Letter	Question	Student Response
G	What letter?	*Capital G.*
w	What letter?	*w.*
K	What letter?	*Capital K.*
L	What letter?	*Capital L.*
k	What letter?	*k.*
g	What letter?	*g.*
W	What letter?	*Capital W.*
l	What letter?	*l.*

Review as needed.

Activity 2 Letter Formation Cumulative Review—g/G, l/L, w/W, k/K

Write g, capital G, l, capital L, w, capital W, k, and capital K on the board in the order shown (with your back to students). **Provide** lined paper to students.
Show me how you can write these letters and capitals.
Guide students as they write the letters and capitals on their paper. **Review** as needed.

 Link letter names to letter sounds as they appear in the program as needed.

Lesson 100 403

Part C: Comprehension Strategies

9 minutes

Teacher Materials:
Narrative trade book
Story Map
My Book Review

Student Materials:
Story Map
My Book Review

Activity 1 Listening Comprehension—A During-Reading Strategy

Direct students to narrative trade book of teacher choice. **Elicit** responses to questions. **Guide** as needed.
Today I'll read the story one last time. Listen to the story to remember all the parts of the story. After you listen to the story, you'll get to tell about the illustrations that you made in the last lesson. You'll tell about the characters, setting, and the beginning, the middle, and the end events.

Elicit correct listening behavior from students. **Reread** trade book. **Model** prosody during read-aloud.

Guide students to focus on story elements that they illustrated. **Elicit** answers to questions about story elements as you read. **Guide** as needed.

Activity 2 Retell the Story—An After-Reading Strategy

Assign student partners. **Provide** copy of Story Map completed in Lesson 99. **Elicit** responses to questions. **Guide** as needed.
You're going to tell a partner all the parts of the story from your pictures. Your partner will listen to you the right way. Then you'll listen politely as your partner tells you about his or her pictures.

When you're done, if there is time, you can show the class your illustrations and tell all the parts of the story.
Monitor students as they retell story.

Share illustrations with class as time permits, or make a class book of story maps.

Activity 3 Connections Through Shared Writing—Express Opinions

Show My Book Review. **Elicit** responses to questions. **Guide** as needed.
Think about the two books we read, _____ and _____. Let's talk about the two books. Which one did you like best and why?

Provide copies of My Book Review to students. **Guide** students through completion of My Book Review. **Share** with class as time permits.

Lesson 101

> **Materials**
> **Teacher:** Narrative trade book (same book for Lessons 101–105), 1-My Prediction Chart
> **Student:** Lined paper, Copy of 1-My Prediction Chart

5 minutes

Part A: Phonemic and Phonological Awareness

Activity 1 Phoneme Isolation—Initial

Elicit responses. **Guide** as needed.
Let's work on a sound at the *beginning* of a word. I'm going to say a list of words. Some of the words will have the **/fr/** sound at the *beginning*, and some will not. I'll say the word first, and then you'll say the word.

Remember, we're listening for the **/fr/** sound at the *beginning* of the word. What sound are we listening for? /fr/.

Listen. **Frog.** Say **frog.** *Frog.*

Give me a thumbs-up if you hear **/fr/** at the *beginning* of **frog.** (Thumbs-up.)

Yes, **frog** begins with the sound **/fr/.**

(Continue the activity with the following lists of words.
Freeze. Frame. Close. Brick. Free. Crime.
Fruit. Frown. Phone. Nose. Freckle. Cough.)

Let's work on another sound at the *beginning* of a word. I'm going to say a list of words. Some of the words will have the **/gl/** sound at the *beginning,* and some will not. I'll say the word first, and then you'll say the word.

Remember, we're listening for the **/gl/** sound at the *beginning* of the word. What sound are we listening for? /gl/.

Listen. **Glove.** Say **glove.** *Glove.*

Give me a thumbs-up if you hear **/gl/** at the *beginning* of **glove.** (Thumbs-up.)

Yes, **glove** begins with the sound **/gl/.**

(Continue the activity with the following lists of words:
Drip. Glow. Glass. Breeze. Smile. Glide.
Glum. Glaze. Purse. Log. Glue. Tent.)

Lesson 101   **405**

Activity 2 Phoneme Categorization—Final

Elicit responses. **Guide** as needed.

We're going to find words that don't belong. I'm going to say three words. Listen closely and see if you can tell which word *does not* belong. In earlier activities, you found words that didn't belong because the beginning sound was different. Today I want you to listen closely to the *last* sound in the words. I'll show you the first one.

My turn. Listen. **Came, home, bus.** Which word *doesn't* belong? **Bus. Bus** *doesn't* belong because **came** and **home** both end with the sound **/mmm/,** and **bus** ends with the sound **/sss/.** So the word **bus** doesn't belong. Your turn. Listen. **Came, home, bus.** Which word *doesn't* belong? *Bus.*

Right, **bus** *doesn't* belong because it ends with **/sss/** and **came** and **home** end with **/mmm/.**

(Continue the activity with the following examples:
Gas, fuss, bear.
Tear, fur, him.
Ham, tame, pear.
Guess, ram, pass.
Year, fair, goose.)

Part B: Letter Recognition and Formation

6 minutes

Student Materials:
Lined paper

Activity 1 Letter Recognition—v

Elicit responses to questions. **Guide** as needed. **Write** v on the board. **Point** to v.
Today you'll learn a new letter.
The name of this letter is **v.** What letter name? *v.*
Again, what letter name? *v.*
Review as needed.

Activity 2 Letter Formation—v

Now we're going to practice writing **v.** When you practice writing, you'll learn not only where to start and stop the letter, but also which way to move your hand when you're making the letter. It's tricky, but you're so smart you'll learn how to write **v** very quickly. Watch.

Here's how you write **v** in the air.
Model v formation in the air (with your back to students).

Watch again.

Now let's practice writing **v** in the air. Hold up your writing hand, and make **v** in the air.
Guide students as they write v in the air.

Let's practice **v** again.

Here's how to write **v** with your writing hand pointer finger.
Model v formation on the board with your finger (with your back to students).

406 Lesson 101

Watch again.

Now let's practice writing **v** on your table without using your pencil. Use your writing hand pointer finger, and make **v** on your table.
Guide students as they write v on their table or desktop.

Let's practice **v** again.

Model writing v on the board (with your back to students).
Remember that every letter has a name.
You learned the name of this letter is **v**. What letter name? v.
Again, what letter name? v.

Provide lined paper to students.
Now let's practice writing **v** with your pencil.
Guide students as they write v on their paper. **Review** as needed.

 Link letter names to letter sounds as they appear in the program as needed.

 Set up a writing center with writing materials and correct models of letters learned so far for students to use in their free time.

Part C: Comprehension Strategies

9 minutes

Teacher Materials:
Narrative trade book

My Prediction Chart

Student Materials:
My Prediction Chart

Activity 1 Title, Author, and Illustrator Identification—A Before-Reading Strategy

 Provide a reading center to display books being read so that students can enjoy them again during free time.

Direct students to narrative trade book of teacher choice. **Elicit** responses to questions. **Guide** as needed.

Show front cover of book and allow student to point to name of title, author, and illustrator as you discuss them.
We'll read a new book today. The title of today's story is _____. What's the title of today's story? (Student response.)

The author of today's story is _____. Who's the author of today's story? (Student response.)

The illustrator of today's story is _____. Who's the illustrator? (Student response.)

Lesson 101 **407**

Activity 2 Activate Background Knowledge—A Before-Reading Strategy

Elicit responses to questions. **Guide** as needed.
The information that you already have in your brain is called background knowledge.

What's the information you have in your brain called? *Background knowledge.*

Choose a topic to activate background knowledge from story you will read.
Tell me your background knowledge for _____ .
Discuss background knowledge of students as it relates to topic chosen.

When you think about your background knowledge before you read, it helps you better understand the story. You can connect what you know to what happens in the story.

Activity 3 Make Predictions—A Before-Reading Strategy

Show title, front and back cover, and pictures inside book. **Elicit** responses to questions.
Guide as needed. **Provide** copies of My Prediction Chart.
The title of today's book is _____ . Write the title in the box labeled "Book Title".

Now that you know the title of today's book, let's look at the cover and pictures inside the book for clues to make some good guesses of what you think the story will be about.

What do you call your good guesses? *Predictions.*

Making predictions helps you get interested in the story before you read it. Let's make some predictions about the story before I read it to you.

What do you predict this story will be about? (Student response.)

Write your prediction in the box labeled "I Predict That".
Guide as needed.

What characters do you predict will be in the story? (Student response.)

What do you predict the setting will be? (Student response.)

What do you predict might happen in the story? (Student response.)

When we read the book you will check your predictions to see whether they're correct.

Elicit correct listening behavior from students. **Read** trade book. **Model** prosody during read-aloud.

Guide students to confirm predictions and/or connect background knowledge as you read story. **Ask** questions to confirm predictions and/or connect background knowledge. **Guide** as needed.

408 *Lesson 101*

Activity 4 Confirm Predictions—An After-Reading Strategy

Elicit responses to questions. **Guide** as needed.

Now let's check your predictions to see whether they were correct. You predicted that the story was about _____.

Was your prediction correct? (Student response.)
Circle whether or not your prediction was correct in the box labeled "Was My Prediction Correct?"

You predicted that _____ were characters in the story. Was your prediction correct? (Student response.)

You predicted that the setting was _____. Was your prediction correct? (Student response.)

You predicted that some events would be _____. Was your prediction correct? (Student response.)

Remember that your predictions don't have to be correct. Just making a prediction and listening to see whether your prediction is correct helps you stay interested in the story.

Lesson 101 **409**

Lesson 102

Materials

Teacher: Narrative trade book (from Lesson 101); Picture-Sound Cards for /s/, /sh/, /f/, /v/, /th/, /ch/, /a/, /o/, /l/, /w/, /e/, and /i/

Student: Lined paper

5 minutes

Teacher Materials:
Picture-Sound Cards for /s/, /sh/, /f/, /v/, /th/, /ch/, /a/, /o/, /l/, /w/, /e/, and /i/

Part A: Phonemic and Phonological Awareness

Activity 1 Phoneme Isolation—Initial

Use IWB interactive cards or picture-sound cards. **Elicit** responses. **Guide** as needed. Let's review some of the Picture Sound Cards that you learned so well. I'm going to show you two cards and name the object on each card. Then I'll tell you a sound. Think about which word starts with that sound. Let's try it. Today we'll be listening for the sound at the *beginning* of a word.

Show /s/ card; use any of four Picture-Sound Cards per phoneme for activity.
This is a _____. What is this? (Student response.)

Show /sh/ card; use any of four Picture-Sound Cards per phoneme for activity.
This is a _____. What is this? (Student response.)

Which word *begins* with **/sss/?** (Student response.)

Show /f/ card; use any of four Picture-Sound Cards per phoneme for activity.
This is a _____. What is this? (Student response.)

Show /v/ card; use any of four Picture-Sound Cards per phoneme for activity.
This is a _____. What is this? (Student response.)

Which word *begins* with **/vvv/?** (Student response.)

(Continue the activity with the following examples:
/th/ and /ch/: Which word begins with /ththth/?
/a/ and /o/: Which word begins with /ooo/?
/l/ and /w/: Which word begins with /www/?
/e/ and /i/: Which word begins with /eee/?)

Activity 2 Phoneme Isolation—Medial

Elicit responses. **Guide** as needed.
We're going to keep working on the *middle* sound of a word. I'm going to say two words. Listen carefully to find out which word has the special sound in the *middle*. One word will have **/āāā/** in the *middle,* and the other word will not. Tell me the word that has **/āāā/** in the *middle* of the word. What sound are we listening for in the *middle* of the word? /āāā/.

410   Lesson 102

Let's try it. Remember to listen for our special sound **/āāā/.** Your turn. Listen. Cane. Cone. Listen again. Cane. Cone. Which word has the *middle* sound **/āāā/?** *Cane.*

Yes, **cane** has the *middle* sound **/āāā/.**

(Continue the activity with the remaining pairs of words:
Run, rain.
Face, fuss.
Game, gum.
Tip, tape.)

Activity 3 Phoneme Identity—Final

Elicit responses. **Guide** as needed.
We're going to play a game and find something the same. I'm going to say three words. Listen closely and see if you can tell which sound is the same.

Your turn. What sound is the same in **love, give,** and **have?** */vvv/.*

Yes, **love, give,** and **have** all end with the last sound **/vvv/.**

(Continue the activity with the following examples:
What sound is the same in lap, stop, and up?
What sound is the same in much, latch, and watch?
What sound is the same in dove, shave, and stove?
What sound is the same in soap, deep, and flip?
What sound is the same in clutch, each, and perch?)

Activity 4 Phoneme Blending

Elicit responses. **Guide** as needed.
Today we're going to put two sounds together and make words. This time you're going to help me say the sounds before we make the word. I'm going to say a word very slowly so you can hear each sound. You need to listen carefully and say the sounds. When you say the sounds, it will sound almost like you're singing them. Then we'll put the sounds together and say the word.

Model holding each continuous sound for two to three seconds. **Hold** up one finger for each phoneme in word, back of hand to students.
My turn. Listen. **/mmm/ /ēēē/.** Say those sounds with me. */mmm/ /ēēē/.*
Now say the sounds by yourself. */mmm/ /ēēē/.*
Your turn again. Say the sounds. */mmm/ /ēēē/.*
Now let's put it together. What word? *Me.*

Let's try some more. My turn. Listen. **/sss/ /ēēē/.**
Say those sounds with me. */sss/ /ēēē/.*
Now say the sounds by yourself. */sss/ /ēēē/.*
Your turn again. Say the sounds. */sss/ /ēēē/.*
Now let's put it together. What word? *See.*

(Continue the activity with the following words:
no [nnn-ōōō], so [sss-ōōō].)

Lesson 102 **411**

6 minutes

Student Materials:
Lined paper

Part B: Letter Recognition and Formation

Activity 1 Letter Recognition Review—v

Elicit responses to questions. **Guide** as needed. **Write** v on the board. **Point** to v.
We learned that this letter is **v.** What letter name? *v.*
Again, what letter name? *v.*
Review as needed.

Activity 2 Letter Formation Review—v

Now we're going to practice writing **v.** When you practice writing, you'll learn not only where to start and stop the letter, but also which way to move your hand when you're making the letter. It's tricky, but you're so smart you'll learn how to write **v** very quickly. Watch.

Here's how you write **v** in the air.
Model v formation in the air (with your back to students).

Watch again.

Now let's practice writing **v** in the air. Hold up your writing hand, and make **v** in the air.
Guide students as they write v in the air.

Let's practice **v** again.

Here's how to write **v** with your writing hand pointer finger.
Model v formation on the board with your finger (with your back to students).

Watch again.

Now let's practice writing **v** on your table without using your pencil. Use your writing hand pointer finger, and make **v** on your table.
Guide students as they write v on their table or desktop.

Let's practice **v** again.

Model writing v on the board (with your back to students).
Remember that every letter has a name.
You learned the name of this letter is **v.** What letter name? *v.*
Again, what letter name? *v.*

Provide lined paper to students.
Now let's practice writing **v** with your pencil.
Guide students as they write v on their paper. **Review** as needed.

 Link letter names to letter sounds as they appear in the program as needed.

412 Lesson 102

9 minutes

Teacher Materials:
Narrative trade book

Part C: Comprehension Strategies

Activity 1 — Listening Comprehension—A During-Reading Strategy

Direct students to narrative trade book of teacher choice. **Elicit** responses to questions. **Guide** as needed.

You've learned all about stories. Stories have characters, a setting, a beginning, a middle, and an end. Listen to the story again and see whether you can tell me all the parts of the story after I read it.

Elicit correct listening behavior from students. **Reread** trade book. **Model** prosody during read-aloud.

Ask questions to elicit identification of story elements. **Guide** as needed.

Activity 2 — Story Elements: Identify Characters, Setting, Beginning, Middle, and End—An After-Reading Strategy

Elicit responses to questions. **Guide** as needed.

You listened to the story. Now you can tell me all the parts of the story that you heard as you listened. What characters are in the story? (Student response.)

Who do you think is the main character? (Student response.)

What's the setting of the story? (Student response.)

Does the setting change or stay the same? (Student response.)

What events happened at the beginning? (Student response.)

What events happened in the middle? (Student responses.)

What events happened at the end? (Student response.)

You told all the parts of the story. Excellent job listening to the story and remembering all the parts.

Lesson 102

Lesson 103

Materials
Teacher: Narrative trade book (from Lesson 101)
Student: Lined paper

Part A: Phonemic and Phonological Awareness

Activity 1   Phoneme Isolation—Initial

Elicit responses. **Guide** as needed.
Let's work on a sound at the *beginning* of a word. I'm going to say a list of words. Some of the words will have the **/gr/** sound at the *beginning,* and some will not. I'll say the word first, and then you'll say the word.

Remember, we're listening for the **/gr/** sound at the *beginning* of the word. What sound are we listening for? */gr/.*

Listen. **Grass.** Say **grass.** *Grass.*

Give me a thumbs-up if you hear **/gr/** at the *beginning* of **grass.** (Thumbs-up.)

Yes, **grass** *begins* with the sound **/gr/.**

(Continue the activity with the following lists of words.
Grease. Grow. Fleet. Blew. Grip. Crumb.
Green. Grape. Clap. Frog. Grain. Grumpy.)

Let's work on another sound at the *beginning* of a word. I'm going to say a list of words. Some of the words will have the **/pl/** sound at the *beginning,* and some will not. I'll say the word first, and then you'll say the word.

Remember, we're listening for the **/pl/** sound at the *beginning* of the word. What sound are we listening for? */pl/.*

Listen. **Plum.** Say **plum.** *Plum.*

Give me a thumbs-up if you hear **/pl/** at the *beginning* of **plum.** (Thumbs-up.)

Yes, **plum** *begins* with the sound **/pl/.**

(Continue the activity with the following lists of words:
Drove. Please. Place. Brown. Twig. Plant.
Play. Plate. Punch. Rug. Pliers. Sap.)

414   Lesson 103

Activity 2 Phoneme Categorization—Final

Elicit responses. **Guide** as needed.
We're going to find words that don't belong. I'm going to say three words. Listen closely and see if you can tell which word *does not* belong. In earlier activities, you found words that didn't belong because the beginning sound was different. Today I want you to listen closely to the *last* sound in the words, and tell me the word that *does not* belong.

Your turn. Listen. **Sad, food, game.** Which word doesn't belong? *Game.*

Right, **game** *doesn't* belong because it ends with **/mmm/** and **sad** and **food** end with **/d/.**

(Continue the activity with the following examples:
Leaf, cough, glass.
Cut, hurt, tear.
Mud, feed, loss.
Knife, ear, half.
Seat, put, home.)

Part B: Letter Recognition and Formation

6 minutes

Student Materials:
Lined paper

Activity 1 Letter Recognition—Capital V

Elicit responses to questions. **Guide** as needed. **Write** capital V on the board. **Point** to capital V.
Today you'll learn another way to write **v.**
The name of this letter is **capital V.** What letter name? *Capital V.*
Again, what letter name? *Capital V.*
Review as needed.

Activity 2 Letter Formation—Capital V

Now we're going to practice writing **capital V.** When you practice writing, you'll learn not only where to start and stop the letter, but also which way to move your hand when you're making the letter. It's tricky, but you're so smart you'll learn how to write **capital V** very quickly. Watch.

Here's how you write **capital V** in the air.
Model capital V formation in the air (with your back to students).

Watch again.

Now let's practice writing **capital V** in the air. Hold up your writing hand, and make **capital V** in the air.
Guide students as they write capital V in the air.

Let's practice **capital V** again.

Lesson 103   **415**

Here's how to write **capital V** with your writing hand pointer finger.
Model capital V formation on the board with your finger (with your back to students).

Watch again.

Now let's practice writing **capital V** on your table without using your pencil.
Use your writing hand pointer finger, and make **capital V** on your table.
Guide students as they write capital V on their table or desktop.

Let's practice **capital V** again.

Model writing capital V on the board (with your back to students).
Remember that every letter has a name.
You learned the name of this letter is **capital V.** What letter name? *Capital V.*
Again, what letter name? *Capital V.*

Provide lined paper to students.
Now let's practice writing **capital V** with your pencil.
Guide students as they write capital V on their paper. **Review** as needed.

 Link letter names to letter sounds as they appear in the program as needed.

Part C: Comprehension Strategies

9 minutes

Teacher Materials:
Narrative trade book

Activity 1 Listening Comprehension—A During-Reading Strategy

Direct students to narrative trade book of teacher choice. **Elicit** response to question. **Guide** as needed.
We'll read the story again today. When we read the story today, I want you to think about anything in the story that reminds you of something that you know or something that has happened to you. We'll connect the story to your life after we read the story. Then we'll play the story.

Elicit correct listening behavior from students. **Reread** trade book. **Model** prosody during read-aloud.

Elicit text-to-self connections. **Guide** as needed.

Activity 2 Make Connections: Text-to-Self—An After-Reading Strategy

Elicit responses to questions. **Guide** as needed.
Making connections helps you understand what you read. It helps make reading more fun and interesting. Let's talk about this story and see how it matches or connects to your own life.

What connections from the story can you make to your life? (Student response.)

Discuss how characters, events, or items in story relate to things in students' lives.

Remember that when you read, making connections to your life helps you better understand and remember the story.

Activity 3 Retell the Story: Play the Story—An After-Reading Strategy

Discuss story elements and assign roles for playing the story. **Try** to assign a role to all students. **Elicit** responses to questions. **Guide** as needed.

Now you'll play the story. I'll need your ideas for how to play the story. Let's start with the setting. What's the setting? (Student response.)

Who would be willing to play the parts of the setting? (Student response.)

Who's the main character? (Student response.)

Who could play the main character? (Student response.)

What other characters are important in the story? (Student response.)

Who would be willing to play those parts? (Student response.)

You're going to play the beginning, the middle, and the end of the story.

What events happened at the beginning of the story? (Student response.)

How would you play those events? (Student response.)

What events happened in the middle of the story? (Student response.)

How would you play those events? (Student response.)

What events happened at the end of the story? (Student responses.)

How would you play those events? (Student response.)

I'll tell the whole story. As I tell the story, the players can do the actions I'm telling about. If there are words to say, I'll help you say them.

Coach all students to play story by telling story very simply and guiding students to play or mime actions. If there is dialogue, say the words and then have students repeat the words or prompt student to say appropriate words.

Praise creativity in playing story. **Prompt** everyone to bow as you applaud them.

Wow, that was fun!

Lesson 103   **417**

Lesson 104

> **Materials**
> **Teacher:** Narrative trade book (from Lesson 101); additional trade book that has similar story elements for text-to-text connection (either from student suggestions or teacher choice); Picture-Sound Cards for /bl/, /br/, /ō/, /u/, /y/, and /ī/
> **Student:** Lined paper

5 minutes

Teacher Materials:
Picture-Sound Cards for /bl/, /br/, /ō/, /u/, /y/, and /ī/

Part A: Phonemic and Phonological Awareness

Activity 1 Phoneme Isolation—Initial

Use IWB interactive cards or picture-sound cards. **Elicit** responses. **Guide** as needed.
I'm going to show you two cards and name the object on each card. Then I'll tell you a sound. Think about which word starts with that sound. Let's try it. Today we'll be listening for the sound at the *beginning* of a word.

Show /bl/ card; use either of two Picture-Sound Cards per phoneme for activity.
This is a _____. What is this? (Student response.)

Show /ō/ card; use any of four Picture-Sound Cards per phoneme for activity.
This is a _____. What is this? (Student response.)

Which word *begins* with **/bl/?** (Student response.)

Show /u/ card; use any of four Picture-Sound Cards per phoneme for activity.
This is a _____. What is this? (Student response.)

Show /br/ card; use either of two Picture-Sound Cards per phoneme for activity.
This is a _____. What is this? (Student response.)

Which word *begins* with **/br/?** (Student response.)

(Continue the activity with the following examples:
/br/ and /y/: Which word begins with /br/?
/ī/ and /bl/: Which word begins with /bl/?)

Activity 2 Phoneme Isolation—Medial

Elicit responses. **Guide** as needed.
We're going to keep working on the *middle* sound of a word. I'm going to say two words. Listen carefully to find out which word has the special sound in the *middle*. One word will have **/uuu/** in the *middle*, and the other word will not. Tell me the word that has **/uuu/** in the *middle* of the word. What sound are we listening for in the *middle* of the word? */uuu/*.

Let's try it. Remember to listen for our special sound **/uuu/.** Your turn. Listen. Bus. Boss. Listen again. Bus. Boss. Which word has the *middle* sound **/uuu/?** *Bus.*

Yes, **bus** has the *middle* sound **/uuu/.**

418 Lesson 104

(Continue the activity with the remaining pairs of words:
Tube, tub.
Cup, keep.
Kite, cut.
Bug, bag.)

Activity 3 Phoneme Identity—Final

Elicit responses. **Guide** as needed.
We're going to play a game and find something the same. I'm going to say three words. Listen closely and see if you can tell which sound is the same.

Your turn. What sound is the same in **tub, grab,** and **rob?** /b/.

Yes, **tub, grab,** and **rob** all end with the last sound **/b/.**

(Continue the activity with the following examples:
What sound is the same in my, fry, and supply?
What sound is the same in mother, her, and over?
What sound is the same in stub, crib, and mob?
What sound is the same in cry, shy, and by?
What sound is the same in cover, stir, and other?)

Activity 4 Phoneme Blending

Elicit responses. **Guide** as needed.
Today we're going to put two sounds together and make words. This time you're going to help me say the sounds before we make the word. I'm going to say a word very slowly so you can hear each sound. You need to listen carefully and say the sounds. When you say the sounds, it will sound almost like you're singing them. Then we'll put the sounds together and say the word.

Hold up one finger for each phoneme in each word (with the back of your hand to students).
My turn. Listen. **/mmm/ /īīī/.**
Say those sounds with me. /mmm/ /īīī/.
Now say the sounds by yourself. /mmm/ /īīī/.
Your turn again Say the sounds. /mmm/ /īīī/.
Now let's put it together. What word? My.

Let's try some more. My turn. Listen. **/shshsh/ /īīī/.**
Say those sounds with me. /shshsh/ /īīī/.
Now say the sounds by yourself. /shshsh/ /īīī/.
Your turn again. Say the sounds. /shshsh/ /īīī/.
Now let's put it together. What word? Shy.

(Continue the activity with the following words:
say (sss-āāā), may (mmm-āāā).

Lesson 104   **419**

6 minutes

Student Materials:
Lined paper

Part B: Letter Recognition and Formation

Activity 1 Letter Recognition Review—Capital V

Elicit responses to questions. **Guide** as needed **Write** capital V on the board. **Point** to capital V.
We learned that this letter is **capital V.** What letter name? *Capital V.*
Again, what letter name? *Capital V.*
Review as needed.

Activity 2 Letter Formation Review—Capital V

Now we're going to practice writing **capital V.** When you practice writing, you'll learn not only where to start and stop the letter, but also which way to move your hand when you're making the letter. It's tricky, but you're so smart you'll learn how to write **capital V** very quickly. Watch.

Here's how you write **capital V** in the air.
Model capital V formation in the air (with your back to students).

Watch again.

Now let's practice writing **capital V** in the air. Hold up your writing hand, and make **capital V** in the air.
Guide students as they write capital V in the air.

Let's practice **capital V** again.

Here's how to write **capital V** with your writing hand pointer finger.
Model capital V formation on the board with your finger (with your back to students).

Watch again.

Now let's practice writing **capital V** on your table without using your pencil. Use your writing hand pointer finger, and make **capital V** on your table.
Guide students as they write capital V on their table or desktop.

Let's practice **capital V** again.

Model writing capital V on the board (with your back to students).
Remember that every letter has a name.
You learned the name of this letter is **capital V.** What letter name? *Capital V.*
Again, what letter name? *Capital V.*

Provide lined paper to students.
Now let's practice writing **capital V** with your pencil.
Guide students as they write capital V on their paper. **Review** as needed.

 Link letter names to letter sounds as they appear in the program as needed.

420 Lesson 104

Part C: Comprehension Strategies

9 minutes

Teacher Materials:
Narrative trade book
Additional trade book

Activity 1 Listening Comprehension—A During-Reading Strategy

Direct students to narrative trade book of teacher choice. **Elicit** responses to questions. **Guide** as needed.

We'll read the story again today. When we read the story today, I want you to think about all the stories you have heard. I want you to think of which story reminds you of this one.

Elicit correct listening behavior from students. **Reread** trade book. **Model** prosody during read-aloud.

Guide students to focus on thinking of another story like this one for a text-to-text connection. **Elicit** responses to questions about text-to-text connections. **Guide** as needed.

You have heard lots of stories this year.

What story have you heard that reminds you of this story? (Student response.)
Elicit names of stories that are like today's story. **Guide** as needed.

Obtain book for text-to-text connection from student suggestions, if possible.

Activity 2 Make Connections Text-to-Text—An After-Reading Strategy

Elicit responses to questions. **Guide** as needed.
When I read this story, it reminded me right away of the story _____.
Listen to that story again, and then we'll make a connection to the story.

When I can connect a story that I am reading to another story that I know, it helps me to understand the story better. Making a connection to another story I have heard is a smart thing to do.
Elicit correct listening behavior from students. **Reread** other story for text-to-text connection. **Model** prosody during read-aloud.

Guide students to think of similarities between stories for text-to-text connection.

Lesson 104   421

Lesson 105

Materials
Teacher: Narrative trade book (from Lesson 101); 5-Story Map; Letter Recognition
Student: Lined paper; copy of 5-Story Map with writing lines

Part A: Phonemic and Phonological Awareness

Activity 1 Phoneme Isolation—Initial

Elicit responses. **Guide** as needed.
Let's work on a sound at the *beginning* of a word. I'm going to say a list of words. Some of the words will have the **/pr/** sound at the *beginning,* and some will not. I'll say the word first, and then you'll say the word.

Remember, we're listening for the **/pr/** sound at the *beginning* of the word. What sound are we listening for? */pr/.*

Listen. **Price.** Say **price.** *Price.*

Give me a thumbs-up if you hear **/pr/** at the *beginning* of **price.** (Thumbs-up.)

Yes, **price** *begins* with the sound **/pr/.**

(Continue the activity with the following lists of words.
Prince. Prune. Dress. Bring. Proud. Closet.
Pretzel. Print. Point. Glow. Prance. Princess.)

Let's work on another sound at the *beginning* of a word. I'm going to say a list of words. Some of the words will have the **/sk/** sound at the *beginning,* and some will not. I'll say the word first, and then you'll say the word.

Remember, we're listening for the **/sk/** sound at the *beginning* of the word. What sound are we listening for? */sk/.*

Listen. **School.** Say **school.** *School.*

Give me a thumbs-up if you hear **/sk/** at the *beginning* of **school.** (Thumbs-up.)

Yes, **school** *begins* with the sound **/sk/.**

(Continue the activity with the following lists of words:
Sky. Scarf. Sold. Blend. Trick. Skin.
Skip. Skirt. Plug. Foggy. Score. Pass.)

Activity 2 Phoneme Categorization—Final

Elicit responses. **Guide** as needed.
We're going to find words that don't belong. I'm going to say three words. Listen closely and see if you can tell which word *does not* belong. I want you to listen closely to the *last* sound in the words.

Your turn. Listen. **Ran, fun, seed.** Which word doesn't belong? *Seed.*

Right, **seed** *doesn't* belong because it ends with **/d/** and **ran** and **fun** end with **/nnn/.**

(Continue the activity with the following examples:
Take, poke, tough.
Bath, moth, suit.
Chain, turn, laugh.
Hike, boot, luck.
Path, earth, food.)

Part B: Letter Recognition and Formation

6 minutes

Activity 1 Letter Recognition Cumulative Review—l/L, w/W, k/K, v/V

Teacher Materials:
Letter Recognition

Student Materials:
Lined paper

Display on IWB or **write** letters and capitals on the board in the order shown. **Elicit** responses to questions. **Guide** as needed.
This week you've learned one letter and one capital—**v** and **capital V.** Let's review all the letters and capitals you've learned. Are you ready?

Letter	Question	Student Response
V	What letter?	Capital V.
L	What letter?	Capital L.
v	What letter?	v.
k	What letter?	k.
W	What letter?	Capital W.
K	What letter?	Capital K.
l	What letter?	l.
w	What letter?	w.

Review as needed.

Lesson 105

Activity 2 | Letter Formation Cumulative Review—l/L, w/W, k/K, v/V

Write l, capital L, w, capital W, k, capital K, v, and capital V on the board in the order shown (with your back to students). **Provide** lined paper to students.

Show me how you can write these letters and capitals.
Guide students as they write the letters and capitals on their paper. **Review** as needed.

 Link letter names to letter sounds as they appear in the program as needed.

Part C: Comprehensive Strategies

 9 minutes

Teacher Materials:
Narrative trade book
Story Map

Student Materials:
Story Map

Activity 1 | Listening Comprehension—A During-Reading Strategy

Direct students to narrative trade book of teacher choice. **Elicit** responses to questions. **Guide** as needed.
Today as I read the story, I want you to think carefully about all the parts of the story. The illustrator made the pictures for you so that the book would be fun to read. Look for what the illustrator did to show all the parts of the story. After I read the story, you'll become an illustrator and draw pictures for all the parts of the story. While I read, think about what you want to draw. Then be ready to retell the story to your neighbor.

Elicit correct listening behavior from students. **Reread** trade book. **Model** prosody during read-aloud.

Guide students to focus on illustrations for all story elements. **Elicit** answers to questions about how illustrator shows all story elements. **Guide** as needed.

Activity 2 | Story Elements: Illustrate and Retell Story—An After-Reading Strategy

Show Story Map. **Provide** copy of Story Map to each student. **Elicit** responses to questions. **Guide** as needed.
This is your new Story Map. It has places for you to make pictures for the characters, setting, and the beginning, the middle, and the end of the story.

Guide students to draw illustrations in the correct boxes and to work quickly.
Touch the box for characters. What will you put in that box? (**Idea:** *Picture(s) of main character(s).*)

Touch the box for setting. What will you put in that box? (Idea: *Picture of the setting.*)

Touch the beginning, middle, and end boxes. What will you put in those boxes? (Idea: *Events that happened at the beginning, the middle, and the end.*)

When you're finished, you can share your illustrations with your neighbor and tell the story from your illustrations.

Share illustrations with class if time permits, or make a class book of Story Maps.

Activity 3 Collaborate to Strengthen Writing

Show Story Map.

Now let's write about what happened in our story. Watch as I write about the beginning, the middle, and the end of the story.

Model writing 3 separate sentences that tell about the beginning, the middle, and the end of the story.

Now it is your turn to write about what happens **first** at the beginning of the story, **then** what happens in the middle of the story, and **finally** what happens at the end of the story. If you need help, ask me.

Monitor students. **Guide** as needed.

Assign student partners.

Share your writing with your neighbor. Add suggestions to make your neighbor's writing better if you think it needs it.

Model how to give feedback on what was written if it needs it. **Monitor** students. **Guide** as needed.

Lesson 105 **425**

Lesson 106

Materials

Teacher: Narrative trade book (same book for Lessons 106–110); Picture-Sound Cards for /cl/, /cr/, /ū/, /j/, /kw/, and /z/, 1-My Prediction Chart
Student: Lined paper

5 minutes

Teacher Materials:
Picture-Sound Cards for /cl/, /cr/, /ū/, /j/, /kw/, and /z/

Part A: Phonemic and Phonological Awareness

Activity 1 Phoneme Isolation—Initial

Use IWB interactive cards or picture-sound cards. **Elicit** responses. **Guide** as needed.
I'm going to show you two cards, and name the object on each card. Then I'll tell you a sound. Think about which word starts with that sound. Let's try it. Today we'll be listening for the sound at the *beginning* of a word.

Show /cl/ card; use either of two Picture-Sound Cards per phoneme for activity.
This is a _____. What is this? (Student response.)

Show /ū/ card; use any of four Picture-Sound Cards per phoneme for activity.
This is a _____. What is this? (Student response.)

Which word *begins* with **/cl/?** (Student response.)

Show /j/ card; use any of four Picture-Sound Cards per phoneme for activity.
This is a _____. What is this? (Student response.)

Show /cr/ card; use either of two Picture-Sound Cards per phoneme for activity.
This is a _____. What is this? (Student response.)

Which word *begins* with **/cr/?** (Student response.)

(Continue the activity with the following examples:
/cr/ and /kw/: Which word begins with /cr/?
/z/ and /cl/: Which word begins with /cl/?)

Activity 2 Phoneme Isolation—Medial

Elicit responses. **Guide** as needed.
We're going to keep working on the *middle* sound of a word. I'm going to say two words. Listen carefully to find out which word has the special sound in the *middle*. One word will have **/ōōō/** in the *middle,* and the other word will not have **/ōōō/** in the *middle*. You're going to tell me the word that has **/ōōō/** in the *middle* of the word. What sound are we listening for in the *middle* of the word? /ōōō/.

426   Lesson 106

Let's try it. Remember to listen for our special sound **/ōōō/.** Your turn. Listen. Cone. Cane. Listen again. Cone. Cane. Which word has the *middle* sound **/ōōō/?** *Cone.*

Yes, **cone** has the *middle* sound **/ōōō/.**

(Continue the activity with the remaining pairs of words:
Cat, coat.
Phone, fine.
Goat, get.
Sip, soap.)

Activity 3 Phoneme Identity—Final

Elicit responses. **Guide** as needed.
We're going to play a game and find something the same. I'm going to say three words. Listen closely and see if you can tell which sound is the same.

Your turn. What sound is the same in **packs, fox,** and **socks?** /ks/.

Yes, **packs, fox,** and **socks** all end with the last sound **/ks/.**

(Continue the activity with the following examples:
What sound is the same in breeze, buzz, and was?
What sound is the same in box, bricks, and locks?
What sound is the same in rise, freeze, and prize?)

Activity 4 Phoneme Blending

Elicit responses. **Guide** as needed.
Today we're going to put two sounds together and make words. This time you're going to help me say the sounds before we make the word. I'm going to say a word very slowly so you can hear each sound. You need to listen carefully and say the sounds. When you say the sounds, it will sound almost like you're singing them. Then we'll put the sounds together and say the word.

Hold up one finger for each phoneme in each word (with the back of your hand to students).
My turn. Listen. **/ēēē/ /t/.**
Say those sounds with me. */ēēē/ /t/.*
Now say the sounds by yourself. */ēēē/ /t/.*
Your turn again. Say the sounds. */ēēē/ /t/.*
Now let's put it together. What word? *Eat.*

Let's try some more. My turn. Listen. **/aaa/ /t/.**
Say those sounds with me. */aaa/ /t/.*
Now say the sounds by yourself. */aaa/ /t/.*
Your turn again. Say the sounds. */aaa/ /t/.*
Now let's put it together. What word? *At.*

(Continue the activity with the following words:
off (ooo-fff), if (iii-fff).

Lesson 106   **427**

6 minutes

Student Materials:
Lined paper

Part B: Letter Recognition and Formation

Activity 1 Letter Recognition—p

Elicit responses to questions. **Guide** as needed. **Write** p on the board. **Point** to p.
Today you'll learn a new letter. The name of this letter is **p.** What letter name? *p.*
Again, what letter name? *p.*
Review as needed.

Activity 2 Letter Formation—p

Now we're going to practice writing **p.** When you practice writing, you'll learn not only where to start and stop the letter, but also which way to move your hand when you're making the letter. It's tricky, but you're so smart you'll learn how to write **p** very quickly. Watch.

Here's how you write **p** in the air.
Model p formation in the air (with your back to students).

Watch again.

Now let's practice writing **p** in the air. Hold up your writing hand, and make **p** in the air.
Guide students as they write p in the air.

Let's practice **p** again.

Here's how to write **p** with your writing hand pointer finger.
Model p formation on the board with your finger (with your back to students).

Watch again.

Now let's practice writing **p** on your table without using your pencil. Use your writing hand pointer finger, and make **p** on your table.
Guide students as they write p on their table or desktop.

Let's practice **p** again.

Model writing p on the board (with your back to students).
Remember that every letter has a name.
You learned the name of this letter is **p.** What letter name? *p.*
Again, what letter name? *p.*

Provide lined paper to students.
Now let's practice writing **p** with your pencil.
Guide students as they write p on their paper. **Review** as needed.

 Link letter names to letter sounds as they appear in the program as needed.

Set up a writing center with writing materials and correct models of letters learned so far for students to use in their free time.

428   Lesson 106

Part C: Comprehension Strategies

9 minutes

Teacher Materials:
Narrative trade book
My Prediction Chart

Student Materials:
Lined paper

Activity 1 — Title, Author, and Illustrator Identification—A Before-Reading Strategy

Provide a reading center to display books being read so that students can enjoy them again during free time.

Direct students to narrative trade book of teacher choice. **Elicit** responses to questions. **Guide** as needed.

Show front cover of book and allow student to point to name of title, author, and illustrator as you discuss them.
We'll read a new story today. The title of today's story is _____. What's the title of today's story? (Student response.)

The author of today's story is _____. Who's the author of today's story? (Student response.)

The illustrator of today's story is _____. Who's the illustrator? (Student response.)

Activity 2 — Activate Background Knowledge—A Before-Reading Strategy

Elicit responses to questions. **Guide** as needed.
The information that you already have in your brain is called background knowledge.

What's the information you have in your brain called? *Background knowledge.*

Choose a topic to activate background knowledge from story you will read.
Tell me your background knowledge for _____.
Discuss background knowledge for topic chosen.

Provide lined paper. **Model** writing a sentence about what you know.
Write a sentence that tells me your background knowledge for _____.
If you need help, ask me.
Monitor students. **Guide** students as needed.

When you think about your background knowledge before you read, it helps you better understand the story. You can connect what you know to what happens in the story.

Lesson 106 **429**

Activity 3 Make Predictions—A Before-Reading Strategy

Show My Prediction Chart and fill in appropriate areas. **Show** title, front and back cover, and pictures inside book. **Elicit** responses to questions. **Guide** as needed.

The title of today's book is _____. Now that you know the title of today's book, let's look at the cover and pictures inside the book for clues to make some good guesses of what you think the story will be about.

What do you call your good guesses? *Predictions.*

Making predictions helps us get interested in the story before we read it. Let's make some predictions about the story before I read it to you.

What do you predict this story will be about? (Student response.)

What characters do you predict will be in the story? (Student response.)

What do you predict the setting will be? (Student response.)

What do you predict might happen in the story? (Student response.)

When we read the book we'll check your predictions to see whether they're correct.

Elicit correct listening behavior from students. **Read** trade book. **Model** prosody during read-aloud.

Guide students to confirm predictions and/or connect background knowledge as you read story. **Ask** questions to confirm predictions and/or connect background knowledge. **Guide** as needed.

Activity 4 Confirm Predictions—An After-Reading Strategy

Show My Prediction Chart and circle whether or not prediction was correct. **Elicit** responses to questions. **Guide** as needed.

Now let's check your predictions to see whether they were correct. You predicted that the story was about _____. Was your prediction correct? (Student response.)

You predicted that _____ were characters in the story. Was your prediction correct? (Student response.)

You predicted that the setting was _____. Was your prediction correct? (Student response.)

You predicted that some events would be _____. Was your prediction correct? (Student response.)

Remember that your predictions don't have to be correct. Just making a prediction and listening to see whether your prediction is correct helps you stay interested in the story.

430 *Lesson 106*

Lesson 107

Materials
Teacher: Narrative trade book (from Lesson 106)
Student: Lined paper

5 minutes

Part A: Phonemic and Phonological Awareness

Activity 1 Phoneme Isolation—Initial

Elicit responses. **Guide** as needed.
Let's work on a sound at the *beginning* of a word. I'm going to say a list of words. Some of the words will have the **/sl/** sound at the *beginning,* and some will not. I'll say the word first, and then you'll say the word.

Remember, we're listening for the **/sl/** sound at the *beginning* of the word. What sound are we listening for? */sl/*.

Listen. **Sleep.** Say **sleep.** *Sleep.*

Give me a thumbs-up if you hear **/sl/** at the *beginning* of **sleep.**
(Thumbs-up.)

Yes, **sleep** *begins* with the sound **/sl/.**

(Continue the activity with the following lists of words.
Slip. Sled. Flag. Bruise. Slipper. Cry.
Slide. Sling Song. Little. Slow. Sleigh.)

Let's work on another sound at the *beginning* of a word. I'm going to say a list of words. Some of the words will have the **/sm/** sound at the *beginning,* and some will not. I'll say the word first, and then you'll say the word.

Remember, we're listening for the **/sm/** sound at the *beginning* of the word. What sound are we listening for? */sm/*.

Listen. **Smile.** Say **smile.** *Smile.*

Give me a thumbs-up if you hear **/sm/** at the *beginning* of **smile.**
(Thumbs-up.)

Yes, **smile** *begins* with the sound **/sm/.**

(Continue the activity with the following lists of words:
Smoke. Smell. Sold. Blend. Send. Smudge.
Smart. Smear. Grip. Mass. Small. Praise.)

Lesson 107   431

Activity 2 | Phoneme Categorization—Final

Elicit responses. **Guide** as needed.
We're going to find words that don't belong. I'm going to say three words. I want you to listen closely and see if you can tell which word *does not* belong. Listen closely to the *last* sound in the words.

Your turn. Listen. **Flag, dog, can.** Which word doesn't belong? *Can.*

Right, **can** *doesn't* belong because it ends with **/nnn/** and **flag** and **dog** end with **/g/.**

(Continue the activity with the following examples:
Pull, tall, stick.
Wish, mash, both.
Pig, log, book.
Mall, with, pill.
Push, cash, fin.)

Part B: Letter Recognition and Formation

6 minutes

Student Materials:
Lined paper

Activity 1 | Letter Recognition Review—p

Elicit responses to questions. **Guide** as needed. **Write** p on the board. **Point** to p.
We learned that this letter is **p.** What letter name? *p.*
Again, what letter name? *p.*
Review as needed.

Activity 2 | Letter Formation Review—p

Now we're going to practice writing **p.** When you practice writing, you'll learn not only where to start and stop the letter, but also which way to move your hand when you're making the letter. It's tricky, but you're so smart you'll learn how to write **p** very quickly. Watch.

Here's how you write **p** in the air.
Model p formation in the air (with your back to students).

Watch again.

Now let's practice writing **p** in the air. Hold up your writing hand, and make **p** in the air.
Guide students as they write p in the air.

Let's practice **p** again.

Here's how to write **p** with your writing hand pointer finger.
Model p formation on the board with your finger (with your back to students).

Watch again.

Now let's practice writing **p** on your table without using your pencil. Use your writing hand pointer finger, and make **p** on your table.
Guide students as they write p on their table or desktop.

Let's practice **p** again.

Model writing p on the board (with your back to students).
Remember that every letter has a name.
You learned the name of this letter is **p.** What letter name? *p.*
Again, what letter name? *p.*

Provide lined paper to students.
Now let's practice writing **p** with your pencil.
Guide students as they write p on their paper. **Review** as needed.

 Link letter names to letter sounds as they appear in the program as needed.

Part C: Comprehension Strategies

9 minutes

Teacher Materials:
Narrative trade book

Student Materials:
Lined paper

Activity 1 Listening Comprehension—A During-Reading Strategy

Direct students to narrative trade book of teacher choice. **Elicit** response to question. **Guide** as needed.
We'll read the story again today. When we read the story today, I want you to think about anything in the story that reminds you of something that you know or something that has happened to you. We'll connect the story to your life after we read the story.

Elicit correct listening behavior from students. **Reread** trade book. **Model** prosody during read-aloud.

Elicit text-to-self connections. **Guide** as needed.

Activity 2 Make Connections: Text-to-Self—An After-Reading Strategy

Elicit responses to questions. **Guide** as needed.
Making connections helps me to understand what I read. It helps make reading more fun and interesting. Let's talk about this story and see how it matches or connects to my own life.

Listen as I make some connections.
Model making text-to-self connections.

What connections from the story can you make to your life? (Student response.)

Lesson 107 **433**

Discuss how characters, events, or items in story relate to things in students' lives.

Provide lined paper. **Model** writing a sentence about a connection you made.
Write a sentence that describes the connection you made to your life. If you need help, ask me.
Monitor students. **Guide** students as needed.

Remember that making connections to your life helps you better understand and remember the story.

Activity 3 Identify Main Idea—An After-Reading Strategy

Elicit responses to questions. **Guide** as needed.
Today we're going to try to learn something that's a little tricky. We're going to figure out what the story is mostly about. When we think about what the story is mostly about, we're thinking about the main idea of the story. The main idea is what the story is mostly about. What's the main idea? (Idea: *What the story is mostly about.*)

It's a little tricky to figure out what the story is mostly about, but the story gives me clues to make it easier.

Model think-aloud for finding main idea of story.

> ### Sample Wording for Think-Aloud
>
> When I figure out what the story is mostly about, I think about all the things in the story. I know the title of our story is _____ . That makes me think about _____ . I know that the story takes place _____ and that the characters are _____ . I know that the most important thing to happen was _____ . I think the story was mostly about _____ . So I think the main idea of the story is _____ .

What's the main idea of our story? (Student response.)
Tell main idea by first naming main character then telling most important event, what main character learned, or how main character changed in story.

434   *Lesson 107*

Lesson 108

Materials

Teacher: Narrative trade book (from Lesson 106); additional trade book that has similar story elements for text-to-text connection (either from student suggestions or teacher choice); Picture-Sound Cards for /dr/, /fl/, /bl/, /br/, /d/, and /f/

Student: Lined paper

5 minutes

Teacher Materials: Picture-Sound Cards for /dr/, /fl/, /bl/, /br/, /d/, and /f/

Part A: Phonemic and Phonological Awareness

Activity 1 Phoneme Isolation—Initial

Use IWB interactive cards or picture-sound cards. **Elicit** responses. **Guide** as needed. I'm going to show you two cards, and name the object on each card. Then I'll tell you a sound. Think about which word starts with that sound. Let's try it. Today we'll be listening for the sound at the *beginning* of a word.

Show /dr/ card; use either of two Picture-Sound Cards per phoneme for activity. This is a _____. What is this? (Student response.)

Show /br/ card; use either of two Picture-Sound Cards per phoneme for activity. This is a _____. What is this? (Student response.)

Which word *begins* with **/dr/?** (Student response.)

Show /bl/ card; use either of two Picture-Sound Cards per phoneme for activity. This is a _____. What is this? (Student response.)

Show /fl/ card; use either of two Picture-Sound Cards per phoneme for activity. This is a _____. What is this? (Student response.)

Which word *begins* with **/fl/?** (Student response.)

(Continue the activity with the following examples:
/fl/ and /f/: Which word begins with /fl/?
/d/ and /dr/: Which word begins with /dr/?)

Activity 2 Phoneme Isolation—Medial

Elicit responses. **Guide** as needed.
We're going to keep working on the *middle* sound of a word. I'm going to say two words. Listen carefully to find out which word has the special sound in the *middle*. One word will have **/eee/** in the *middle*, and the other word will not. You're going to tell me the word that has **/eee/** in the *middle* of the word. What sound are we listening for in the *middle* of the word? /eee/.

Let's try it. Remember to listen for our special sound **/eee/.** Your turn. Listen. Shed. Shade. Listen again. Shed. Shade. Which word has the middle sound **/eee/?** *Shed.*

Yes, **shed** has the *middle* sound **/eee/.**

(Continue the activity with the remaining pairs of words:
Vote, vet.
Bed, bad.
Head, hide.
Late, let.)

Activity 3 Phoneme Identity—Initial

Elicit responses. **Guide** as needed.
You've worked so hard to tell me the sounds that are the same in different words. Today you're going to tell me the *first* sound you hear in my special words. I'll tell you a word.

Model phoneme sounds.
Your turn. What is the first sound you hear in **mother?** */mmm/.*

What is the first sound you hear in **sand?** */sss/.*

What is the first sound you hear in **apple?** */aaa/.*

What is the first sound you hear in **eagle?** */ēēē/.*

What is the first sound you hear in **saddle?** */sss/.*

What is the first sound you hear in **easy?** */ēēē/.*

What is the first sound you hear in **mind?** */mmm/.*

What is the first sound you hear in **add?** */aaa/.*

Activity 4 Phoneme Blending

Elicit responses. **Guide** as needed.
Let's put some sounds together and make words. I'm going to say a word very slowly so you can hear each sound. You need to listen carefully and say the sounds. When you say the sounds, it will sound almost like you're singing them. Then we'll put the sounds together and say the word.

My turn. Listen. **/shshsh/ /ōōō/.**
Say those sounds with me. */shshsh/ /ōōō/.*
Now say the sounds by yourself. */shshsh/ /ōōō/.*
Your turn again. Say the sounds. */shshsh/ /ōōō/.*
Now let's put it together. What word? *Show.*

436   *Lesson 108*

Let's try some more. My turn. Listen. **/lll/ /ōōō/.**
Say those sounds with me. /lll/ /ōōō/.
Now say the sounds by yourself. /lll/ /ōōō/.
Your turn again. Say the sounds. /lll/ /ōōō/.
Now let's put it together. What word? *Low.*

(Continue the activity with the following words:
moo (mmm-oooooo), zoo (zzz-oooooo).

Part B: Letter Recognition and Formation

6 minutes

Student Materials:
Lined paper

Activity 1 Letter Recognition—Capital P

Elicit responses to questions. **Guide** as needed. **Write** capital P on the board. **Point** to capital P.
Today you'll learn another way to write **p.**
The name of this letter is **capital P.** What letter name? *Capital P.*
Again, what letter name? *Capital P.*
Review as needed.

Activity 2 Letter Formation—Capital P

Now we're going to practice writing **capital P.** When you practice writing, you'll learn not only where to start and stop the letter, but also which way to move your hand when you're making the letter. It's tricky, but you're so smart you'll learn how to write **capital P** very quickly. Watch.

Here's how you write **capital P** in the air.
Model capital P formation in the air (with your back to students).

Watch again.

Now let's practice writing **capital P** in the air. Hold up your writing hand, and make **capital P** in the air.
Guide students as they write capital P in the air.

Let's practice **capital P** again.

Here's how to write **capital P** with your writing hand pointer finger.
Model capital P formation on the board with your finger (with your back to students).

Watch again.

Now let's practice writing **capital P** on your table without using your pencil. Use your writing hand pointer finger, and make **capital P** on your table.
Guide students as they write capital P on their table or desktop.

Let's practice **capital P** again.

Lesson 108   **437**

Model writing capital P on the board (with your back to students).
Remember that every letter has a name.
You learned the name of this letter is **capital P.** What letter name? *Capital P.*
Again, what letter name? *Capital P.*

Provide lined paper to students.
Now let's practice writing **capital P** with your pencil.
Guide students as they write capital P on their paper. **Review** as needed.

 Link letter names to letter sounds as they appear in the program as needed.

Part C: Comprehension Strategies

9 minutes

Teacher Materials:
Narrative trade book
Additional trade book

Activity 1 Listening Comprehension—A During-Reading Strategy

Direct students to narrative trade book of teacher choice. **Elicit** responses to questions. **Guide** as needed.
We'll read the story again today. When we read the story today, I want you to think about all the stories you have heard. I want you to think of which story reminds you of this one.

Elicit correct listening behavior from students. **Reread** trade book. **Model** prosody during read-aloud.

Guide students to focus on thinking of another story like this one for a text-to-text connection. **Elicit** responses to questions about text-to-text connections. **Guide** as needed.

You have heard lots of stories this year. What story have you heard that reminds you of this story? (Student response.)
Elicit names of stories that are like today's story. **Guide** as needed.

Obtain book for text-to-text connection from student suggestions, if possible.

Activity 2 Make Connections: Text-to-Text—An After-Reading Strategy

Elicit responses to questions. **Guide** as needed.
When I read this story, it reminded me right away of the time I read _____. Listen as I show you what I mean.

When I can connect a story that I am reading to another story that I know, it helps me to understand the story better. Making a connection to another story I have heard is a smart thing to do.

Elicit correct listening behavior from students. **Reread** other story for text-to-text connection. **Model** prosody during read-aloud.

Guide students to think of similarities between stories for text-to-text connection.

438   Lesson 108

Activity 3 | Identify Main Idea—An After-Reading Strategy

Direct students to second text used for text-to-text connection and use again to find main idea. **Elicit** responses to questions. **Guide** as needed.

Today we're going to work on something that's a little tricky. We're going to figure out what the story is mostly about. When we think about what the story is mostly about we're thinking about the main idea of the story. The main idea is what the story is mostly about.

What's the main idea? (Idea: *What the story is mostly about.*)

What do we call what the story is mostly about? *The main idea.*

It's a little tricky to figure out the main idea, but the story gives me clues to make it easier.

The main idea of this story is _____. What's the main idea of our story? (Student response.)

Model finding main idea of story. **Tell** main idea by first naming main character, then telling most important event, what main character learned, or how main character changed in story.

Lesson 108 **439**

Lesson 109

Materials
Teacher: Narrative trade book (from Lesson 106); 5-Story Map
Student: Lined paper; copy of 5-Story Map

Part A: Phonemic and Phonological Awareness

 5 minutes

Activity 1 Phoneme Isolation—Initial

Elicit responses. **Guide** as needed.
Let's work on a sound at the *beginning* of a word. I'm going to say a list of words. Some of the words will have the **/sn/** sound at the *beginning,* and some will not. I'll say the word first, and then you'll say the word.

Remember, we're listening for the **/sn/** sound at the *beginning* of the word. What sound are we listening for? */sn/.*

Listen. **Snow.** Say **snow.** *Snow.*

Give me a thumbs-up if you hear **/sn/** at the *beginning* of **snow.** (Thumbs-up.)

Yes, **snow** *begins* with the sound **/sn/.**

(Continue the activity with the following lists of words.
Snake. Snap. Drop. Clock. Snack. Froze.
Sneak. Snail. Name. Tease. Sneeze. Sniff.)

Let's work on another sound at the *beginning* of a word. I'm going to say a list of words. Some of the words will have the **/sp/** sound at the *beginning,* and some will not. I'll say the word first, and then you'll say the word.

Remember, we're listening for the **/sp/** sound at the *beginning* of the word. What sound are we listening for? */sp/.*

Listen. **Spoon.** Say **spoon.** *Spoon.*

Give me a thumbs-up if you hear **/sp/** at the *beginning* of **spoon.** (Thumbs-up)

Yes, **spoon** *begins* with the sound **/sp/.**

(Continue the activity with the following lists of words:
Spider. Spell. Sold. Ski. Place. Spice.
Speak. Spot. Print. Map. Spend. Slide.)

Activity 2 Phoneme Categorization—Final

Elicit responses. **Guide** as needed.
We're going to find words that don't belong. I'm going to say three words. Listen closely and see if you can tell which word *does not* belong. I want you to listen closely to the *last* sound in the words.

Your turn. Listen. **Love, have, bug.** Which word doesn't belong? *Bug.* Right, **bug** *doesn't* belong because it ends with **/g/** and **love** and **have** end with **/vvv/.**

(Continue the activity with the following examples:
Lip, rope, pull.
Match, witch, smash.
Gave, dive, mill.
Flop, wish, keep.
Such, catch, leg.)

Part B: Letter Recognition and Formation

6 minutes

Student Materials:
Lined paper

Activity 1 Letter Recognition Review—Capital P

Elicit responses to questions. **Guide** as needed. **Write** capital P on the board. **Point** to capital P.
We learned that this letter is **capital P.** What letter name? *Capital P.*
Again, what letter name? *Capital P.*
Review as needed.

Activity 2 Letter Formation Review—Capital P

Now we're going to practice writing **capital P.** When you practice writing, you'll learn not only where to start and stop the letter, but also which way to move your hand when you're making the letter. It's tricky, but you're so smart you'll learn how to write **capital P** very quickly. Watch.

Here's how you write **capital P** in the air.
Model capital P formation in the air (with your back to students).

Watch again.

Now let's practice writing **capital P** in the air. Hold up your writing hand, and make **capital P** in the air.
Guide students as they write capital P in the air.

Let's practice **capital P** again.

Here's how to write **capital P** with your writing hand pointer finger.
Model capital P formation on the board with your finger (with your back to students).

Watch again.

Lesson 109   **441**

Now let's practice writing **capital P** on your table without using your pencil. Use your writing hand pointer finger, and make **capital P** on your table.
Guide students as they write capital P on their table or desktop.

Let's practice **capital P** again.

Model writing capital P on the board (with your back to students).
Remember that every letter has a name.
You learned the name of this letter is **capital P.** What letter name? *Capital P.*
Again, what letter name? *Capital P.*

Provide lined paper to students.
Now let's practice writing **capital P** with your pencil.
Guide students as they write capital P on their paper. **Review** as needed.

 Link letter names to letter sounds as they appear in the program as needed.

Part C: Comprehension Strategies

 9 minutes

Teacher Materials:
Narrative trade book

Story Map

Student Materials:
Story Map

Activity 1 Listening Comprehension—A During-Reading Strategy

Direct students to narrative trade book of teacher choice. **Elicit** responses to questions. **Guide** as needed.
Today as I read the story, I want you to look carefully at the pictures of all the parts of the story. The illustrator made the pictures for you so that the book would be fun to read. Look for what the illustrator did to show the parts of the story. After I read the story, you'll become an illustrator and draw pictures of all the parts.

Elicit correct listening behavior from students. **Reread** trade book. **Model** prosody during read-aloud.

Guide students to focus on illustrations for all story elements. **Elicit** responses to questions about how illustrator shows all story elements. **Guide** as needed.

Activity 2 Identify Main Idea—An After-Reading Strategy

Elicit responses to questions. **Guide** as needed.
Before you illustrate the parts of the story, let's think about what the story is mostly about. We're thinking about the main idea of the story. The main idea is what the story is mostly about. What's the main idea? (Idea: *What the story is mostly about.*)

What do we call what the story is mostly about? *The main idea.*

It's a little tricky to figure out the main idea, but the story gives me clues to make it easier.
Guide students to find main idea using clues from the story.

What's the title of the story? (**Student response.**)

Who are the main characters in the story? (**Student response.**)

Select from following questions those that will help you elicit the main idea from students.

What was the main thing that happened in the story? (**Student response.**)

How did the main character change? (**Student response.**)

What did the main character learn? (**Student response.**)

So the main idea of this story is _____.

What's the main idea of our story? (**Student response.**)
Tell main idea by first naming main character. Then tell most important event, what main character learned, or how main character changed in story.

Activity 3 Story Elements: Illustrate Story—An After-Reading Strategy

Show Story Map. **Provide** Story Map to each student. **Elicit** responses to questions. **Guide** as needed.
Now you'll become an illustrator. Make pictures to show all the parts of the story.

Monitor students and provide assistance in filling Story Map as needed.

In the next lesson, you'll get to tell about your illustration.
Save student copies of Story Map for Lesson 110.

Lesson 109 **443**

Lesson 110

Materials

Teacher: Narrative trade book (from Lesson 106); 5-Story Map (from Lesson 109); Picture-Sound Cards for /fr/, /gl/, /cl/, /cr/, /f/, and /g/; Letter Recognition; 8-My Book Review

Student: Lined paper; copy of 5-Story Map (from Lesson 109); copy of 8-My Book Review

5 minutes

Teacher Materials:
Picture-Sound Cards for /fr/, /gl/, /cl/, /cr/, /f/, and /g/

Part A: Phonemic and Phonological Awareness

Activity 1 Phoneme Isolation—Initial

Use IWB interactive cards or picture-sound cards. **Elicit** responses. **Guide** as needed.
I'm going to show you two cards and name the object on each card. Then I'll tell you a sound. Think about which word starts with that sound. Let's try it. Today we'll be listening for the sound at the *beginning* of a word.

Show /fr/ card; use either of two Picture-Sound Cards per phoneme for activity.
This is a _____. What is this? (Student response.)

Show /cr/ card; use either of two Picture-Sound Cards per phoneme for activity.
This is a _____. What is this? (Student response.)

Which word *begins* with **/fr/?** (Student response.)

Show /cl/ card; use either of two Picture-Sound Cards per phoneme for activity.
This is a _____. What is this? (Student response.)

Show /gl/ card; use either of two Picture-Sound Cards per phoneme for activity.
This is a _____. What is this? (Student response.)

Which word *begins* with **/gl/?** (Student response.)

(Continue the activity with the following examples.
/gl/ and /g/: Which word begins with /gl/?
/f/ and /fr/: Which word begins with /fr/?)

Activity 2 Phoneme Isolation—Medial

Elicit responses. **Guide** as needed.
We're going to keep working on the *middle* sound of a word. I'm going to say two words. Listen carefully to find out which word has the special sound in the *middle*. One word will have **/iii/** in the *middle,* and the other word will not. You're going to tell me the word that has **/iii/** in the *middle* of the word. What sound are we listening for in the *middle* of the word? /iii/.

444   Lesson 110

Let's try it. Remember to listen for our special sound /īīī/. Your turn. Listen. Pipe. Pop. Listen again. Pipe. Pop. Which word has the middle sound /īīī/? *Pipe.*

Yes, **pipe** has the *middle* sound /īīī/.

(Continue the activity with the remaining pairs of words:
Dime, dim.
Moose, mice.
Have, hive.
Bike, bake.)

Activity 3 Phoneme Identity—Initial

Elicit responses. **Guide** as needed.
You've worked so hard to tell me the sounds that are the same in different words. Today you're going to tell me the *first* sound you hear in my special words. I'll say a word.

Model phoneme sounds.
Your turn. What is the first sound you hear in **raft?** */rrr/.*

What is the first sound you hear in **dinner?** */d/.*

What is the first sound you hear in **fire?** */fff/.*

What is the first sound you hear in **insect?** */iii/.*

What is the first sound you hear in **doctor?** */d/.*

What is the first sound you hear in **itch?** */iii/.*

What is the first sound you hear in **ribbon?** */rrr/.*

What is the first sound you hear in **folder?** */fff/.*

Activity 4 Phoneme Blending

Elicit responses. **Guide** as needed.
Let's put some sounds together and make words. I'm going to say a word very slowly so you can hear each sound. You need to listen carefully and say the sounds. When you say the sounds, it will sound almost like you're singing them. Then we'll put the sounds together and say the word.

My turn. Listen. **/www/ /ēēē/.**
Say those sounds with me. */www/ /ēēē/.*
Now say the sounds by yourself. */www/ /ēēē/.*
Your turn again. Say the sounds. */www/ /ēēē/.*
Now let's put it together. What word? *We.*

Lesson 110   **445**

Let's try some more. My turn. Listen. **/shshsh/ /ēēē/.**
Say those sounds with me. */shshsh/ /ēē /.*
Now say the sounds by yourself. */shshsh/ /ēēē/.*
Your turn again. Say the sounds. */shshsh/ /ēēē/.*
Now let's put it together. What word? *She.*

(Continue the activity with the following words:
ear (ēēē–rrr), each (ēēē–ch).

Part B: Letter Recognition and Formation

6 minutes

Teacher Materials:
Letter Recognition

Student Materials:
Lined paper

Activity 1 Letter Recognition Cumulative Review—w/W, k/K, v/V, p/P

Display on IWB or **write** letters and capitals on the board in the order shown. **Elicit** responses to questions. **Guide** as needed.

This week you've learned one letter and one capital—**p** and **capital P**. Let's review all the letters and capitals you've learned. Are you ready?

Letter	Question	Student Response
v	What letter?	v.
K	What letter?	Capital K.
p	What letter?	p.
w	What letter?	w.
V	What letter?	Capital V.
k	What letter?	k.
P	What letter?	Capital P.
W	What letter?	Capital W.

Review as needed.

446 Lesson 110

Activity 2 | Letter Formation Cumulative Review—w/W, k/K, v/V, p/P

Write w, capital W, k, capital K, v, capital V, p, and capital P on the board in the order shown (with your back to students). **Provide** lined paper to students.

Show me how you can write these letters and capitals.
Guide students as they write the letters and capitals on their paper. **Review** as needed.

 Link letter names to letter sounds as they appear in the program as needed.

Part C: Comprehension Strategies

 9 minutes

Activity 1 | Listening Comprehension—A During-Reading Strategy

Teacher Materials:
Narrative trade book
Story Map
My Book Review

Student Materials:
Story Map
My Book Review

Direct students to narrative trade book of teacher choice. **Elicit** responses to questions. **Guide** as needed.
Today I will read the story one last time. Listen to the story to remember all the parts of the story. Then you will get to tell about the illustrations that you made in the last lesson. You will tell about the characters, setting, and the events from the beginning, the middle, and the end of the story.

Elicit correct listening behavior from students. **Reread** trade book. **Model** prosody during read-aloud.

Guide students to focus on story elements. **Elicit** responses to questions about story elements. **Guide** as needed.

Lesson 110

Activity 2 **Retell the Story—An After-Reading Strategy**

Assign student partners. **Provide** copy of Story Map completed in Lesson 109. **Elicit** responses to questions. **Guide** as needed.

You are going to tell a partner all the parts of the story from your pictures. Your partner will listen to you the right way. Then you will listen politely as your partner tells you about his or her pictures.

When you're done, if there is time, you can show the class your illustrations and tell all the parts of the story.

Monitor students as they retell the story.

Share Story Maps with class as time permits, or make a class book of Story Maps.

Activity 3 **Connections Through Shared Writing— Express Opinions**

Show My Book Review. **Elicit** responses to questions. **Guide** as needed.

Think about the two books we read, _____ and _____. Let's talk about the two books. Which one did you like best and why?

Provide copies of My Book Review to students. **Guide** students through completion of My Book Review. **Share** with class as time permits.

448 *Lesson 110*

Lesson 111

Materials
Teacher: Narrative trade book (same book for Lessons 111–115), 1-My Prediction Chart
Student: Lined paper, Copy of 1-My Prediction Chart

Part A: Phonemic and Phonological Awareness

Activity 1 Phoneme Isolation—Initial

Elicit responses. **Guide** as needed.
Let's work on a sound at the *beginning* of a word. I'm going to say a list of words. Some of the words will have the **/st/** sound at the *beginning*, and some will not. I'll say the word first, and then you'll say the word.

Remember, we're listening for the **/st/** sound at the *beginning* of the word. What sound are we listening for? */st/*.

Listen. **Star.** Say **star.** *Star.*

Give me a thumbs-up if you hear **/st/** at the *beginning* of **star.** (Thumbs-up.)

Yes, **star** *begins* with the sound **/st/.**

(Continue the activity with the following lists of words.
Stove. Sting. Drip. Flame. Steal. Sick.
Stink. Steam. Nose. Snow. Stool. Stack.)

Let's work on another sound at the *beginning* of a word. I'm going to say a list of words. Some of the words will have the **/sw/** sound at the *beginning*, and some will not. I'll say the word first, and then you'll say the word.

Remember, we're listening for the **/sw/** sound at the *beginning* of the word. What sound are we listening for? */sw/*.

Listen. **Swing.** Say **swing.** *Swing.*

Give me a thumbs-up if you hear **/sw/** at the *beginning* of **swing.** (Thumbs-up.)

Yes, **swing** *begins* with the sound **/sw/.**

(Continue the activity with the following lists of words:
Swim. Swell. Win. Sleep. Grease. Swallow.
Swift. Swipe. Proud. Sister. Sweet. Sweater.)

Lesson 111   **449**

Activity 2 Phoneme Blending

Elicit responses. **Guide** as needed. **Fade** model when students are performing well.
Let's put some sounds together and make words. I'm going to say a word very slowly so you can hear each sound. You need to listen carefully and say the sounds. When you say the sounds, it will sound almost like you're singing them. Then we'll put the sounds together and say the word.

My turn. Listen. **/aaa/ /t/.**
Say those sounds with me. */aaa/ /t/.*
Now say the sounds by yourself. */aaa/ /t/.*
Your turn again. Say the sounds. */aaa/ /t/.*
Now let's put it together. What word? *At.*

Let's make a bigger word. My turn. Listen. **/mmm/ /aaa/ /t/.**
Say those sounds with me. */mmm/ /aaa/ /t/.*
Now say the sounds by yourself. */mmm/ /aaa/ /t/.*
Your turn again. Say the sounds. */mmm/ /aaa/ /t/.*
Now let's put it together. What word? *Mat.*

(Continue the activity with the following words.
sat [sss-aaa-t], rat [rrr-aaa-t], fat [fff-aaa-t].)

Part B: Letter Recognition and Formation

6 minutes

Student Materials:
Lined paper

Activity 1 Letter Recognition—b

Elicit responses to questions. **Guide** as needed. **Write** b on the board. **Point** to b.
Today you'll learn a new letter.
The name of this letter is **b.** What letter name? *b.*
Again, what letter name? *b.*
Review as needed.

Activity 2 Letter Formation—b

Now we're going to practice writing **b.** When you practice writing, you'll learn not only where to start and stop the letter, but also which way to move your hand when you're making the letter. It's tricky, but you're so smart you'll learn how to write **b** very quickly. Watch.

Here's how you write **b** in the air.
Model b formation in the air (with your back to students).

Watch again.

Now let's practice writing **b** in the air. Hold up your writing hand, and make **b** in the air.
Guide students as they write b in the air.

Let's practice **b** again.

450 Lesson 111

Here's how to write **b** with your writing hand pointer finger.
Model b formation on the board with your finger (with your back to students).

Watch again.

Now let's practice writing **b** on your table without using your pencil. Use your writing hand pointer finger, and make **b** on your table.
Guide students as they write b on their table or desktop.

Let's practice **b** again.

Model writing b on the board (with your back to students).
Remember that every letter has a name.
You learned the name of this letter is **b.** What letter name? *b.*
Again, what letter name? *b.*

Provide lined paper to students.
Now let's practice writing **b** with your pencil.
Guide students as they write b on their paper. **Review** as needed.

 Link letter names to letter sounds as they appear in the program as needed.

Set up a writing center with writing materials and correct models of letters learned so far for students to use in their free time.

Part C: Comprehension Strategies

9 minutes

Teacher Materials:
Narrative trade book

My Prediction Chart

Student Materials:
My Prediction Chart

Activity 1 Title, Author, and Illustrator Identification—A Before-Reading Strategy

Provide a reading center to display books being read so that students can enjoy them again during free time.

Direct students to narrative trade book of teacher choice. **Elicit** responses to questions. **Guide** as needed.

Show front cover of book, and allow student to point to name of title, author, and illustrator as you discuss them.
We'll read a new book today. The title of today's story is _____. What's the title of today's story? (Student response.)

The author of today's story is _____. Who's the author of today's story? (Student response.)

The illustrator of today's story is _____. Who's the illustrator? (Student response.)

Lesson 111   **451**

Activity 2 Activate Background Knowledge—A Before-Reading Strategy

Elicit responses to questions. **Guide** as needed.
The information that you already have in your brain is called background knowledge. What's the information you already have in your brain called? *Background knowledge.*

Choose a topic to activate background knowledge from story you will read.
Tell me your background knowledge for _____.
Discuss background knowledge of students as it relates to topic chosen.

When you think about your background knowledge before you read, it helps you better understand the story. You can connect what you know to what happens in the story.

Activity 3 Make Predictions—A Before-Reading Strategy

Show My Prediction Chart and provide copies for students. **Show** title, front and back cover, and pictures inside book. **Elicit** responses to questions. **Guide** as needed.

The title of today's book is _____. Write the book title in the box labeled "Book Title".

Now that you know the title of today's book, let's look at the cover and pictures inside the book for clues to make some good guesses of what you think the story will be about.

What do you call your good guesses? *Predictions.*

Making predictions helps you get interested in the story before you read it. Let's make some predictions about the story before I read it to you.

What do you predict this story will be about? (Student response.)
Write your prediction in the box labeled "I Predict That."

What characters do you predict will be in the story? (Student response.)

What do you predict the setting will be? (Student response.)

What do you predict might happen in the story? (Student response.)

When we read the book you will check your predictions to see whether they are correct.

Elicit correct listening behavior from students. **Read** trade book. **Model** prosody during read-aloud.

Guide students to confirm predictions and/or connect background knowledge as you read story. **Ask** questions to confirm predictions and/or connect background knowledge. **Guide** as needed.

452 *Lesson 111*

Activity 4 Confirm Predictions—An After-Reading Strategy

Elicit responses to questions. **Guide** as needed.

Now let's check your predictions to see whether they were correct. You predicted that the story was about _____. Was your prediction correct? (Student response.)

Circle whether or not your prediction was correct in the box labeled "Was My Prediction Correct?".

You predicted that _____ were characters in the story. Was your prediction correct? (Student response.)

You predicted that the setting was _____. Was your prediction correct? (Student response.)

You predicted that some events would be _____. Was your prediction correct? (Student response.)

Remember that your predictions don't have to be correct. Just making a prediction and listening to see whether your prediction is correct helps you stay interested in the story.

Lesson 111

Lesson 112

Materials
Teacher: Narrative trade book (from Lesson 111); Picture-Sound Cards for /gr/, /pl/, /dr/, /fl/, /g/, and /p/
Student: Lined paper

5 minutes

Teacher Materials:
Picture-Sound Cards for /gr/, /pl/, /dr/, /fl/, /g/, and /p/

Part A: Phonemic and Phonological Awareness

Activity 1 Phoneme Isolation—Initial

Use IWB interactive cards or picture-sound cards. **Elicit** responses. **Guide** as needed.
I'm going to show you two cards and name the object on each card. Then I'll tell you a sound. Think about which word starts with that sound. Let's try it. Today we'll be listening for the sound at the *beginning* of a word.

Show /gr/ card; use either of two Picture-Sound Cards per phoneme for activity.
This is a _____. What is this? (Student response.)

Show /dr/ card; use either of two Picture-Sound Cards per phoneme for activity.
This is a _____. What is this? (Student response.)

Which word *begins* with **/gr/?** (Student response.)

Show /fl/ card; use either of two Picture-Sound Cards per phoneme for activity.
This is a _____. What is this? (Student response.)

Show /pl/ card; use either of two Picture-Sound Cards per phoneme for activity.
This is a _____. What is this? (Student response.)

Which word *begins* with **/pl/?** (Student response.)

(Continue the activity with the following examples:
/pl/ and /p/: Which word begins with /pl/?
/g/ and /gr/: Which word begins with /gr/?)

Activity 2 Phoneme Identity—Initial

Elicit responses. **Guide** as needed.
Let's find the *first* sound in a word. I'll say a word, and you tell me the *first* sound in that word.

What is the first sound you hear in **turtle?** */t/.*

What is the first sound you hear in **number?** */nnn/.*

What is the first sound you hear in **calendar?** */k/.*

What is the first sound you hear in **olive?** */ooo/.*

454   Lesson 112

What is the first sound you hear in **heavy?** /h/.

What is the first sound you hear in **kitchen?** /k/.

What is the first sound you hear in **tickle?** /t/.

What is the first sound you hear in **hanger?** /h/.

What is the first sound you hear in **neighbor?** /nnn/.

What is the first sound you hear in **often?** /ooo/.

Activity 3 Phoneme Categorization—Final

Elicit responses. **Guide** as needed.
We're going to find words that don't belong. I'm going to say three words. Listen closely and see if you can tell which word *does not* belong. I want you to listen closely to the *last* sound in the words.

Your turn. Listen. **Tub, grab, cove.** Which word doesn't belong? *Cove.*

Right, **cove** *doesn't* belong because it ends with **/vvv/** and **tub** and **grab** end with **/b/.**

(Continue the activity with the following examples:
Purr, were, snap.
Prize, lose, catch.
Snob, club, sip.
Her, beach, blur.
Maze, breeze, five.)

Activity 4 Phoneme Segmentation

Elicit responses. **Guide** as needed.
You've learned to blend sounds together to make words. Now we're going to try something a little harder. We're going to break words apart by each sound. I'm going to tell you a word. You'll need to listen closely and tell me the different sounds you hear in the word. I'll show you how to do the first one.

Pause briefly between each sound so students can hear each phoneme as an individual sound. **Model** holding each continuous sound for 2 to 3 seconds. **Say** stop sounds quickly. **Hold** up one finger for each phoneme in word, back of hand to students.
My turn. The word is **me.** I can say the sounds in **me. /mmm/ /ēēē/.**
Those are the sounds in the word **me.**
Try it with me. The word is **me.** Tell me the sounds you hear in **me.** /mmm/ /ēēē/.
Your turn by yourself. The word is **me.** Tell me the sounds you hear in **me.** /mmm/ /ēēē/.
Yes. You said the sounds in the word **me.**

(Continue the activity with the following words:
see [sss-ēēē], we [www-ēēē].)

Lesson 112 **455**

6 minutes

Student Materials:
Lined paper

Part B: Letter Recognition and Formation

Activity 1 Letter Recognition Review—b

Elicit responses to questions. **Guide** as needed. **Write** b on the board. **Point** to b.
We learned that this letter is **b.** What letter name? *b.*
Again, what letter name? *b.*
Review as needed.

Activity 2 Letter Formation Review—b

Now we're going to practice writing **b.** When you practice writing, you'll learn not only where to start and stop the letter, but also which way to move your hand when you're making the letter. It's tricky, but you're so smart you'll learn how to write **b** very quickly. Watch.

Here's how you write **b** in the air.
Model b formation in the air (with your back to students).

Watch again.

Now let's practice writing **b** in the air. Hold up your writing hand, and make **b** in the air.
Guide students as they write b in the air.

Let's practice **b** again.

Here's how to write **b** with your writing hand pointer finger.
Model b formation on the board with your finger (with your back to students).

Watch again.

Now let's practice writing **b** on your table without using your pencil. Use your writing hand pointer finger, and make **b** on your table.
Guide students as they write b on their table or desktop.

Let's practice **b** again.

Model writing b on the board (with your back to students).
Remember that every letter has a name.
You learned the name of this letter is **b.** What letter name? *b.*
Again, what letter name? *b.*

Provide lined paper to students.
Now let's practice writing **b** with your pencil.
Guide students as they write b on their paper. **Review** as needed.

 Link letter names to letter sounds as they appear in the program as needed.

456 Lesson 112

Part C: Comprehension Strategies

9 minutes

Teacher Materials:
Narrative trade book

Activity 1 Listening Comprehension—A During-Reading Strategy

Direct students to narrative trade book of teacher choice. **Elicit** responses to questions. **Guide** as needed.

You've learned all about stories. Stories have characters, a setting, a beginning, a middle, and an end. Listen to the story again and see whether you can tell me all the parts of the story after I read it.

Elicit correct listening behavior from students. **Reread** trade book. **Model** prosody during read-aloud.

Ask questions to elicit identification of characters, setting, and events. **Guide** as needed.

Activity 2 Story Elements: Identify Characters, Setting, Beginning, Middle, and End—An After-Reading Strategy

Elicit responses to questions. **Guide** as needed.
You listened to the story. Now you can tell me all the parts of the story that you heard as you listened. Who are the characters in the story? (Student response.)

Who do you think is the main character? (Student response.)

What's the setting of the story? (Student response.)

Does the setting change or stay the same? (Student response.)

What events happened at the beginning? (Student response.)

What events happened in the middle? (Student response.)

What events happened at the end? (Student response.)

You told all the parts of the story. Excellent job listening to the story and remembering all the parts.

Activity 3 Identify Main Idea—An After-Reading Strategy

Elicit responses to questions. **Guide** as needed.
Now let's think about what the story is mostly about. We're thinking about the main idea of the story. What's the main idea? (Idea: *What the story is mostly about.*)

What do we call what the story is mostly about? *The main idea.*

It's a little tricky to figure out the main idea, but the story gives me clues to make it easier.

Guide students to find main idea using clues from story. **Select** from following questions the ones that will help you elicit main idea from students.

What's the title of the story? (Student response.)

Who are the main characters in the story? (Student response.)

What was the main thing that happened in the story? (Student response.)

How did the main character change? (Student response.)

What did the main character learn? (Student response.)

To tell the main idea, I want you to think about the main character and then tell about _____ .

What do you think is the main idea? (Student response.)

Yes, the main idea is _____ .

What's the main idea of our story? (Student response.)

Guide students to find main idea by first naming main character, then telling most important event, what main character learned, or how main character changed in story.

458   *Lesson 112*

Lesson 113

> **Materials**
> **Teacher:** Narrative trade book (from Lesson 111)
> **Student:** Lined paper

Part A: Phonemic and Phonological Awareness

Activity 1 Phoneme Isolation—Initial

Elicit responses. **Guide** as needed.
Let's work on a sound at the *beginning* of a word. I'm going to say a list of words. Some of the words will have the **/tr/** sound at the *beginning,* and some will not. I'll say the word first, and then you'll say the word.

Remember, we're listening for the **/tr/** sound at the *beginning* of the word. What sound are we listening for? */tr/.*

Listen. **Tree.** Say **tree.** *Tree.*

Give me a thumbs-up if you hear **/tr/** at the *beginning* of **tree.** (Thumbs-up.)

Yes, **tree** *begins* with the sound **/tr/.**

(Continue the activity with the following lists of words.
Trace. Trip. Flat. Glow. Train. Treat.
Try. Tummy. Trunk. Swing. Tread. Trouble.)

Let's work on another sound at the *beginning* of a word. I'm going to say a list of words. Some of the words will have the **/tw/** sound at the *beginning,* and some will not. I'll say the word first, and then you'll say the word.

Remember, we're listening for the **/tw/** sound at the *beginning* of the word. What sound are we listening for? */tw/.*

Listen. **Twig.** Say **twig.** *Twig.*

Give me a thumbs-up if you hear **/tw/** at the *beginning* of **twig.** (Thumbs-up.)

Yes, **twig** *begins* with the sound **/tw/.**

(Continue the activity with the following lists of words:
Twelve. Twice. Ten. Smoke. Plead. Twenty.
Twin. Twirl. Spin. Want. Start. Twist.)

Lesson 113   459

Activity 2 Phoneme Blending

Elicit responses. **Guide** as needed. **Fade** model when students are performing well.
Let's put some sounds together and make words. I'm going to say a word very slowly so you can hear each sound. You need to listen carefully and say the sounds. When you say the sounds, it will sound almost like you're singing them. Then we'll put the sounds together and say the word.

My turn. Listen. **/aaa/ /nnn/.**
Now say the sounds by yourself. */aaa/ /nnn/.*
Your turn again. Say the sounds. */aaa/ /nnn/.*
Now let's put it together. What word? *An.*

Let's make a bigger word. My turn. Listen. **/mmm/ /aaa/ /nnn/.**
Now say the sounds by yourself. */mmm/ /aaa/ /nnn/.*
Your turn again. Say the sounds. */mmm/ /aaa/ /nnn/.*
Now let's put it together. What word? *Man.*

(Continue the activity with the following words.
ran [rrr-aaa-nnn], fan [fff-aaa-nnn], than [ththth-aaa-nnn].)

Part B: Letter Recognition and Formation

6 minutes

Student Materials:
Lined paper

Activity 1 Letter Recognition—Capital B

Elicit responses to questions. **Guide** as needed. **Write** capital B on the board.
Point to capital B.
Today you'll learn another way to write **b.**
The name of this letter is **capital B.** What letter name? *Capital B.*
Again, what letter name? *Capital B.*
Review as needed.

Activity 2 Letter Formation—Capital B

Now we're going to practice writing **capital B.** When you practice writing, you'll learn not only where to start and stop the letter, but also which way to move your hand when you're making the letter. It's tricky, but you're so smart you'll learn how to write **capital B** very quickly. Watch.

Here's how you write **capital B** in the air.
Model capital B formation in the air (with your back to students).

Watch again.

Now let's practice writing **capital B** in the air. Hold up your writing hand, and make **capital B** in the air.
Guide students as they write capital B in the air.

Let's practice **capital B** again.

460 Lesson 113

Here's how to write **capital B** with your writing hand pointer finger.
Model capital B formation on the board with your finger (with your back to students).

Watch again.

Now let's practice writing **capital B** on your table without using your pencil. Use your writing hand pointer finger, and make **capital B** on your table.
Guide students as they write capital B on their table or desktop.

Let's practice **capital B** again.
Model writing capital B on the board (with your back to students).
Remember that every letter has a name.
You learned the name of this letter is **capital B.** *What letter name? Capital B. Again, what letter name? Capital B.*

Provide lined paper to students.
Now let's practice writing **capital B** with your pencil.
Guide students as they write capital B on their paper. **Review** as needed.

 Link letter names to letter sounds as they appear in the program as needed.

Part C: Comprehension Strategies

9 minutes

Teacher Materials:
Narrative trade book

Student Materials:
Lined paper

Activity 1 Listening Comprehension—A During-Reading Strategy

Direct students to narrative trade book of teacher choice. **Elicit** response to question. **Guide** as needed.
We'll read the story again today. When we read the story today, I want you to think about anything in the story that reminds you of something that you know or something that has happened to you. We'll connect the story to your life after we read the story. Then we will talk about the main idea of the story.

Elicit correct listening behavior from students. **Reread** trade book. **Model** prosody during read-aloud.

Elicit text-to-self connections and clues for identifying main idea. **Guide** as needed.

Activity 2 Make Connections: Text-to-Self—An After-Reading Strategy

Elicit responses. **Guide** as needed.
Making connections helps you to understand what you read. It helps make reading more fun and interesting. Let's talk about this story and see how it matches or connects to your own life. What connections from the story can you make to your life? (Student response.)
Discuss how characters, events, or items in story relate to things in students' lives.

Lesson 113   **461**

Provide lined paper. **Model** writing a sentence about a connection you made.
Write a sentence that describes the connection you made to your life. If you
need help, ask me.
Monitor students. **Guide** students as needed.

Remember that when you read, making connections to your life helps you
better understand and remember the story.

Activity 3 Identify Main Idea—An After-Reading Strategy

Elicit responses to questions. **Guide** as needed.
Now let's think about what the story is mostly about. We're thinking about
the main idea of the story. What's the main idea? (Idea: *What the story is
mostly about.*)

What do we call what the story is mostly about? *The main idea.*

It's a little tricky to figure out the main idea, but the story gives me clues to
make it easier.

Guide students to find main idea using clues from story. **Select** from following
questions the ones that will help you elicit main idea from students.

What's the title of the story? (Student response.)

Who are the main characters in the story? (Student response.)

What was the main thing that happened in the story? (Student response.)

How did the main character change? (Student response.)

What did the main character learn? (Student response.)

To tell the main idea, I want you to think about the main character and then
tell about _____ .

What do you think is the main idea? (Student response.)

Yes, the main idea is _____ .

What's the main idea of our story? (Student response.)
Guide students to find main idea by first naming main character, then telling most
important event, what main character learned, or how main character changed in story.

462   *Lesson 113*

Lesson 114

Materials

Teacher: Narrative trade book (from Lesson 111); additional trade book that has similar story elements for text-to-text connection (either from student suggestions or teacher choice); Picture-Sound Cards for /pr/, /sk/, /fr/, /gl/, /p/, and /s/; 14-Phonemic Awareness

Student: Lined paper, copy of 14-Phonemic Awareness

5 minutes

Teacher Materials:
Picture-Sound Cards for /pr/, /sk/, /fr/, /gl/, /p/, and /s/

Phonemic Awareness

Part A: Phonemic and Phonological Awareness

Activity 1 Phoneme Isolation—Initial

Use IWB interactive cards or picture-sound cards. **Elicit** responses. **Guide** as needed.
I'm going to show you two cards and name the object on each card. Then I'll tell you a sound. Think about which word starts with that sound. Let's try it. Today we'll be listening for the sound at the *beginning* of a word.

Show /pr/ card; use either of two Picture-Sound Cards per phoneme for activity.
This is a _____. What is this? (Student response.)

Show /fr/ card; use either of two Picture-Sound Cards per phoneme for activity.
This is a _____. What is this? (Student response.)

Which word *begins* with **/pr/?** (Student response.)

Show /gl/ card; use either of two Picture-Sound Cards per phoneme for activity.
This is a _____. What is this? (Student response.)

Show /sk/ card; use either of two Picture-Sound Cards per phoneme for activity.
This is a _____. What is this? (Student response.)

Which word *begins* with **/sk/?** (Student response.)

(Continue the activity with the following examples:
/sk/ and /s/: Which word begins with /sk/?
/p/ and /pr/: Which word begins with /pr/?)

Activity 2 Phoneme Identity—Initial

Elicit responses. **Guide** as needed.
Let's find the *first* sound in a word. I'll say a word, and you tell me the *first* sound in that word.

What is the first sound you hear in **acorn?** /āāā/.

What is the first sound you hear in **thimble?** /thththth/.

What is the first sound you hear in **umbrella?** /uuu/.

What is the first sound you hear in **garage?** /g/.

Lesson 114   463

What is the first sound you hear in **lumber?** /lll/.

What is the first sound you hear in **unhappy?** /uuu/.

What is the first sound you hear in **able?** /āāā/.

What is the first sound you hear in **letter?** /lll/.

What is the first sound you hear in **theater?** /ththth/.

What is the first sound you hear in **gallon?** /g/.

Activity 3 Phoneme Categorization—Initial

Show Phonemic Awareness. **Distribute** copy of Phonemic Awareness. **Elicit** responses. **Guide** as needed.

You've worked hard to find words that don't belong with other words. We're going to try something new today. We're going to look at a picture on this page and find other pictures to match our sounds. I'm going to name each picture. I want you to touch each picture after I name it and repeat the name. We're going to find words that have the same *first* sound. If the word has the same *first* sound as the word in the top picture, we can circle it to show that they go together.

Model use of Phonemic Awareness; point to each picture as word is said.
Let's try it.
Point to picture at top of page.
Touch the picture at the top of the page. This is a **mouse.** What is this? *Mouse.*

That's right. The picture shows a **mouse.** So what is the *first* sound in **mouse?** /mmm/.

Yes, **/mmm/.** So now we need to look at the other pictures and see which ones have the same *first* sound as **mouse.**
Point to first picture in first row.
Touch the first picture in the first row. This is a **mat.** What is this? *Mat.*

Does **mat** have the same *first* sound as **mouse?** *Yes.*

Then we can circle the picture of the **mat.**
Point to second picture in first row.
Touch the next picture. This is a **bone.** What is this? *Bone.*

Does **bone** have the same *first* sound as **mouse?** *No.*

So we don't want to circle the picture of the **bone** because the *first* sound in **bone** is **/b/,** not **/mmm/.**
Point to third picture in first row.
Touch the next picture. This is a **moon.** What is this? *Moon.*

Does **moon** have the same *first* sound as **mouse?** *Yes.*

464 *Lesson 114*

Then we can circle the picture of the **moon.** When we're finished with our lesson, you'll color the pictures you circled to show they have the same first sound.

(Continue the activity with the second row of pictures:
Second row: mop, money, comb.)

(Use the same procedure to find the pictures of words that have the same first sound as the next key word: sock.
Third row: ear, saw, seven.
Fourth row: sun, bus, sad.)

Activity 4 Phoneme Segmentation

Elicit responses. **Guide** as needed.
Let's work on our new activity. We're going to break words apart by each sound. I'm going to say a word. You'll need to listen closely and tell me the different sounds you hear in the word. I'll show you how to do the first one.

Pause briefly between each sound so students can hear each phoneme as an individual sound.
My turn. The word is **may.** I can say the sounds in **may.** /mmm/ /āāā/.
Those are the sounds in the word **may.**
Try it with me. The word is **may.** Tell me the sounds you hear in **may.** /mmm/ /āāā/.
Your turn by yourself. The word is **may.** Tell me the sounds you hear in **may.** /mmm/ /āāā/.
Yes, you said the sounds in the word **may.**

(Continue the activity with the following words:
say [sss-āāā], way [www-āāā].)

Part B: Letter Recognition and Formation

6 minutes

Student Materials:
Lined paper

Activity 1 Letter Recognition Review—Capital B

Elicit responses to questions. **Guide** as needed. **Write** capital B on the board. **Point** to capital B.
We learned that this letter is **capital B.** What letter name? *Capital B.*
Again, what letter name? *Capital B.*
Review as needed.

Activity 2 Letter Formation Review—Capital B

Now we're going to practice writing **capital B.** When you practice writing, you'll learn not only where to start and stop the letter, but also which way to move your hand when you're making the letter. It's tricky, but you're so smart you'll learn how to write **capital B** very quickly. Watch.

Here's how you write **capital B** in the air.
Model capital B formation in the air (with your back to students).

Lesson 114   **465**

Watch again.

Now let's practice writing **capital B** in the air. Hold up your writing hand, and make **capital B** in the air.
Guide students as they write capital B in the air.

Let's practice **capital B** again.

Here's how to write **capital B** with your writing hand pointer finger.
Model capital B formation on the board with your finger (with your back to students).

Watch again.

Now let's practice writing **capital B** on your table without using your pencil. Use your writing hand pointer finger, and make **capital B** on your table.
Guide students as they write capital B on their table or desktop.

Let's practice **capital B** again.

Model writing capital B on the board (with your back to students).
Remember that every letter has a name.
You learned the name of this letter is **capital B.** What letter name? *Capital B.*
Again, what letter name? *Capital B.*

Provide lined paper to students.
Now let's practice writing **capital B** with your pencil.
Guide students as they write capital B on their paper. **Review** as needed.

 Link letter names to letter sounds as they appear in the program as needed.

Part C: Comprehension Strategies

 9 minutes

Teacher Materials:
Narrative trade book
Additional trade book

Activity 1 Listening Comprehension—A During-Reading Strategy

Direct students to narrative trade book of teacher choice. **Elicit** response to question. **Guide** as needed.
We'll read the story again today. When we read the story today, I want you to think about all the stories you've heard. I want you to think of which story reminds you of this one.

Elicit correct listening behavior from students. **Reread** trade book. **Model** prosody during read-aloud.

Guide students to focus on thinking of another story like this one for a text-to-text connection. **Elicit** responses to questions about text-to-text connections. **Guide** as needed.

You've heard lots of stories this year. What story have you heard that reminds you of this story? (Student response.)
Elicit names of stories that are like today's story. **Guide** as needed.

Obtain book for text-to-text connection from student suggestions, if possible.

466 Lesson 114

Activity 2 **Make Connections: Text-to-Text—An After-Reading Strategy**

Elicit responses to questions. **Guide** as needed.

When you heard this story, it reminded you of the story _____. Listen to that story again and then we'll make a connection to the story.

When you can connect a story that you are reading to another story that you know, it helps you to understand the story better. Making a connection to another story you've heard is a smart thing to do.

Elicit correct listening behavior from students. **Reread** other story for text-to-text connection. **Model** prosody during read-aloud.

Guide students to think of similarities between stories for text-to-text connection.

Lesson 114   **467**

Lesson 115

Materials

Teacher: Narrative trade book (from Lesson 111); Picture-Sound Cards for /sl/, /sm/, /sn/, /pl/, /pr/, and /s/; Letter Recognition
Student: Lined paper

5 minutes

Teacher Materials:
Picture-Sound Cards for /sl/, /sm/, /sn/, /pl/, /pr/, and /s/

Part A: Phonemic and Phonological Awareness

Activity 1 Phoneme Isolation—Initial

Use IWB interactive cards or picture-sound cards. **Elicit** responses. **Guide** as needed.
I'm going to show you two cards and name the object on each card. Then I'll tell you a sound. Think about which word starts with that sound. Let's try it. Today we'll be listening for the sound at the *beginning* of a word.

Show /sl/ card; use either of two Picture-Sound Cards per phoneme for activity.
This is a _____. What is this? (Student response.)

Show /pl/ card; use either of two Picture-Sound Cards per phoneme for activity.
This is a _____. What is this? (Student response.)

Which word *begins* with **/sl/**? (Student response.)

Show /pr/ card; use either of two Picture-Sound Cards per phoneme for activity.
This is a _____. What is this? (Student response.)

Show /sm/ card; use either of two Picture-Sound Cards per phoneme for activity.
This is a _____. What is this? (Student response.)

Which word *begins* with **/sm/**? (Student response.)

(Continue the activity with the following examples:
/sn/ and /s/: Which word begins with /sn/?
/pr/ and /sl/: Which word begins with /sl/?
/s/ and /sm/: Which word begins with /sm/?
/sn/ and /pl/: Which word begins with /sn/?)

Activity 2 Phoneme Segmentation

Elicit responses. **Guide** as needed. **Pause** briefly between each sound so students can hear each phoneme as an individual sound.
Let's work on our new activity. We're going to break words apart by each sound. I'm going to say a word. You'll need to listen closely and tell me the different sounds you hear in the word. I'll show you how to do the first one.

My turn. The word is **my.** I can say the sounds in **my.** /mmm/ /īī/. Those are the sounds in the word **my.**
Try it with me. The word is **my.** Tell me the sounds you hear in **my.** /mmm/ /īī/.
Your turn by yourself. The word is **my.** Tell me the sounds you hear in **my.** /mmm/ /īī/.
Yes, you said the sounds in the word **my.**

(Continue the activity with the following words: shy [shshsh-īī], lie [lll-īī].)

Part B: Letter Recognition and Formation

6 minutes

Activity 1 Letter Recognition Cumulative Review—k/K, v/V, p/P, b/B

Teacher Materials:
Letter Recognition

Student Materials:
Lined paper

Display on IWB or **write** letters and capitals on the board in the order shown. **Elicit** responses to questions. **Guide** as needed.
This week you've learned one letter and one capital—**b** and **capital B.**
Let's review all the letters and capitals you've learned. Are you ready?

Letter	Question	Student Response
b	What letter?	b.
V	What letter?	Capital V.
k	What letter?	k.
P	What letter?	Capital P.
K	What letter?	Capital K.
v	What letter?	v.
B	What letter?	Capital B.
p	What letter?	p.

Review as needed.

Activity 2 Letter Formation Cumulative Review—k/K, v/V, p/P, b/B

Write k, capital K, v, capital V, p, capital P, b, and capital B on the board in the order shown (with your back to students). **Provide** lined paper to students.

Show me how you can write these letters and capitals.
Guide students as they write the letters and capitals on their paper. **Review** as needed.

 Link letter names to letter sounds as they appear in the program as needed.

Lesson 115 **469**

9 minutes

Teacher Materials:
Narrative trade book

Part C: Comprehension Strategies

Activity 1 Listening Comprehension—A During-Reading Strategy

Direct students to narrative trade book of teacher choice. **Elicit** responses to questions. **Guide** as needed.
We'll read the story again today. After we have read the story, we'll play the story. Think of some good ideas for how to play the story.

Elicit correct listening behavior from students. **Reread** trade book. **Model** prosody during read-aloud.

Guide students to focus on ideas for playing story. **Elicit** responses to questions about how to play story. **Guide** as needed.

Activity 2 Retell the Story: Play the Story—An After-Reading Strategy

Elicit responses to questions. **Guide** as needed.
Now you'll play the story. I'll need your ideas for how to play the story.

Let's start with the setting. What's the setting? (Student response.)

Who would be willing to play the parts of the setting? (Student response.)

Who's the main character? (Student response.)

Who could play the main character? (Student response.)

What other characters are important in the story? (Student response.)

Who would be willing to play those parts? (Student response.)

You're going to play the beginning, the middle, and the end of the story. What events happened at the beginning of the story? (Student response.)

How would you play those events? (Student response.)

What events happened in the middle of the story? (Student response.)

How would you play those events? (Student response.)

What events happened at the end of the story? (Student response.)

How would you play those events? (Student response.)

Discuss story elements and assign roles for playing story. Try to assign roles to all students.
I'll tell the whole story. As I tell the story, the players can do the actions I'm telling about. If there are words to say, I'll help you say them.

Coach all students to play story by telling story and guiding students to play or mime actions. If there is dialogue, say words and then have students repeat words or prompt student to say appropriate words.

Praise creativity in playing story. **Prompt** everyone to bow as you applaud them.

Wow, that was fun!

Lesson 116

Materials
Teacher: Narrative trade book (same book for Lessons 116–120); 15-Phonemic Awareness
Student: Lined paper; copy of 15-Phonemic Awareness

Part A: Phonemic and Phonological Awareness

5 minutes

Teacher Materials:
Phonemic Awareness

Student Materials:
Phonemic Awareness

Activity 1 Phoneme Identity—Initial

Elicit responses. **Guide** as needed.
Let's find the *first* sound in a word. I'll tell you a word, and you tell me the *first* sound in that word.

What is the first sound you hear in **winter?** /www/.

What is the first sound you hear in **shampoo?** /shshsh/.

What is the first sound you hear in **opening?** /ōōō/.

What is the first sound you hear in **victory?** /vvv/.

What is the first sound you hear in **pumpkin?** /p/.

What is the first sound you hear in **overtime?** /ōōō/.

What is the first sound you hear in **washcloth?** /www/.

What is the first sound you hear in **pencil?** /p/.

What is the first sound you hear in **shoulder?** /shshsh/.

What is the first sound you hear in **volcano?** /vvv/.

Activity 2 Phoneme Categorization—Initial

Show Phonemic Awareness. **Distribute** copy of Phonemic Awareness. **Elicit** responses. **Guide** as needed.
We're going to look at a picture on this page and find other pictures to match our sounds. I'm going to name each picture. I want you to touch each picture after I name it and repeat the name. We're going to find words that have the same *first* sound. If the word has the same *first* sound as the word in the top picture, we can circle the picture to show that they go together.

Model use of Phonemic Awareness; point to each picture as word is said.
Let's try it.
Point to picture at top of page.

Lesson 116 **471**

Touch the picture at the top of the page. This is a **rake.** What is this? *Rake.*

That's right. The picture shows a **rake.** What is the *first* sound in **rake?** /rrr/.

Yes, **/rrr/.** We need to look at the other pictures and see which words have the same *first* sound as **rake.**
Point to first picture in first row.
Touch the first picture in the first row. This is a **ring.** What is this? *Ring.*

Does **ring** have the same *first* sound as **rake?** *Yes.*

Then we can circle the picture of the **ring.**
Point to second picture in first row.
Touch the next picture. This is a **jar.** What is this? *Jar.*

Does **jar** have the same *first* sound as **rake?** *No.*

We don't want to circle the picture of the **jar** because the *first* sound in **jar** is **/j/,** not **/rrr/.**
Point to third picture in first row.
Touch the next picture. This is a **rope.** What is this? *Rope.*

Does **rope** have the same *first* sound as **rake?** *Yes.*

Then we can circle the picture of the **rope.** When we're finished with our lesson, you'll color the pictures you circled to show they have the same first sound.

(Continue the activity with the second row of pictures.
Second row: rabbit, crab, roof.)

(Use the same procedure to find the pictures of words that have the same first sound as the next key word: door.
Third row: doll, desk, ball.
Fourth row: dog, duck, hand.)

Activity 3 Phoneme Blending

Elicit responses. **Guide** as needed.
Let's put some sounds together and make words. I'm going to say a word very slowly so you can hear each sound. You need to listen carefully and say the sounds. When you say the sounds, it will sound almost like you're singing them. Then we'll put the sounds together and say the word.

My turn. Listen. **/iii/ /t/.**
Say the sounds. */iii/ /t/.*
Again, say the sounds. */iii/ /t/.*
Now let's put it together. What word? *It.*

Let's make a bigger word. My turn. Listen. **/mmm/ /iii/ /t/.**
Say the sounds. */mmm/ /iii/ /t/.*
Again, say the sounds. */mmm/ /iii/ /t/.*
Now let's put it together. What word? *Mitt.*

(Continue the activity with the following words:
sit [sss-iii-t], fit [fff-iii-t], knit [nnn-iii-t].)

472   *Lesson 116*

6 minutes

Student Materials:
Lined paper

Part B: Letter Recognition and Formation

Activity 1 Letter Recognition—y

Elicit responses to questions. **Guide** as needed. **Write** y on the board. **Point** to y.
Today you'll learn a new letter.
The name of this letter is **y.** What letter name? *y.*
Again, what letter name? *y.*
Review as needed.

Activity 2 Letter Formation—y

Now we're going to practice writing **y.** When you practice writing, you'll learn not only where to start and stop the letter, but also which way to move your hand when you're making the letter. It's tricky, but you're so smart you'll learn how to write **y** very quickly. Watch.

Here's how you write **y** in the air.
Model y formation in the air (with your back to students).

Watch again.

Now let's practice writing **y** in the air. Hold up your writing hand, and make **y** in the air.
Guide students as they write y in the air.

Let's practice **y** again.

Here's how to write **y** with your writing hand pointer finger.
Model y formation on the board with your finger (with your back to students).

Watch again.

Now let's practice writing **y** on your table without using your pencil. Use your writing hand pointer finger, and make **y** on your table.
Guide students as they write y on their table or desktop.

Let's practice **y** again.

Model writing y on the board (with your back to students).
Remember that every letter has a name.
You learned the name of this letter is **y.** What letter name? *y.*
Again, what letter name? *y.*

Provide lined paper to students.
Now let's practice writing **y** with your pencil.
Guide students as they write y on their paper. **Review** as needed.

 Link letter names to letter sounds as they appear in the program as needed.

Set up a writing center with writing materials and correct models of letters learned so far for students to use in their free time.

Lesson 116   **473**

9 minutes

Teacher Materials:
Narrative trade book

Student Materials:
Lined paper

Part C: Comprehension Strategies

Activity 1 Title, Author, and Illustrator Identification—A Before-Reading Strategy

Provide a reading center to display books being read so that students can enjoy them again during free time.

Direct students to narrative trade book of teacher choice. **Elicit** responses to questions. **Guide** as needed.

Show front cover of book, and allow student to point to name of title, author, and illustrator as you discuss them.

We'll read a new story today. The title of today's story is _____. What's the title of today's story? (Student response.)

The author of today's story is _____. Who's the author of today's story? (Student response.)

The illustrator of today's story is _____. Who's the illustrator? (Student response.)

Activity 2 Activate Background Knowledge—A Before-Reading Strategy

Elicit responses to questions. **Guide** as needed.
The information that you already have in your brain is called background knowledge.

What's the information you already have in your brain called? *Background knowledge.*

Choose a topic to activate background knowledge from story you will read.
Tell me your background knowledge for _____.
Discuss background knowledge for topic chosen.

Provide lined paper. **Model** writing a sentence about what you know.
Write a sentence that tells me your background knowledge for _____.
If you need help, ask me.
Monitor students. **Guide** students as needed.

When you think about your background knowledge before you read, it helps you better understand the story. You can connect what you know to what happens in the story.

474　Lesson 116

Activity 3 Make Predictions—A Before-Reading Strategy

Show title, front and back cover, and pictures inside book. **Elicit** responses to questions. **Guide** as needed.

The title of today's book is _____. Now that you know the title of today's book, let's look at the cover and pictures inside the book for clues to make some good guesses of what you think the story will be about. What do you call your good guesses? *Predictions.*

Making predictions helps us get interested in the story before we read it. Let's make some predictions about the story before I read it to you. What do you predict this story will be about? (Student response.)

What characters do you predict will be in the story? (Student response.)

What do you predict the setting will be? (Student response.)

What do you predict might happen in the story? (Student response.)

When we read the book, we'll check your predictions to see whether they're correct.

Elicit correct listening behavior from students. **Read** trade book. **Model** prosody during read-aloud.

Guide students to confirm predictions and/or connect background knowledge as you read story. **Ask** questions to confirm predictions and/or connect background knowledge. **Guide** as needed.

Activity 4 Confirm Predictions—An After-Reading Strategy

Elicit responses to questions. **Guide** as needed.

Now let's check your predictions to see whether they were correct. You predicted that the story was about _____. Was your prediction correct? (Student response.)

You predicted that _____ were characters in the story. Was your prediction correct? (Student response.)

You predicted that the setting was _____. Was your prediction correct? (Student response.)

You predicted that some events would be _____. Was your prediction correct? (Student response.)

Remember that your predictions don't have to be correct. Just making a prediction and listening to see whether your prediction is correct helps you stay interested in the story.

Lesson 116

Lesson 117

Materials
Teacher: Narrative trade book (from Lesson 116); Picture-Sound Cards for /sp/, /st/, /sw/, /sk/, /sl/, and /s/
Student: Lined paper

5 minutes

Teacher Materials:
Picture-Sound Cards for /sp/, /st/, /sw/, /sk/, /sl/, and /s/

Part A: Phonemic and Phonological Awareness

Activity 1 Phoneme Isolation—Initial

Elicit responses. **Guide** as needed.
I'm going to show you two cards and name the object on each card. Then I'll tell you a sound. Think about which word starts with that sound. Let's try it. Today we'll be listening for the sound at the *beginning* of a word.

Show /sp/ card; use either of two Picture-Sound Cards per phoneme for activity.
This is a _____. What is this? (Student response.)

Show /sk/ card; use either of two Picture-Sound Cards per phoneme for activity.
This is a _____. What is this? (Student response.)

Which word *begins* with **/sp/?** (Student response.)

Show /sl/ card; use either of two Picture-Sound Cards per phoneme for activity.
This is a _____. What is this? (Student response.)

Show /st/ card; use either of two Picture-Sound Cards per phoneme for activity.
This is a _____. What is this? (Student response.)

Which word *begins* with **/st/?** (Student response.)

(Continue the activity with the following examples:
/sw/ and /s/: Which word begins with /sw/?
/sl/ and /sp/: Which word begins with /sp/?
/s/ and /st/: Which word begins with /st/?
/sw/ and /sk/: Which word begins with /sw/?)

Activity 2 Phoneme Identity—Initial

Elicit responses. **Guide** as needed.
Let's find the *first* sound in a word. I'll tell you a word, and you tell me the *first* sound in that word.

What is the first sound you hear in **chisel?** /ch/.

What is the first sound you hear in **enemy?** /eee/.

What is the first sound you hear in **barrel?** /b/.

What is the first sound you hear in **iceberg?** /īī/.

476   Lesson 117

What is the first sound you hear in **yesterday**? */yyy/*.

What is the first sound you hear in **bother**? */b/*.

What is the first sound you hear in **charcoal**? */ch/*.

What is the first sound you hear in **yogurt**? */yyy/*.

What is the first sound you hear in **eggplant**? */eee/*.

What is the first sound you hear in **identify**? */īīī/*.

Activity 3 Phoneme Blending

Elicit responses. **Guide** as needed.
Let's put some sounds together and make words. I'm going to say a word very slowly so you can hear each sound. You need to listen carefully and say the sounds. When you say the sounds, it will sound almost like you're singing them. Then we'll put the sounds together and say the word.

My turn. Listen. **/ēēē/ /t/.**
Say the sounds. */ēēē/ /t/.*
Again, say the sounds. */ēēē/ /t/.*
Now let's put it together. What word? *Eat.*

Let's make a bigger word. My turn. Listen. **/mmm/ /ēēē/ /t/.**
Say the sounds. */mmm/ /ēēē/ /t/.*
Again, say the sounds. */mmm/ /ēēē/ /t/.*
Now let's put it together. What word? *Meat.*

(Continue the activity with the following words:
seat [sss-ēēē-t], feet [fff-ēēē-t], sheet [shshsh-ēēē-t].)

Part B: Letter Recognition and Formation

6 minutes

Student Materials:
Lined paper

Activity 1 Letter Recognition Review—y

Elicit responses to questions. **Guide** as needed. **Write** y on the board. **Point** to y.
We learned that this letter is **y.** What letter name? *y.*
Again, what letter name? *y.*
Review as needed.

Activity 2 Letter Formation Review—y

Now we're going to practice writing **y.** When you practice writing, you'll learn not only where to start and stop the letter, but also which way to move your hand when you're making the letter. It's tricky, but you're so smart you'll learn how to write **y** very quickly. Watch.

Here's how you write **y** in the air.
Model y formation in the air (with your back to students).

Lesson 117   **477**

Watch again.

Now let's practice writing **y** in the air. Hold up your writing hand, and make **y** in the air.
Guide students as they write y in the air.

Let's practice **y** again.

Here's how to write **y** with your writing hand pointer finger.
Model y formation on the board with your finger (with your back to students).

Watch again.

Now let's practice writing **y** on your table without using your pencil. Use your writing hand pointer finger, and make **y** on your table.
Guide students as they write y on their table or desktop.

Let's practice **y** again.

Model writing y on the board (with your back to students).
Remember that every letter has a name.
You learned the name of this letter is **y.** What letter name? *y.*
Again, what letter name? *y.*

Provide lined paper to students.
Now let's practice writing **y** with your pencil.
Guide students as they write y on their paper. **Review** as needed.

 Link letter names to letter sounds as they appear in the program as needed.

Part C: Comprehension Strategies

9 minutes

Teacher Materials:
Narrative trade book

Activity 1 Listening Comprehension—A During-Reading Strategy

Direct students to narrative trade book of teacher choice. **Elicit** responses to questions. **Guide** as needed.
We'll read the story again today. When we read the story today, I want you to think about anything in the story that reminds you of something that you know or something that has happened to you. We'll connect the story to your life after we read the story. Then we'll talk about the main idea.

Elicit correct listening behavior from students. **Reread** trade book. **Model** prosody during read-aloud.

Elicit text-to-self connections and clues for main idea. **Guide** as needed.

478 Lesson 117

Activity 2 Make Connections: Text-to-Self—An After-Reading Strategy

Elicit responses to questions. **Guide** as needed. **Model** making text-to-self connections.
Making connections helps me to understand what I read. It helps make reading more fun and interesting. Let's talk about this story and see how it matches or connects to my own life. Listen as I make some connections.

What connections from the story can you make to your life? (Student response.)
Discuss how characters, events, or items in story relate to things in students' lives.

Remember that making connections to your life helps you better understand and remember the story.

Activity 3 Identify Main Idea—An After-Reading Strategy

Elicit responses to questions. **Guide** as needed.
Now let's think about what the story is mostly about. We're thinking about the main idea of the story. What's the main idea? (Idea: *What the story is mostly about*.)

What do we call what the story is mostly about? *The main idea.*

It's a little tricky to figure out the main idea, but the story gives me clues to make it easier.

Guide students to find main idea using clues from story. **Select** from following questions ones that will help you elicit main idea from students.

What's the title of the story? (Student response.)

Who are the main characters in the story? (Student response.)

What was the main thing that happened in the story? (Student response.)

How did the main character change? (Student response.)

What did the main character learn? (Student response.)

To tell the main idea, I want you to think about the main character and then tell about _____.

What do you think is the main idea? (Student response.)

Yes, the main idea is _____.

What's the main idea of our story? (Student response.)
Guide students to find main idea by first naming main character, then telling most important event, what main character learned, or how main character changed in story.

Lesson 117 **479**

Lesson 118

Materials

Teacher: Narrative trade book (from Lesson 116); additional trade book that has similar story elements for text-to-text connection (either from student suggestions or teacher choice); 16-Phonemic Awareness

Student: Lined paper; copy of 16-Phonemic Awareness

5 minutes

Teacher Materials:
Phonemic Awareness

Student Materials:
Phonemic Awareness

Part A: Phonemic and Phonological Awareness

Activity 1 Phoneme Categorization—Initial

Show Phonemic Awareness. **Distribute** copy of Phonemic Awareness. **Elicit** responses. **Guide** as needed.
We're going to look at a picture on this page, and find other pictures to match our sounds. I'm going to name each picture. I want you to touch each picture after I name it and repeat the name. We're going to find words that have the same *first* sound. If the word has the same *first* sound as the word in the top picture, we can circle the picture to show that they go together.

Model use of Phonemic Awareness; point to each picture as word is said.
Let's try it.
Point to picture at top of page.
Touch the picture at the top of the page. This is a **fan.** What is this? *Fan.*

That's right. The picture shows a **fan.** So what is the *first* sound in **fan?** */fff/.*

Yes, **/fff/.** We need to look at the other pictures and see which words have the same *first* sound as **fan.**
Point to first picture in first row.
Touch the first picture in the first row. This is a **canoe.** What is this? *canoe.*

Does **canoe** have the same *first* sound as **fan?** *No.*

We don't want to circle the picture of the **canoe** because the *first* sound in **canoe** is **/k/,** not **/fff/.**
Point to second picture in first row.
Touch the next picture. This is a **five.** What is this? *Five.*

Does **five** have the same *first* sound as **fan?** *Yes.*

Then we can circle the picture of the **five.**
Point to third picture in first row.
Touch the next picture. This is a **football.** What is this? *Football.*

Does **football** have the same *first* sound as **fan?** *Yes.*

Then we can circle the picture of the **football.** When we're finished with our lesson, you'll color the pictures you circled to show they have the same first sound.

(Continue the activity with the second row of pictures.
Second row: knife, fish, fire.)

(Use the same procedure to find the pictures of words that have the same first sound as the next key word: tape.
Third row: teeth, dog, tire.
Fourth row: tie, nest, ten.)

Activity 2 Phoneme Segmentation

Elicit responses to questions. **Guide** as needed.
Let's work on breaking words apart by each sound. I'm going to say a word. You'll need to listen closely and tell me the different sounds you hear in the word. I'll show you how to do the first one.

My turn. The word is **so.** I can say the sounds in **so.** /sss/ /ōōō/. Those are the sounds in the word **so.**
Try it with me. The word is **so.** Tell me the sounds you hear in **so.** /sss/ /ōōō/.
Your turn by yourself. The word is **so.** Tell me the sounds you hear in **so.** /sss/ /ōōō/.
Yes, you said the sounds in the word **so.**

(Continue the activity with the following words:
no [nnn-ōōō], show [shshsh-ōōō].)

Part B: Letter Recognition and Formation

6 minutes

Student Materials:
Lined paper

Activity 1 Letter Recognition—Capital Y

Elicit responses to questions. **Guide** as needed. **Write** capital <u>Y</u> on the board. **Point** to capital <u>Y</u>.
Today you'll learn another way to write **y.**
The name of this letter is **capital Y.** What letter name? *Capital Y.*
Again, what letter name? *Capital Y.*
Review as needed.

Activity 2 Letter Formation—Capital Y

Now we're going to practice writing **capital Y.** When you practice writing, you'll learn not only where to start and stop the letter, but also which way to move your hand when you're making the letter. It's tricky, but you're so smart you'll learn how to write **capital Y** very quickly. Watch.

Here's how you write **capital Y** in the air.
Model capital <u>Y</u> formation in the air (with your back to students).

Lesson 118   **481**

Watch again.

Now let's practice writing **capital Y** in the air. Hold up your writing hand, and make **capital Y** in the air.
Guide students as they write capital Y in the air.

Let's practice **capital Y** again.

Here's how to write **capital Y** with your writing hand pointer finger.
Model capital Y formation on the board with your finger (with your back to students).

Watch again.

Now let's practice writing **capital Y** on your table without using your pencil. Use your writing hand pointer finger, and make **capital Y** on your table.
Guide students as they write capital Y on their table or desktop.

Let's practice **capital Y** again.

Model writing capital Y on the board (with your back to students).
Remember that every letter has a name.
You learned the name of this letter is **capital Y.** What letter name? *Capital Y.*
Again, what letter name? *Capital Y.*

Provide lined paper to students.
Now let's practice writing **capital Y** with your pencil.
Guide students as they write capital Y on their paper. **Review** as needed.

 Link letter names to letter sounds as they appear in the program as needed.

Part C: Comprehension Strategies

9 minutes

Teacher Materials:
Narrative trade book

Additional trade book

Activity 1 Listening Comprehension—A During-Reading Strategy

Direct students to narrative trade book of teacher choice. **Elicit** responses to questions. **Guide** as needed.
We'll read the story again today. When we read the story today, I want you to think about all the stories you've heard. I want you to think of which story reminds you of this one.

Elicit correct listening behavior from students. **Reread** trade book. **Model** prosody during read-aloud.

Guide students to focus on thinking of another story like this one for a text-to-text connection. **Elicit** responses to questions about text-to-text connections. **Guide** as needed.

You've heard lots of stories this year. What story have you heard that reminds you of this story? (Student response.)
Elicit names of stories that are like today's story. **Guide** as needed.

Obtain book for text-to-text connection from student suggestions, if possible.

482 Lesson 118

Activity 2 Make Connections: Text-to-Text—An After-Reading Strategy

Elicit responses to questions. **Guide** as needed.

When I read this story, it reminded me right away of the time I read
_____. Listen as I show you what I mean.

When I can connect a story that I'm reading to another story that I know, it helps me to understand the story better. Making a connection to another story I have heard is a smart thing to do.

Elicit correct listening behavior from students. **Reread** other story for text-to-text connection. **Model** prosody during read-aloud. **Guide** students to think of similarities between stories for text-to-text connection.

Activity 3 Identify Main Idea—An After-Reading Strategy

Direct students to second text used for text-to-text connection and use again to find main idea. **Elicit** responses to questions. **Guide** as needed.

Now let's think about what the story is mostly about. We're thinking about the main idea of the story. What's the main idea? (Idea: *What the story is mostly about.*)

What do we call what the story is mostly about? *The main idea.*

It's a little tricky to figure out the main idea, but the story gives me clues to make it easier.

Guide students to find main idea using clues from story. **Select** from following questions the ones that will help you elicit main idea from students.

What's the title of the story? (Student response.)

Who are the main characters in the story? (Student response.)

What was the main thing that happened in the story? (Student response.)

How did the main character change? (Student response.)

What did the main character learn? (Student response.)

To tell the main idea, I want you to think about the main character and then tell about _____.

What do you think is the main idea? (Student response.)

Yes, the main idea is _____.

What's the main idea of our story? (Student response.)

Guide students to find main idea by first naming main character, then telling most important event, what main character learned, or how main character changed in story.

Lesson 118   **483**

Lesson 119

Materials

Teacher: Narrative trade book (from Lesson 116); 5-Story Map; Picture-Sound Cards for /tr/, /tw/, /sm/, /sn/, /r/, and /t/

Student: Lined paper; copy of 5-Story Map with writing lines

5 minutes

Teacher Materials:
Picture-Sound Cards for /tr/, /tw/, /sm/, /sn/, /r/, and /t/

Part A: Phonemic and Phonological Awareness

Activity 1 Phoneme Isolation—Initial

Use IWB interactive cards or picture-sound cards. **Elicit** responses. **Guide** as needed.
I'm going to show you two cards and name the object on each card. Then I'll tell you a sound. Think about which word starts with that sound. Let's try it. Today we'll be listening for the sound at the *beginning* of a word.

Show /tr/ card; use either of two Picture-Sound Cards per phoneme for activity.
This is a _____. What is this? (Student response.)

Show /sm/ card; use either of two Picture-Sound Cards per phoneme for activity.
This is a _____. What is this? (Student response.)

Which word *begins* with **/tr/**? (Student response.)

Show /sn/ card; use either of two Picture-Sound Cards per phoneme for activity.
This is a _____. What is this? (Student response.)

Show /tw/ card; use either of two Picture-Sound Cards per phoneme for activity.
This is a _____. What is this? (Student response.)

Which word *begins* with **/tw/**? (Student response.)

(Continue the activity with the following examples:
/tw/ and /t/: Which word begins with /tw/?
/r/ and /tr/: Which word begins with /tr/?)

Activity 2 Phoneme Identity—Initial

Elicit responses. **Guide** as needed.
Let's find the *first* sound in a word. I'll tell you a word, and you tell me the *first* sound in that word.

What is the first sound you hear in **January**? /j/.

What is the first sound you hear in **unique**? /ūūū/.

What is the first sound you hear in **quickly**? /kw/.

What is the first sound you hear in **zucchini**? /zzz/.

484 Lesson 119

What is the first sound you hear in **question?** /kw/.

What is the first sound you hear in **gymnastics?** /j/.

What is the first sound you hear in **universe?** /ūūū/.

What is the first sound you hear in **zillion?** /zzz/.

Activity 3: Phoneme Blending

Elicit responses. **Guide** as needed.
Let's put some sounds together and make words. I'm going to say a word very slowly so you can hear each sound. You need to listen carefully and say the sounds. When you say the sounds, it will sound almost like you're singing them. Then we'll put the sounds together and say the word.

My turn. Listen. **/iii/ /nnn/.**
Say the sounds. /iii/ /nnn/.
Again, say the sounds. /iii/ /nnn/.
Now let's put it together. What word? *In.*

Let's make a bigger word. My turn. Listen. **/fff/ /iii/ /nnn/.**
Say the sounds. /fff/ /iii/ /nnn/.
Again, say the sounds. /fff/ /iii/ /nnn/.
Now let's put it together. What word? *Fin.*

(Continue the activity with the following words:
shin [shshsh-iii-nnn], win [www-iii-nnn], thin [ththth-iii-nnn].)

Part B: Letter Recognition and Formation

6 minutes

Student Materials:
Lined paper

Activity 1: Letter Recognition Review—Capital Y

Elicit responses to questions. **Guide** as needed. **Write** capital Y on the board. **Point** to capital Y.
We learned that this letter is **capital Y.** What letter name? *Capital Y.*
Again, what letter name? *Capital Y.*
Review as needed.

Activity 2: Letter Formation Review—Capital Y

Now we're going to practice writing **capital Y.** When you practice writing, you'll learn not only where to start and stop the letter, but also which way to move your hand when you're making the letter. It's tricky, but you're so smart you'll learn how to write **capital Y** very quickly. Watch.

Here's how you write **capital Y** in the air.
Model capital Y formation in the air (with your back to students).

Watch again.

Lesson 119

Now let's practice writing **capital Y** in the air. Hold up your writing hand, and make **capital Y** in the air.
Guide students as they write capital Y in the air.

Let's practice **capital Y** again.

Here's how to write **capital Y** with your writing hand pointer finger.
Model capital Y formation on the board with your finger (with your back to students).

Watch again.

Now let's practice writing **capital Y** on your table without using your pencil. Use your writing hand pointer finger, and make **capital Y** on your table.
Guide students as they write capital Y on their table or desktop.

Let's practice **capital Y** again.

Model writing capital Y on the board (with your back to students).
Remember that every letter has a name.
You learned the name of this letter is **capital Y.** What letter name? *Capital Y.*
Again, what letter name? *Capital Y.*

Provide lined paper to students.
Now let's practice writing **capital Y** with your pencil.
Guide students as they write capital Y on their paper. **Review** as needed.

 Link letter names to letter sounds as they appear in the program as needed.

Part C: Comprehension Strategies

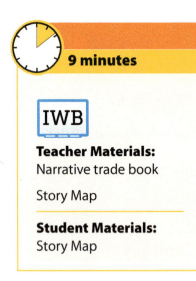

9 minutes

Teacher Materials:
Narrative trade book
Story Map

Student Materials:
Story Map

Activity 1 Listening Comprehension—A During-Reading Strategy

Direct students to narrative trade book of teacher choice.
Today as I read the story, I want you to look carefully at the pictures of all the parts of the story. Look for what the illustrator did to show the parts of the story. After I read the story, you'll become an illustrator and draw pictures of all the parts.

Elicit correct listening behavior from students. **Reread** trade book. **Model** prosody during read-aloud.

Guide students to focus on illustrations for all story elements. **Elicit** responses to questions about how illustrator shows all story elements. **Guide** as needed.

486 Lesson 119

Activity 2 **Story Elements: Illustrate Story—An After-Reading Strategy**

Show Story Map. Provide Story Map to each student. **Elicit** responses to questions. **Guide** as needed.

Now you'll become an illustrator. Make pictures to show all the parts of the story.

Monitor students and provide assistance in filling in Story Map as needed. **Save** student copies of Story Map for Lesson 120.

Activity 3 **Collaborate to Strengthen Writing**

Show Story Map.

Now let's write about what happened in our story. Watch as I write about the beginning, the middle, and the end of the story.

Model writing 3 separate sentences that tell about the beginning, the middle, and the end of the story.

Now it is your turn to write about what happens **first** at the beginning of the story, **then** what happens in the middle of the story, and **finally** what happens at the end of the story. If you need help, ask me.

Monitor students. **Guide** as needed.

Assign student partners.

Share your writing with your neighbor. Add suggestions to make your neighbor's writing better if you think it needs it.

Model how to give feedback on what was written if it needs it. **Monitor** students. **Guide** as needed.

Lesson 119 **487**

Lesson 120

> **Materials**
> **Teacher:** Narrative trade book (from Lesson 116); 5-Story Map (from Lesson 119); 17-Phonemic Awareness; Letter Recognition; 8-My Book Review
> **Student:** Lined paper; copy of 5-Story Map (from Lesson 119); 17-Phonemic Awareness; copy of 8-My Book Review

5 minutes

Part A: Phonemic and Phonological Awareness

Teacher Materials:
Phonemic Awareness

Student Materials:
Phonemic Awareness

Activity 1 Phoneme Categorization—Initial

Show Phonemic Awareness. **Distribute** copy of Phonemic Awareness. **Elicit** responses. **Guide** as needed.
We're going to look at a picture on this page and find other pictures to match our sounds. I'm going to name each picture. I want you to touch each picture after I name it and repeat the name. We're going to find words that have the same *first* sound. If the word has the same *first* sound as the word in the top picture, we can circle the picture to show that they go together.

Model use of Phonemic Awareness; point to each picture as word is said.
Let's try it.
Point to picture at top of page.
Touch the picture at the top of the page. This is a **kite.** What is this? *Kite.*

That's right. The picture shows a **kite.** So what is the *first* sound in **kite?** */k/.*

Yes, **/k/.** We need to look at the other pictures and see which words have the same *first* sound as **kite.**
Point to first picture in first row.
Touch the first picture in the first row. This is a **cone.** What is this? *Cone.*

Does **cone** have the same *first* sound as **kite?** *Yes.*

Then we can circle the picture of the **cone.**
Point to second picture in first row.
Touch the next picture. This is a **king.** What is this? *King.*

Does **king** have the same *first* sound as **kite?** *Yes.*

Then we can circle the picture of the **king.**
Point to third picture in first row.
Touch the next picture. This is a **hook.** What is this? *Hook.*

Does **hook** have the same *first* sound as **kite?** *No.*

We don't want to circle the picture of the **hook** because the *first* sound in **hook** is **/h/,** not **/k/.** When we're finished with our lesson, you'll color the pictures you circled to show they have the same first sound.

(Continue the activity with the second row of pictures.
Second row: cage, flag, key.)

(Use the same procedure to find the pictures of words that have the same first sound as the next key word: girl.
Third row: log, goat, gum.
Fourth row: gate, door, gift.)

Activity 2 Phoneme Segmentation

Elicit responses to questions. **Guide** as needed.
Let's work on breaking words apart by each sound. I'm going to say a word. You'll need to listen closely and tell me the different sounds you hear in the word. I'll show you how to do the first one.

My turn. The word is **shoe.** I can say the sounds in **shoe.** /shshsh/ /oooooo/. Those are the sounds in the word **shoe.**
Your turn by yourself. The word is **shoe.** Tell me the sounds you hear in **shoe.** /shshsh/ (pause) /oooooo/.
Yes, you said the sounds in the word **shoe.**

(Continue the activity with the following words:
zoo [zzz- uuu], moo [mmm- uuu].)

Part B: Letter Recognition and Formation

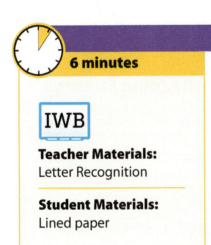

6 minutes

IWB

Teacher Materials:
Letter Recognition

Student Materials:
Lined paper

Activity 1 Letter Recognition Cumulative Review—v/V, p/P, b/B, y/Y

Display on IWB or **write** letters and capitals on the board in the order shown. **Elicit** responses to questions. **Guide** as needed.
This week you've learned one letter and one capital— **y** and **capital Y.** Let's review all the letters and capitals you've learned. Are you ready?

Letter	Question	Student Response
p	What letter?	p.
B	What letter?	Capital B.
v	What letter?	v.
y	What letter?	y.
P	What letter?	Capital P.
V	What letter?	Capital V.
b	What letter?	b.
Y	What letter?	Capital Y.

Review as needed.

Lesson 120   489

Activity 2 Letter Formation Cumulative Review—v/V, p/P, b/B, y/Y

Write v, capital V, p, capital P, b, capital B, y, and capital Y on the board in the order shown (with your back to students). **Provide** lined paper to students.

Show me how you can write these letters and capitals.
Guide students as they write the letters and capitals on their paper. **Review** as needed.

 Link letter names to letter sounds as they appear in the program as needed.

Part C: Comprehension Strategies

9 minutes

Teacher Materials:
Narrative trade book
Story Map
My Book Review

Student Materials:
Story Map
My Book Review

Activity 1 Listening Comprehension—A During-Reading Strategy

Direct students to trade book. **Elicit** responses to questions. **Guide** as needed.
Today I will read the story one last time. Listen to the story to remember all the parts of the story. Then you will get to tell about the illustrations that you made in the last lesson. You will tell about the characters, the setting, and the events for the beginning, the middle, and the end of the story.

Elicit correct listening behavior from students. **Reread** trade book. **Model** prosody. **Guide** students to focus on story elements. **Elicit** responses.

Activity 2 Retell the Story—An After-Reading Strategy

Assign student partners. **Provide** copy of Story Map completed in Lesson 119. **Elicit** responses to questions. **Guide** as needed.
You're going to tell a partner all the parts of the story from your pictures. Your partner will listen to you the right way. Then you'll listen politely as your partner tells you about his or her pictures.

When you're done, if there is time, you can show the class your illustrations and tell all the parts of the story.
Monitor students as they retell story. **Share** Story Maps with class as time permits, or make a class book of Story Maps.

Activity 3 Connections Through Shared Writing—Express Opinions

Show My Book Review. **Elicit** responses to questions. **Guide** as needed.
Think about the two books we read, _____ and _____. Let's talk about the two books. Which one did you like best and why?

Provide copies of My Book Review to students. **Guide** students through completion of My Book Review. **Share** with class as time permits.

490   Lesson 120

Lesson 121

Materials
Teacher: Narrative trade book (same book for Lessons 121–125), 1-My Prediction Chart
Student: Lined paper, Copy of 1-My Prediction Chart

5 minutes

Part A: Phonemic and Phonological Awareness

Activity 1 Phoneme Identity—Final

Elicit responses. **Guide** as needed.
Let's find the *last* sound in a word. I'll say a word, and you tell me the *last* sound in that word.

What is the last sound you hear in **stadium?** /mmm/.

What is the last sound you hear in **pillowcase?** /sss/.

What is the last sound you hear in **especially?** /ēēē/.

What is the last sound you hear in **choir?** /rrr/.

What is the last sound you hear in **apostrophe?** /ēēē/.

What is the last sound you hear in **calcium?** /mmm/.

What is the last sound you hear in **campfire?** /rrr/.

What is the last sound you hear in **compass?** /sss/.

Activity 2 Phoneme Blending

Elicit responses. **Guide** as needed.
Let's put some sounds together and make words. I'm going to say a word very slowly so you can hear each sound. You need to listen carefully and say the sounds. When you say the sounds, it will sound almost like you're singing them. Then we'll put the sounds together and say the word.

My turn. Listen. **/ooo/ /p/.**
Say the sounds. */ooo/ /p/.*
Again, say the sounds. */ooo/ /p/.*
Now let's put it together. *op.*

Lesson 121   491

Let's make a bigger word. My turn. Listen. **/mmm/ /ooo/ /p/.**
Say the sounds. /mmm/ /ooo/ /p/.
Again, say the sounds. /mmm/ /ooo/ /p/.
Now let's put it together. What word? *Mop.*

(Continue the activity with the following words:
shop [shshsh-ooo-p], ut [uuu-t], nut [nnn-uuu-t], shut [shshsh-uuu-t].)

6 minutes

Student Materials:
Lined paper

Part B: Letter Recognition and Formation

Activity 1 Letter Recognition—x

Elicit responses to questions. **Guide** as needed. **Write** x on the board.
Today you'll learn a new letter.
The name of this letter is **x.** What letter name? *x.*
Again, what letter name? *x.*
Review as needed.

Activity 2 Letter Formation—x

Now we're going to practice writing **x.** When you practice writing, you'll learn not only where to start and stop the letter, but also which way to move your hand when you're making the letter. It's tricky, but you're so smart you'll learn how to write **x** very quickly. Watch.

Here's how you write **x** in the air.
Model x formation in the air (with your back to students).

Watch again.

Now let's practice writing **x** in the air. Hold up your writing hand, and make **x** in the air.
Guide students as they write x in the air.

Let's practice **x** again.

Here's how to write **x** with your writing hand pointer finger.
Model x formation on the board with your finger (with your back to students).

Watch again.

Now let's practice writing **x** on your table without using your pencil. Use your writing hand pointer finger, and make **x** on your table.
Guide students as they write x on their table or desktop.

Let's practice **x** again.

492 Lesson 121

Model writing x on the board (with your back to students).
Remember that every letter has a name.
You learned the name of this letter is **x.** What letter name? *x.*
Again, what letter name? *x.*

Provide lined paper to students.
Now let's practice writing **x** with your pencil.
Guide students as they write x on their paper. **Review** as needed.

 Link letter names to letter sounds as they appear in the program as needed.

 Set up a writing center with writing materials and correct models of letters learned so far for students to use in their free time.

Part C: Comprehension Strategies

9 minutes

Teacher Materials:
Narrative trade book

My Prediction Chart

Student Materials:
My Prediction Chart

Activity 1 Title, Author, and Illustrator Identification—A Before-Reading Strategy

 Provide a reading center to display books being read so that students can enjoy them again during free time.

Direct students to narrative trade book of teacher choice. **Elicit** responses to questions. **Guide** as needed.

Show front cover of book, and allow student to point to name of title, author, and illustrator as you discuss them.

We'll read a new book today. The title of today's story is _____.
What's the title of today's story? (Student response.)

The author of today's story is _____. Who's the author of today's story? (Student response.)

The illustrator of today's story is _____. Who's the illustrator? (Student response.)

Activity 2 Establish Purpose for Reading—A Before-Reading Strategy

Elicit responses to questions. **Guide** as needed.
We've read lots of stories. The stories we have read have characters, setting, and events that happened. These kinds of stories are called narrative stories. Narrative text is written to tell stories. Stories are written for us to enjoy. Why do we read narrative stories? (Idea: *To enjoy them.*)

When we look at a story and see that it has characters, setting, and events, we know we'll be reading a narrative story and we can get ready to enjoy it. We'll read a narrative story today. Why will we read this narrative story? (Idea: *To enjoy it.*)

Lesson 121 **493**

Activity 3 Make Predictions—A Before-Reading Strategy

Show My Prediction Chart and provide copies to students. **Show** title, front and back cover, and pictures inside book. **Elicit** responses to questions. **Guide** as needed.
The title of today's book is _____. Write the book title in the box labeled "Book Title".

Now that you know the title of today's book, let's look at the cover and pictures inside the book for clues to make some predictions for the story. What do you predict this story will be about? (Student response.) Write your prediction in the box labeled "I Predict That."

What characters do you predict will be in the story? (Student response.)

What do you predict the setting will be? (Student response.)

What do you predict might happen in the story? (Student response.)

When we read the book, you'll check your predictions to see whether they're correct.

Elicit correct listening behavior from students. **Read** trade book. **Model** prosody during read-aloud.

Guide students to confirm predictions and/or connect background knowledge as you read story. **Ask** questions to confirm predictions and/or connect background knowledge. **Guide** as needed.

Activity 4 Confirm Predictions—An After-Reading Strategy

Elicit responses to questions. **Guide** as needed.
Now let's check your predictions to see whether they were correct. You predicted that the story was about _____. Was your prediction correct? (Student response.)
Circle whether or not your prediction was correct in the box labeled "Was My Prediction Correct?".

You predicted that _____ were characters in the story. Was your prediction correct? (Student response.)

You predicted that the setting was _____. Was your prediction correct? (Student response.)

You predicted that some events would be _____. Was your prediction correct? (Student response.)

Remember that your predictions don't have to be correct. Just making a prediction and listening to see whether your prediction is correct helps you stay interested in the story.

494 *Lesson 121*

Lesson 122

Materials
Teacher: Narrative trade book (from Lesson 121); 18-Phonemic Awareness
Student: Lined paper; copy of 18-Phonemic Awareness

Part A: Phonemic and Phonological Awareness

5 minutes

Teacher Materials:
Phonemic Awareness

Student Materials:
Phonemic Awareness

Activity 1 Phoneme Categorization—Initial

Show Phonemic Awareness. **Distribute** copy of Phonemic Awareness. **Elicit** responses. **Guide** as needed.
We're going to look at a picture on this page and find other pictures to match our sounds. I'm going to name each picture. I want you to touch each picture after I name it and repeat the name. We're going to find words that have the same *first* sound. If the word has the same *first* sound as the word in the top picture, we can circle the picture to show that they go together.

Model use of Phonemic Awareness; point to each picture as word is said.
Let's try it.
Point to picture at top of page.
Touch the picture at the top of the page. This is a **pig.** What is this? *Pig.*

That's right. The picture shows a **pig.** What is the *first* sound in **pig?** */p/.*

Yes, **/p/.** We need to look at the other pictures and see which ones have the same *first* sound as **pig.**
Point to first picture in first row.
Touch the first picture in the first row. This is a **pen.** What is this? *Pen.*

Does **pen** have the same *first* sound as **pig?** *Yes.*

Then we can circle the picture of the **pen.** When we're finished with our lesson, you'll color the pictures you circled to show they have the same first sound.

(Continue the activity with the rest of the pictures in the first and second rows.
First row: napkin, pizza.
Second row: piano, tape, pie.)

(Then use the same procedure to find the pictures of words that have the same first sound as the next key word: lock.
Third row: shell, lamp, ladder.
Fourth row: leaf, balloon, lips.)

Lesson 122   **495**

Activity 2 Phoneme Segmentation

Elicit responses. **Guide** as needed. **Model** segmentation only if students have difficulty without this step.
Let's work on breaking words apart by each sound. I'm going to tell you a word. You'll need to listen closely and tell me the different sounds you hear in the word.

Listen. The word is **she.** What word? *She.*
Your turn. Tell me the sounds you hear in **she.** */shshsh/ /ēēē/.*
Yes, you said the sounds in the word **she.**

(Continue the activity with the following words:
knee [nnn-ēēē], fee [fff-ēēē].
If children need more practice, continue with me, see, and we.)

Part B: Letter Recognition and Formation

6 minutes

Student Materials:
Lined paper

Activity 1 Letter Recognition Review—x

Elicit responses to questions. **Guide** as needed. **Write** x on the board. **Point** to x.
We learned that this letter is **x.** What letter name? *x.*
Again, what letter name? *x.*
Review as needed.

Activity 2 Letter Formation Review—x

Now we're going to practice writing **x.** When you practice writing, you'll learn not only where to start and stop the letter, but also which way to move your hand when you're making the letter. It's tricky, but you're so smart you'll learn how to write **x** very quickly. Watch.

Here's how you write **x** in the air.
Model x formation in the air (with your back to students).

Watch again.

Now let's practice writing **x** in the air. Hold up your writing hand, and make **x** in the air.
Guide students as they write x in the air.

Let's practice **x** again.

Here's how to write **x** with your writing hand pointer finger.
Model x formation on the board with your finger (with your back to students).

Watch again.

Now let's practice writing **x** on your table without using your pencil. Use your writing hand pointer finger, and make **x** on your table.
Guide students as they write x on their table or desktop.

Let's practice **x** again.

496 Lesson 122

Model writing x on the board (with your back to students).
Remember that every letter has a name.
You learned the name of this letter is **x.** What letter name? *x.*
Again, what letter name? *x.*

Provide lined paper to students.
Now let's practice writing **x** with your pencil.
Guide students as they write x on their paper. **Review** as needed.

 Link letter names to letter sounds as they appear in the program as needed.

Part C: Comprehension Strategies

9 minutes

Teacher Materials:
Narrative trade book

Activity 1 Listening Comprehension—A During-Reading Strategy

Direct students to narrative trade book of teacher choice. **Elicit** responses to questions. **Guide** as needed.

You've learned all about stories. Stories have characters, a setting, a beginning, a middle, and an end. We call these stories narratives. Narratives are written for us to enjoy. Why do you read narrative stories? (Idea: *To enjoy them.*)

Enjoy listening to the story again and see whether you can tell me all the parts of the story after I read it.

Elicit correct listening behavior from students. **Reread** trade book. **Model** prosody during read-aloud.

Ask questions to elicit identification of characters, setting, and events. **Guide** as needed.

Activity 2 Story Elements: Identify Characters, Setting, Beginning, Middle, and End—An After-Reading Strategy

Elicit responses to questions. **Guide** as needed.
You listened to the story. Now you can tell me all the parts of the story that you heard as you listened. What characters are in the story? (Student response.)

Who do you think is the main character? (Student response.)

What's the setting of the story? (Student response.)

Does the setting change or stay the same? (Student response.)

What events happened at the beginning? (Student response.)

Lesson 122   **497**

What events happened in the middle? (Student response.)

What events happened at the end? (Student response.)

You told all the parts of the story. Excellent job listening to the story and remembering all the parts.

Activity 3 Identify Main Idea—An After-Reading Strategy

Elicit responses to questions. **Guide** as needed.
Now let's think about what the story is mostly about. We're thinking about the main idea of the story. What's the main idea? (Idea: *What the story is mostly about.*)

What do we call it when we are trying to think of what the story is mostly about? *The main idea.*

It's a little tricky to figure out the main idea, but the story gives me clues to make it easier.

Guide students to find main idea using clues from story. **Select** from following questions ones that will help you elicit main idea from students.

What's the title of the story? (Student response.)

Who are the main characters in the story? (Student response.)

What was the main thing that happened in the story? (Student response.)

How did the main character change? (Student response.)

What did the main character learn? (Student response.)

To tell the main idea, I want you to think about the main character and then tell about _____.

What do you think is the main idea? (Student response.)

Yes, the main idea is _____.

What's the main idea of the story? (Student response.)
Guide students to find main idea by first naming main character, then telling most important event, what main character learned, or how main character changed in story.

498 *Lesson 122*

Lesson 123

Materials
Teacher: Narrative trade book (from Lesson 121)
Student: Lined paper

5 minutes

Part A: Phonemic and Phonological Awareness

Activity 1 Phoneme Identity—Final

Elicit responses. **Guide** as needed.
Let's find the *last* sound in a word. I'll say a word and you tell me the *last* sound in that word.

What is the last sound you hear in **island?** /d/.

What is the last sound you hear in **paragraph?** /fff/.

What is the last sound you hear in **August?** /t/.

What is the last sound you hear in **teaspoon?** /nnn/.

What is the last sound you hear in **chocolate?** /t/.

What is the last sound you hear in **thousand?** /d/.

What is the last sound you hear in **question?** /nnn/.

What is the last sound you hear in **enough?** /fff/.

Activity 2 Phoneme Blending

Elicit responses. **Guide** as needed.
Let's put some sounds together and make words. I'm going to say a word very slowly so you can hear each sound. You need to listen carefully and say the sounds. When you say the sounds, it will sound almost like you're singing them. Then we'll put the sounds together and say the word.

My turn. Listen. **/aaa/ /d/.**
Say the sounds. /aaa/ /d/.
Again, say the sounds. /aaa/ /d/.
Now let's put it together. *ad.*

Let's make a bigger word. My turn. Listen. **/mmm/ /aaa/ /d/.**
Say the sounds. /mmm/ /aaa/ /d/.
Again, say the sounds. /mmm/ /aaa/ /d/.
Now let's put it together. What word? *Mad.*

(Continue the activity with the following words:
sad [sss-aaa-d], ear [ēēē-r], near [nnn-ēēē-r], fear [fff-ēēē-r].

Lesson 123   **499**

6 minutes

Student Materials:
Lined paper

Part B: Letter Recognition and Formation

Activity 1 Letter Recognition—Capital X

Elicit responses to questions. **Guide** as needed **Write** capital X on the board. **Point** to capital X.
Today you'll learn another way to write **x.**
The name of this letter is **capital X.** What letter name? *Capital X.*
Again, what letter name? *Capital X.*
Review as needed.

Activity 2 Letter Formation—Capital X

Now we're going to practice writing **capital X.** When you practice writing, you'll learn not only where to start and stop the letter, but also which way to move your hand when you're making the letter. It's tricky, but you're so smart you'll learn how to write **capital X** very quickly. Watch.

Here's how you write **capital X** in the air.
Model capital X formation in the air (with your back to students).

Watch again.

Now let's practice writing **capital X** in the air. Hold up your writing hand, and make **capital X** in the air.
Guide students as they write capital X in the air.

Let's practice **capital X** again.

Here's how to write **capital X** with your writing hand pointer finger.
Model capital X formation on the board with your finger (with your back to students).

Watch again.

Now let's practice writing **capital X** on your table without using your pencil. Use your writing hand pointer finger, and make **capital X** on your table.
Guide students as they write capital X on their table or desktop.

Let's practice **capital X** again.

Model writing capital X on the board (with your back to students).
Remember that every letter has a name.
You learned the name of this letter is **capital X.** What letter name? *Capital X.*
Again, what letter name? *Capital X.*

Provide lined paper to students.
Now let's practice writing **capital X** with your pencil.
Guide students as they write capital X on their paper. **Review** as needed.

 Link letter names to letter sounds as they appear in the program as needed.

500   Lesson 123

Part C: Comprehension Strategies

9 minutes

Teacher Materials:
Narrative trade book

Student Materials:
Lined paper

Activity 1 Listening Comprehension—A During-Reading Strategy

Direct students to narrative trade book of teacher choice. **Elicit** response to question. **Guide** as needed.
We'll read the story again today. When we read the story today, I want you to think about anything in the story that reminds you of something that you know or something that has happened to you. We'll connect the story to your life after we read the story. Then we'll talk about the main idea of the story.

Elicit correct listening behavior from students. **Reread** trade book. **Model** prosody during read-aloud.

Elicit text-to-self connections and clues for identifying main idea. **Guide** as needed.

Activity 2 Make Connections: Text-to-Self—An After-Reading Strategy

Elicit responses to questions. **Guide** as needed.
Making connections helps you to understand what you read. It helps make reading more fun and interesting. Let's talk about this story and see how it matches or connects to your own life. What connections from the story can you make to your life? (**Student response.**)
Discuss how characters, events, or items in story relate to things in students' lives.

Provide lined paper. **Model** writing a sentence about a connection you made.
Write a sentence that describes the connection you made to your life. If you need help, ask me.
Monitor students. **Guide** students as needed.

Remember that when you read, making connections to your life helps you better understand and remember the story.

Lesson 123

Activity 3 Identify Main Idea—An After-Reading Strategy

Elicit responses to questions. **Guide** as needed.

Now let's think about what the story is mostly about. We're thinking about the main idea of the story. What's the main idea? (Idea: *What the story is mostly about.*)

What do we call what the story is mostly about? *The main idea.*

It's a little tricky to figure out the main idea, but the story gives me clues to make it easier.

Guide students to find main idea using clues from story. **Select** from following questions ones that will help you elicit main idea from students.

What's the title of the story? (Student response.)

Who are the main characters in the story? (Student response.)

What was the main thing that happened in the story? (Student response.)

How did the main character change? (Student response.)

What did the main character learn? (Student response.)

To tell the main idea, I want you to think about the main character and then tell about _____.

Talk to your neighbor and tell them what you think the main idea is. Then listen to your neighbor tell you his or her idea for the main idea.

Share what you talked about. What do you think is the main idea? (Student response.)

Guide student partners to find main idea by first naming main character, then telling most important event, what main character learned, or how main character changed in story.

Yes, the main idea is _____.

502 *Lesson 123*

Lesson 124

Materials

Teacher: Narrative trade book (from Lesson 121); additional trade book that has similar story elements for text-to-text connection (either from student suggestions or teacher choice); 19-Phonemic Awareness

Student: Lined paper; copy of 19-Phonemic Awareness

5 minutes

Part A: Phonemic and Phonological Awareness

Activity 1 Phoneme Categorization—Initial

Teacher Materials:
Phonemic Awareness

Student Materials:
Phonemic Awareness

Show Phonemic Awareness. **Distribute** copy of Phonemic Awareness. **Elicit** responses. **Guide** as needed.
We're going to look at a picture on this page and find other pictures to match our sounds. I'm going to name each picture. I want you to touch each picture after I name it and repeat the name. We're going to find words that have the same *first* sound. If the word has the same *first* sound as the word in the top picture, we can circle the picture to show that they go together.

Model use of Phonemic Awareness; point to each picture as word is said.
Let's try it.
Point to picture at top of page.
Touch the picture at the top of the page. This is a **bell.** What is this? *Bell.*

That's right. The picture shows a **bell.** What is the *first* sound in **bell?** */b/.*

Yes, **/b/.** We need to look at the other pictures and see which words have the same *first* sound as **bell.**
Point to first picture in first row.

Touch the first picture in the first row. This is a **globe.** What is this? *Globe.*

Does **globe** have the same *first* sound as **bell?** *No.*

Then we can't circle the picture of the **globe.** When we're finished with our lesson, you'll color the pictures you circled to show they have the same first sound.

(Continue the activity with the rest of the pictures in the first and second rows.
First row: bike, rabbit.
Second row: bottle, balloon, bone.)

(Then use the same procedure to find the pictures of words that have the same first sound as the next key word: vase.
Third row: vacuum, van, stove.
Fourth row: seven, violin, vest.)

Lesson 124   503

Activity 2 Phoneme Segmentation

Elicit responses. **Guide** as needed.
Let's work on breaking words apart by each sound. I'm going to tell you a word. You'll need to listen closely and tell me the different sounds you hear in the word.

Listen. The word is **ray.** What word? *Ray.*
Your turn. Tell me the sounds you hear in **ray.** /rrr/ /āāā/.
Yes, you said the sounds in the word **ray.**

(Continue the activity with the following words:
they [ththth-āāā], lay [lll-āāā].
If children need more practice, continue with may, say, and way.)

Part B: Letter Recognition and Formation

6 minutes

Student Materials:
Lined paper

Activity 1 Letter Recognition Review—Capital X

Elicit responses to questions. **Guide** as needed. **Write** capital X on the board. **Point** to capital X.
We learned that this letter is **capital X.** What letter name? *Capital X.*
Again, what letter name? *Capital X.*
Review as needed.

Activity 2 Letter Formation Review—Capital X

Now, we're going to practice writing **capital X.** When you practice writing, you'll learn not only where to start and stop the letter, but also which way to move your hand when you're making the letter. It's tricky, but you're so smart you'll learn how to write **capital X** very quickly. Watch.

Here's how you write **capital X** in the air.
Model capital X formation in the air (with your back to students).

Watch again.

Now let's practice writing **capital X** in the air. Hold up your writing hand, and make **capital X** in the air.
Guide students as they write capital X in the air.

Let's practice **capital X** again.

Here's how to write **capital X** with your writing hand pointer finger.
Model capital X formation on the board with your finger (with your back to students).

Watch again.

Now let's practice writing **capital X** on your table without using your pencil.
Use your writing hand pointer finger, and make **capital X** on your table.
Guide students as they write capital X on their table or desktop.

Let's practice **capital X** again.

Model writing capital X on the board (with your back to students).
Remember that every letter has a name.
You learned the name of this letter is **capital X.** What letter name? *Capital X.*
Again, what letter name? *Capital X.*

Provide lined paper to students.
Now let's practice writing **capital X** with your pencil.
Guide students as they write capital X on their paper. **Review** as needed.

 Link letter names to letter sounds as they appear in the program as needed.

Part C: Comprehension Strategies

9 minutes

Teacher Materials:
Narrative trade book

Additional trade book

Activity 1 Listening Comprehension—A During-Reading Strategy

Direct students to narrative trade book of teacher choice. **Elicit** responses to questions. **Guide** as needed.
We'll read the story again today. When we read the story today, I want you to think about all the stories you've heard. I want you to think about which story reminds you of this one.

Elicit correct listening behavior from students. **Reread** trade book. **Model** prosody during read-aloud.

Guide students to focus on thinking of another story like this one for a text-to-text connection. **Elicit** responses to questions about text-to-text connections. **Guide** as needed.

You've heard lots of stories this year. What story have you heard that reminds you of this story? (Student response.)
Elicit names of stories that are like today's story. **Guide** as needed.

Obtain book for text-to-text connection from student suggestions, if possible.

Lesson 124   505

Activity 2 **Make Connections: Text-to-Text—An After-Reading Strategy**

Elicit responses to questions. **Guide** as needed.

When you heard this story, it reminded you of the story _____ . Listen to that story again and then we'll make a connection to the story.

Elicit correct listening behavior from students. **Reread** other story for text-to-text connection. **Model** prosody during read-aloud. **Guide** students to think of similarities between stories for text-to-text connection.

When you can connect a story that you're reading to another story that you know, it helps you to understand the story better. Making a connection to another story you've heard is a smart thing to do.

Lesson 125

Materials
Teacher: Narrative trade book (from Lesson 121); Letter Recognition
Student: Lined paper

5 minutes

Part A: Phonemic and Phonological Awareness

Activity 1 Phoneme Identity—Final

Elicit responses. **Guide** as needed.
Let's find the *last* sound in a word. I'll say a word, and you tell me the *last* sound in that word.

What is the last sound you hear in **music?** /k/.

What is the last sound you hear in **cereal?** /lll/.

What is the last sound you hear in **birdbath?** /thththt/.

What is the last sound you hear in **beanbag?** /g/.

What is the last sound you hear in **underneath?** /ththth/.

What is the last sound you hear in **stomach?** /k/.

What is the last sound you hear in **catalog?** /g/.

What is the last sound you hear in **hospital?** /lll/.

Activity 2 Phoneme Blending

Elicit responses. **Guide** as needed.
Let's put some sounds together and make words. I'm going to say a word very slowly so you can hear each sound. You need to listen carefully and say the sounds. When you say the sounds, it will sound almost like you're singing them. Then we'll put the sounds together and say the word.

My turn. Listen. **/iii/ /k/.**
Say the sounds. /iii/ /k/.
Again, say the sounds. /iii/ /k/.
Now let's put it together. *ick.*

Lesson 125   507

Let's make a bigger word. My turn. Listen. **/sss/ /iii/ /k/.**
Say the sounds. /sss/ /iii/ /k/.
Again, say the sounds. /sss/ /iii/ /k/.
Now let's put it together. What word? *Sick.*

(Continue the activity with the following words:
lick [lll-iii-k], et [eee-t], net [nnn-eee-t], vet [vvv-eee-t].)

6 minutes

Teacher Materials:
Letter Recognition

Student Materials:
Lined paper

Part B: Letter Recognition and Formation

Activity 1 — Letter Recognition Cumulative Review— p/P, b/B, y/Y, x/X

Display on IWB or **write** letters and capitals on the board in the order shown. **Elicit** responses to questions. **Guide** as needed.

This week you've learned one letter and one capital—**x** and **capital X.** Let's review all the letters and capitals you've learned. Are you ready?

Letter	Question	Student Response
x	What letter?	x.
Y	What letter?	Capital Y.
B	What letter?	Capital B.
y	What letter?	y.
b	What letter?	b.
P	What letter?	Capital P.
X	What letter?	Capital X.
p	What letter?	p.

Review as needed.

Activity 2 — Letter Formation Cumulative Review—p/P, b/B, y/Y, x/X

Write p, capital P, b, capital B, y, capital Y, x, and capital X on the board in the order shown (with your back to students). **Provide** lined paper to students.

Show me how you can write these letters and capitals.
Guide students as they write the letters and capitals on their paper. **Review** as needed.

 Link letter names to letter sounds as they appear in the program as needed.

508   Lesson 125

9 minutes

Teacher Materials:
Narrative trade book

Part C: Comprehension Strategies

Activity 1 Listening Comprehension—A During-Reading Strategy

Direct students to narrative trade book of teacher choice. **Elicit** responses to questions. **Guide** as needed.
We'll read the story again today. After we have read the story, we'll play the story. Think of some good ideas for how to play the story.

Elicit correct listening behavior from students. **Reread** trade book. **Model** prosody during read-aloud.

Guide students to focus on ideas for playing story. **Elicit** responses to questions about how to play story. **Guide** as needed.

Activity 2 Retell the Story: Play the Story—An After-Reading Strategy

Elicit responses to questions. **Guide** as needed.
Now you'll play the story. I'll need your ideas for how to play the story.

Discuss story elements and assign roles for playing story. **Try** to assign roles to all students.
Let's start with the setting. What's the setting? (Student response.)

Who would be willing to play the parts of the setting? (Student response.)

Who is the main character? (Student response.)

Who could play the main character? (Student response.)

What other characters are important in the story? (Student response.)

Who would be willing to play those parts? (Student response.)

You're going to play the beginning, the middle, and the end of the story. What events happened at the beginning of the story? (Student response.)

How would you play those events? (Student response.)

What events happened in the middle of the story? (Student response.)

How would you play those events? (Student response.)

What events happened at the end of the story? (Student response.)

How would you play those events? (Student response.)

I'll tell the whole story. As I tell the story, the players can do the actions I'm telling about. If there are words to say, I'll help you say them.

Coach all students to play story by telling story very simply and guiding students to play or mime actions. If there is dialogue, say the words and then have students repeat words or prompt student to say appropriate words.

Praise creativity in playing story. **Prompt** everyone to bow as you applaud them.

Wow, that was fun!

Lesson 125

Lesson 126

Materials
Teacher: Expository trade book (same book for Lessons 126–130); 6-KWL Chart; 20-Phonemic Awareness
Student: Lined paper; copy of 20-Phonemic Awareness

Part A: Phonemic and Phonological Awareness

5 minutes

Teacher Materials:
Phonemic Awareness

Student Materials:
Phonemic Awareness

Activity 1 Phoneme Categorization—Initial

Show Phonemic Awareness. **Distribute** copy of Phonemic Awareness. **Elicit** responses. **Guide** as needed.
We're going to look at a picture on this page and find other pictures to match our sounds. I'm going to name each picture. I want you to touch each picture after I name it and repeat the name. We're going to find words that have the same *first* sound. If the word has the same *first* sound as the word in the top picture, we can circle the picture to show that they go together.

Model use of Phonemic Awareness; point to each picture as word is said.
Let's try it.
Point to picture at top of page.
Touch the picture at the top of the page. This is a **jar.** What is this? *Jar.*

That's right. The picture shows a **jar.** So what is the *first* sound in **jar?** */j/.*

Yes, **/j/.** So we need to look at the other pictures and see which words have the same first sound as **jar.**
Point to first picture in first row.
Touch the first picture in the first row. This is a **giraffe.** What is this? *Giraffe.*

Does **giraffe** have the same *first* sound as **jar?** *Yes.*

Then we can circle the picture of the **giraffe.** When we're finished with our lesson, you'll color the pictures you circled to show they have the same first sound

(Continue the activity with the rest of the pictures in the first and second rows.
First row: cage, jaw.
Second row: elf, jeans, jacket.)

(Then use the same procedure to find the pictures of words that have the same first sound as the next key word: chair.
Third row: cheese, checkers, watch.
Fourth row: cheek, chicken, crutches.)

Activity 2 Phoneme Segmentation

Elicit responses. **Guide** as needed.
Let's work on breaking words apart by each sound. I'm going to tell you a word. You'll need to listen closely and tell me the different sounds you hear in the word.
Listen. The word is **mow.** What word? *Mow.*
Your turn. Tell me the sounds you hear in **mow.** */mmm/ /ōō/.*
Yes, you said the sounds in the word **mow.**

(Continue the activity with the following words:
low [lll-ōōō], row [rrr-ōōō].
If children need more practice, continue with so, no, and show.)

Part B: Letter Recognition and Formation

6 minutes

Student Materials:
Lined paper

Activity 1 Letter Recognition—j

Elicit responses to questions. **Guide** as needed. **Write** j on the board. **Point** to j.
Today you'll learn a new letter.
The name of this letter is **j.** What letter name? *j.*
Again, what letter name? *j.*
Review as needed.

Activity 2 Letter Formation—j

Now we're going to practice writing **j.** When you practice writing, you'll learn not only where to start and stop the letter, but also which way to move your hand when you're making the letter. It's tricky, but you're so smart you'll learn how to write **j** very quickly. Watch.

Here's how you write **j** in the air.
Model j formation in the air (with your back to students).

Watch again.

Now let's practice writing **j** in the air. Hold up your writing hand, and make **j** in the air.
Guide students as they write j in the air.

Let's practice **j** again.

Here's how to write **j** with your writing hand pointer finger.
Model j formation on the board with your finger (with your back to students).

Watch again.

Now let's practice writing **j** on your table without using your pencil. Use your writing hand pointer finger, and make **j** on your table.
Guide students as they write j on their table or desktop.

Lesson 126   **511**

Let's practice **j** again.

Model writing j on the board (with your back to students).
Remember that every letter has a name.
You learned the name of this letter is **j.** What letter name? *j.*
Again, what letter name? *j.*

Provide lined paper to students.
Now let's practice writing **j** with your pencil.
Guide students as they write j on their paper. **Review** as needed.

 Link letter names to letter sounds as they appear in the program as needed.

Set up a writing center with writing materials and correct models of letters learned so far for students to use in their free time.

Part C: Comprehension Strategies

9 minutes

IWB

Teacher Materials:
Expository trade book

KWL Chart

Activity 1 Establish Purpose for Reading—A Before-Reading Strategy

 Provide a reading center to display books being read so that students can enjoy them again during free time.

Direct students to expository trade book of teacher choice. **Elicit** responses to questions. **Guide** as needed.

Today you'll hear a new kind of story. Today's story is called expository text. Expository stories teach you new information. They tell about things that are true.

Expository stories are different from narrative stories. These stories usually don't have characters, a setting, a beginning, a middle, or an end. Instead, expository stories are organized around topics. We read expository stories to learn new things.

Why do we read expository stories? (Idea: *To learn new things.*)

Why will we read this story today? (Idea: *To learn new things.*)

512 Lesson 126

Activity 2 Title, Author, and Illustrator Identification—A Before-Reading Strategy

Show front cover of book, and allow student to point to name of title, author, and illustrator as you discuss them. **Elicit** responses to questions. **Guide** as needed.

The title of today's story is _____ . What's the title of today's story? (Student response.)

The topic we'll learn about in this story is _____ . What is the topic we'll learn about in this story? (Student response.)

The author of today's story is _____ . Who's the author of today's story? (Student response.)

The illustrator of today's story is _____ . Who's the illustrator? (Student response.)

Expository stories, like this story about _____ , are written to help you to learn new things. Why will we read this expository story? (Idea: *To learn new things about _____ .*)

Activity 3 KWL Chart: What I Know—A Before-Reading Strategy

When we read expository stories, we need to stop and think about what we know before we read. I have a new chart here that will help me think about and write what I already know about _____ . I'll write what I know in the section called "What I Know."

Listen as I think about what I know and fill in my chart.
Model think-aloud for writing What I Know about topic on KWL Chart. **Write** three items on What I Know section of chart.

Sample Wording for Think-Aloud

When I think of _____ , I remember that I learned _____ , so I'll write that on my chart.

I remember that one time I saw a _____ and it looked _____ , so I'll write that on my chart.

Someone told me that _____ and I think it is true, so I'll write that on my chart.

One time I saw a program on TV about _____ and they said _____ , so I'll write that on my chart.

Now I have written the facts that I know about _____ .

Lesson 126 **513**

Activity 4 KWL Chart: What I Wonder—A Before-Reading Strategy

The next part of the chart says, "What I Wonder." This is where I'll write what I want to learn about the topic _____. Listen as I think and write the questions I have for what I wonder.

Model think-aloud for filling in What I Wonder section of KWL Chart. **Write** three questions.

Sample Wording for Think-Aloud

When I think about _____ I have a lot of questions. I want to know the answers to my question. So I'll write my questions to help me remember what I want to know.

I wonder where _____?

I wonder what _____?

I wonder how _____?

I wonder when _____?

I'll write those questions on my KWL Chart.

In the next lesson, we'll finish our KWL Chart by filling in the new information we learned from the book.

Elicit correct listening behavior from students. **Read** expository trade book. **Model** prosody during read-aloud.

Guide students to listen for information or facts about topic. **Ask** questions to elicit new information or facts that students are learning. **Guide** as needed.

Activity 5 Identify Reasons to Support Statements—An After-Reading Strategy

Select a general statement from the expository text (e.g., "Cheetahs are amazing animals.") that is followed by several reasons (e.g., "runs fast, is endangered, has keen senses"). **Elicit** responses to questions. **Guide** as needed.
What reasons does the author give to support the following sentence "_____ _____"?

514 *Lesson 126*

Lesson 127

> **Materials**
> **Teacher:** Expository trade book (from Lesson 126); 6-KWL Chart (from Lesson 126)
> **Student:** Lined paper

5 minutes

Part A: Phonemic and Phonological Awareness

Activity 1 Phoneme Identity—Final

Elicit responses. **Guide** as needed.
Let's find the *last* sound in a word. I'll say a word, and you tell me the *last* sound in that word.

What is the last sound you hear in **finish?** /shshsh/.

What is the last sound you hear in **mosquito?** /ōōō/.

What is the last sound you hear in **microwave?** /vvv/.

What is the last sound you hear in **envelope?** /p/.

What is the last sound you hear in **arrive?** /vvv/.

What is the last sound you hear in **moustache?** /shshsh/.

What is the last sound you hear in **telescope?** /p/.

What is the last sound you hear in **gazebo?** /ōōō/.

Activity 2 Phoneme Blending

Elicit responses. **Guide** as needed.
Let's put some sounds together and make words. I'm going to say a word very slowly so you can hear each sound. You need to listen carefully and say the sounds. When you say the sounds, it will sound almost like you're singing them. Then we'll put the sounds together and say the word.

My turn. Listen. **/āāā/ /k/.**
Say the sounds. /āāā/ /k/.
Again, say the sounds. /āāā/ /k/.
Now let's put it together. *āke.*

Lesson 127   515

Let's make a bigger word. My turn. Listen. **/mmm/ /āāā/ /k/.**
Say the sounds. /mmm/ /āāā/ /k/.
Again, say the sounds. /mmm/ /āāā/ /k/.
Now let's put it together. What word? *Make.*

(Continue the activity with the following words:
rake [rrr-āāā-k], shake [shshsh-āāā-k], ice [ĪĪĪ- sss], nice [nnn-ĪĪĪ-sss],
mice [mmm-ĪĪĪ-sss], rice [rrr-ĪĪĪ-sss].)

Part B: Letter Recognition and Formation

6 minutes

Student Materials:
Lined paper

Activity 1 Letter Recognition Review—j

Elicit responses to questions. **Guide** as needed. **Write** j on the board. **Point** to j.
We learned that this letter is **j.** What letter name? *j.*
Again, what letter name? *j.*
Review as needed.

Activity 2 Letter Formation Review—j

Now we're going to practice writing **j.** When you practice writing, you'll learn not only where to start and stop the letter, but also which way to move your hand when you're making the letter. It's tricky, but you're so smart you'll learn how to write **j** very quickly. Watch.

Here's how you write **j** in the air.
Model j formation in the air (with your back to students).

Watch again.

Now let's practice writing **j** in the air. Hold up your writing hand, and make **j** in the air.
Guide students as they write j in the air.

Let's practice **j** again.

Here's how to write **j** with your writing hand pointer finger.
Model j formation on the board with your finger (with your back to students).

Watch again.

Now let's practice writing **j** on your table without using your pencil.
Use your writing hand pointer finger, and make **j** on your table.
Guide students as they write j on their table or desktop.

Let's practice **j** again.

Model writing j on the board (with your back to students).
Remember that every letter has a name.
You learned the name of this letter is **j.** What letter name? *j.*
Again, what letter name? *j.*

516 Lesson 127

Provide lined paper to students.
Now let's practice writing **j** with your pencil.
Guide students as they write j on their paper. **Review** as needed.

 Link letter names to letter sounds as they appear in the program as needed.

Part C: Comprehension Strategies

9 minutes

Teacher Materials:
Expository trade book
KWL Chart

Activity 1 Listening Comprehension—A During-Reading Strategy

Direct students to expository trade book of teacher choice. **Elicit** responses to questions. **Guide** as needed.

We'll read the story again today. Remember that we are reading an expository book. Expository text is written to teach us new information or new facts. Why will we read this book about _____? (Idea: *To learn new information or facts.*)

When we read the story today, I want you to think about the new facts you are learning from this book. Then we'll fill in the last part of our KWL Chart.

Elicit correct listening behavior from students. **Reread** trade book. **Model** prosody during read-aloud.

Elicit new information that students are learning from text. **Guide** as needed.

Activity 2 KWL Chart: What I Learned—An After-Reading Strategy

Show KWL Chart. **Elicit** responses to questions. **Guide** as needed.

Now we get to fill in the last part of the KWL Chart. That section is called "What I Learned." I love to learn new things, so this is my favorite part of the chart.

Watch me as I show you how I fill in something I learned from the book.

Model think-aloud for filling What I Learned section of the KWL Chart. **Write** three facts that you learned.

Sample Wording for Think-Aloud
I learned _____ about this topic so I'll write that on the chart.

Tell me something you learned from the book that I can write on my chart. (Student response.)

Lesson 127   517

Activity 3 Identify Main Idea—An After-Reading Strategy

Now let's think about the main idea of this story. Finding the main idea of expository stories is easier than narrative stories because we already know the topic of the book. To tell the main idea, I just have to say the topic and an important thing I learned.

Listen as I show you how I think about the main idea for expository stories.

Model think-aloud for finding main idea in expository text.

Sample Wording for Think-Aloud
I know the topic is _____. An important thing I learned is _____. So I put those two things together and say the main idea is _____.

What's the main idea of this story? (**Student response.**)

Activity 4 Identify Reasons to Support Statements—An After-Reading Strategy

Select a general statement from the expository text (e.g., "Cheetahs are amazing animals.") that is followed by several reasons (e.g., "runs fast, is endangered, has keen senses"). **Elicit** responses to questions. **Guide** as needed.

What reasons does the author give to support the following sentence "_____ _____"?

Lesson 128

Materials

Teacher: Expository trade book (from Lesson 126); additional expository trade book on same topic; 6-KWL Chart (from Lessons 126 and 127); 21-Phonemic Awareness

Student: Lined paper; copy of 21-Phonemic Awareness

Part A: Phonemic and Phonological Awareness

5 minutes

Teacher Materials:
Phonemic Awareness

Student Materials:
Phonemic Awareness

Activity 1 Phoneme Categorization—Initial

Show Phonemic Awareness. **Distribute** copy of Phonemic Awareness. **Elicit** responses. **Guide** as needed.
We're going to look at a picture on this page and find other pictures to match our sounds. I'm going to name each picture. I want you to touch each picture after I name it and repeat the name. We're going to find words that have the same *first* sound. If the word has the same *first* sound as the word in the top picture, we can circle the picture to show that they go together.

Model use of Phonemic Awareness; point to each picture as word is said.
Let's try it.

Point to picture at top of page.
Touch the picture at the top of the page. This is a **shell.** What is this? *Shell.*

That's right. The picture shows a **shell.** So what is the *first* sound in **shell?** */shshsh/.*

Yes, **/shshsh/.** So we need to look at the other pictures and see which words have the same first sound as **shell.**
Point to first picture in first row.
Touch the first picture in the first row. This is a **sheep.** What is this? *Sheep.*

Does **sheep** have the same *first* sound as **shell?** *Yes.*

Then we can circle the picture of the **sheep.** When we're finished with our lesson, you'll color the pictures you circled to show they have the same first sound.

(Continue the activity with the rest of the pictures in the first and second rows.
First row: shoe, brush.
Second row: shark, mushroom, shovel.)

(Then use the same procedure to find the pictures of words that have the same first sound as the next key word: thumb.
Third row: tooth, thorn, thigh.
Fourth row: toothbrush, thermos, thirteen.)

Lesson 128   519

Activity 2 Phoneme Segmentation

Elicit responses. **Guide** as needed.
Let's work on breaking words apart by each sound. I'm going to say a word. You'll need to listen closely and tell me the different sounds you hear in the word.

Listen. The word is **eat.** What word? *Eat.*
Your turn. Tell me the sounds you hear in **eat.** /ēēē/ /t/.
Yes, you said the sounds in the word **eat.**

(Continue the activity with the following words:
ear [ēēē-rrr], each [ēēē-ch].)

Part B: Letter Recognition and Formation

6 minutes

Student Materials:
Lined paper

Activity 1 Letter Recognition—Capital J

Elicit responses to questions. **Guide** as needed. **Write** capital J on the board.
Point to capital J.
Today you'll learn another way to write **j.**
The name of this letter is **capital J.** What letter name? *Capital J.*
Again, what letter name? *Capital J.*
Review as needed.

Activity 2 Letter Formation—Capital J

Now we're going to practice writing **capital J.** When you practice writing, you'll learn not only where to start and stop the letter, but also which way to move your hand when you're making the letter. It's tricky, but you're so smart you'll learn how to write **capital J** very quickly. Watch.

Here's how you write **capital J** in the air.
Model capital J formation in the air (with your back to students).

Watch again.

Now let's practice writing **capital J** in the air. Hold up your writing hand, and make **capital J** in the air.
Guide students as they write capital J in the air.

Let's practice **capital J** again.

Here's how to write **capital J** with your writing hand pointer finger.
Model capital J formation on the board with your finger (with your back to students).

Watch again.

520   Lesson 128

Now let's practice writing **capital J** on your table without using your pencil. Use your writing hand pointer finger, and make **capital J** on your table.
Guide students as they write capital J on their table or desktop.

Let's practice **capital J** again.

Model writing capital J on the board (with your back to students).
Remember that every letter has a name.
You learned the name of this letter is **capital J.** What letter name? *Capital J.*
Again, what letter name? *Capital J.*

Provide lined paper to students.
Now let's practice writing **capital J** with your pencil.
Guide students as they write capital J on their paper. **Review** as needed.

 Link letter names to letter sounds as they appear in the program as needed.

Part C: Comprehension Strategies

9 minutes

Teacher Materials:
Expository trade book

Additional expository trade book on same topic

KWL Chart

Activity 1 Listening Comprehension—A During-Reading Strategy

Direct students to expository trade book of teacher choice. **Elicit** response to question. **Guide** as needed.

We'll read the story again today. Remember that we are reading an expository story. We read expository stories to learn new information or new facts. Why do we read expository stories? (Idea: *To learn new information or new facts.*)

When we read the story today, I want you to remember all the things you learned from the story. Then I'll read another story on the same topic. I'll read another book about _____. This book might have the same information as the last one or it might have new information. If it has new information, we'll add the new information to our KWL Chart.

Elicit correct listening behavior from students. **Reread** expository trade book. **Read** second expository text on topic. **Model** prosody during read-aloud.

Guide students to focus on learning new facts or information on topic. **Elicit** responses to questions about new facts learned. **Guide** as needed.

Lesson 128 **521**

Activity 2 KWL Chart: What I Learned—An After-Reading Strategy

Show KWL Chart. **Elicit** responses to questions. **Guide** as needed.

Now that we have read both books on the topic of _____ , we're ready to add any new things we learned to the "What I Learned" section of our KWL Chart.

Tell me some new things you've learned about the topic and I'll write the new facts on our KWL Chart. (**Student response.**)

Let's review the things we learned about _____ .

Review new facts learned about topic.

Activity 3 Identify Reasons to Support Statements—An After-Reading Strategy

Select a general statement from the expository text (e.g., "Cheetahs are amazing animals.") that is followed by several reasons (e.g., "runs fast, is endangered, has keen senses"). **Elicit** responses to questions. **Guide** as needed.

What reasons does the author give to support the following sentence "_____ _____"?

Lesson 129

Materials
Teacher: Expository trade book (from Lesson 126)
Student: Lined and drawing paper

5 minutes

Part A: Phonemic and Phonological Awareness

Activity 1 Phoneme Identity—Final

Elicit responses. **Guide** as needed.
Let's find the *last* sound in a word. I'll say a word, and you tell me the *last* sound in that word.

What is the last sound you hear in **sandwich?** /ch/.

What is the last sound you hear in **doorknob?** /b/.

What is the last sound you hear in **lullaby?** /īīī/.

What is the last sound you hear in **mayonnaise?** /zzz/.

What is the last sound you hear in **rock-a-bye?** /īīī/.

What is the last sound you hear in **attach?** /ch/.

What is the last sound you hear in **exercise?** /zzz/.

What is the last sound you hear in **describe?** /b/.

Activity 2 Phoneme Blending

Elicit responses. **Guide** as needed.
Let's put some sounds together and make words. I'm going to say a word very slowly so you can hear each sound. You need to listen carefully and say the sounds. When you say the sounds, it will sound almost like you're singing them. Then we'll put the sounds together and say the word.

My turn. Listen. **/īīī/ /d/.**
Say the sounds. /īīī/ /d/.
Again, say the sounds. /īīī/ /d/.
Now let's put it together. *īde.*

Lesson 129   523

Let's make a bigger word. My turn. Listen. **/sss/ /īīī/ /d/.**
Say the sounds. /sss/ /īīī/ /d/.
Again, say the sounds. /sss/ /īīī/ /d/.
Now let's put it together. What word? *Side.*

(Continue the activity with the following words:
ride [rrr-īīī-d], wide [www-īīī-d], ine [īīī-nnn], shine [shshsh-īīī-nnn],
line [lll-īīī-nnn], fine [fff-īīī-nnn].)

Part B: Letter Recognition and Formation

6 minutes

Student Materials:
Lined paper

Activity 1 Letter Recognition Review—Capital J

Elicit responses to questions. **Guide** as needed. **Write** capital J on the board. **Point** to capital J.
We learned that this letter is **capital J.** What letter name? *Capital J.*
Again, what letter name? *Capital J.*
Review as needed.

Activity 2 Letter Formation Review—Capital J

Now we're going to practice writing **capital J.** When you practice writing, you'll learn not only where to start and stop the letter, but also which way to move your hand when you're making the letter. It's tricky, but you're so smart you'll learn how to write **capital J** very quickly. Watch.

Here's how you write **capital J** in the air.
Model capital J formation in the air (with your back to students).

Watch again.

Now let's practice writing **capital J** in the air. Hold up your writing hand, and make **capital J** in the air.
Guide students as they write capital J in the air.

Let's practice **capital J** again.

Here's how to write **capital J** with your writing hand pointer finger.
Model capital J formation on the board with your finger (with your back to students).

Watch again.

Now let's practice writing **capital J** on your table without using your pencil. Use your writing hand pointer finger, and make **capital J** on your table.
Guide students as they write capital J on their table or desktop.

Let's practice **capital J** again.

Lesson 129

Model writing capital J on the board (with your back to students).
Remember that every letter has a name.
You learned the name of this letter is **capital J.** What letter name? *Capital J.*
Again, what letter name? *Capital J.*

Provide lined paper to students.
Now let's practice writing **capital J** with your pencil.
Guide students as they write capital J on their paper. **Review** as needed.

 Link letter names to letter sounds as they appear in the program as needed.

Part C: Comprehension Strategies

9 minutes

Teacher Materials:
Expository trade book

Student Materials:
Drawing paper

Activity 1 Listening Comprehension—A During-Reading Strategy

Direct students to expository trade book of teacher choice. **Elicit** responses to questions. **Guide** as needed.

Today as I read the story, I want you to look carefully at all the pictures of the story. The illustrator is trying to teach new facts or information to you with the pictures. Lots of times, pictures in expository books are photographs of real things to teach you what things really look like. After we read the story, you can draw a picture of your favorite part of the story.

Elicit correct listening behavior from students. **Reread** trade book. **Model** prosody during read-aloud.

Guide students to focus on illustrations to learn new information. **Elicit** responses to questions about how illustrator shows new facts or information. **Guide** as needed.

Activity 2 Summarize Expository Text—An After-Reading Strategy

Elicit responses to questions. **Guide** as needed.
One way to remember new facts is to say them to yourself in your own words. If you want to remember facts from expository stories, it will help you remember the fact if you say the fact in your own words.

Why do we say the fact in our own words? (Idea: *To help us remember the new fact.*)

When I tell the fact I'm learning in my own words I am summarizing.

I'll show you how I summarize a fact from page _____ of our expository story. First I'll read the fact, and then I'll summarize it.

Model think-aloud for summarizing a fact from expository text.

Lesson 129 **525**

Sample Wording for Think-Aloud

When I summarize this fact, I'll tell the new fact I'm learning in my own words. (Idea: *Retell a fact of choice in your own words.*)

Notice that I told the fact I want to remember in my own words. I didn't tell all the words exactly like the words in the story. I summarized the fact.

Activity 3 Illustrate Expository Text—An After-Reading Strategy

Provide drawing paper to students.

Now you get to think of your favorite page of the expository story, and draw a picture of the new fact you learned from that page.

When you're finished, tell your neighbor about your illustration and the new fact you learned.

Share illustrations of new facts learned with class as time permits, or make a class book of new facts learned from expository text.

Lesson 130

Materials

Teacher: Expository trade book (from Lesson 126); 22-Phonemic Awareness; Letter Recognition; 8-My Book Review

Student: Lined and drawing paper; copy of 22-Phonemic Awareness; copy of 8-My Book Review

5 minutes

Teacher Materials:
Phonemic Awareness

Student Materials:
Phonemic Awareness

Part A: Phonemic and Phonological Awareness

Activity 1 Phoneme Categorization—Initial

Show Phonemic Awareness. **Distribute** copy of Phonemic Awareness. **Elicit** responses. **Guide** as needed.

We're going to look at a picture on this page and find other pictures to match our sounds. I'm going to name each picture. I want you to touch each picture after I name it and repeat the name. We're going to find words that have the same *first* sound. If the word has the same *first* sound as the word in the top picture, we can circle the picture to show that they go together.

Model use of Phonemic Awareness; point to each picture as word is said. **Point** to picture at top of page.

Touch the picture at the top of the page. This is a **nose.** What is this? *Nose.* That's right. The picture shows a **nose.** What is the *first* sound in **nose?** /nnn/. Yes, **/nnn/.** We need to look at the other pictures and see which words have the same *first* sound as **nose.**

Point to first picture in first row.
Touch the first picture in the first row. This is a **neck.** What is this? *Neck.* Does **neck** have the same *first* sound as **nose?** *Yes.*

Then we can circle the picture of the **neck.** When we're finished with our lesson, you'll color the pictures you circled to show they have the same first sound.

Lesson 130   **527**

(Continue the activity with the rest of the pictures in the first and second rows.
First row: sun, net.
Second row: nurse, nut, candle.)

(Then use the same procedure to find the pictures of words that have the same first sound as the next key word: horse.
Third row: hill, hand, umbrella.
Fourth row: tent, house, hat.)

Activity 2 Phoneme Segmentation

Elicit responses. **Guide** as needed.
Let's work on breaking words apart by each sound. I'm going to say a word. You'll need to listen closely and tell me the different sounds you hear in the word.

Listen. The word is **ate.** What word? *Ate.*
Your turn. Tell me the sounds you hear in **ate.** /ā ā ā/ /t/.
Yes, you said the sounds in the word **ate.**

(Continue the activity with the following words:
age [ā ā ā-j], ape [ā ā ā-p].)

Part B: Letter Recognition and Formation

6 minutes

Teacher Materials:
Letter Recognition

Student Materials:
Lined paper

Activity 1 Letter Recognition Cumulative Review— b/B, y/Y, x/X, j/J

Display on IWB or **write** letters and capitals on the board in the order shown. **Elicit** responses to questions. **Guide** as needed.
This week you've learned one letter and one capital—**j** and **capital J.** Let's review all the letters and capitals you've learned. Are you ready?

Letter	Question	Student Response
B	What letter?	Capital B.
x	What letter?	x.
j	What letter?	j.
Y	What letter?	Capital Y.
b	What letter?	b.
y	What letter?	y.
X	What letter?	Capital X.
J	What letter?	Capital J.

Review as needed.

Activity 2 | Letter Formation Cumulative Review—b/B, y/Y, x/X, j/J

Write <u>b</u>, capital <u>B</u>, <u>y</u>, capital <u>Y</u>, <u>x</u>, capital <u>X</u>, <u>j</u>, and capital <u>J</u> on the board in the order shown (with your back to students). **Provide** lined paper to students.

Show me how you can write these letters and capitals.
Guide students as they write the letters and capitals on their paper. **Review** as needed.

 Link letter names to letter sounds as they appear in the program as needed.

Part C: Comprehension Strategies

9 minutes

Teacher Materials:
Expository trade book
My Book Review

Student Materials:
Drawing paper
My Book Review

Activity 1 | Listening Comprehension—A During-Reading Strategy

Direct students to expository trade book of teacher choice. **Elicit** responses to questions. **Guide** as needed.

Today as I read the story, I want you to look carefully at all the pictures of the story. The illustrator is trying to teach new facts or information to you with the pictures. Lots of times, pictures in expository books are photographs of real things to teach you what things really look like. After we read the story, you can draw another picture of a new fact that you learned from the story. We'll also summarize a fact that we learned by telling the fact in our own words.

Elicit correct listening behavior from students. **Reread** trade book. **Model** prosody during read-aloud.

Guide students to focus on illustrations to learn new information. **Elicit** responses to questions about how illustrator shows new facts or information. **Guide** as needed.

Activity 2 | Summarize Expository Text—An After-Reading Strategy

Elicit responses to questions. **Guide** as needed.
One way to remember new facts is to say them to yourself in your own words. If you want to remember facts from expository stories, it will help you remember the fact if you say the fact in your own words. Why do we say the fact in our own words? (**Idea:** *To help us remember the new fact.*)

When I tell the fact I'm learning in my own words, I'm summarizing.

I'll show you how I summarize a fact from page _____ of our expository story. First I'll read the fact, and then I'll summarize it.
Model summarizing a fact from expository text.

Notice that I told the fact I want to remember in my own words. I didn't tell all the words exactly like the words in the story. I summarized the fact.

Lesson 130 **529**

Now I'll tell you a fact. Let's think together about how to say the fact in our own words.

How can you say that fact in your own words? (**Student response.**)
Guide students to summarize a fact from the text in their own words.

When you can say a fact in your own words, you are learning to summarize.

Activity 3 Illustrate Expository Text—An After-Reading Strategy

Provide drawing paper to students.
Now you get to think of your favorite page of the expository story, and draw a picture of the new fact you learned from that page.

When you're finished, tell your neighbor about your illustration and the new fact you learned.
Share illustrations of new facts learned with class as time permits, or make a class book of new facts learned from expository text.

Activity 4 Connections Through Shared Writing— Express Opinions

Show My Book Review. **Elicit** responses to questions. **Guide** as needed.
Think about the two books we read, _____ and _____. Let's talk about the two books. Which one did you like best and why?

Provide copies of My Book Review to students. **Guide** students through completion of My Book Review. **Share** with class as time permits.

530   *Lesson 130*

Lesson 131

Materials
Teacher: Expository trade book (same book for Lessons 131–135); 6-KWL Chart
Student: Lined paper

 5 minutes

Part A: Phonemic and Phonological Awareness

Activity 1 Phoneme Identity—Middle

Elicit responses. **Guide** as needed.
Let's find the *middle* sound in a word. I'll say a word, and you tell me the *middle* sound in that word.

What is the *middle* sound you hear in **meat?** /ēēē/.

What is the *middle* sound you hear in **game?** /āāā/.

What is the *middle* sound you hear in **shake?** /āāā/.

What is the *middle* sound you hear in **keep?** /ēēē/.

What is the *middle* sound you hear in **late?** /āāā/.

What is the *middle* sound you hear in **team?** /ēēē/.

Activity 2 Phoneme Blending

Elicit responses. **Guide** as needed.
Let's put some sounds together and make words. I'm going to say a word very slowly so you can hear each sound. You need to listen carefully and say the sounds. When you say the sounds, it will sound almost like you're singing them. Then we'll put the sounds together and say the word.

My turn. Listen. **/aaa/ /t/.**
Say the sounds. /aaa/ /t/.
Again, say the sounds. /aaa/ /t/.
Now let's put it together. What word? *at.*

Let's make a bigger word. My turn. Listen. **/mmm/ /aaa/ /t/.**
Say the sounds. /mmm/ /aaa/ /t/.
Again, say the sounds. /mmm/ /aaa/ /t/.
Now let's put it together. What word? *Mat.*

Now we're going to make a bigger word that has a quick sound at the beginning. Listen closely. My turn. Listen. **/k/ /aaa/ /t/.**
Say the sounds. /k/ /aaa/ /t/.
Again, say the sounds. /k/ /aaa/ /t/.
Now let's put it together. What word? *Cat.*

(Continue the activity with the following words:
sat [sss-aaa-t], hat [h-aaa-t], bat [b-aaa-t], pat p[-aaa-t].)

Part B: Letter Recognition and Formation

6 minutes

Student Materials:
Lined paper

Activity 1 Letter Recognition—q

Elicit responses to questions. **Guide** as needed. **Write** q on the board. **Point** to q.
Today you'll learn a new letter.
The name of this letter is **q.** What letter name? *q.*
Again, what letter name? *q.*
Review as needed.

Activity 2 Letter Formation—q

Now we're going to practice writing **q.** When you practice writing, you'll learn not only where to start and stop the letter, but also which way to move your hand when you're making the letter. It's tricky, but you're so smart you'll learn how to write **q** very quickly. Watch.

Here's how you write **q** in the air.
Model q formation in the air (with your back to students).

Watch again.

Now let's practice writing **q** in the air. Hold up your writing hand, and make **q** in the air.
Guide students as they write q in the air.

Let's practice **q** again.

Here's how to write **q** with your writing hand pointer finger.
Model q formation on the board with your finger (with your back to students).

Watch again.

Now let's practice writing **q** on your table without using your pencil. Use your writing hand pointer finger, and make **q** on your table.
Guide students as they write q on their table or desktop.

Let's practice **q** again.

Model writing q on the board (with your back to students).
Remember that every letter has a name.
You learned the name of this letter is **q.** What letter name? *q.*
Again, what letter name? *q.*

532   Lesson 131

Provide lined paper to students.
Now let's practice writing **q** with your pencil.
Guide students as they write q on their paper. **Review** as needed.

 Link letter names to letter sounds as they appear in the program as needed.

Set up a writing center with writing materials and correct models of letters learned so far for students to use in their free time.

Part C: Comprehension Strategies

Teacher Materials:
Expository trade book
KWL Chart

Activity 1 Establish Purpose for Reading—A Before-Reading Strategy

Provide a reading center to display books being read so that students can enjoy them again during free time.

Direct students to expository trade book of teacher choice. **Elicit** responses to questions. **Guide** as needed.
Today you'll hear an expository story. Expository stories teach you new information. They tell about things that are true.

Expository stories are different from narrative stories. These stories don't usually have characters, a setting, a beginning, a middle, or an end. Instead, expository stories are organized around topics. We read expository stories to learn new things. Why do we read expository stories? (Idea: *To learn new things.*)

Why will we read this story today? (Idea: *To learn new things.*)

Activity 2 Title, Author, and Illustrator Identification—A Before-Reading Strategy

Show front cover of book, and allow a student to point to name of title, author, and illustrator as you discuss them. **Elicit** responses to questions. **Guide** as needed.
The title of today's story is _____. What's the title of today's story? (**Student response.**)

The topic we'll learn about in this story is _____. What's the topic we'll learn about in this story? (**Student response.**)

The author of today's story is _____. Who's the author of today's story? (**Student response.**)

The illustrator of today's story is _____. Who's the illustrator? (**Student response.**)

Expository stories, like this story about _____, are written to help you to learn new things. Why will we read this expository story? *To learn new things about* _____.

Lesson 131   **533**

Activity 3 KWL Chart: What I Know—A Before-Reading Strategy

Elicit responses to questions. **Guide** as needed.

When we read expository stories, we need to stop and think about what we know before we read. I have a KWL Chart here that will help me think about and write what I already know about _____ . I'll write what I know in the section called, "What I Know."

Listen as I think about what I know and fill in my chart.

Model writing What I Know about the topic on KWL Chart. **Write** three items on What I Know section of chart.

Now I have written the facts that I know about _____ .

Activity 4 KWL Chart: What I Wonder—A Before-Reading Strategy

The next part of the chart says, "What I Wonder." This is where I will write what I want to learn about the topic _____ .

Listen as I think and write the questions I have for what I wonder.

Model filling in What I Wonder section of KWL Chart. **Write** three questions.

Elicit correct listening behavior from students. **Read** expository trade book. **Model** prosody during read-aloud.

Guide students to listen for information or facts about the topic. **Ask** questions to elicit new information or facts that students are learning. **Guide** as needed.

534 *Lesson 131*

Lesson 132

Materials
Teacher: Expository trade book (from Lesson 131); 6-KWL Chart (from Lesson 131); 23-Phonemic Awareness
Student: Lined paper; copy of 23-Phonemic Awareness

5 minutes

Teacher Materials:
Phonemic Awareness

Student Materials:
Phonemic Awareness

Part A: Phonemic and Phonological Awareness

Activity 1 Phoneme Categorization—Final

Show Phonemic Awareness. **Distribute** copy of Phonemic Awareness. **Elicit** responses. **Guide** as needed.
We're going to look at a picture on this page and find other pictures to match our sounds. I'm going to name each picture. I want you to touch each picture after I name it and repeat the name. In other lessons, we were looking for words that have the same *first* sound. Now we're going to find words that have the same *last* sound. If the word has the same *last* sound as the word in the top picture, then we can circle the picture to show that they go together.

Model use of Phonemic Awareness; point to each picture as word is said.
Let's try it.
Point to picture at top of page.
Touch the picture at the top of the page. This is a **crab.** What is this? *Crab.* That's right. The picture shows a **crab.** What is the *last* sound in **crab?** */b/.* Yes, **/b/.** We need to look at the other pictures and see which words have the same *last* sound as **crab.**

Point to first picture in first row.
Touch the first picture in the first row. This is a **globe.** What is this? *Globe.*

Does **globe** have the same *last* sound as **crab?** *Yes.*

Then we can circle the picture of the **globe.**

Point to second picture in first row.
Touch the next picture. This is a **ball.** What is this? *Ball.*

Does **ball** have the same *last* sound as **crab?** *No.*

Then we can't circle the picture of the **ball** because the *last* sound in **ball** is **/lll/** and the *last* sound in **crab** is **/b/.** When we're finished with our lesson, you'll color the pictures you circled to show they have the same *last* sound.

(Continue the activity with the rest of the pictures in the first and second rows.
First row: web
Second row: zebra, robe, crib.)

Lesson 132   535

(Then use the same procedure to find the pictures of words that have the same last sound as the next key word: cup.
Third row: ship, tape, pig.
Fourth row: soap, mop, compass.)

Activity 2 Phoneme Segmentation

Elicit responses. **Guide** as needed.
Let's work on breaking words apart by each sound. I'm going to tell you a word. You'll need to listen closely and tell me the different sounds you hear in the word.

Listen. The word is **it.** What word? *It.*
Your turn. Tell me the sounds you hear in **it.** */iii/ /t/.*
Yes, you said the sounds in the word **it.**

Listen. My turn. The word is **sit.** What word? *Sit.*
I'll say the sounds in **sit. /sss/ /iii/ /t/.**
Your turn. Tell me the sounds you hear in **sit.** */sss/ /iii/ /t/.*
Yes, you said the sounds in the word **sit.**

(Continue the activity with the following words: mitt [mmm-iii-t], fit [fff-iii-t], knit [nnn-iii-t].)

Part B: Letter Recognition and Formation

6 minutes

Student Materials:
Lined paper

Activity 1 Letter Recognition Review—q

Elicit responses to questions. **Guide** as needed. **Write** q on the board. **Point** to q.
We learned that this letter is **q.** What letter name? *q.*
Again, what letter name? *q.*
Review as needed.

Activity 2 Letter Formation Review—q

Now we're going to practice writing **q.** When you practice writing, you'll learn not only where to start and stop the letter, but also which way to move your hand when you're making the letter. It's tricky, but you're so smart you'll learn how to write **q** very quickly. Watch.

Here's how you write **q** in the air.
Model q formation in the air (with your back to students).

Watch again.

536   Lesson 132

Now let's practice writing **q** in the air. Hold up your writing hand, and make **q** in the air.
Guide students as they write q in the air.

Let's practice **q** again.

Here's how to write **q** with your writing hand pointer finger.
Model q formation on the board with your finger (with your back to students).

Watch again.

Now let's practice writing **q** on your table without using your pencil. Use your writing hand pointer finger, and make **q** on your table.
Guide students as they write q on their table or desktop.

Let's practice **q** again.

Model writing q on the board (with your back to students).
Remember that every letter has a name.
You learned the name of this letter is **q.** What letter name? *q.*
Again, what letter name? *q.*

Provide lined paper to students.
Now let's practice writing **q** with your pencil.
Guide students as they write q on their paper. **Review** as needed.

 Link letter names to letter sounds as they appear in the program as needed.

Part C: Comprehension Strategies

 9 minutes

Teacher Materials:
Expository trade book

KWL Chart

Activity 1 Listening Comprehension—A During-Reading Strategy

Direct students to expository trade book of teacher choice. **Elicit** responses to questions. **Guide** as needed.

We'll read the story again today. Remember that we are reading an expository book. Expository text is written to teach us new information or new facts. Why will we read this book about _____? (Idea: *To learn new information or facts.*)

When we read the story today, I want you to think about the new facts you are learning from this book. Then we'll fill in the last part of our KWL Chart.

Elicit correct listening behavior from students. **Reread** trade book. **Model** prosody during read-aloud.

Elicit new information or facts that students are learning from text. **Guide** as needed.

Lesson 132   **537**

Activity 2 KWL Chart: What I Learned—An After-Reading Strategy

Show KWL Chart. **Elicit** responses to questions. **Guide** as needed.
Now we get to fill in the last part of the KWL Chart. That section is called "What I Learned." I love to learn new things, so this is my favorite part of the chart.

Watch me as I show you how I fill in something I learned from the book.
Model filling What I Learned section of KWL Chart. **Write** three facts that you learned.

Tell me something you learned from the book that I can write on my chart. (Student response.)

Activity 3 Identify Main Idea—An After-Reading Strategy

Elicit responses to questions. **Guide** as needed.
Now let's think about the main idea of this story. Finding the main idea of expository stories is easier than in narrative stories because we already know the topic of the book. To tell the main idea, I just have to say the topic and an important thing I learned.

Listen as I show you how I think about the main idea for expository stories.
Model finding main idea in expository text.

The main idea of this expository story is _____. What's the main idea of this story? (Student response.)

Activity 4 Identify Reasons to Support Statements—An After-Reading Strategy

Select a general statement from the expository text (e.g., "Cheetahs are amazing animals.") that is followed by several reasons (e.g., "runs fast, is endangered, has keen senses"). **Elicit** responses to questions. **Guide** as needed.
What reasons does the author give to support the following sentence "_____ _____"?

538   *Lesson 132*

Lesson 133

Materials
Teacher: Expository trade book (from Lesson 131); additional expository trade book on same topic; KWL Chart (from Lessons 131 and 132)
Student: Lined paper

5 minutes

Part A: Phonemic and Phonological Awareness

Activity 1 Phoneme Identity—Middle

Elicit responses. **Guide** as needed.
Let's find the *middle* sound in a word. I'll tell you a word, and you tell me the *middle* sound in that word.

What is the *middle* sound you hear in **dime**? /īīī/.

What is the *middle* sound you hear in **phone**? /ōōō/.

What is the *middle* sound you hear in **rose**? /ōōō/.

What is the *middle* sound you hear in **mice**? /īīī/.

What is the *middle* sound you hear in **goat**? /ōōō/.

What is the *middle* sound you hear in **hide**? /īīī/.

Activity 2 Phoneme Blending

Elicit responses. **Guide** as needed.
Let's put some sounds together and make words. I'm going to say a word very slowly so you can hear each sound. You need to listen carefully and say the sounds. When you say the sounds, it will sound almost like you're singing them. Then we'll put the sounds together and say the word.

My turn. Listen. **/ēēē/ /t/.**
Say the sounds. /ēēē/ /t/.
Again, say the sounds. /ēēē/ /t/.
Now let's put it together. What word? *Eat.*

Let's make a bigger word. My turn. Listen. **/sss/ /ēēē/ /t/.**
Say the sounds. /sss/ /ēēē/ /t/.
Again, say the sounds. /sss/ /ēēē/ /t/.
Now let's put it together. What word? *Seat.*

Lesson 133   **539**

Now we're going to make a bigger word that has a quick sound at the beginning. Listen closely. My turn. Listen. **/b/ /ēēē/ /t/.**
Say the sounds. /b/ /ēēē/ /t/.
Again, say the sounds. /b/ /ēēē/ /t/.
Now let's put it together. What word? *Beat.*

(Continue the activity with the following words:
meat [mmm-ēēē-t], heat [h-ēēē-t], cheat [ch-ēēē-t].)

Part B: Letter Recognition and Formation

6 minutes

Student Materials:
Lined paper

Activity 1 Letter Recognition—Capital Q

Elicit responses to questions. **Guide** as needed. **Write** capital Q on the board.
Point to capital Q.
Today you'll learn another way to write **q.**
The name of this letter is **capital Q.** What letter name? *Capital Q.*
Again, what letter name? *Capital Q.*
Review as needed.

Activity 2 Letter Formation—Capital Q

Now we're going to practice writing **capital Q.** When you practice writing, you'll learn not only where to start and stop the letter, but also which way to move your hand when you're making the letter. It's tricky, but you're so smart you'll learn how to write **capital Q** very quickly. Watch.

Here's how you write **capital Q** in the air.
Model capital Q formation in the air (with your back to students).

Watch again.

Now let's practice writing **capital Q** in the air. Hold up your writing hand, and make **capital Q** in the air.
Guide students as they write capital Q in the air.

Let's practice **capital Q** again.

Here's how to write **capital Q** with your writing hand pointer finger.
Model capital Q formation on the board with your finger (with your back to students).

Watch again.

Now let's practice writing **capital Q** on your table without using your pencil. Use your writing hand pointer finger, and make **capital Q** on your table.
Guide students as they write capital Q on their table or desktop.

Let's practice **capital Q** again.

Model writing capital Q on the board (with your back to students).
Remember that every letter has a name.
You learned the name of this letter is **capital Q.** What letter name? *Capital Q.*
Again, what letter name? *Capital Q.*

540   Lesson 133

Provide lined paper to students.
Now let's practice writing **capital Q** with your pencil.
Guide students as they write capital Q on their paper. **Review** as needed.

 Link letter names to letter sounds as they appear in the program as needed.

Part C: Comprehension Strategies

9 minutes

Teacher Materials:
Expository trade book

Additional expository trade book

KWL Chart

Activity 1 Listening Comprehension—A During-Reading Strategy

Direct students to expository trade book of teacher choice. **Elicit** responses to questions. **Guide** as needed.
We'll read the story again today. Remember that we are reading an expository story. We read expository stories to learn new information or new facts.

Why do we read expository stories? (Idea: *To learn new information or new facts.*)

When we read the story today, I want you to remember all the things you learned from the story. Then I will read another story on the same topic. I will read another story about _____. This story might have the same information as the last one, or it might have new information. If it has new information, we will add the new information to our KWL Chart.

Elicit correct listening behavior from students. **Reread** expository trade book.
Read second expository text on topic. **Model** prosody during read-aloud.

Guide students to focus on learning new facts or information on the topic.
Elicit responses to questions about new facts learned. **Guide** as needed.

Activity 2 KWL Chart: What I Learned—An After-Reading Strategy

Show KWL Chart partially completed in Lessons 131 and 132. **Elicit** responses to questions. **Guide** as needed.
Now that we have read both books on the topic of _____, we're ready to add any new things we learned to the "What I Learned" section of our KWL Chart.

Tell me some new things you have learned about the topic and I will write the new facts on our KWL Chart. (Student response.)
Guide students to think of new facts learned to write in What I Learned section of KWL Chart. **Write** new information or facts.

Let's review the things we learned about _____.
Review all facts learned about the topic and written on the chart.

Lesson 133   **541**

Lesson 134

Materials
Teacher: Expository trade book (from Lesson 131); 24-Phonemic Awareness
Student: Lined and drawing paper; copy of 24-Phonemic Awareness

Part A: Phonemic and Phonological Awareness

 5 minutes

Teacher Materials:
Phonemic Awareness

Student Materials:
Phonemic Awareness

Activity 1 Phoneme Categorization—Final

Show Phonemic Awareness. **Distribute** copy of Phonemic Awareness. **Elicit** responses. **Guide** as needed.
We're going to look at a picture on this page and find other pictures to match our sounds. I'm going to name each picture. I want you to touch each picture after I name it and repeat the name. In other lessons, we were looking for words that have the same *first* sound. Now we're going to find words that have the same *last* sound. If the word has the same *last* sound as the word in the top picture, then we can circle the picture to show that they go together.

Model use of Phonemic Awareness; point to each picture as word is said.
Let's try it.
Point to picture at top of page.
Touch the picture at the top of the page. This is a **cat.** What is this? *Cat.* That's right. The picture shows a **cat.** What is the *last* sound in **cat?** /t/. Yes, **/t/.** We need to look at the other pictures and see which ones have the same *last* sound as **cat.**

Point to first picture in the first row.
Touch the first picture in the first row. This is a **foot.** What is this? *Foot.* Does **foot** have the same *last* sound as **cat?** *Yes.*
Then we can circle the picture of the **foot.** When we're finished with our lesson, you'll color the pictures you circled to show they have the same *last* sound.

(Continue the activity with the rest of the pictures in the first and second rows.
First row: nest, table.
Second row: peanut, salt, butterfly.)

(Then use the same procedure to find the pictures of words that have the same last sound as the next key word: hand.
Third row: door, sad, wood.
Fourth row: bed, needle, bird.)

542 Lesson 134

Activity 2 Phoneme Segmentation

Elicit responses. **Guide** as needed.
Let's work on breaking words apart by each sound. I'm going to say a word. You'll need to listen closely and tell me the different sounds you hear in the word.

Listen. The word is **an.** What word? *An.*
Your turn. Tell me the sounds you hear in **an.** */aaa/ /nnn/.*
Yes, you said the sounds in the word **an.**

Listen. My turn. The word is **ran.** What word? *Ran.*
I'll say the sounds in **ran. /rrr/ /aaa/ /nnn/.**
Your turn. Tell me the sounds you hear in **ran.** */rrr/ /aaa/ /nnn/.*
Yes, you said the sounds in the word **ran.**

(Continue the activity with the following words:
man [mmm-aaa-nnn], fan [fff-aaa-nnn], than [ththth-aaa-nnn].)

Part B: Letter Recognition and Formation

6 minutes

Student Materials:
Lined paper

Activity 1 Letter Recognition Review—Capital Q

Elicit responses to questions. **Guide** as needed. **Write** capital Q on the board.
Point to capital Q.
We learned that this letter is **capital Q.** What letter name? *Capital Q.*
Again, what letter name? *Capital Q.*
Review as needed.

Activity 2 Letter Formation Review—Capital Q

Now we're going to practice writing **capital Q.** When you practice writing, you'll learn not only where to start and stop the letter, but also which way to move your hand when you're making the letter. It's tricky, but you're so smart you'll learn how to write **capital Q** very quickly. Watch.

Here's how you write **capital Q** in the air.
Model capital Q formation in the air (with your back to students).

Watch again.

Lesson 134 **543**

Now let's practice writing **capital Q** in the air. Hold up your writing hand, and make **capital Q** in the air.
Guide students as they write capital Q in the air.

Let's practice **capital Q** again.

Here's how to write **capital Q** with your writing hand pointer finger.
Model capital Q formation on the board with your finger (with your back to students).

Watch again.

Now let's practice writing **capital Q** on your table without using your pencil. Use your writing hand pointer finger, and make **capital Q** on your table.
Guide students as they write capital Q on their table or desktop.

Let's practice **capital Q** again.

Model writing capital Q on the board (with your back to students).
Remember that every letter has a name.
You learned the name of this letter is **capital Q.** What letter name? *Capital Q.*
Again, what letter name? *Capital Q.*

Provide lined paper to students.
Now let's practice writing **capital Q** with your pencil.
Guide students as they write capital Q on their paper. **Review** as needed.

 Link letter names to letter sounds as they appear in the program as needed.

Part C: Comprehension Strategies

9 minutes

Teacher Materials:
Expository trade book

Student Materials:
Drawing paper

Activity 1 Listening Comprehension—A During-Reading Strategy

Direct students to expository trade book of teacher choice. **Elicit** responses to questions. **Guide** as needed.
Today as I read the story, I want you to look carefully at all the pictures of the story. The illustrator is trying to teach you new facts or information with the pictures. Lots of times, pictures in expository books are photographs of real things to teach you what things really look like. After we read the story, you can draw a picture of your favorite part of the story.

Elicit correct listening behavior from students. **Reread** trade book. **Model** prosody during read-aloud.

Guide students to focus on illustrations to learn new information. **Elicit** responses to questions about how illustrator shows new facts or information. **Guide** as needed.

544   Lesson 134

Activity 2 Summarize Expository Text—An After-Reading Strategy

Elicit responses to questions. **Guide** as needed.
One way to remember new facts is to say them to yourself in your own words. To remember facts from expository stories, it helps you remember a fact if you say the fact in your own words. Why do we say the fact in our own words? (Idea: *To help us remember the new fact.*)

When I summarize a whole page, I want to tell only the important idea about what I am learning.

I'll show you how I summarize page _____ of our expository story. First I'll read the page, and then I'll tell the important idea in my own words.
Model summarizing a page from expository text.

Notice that I told about the page that I want to remember in my own words. I didn't tell all the information. I just told the important idea in my own words. I summarized the page.

Activity 3 Illustrate and Retell Expository Text—An After-Reading Strategy

Provide drawing paper to students. **Elicit** responses to questions. **Guide** as needed.
Now you get to think of your favorite page of the expository story, and draw a picture of the new fact you learned from that page.

When you're finished, tell your neighbor about your illustration and the new fact you learned.
Share illustrations of new facts learned with class as time permits, or make a class book of new facts learned from expository text.

Lesson 134   **545**

Lesson 135

Materials
Teacher: Expository trade book (from Lesson 131); Letter Recognition
Student: Lined and drawing paper

5 minutes

Part A: Phonemic and Phonological Awareness

Activity 1 Phoneme Identity—Middle

Elicit responses. **Guide** as needed.
Let's find the *middle* sound in a word. I'll tell you a word, and you tell me the *middle* sound in that word.

What is the *middle* sound you hear in **shack**? /aaa/.

What is the *middle* sound you hear in **log**? /ooo/.

What is the *middle* sound you hear in **shop**? /ooo/.

What is the *middle* sound you hear in **jam**? /aaa/.

What is the *middle* sound you hear in **dock**? /ooo/.

What is the *middle* sound you hear in **nap**? /aaa/.

Activity 2 Phoneme Blending

Elicit responses. **Guide** as needed.
Let's put some sounds together and make words. I'm going to say a word very slowly so you can hear each sound. You need to listen carefully and say the sounds. When you say the sounds, it will sound almost like you're singing them. Then we'll put the sounds together and say the word.

My turn. Listen. **/iii/ /t/.**
Say the sounds. /iii/ /t/.
Again, say the sounds. /iii/ /t/.
Now let's put it together. What word? *it.*

Let's make a bigger word. My turn. Listen. **/sss/ /iii/ /t/.**
Say the sounds. /sss/ /iii/ /t/.
Again, say the sounds. /sss/ /iii/ /t/.
Now let's put it together. What word? *Sit.*

Now we're going to make a bigger word that has a quick sound at the beginning. Listen. My turn. The word is **ran**. What word? *Ran.*
I'll say the sounds in **ran**. **/rrr/ /aaa/ /nnn/.**
Your turn. Tell me the sounds you hear in **ran**. /rrr/ /aaa/ /nnn/.
Yes, you said the sounds in the word **ran**.

546 Lesson 135

(Continue the activity with the following words:
hit [h-iii-t], pit [p-iii-t], mitt [mmm-iii-t].)

Part B: Letter Recognition and Formation

6 minutes

Teacher Materials:
Letter Recognition

Student Materials:
Lined paper

Activity 1 Letter Recognition Cumulative Review—y/Y, x/X, j/J, q/Q

Display on IWB or **write** letters and capitals on the board in the order shown. **Elicit** responses to questions. **Guide** as needed.

This week you've learned one letter and one capital—**q** and **capital Q.**
Let's review all the letters and capitals you've learned. Are you ready?

Letter	Question	Student Response
Y	What letter?	Capital Y.
j	What letter?	j
q	What letter?	q
Q	What letter?	Capital Q.
x	What letter?	x.
J	What letter?	Capital J.
y	What letter?	y.
X	What letter?	Capital X.

Review as needed.

Activity 2 Letter Formation Cumulative Review—y/Y, x/X, j/J, q/Q

Write y, capital Y, x, capital X, j, capital J, q, and capital Q on the board in the order shown (with your back to students). **Provide** lined paper to students.

Show me how you can write these letters and capitals.
Guide students as they write the letters and capitals on their paper. **Review** as needed.

 Link letter names to letter sounds as they appear in the program as needed.

Part C: Comprehension Strategies

9 minutes

Teacher Materials:
Expository trade book

Student Materials:
Drawing paper

Activity 1 Listening Comprehension—A During-Reading Strategy

Direct students to expository trade book of teacher choice. **Elicit** responses to questions. **Guide** as needed.
Today as I read the story, I want you to look carefully at all the pictures of the story. The illustrator is trying to teach you new facts or information with the pictures. Lots of times, pictures in expository books are photographs of real things to teach you what things really look like. After we read the story,

Lesson 135 **547**

you can draw another picture of a new fact that you learned from the story. We will also summarize a page from the story by telling the important idea in our own words.

Elicit correct listening behavior from students. **Reread** trade book. **Model** prosody during read-aloud.

Guide students to focus on illustrations to learn new information. **Elicit** responses to questions about how illustrator shows new facts or information. **Guide** as needed.

Activity 2 Summarize Expository Text—An After-Reading Strategy

Elicit responses to questions. **Guide** as needed.
One way to remember new facts is to say them to yourself in your own words. To remember facts from expository stories, it helps you remember a fact if you say the fact in your own words.

Why do we say the fact in our own words? (Idea: *To help us remember the new fact.*)

When I summarize a whole page, I want to tell only the important idea about what I am learning. Today we will practice summarizing a page from our story.

Let's summarize page _____ of our expository story. First I'll read the page, and then we'll work together to summarize the page.

Guide students to summarize a page from expository text.
What do you think is the important idea from this page? (**Student response.**)

So how could we say that idea in our own words? (**Student response.**)

Yes, I think if we summarize this page we could say _____. What's a good summary of this page? (**Student response.**)

Notice that we told about the page that we want to remember in our own words. We didn't tell everything on the page. We just told the important idea.

Activity 3 Illustrate and Retell Expository Text—An After-Reading Strategy

Provide drawing paper to students.
Now you get to think of your favorite page of the expository story, and draw a picture of the new fact you learned from that page.

When you're finished, tell your neighbor about your illustration and the new fact you learned.
Share illustrations of new facts learned with class as time permits, or make a class book of new facts learned from expository text.

548 *Lesson 135*

Lesson 136

Materials
Teacher: Expository trade book (same book for Lessons 136–140); 6-KWL Chart; 25-Phonemic Awareness
Student: Lined paper; copy of 25-Phonemic Awareness, copy of 6-KWL Chart

5 minutes

Teacher Materials:
Phonemic Awareness

Student Materials:
Phonemic Awareness

Part A: Phonemic and Phonological Awareness

Activity 1 Phoneme Categorization—Final

Show Phonemic Awareness. **Distribute** copy of Phonemic Awareness. **Elicit** responses. **Guide** as needed.

We're going to look at a picture on this page and find other pictures to match our sounds. I'm going to name each picture. I want you to touch each picture after I name it and repeat the name. We're going to find words that have the same *last* sound. If the word has the same *last* sound as the word in the top picture, then we can circle the picture to show that they go together.

Model use of Phonemic Awareness; point to each picture as word is said.
Let's try it.
Point to picture at top of page.
Touch the picture at the top of the page. This is a **drum.** What is this? *Drum.*
That's right. The picture shows a **drum.** So what is the *last* sound in **drum?**
/mmm/.
Yes, **/mmm/.** So we need to look at the other pictures and see which ones have the same *last* sound as **drum.**

Point to first picture in first row.
Touch the first picture in the first row. This is a **camel.** What is this? *Camel.*
Does **camel** have the same *last* sound as **drum?** *No.*
Then we can't circle the picture of the **camel.** When we're finished with our lesson, you'll color the pictures you circled to show they have the same *last* sound.

(Continue the activity with the rest of the pictures in the first and second rows.
First row: broom, comb.
Second row: moon, thumb, dime.)

(Then use the same procedure to find the pictures of words that have the same last sound as the next key word: pen.
Third row: bone, moon, nail.
Fourth row: candle, man, cone.)

Activity 2 Phoneme Segmentation

Elicit responses. **Guide** as needed.
Let's work on breaking words apart by each sound. I'm going to say a word. You'll need to listen closely and tell me the different sounds you hear in the word.

Lesson 136   **549**

Listen. The word is **eat.** What word? *Eat.*
Your turn. Tell me the sounds you hear in **eat.** */ēēē/ /t/.*
Yes, you said the sounds in the word **eat.**

Listen. My turn. The word is **meat.** What word? *Meat.*
I'll say the sounds in **meat.** */mmm/ /ēēē/ /t/.*
Your turn. Tell me the sounds you hear in **meat.** */mmm/ /ēēē/ /t/.*
Yes, you said the sounds in the word **meat.**

(Continue the activity with the following words:
seat [sss-ēēē-t], feet [fff-ēēē-t], sheet [shshsh-ēēē-t].)

6 minutes

Student Materials:
Lined paper

Part B: Letter Recognition and Formation

Activity 1 Letter Recognition—z

Elicit responses to questions. **Guide** as needed. **Write** z on the board. **Point** to z.
Today you'll learn a new letter.
The name of this letter is **z.** What letter name? *z.*
Again, what letter name? *z.*
Review as needed.

Activity 2 Letter Formation—z

Now we're going to practice writing **z.** When you practice writing, you'll learn not only where to start and stop the letter, but also which way to move your hand when you're making the letter. It's tricky, but you're so smart you'll learn how to write **z** very quickly. Watch.

Here's how you write **z** in the air.
Model z formation in the air (with your back to students).

Watch again.

Now let's practice writing **z** in the air. Hold up your writing hand, and make **z** in the air.
Guide students as they write z in the air.

Let's practice **z** again.

Here's how to write **z** with your writing hand pointer finger.
Model z formation on the board with your finger (with your back to students).

Watch again.

Now let's practice writing **z** on your table without using your pencil. Use your writing hand pointer finger, and make **z** on your table.
Guide students as they write z on their table or desktop.

Let's practice **z** again.

Model writing z on the board (with your back to students).
Remember that every letter has a name.

550 Lesson 136

You learned the name of this letter is **z.** What letter name? z.
Again, what letter name? z.

Provide lined paper to students.
Now let's practice writing **z** with your pencil.
Guide students as they write z on their paper. **Review** as needed.

Link letter names to letter sounds as they appear in the program as needed.

Set up a writing center with writing materials and correct models of letters learned so far for students to use in their free time.

Part C: Comprehension Strategies

9 minutes

Teacher Materials:
Expository trade book
KWL Chart

Student Materials:
KWL Chart

Activity 1 Establish Purpose for Reading—A Before-Reading Strategy

Provide a reading center to display books being read so that students can enjoy them again during free time.

Direct students to expository trade book of teacher choice. **Elicit** responses to questions. **Guide** as needed.
Today you'll hear an expository story. Expository stories teach you new information. They tell about things that are true. We read expository stories to learn new things. Why do we read expository stories? (Idea: *To learn new things.*)

Why will we read this story today? (Idea: *To learn new things.*)

Activity 2 Title, Author, and Illustrator Identification—A Before-Reading Strategy

Show front cover of book, and allow student to point to name of title, author, and illustrator as you discuss them. **Elicit** responses to questions. **Guide** as needed.
The title of today's story is _____. What's the title of today's story? (Student response.)

The topic we'll learn about in this story is _____. What's the topic we will learn about in this story? (Student response.)

The author of today's story is _____. Who's the author of today's story? (Student response.)

The illustrator of today's story is _____. Who's the illustrator? (Student response.)

Expository stories like this story about _____ are written to help you to learn new things.

Why will we read this expository story? *To learn new things about _____.*

Lesson 136   551

Activity 3 KWL Chart: What I Know—A Before-Reading Strategy

Elicit responses to questions. **Guide** as needed.
When you read expository stories, you need to stop and think about what you know before you read. This KWL Chart will help you think about what you already know about _____. I'll write what you know in the section called, "What I Know."

Let's work together to think about what you know to fill in the chart. (Student response.)

Guide students to share what they know about topic for What I Know section of KWL Chart. **Write** three items on What I Know section of chart.

Now I have written some facts that you know about _____, it is your turn to write one fact that you know about _____ on the "What I Know" section of the chart.
Guide as needed.

Assign partners. **Guide** as needed.
Now share your fact with your partner and add suggestions to make your neighbor's writing better if you think it needs it.

Activity 4 KWL Chart: What I Wonder—A Before-Reading Strategy

Elicit responses to questions. **Guide** as needed.
The next part of the chart says, "What I Wonder." This is where I will write what you want to learn about the topic _____.

Think of what you wonder about _____, and then we'll write the questions you have on the chart. (Student response.)
Guide students to think of questions for What I Wonder section of KWL Chart. **Write** three questions.

Now I have written what you wonder about _____, it is your turn to write one thing you wonder about _____ on the "What I Wonder" section of the chart.
Guide as needed.

In the next lesson, we'll finish our KWL Chart by filling in the new information we learned from the book.

Elicit correct listening behavior from students. **Read** expository trade book.
Model prosody during read-aloud.

Guide students to listen for information or facts about topic. **Ask** questions to elicit new information or facts that students are learning. **Guide** as needed.

552 Lesson 136

Lesson 137

Materials
Teacher: Expository trade book (from Lesson 136); 6-KWL Chart (from Lesson 136)
Student: Lined paper, Copy of 5-KWL Chart (from Lesson 136)

5 minutes

Part A: Phonemic and Phonological Awareness

Activity 1 Phoneme Identity—Middle

Elicit responses. **Guide** as needed.
Let's find the *middle* sound in a word. I'll say a word, and you tell me the *middle* sound in that word.

What is the middle sound you hear in **shed?** /eee/.

What is the middle sound you hear in **lip?** /iii/.

What is the middle sound you hear in **pig?** /iii/.

What is the middle sound you hear in **hen?** /eee/.

What is the middle sound you hear in **chin?** /iii/.

What is the middle sound you hear in **sell?** /eee/.

Activity 2 Phoneme Blending

Elicit responses. **Guide** as needed.
Let's put some sounds together and make words. I'm going to say a word very slowly so you can hear each sound. You need to listen carefully and say the sounds. When you say the sounds, it will sound almost like you're singing them. Then we'll put the sounds together and say the word.

My turn. Listen. **/ooo/ /t/.**
Say the sounds. /ooo/ /t/.
Again, say the sounds. /ooo/ /t/.
Now let's put it together. *ot.*

Let's make a bigger word. My turn. Listen. **/nnn/ /ooo/ /t/.**
Say the sounds. /nnn/ /ooo/ /t/.
Again, say the sounds. /nnn/ /ooo/ /t/.
Now let's put it together. What word? *Not.*

Now we're going to make a bigger word that has a quick sound at the beginning. Listen closely. My turn. Listen. **/h/ /ooo/ /t/.**
Say the sounds. /h/ /ooo/ /t/.
Again, say the sounds. /h/ /ooo/ /t/.
Now let's put it together. What word? *Hot.*

(Continue the activity with the following words:
cot [c-ooo-t], pot [p-ooo-t], lot [lll-ooo-t].)

Part B: Letter Recognition and Formation

6 minutes

Student Materials:
Lined paper

Activity 1 Letter Recognition Review—z

Elicit responses to questions. **Guide** as needed. **Write** z on the board. **Point** to z.
We learned that this letter is **z.** What letter name? *z.*
Again, what letter name? *z.*
Review as needed.

Activity 2 Letter Formation Review—z

Now we're going to practice writing **z.** When you practice writing, you'll learn not only where to start and stop the letter, but also which way to move your hand when you're making the letter. It's tricky, but you're so smart you'll learn how to write **z** very quickly. Watch.

Here's how you write **z** in the air.
Model z formation in the air (with your back to students).

Watch again.

Now let's practice writing **z** in the air. Hold up your writing hand, and make **z** in the air.
Guide students as they write z in the air.

Let's practice **z** again.

Here's how to write **z** with your writing hand pointer finger.
Model z formation on the board with your finger (with your back to students).

Watch again.

Now let's practice writing **z** on your table without using your pencil. Use your writing hand pointer finger, and make **z** on your table.
Guide students as they write z on their table or desktop.

Let's practice **z** again.

554 Lesson 137

Model writing z on the board (with your back to students).
Remember that every letter has a name.
You learned the name of this letter is **z.** What letter name? z.
Again, what letter name? z.

Provide lined paper to students.
Now let's practice writing **z** with your pencil.
Guide students as they write z on their paper. **Review** as needed.

 Link letter names to letter sounds as they appear in the program as needed.

Part C: Comprehension Strategies

 9 minutes

Teacher Materials:
Expository trade book
KWL Chart

Student Materials:
KWL Chart

Activity 1 Listening Comprehension—A During-Reading Strategy

Direct students to expository trade book of teacher choice. **Elicit** responses to questions. **Guide** as needed.
We'll read the story again today. Remember that we are reading an expository book. Expository text is written to teach us new information or new facts. Why will we read this book about _____? (Idea: *To learn new information or facts.*)

When we read the story today, I want you to think about the new facts you are learning from this book. Then we'll fill in the last part of our KWL Chart.

Elicit correct listening behavior from students. **Reread** trade book. **Model** prosody during read-aloud.

Elicit new information or facts that students are learning from text. **Guide** as needed.

Activity 2 KWL Chart: What I Learned—An After-Reading Strategy

Show KWL Chart. **Elicit** responses to questions. **Guide** as needed.
Now we get to fill in the last part of the KWL Chart. That section is called "What I Learned."

Let's work together to fill in the last section of the chart.
Guide students to tell new facts learned for What I Learned section of KWL Chart.
Write three facts that you learned.
Tell me some new facts that you learned from this book and I will write them on the chart. (Student response.)

Now I have written what you learned about _____, it is your turn to write one thing you learned about _____ on the "What I Learned" section of the chart.
Guide as needed.

Lesson 137 **555**

Assign partners. **Guide** as needed.
Now share what you learned with your partner and add suggestions to make your neighbor's writing better if you think it needs it.

Activity 3 Identify Main Idea—An After-Reading Strategy

Elicit responses to questions. **Guide** as needed.
Now let's think about the main idea of this story. Finding the main idea of expository stories is easier than narrative because we already know the topic of the story. To tell the main idea, I just have to say the topic and an important thing I learned.

Guide students to find main idea of expository text.
What's the topic of this book? (**Student response.**)

What very important fact did this story teach you? (**Student response.**)

Put the topic and the important information together to get the main idea. So what do you think the main idea is of this story? (**Student response.**)

Yes, the main idea of this expository story is _____ . What's the main idea of this story? (**Student response.**)

556 *Lesson 137*

Lesson 138

Materials

Teacher: Expository trade book (from Lesson 136); additional expository trade book on same topic; 6-KWL Chart (from Lesson 136–137); 26-Phonemic Awareness

Student: Lined paper; copy of 26-Phonemic Awareness

Part A: Phonemic and Phonological Awareness

5 minutes

Teacher Materials:
Phonemic Awareness

Student Materials:
Phonemic Awareness

Activity 1 Phoneme Categorization—Final

Show Phonemic Awareness. **Distribute** copy of Phonemic Awareness. **Elicit** responses. **Guide** as needed.
We're going to look at a picture on this page and find other pictures to match our sounds. I'm going to name each picture. Touch each picture after I name it, and repeat the name. We're going to find words that have the same *last* sound. If the picture has the same *last* sound as the top picture, we can circle it to show that they go together.

Model use of Phonemic Awareness; point to each picture as word is said.
Let's try it.
Point to picture at top of page.
Touch the picture at the top of the page. This is a **hook.** What is this? *Hook.* That's right. The picture shows a **hook**. What is the *last* sound in **hook?** /k/. Yes, **/k/.** Look at the other pictures and see which ones have the same *last* sound as **hook.**

Point to first picture in first row.
Touch the first picture in the first row. This is a **rake.** What is this? *Rake.*
Does **rake** have the same *last* sound as **hook?** *Yes.*
Then we can circle the picture of the **rake.** When we're finished with our lesson, you can color the pictures that you circled to show they have the same *last* sound.

(Continue the activity with the rest of the pictures in the first and second rows.
First row: sock, bucket.
Second row: bike, duck, king.)

(Then use the same procedure to find the pictures of words that have the same last sound as the next key word: bench.
Third row: watch, wheelchair, wrench.
Fourth row: cheese, couch, branch.)

Lesson 138   557

Activity 2 Phoneme Segmentation

Model activity if students require assistance. **Elicit** responses. **Guide** as needed.
Let's work on breaking words apart by each sound. I'm going to say a word. Listen closely, and tell me the different sounds you hear in the word.

Listen. The word is **at**. What word? *At.*
Your turn. Tell me the sounds you hear in **at**. */aaa/ /t/.*
Yes. You said the sounds in the word **at.**

Listen. My turn. The word is **mat**. What word? *Mat.*
Your turn. Tell me the sounds you hear in **mat**. */mmm/ /aaa/ /t/.*
Yes. You said the sounds in the word **mat.**

(Continue the activity with the following words:
rat [rrr-aaa-t], fat [fff-aaa-t], sat [sss-aaa-t].)

Part B: Letter Recognition and Formation

6 minutes

Student Materials:
Lined paper

Activity 1 Letter Recognition—Capital Z

Elicit responses to questions. **Guide** as needed. **Write** capital Z on the board.
Point to capital Z.
Today you'll learn another way to write **z.**
The name of this letter is **capital Z.** What letter name? *Capital Z.*
Again, what letter name? *Capital Z.*
Review as needed.

Activity 2 Letter Formation—Capital Z

Now we're going to practice writing **capital Z.** When you practice writing, you'll learn not only where to start and stop the letter, but also which way to move your hand when you're making the letter. It's tricky, but you're so smart you'll learn how to write **capital Z** very quickly. Watch.

Here's how you write **capital Z** in the air.
Model capital Z formation in the air (with your back to students).

Watch again.

Now let's practice writing **capital Z** in the air. Hold up your writing hand, and make **capital Z** in the air.
Guide students as they write capital Z in the air.

Let's practice **capital Z** again.

Here's how to write **capital Z** with your writing hand pointer finger.
Model capital Z formation on the board with your finger (with your back to students).

558 Lesson 138

Watch again.

Now let's practice writing **capital Z** on your table without using your pencil. Use your writing hand pointer finger, and make **capital Z** on your table.
Guide students as they write capital Z on their table or desktop.

Let's practice **capital Z** again.

Model writing capital Z on the board (with your back to students).
Remember that every letter has a name.
You learned the name of this letter is **capital Z.** What letter name? *Capital Z.*
Again, what letter name? *Capital Z.*

Provide lined paper to students.
Now let's practice writing **capital Z** with your pencil.
Guide students as they write capital Z on their paper. **Review** as needed.

 Link letter names to letter sounds as they appear in the program as needed.

Part C: Comprehension Strategies

 9 minutes

Activity 1 Listening Comprehension—A During-Reading Strategy

Teacher Materials:
Expository trade book

Additional expository trade book

KWL Chart

Student Materials:
KWL Chart

Direct students to expository trade book of teacher choice. **Elicit** responses to questions. **Guide** as needed.
We'll read the story again today. Remember that we are reading an expository story. We read expository stories to learn new information or new facts.
Why do we read expository stories? (Idea: *To learn new information or new facts.*)

When we read the story today, I want you to remember all the things you learned from the story. Then I will read another story on the same topic. I will read another story about _____. This story might have the same information as the last one, or it might have new information. If it has new information, we will add the new information to our KWL Chart.

Elicit correct listening behavior from students. **Reread** expository trade book.
Read second expository text on topic. **Model** prosody during read-aloud.

Guide students to focus on learning new facts or information on topic. **Elicit** responses to questions about new facts learned. **Guide** as needed.

Lesson 138 **559**

Activity 2 KWL Chart: What I Learned—An After-Reading Strategy

Show KWL Chart. **Elicit** responses to questions. **Guide** as needed.

Now that we have read both books on the topic of _____, we are ready to add any new things we learned to the "What I Learned" section of our KWL Chart.

Tell me some new things you have learned about the topic, and I will write the new facts on our KWL Chart. (Student response.)

Write new information or facts on What I Learned section of KWL Chart.

Let's review all the things we learned about _____.

Review all facts learned about the topic and written on chart.

Activity 3 Identify Reasons to Support Statements—An After-Reading Strategy

Select a general statement from the expository text (e.g., "Cheetahs are amazing animals.") that is followed by several reasons (e.g., "runs fast, is endangered, has keen senses"). **Elicit** responses to questions. **Guide** as needed.

What reasons does the author give to support the following sentence "_____ _____"?

560 *Lesson 138*

Lesson 139

> **Materials**
> **Teacher:** Expository trade book (from Lesson 136)
> **Student:** Lined and drawing paper

5 minutes

Part A: Phonemic and Phonological Awareness

Activity 1 Phoneme Identity—Middle

Elicit responses. **Guide** as needed.
Let's find the *middle* sound in a word. I'll say a word, and you tell me the *middle* sound in that word.

What is the middle sound you hear in **bug**? /uuu/.

What is the middle sound you hear in **pure**? /ūūū/.

What is the middle sound you hear in **mule**? /ūūū/.

What is the middle sound you hear in **gum**? /uuu/.

What is the middle sound you hear in **fuel**? /ūūū/.

What is the middle sound you hear in **cut**? /uuu/.

Activity 2 Phoneme Blending

Elicit responses. **Guide** as needed.
Let's put some sounds together and make words. I'm going to say a word very slowly so you can hear each sound. You need to listen carefully and say the sounds. When you say the sounds, it will sound almost like you're singing them. Then we'll put the sounds together and say the word.

My turn. Listen. **/aaa/ /k/.**
Say the sounds. /aaa/ /k/.
Again, say the sounds. /aaa/ /k/.
Now let's put it together. *ack.*

Let's make a bigger word. My turn. Listen. **/sss/ /aaa/ /k/.**
Say the sounds. /sss/ /aaa/ /k/.
Again, say the sounds. /sss/ /aaa/ /k/.
Now let's put it together. What word? *Sack.*

Now we're going to make a bigger word that has a quick sound at the beginning. Listen closely. My turn. Listen. **/b/ /aaa/ /k/.**
Say the sounds. /b/ /aaa/ /k/.
Again, say the sounds. /b/ /aaa/ /k/.
Now let's put it together. What word? *Back.*

Lesson 139   561

(Continue the activity with the following words:
tack [t-aaa-k], pack [p-aaa-k], rack [rrr-aaa-k].)

6 minutes

Student Materials:
Lined paper

Part B: Letter Recognition and Formation

Activity 1 Letter Recognition Review—Capital Z

Elicit responses to questions. **Guide** as needed. **Write** capital Z on the board.
Point to capital Z.
We learned that this letter is **capital Z.** What letter name? *Capital Z.*
Again, what letter name? *Capital Z.*
Review as needed.

Activity 2 Letter Formation Review—Capital Z

Now we're going to practice writing **capital Z.** When you practice writing, you'll learn not only where to start and stop the letter, but also which way to move your hand when you're making the letter. It's tricky, but you're so smart you'll learn how to write **capital Z** very quickly. Watch.

Here's how you write **capital Z** in the air.
Model capital Z formation in the air (with your back to students).

Watch again.

Now let's practice writing **capital Z** in the air. Hold up your writing hand, and make **capital Z** in the air.
Guide students as they write capital Z in the air.

Let's practice **capital Z** again.

Here's how to write **capital Z** with your writing hand pointer finger.
Model capital Z formation on the board with your finger (with your back to students).

Watch again.

Now let's practice writing **capital Z** on your table without using your pencil. Use your writing hand pointer finger, and make **capital Z** on your table.
Guide students as they write capital Z on their table or desktop.

Let's practice **capital Z** again.

Model writing capital Z on the board (with your back to students).
Remember that every letter has a name.
You learned the name of this letter is **capital Z.** What letter name? *Capital Z.*
Again, what letter name? *Capital Z.*

Provide lined paper to students.
Now let's practice writing **capital Z** with your pencil.
Guide students as they write capital Z on their paper. **Review** as needed.

 Link letter names to letter sounds as they appear in the program as needed.

562   Lesson 139

Part C: Comprehension Strategies

9 minutes

Teacher Materials:
Expository trade book

Student Materials:
Drawing paper

Activity 1 Listening Comprehension—A During-Reading Strategy

Today as I read the story, I want you to look carefully at all the pictures of the story. The illustrator is trying to teach you new facts or information with the pictures. Lots of times, pictures in expository books are photographs of real things to teach you what things really look like. After we read the story, you can draw another picture of a new fact that you learned from the story. We will also summarize a page from the story by telling the important idea in our own words.

Elicit correct listening behavior from students. **Reread** trade book. **Model** prosody during read-aloud.

Guide students to focus on illustrations to learn new information. **Elicit** responses to questions about how illustrator shows new facts or information. **Guide** as needed.

Activity 2 Summarize Expository Text—An After-Reading Strategy

Elicit responses to questions. **Guide** as needed.
When I summarize, I want to tell only the important idea about what I am learning. Today, we will practice summarizing a page from our story.

Guide students to summarize a page from expository text.
Let's summarize page _____ of our expository story. First I'll read the page, and then we'll work together to tell the important idea from the page in our own words.

What do you think is the important idea from this page? (Student response.)

So how could we say that idea in our own words? (Student response.)

Yes, I think that if we summarize this page we could say _____. What's a good summary of this page? (Student response.)

Notice that we told about the page what we want to remember in our own words. We didn't tell everything on the page. We just told the important ideas.

Activity 3 Illustrate and Retell Expository Text—An After-Reading Strategy

Provide drawing paper to students. **Elicit** responses to questions. **Guide** as needed.
Now you get to think of your favorite page of the expository story and draw a picture of the new fact you learned from that page.

When you're finished, tell your neighbor about your illustration and the new fact you learned.

Share illustrations of new facts learned with class as time permits, or make a class book of new facts learned from expository text.

Lesson 139 **563**

Lesson 140

Materials

Teacher: Expository trade book (from Lesson 136); 27-Phonemic Awareness; Letter Recognition; 8-My Book Review

Student: Lined and drawing paper; copy of 27-Phonemic Awareness; copy of 8-My Book Review

Part A: Phonemic and Phonological Awareness

5 minutes

Teacher Materials:
Phonemic Awareness

Student Materials:
Phonemic Awareness

Activity 1 Phoneme Categorization—Final

Show Phonemic Awareness. **Distribute** copy of Phonemic Awareness. **Elicit** responses. **Guide** as needed.
We're going to look at a picture on this page and find other pictures to match our sounds. I'm going to name each picture. Touch each picture after I name it, and repeat the name. We're going to find words that have the same *last* sound. If the picture has the same *last* sound as the top picture, we can circle it to show that they go together.

Model use of Phonemic Awareness; point to each picture as word is said.
Let's try it.
Point to picture at top of page.
Touch the picture at the top of the page. This is a **flag.** What is this? *Flag.* That's right. The picture shows a **flag.** What is the *last* sound in **flag?** /g/. Yes, **/g/.** Look at the other pictures and see which ones have the same *last* sound as **flag.**

Point to first picture in first row.
Touch the first picture in the first row. This is an **egg.** What is this? *Egg.* Does **egg** have the same *last* sound as **flag?** *Yes.*
Then we can circle the picture of the **egg.** When we're finished with our lesson, you'll color the pictures you circled to show they have the same *last* sound.

(Continue the activity with the rest of the pictures in the first and second rows.
First row: log, eagle.
Second row: goat, twig, dog.)

(Then use the same procedure to find the pictures of words that have the same last sound as the next key word: bridge.
Third row: cage, igloo, orange.
Fourth row: page, jar, badge.)

Activity 2 Phoneme Segmentation

Model activity if students require assistance. **Elicit** responses. **Guide** as needed.
Let's work on breaking words apart by each sound. I'm going to say a word. Listen closely, and tell me the different sounds you hear in the word.

Listen. The word is **in.** What word? *In.*
Your turn. Tell me the sounds you hear in **in.** */iii/ /nnn/.*
Yes, you said the sounds in the word **in.**

Listen. My turn. The word is **shin.** What word? *Shin.*
Your turn. Tell me the sounds you hear in **shin.** */shshsh/ /iii/ /nnn/.*
Yes, you said the sounds in the word **shin.**

(Continue the activity with the following words:
fin [fff-iii-nnn], win [www-iii-nnn], thin [ththth-iii-nnn].)

Part B: Letter Recognition and Formation

6 minutes

Teacher Materials:
Letter Recognition

Student Materials:
Lined paper

Activity 1 Letter Recognition Cumulative Review—x/X, j/J, q/Q, z/Z

Display on IWB or **write** letters and capitals on the board in the order shown.
Elicit responses to questions. **Guide** as needed.
This week you've learned one letter and one capital—**z** and **capital Z.**
Let's review all the letters and capitals you've learned. Are you ready?

Letter	Question	Student Response
J	What letter?	Capital J.
q	What letter?	q.
z	What letter?	z.
X	What letter?	Capital X.
j	What letter?	j.
x	What letter?	x.
z	What letter?	Capital Z.
Q	What letter?	Capital Q.

Review as needed.

Activity 2 Letter Formation Cumulative Review—x/X, j/J, q/Q, z/Z

Write x, capital X, j, capital J, q, capital Q, z, and capital Z on the board in the order shown (with your back to students). **Provide** lined paper to students.

Show me how you can write these letters and capitals.
Guide students as they write the letters and capitals on their paper. **Review** as needed.

 Link letter names to letter sounds as they appear in the program as needed.

Lesson 140   **565**

Part C: Comprehension Strategies

9 minutes

Teacher Materials:
Expository trade book
My Book Review

Student Materials:
Drawing paper
My Book Review

Activity 1 Listening Comprehension—A During-Reading Strategy

Direct students to expository trade book of teacher choice.
Today as I read the story, I want you to look carefully at all the pictures of the story. The illustrator is trying to teach you new facts or information with the pictures. After we read the story, you can draw another picture of a new fact that you learned from the story. We'll also summarize a page from the story by telling the important idea in our own words.

Elicit correct listening behavior from students. **Reread** trade book. **Model** prosody during read-aloud.

Guide students to focus on illustrations to learn new information. **Elicit** responses to questions about how illustrator shows new facts or information. **Guide** as needed.

Activity 2 Summarize Expository Text—An After-Reading Strategy

Elicit responses to questions. **Guide** as needed.
When I summarize, I want to tell only the important idea about what I'm learning. Today we will practice summarizing a page from our story.

Guide students to summarize a page from expository text.
Let's summarize page _____ of our expository story. First I'll read the page, and then we'll work together to tell the important idea from the page in our own words.

What do you think is the important idea from this page? (Student response.)

So how could we say that idea in our own words? (Student response.)

Yes, I think if we summarize this page we could say, _____. What's a good summary of this page? (Student response.)

Notice that we told about the page what we want to remember in our own words. We didn't tell everything on the page. We just told the important ideas.

566 Lesson 140

Activity 3 Illustrate and Retell Expository Text—An After-Reading Strategy

Provide drawing paper to students.

Now you get to think of your favorite page of the expository story and draw a picture of the new fact you learned from that page.

When you're finished, tell your neighbor about your illustration and the new fact you learned.

Share illustrations of new facts learned with class as time permits, or make a class book of new facts learned from expository text.

Activity 4 Connections Through Shared Writing— Express Opinions

Show My Book Review. **Elicit** responses to questions. **Guide** as needed.

Think about the two books we read, _____ and _____. Let's talk about the two books. Which one did you like best and why?

Provide copies of My Book Review to students. **Guide** students through completion of My Book Review. **Share** with class as time permits.

Lesson 140   **567**

Lesson 141

Materials
Teacher: Expository trade book (same book for Lessons 141–145); 6-KWL Chart; 28-Phonemic Awareness; Letter Recognition
Student: Lined paper; copy of 28-Phonemic Awareness, Copy of 6-KWL Chart

5 minutes

Part A: Phonemic and Phonological Awareness

Teacher Materials:
Phonemic Awareness

Student Materials:
Phonemic Awareness

Activity 1 Phoneme Categorization—Middle

Show Phonemic Awareness. **Distribute** copy of Phonemic Awareness. **Elicit** responses.
We're going to look at a picture on this page and find other pictures to match our sounds. In other lessons, we were looking for pictures that have the same *first* or *last* sound. Now we're going to find pictures that have the same *middle* sound. If the picture has the same *middle* sound as the top picture, we can circle it to show that they go together.
Point to picture at top of page.
Touch the picture at the top of the page. This is a **mat.** What is this? *Mat.*
The picture shows a **mat.** What is the *middle* sound in **mat?** */aaa/.*
Yes, **/aaa/.** See which other pictures have the same *middle* sound as **mat.**
Point to first picture in first row.
Touch the first picture in the first row. This is a **fan.** What is this? *Fan.*
Does **fan** have the same *middle* sound as **mat?** *Yes.*
We can circle the **fan.** When we're finished, you can color the pictures you circled to show they have the same *middle* sound.
(Continue the activity with the rest of the pictures in the first and second rows.
First row: hat, cage. Second row: rope, man, kite.)
(Then use the same procedure to find the pictures of words that have the same middle sound as the next key word: leaf. Third row: sheep, vest, cheese. Fourth row: teeth, duck, bone.)

Activity 2 Phoneme Blending

Elicit responses. **Guide** as needed.
I'm going to say a word slowly so you can hear each sound. Listen carefully and say the sounds. When you say the sounds, it will sound almost like you're singing. Then we'll put the sounds together and say the word.
My turn. Listen. **/ōōō/ /nnn/.** Say the sounds. */ōōō/ /nnn/.* Again, say the sounds. */ōōō/ /nnn/.* Now let's put it together. *ōne.*
Let's make a bigger word. My turn. Listen. **/fff/ /ōōō/ /nnn/.**
Say the sounds. */fff/ /ōōō/ /nnn/.* Again, say the sounds. */fff/ /ōōō/ /nnn/.* Now let's put it together. What word? *Phone.*
Now we're going to make a bigger word that has a quick sound at the beginning. Listen closely. My turn. Listen. **/b/ /ōōō/ /nnn/.**
Say the sounds. */b/ /ōōō/ /nnn/.* Again, say the sounds. */b/ /ōōō/ /nnn/.*
Now let's put it together. What word? *Bone.*
(Continue the activity with cone [c-ōōō-nnn].
Then blend the following:
eep [ēēē-p], sheep [shshsh-ēēē-p], deep [d- ēēē-p], peep [p-ēēē-p].)

Activity 3 Phoneme Segmentation

Model activity if students have difficulty. **Elicit** responses. **Guide** as needed.
Let's work on breaking words apart by each sound. I'm going to say a word. Listen closely, and tell me the different sounds you hear in the word.

Listen. The word is **add.** What word? *Add.*
Your turn. Tell me the sounds you hear in **add.** */aaa/ /d/.*
Yes. You said the sounds in the word **add.**

Listen. My turn. The word is **mad.** What word? *Mad.*
Your turn. Tell me the sounds you hear in **mad.** */mmm/ /aaa/ /d/.*
Yes. You said the sounds in the word **mad.**

(Continue the activity with the following words:
sad [sss-aaa-d], fad [fff-aaa-d], lad [lll-aaa-d].)

Part B: Letter Recognition and Formation

6 minutes

Teacher Materials:
Letter Recognition

Student Materials:
Lined paper

Activity 1 Letter Recognition Cumulative Review—a/A, m/M, s/S, e/E, r/R, d/D

Display on IWB or **write** letters and capitals on the board in the order shown.
Elicit responses to questions. **Guide** as needed.
You've learned all the letters and capital letters. Let's review some of the letters and capital letters you've learned. Are you ready?

Letter	Question	Student Response
s	What letter?	*s.*
m	What letter?	*m.*
E	What letter?	*Capital E.*
D	What letter?	*Capital D.*
a	What letter?	*a.*
e	What letter?	*e.*
R	What letter?	*Capital R.*
M	What letter?	*Capital M.*
S	What letter?	*Capital S.*
A	What letter?	*Capital A.*
r	What letter?	*r.*
d	What letter?	*d.*

Review as needed.

Lesson 141   569

Activity 2 Letter Formation Cumulative Review—a/A, m/M, s/S, e/E, r/R, d/D

Write a, capital A, m, capital M, s, capital S, e, capital E, r, capital R, d, and capital D on the board in the order shown (with your back to students). **Provide** lined paper to students.

Show me how you can write these letters and capitals.
Guide students as they write the letters and capitals on their paper. **Review** as needed.

 Link letter names to letter sounds as they appear in the program as needed.

Set up a writing center with writing materials and correct models of letters learned so far for students to use in their free time.

Part C: Comprehension Strategies

9 minutes

Teacher Materials:
Expository trade book

KWL Chart

Student Materials:
KWL Chart

Activity 1 Establish Purpose for Reading—A Before-Reading Strategy

 Provide a reading center to display books being read so that students can enjoy them again during free time.

Direct students to expository trade book of teacher choice. **Elicit** responses to questions. **Guide** as needed.
Today you'll hear an expository story. Expository stories teach you new information. They tell about things that are true. Why do we read expository stories? (Idea: *To learn new things.*)

Why will we read this story today? (Idea: *To learn new things.*)

570   Lesson 141

Activity 2 Title, Author, and Illustrator Identification—A Before-Reading Strategy

Show front cover of book and allow student to point to name of title, author, and illustrator as you discuss them. **Elicit** responses to questions. **Guide** as needed.

The title of today's story is _____. What's the title of today's story? (Student response.)

The topic we'll learn about in this story is _____. What's the topic we'll learn about in this story? (Student response.)

The author of today's story is _____. Who's the author of today's story? (Student response.)

The illustrator of today's story is _____. Who's the illustrator? (Student response.)

Expository stories, like this story about _____, help you learn new things. Why will we read this story? *To learn new things about* _____.

Activity 3 KWL Chart: What I Know—A Before-Reading Strategy

Elicit responses to questions. **Guide** as needed.

When you read expository stories, think about what you know before you read. This KWL Chart will help you think what you already know about _____. I'll write what you know in the section called "What I Know."

Tell me what you know about _____, and I'll write it on the chart. (Student response.)

Elicit what students know about topic for What I Know section of KWL Chart. **Write** three items on What I Know section of chart.

Now I have written some facts that you know about _____. It is your turn to write one fact that you know about _____.

Activity 4 KWL Chart: What I Wonder—A Before-Reading Strategy

Elicit responses to questions. **Guide** as needed.

The next part of the chart says, "What I Wonder." This is where I'll write what you want to learn about the topic _____. Think of what you wonder about _____, and then we'll write the questions you have on the chart. (Student response.)

Elicit three questions from students for What I Wonder section of KWL Chart.

Now I have written some things that you wonder about _____. It is your turn to write one thing that you wonder about _____.

In the next lesson, we'll finish our KWL Chart by filling in new information.

Elicit correct listening behavior. **Read** trade book. **Model** prosody.

Guide students to listen for information or facts about topic. **Ask** questions to elicit new information or facts that students are learning. **Guide** as needed.

Lesson 141 **571**

Lesson 142

Materials

Teacher: Expository trade book (from Lesson 141); 6-KWL Chart (from Lesson 141); 29-Phonemic Awareness; Letter Recognition

Student: Lined paper; copy of 29-Phonemic Awareness, Copy of 6-KWL Chart (from Lesson 141)

Part A: Phonemic and Phonological Awareness

5 minutes

Teacher Materials:
Phonemic Awareness

Student Materials:
Phonemic Awareness

Activity 1 Phoneme Categorization—Middle

Show Phonemic Awareness. **Distribute** copy of Phonemic Awareness. **Elicit** responses. **Guide** as needed.

We're going to look at a picture on this page and find other pictures to match our sounds. I'm going to name each picture. Touch each picture after I name it, and repeat the name. We're going to find pictures that have the same *middle* sound. If the picture has the same *middle* sound as the top picture, we can circle it to show that they go together.

Model use of Phonemic Awareness; point to each picture as word is said.
Let's try it.
Point to picture at top of page.
Touch the picture at the top of the page. This is a **pig.** What is this? *Pig.*
That's right. The picture shows a **pig.** So what is the *middle* sound in **pig?** /iii/.
Yes, **/iii/.** Let's look at the other pictures and see which ones have the same *middle* sound as **pig.**

Point to first picture in first row.
Touch the first picture in the first row. This is a **bike.** What is this? *Bike.*
Does **bike** have the same *middle* sound as **pig?** *No.*
Then we can't circle the picture of the **bike** because bike and **pig** don't have the same *middle* sound. When we're finished with our lesson, you'll color the pictures you circled to show they have the same *middle* sound.

(Continue the activity with the rest of the pictures in the first and second rows.
First row: hill, mop.
Second row: chair, ship, crib.)

(Then use the same procedure to find the pictures of words that have the same middle sound as the next key word: sock.
Third row: mop, fox, shell.
Fourth row: bone, dog, broom.)

572 Lesson 142

Activity 2 **Phoneme Blending**

Elicit responses. **Guide** as needed.
Let's put some sounds together and make words. I'm going to say a word very slowly so you can hear each sound. You need to listen carefully and say the sounds. Then we'll put the sounds together and say the word.

My turn. Listen. **/uuu/ /nnn/.**
Say the sounds. */uuu/ /nnn/.*
Again, say the sounds. */uuu/ /nnn/.*
Now let's put it together. *un.*

Let's make a bigger word. My turn. Listen. **/sss/ /uuu/ /nnn/.**
Say the sounds. */sss/ /uuu/ /nnn/.*
Again, say the sounds. */sss/ /uuu/ /nnn/.*
Now let's put it together. What word? *Sun.*

(Continue the activity with the following words:
bun [b-uuu-nnn], ton [t-uuu-nnn].

Then blend the following:
ig [iii-g], wig [www-iii-g], pig [p-iii-g], jig [j-iii-g].)

Activity 3 **Phoneme Segmentation**

Elicit responses. **Guide** as needed.
Let's work on breaking words apart by each sound. I'm going to say a word. Listen closely, and tell me the different sounds you hear in the word.

Listen. Say **ip.** *ip.*
Your turn. Tell me the sounds you hear in **ip.** */iii/ /p/.*
Yes. You said the sounds in **ip.**

Listen. The word is **sip.** What word? *Sip.*
Your turn. Tell me the sounds you hear in **sip.** */sss/ /iii/ /p/.*
Yes. You said the sounds in the word **sip.**

(Continue the activity with the following words:
lip [lll-iii-p], zip [zzz-iii-p], ship [shshsh-iii-p].)

Lesson 142 **573**

6 minutes

Teacher Materials:
Letter Recognition

Student Materials:
Lined paper

Part B: Letter Recognition and Formation

Activity 1 Letter Recognition Cumulative Review—f/F, i/I, t/T, n/N, c/C, o/O

Display on IWB or **write** letters and capitals on the board in the order shown. **Elicit** responses to questions. **Guide** as needed.

Let's review some of the other letters and capital letters you've learned. Are you ready?

Letter	Question	Student Response
c	What letter?	c.
N	What letter?	Capital N.
i	What letter?	i.
O	What letter?	Capital O.
T	What letter?	Capital T.
f	What letter?	f.
n	What letter?	n.
C	What letter?	Capital C.
t	What letter?	t.
o	What letter?	o.
I	What letter?	Capital I.
F	What letter?	Capital F.

Review as needed.

Activity 2 Letter Formation Cumulative Review— f/F, i/I, t/T, n/N, c/C, o/O

Write f, capital F, i, capital I, t, capital T, n, capital N, c, capital C, o, and capital O on the board in the order shown (with your back to students). **Provide** lined paper to students.

Show me how you can write these letters and capitals.

Guide students as they write the letters and capitals on their paper. **Review** as needed.

 Link letter names to letter sounds as they appear in the program as needed.

574 Lesson 142

Part C: Comprehension Strategies

9 minutes

Teacher Materials:
Expository trade book
KWL Chart

Student Materials:
KWL Chart

Activity 1 Listening Comprehension—A During-Reading Strategy

Direct students to expository trade book of teacher choice. **Elicit** response to question. **Guide** as needed.

We'll read the story again today. Remember that we're reading an expository book. Expository stories are written to teach us new information or new facts. Why will we read this book about _____? (Idea: *To learn new information or facts.*)

When we read the story today, I want you to think about the new facts you are learning from this book. Then we'll fill in the last part of our KWL Chart.

Elicit correct listening behavior from students. **Reread** trade book. **Model** prosody during read-aloud.

Elicit new information or facts that students are learning from text. **Ask** questions to identify new facts learned. **Guide** as needed.

Activity 2 KWL Chart: What I Learned—An After-Reading Strategy

Show KWL Chart. **Elicit** responses to questions. **Guide** as needed.
Now we get to fill in the last part of the KWL Chart. That section is called "What I Learned."

Let's work together to fill in the last section of the chart.

Tell me some new facts that you learned from this book, and I'll write them on the chart. (Student response.)

Elicit new facts learned from students for What I Learned section of KWL Chart. **Write** three facts that you learned.

Now I have written some facts that you learned about _____. It is your turn to write one fact that you learned about _____.
Guide as needed

Assign partners. **Guide** as needed.
Now share what you learned with your partner and add suggestions to make your neighbor's writing better if you think it needs it.

Lesson 142 575

Activity 3 **Identify Main Idea—An After-Reading Strategy**

Elicit responses to questions. **Guide** as needed.

Now let's think about the main idea of this story. Finding the main idea in expository stories is easier than in narrative stories because we already know the topic of the story. To tell the main idea, I just have to say the topic and an important thing I learned.

Guide students to find main idea of expository text.

What's the topic of this book? (Student response.)

What very important fact did this story teach you? (Student response.)

Put the topic and the important information together to get the main idea.

So what do you think is the main idea of this story? (Student response.)

Yes, the main idea of this expository story is, _____. What's the main idea of this story? (Student response.)

Lesson 143

Materials

Teacher: Expository trade book (from Lesson 141); additional expository trade book on same topic; 6-KWL Chart (from Lessons 141 and 142); 30-Phonemic Awareness; Letter Recognition

Student: Lined paper; copy of 30-Phonemic Awareness

Part A: Phonemic and Phonological Awareness

5 minutes

Teacher Materials:
Phonemic Awareness

Student Materials:
Phonemic Awareness

Activity 1 Phoneme Categorization—Middle

Show Phonemic Awareness. **Distribute** copy of Phonemic Awareness. **Elicit** responses. **Guide** as needed.

We're going to look at a picture on this page and find other pictures to match our sounds. I'm going to name each picture. Touch each picture after I name it, and repeat the name. We're going to find pictures that have the same *middle* sound. If the picture has the same *middle* sound as the top picture, we can circle it to show that they go together.

Model use of Phonemic Awareness; point to each picture as word is said.
Point to picture at top of page.
Touch the picture at the top of the page. This is **tape.** What is this? *Tape.*
That's right. The picture shows **tape.** So what is the *middle* sound in **tape?** /āāā/.
Yes, **/āāā/.** Let's look at the other pictures and see which ones have the same *middle* sound as **tape.**

Point to first picture in first row.
Touch the first picture in the first row. This is a **vase.** What is this? *Vase.*
Does **vase** have the same *middle* sound as **tape?** *Yes.*
Then we can circle the picture of the **vase.** When we're finished with our lesson, you'll color the pictures you circled to show they have the same middle sound.

(Continue the activity with the rest of the pictures in the first and second rows.
First row: comb, flag.
Second row: shirt, cage, nail.)

(Then use the same procedure to find the pictures of words that have the same middle sound as the next key word: nut.
Third row: soap, cup, thumb.
Fourth row: glass, sun, fire.)

Lesson 143   577

Activity 2 Phoneme Blending

Elicit responses. **Guide** as needed.
Let's put some sounds together and make words. I'm going to say a word very slowly so you can hear each sound. You need to listen carefully and say the sounds. Then we'll put the sounds together and say the word.

My turn. Listen. **/uuu/ /g/.**
Say the sounds. /uuu/ /g/.
Again, say the sounds. /uuu/ /g/.
Now let's put it together. ug.

Let's make a bigger word. My turn. Listen. **/b/ /uuu/ /g/.**
Say the sounds. /b/ /uuu/ /g/.
Again, say the sounds. /b/ /uuu/ /g/.
Now let's put it together. What word? Bug.

(Continue the activity with the following words:
rug [rrr-uuu-g], hug [h-uuu-g].)

Then blend the following:
op [ooo-p], chop [ch-ooo-p], mop [mmm-ooo-p], hop [h-ooo-p].)

Activity 3 Phoneme Segmentation

Elicit responses. **Guide** as needed.
Let's work on breaking words apart by each sound. I'm going to say a word. Listen closely, and tell me the different sounds you hear in the word.

Listen. Say **ine.** ine.
Your turn. Tell me the sounds you hear in **ine.** /īīī/ /nnn/.
Yes, you said the sounds in **ine.**

Listen. The word is **line.** What word? Line.
Your turn. Tell me the sounds you hear in **line.** /lll/ /īīī/ /nnn/.
Yes, you said the sounds in the word **line.**

(Continue the activity with the following words:
shine [shshsh-iii-nnn], vine [vvv-iii-nnn], mine [mmm-iii-nnn].)

Part B: Letter Recognition and Formation

6 minutes

Activity 1 Letter Recognition Cumulative Review—h/H, u/U, g/G, l/L, w/W, k/K, v/V

Teacher Materials:
Letter Recognition

Student Materials:
Lined paper

Display on IWB or **write** letters and capitals on the board in the order shown.
Elicit responses to questions. **Guide** as needed.
Let's review some of the other letters and capital letters you've learned. Are you ready?

578 Lesson 143

Letter	Question	Student Response
g	What letter?	g.
U	What letter?	Capital U.
W	What letter?	Capital W.
l	What letter?	l.
G	What letter?	Capital G.
h	What letter?	h.
w	What letter?	w.
V	What letter?	Capital V.
u	What letter?	u.
L	What letter?	Capital L.
k	What letter?	k.
H	What letter?	Capital H.
K	What letter?	Capital K.
v	What letter?	v.

Review as needed.

Activity 2 Letter Formation Cumulative Review— h/H, u/U, g/G, I/L, w/W, k/K, v/V

Write h, capital H, u, capital U, g, capital G, l, capital L, w, capital W, k, capital K, v, and capital V on the board in the order shown (with your back to students). **Provide** lined paper to students.

Show me how you can write these letters and capitals.
Guide students as they write the letters and capitals on their paper. **Review** as needed.

 Link letter names to letter sounds as they appear in the program as needed.

Lesson 143

Part C: Comprehension Strategies

9 minutes

Teacher Materials:
Expository trade book

Additional expository trade book

KWL Chart

Activity 1 Listening Comprehension—A During-Reading Strategy

Direct students to expository trade book of teacher choice. **Elicit** response to question. **Guide** as needed.

We'll read the story again today. Remember that we are reading an expository story. We read expository stories to learn new information or new facts. Why do we read expository stories? (Idea: *To learn new information or new facts.*)

When we read the story today, I want you to remember all the things you learned from the story. Then I will read another story on the same topic. I will read another story about _____. This story might have the same information as the last one, or it might have new information. If it has new information, we will add the new information to our KWL Chart.

Elicit correct listening behavior from students. **Reread** expository trade book. **Read** second expository text on topic. **Model** prosody during read-aloud.

Guide students to focus on learning new facts or information on the topic.
Elicit answers to questions about new facts learned. **Guide** as needed.

Activity 2 KWL Chart: What I Learned—An After-Reading Strategy

Show KWL Chart. **Elicit** responses to questions. **Guide** as needed.
Now that we've read both books on the topic of _____ we are ready to add any new things we learned to the "What I Learned" section of our KWL Chart.

Tell me some new things you have learned about the topic, and I'll write the new facts on our KWL Chart. (**Student response.**)

Write new information or facts on What I Learned section of KWL Chart.

Let's review all the things we learned about _____.
Review all facts learned about topic and written on chart.

Lesson 144

Materials

Teacher: Expository trade book (from Lesson 141); 31-Phonemic Awareness; Letter Recognition

Student: Lined and drawing paper; copy of 31-Phonemic Awareness

5 minutes

Teacher Materials:
Phonemic Awareness

Student Materials:
Phonemic Awareness

Part A: Phonemic and Phonological Awareness

Activity 1 Phoneme Categorization—Middle

Show Phonemic Awareness. **Distribute** copy of Phonemic Awareness. **Elicit** responses. **Guide** as needed.

We're going to look at a picture on this page, and find other pictures to match our sounds. I'm going to name each picture. Touch each picture after I name it, and repeat the name. We're going to find pictures that have the same *middle* sound. If the picture has the same *middle* sound as the top picture, we can circle it to show that they go together.

Model use of Phonemic Awareness; point to each picture as word is said.
Point to picture at top of page.
Touch the picture at the top of the page. This is a **rope.** What is this? *Rope.* That's right. The picture shows a **rope.** What is the *middle* sound in **rope?** /ōōō/.
Yes, **/ōōō/.** We need to look at the other pictures and see which ones have the same *middle* sound as **rope.**

Point to first picture in first row.
Touch the first picture in the first row. This is a **horse.** What is this? *Horse.* Does **horse** have the same *middle* sound as **rope?** *Yes.*
Then we can circle the picture of the **horse.** When we're finished with our lesson, you'll color the pictures you circled to show they have the same *middle* sound.

(Continue the activity with the rest of the pictures in the first and second rows.
First row: nose, king.
Second row: globe, box, coat.)

(Then use the same procedure to find the pictures of words that have the same middle sound as the next key word: bed.
Third row: pen, goat, shell.
Fourth row: clock, mouse, neck.)

Lesson 144   581

Activity 2 Phoneme Blending

Elicit responses. **Guide** as needed.

Let's put some sounds together and make words. I'm going to say a word very slowly so you can hear each sound. You need to listen carefully and say the sounds. Then we'll put the sounds together and say the word.

My turn. Listen. **/āāā/ /nnn/.**
Say the sounds. */āāā/ /nnn/.*
Again, say the sounds. */āāā/ /nnn/.*
Now let's put it together. *ain.*

Let's make a bigger word. My turn. Listen. **/rrr/ /āāā/ /nnn/.**
Say the sounds. */rrr/ /āāā/ /nnn/.*
Again, say the sounds. */rrr/ /āāā/ /nnn/.*
Now let's put it together. What word? *Rain.*

(Continue the activity with the following words:
pain [p-āāā-nnn], cane [c-āāā-nnn].

Then blend the following:
ive [iii-vvv], dive [d-iii-vvv], hive [h-iii-vvv], five [fff-iii-vvv].)

Activity 3 Phoneme Segmentation

Elicit responses. **Guide** as needed.

Let's work on breaking words apart by each sound. I'm going to say a word. You'll need to listen closely and tell me the different sounds you hear in the word.

Listen. Say **ock?** *ock.*
Your turn. Tell me the sounds you hear in **ock.** */ooo/ /k/.*
Yes, you said the sounds in **ock.**

Listen. The word is **sock.** What word? *Sock.*
Your turn. Tell me the sounds you hear in **sock.** */sss/ /ooo/ /k/.*
Yes, you said the sounds in the word **sock.**

(Continue the activity with the following words:
lock [lll-ooo-k], rock [rrr-ooo-k], shock [shshsh-ooo-k].)

582 *Lesson 144*

Part B: Letter Recognition and Formation

6 minutes

Teacher Materials:
Letter Recognition

Student Materials:
Lined paper

Activity 1 Letter Recognition Cumulative Review—p/P, b/B, y/Y, x/X, j/J, q/Q, z/Z

Display on IWB or **write** letters and capitals on the board in the order shown.
Elicit responses to questions. **Guide** as needed.

Let's review some of the other letters and capital letters you've learned. Are you ready?

Letter	Question	Student Response
b	What letter?	b.
Y	What letter?	Capital Y.
j	What letter?	j.
z	What letter?	z.
P	What letter?	Capital P.
x	What letter?	x.
J	What letter?	Capital J.
B	What letter?	Capital B.
q	What letter?	q.
Z	What letter?	Capital Z.
p	What letter?	p.
y	What letter?	y.
Q	What letter?	Capital Q.
X	What letter?	Capital X.

Review as needed.

Lesson 144

Activity 2 — Letter Formation Cumulative Review— p/P, b/B, y/Y, x/X, j/J, q/Q, z/Z

Write p, capital P, b, capital B, y, capital Y, x, capital X, j, capital J, q, capital Q, z and capital Z on the board in the order shown (with your back to students). **Provide** lined paper to students.

Show me how you can write these letters and capitals.
Guide students as they write the letters and capitals on their paper. **Review** as needed.

 Link letter names to letter sounds as they appear in the program as needed.

Part C: Comprehensive Strategies

9 minutes

Teacher Materials:
Expository trade book

Student Materials:
Drawing paper

Activity 1 — Listening Comprehension—A During-Reading Strategy

Direct students to expository trade book of teacher choice. **Elicit** responses to questions. **Guide** as needed.
Today as I read the story, I want you to look carefully at all the pictures of the story. The illustrator is trying to teach you new facts or information with the pictures. After we read the story, you can draw a picture of a new fact that you learned from the story. We'll also summarize a page from the story by telling the important idea in our own words.

Elicit correct listening behavior from students. **Reread** trade book. **Model** prosody during read-aloud.

Guide students to focus on illustrations to learn new information. **Elicit** responses to questions about how illustrator shows new facts or information. **Guide** as needed.

Activity 2 — Summarize Expository Text—An After Reading Strategy

Elicit responses to questions. **Guide** as needed.
When you summarize, I want you to tell only the important idea about what you are learning. Today you'll practice summarizing a page from the story.

You'll summarize page _____ of the expository story. First I'll read the page, and then you'll work with a partner to tell the important idea from the page in your own words.

What two things do you need to do to summarize a page? (Idea: *Think of the important idea and tell it in your own words.*)

Assign student partners. **Monitor** student partners as they work.
Talk to your partner, and think of the important idea on this page. What did you and your partner think was the important idea? (Student response.)

Monitor student partners as they work.

Talk with your partner about how to put that idea in your own words.

How did you and your partner put the important idea in your own words? (Student response.)

Yes, I think a good summary of this page is _____. What's a good summary of this page? (Student response.)

Notice that you told about the page what you want to remember in your own words. You didn't tell everything on the page. You just told the important ideas.

Activity 3 Illustrate and Retell Expository Text—An After-Reading Strategy

Provide drawing paper to students.

Now you get to think of your favorite page of the expository story and draw a picture of the new fact you learned from that page.

When you're finished, tell your neighbor about your illustration and the new fact you learned.

Share illustrations of new facts learned with class as time permits, or make a class book of new facts learned from expository text.

Lesson 144

Lesson 145

> **Materials**
> **Teacher:** Expository trade book (from Lesson 141); 32-Phonemic Awareness; Letter Recognition
> **Student:** Lined and drawing paper; copy of 32-Phonemic Awareness

5 minutes

Teacher Materials:
Phonemic Awareness

Student Materials:
Phonemic Awareness

Part A: Phonemic and Phonological Awareness

Activity 1 Phoneme Categorization—Middle

Show Phonemic Awareness. **Distribute** copy of Phonemic Awareness. **Elicit** responses. **Guide** as needed.
We're going to look at a picture on this page and find other pictures to match our sounds. I'm going to name each picture. Touch each picture after I name it, and repeat the name. We're going to find pictures that have the same *middle* sound. If the picture has the same *middle* sound as the top picture, we can circle it to show that they go together.

Model use of Phonemic Awareness; point to each picture as word is said.
Point to picture at top of page.
Touch the picture at the top of the page. This is a **bike.** What is this? *Bike.* That's right. The picture shows a bike. What is the *middle* sound in **bike?** /ī/. Yes, /ī/. Let's look at the other pictures and see which ones have the same *middle* sound as **bike.**

Point to first picture in first row.
Touch the first picture in the first row. This is a **tire.** What is this? *Tire.* Does **tire** have the same *middle* sound as **bike?** *Yes.*
Then we can circle the picture of the **tire.** When we're finished with our lesson, you'll color the pictures you circled to show they have the same *middle* sound.

(Continue the activity with the rest of the pictures in the first and second rows.
First row: watch, page.
Second row: comb, knife, five.)

(Then use the same procedure to find the pictures of words that have the same middle sound as the next key word: moon.
Third row: lamb, broom, flag.
Fourth row: spoon, roof, brush.)

Activity 2 Phoneme Blending

Elicit responses. **Guide** as needed.
Let's put some sounds together and make words. I'm going to say a word very slowly so you can hear each sound. You need to listen carefully and say the sounds. Then we'll put the sounds together and say the word.

My turn. Listen. **/ōōō/ /zzz/.**
Say the sounds. /ōōō/ /zzz/.
Again, say the sounds. /ōōō/ /zzz/.
Now let's put it together. *ose.*

Let's make a bigger word. My turn. Listen. **/h/ /ōōō/ /zzz/.**
Say the sounds. /h/ /ōōō/ /zzz/.
Again, say the sounds. /h/ /ōōō/ /zzz/.
Now let's put it together. What word? *Hose.*

(Continue the activity with the following words:
rose [rrr-ōōō-zzz], those [ththth-ōōō-zzz].

Then blend the following: ed [eee-d], bed [b-eee-d], red [rrr-eee-d], shed [shshsh-eee-d].)

Activity 3 Phoneme Segmentation

Elicit responses. **Guide** as needed.
Let's work on breaking words apart by each sound. I'm going to say a word. You'll need to listen closely and tell me the different sounds you hear in the word.

Listen. Say **ight.** *ight.*
Your turn. Tell me the sounds you hear in **ight.** */īīī/ /t/.*
Yes, you said the sounds in **ight.**

Listen. The word is **right.** What word? *Right.*
Your turn. Tell me the sounds you hear in **right.** */rrr/ /īīī/ /t/.*
Yes, you said the sounds in the word **right.**

(Continue the activity with the following words:
night [nnn-iii-t], light [lll-iii-t], fight [fff-iii-t].)

Part B: Letter Recognition and Formation

6 minutes

Teacher Materials:
Letter Recognition

Student Materials:
Lined paper

Activity 1 Letter Recognition Cumulative Review—j/J, q/Q, z/Z

Display on IWB or **write** letters and capitals on the board in the order shown.
Elicit responses to questions. **Guide** as needed.
This week you've shown you know the letters and capital letters. Let's review three letters and capital letters you have learned. Are you ready?

Lesson 145   587

Letter	Question	Student Response
J	What letter?	Capital J.
z	What letter?	z.
Q	What letter?	Capital Q.
Z	What letter?	Capital Z.
q	What letter?	q.
j	What letter?	j.

Review as needed.

Activity 2 Letter Formation Cumulative Review—j/J, q/Q, z/Z

Write j, capital J, q, capital Q, z, and capital Z on the board in the order shown (with your back to students). **Provide** lined paper to students.

Show me how you can write these letters and capitals.
Guide students as they write the letters and capitals on their paper. **Review** as needed.

 Link letter names to letter sounds as they appear in the program as needed.

Part C: Comprehension Strategies

9 minutes

Teacher Materials:
Expository trade book

Student Materials:
Drawing paper

Activity 1 Listening Comprehension—A During-Reading Strategy

Direct students to expository trade book of teacher choice. **Elicit** responses to questions. **Guide** as needed.
Today as I read the story, I want you to look carefully at all the pictures of the story. The illustrator is trying to teach you new facts or information with the pictures. After we read the story, you can draw another picture of a new fact that you learned from the story. We'll also summarize a page from the story by telling the important idea in our own words.

Elicit correct listening behavior from students. **Reread** trade book. **Model** prosody during read-aloud.

Guide students to focus on illustrations to learn new information. **Elicit** responses to questions about how illustrator shows new facts or information. **Guide** as needed.

588 Lesson 145

Activity 2 Summarize Expository Text—An After-Reading Strategy

Assign student partners. **Elicit** responses to questions. **Guide** as needed.

When you summarize, I want you to tell only the important idea about what you are learning. Today you'll practice summarizing a page from the story. You'll summarize page _____ of the expository story. First I'll read the page, and then you'll work with a partner to tell the important idea from the page in your own words.

What two things do you need to do to summarize a page? (Idea: *Think of the important idea and tell it in your own words.*)

Talk to your partner, and think of the important idea on this page.
Monitor student partners as they work.

What did you and your partner think was the important idea?
(**Student response.**)

Talk with your partner about how to put that idea in your own words.
Monitor student partners as they work.

How did you and your partner put the important idea in your own words?
(**Student response.**)

Yes, I think a good summary of this page is _____. What's a good summary of this page? (**Student response.**)

Notice that you told about the page what you want to remember in your own words. You didn't tell everything on the page. You just told the important idea.

Activity 3 Illustrate and Retell Expository Text—An After-Reading Strategy

Provide drawing paper to students.

Now you get to think of your favorite page of the expository story and draw a picture of the new fact you learned from that page.

When you're finished, tell your neighbor about your illustration and the new fact you learned.

Share illustrations of new facts learned with class as time permits, or make a class book of new facts learned from expository text.

Lesson 145 **589**

Lesson 146

Materials

Teacher: *Storybook;* IWB-Sequence Events or write 3 main events on 3 large index cards; 7-Mental Images; 1-Phonemic Awareness; 3 manipulatives such as blocks, discs, chips, counters (if not using IWB)

Student: Lined paper; *Storybook;* copy of 1-Phonemic Awareness; 3 manipulatives such as blocks, discs, chips, counters

Part A: Phonemic and Phonological Awareness

5 minutes

Teacher Materials:
Phonemic Awareness

3 manipulatives such as blocks, discs, chips, counters

Student Materials:
Phonemic Awareness

3 manipulatives such as blocks, discs, chips, counters

Activity 1 Phoneme Blending

Elicit responses. **Guide** as needed.
Let's put some sounds together and make words. I'm going to say a word very slowly so you can hear each sound. You need to listen carefully and say the sounds. Then we'll put the sounds together and say the word.

My turn. Listen. **/mmm/ /āāā/ /k/.**
Say the sounds. /mmm/ /āāā/ /k/.
Again, say the sounds. /mmm/ /āāā/ /k/.
Let's put it together. What word? *Make.*

My turn. Listen. **/mmm/ /aaa/ /p/.**
Say the sounds. /mmm/ /aaa/ /p/.
Again, say the sounds. /mmm/ /aaa/ /p/.
Let's put it together. What word? *Map.*

(Continue the activity with the following words:
meal [mmm-ēēē-lll], met [mmm-eee-t], mice [mmm-īīī-sss], mitt [mmm-iii-t], moon [mmm-oooooo-nnn], mop [mmm-ooo-p], moth [mmm-ooo-ththth], mud [mmm-uuu-d].)

Activity 2 Phoneme Segmentation

Show Phonemic Awareness. **Elicit** responses. **Guide** as needed.
You've done such a great job breaking words apart by each sound. Today we're going to use chips to show how many sounds there are in a word. For each sound in the word, we'll push one chip up to the arrow on the page. I'll show you how to do the first one.

Model use of the chips by moving the chips to the arrow for each word and then back to the bottom when finished. **Remind** students that each chip represents one phoneme.
Listen. I can say a word and move a chip for each sound in the word.
At. /aaa/ /t/. At. Say the sounds in **at** with me, and move a chip for each sound. /aaa/ /t/.

590   Lesson 146

Now bring your finger back to the dot of the arrow. Let's slide our fingers under the chips and say the word. *At.* Let's move our chips back to the bottom so you can try it by yourselves. Say the sounds you hear in **at,** and move a chip for each sound. */aaa/ /t/.*

Move your finger back to the dot. What word? *At.*
Great job. Now move our chips back to the bottom, and let's try another one.

(Continue the activity with the following words: mat, sat, rat, fat.)

6 minutes

Student Materials:
Lined paper

Part B: Letter Recognition and Formation

Activity 1 Letter Recognition—School Name

Write (name of school) on board. **Elicit** responses to questions. **Guide** as needed.
You've learned all the letters and capital letters. Now we're going to learn to put the letters and capital letters together to write important names. The first name we're going to write is the name of our school.

Point to (name of school).
The name of our school is _____.

What's the name of our school? (Student response.)

Good. The name of our school is _____.

Now I'm going to point to each letter or capital letter in our school's name. I want you to tell me the letter or capital letter. Ready?
Point to each letter or capital letter in (school name).

Activity 2 Letter Formation—School Name

Provide lined paper to students.
Now we're going to practice writing our school's name.

Here's how you write our school's name.
Model writing (school's name) on the board (with your back to students).

Let's practice writing our school's name.
Guide students as they write (school's name) on their paper using a pencil.
Review as needed.

 Link letter names to letter sounds as they appear in the program as needed.

Set up a writing center with writing materials and correct models of letters learned so far for students to use in their free time.

Lesson 146   **591**

9 minutes

Teacher Materials:
Storybook

Sequence Events

Mental Images

Student Materials:
Storybook

Part C: Comprehension Strategies

Activity 1 Establish Purpose for Reading—A Before-Reading Strategy

  Direct students to Lesson 145, pages 145–147, in *Storybook*.

Elicit responses to questions. **Guide** as needed.
You know that when you read a story with characters, setting, and events that happen, you are reading narrative text. Narrative text is written to tell a story for you to enjoy. Why is narrative text written? (Idea: *To tell a story for you to enjoy.*)

Expository text is written to teach you new facts. Why is expository text written? (Idea: *To teach you new facts.*)

In the last lesson, you read "The Pig That Bit His Leg." Do you think that story is a narrative or expository text? *Narrative.*

Why do you think it is narrative text? (Idea: *It has characters, setting, and events that happen.*)

Why was that narrative text written? (Idea: *To tell a story for you to enjoy.*)

Activity 2 Sequence and Retell the Story—An After-Reading Strategy

Elicit responses to questions. **Guide** as needed.
I'll tell the events that happened in the story from the last lesson. But I'll tell you the events in the wrong order. Listen carefully to see whether you can figure out what I do wrong. Then you can help me fix it.

I wrote the events on these cards. I'll put them up on the board as I tell them to you. See if you can put the cards in the right order.

The pig gave his leg a bite.

The bug and pig met on the road.

The bug bit a log.

I'll read the events again.
Reread events in the same order.
Oops! Those events are not in the right order.
Watch me as I put them in the right order.
Model rearranging cards on IWB board in the right order.

Now I can retell the events because they're in the right order. Listen as I retell the events.
Model retelling events in the right order.

We'll play the "Put the Cards in the Right Order" game in the next lesson.

592 Lesson 146

Activity 3 **Comprehension Monitoring: Mental Imaging—A During-Reading Strategy**

Elicit responses to questions. **Guide** as needed.

When good readers read stories, they make pictures in their minds of the words they're reading. Listen to how I make a picture in my mind when I read a sentence.

Model think-aloud for mental imaging.

Sample Wording for Think-Aloud

When I read about the bug and the pig meeting on the road, I made a picture in my mind. I thought of a black road with lines on it. Then I thought of a tiny bug like a small beetle on one side of the road. Then I thought of a big, fat, pink pig on the other side of the road. I made a picture of them looking at each other in my mind.

When you're reading a story, it's a good idea to make a picture in your mind of the words you're reading.

Show Mental Images. **Model** completing organizer by writing sentence and making picture for mental image.

Lesson 146 **593**

Lesson 147

Materials

Teacher: *Storybook;* write IWB-Sequence Events or write 3 main events on 3 large index cards; 7-Mental Images; 1-Phonemic Awareness; 3 manipulatives such as blocks, discs, chips, counters (if not using IWB)

Student: Lined paper; *Storybook;* 1-Phonemic Awareness; 3 manipulatives such as blocks, discs, chips, counters

5 minutes

Teacher Materials:
Phonemic Awareness

3 manipulatives such as blocks, discs, chips, counters

Student Materials:
Phonemic Awareness;

3 manipulatives such as blocks, discs, chips, counters

Part A: Phonemic and Phonological Awareness

Activity 1 Phoneme Blending

Elicit responses. **Guide** as needed.
Let's put some sounds together and make words. I'm going to say a word very slowly so you can hear each sound. You need to listen carefully and say the sounds. Then we'll put the sounds together and say the word.

My turn. Listen. **/sss/ /āāā/ /fff/.**
Say the sounds. */sss/ /āāā/ /fff/.*
Again, say the sounds. */sss/ /āāā/ /fff/.*
Let's put it together. What word? *Safe.*

My turn. Listen. **/sss/ /aaa/ /t/.**
Say the sounds. */sss/ /aaa/ /t/.*
Again, say the sounds. */sss/ /aaa/ /t/.*
Let's put it together. What word? *Sat.*

(Continue the activity with the following words:
seed [sss-ēēē-d], set [sss-eee-t], side [sss-iii-d], sick [sss-iii-k], soon [sss-üüü-nnn], soap [sss-ōōō-p], sod [sss-ooo-d], sun [sss-uuu-nnn].)

Activity 2 Phoneme Segmentation

Show Phonemic Awareness. **Elicit** responses. **Guide** as needed.
You've done such a great job breaking words apart by each sound. Today we're going to use chips to show how many sounds there are in a word. For each sound in the word, we'll push one chip up to the arrow on the page. I'll show you how to do the first one.

Model use of the chips by moving the chips to the arrow for each word and then back to the bottom when finished. **Remind** students that each chip represents one phoneme.
Listen. I can say a word and move a chip for each sound in the word. **It. /iii/ /t/.** *It.*

Say the sounds in **it** with me, and move a chip for each sound. */iii/ /t/.* Now bring your finger back to the dot of the arrow. Let's slide our fingers under the chips and say the word. *It.* Let's move our chips back to the bottom so you can try it by yourselves. Say the sounds you hear in **it,** and move a chip for each sound. */iii/ /t/.*

594 Lesson 147

Move your finger back to the dot. What word? *It.*

Great job. Now move your chips back to the bottom, and let's try another one.

(Continue the activity with the following words: mitt, sit, in, win, fin.)

Part B: Letter Recognition and Formation

6 minutes

Student Materials:
Lined paper

Activity 1 Letter Recognition Review—School Name

Write (name of school) on board. **Elicit** responses to questions. **Guide** as needed.
You've learned how to write the name of our school.

Point to (name of school).
The name of our school is _____.

What's the name of our school? (**Student response.**)

Now I'm going to point to each letter or capital letter in our school's name.
I want you to tell me the letter or capital letter. Ready?
Point to each letter or capital letter in (school name).

Activity 2 Letter Formation Review—School Name

Provide lined paper to students.
Now we're going to practice writing our school's name.

Here's how you write our school's name.
Model writing (school's name) on the board (with your back to students).

Let's practice writing our school's name.
Guide students as they write (school's name) on their paper using a pencil.
Review as needed.

 Link letter names to letter sounds as they appear in the program as needed.

Part C: Comprehension Strategies

9 minutes

IWB

Student Materials:
Storybook

Sequence Events

Mental Images

Student Materials:
Storybook

Activity 1 Sequence and Retell the Story—An After-Reading Strategy

 Direct students to Lesson 146, pages 148 and 149, in *Storybook*.

Elicit responses to questions. **Guide** as needed.

Let's play "Put the Cards in the Right Order." I wrote the events on these cards. I will put them up on the board as I tell them to you. See whether you can put the cards in the right order.

The cat talked to the girl.

A girl went to the park with her cat.

Lesson 147   **595**

The girl was sad because the cat did not talk.

I'll read the events again.
Reread events in the same order.
Oops! Those events are not in the right order.
Help me put them in the right order.

Guide students to help in rearranging cards on board in the right order.

Now we can retell the events because they're in the right order. Listen as I retell the events.

Model retelling events in the right order.

Assign student partners.
Your turn to tell the events in the right order to your partner. Then listen as your partner tells the events in the right order. Help each other if you get mixed up.
Monitor student partners as they retell events in the right order.

Activity 2 Comprehension Monitoring: Mental Imaging—A During-Reading Strategy

Elicit responses to questions. **Guide** as needed.
When good readers read stories, they make pictures in their minds of the words they are reading. Listen to how I make a picture in my mind when I read a sentence.

Model mental imaging for a sentence in story.

Elicit ideas from students for how to draw mental image on Mental Image organizer.

When you're reading a story, it's a good idea to make a picture in your mind of the words you're reading.

Activity 3 Establish Purpose for Reading—A Before-Reading Strategy

Elicit responses to questions. **Guide** as needed.
You know that when you read a story with characters, setting, and events that happen, you're reading narrative text. Narrative text is written to tell a story for you to enjoy. Why is narrative text written? (Idea: *To tell a story for you to enjoy.*)

The next story you'll read has characters, setting, and events that happen. Is that story narrative or expository text? *Narrative*

Why will you read that narrative text? (Idea: *To enjoy it.*)

596 *Lesson 147*

Lesson 148

Materials

Teacher: *Storybook;* IWB-Sequence Events or write 3 main events on 3 large index cards; 7-Mental Images; 1-Phonemic Awareness; 3 manipulatives such as blocks, discs, chips, counters (if not using IWB)

Student: Lined paper; *Storybook;* copy of 7-Mental Images; copy of 1-Phonemic Awareness; 3 manipulatives such as blocks, discs, chips, counters

Part A: Phonemic and Phonological Awareness

5 minutes

Teacher Materials:
Phonemic Awareness

3 manipulatives such as blocks, discs, chips, counters

Student Materials:
Phonemic Awareness

3 manipulatives such as blocks, discs, chips, counters

Activity 1 Phoneme Blending

Elicit responses. **Guide** as needed.
Let's put some sounds together and make words. I'm going to say a word very slowly so you can hear each sound. You need to listen carefully and say the sounds. Then we'll put the sounds together and say the word.

My turn. Listen. **/rrr/ /āāā/ /sss/.**
Say the sounds. /rrr/ /āāā/ /sss/.
Again, say the sounds. /rrr/ /āāā/ /sss/.
Let's put it together. What word? *Race.*

My turn. Listen. **/rrr/ /aaa/ /t/.**
Say the sounds. /rrr/ /aaa/ /t/.
Again, say the sounds. /rrr/ /aaa/ /t/.
Let's put it together. What word? *Rat.*

(Continue the activity with the following words:
read [rrr-ēēē-d], red [rrr-eee-d], ride [rrr-īīī-d], rib [rrr-iii-b], road [rrr-ōōō-d], rock [rrr-ooo-k], row [rrr-ōōō], rug [rrr-uuu-g].)

Activity 2 Phoneme Segmentation

Show Phonemic Awareness. **Elicit** responses. **Guide** chip placement as needed.
Let's use our chips to show how many sounds there are in a word. For each sound in the word, we'll push one chip up to the arrow on the page. When we finish, we'll read the whole word.

Model use of the chips by moving the chips to the arrow for each word and then back to the bottom when finished. **Remind** students that each chip represents one phoneme.
Listen. I can say a word and move a chip for each sound in the word.
An. /aaa/ /nnn/. An. Your turn. Say the sounds you hear in **an,** and move a chip for each sound. /aaa/ /n/.

Move your finger back to the dot. What word? *An.*

How many chips did you move for the word **an?** *Two.*

Yes, you moved two chips, so there are two sounds in the word **an.**
Great job. Now move your chips back to the bottom, and let's try another one.

(Continue the activity with the following words: man, fan, eat, feet, seat.)

Lesson 148   **597**

6 minutes

Student Materials:
Lined paper

Part B: Letter Recognition and Formation

Activity 1 Letter Recognition—City Name

Write (name of city) on board. **Elicit** responses to questions. **Guide** as needed.
You've learned all the letters and capital letters. You've also learned how to write our school's name. Now we're going to learn to write the name of our city.

Point to (name of city).
The name of our city is _____.

What's the name of our city? (Student response.)

Good. The name of our city is _____.

Now I'm going to point to each letter or capital letter in our city's name. I want you to tell me the letter or capital letter. Ready?
Point to each letter or capital letter in (city's name).

Activity 2 Letter Formation—City Name

Provide lined paper to students.
Now we're going to practice writing our city's name.

Here's how you write our city's name.
Model writing (city's name) on the board (with your back to students).

Let's practice writing our city's name.
Guide students as they write (city's name) on their paper using a pencil.
Review as needed.

  Link letter names to letter sounds as they appear in the program as needed.

9 minutes

IWB

Teacher Materials:
Storybook
Sequence Events
Mental Images

Student Materials:
Storybook
Mental Images

Part C: Comprehension Strategies

Activity 1 Sequence and Retell the Story—An After-Reading Strategy

  Direct students to Lesson 147, pages 150–152, in *Storybook*.

Elicit responses to questions. **Guide** as needed.
Let's play "Put the Cards in the Right Order." I wrote the events on these cards. I'll put them up on the board as I tell them to you. See whether you can put the cards in the right order.

The cat and the girl talked and talked.

Ann left the park because the cat talked.

Ann came to the park and wanted the cat.

I'll read the events again.
Reread events in the same order.
Oops! Those events are not in the right order.
Help me put them in the right order.

Guide students to help in rearranging cards on board in the right order.

Now we can retell the events because they're in the right order.
Listen as I retell the events.
Model retelling events in the right order.

Assign student partners.
Your turn to tell the events in the right order to your partner. Then listen as your partner tells the events in the right order. Help each other if you get mixed up.

Monitor student partners as they retell events in the right order.

Activity 2 Comprehension Monitoring: Mental Imaging—A During-Reading Strategy

Elicit responses to questions. **Guide** as needed.
When good readers read stories, they make pictures in their minds of the words they're reading. Let's see whether you can make a picture in your mind when you read a sentence. Think about the sentence, "The girl and the cat talked and talked."

What pictures do you see in your mind when you read that sentence? (Student response.)
Guide students to make mental images for a sentence in story. **Guide** students to fill in Mental Image organizer.

When you are reading a story, it's a good idea to make a picture in your mind of the words you are reading.

Activity 3 Establish Purpose for Reading—A Before-Reading Strategy

Elicit responses to questions. **Guide** as needed.
You know that when you read a story with characters, setting, and events that happen, you're reading narrative text. Narrative text is written to tell a story for you to enjoy. Why is narrative text written? (Idea: *To tell a story for you to enjoy.*)

The next story you will read has characters, setting, and events that happen. Is that story narrative or expository text? *Narrative.*

Why will you read that narrative story? (Idea: *To enjoy it.*)

Lesson 148 **599**

Lesson 149

Materials

Teacher: *Storybook;* IWB-Sequence Events or write 3 main events on 3 large index cards; 7-Mental Images; 1-Phonemic Awareness; 3 manipulatives such as blocks, discs, chips, counters (if not using IWB)

Student: Lined paper; copy of 7-Mental Images; *Storybook;* copy of 1-Phonemic Awareness; 3 manipulatives such as blocks, discs, chips, counters

Part A: Phonemic and Phonological Awareness

5 minutes

Teacher Materials:
Phonemic Awareness

3 manipulatives such as blocks, discs, chips, counters

Student Materials:
Phonemic Awareness

3 manipulatives such as blocks, discs, chips, counters

Activity 1 Phoneme Blending

Elicit responses. **Guide** as needed.
Let's put some sounds together and make words. I'm going to say a word very slowly so you can hear each sound. You need to listen carefully and say the sounds. Then we'll put the sounds together and say the word.

My turn. Listen. **/d/ /āāā/ /t/.**
Say the sounds. /d/ /āāā/ /t/.
Again, say the sounds. /d/ /āāā/ /t/.
Let's put it together. What word? *Date.*

My turn. Listen. **/d/ /aaa/ /shshsh/.**
Say the sounds. /d/ /aaa/ /shshsh/.
Again, say the sounds. **/d/ /aaa/ /shshsh/.**
Let's put it together. What word? *Dash.*

(Continue the activity with the following words:
deep [d-ēēē-p], deck [d-eee-k], dime [d-īīī-mmm], ditch [d-iii-ch], dove [d-ōōō-vvv], doll [d-ooo-lll], dough [d-ōōō], duck [d-uuu-k].)

Activity 2 Phoneme Segmentation

Show Phonemic Awareness. **Elicit** responses. **Guide** chip placement as needed.
Let's use our chips to show how many sounds there are in a word. For each sound in the word, we'll push one chip up to the arrow on the page. When we finish, we'll read the whole word.

Model use of the chips by moving the chips to the arrow for each word and then back to the bottom when finished. **Remind** students that each chip represents one phoneme.
Listen. I can say a word and move a chip for each sound in the word.
Am. /aaa/ /mmm/. Am. Your turn. Say the sounds you hear in **am,** and move a chip for each sound. /aaa/ /mmm/.

Move your finger back to the dot. What word? *Am.*

How many chips did you move for the word **am?** *Two.*

Yes, you moved two chips, so there are two sounds in the word **am.**
Great job. Now move your chips back to the bottom, and let's try another one.

(Continue the activity with the following words: ram, sam, ice, nice, mice.)

600   Lesson 149

Part B: Letter Recognition and Formation

6 minutes

Student Materials:
Lined paper

Activity 1 Letter Recognition Review—City Name

Write (name of city) on board. **Elicit** responses to questions. **Guide** as needed.
You've learned how to write the name of our city.

Point to (name of city).
The name of our city is _____.

What's the name of our city? (Student response.)

Now I'm going to point to each letter or capital letter in our city's name. I want you to tell me the letter or capital letter. Ready?
Point to each letter or capital letter in (city's name).

Activity 2 Letter Formation Review—City Name

Provide lined paper to students.
Now we're going to practice writing our city's name.

Here's how you write our city's name.
Model writing (city's name) on the board (with your back to students).

Let's practice writing our city's name.
Guide students as they write (city's name) on their paper using a pencil.
Review as needed.

 Link letter names to letter sounds as they appear in the program as needed.

Part C: Comprehension Strategies

9 minutes

Teacher Materials:
Storybook
Sequence Events
Mental Images

Student Materials:
Storybook
Mental Images

Activity 1 Sequence and Retell the Story—An After-Reading Strategy

 Direct students to Lesson 148, pages 153–155, in *Storybook*.

Elicit responses to questions. **Guide** as needed.
Let's play "Put the Cards in the Right Order." I wrote the events on these cards. I will put them up on the board as I tell them to you. See whether you can put the cards in the right order.

The moon cow jumped in the pool.

The girl went swimming with the moon cow.

Some girls went to the moon in a moon ship.

I'll read the events again.
Reread events in the same order.

Lesson 149   601

Oops! Those events are not in the right order.
Put them in the right order.

Monitor students as they rearrange cards on board in the right order.

Assign student partners.
Now you can retell the events because they're in the right order. Your turn to tell the events in the right order to your partner. Then listen as your partner tells the events in the right order. Help each other if you get mixed up.
Monitor student partners as they retell events in the right order.

Activity 2 Comprehension Monitoring: Mental Imaging—A During-Reading Strategy

Elicit responses to questions. **Guide** as needed.
When good readers read stories, they make pictures in their minds of the words they're reading. Let's see whether you can make a picture in your mind when you read a sentence. Think about the sentence, "The girl went with the moon cow to a pool."

What pictures do you see in your mind when you read that sentence? (Student response.)

Guide students to make mental images for a sentence in story and fill in Mental Image organizer.

When you're reading a story, it is a good idea to make a picture in your mind of the words you are reading.

Activity 3 Establish Purpose for Reading—A Before-Reading Strategy

Elicit responses to questions. **Guide** as needed.
You know that when you read a story with characters, setting, and events that happen, you are reading narrative text. Narrative text is written to tell a story for you to enjoy. Why is narrative text written? (Idea: *To tell a story for you to enjoy.*)

The next story you will read has characters, setting, and events that happen. Is that story narrative or expository text? *Narrative.*

Why will you read that narrative story? (Idea: *To enjoy it.*)

602 *Lesson 149*

Lesson 150

Materials

Teacher: *Storybook;* IWB-Sequence Events or write 3 main events on 3 large index cards; 7-Mental Images; 1-Phonemic Awareness; 3 manipulatives such as blocks, discs, chips, counters (if not using IWB); Letter Recognition

Student: Lined paper; *Storybook;* copy of 7-Mental Images; copy of 1-Phonemic Awareness; 3 manipulatives such as blocks, discs, chips, counters

5 minutes

Part A: Phonemic and Phonological Awareness

Teacher Materials:
Phonemic Awareness

3 manipulatives such as blocks, discs, chips, counters

Student Materials:
Phonemic Awareness

3 manipulatives such as blocks, discs, chips, counters

Activity 1 Phoneme Blending

Elicit responses. **Guide** as needed.
Let's put some sounds together and make words. I'm going to say a word very slowly so you can hear each sound. You need to listen carefully and say the sounds. Then we'll put the sounds together and say the word.

My turn. Listen. **/fff/ /āāā/ /sss/.**
Say the sounds. /fff/ /āāā/ /sss/.
Again, say the sounds. /fff/ /āāā/ /sss/.
Let's put it together. What word? *Face.*

My turn. Listen. **/fff/ /aaa/ /t/.**
Say the sounds. /fff/ /aaa/ /t/.
Again, say the sounds. /fff/ /aaa/ /t/.
Let's put it together. What word? *Fat.*

(Continue the activity with the following words:
feet [fff-ēēē-t], fed [fff-eee-d], fight [fff-īīī-t], fill [fff-iii-lll], foam [fff-ōōō-mmm], fog [fff-ooo-g], food [fff-oooooo-d], fun [fff-uuu-nnn].)

Activity 2 Phoneme Segmentation

Show Phonemic Awareness. **Elicit** responses. **Guide** chip placement as needed.
Let's use our chips to show how many sounds there are in a word. For each sound in the word, we'll push one chip up to the arrow on the page. When we finish, we'll read the whole word.

Model use of the chips by moving the chips to the arrow for each word and then back to the bottom when finished.
Listen. I can say a word and move a chip for each sound in the word.
Add. /aaa/ /d/. Add. Your turn. Say the sounds you hear in **add,** and move a chip for each sound. */aaa/ /d/.*

Lesson 150   **603**

Move your finger back to the dot. What word? *Add.*

How many chips did you move for the word **add?** *Two.*

Yes, you moved two chips, so there are two sounds in the word **add.**
Great job. Now move your chips back to the bottom, and let's try another one.

(Continue the activity with the following words: mad, sad, ate, late, wait.)

Part B: Letter Recognition and Formation

6 minutes

Teacher Materials:
Letter Recognition

Student Materials:
Lined paper

Activity 1 — Letter Recognition Cumulative Review—q/Q, z/Z, school's name, city's name

Display on IWB or **write** letters and capitals and (school) and (city) names on the board in the order shown. **Elicit** responses to questions. **Guide** as needed.

This week you've learned how to put letters and capital letters together to form the names of our school and city. Let's review some letters and capital letters you've learned. Are you ready?

Letter	Question	Student Response
Q	What letter?	Capital Q.
(school's name)	(Repeat for each letter:) What letter?	(Appropriate letters.)
z	What letter?	z.
(city's name)	(Repeat for each letter:) What letter?	(Appropriate letters.)
q	What letter?	q.
Z	What letter?	Capital Z.

Review as needed.

Activity 2 — Letter Formation Cumulative Review—q/Q, z/Z, school's name, city's name

Write letters and capitals and (school) and (city) names on the board in the order shown. **Provide** lined paper to students.

Show me how you can write these letters and capitals.

Guide students as they write the letters and capitals on their paper. **Review** as needed.

 Link letter names to letter sounds as they appear in the program as needed.

604   Lesson 150

9 minutes

IWB

Teacher Materials:
Storybook

Sequence Events

Mental Images

Student Materials:
Storybook

Mental Images

Part C: Comprehension Strategies

Activity 1 Sequence and Retell the Story—An After-Reading Strategy

 Direct students to Lesson 149, pages 156–158, in *Storybook*.

Elicit responses to questions. **Guide** as needed.
Let's play "Put the Cards in the Right Order." I wrote the events on these cards. I'll put them up on the board as I tell them to you. See whether you can put the cards in the right order.

The big man made the car start.

The man asked the big man to start the car.

A man had a car that would not start.

I'll read the events again.
Reread events in the same order.
Oops! Those events are not in the right order.
Put them in the right order.

Monitor students as they rearrange cards on board in the right order.

Assign student partners.
Now you can retell the events because they're in the right order. Your turn to tell the events in the right order to your partner. Then listen as your partner tells the events in the right order. Help each other if you get mixed up.

Tell me the events in the right order for the whole class. (**Student response.**)
Monitor student partners as they retell events in the right order.

Activity 2 Comprehension Monitoring: Mental Imaging—A During-Reading Strategy

Elicit responses to questions. **Guide** as needed.
When good readers read stories, they make pictures in their minds of the words they are reading. Let's see whether you can make a picture in your mind when you read a sentence. Think about the sentence, "The man had an old car."

Tell your partner the picture you see in your mind when you read that sentence. (**Student response.**)

Monitor students as they tell mental images for a sentence in story to each other and fill in Mental Image organizer.

Assign partners. **Guide** as needed.
Now share your chart with your partner and add suggestions to make your neighbor's writing better if you think it needs it.

When you're reading a story, it is a good idea to make a picture in your mind of the words you're reading.

Lesson 150 **605**

Activity 3 Establish Purpose for Reading—A Before-Reading Strategy

 Direct students to Lesson 150, pages 31–33, in *Storybook*.

Elicit responses to questions. **Guide** as needed.

Look at the story on page 31. Do you think that story is narrative or expository text? *Narrative.*

Why do you think it is narrative text? (Idea: *It has characters, setting and events that happen.*)

So why will you read this narrative story? (Idea: *To enjoy it.*)

Lesson 151

Materials

Teacher: *Storybook*; 5-Story Map; 1-Phonemic Awareness; 3 manipulatives such as blocks, discs, chips, counters (if not using IWB)

Student: Lined paper; copy of 5-Story Map; *Storybook*; copy of 1-Phonemic Awareness; 3 manipulatives such as blocks, discs, chips, counters

Part A: Phonemic and Phonological Awareness

5 minutes

Teacher Materials:
Phonemic Awareness

3 manipulatives such as blocks, discs, chips, counters

Student Materials:
Phonemic Awareness

3 manipulatives such as blocks, discs, chips, counters

Activity 1 Phoneme Blending

Elicit responses. **Guide** as needed.
Let's put some sounds together and make words. I'm going to say a word very slowly so you can hear each sound. You need to listen carefully and say the sounds. Then we'll put the sounds together and say the word. Listen for some longer words today.

My turn. Listen. **/t/ /āāā/ /sss/ /t/.**
Say the sounds. /t/ /āāā/ /sss/ /t/.
Again, say the sounds. /t/ /āāā/ /sss/ /t/.
Let's put it together. What word? *Taste.*

My turn. Listen. **/t/ /aaa/ /p/.**
Say the sounds. /t/ /aaa/ /p/.
Again, say the sounds. /t/ /aaa/ /p/.
Let's put it together. What word? *Tap.*

(Continue the activity with the following words:
team [t-ēēē-mmm], ten [t-eee-nnn], tiny [t-īīī-nnn-ēēē], tip [t-iii-p], toad [t-ōōō-d], top [t-ooo-p], town [t-ow-nnn], tug [t-uuu-g].)

Activity 2 Phoneme Segmentation

Show Phonemic Awareness. **Elicit** responses. **Guide** as needed.
Let's use our chips to show how many sounds there are in a word. For each sound in the word, you'll push one chip up to the arrow on the page. When we finish, we'll read the whole word.

Model use of the chips by moving the chips to the arrow for each word and then back to the bottom when finished.
Your turn. Say the sounds you hear in **sack,** and move a chip for each sound. /sss/ /aaa/ /k/.

Move your finger back to the dot. What word? *Sack.*

How many chips did you move for the word **sack?** *Three.*

Lesson 151   607

Yes, you moved three chips. So how many **sounds** are in the word **sack?** *Three.*

Excellent. Now move your chips back to the bottom, and let's try another one.

(Continue the activity with the following words: back, pack, shack, tack, meat, beat, heat, sheet.)

6 minutes

Student Materials:
Lined paper

Part B: Letter Recognition and Formation

Activity 1 Letter Recognition—State Name

Write (name of state) on board. **Elicit** responses to questions. **Guide** as needed.
You've learned all the letters and capital letters. You've also learned how to write our school's name and our city's name. Now we're going to learn to write the name of our state.

Point to (name of state).
The name of our state is _____.

What's the name of our state? (Student response.)

Good. The name of our state is _____.

Now I'm going to point to each letter or capital letter in our state's name. I want you to tell me the letter or capital letter. Ready?
Point to each letter or capital letter in (state's name).

Activity 2 Letter Formation—State Name

Provide lined paper to students.
Now we're going to practice writing our state's name.

Here's how you write our state's name.
Model writing (state's name) on the board (with your back to students).

Let's practice writing our state's name.
Guide students as they write (state's name) on their paper using a pencil.
Review as needed.

Link letter names to letter sounds as they appear in the program as needed.

Set up a writing center with writing materials and correct models of letters learned so far for students to use in their free time.

608   Lesson 151

Part C: Comprehension Strategies

9 minutes

Student Materials:
Storybook
Story Map

Student Materials:
Storybook
Story Map
lined paper

Activity 1 Identify Story Elements and Retell the Story—An After-Reading Strategy

 Direct students to Lesson 150, pages 159–161, in *Storybook*.

Elicit responses to questions. **Guide** as needed.
Today we will work together to fill in all the parts of a Story Map for the story you read in the last lesson. Look at the story on pages 159–161.

Model filling in Story Map. **Monitor** students as they copy on their Story Maps.
What's the title of the story? *"The Old Man Finds a Horse."*

Let's copy the title at the top of our maps.

Who are the main characters in the story? *The old horse and the old man.*

Let's write their names in the box for characters.

What's the setting of the story? *A barn.*

Let's write that in the box for setting.

What happened first in the story? (**Idea:** *The old horse wanted a man to ride on him.*)

Let's draw a quick sketch of that event in the box for Beginning.

What happened next in the story? (**Idea:** *An old man wanted a horse to ride.*)

Let's draw a quick sketch of that event in the box for Middle.

What happened last in the story? (**Idea:** *The man and the horse went riding.*)

Let's draw a quick sketch of that event in the box for End.

Now listen as I retell the story to you from the words and pictures on my Story Map.

Model retelling story by using the Story Map to remind you of parts.

Lesson 151 **609**

Activity 2 Comprehension Monitoring: Reread—A During-Reading Strategy

When you read, you need to understand what you're reading. You read to learn or to enjoy a story but you have to understand what you are reading. One of the things you should do while you're reading is to be thinking, "Does this make sense?"

Let me show you what I mean.

Model think-aloud for rereading text.

Sample Wording for Think-Aloud

I'm reading on the second page of the story. (**Read aloud second line on page 160.**) Stop. That did not make sense to me. Who is in the barn? I'll stop and reread the last paragraph again. (**Reread paragraph.**) Okay. Now it makes sense. The horse is in the barn. Now I can go on and read some more.

When what you are reading does not make sense, stop and reread to help you understand the story.

Activity 3 Activate Background Knowledge—A Before-Reading Strategy

Elicit responses to questions. **Guide** as needed.
In the next story, you'll read about going fishing. Tell me what you know about fishing. (**Student response.**)

Write a sentence that tells me what you know about going fishing.

When you connect what you know to the story you'll read, you'll better understand the story.

610 *Lesson 151*

Lesson 152

Materials

Teacher: *Storybook;* 5-Story Map; 1-Phonemic Awareness; 3 manipulatives such as blocks, discs, chips, counters (if not using IWB)

Student: Lined paper; copy of 5-Story Map for each set of student partners; *Storybook;* copy of 1-Phonemic Awareness; 3 manipulatives such as blocks, discs, chips, counters

Part A: Phonemic and Phonological Awareness

5 minutes

Teacher Materials:
Phonemic Awareness

3 manipulatives such as blocks, discs, chips, counters

Student Materials:
Phonemic Awareness

3 manipulatives such as blocks, discs, chips, counters

Activity 1 Phoneme Blending

Elicit responses. **Guide** as needed.
Let's put some sounds together and make words. I'm going to say a word very slowly so you can hear each sound. You need to listen carefully and say the sounds. Then we'll put the sounds together and say the word. Listen for some longer words today.

My turn. Listen. **/nnn/ /āāā/ /mmm/.**
Say the sounds. */nnn/ /āāā/ /mmm/.*
Again, say the sounds. */nnn/ /āāā/ /mmm/.*
Let's put it together. What word? *Name.*

My turn. Listen. **/nnn/ /aaa/ /p/.**
Say the sounds. */nnn/ /aaa/ /p/.*
Again, say the sounds. */nnn/ /aaa/ /p/.*
Let's put it together. What word? *Nap.*

(Continue the activity with the following words:
needle [nnn-ēēē-d-lll], near [nnn- ēēē-rrr], nest [nnn-eee-sss-t], nice [nnn-īīī-sss], nibble [nnn-iii-b-lll], note [nnn-ōōō-t], nod [nnn-ooo-d], nut [nnn-uuu-t].)

Activity 2 Phoneme Segmentation

Show Phonemic Awareness. **Elicit** responses. **Guide** as needed.
Let's use our chips to show how many sounds there are in a word. For each sound in the word, you'll push one chip up to the arrow on the page. When we finish, we'll read the whole word.

Your turn. Say the sounds you hear in **sick,** and move a chip for each sound. */sss/ /iii/ /k/.*

Move your finger back to the dot. What word? *Sick.*

How many **sounds** are in the word **sick?** *Three.*

Correct. Now move your chips back to the bottom, and let's try another one.

(Continue the activity with the following words: kick, lick, chick, thick, phone, bone, cone, tone, zone.)

6 minutes

Student Materials:
Lined paper

Part B: Letter Recognition and Formation

Activity 1 Letter Recognition Review—State Name

Write (name of state) on board. **Elicit** responses to questions. **Guide** as needed.
You've learned how to write the name of our state.
Point to (name of state).

The name of our state is _____.

What's the name of our state? (Student response.)

Now I'm going to point to each letter or capital letter in our state's name. I want you to tell me the letter or capital letter. Ready?
Point to each letter or capital letter in (state's name).

Activity 2 Letter Formation Review—State Name

Provide lined paper to students.
Now we're going to practice writing our state's name.

Here's how you write our state's name.
Model writing (state's name) on the board (with your back to students).

Let's practice writing our state's name.
Guide students as they write (state's name) on their paper using a pencil.
Review as needed.

 Link letter names to letter sounds as they appear in the program as needed.

9 minutes

Teacher Materials:
Storybook

Story Map

Student Materials:
Storybook

Story Map

Part C: Comprehension Strategies

Activity 1 Identify Story Elements and Retell the Story—An After-Reading Strategy

 Assign student partners. **Direct** students to Lesson 151, page 162, in *Storybook*.

Elicit responses to questions. **Guide** as needed.
Today you'll work with a partner to fill in all the parts of a Story Map for the story you read in the last lesson. Look at the story on page 162. Work with your partner to write the title, names of characters, and setting in the correct boxes. Then draw pictures for the beginning, the middle and the end of the story.

Monitor student partners as they complete their Story Maps.
Now let's check what you put on your Story Map.
Complete your Story Map as students tell you answers.

What's the title of the story? *"Bill Went Fishing."*

Who's the main character in the story? *Bill.*

612 Lesson 152

What's the setting of the story? *A lake or river.*

What picture did you draw for what happened first in the story? (Idea: *Bill did not get fish when he was fishing.*)

What picture did you draw for what happened next in the story? (Idea: *The other boys got fish.*)

What picture did you draw for what happened last in the story? (Idea: *Bill had a tug on his line.*)

Now let's retell the story from the words and pictures on our Story Map. I'll tell the first part about the title, characters, and setting. Then you can tell your partner the events that happened in order.

Guide retelling story by using Story Map to remind you of parts. Retell first part and allow student partners to tell each other events in order.

Activity 2 Comprehension Monitoring: Reread—A During-Reading Strategy

Elicit responses to questions. **Guide** as needed.

When you read, you need to understand what you are reading. You read to learn or to enjoy a story, but you have to understand what you're reading. One of the things you should do while you are reading is to be thinking, "Does this make sense?"

Let me show you what I mean.

Model rereading text for meaning.

When what you're reading does not make sense, stop and reread part of the story to help you understand what you are reading.

What should you do when you don't understand what you're reading? (Idea: *Reread part of the story.*)

Activity 3 Activate Background Knowledge—A Before-Reading Strategy

Elicit responses to questions. **Guide** as needed.

In the next story, you'll read about finding gold.

Tell me what you know about finding gold? (Student response.)

When you connect what you know to the story you'll read, you will better understand the story.

Lesson 152   **613**

Lesson 153

Materials

Teacher: *Storybook;* 5-Story Map; 1-Phonemic Awareness; 3 manipulatives such as blocks, discs, chips, counters (if not using IWB)

Student: Lined paper; copy of 5-Story Map with writing lines; *Storybook;* copy of 1-Phonemic Awareness; 3 manipulatives such as blocks, discs, chips, counters

Part A: Phonemic and Phonological Awareness

5 minutes

Teacher Materials:
Phonemic Awareness

3 manipulatives such as blocks, discs, chips, counters

Student Materials:
Phonemic Awareness

3 manipulatives such as blocks, discs, chips, counters

Activity 1 Phoneme Blending

Elicit responses. **Guide** as needed.
Let's put some sounds together and make words. I'm going to say a word very slowly so you can hear each sound. You need to listen carefully and say the sounds. Then we'll put the sounds together and say the word. Listen for some longer words today.

My turn. Listen. **/k/ /āāā/ /j/.**
Say the sounds. /k/ /āāā/ /j/.
Again, say the sounds. /k/ /āāā/ /j/.
Let's put it together. What word? *Cage.*

My turn. Listen. **/k/ /aaa/ /mmm/ /p/.**
Say the sounds. /k/ /aaa/ /mmm/ /p/.
Again, say the sounds. /k/ /aaa/ /mmm/ /p/.
Let's put it together. What word? *Camp.*

(Continue the activity with the following words:
cattle [k-aaa-t-lll], coast [k-ōōō-sss-t], comb [k-ōōō-mmm], cow [k-ow], kiss [k-iii-sss], kind [k-īīī-nnn-d], key [k-ēēē], cozy [k-ōōō-zzz-ēēē].)

Activity 2 Phoneme Segmentation

Show Phonemic Awareness. **Elicit** responses. **Guide** as needed.
Let's use our chips to show how many sounds there are in a word. For each sound in the word, you'll push one chip up to the arrow on the page. When we finish, we'll read the whole word.

Your turn. Say the sounds you hear in **dog,** and move a chip for each sound. /d/ /ooo/ /g/.

Move your finger back to the dot. What word? *Dog.*

How many **sounds** are in the word **dog?** *Three.*

Correct. Now move your chips back to the bottom, and let's try another one.

(Continue the activity with the following words: fog, log, jog, hog, five, live, hive, dive.)

614 Lesson 153

6 minutes

Student Materials:
Lined paper

Part B: Letter Recognition and Formation

Activity 1 Letter Recognition—United States

Write United States on board. **Elicit** responses to questions. **Guide** as needed.
You've learned all the letters and capital letters. You've also learned how to write our school's name, our city's name, and our state's name. Now we're going to learn to write the name of our country.

Point to United States.
The name of our country is the **United States.**

What's the name of our country? *The United States.*

Good. The name of our country is the **United States.**

Now I'm going to point to each letter or capital letter in **United States.**
I want you to tell me the letter or capital letter. Ready?
Point to each letter or capital letter in United States.

Activity 2 Letter Formation—United States

Provide lined paper to students.
Now we're going to practice writing **United States.**

Here's how you write **United States.**
Model writing United States on the board (with your back to students).

Let's practice writing **United States.**
Guide students as they write United States on their paper using a pencil.
Review as needed.

 Link letter names to letter sounds as they appear in the program as needed.

9 minutes

Teacher Materials:
Storybook

Story Map

Student Materials:
Storybook

Story Map

Part C: Comprehension Strategies

Activity 1 Identify Story Elements and Retell the Story—An After-Reading Strategy

 Assign student partners. **Direct** students to Lesson 152, pages 163–167, in *Storybook*.

Elicit responses to questions. **Guide** as needed.
Today you'll work with a partner to fill in all the parts of a Story Map for the story you read in the last lesson. Look at the story on pages 163–167. Work with your partner to write the title, names of characters, and setting in the correct boxes. Then write sentences for the beginning, the middle, and the end of the story. Add suggestions to make your neighbor's writing better if you think it needs it.

Monitor student partners as they complete their Story Maps.

Lesson 153   **615**

Now let's check what you put on your Story Map.
Complete your Story Map as students tell you answers.

What's the title of the story? *"Bill Went Fishing."*

Who's the main character in the story? *Bill.*

What's the setting of the story? *A lake or river.*

What picture did you draw for what happened first in the story? (Idea: *Bill had a tug on his line.*)

What picture did you draw for what happened next in the story? (Idea: *Bill pulled in an old box and was sad.*)

What picture did you draw for what happened last in the story? (Idea: *Bill had gold in his box and was happy.*)

Now retell the story from the words and pictures on your Story Map. One of you can retell the first part about the title, characters and setting. Then your partner can retell the events that happened in order. Decide who will go first, and then retell the story.
Guide student partners to retell story using Story Map as a guide.

Activity 2 Comprehension Monitoring: Reread—A During-Reading Strategy

Elicit responses to questions. **Guide** as needed.
When you read, you need to understand what you're reading. You might be reading to learn or you might be reading to enjoy a story, but you have to understand what you are reading. One of the things you should do while you are reading is to be thinking, "Does this make sense?" When what you're reading does not make sense, stop and reread part of the story to help you understand what you're reading.

What should you do when you don't understand what you're reading? (Idea: *Reread part of the story.*)

Activity 3 Activate Background Knowledge—A Before-Reading Strategy

Elicit responses to questions. **Guide** as needed.
In the next story, you'll read about an eagle. Tell me what you know about an eagle. (Student response.)

When you connect what you know to the story you'll read, you'll better understand the story.

616   *Lesson 153*

Lesson 154

Materials

Teacher: *Storybook*; 5-Story Map; 1-Phonemic Awareness; 3 manipulatives such as blocks, discs, chips, counters (if not using IWB)

Student: Lined paper; copy of 5-Story Map for each set of student partners; *Storybook*; copy of 1-Phonemic Awareness; 3 manipulatives such as blocks, discs, chips, counters

5 minutes

Teacher Materials:
Phonemic Awareness

3 manipulatives such as blocks, discs, chips, counters

Student Materials:
Phonemic Awareness

3 manipulatives such as blocks, discs, chips, counters

Part A: Phonemic and Phonological Awareness

Activity 1 Phoneme Blending

Elicit responses. **Guide** as needed.
Let's put some sounds together and make words. I'm going to say a word very slowly so you can hear each sound. You need to listen carefully and say the sounds. Then we'll put the sounds together and say the word. Listen for some longer words today.

My turn. Listen. **/h/ /āāā/ /lll/.**
Say the sounds. /h/ /āāā/ /lll/.
Again, say the sounds. /h/ /āāā/ /lll/.
Let's put it together. What word? *Hail.*

My turn. Listen. **/h/ /aaa/ /p/ /ēēē/.**
Say the sounds. /h/ /aaa/ /p/ /ēēē/.
Again, say the sounds. /h/ /aaa/ /p/ /ēēē/.
Let's put it together. What word? *Happy.*

(Continue the activity with the following words:
he [h-ēēē], head [h-eee-d], hive [h-īīī-vvv], hits [h-iii-t-sss], hope [h-ōōō-p], holly [h-ooo-lll-ēēē], hug [h-uuu-g], howl [h-ow-lll].)

Activity 2 Phoneme Segmentation

Show Phonemic Awareness. **Elicit** responses. **Guide** as needed.
Let's use our chips to show how many sounds there are in a word. For each sound in the word, you'll push one chip up to the arrow on the page. When we finish, we'll read the whole word.

Your turn. Say the sounds you hear in **sell,** and move a chip for each sound. /sss/ /eee/ /lll/.

Move your finger back to the dot. What word? *Sell.*

How many **sounds** are in the word **sell?** *Three.*

Correct. Now move your chips back to the bottom, and let's try another one.

(Continue the activity with the following words: bell, well, fell, shell, beep, jeep, keep, weep, sheep.)

Lesson 154   **617**

6 minutes

Student Materials:
Lined paper

Part B: Letter Recognition and Formation

Activity 1 Letter Recognition Review—United States

Write United States on board. **Elicit** responses to questions. **Guide** as needed.
You've learned how to write the name of our country.

Point to United States.
The name of our country is the **United States.**

What's the name of our country? *The United States.*

Now I'm going to point to each letter or capital letter in our country's name. I want you to tell me the letter or capital letter. Ready?
Point to each letter or capital letter in United States.

Activity 2 Letter Formation Review—United States

Provide lined paper to students.
Now we're going to practice writing **United States.**

Here's how you write **United States.**
Model writing United States on the board (with your back to students).

Let's practice writing **United States.**
Guide students as they write United States on their paper using a pencil.
Review as needed.

 Link letter names to letter sounds as they appear in the program as needed.

9 minutes

Teacher Materials:
Storybook
Story Map

Student Materials:
Storybook
Story Map

Part C: Comprehension Strategies

Activity 1 Identify Story Elements and Retell the Story—An After-Reading Strategy

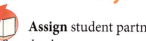 **Assign** student partners. **Direct** students to Lesson 153, pages 168–170, in *Storybook*.

Elicit responses to questions. **Guide** as needed.
Today you'll work with a partner to fill in all the parts of a Story Map for the story you read in the last lesson. Look at the story on pages 168–170. Work with your partner to write the title, names of characters, and setting in the correct boxes. Then write sentences for the beginning, the middle, and the end of the story. Add suggestions to make your neighbor's writing better if you think it needs it.

Monitor student partners as they complete their Story Maps.

Now let's check what you put on your Story Map.
Complete your Story Map as students tell you answers.
What's the title of the story? *"An Old Horse and An Eagle."*

Who are the main characters in the story? *The old horse and the eagle.*

618 Lesson 154

What's the setting of the story? *A hill.*

What picture did you draw for what happened first in the story?
(Idea: *The horse asked the eagle to teach him to fly.*)

What picture did you draw for what happened next in the story?
(Idea: *The eagle flew to the top of the barn.*)

What picture did you draw for what happened last in the story?
(Idea: *The horse ran into the side of the barn.*)

Now retell the whole story to your partner from the words and pictures on your Story Map. Then your partner can retell the whole story to you. Decide who will go first, and then retell the whole story.

Guide student partners to retell story using Story Map as a guide.

Activity 2 Comprehension Monitoring: Reread—A During-Reading Strategy

Elicit responses to questions. **Guide** as needed.
When you read, you need to understand what you're reading. You read to learn or to enjoy a story, but you have to understand what you are reading. One of the things you should do while you're reading is to be thinking, "Does this make sense?" When what you're reading does not make sense, stop and reread part of the story to help you understand what you're reading.

What should you do when you don't understand what you're reading?
(Idea: *Reread part of the story.*)

Activity 3 Activate Background Knowledge—A Before-Reading Strategy

Elicit responses to questions. **Guide** as needed.
In the next story, you'll read about riding on a horse. Tell me what you know about riding on a horse. (**Student response.**)

When you connect what you know to the story you'll read, you'll better understand the story.

Lesson 154   **619**

Lesson 155

Materials

Teacher: *Storybook*; 5-Story Map; 1-Phonemic Awareness; 3 manipulatives such as blocks, discs, chips, counters (if not using IWB); Letter Recognition

Student: Lined paper; copy of 5-Story Map; *Storybook*; copy of 1-Phonemic Awareness; 3 manipulatives such as blocks, discs, chips, counters

5 minutes

Teacher Materials:
Phonemic Awareness

3 manipulatives such as blocks, discs, chips, counters

Student Materials:
Phonemic Awareness

3 manipulatives such as blocks, discs, chips, counters

Part A: Phonemic and Phonological Awareness

Activity 1 Phoneme Blending

Elicit responses. **Guide** as needed.
Let's put some sounds together and make words. I'm going to say a word very slowly so you can hear each sound. You need to listen carefully and say the sounds. Then we'll put the sounds together and say the word. Listen for some longer words today.

My turn. Listen. **/ththth/ /iii/ /k/.**
Say the sounds. */ththth/ /iii/ /k/.*
Again, say the sounds. */ththth/ /iii/ /k/.*
Let's put it together. What word? *Thick.*

My turn. Listen. **/ththth/ /iririr/ /sss/ /t/.**
Say the sounds. */ththth/ /iririr/ /sss/ /t/.*
Again, say the sounds. */ththth/ /iririr/ /sss/ /t/.*
Let's put it together. What word? *Thirst.*

(Continue the activity with the following words:
theme [ththth-ēēē-mmm], thief [ththth-ēēē-fff], thin [ththth-iii-nnn], thumb [ththth-uuu-mmm], thorn [ththth-or-nnn], thud [ththth-uuu-d], thump [ththth-uuu-mmm-p].)

Activity 2 Phoneme Segmentation

Show Phonemic Awareness. **Elicit** responses. **Guide** as needed.
Let's use our chips to show how many sounds there are in a word. For each sound in the word, you'll push one chip up to the arrow on the page. When we finish, we'll read the whole word.

Your turn. Say the sounds you hear in **cut,** and move a chip for each sound. /c/ /uuu/ /t/.

Move your finger back to the dot. What word? *Cut.*

How many **sounds** are in the word **cut?** *Three.*

Correct. Now move your chips back to the bottom, and let's try another one.

(Continue the activity with the following words: hut, shut, rut, nut, mail, sail, tail, pail, nail.)

620 *Lesson 155*

6 minutes

Teacher Materials:
Letter Recognition

Student Materials:
Lined paper

Part B: Letter Recognition and Formation

Activity 1 Letter Recognition Cumulative Review—z/Z, (state name), United States

Display on IWB or **write** z, capital Z, (state's name) and United States on the board in the order shown. **Elicit** responses to questions. **Guide** as needed.

This week you've how to put letters and capital letters together to form the names of our state and country. Let's review some letters and capital letters you've learned. Are you ready?

Letter	Question	Student Response
(state's name)	(Repeat for each letter:) What letter?	(Appropriate letters.)
Z	What letter?	Capital Z.
z	What letter?	z.
United States	(Repeat for each letter:) What letter?	U-n-i-t-e-d S-t-a-t-e-s.

Review as needed.

Activity 2 Letter Formation Cumulative Review—z/Z, (state's name), United States

Write (state's name) and United States on the board. **Provide** lined paper to students.

Show me how you can write these letters and capitals.
Guide students as they write the letters and capitals on their paper. **Review** as needed.

 Link letter names to letter sounds as they appear in the program as needed.

9 minutes

Teacher Materials:
Storybook

Story Map

Student Materials:
Storybook

Story Map

Lined paper

Part C: Comprehension Strategies

Activity 1 Identify Story Elements and Retell the Story—An After-Reading Strategy

 Direct students to Lesson 154, pages 171–173, in *Storybook*.

Elicit responses to questions. **Guide** as needed.
Today you'll work by yourself to fill in all the parts of a Story Map for the story you read in the last lesson. Look at the story on pages 171–173. Write the title, names of characters, and setting in the correct boxes. Then draw pictures for the beginning, the middle and the end of the story.

Monitor student as they complete their Story Maps.

Lesson 155   **621**

Now let's check what you put on your Story Map.
Complete your Story map as students tell you answers.

What's the title of the story? *"An Old Horse and An Eagle."*

Who are the main characters in the story? *The old horse and the eagle.*

What's the setting of the story? *A hill.*

What picture did you draw for what happened first in the story? (Idea: *The eagle flew to the top of a car.*)

What picture did you draw for what happened next in the story? (Idea: *The horse ran into the side of the car.*)

What picture did you draw for what happened last in the story? (Idea: *The horse ran with the eagle on his back.*)

Assign student partners.
Now retell the whole story to your partner from the words and pictures on your Story Map. Then your partner can retell the whole story to you. Decide who will go first, and then retell the whole story.
Monitor student partners as they retell story using Story Map as a guide.

Activity 2 Comprehension Monitoring: Reread—A During-Reading Strategy

Elicit responses to questions. **Guide** as needed.
When you read, you need to understand what you're reading. You read for different reasons, but you have to understand what you are reading. One of the things you should do while you are reading is to be thinking, "Does this make sense?" When what you're reading does not make sense, stop and reread part of the story to help you understand what you're reading.

What should you do when you don't understand what you're reading? (Idea: *Reread part of the story.*)

Activity 3 Activate Background Knowledge—A Before-Reading Strategy

Elicit responses to questions. **Guide** as needed.
In the next story, you'll read about brushing teeth. Tell me what you know about brushing teeth? (Student response.)

Write a sentence that tells me what you know about going fishing. If you need help, ask me.

When you connect what you know to the story you'll read, you'll better understand the story.

622   *Lesson 155*

Lesson 156

Materials

Teacher: *Storybook*; 1-Phonemic Awareness; 3 manipulatives such as blocks, discs, chips, counters (if not using IWB), 1-My Prediction Chart; Letter Recognition

Student: Lined paper; *Storybook*; copy of 1-Phonemic Awareness; 3 manipulatives such as blocks, discs, chips, counters

5 minutes

Part A: Phonemic and Phonological Awareness

Teacher Materials:
Phonemic Awareness

3 manipulatives such as blocks, discs, chips, counters

Student Materials:
Phonemic Awareness

3 manipulatives such as blocks, discs, chips, counters

Activity 1 Phoneme Blending

Elicit responses. **Guide** as needed.
Let's put some sounds together and make words. I'm going to say a word very slowly so you can hear each sound. You need to listen carefully and say the sounds. Then we'll put the sounds together and say the word.

My turn. Listen. **/g/ /āāā/ /mmm/.**
Say the sounds. /g/ /āāā/ /mmm/.
Again, say the sounds. /g/ /āāā/ /mmm/.
Let's put it together. What word? *Game.*

My turn. Listen. **/g/ /aaa/ /sss/.**
Say the sounds. /g/ /aaa/ /sss/.
Again, say the sounds. /g/ /aaa/ /sss/.
Let's put it together. What word? *Gas.*

(Continue the activity with the following words: geese [g-ēēē-sss], get [g-eee-t], gift [g-iii-fff-t], go [g-ōōō], got [g-ooo-t], gown [g-ow-nnn], guest [g-eee-sss-t], gum [g-uuu-mmm].)

Activity 2 Phoneme Segmentation

Show Phonemic Awareness. **Elicit** responses. **Guide** as needed.
Let's use our chips to show how many sounds there are in a word. For each sound in the word, you'll push one chip up to the arrow on the page. When we finish, we'll read the whole word.

Your turn. Say the sounds you hear in **map,** and move a chip for each sound. /mmm/ /aaa/ /p/.

Move your finger back to the dot. What word? *Map.*

How many **sounds** are in the word **map?** *Three.*

Correct. Now move your chips back to the bottom, and let's try another one.

(Continue the activity with the following words: rap, cap, tap, zap, side, ride, hide, wide, tide.)

Lesson 156   623

6 minutes

Teacher Materials:
Letter Recognition

Student Materials:
Lined paper

Part B: Letter Recognition and Formation

Activity 1 Letter Recognition Cumulative Review—a/A, m/M, s/S, e/E, r/R, d/D, (school's name)

Display on IWB or **write** letters and capitals and (school) and (city) names on the board in the order shown. **Elicit** responses to questions. **Guide** as needed.

You've learned all the letters and capital letters. You've also learned the names of our school, city, state, and country. Let's review some of the letters and capital letters you've learned. Are you ready?

Letter	Question	Student Response
E	What letter?	Capital E.
m	What letter?	m.
a	What letter?	a.
D	What letter?	Capital D.
R	What letter?	Capital R.
e	What letter?	e.
d	What letter?	d.
(school's name)	(Repeat for each letter:) What letter?	(Appropriate letters.)
S	What letter?	Capital S.
A	What letter?	Capital A.
r	What letter?	r.
M	What letter?	Capital M.
s	What letter?	s.

Review as needed.

Activity 2 Letter Formation Cumulative Review—a/A, m/M, s/S, e/E, r/R, d/D, school's name

Write a, capital A, m, capital M, s, capital S, e, capital E, r, capital R, d, capital D, and (school's name) on the board. **Provide** lined paper to students.

Show me how you can write these letters and capitals.

 Link letter names to letter sounds as they appear in the program as needed.

624   Lesson 156

Part C: Comprehension Strategies

9 minutes

Teacher Materials:
Storybook
My Prediction Chart

Student Materials:
Storybook

Activity 1 Summarize Narrative Text—An After-Reading Strategy

 Direct students to Lesson 155, pages 174–176, in *Storybook*.

When I want to summarize a story, I need to tell the most important part of the story and leave out the details. You have summarized a page of expository stories. Now we are going to summarize a narrative story.

Let me show you how I summarize a narrative story.

Model think-aloud for summarizing narrative.

> **Sample Wording for Think-Aloud**
>
> I want to summarize the story, "The Red Toothbrush." I want to tell only the most important parts in my own words. As I look at the story, I can see that there are lots of details, but I need to tell only the most important parts. I need to tell about the character and the main thing that happens. So I will say, "There was a girl with a red toothbrush who lost her toothbrush."

I summarized the story in my own words and I told the most important part of the story.

Activity 2 Comprehension Monitoring: Read with Prosody—A During-Reading Strategy

Elicit responses to questions. **Guide** as needed.
When you read stories, you will understand the story better if you read the story the right way. You need to look for the end marks of the sentences and take a little breath after each sentence. If you don't stop after each sentence, the story will not make sense.

Listen to me read the wrong way and see whether the story makes sense.

Model reading story for a few sentences in a monotone voice and run sentences together.

Was it easy to understand the story? **(Student response.)**

Now listen to me read the story the right way.
Model reading story with prosody.

Was it easier to understand the story?
Discuss difference between reading with or without prosody.

Remember that reading the story the right way will help you understand the story.

Lesson 156 **625**

Activity 3 Make Predictions—A Before-Reading Strategy

 Direct students to Lesson 156, pages 177–179, in *Storybook*.

Show My Prediction Chart. **Elicit** response to question. **Guide** as needed.
You have made predictions for stories before. Today you'll make a prediction for what the next story is about. When you make a prediction, you make a good guess.

What did you use before for clues to make a good guess? (**Idea:** *The title, the pictures and the cover.*)

Today you'll use clues from the title, the picture, and the story you already read to make a prediction about the next story.

After you read the title, look at the picture, and think of the story you read in the last lesson, what do you predict will happen in the next story? (**Student response.**)
Elicit prediction from student. **Record** prediction for Lesson 157.

As you read the next story, check to see whether your prediction is correct. Making and checking predictions helps you stay interested in the story you are reading.

Lesson 157

Materials

Teacher: *Storybook;* predictions recorded in Lesson 156; 1-Phonemic Awareness; 3 manipulatives such as blocks, discs, chips, counters (if not using IWB); 1-My Prediction Chart; Letter Recognition

Student: Lined paper; *Storybook;* copy of 1-Phonemic Awareness; 3 manipulatives such as blocks, discs, chips, counters

5 minutes

Teacher Materials:
Phonemic Awareness

3 manipulatives such as blocks, discs, chips, counters

Student Materials:
Phonemic Awareness

3 manipulatives such as blocks, discs, chips, counters

Part A: Phonemic and Phonological Awareness

Activity 1 Phoneme Blending

Elicit responses. **Guide** as needed.
Let's put some sounds together and make words. I'm going to say a word very slowly so you can hear each sound. You need to listen carefully and say the sounds. Then we'll put the sounds together and say the word.

My turn. Listen. **/lll/ /āāā/ /sss/.**
Say the sounds. /lll/ /āāā/ /sss/.
Again, say the sounds. /lll/ /āāā/ /sss/.
Let's put it together. What word? *Lace.*

My turn. Listen. **/lll/ /aaa/ /mmm/ /p/.**
Say the sounds. /lll/ /aaa/ /mmm/ /p/.
Again, say the sounds. /lll/ /aaa/ /mmm/ /p/.
Let's put it together. What word? *Lamp.*

(Continue the activity with the following words:
leaf [lll-ēēē-f], leg [lll-eee-g], life [lll-īīī-fff], lift [lll-iii-fff-t], lip [lll-iii-p], lost [lll-ooo-sss-t], loop [lll-oooooo-p], luck [lll-uuu-k].)

Activity 2 Phoneme Segmentation

Show Phonemic Awareness. **Elicit** responses. **Guide** as needed.
Let's use our chips to show how many sounds there are in a word. For each sound in the word, you'll push one chip up to the arrow on the page. When we finish, we'll read the whole word.

Your turn. Say the sounds you hear in **met,** and move a chip for each sound. /mmm/ /eee/ /t/.

Move your finger back to the dot. What word? *Met.*

How many **sounds** are in the word **met?** *Three.*

Correct. Now move your chips back to the bottom, and let's try another one.

(Continue the activity with the following words: jet, vet, pet, wet, nose, rose, those, hose, chose.)

Lesson 157   **627**

6 minutes

Teacher Materials:
Letter Recognition

Student Materials:
Lined paper

Part B: Letter Recognition and Formation

Activity 1 Letter Recognition Cumulative Review—f/F, i/I, t/T, n/N, c/C, o/O, (city's name)

Display on IWB or **write** letters, capitals and (city's name) on the board in the order shown. **Elicit** responses to questions. **Guide** as needed.

Let's review some of the other letters and capital letters you've learned. Are you ready?

Letter	Question	Student Response
c	What letter?	c.
f	What letter?	f.
i	What letter?	i.
(city's name)	(Repeat for each letter:) What letter?	(Appropriate letters.)
O	What letter?	Capital O.
T	What letter?	Capital T.
t	What letter?	t.
F	What letter?	Capital F.
n	What letter?	n.
C	What letter?	Capital C.
N	What letter?	Capital N.
o	What letter?	o.
I	What letter?	Capital I.

Review as needed.

Activity 2 Letter Formation Cumulative Review—f/F, i/I, t/T, n/N, c/C, o/O, (city's name)

Write f, capital F, i, capital I, t, capital T, n, capital N, c, capital C, o, capital O, and (city's name) on the board. **Provide** lined paper to students.

Show me how you can write these letters and capitals.

Guide students as they write the letters and capitals on their paper. **Review** as needed.

 Link letter names to letter sounds as they appear in the program as needed.

628   Lesson 157

Part C: Comprehension Strategies

9 minutes

Teacher Materials:
Storybook

My Prediction Chart

Student Materials:
Storybook

Activity 1 Confirm Predictions—An After-Reading Strategy

 Direct students to Lesson 156, pages 177–179, in *Storybook*.

Show My Prediction Chart. **Elicit** responses to questions. **Guide** as needed.
In the last lesson, you made a prediction. Let's check that prediction to see whether it is correct.

Discuss accuracy of predictions from Lesson 156.

Remember that it doesn't matter whether your prediction was correct. Just making and checking predictions as you read keeps you interested in what you are reading.

Activity 2 Summarize Narrative Text—An After-Reading Strategy

Elicit responses to questions. **Guide** as needed.
When I want to summarize a story, I need to tell the most important part of the story and leave out the details. You have summarized a page of expository stories. Now you're going to summarize a narrative story.

When you summarize, you should tell about the main character and only the important parts of the story.

What parts do you tell when you summarize? (Idea: *Tell about the main character and only the important parts of the story.*)

Guide students to summarize story.

Who are the main characters in the story? (Idea: *The girl and the dog.*)

What are the most important parts of the story? (Idea: *The dog had the toothbrush and he used the girl's toothbrush. Now they both have teeth that shine like the moon.*)

How can you put those ideas into a summary? (Idea: *The girl found her toothbrush when she found her dog using it. Now they both have shiny teeth.*)

You summarized the story in your own words, and you told the most important part of the story.

Lesson 157 **629**

Activity 3 Comprehension Monitoring: Read with Prosody—A During-Reading Strategy

Elicit responses to questions. **Guide** as needed.

When you read stories, you'll understand the story better if you read the story the right way. You need to look for the end marks of the sentences and take a little breath after each sentence. If you don't stop after each sentence, the story will not make sense.

Listen to me read the first page of the story the right way. Then we'll read the second page of the story together the right way by taking a little breath after each sentence.

Model reading first page of story with prosody.

Read second page of story with students to help them practice reading with prosody.

Remember that reading the story the right way will help you understand the story.

Lesson 158

Materials

Teacher: *Storybook*; 1-Phonemic Awareness; 3 manipulatives such as blocks, discs, chips, counters (if not using IWB), 1-My Prediction Chart; Letter Recognition

Student: Lined paper; *Storybook*; copy of 1-Phonemic Awareness; 3 manipulatives such as blocks, discs, chips, counters, Copy of 1-My Prediction Chart

5 minutes

Part A: Phonemic and Phonological Awareness

Teacher Materials:
Phonemic Awareness

3 manipulatives such as blocks, discs, chips, counters

Student Materials:
Phonemic Awareness

3 manipulatives such as blocks, discs, chips, counters

Activity 1 Phoneme Blending

Elicit responses. **Guide** as needed.
Let's put some sounds together and make words. I'm going to say a word very slowly so you can hear each sound. You need to listen carefully and say the sounds. Then we'll put the sounds together and say the word.

My turn. Listen. **/www/ /āāā/ /t/.**
Say the sounds. */www/ /āāā/ /t/.*
Again, say the sounds. */www/ /āāā/ /t/.*
Let's put it together. What word? *Wait.*

My turn. Listen. **/www/ /aaa/ /g/.**
Say the sounds. */www/ /aaa/ /g/.*
Again, say the sounds. */www/ /aaa/ /g/.*
Let's put it together. What word? *Wag.*

(Continue the activity with the following words:
week [www-ēēē-k], we [www-ēēē], west [www-eee-sss-t], went [www-eee-nnn-t], wish [www-iii-shshsh], will [www-iii-lll], wide [www- īīī -d], woke [www-ōōō-k].)

Activity 2 Phoneme Segmentation

Show Phonemic Awareness. **Elicit** responses. **Guide** chip placement as needed.
Let's use our chips to show how many sounds there are in a word. For each sound in the word, you'll push one chip up to the arrow on the page. When we finish, we'll read the whole word.

Your turn. Say the sounds you hear in **ship,** and move a chip for each sound. */shshsh/ /iii/ /p/.*

Move your finger back to the dot. What word? *Ship.*

How many **sounds** are in the word **ship?** *Three.*

Correct. Now move your chips back to the bottom, and let's try another one.

(Continue the activity with the following words: hip, chip, sip, tip, rake, cake, take, make, bake.)

Lesson 158   631

Part B: Letter Recognition and Formation

6 minutes

Teacher Materials: Letter Recognition

Student Materials: Lined paper

Activity 1 Letter Recognition Cumulative Review—h/H, u/U, g/G, l/L, w/W, k/K, v/V, (state's name)

Display on IWB or **write** letters, capitals and (state's name) on the board in the order shown. **Elicit** responses to questions. **Guide** as needed.

Let's review some of the other letters and capital letters you've learned. Are you ready?

Letter	Question	Student Response
L	What letter?	Capital L.
G	What letter?	Capital G.
W	What letter?	Capital W.
l	What letter?	l.
u	What letter?	u.
V	What letter?	Capital V.
w	What letter?	w.
H	What letter?	Capital H.
v	What letter?	v.
U	What letter?	Capital U.
k	What letter?	k.
h	What letter?	h.
(state's name)	(Repeat for each letter:) What letter?	(Appropriate letters.)
K	What letter?	Capital K.
g	What letter?	g.

Review as needed.

Activity 2 Letter Formation Cumulative Review— h/H, u/U, g/G, l/L, w/W, k/K, v/V, state's name

Write h, capital H, u, capital U, g, capital G, l, capital L, w, capital W, k, capital K, v, capital V, and (state's name) on the board. **Provide** lined paper to students.

Show me how you can write these letters and capitals.

Guide students as they write the letters and capitals on their paper. **Review** as needed.

 Link letter names to letter sounds as they appear in the program as needed.

632 Lesson 158

Part C: Comprehension Strategies

9 minutes

Teacher Materials:
Storybook

My Prediction Chart

Student Materials:
Storybook

My Prediction Chart

Activity 1 Summarize Narrative Text—An After-Reading Strategy

Direct students to Lesson 157, pages 180–182, in *Storybook*.

Elicit responses to questions. **Guide** as needed.
When I want to summarize a story, I need to tell the most important part of the story and leave out the details. When you summarize, you should tell about the main character and only the important parts of the story.

What parts do you tell when you summarize? (Idea: *Tell about the main character and only the important parts of the story.*)

Guide students to summarize story.

Who are the main characters in the story? (Idea: *The fat eagle, the little eagle and the tiger.*)

What are the most important parts of the story? (Idea: *The fat eagle was so fat he couldn't fly. A tiger came hunting for eagles while a little eagle was under a tree. The little eagle did not hear the eagles calling him.*)

How can you put those ideas into a summary? (Idea: *The little eagle was sitting under a tree when a tiger came hunting for him but nobody could help him.*)

You summarized the story in your own words, and you told the most important part of the story.

Activity 2 Comprehension Monitoring: Read with Prosody—A During-Reading Strategy

Elicit responses to questions. **Guide** as needed.
When you read stories, you will understand the story better if you read the story the right way. You need to look for the end marks of the sentences and take a little breath after each sentence. If you don't stop after each sentence, the story will not make sense.

Listen to me read the first page of the story the right way. Then we'll read the second page of the story together the right way by taking a little breath after each sentence.

Model reading first page of story with prosody.

Read second page of story with students to help them practice reading with prosody.

Remember that reading the story the right way will help you understand the story.

Lesson 158   **633**

Activity 3 Make Predictions—A Before-Reading Strategy

 Direct students to Lesson 158, pages 183–185, in *Storybook*.

Show My Prediction Chart and provide copies for students. **Elicit** response to question. **Guide** as needed.

You have made predictions for stories before. Today you'll make a prediction for what the next story is about.

When you make a prediction, you make a good guess.

Today you'll use clues from the title, the picture, and the story you already read to make a prediction about the next story.

After you read the title, look at the picture, and think of the story you read in the last lesson, what do you predict will happen in the next story? Fill in your Prediction Chart with the story title and your prediction

Elicit prediction from student. **Record** prediction for Lesson 159.

As you read the next story, check to see whether your prediction is correct. Making and checking predictions helps you stay interested in the story you are reading.

Lesson 159

Materials

Teacher: *Storybook;* 1-My Prediction Chart (from Lesson 158); 5-Story Map; 1-Phonemic Awareness; 3 manipulatives such as blocks, discs, chips, counters (if not using IWB); Letter Recognition

Student: Lined paper; Copy of 1-My Prediction Chart (from Lesson 158), copy of 5-Story Map; *Storybook;* copy of 1-Phonemic Awareness; 3 manipulatives such as blocks, discs, chips, counters

Part A: Phonemic and Phonological Awareness

5 minutes

Teacher Materials:
Phonemic Awareness

3 manipulatives such as blocks, discs, chips, counters

Student Materials:
Phonemic Awareness

3 manipulatives such as blocks, discs, chips, counters

Activity 1 Phoneme Blending

Elicit responses. **Guide** as needed.
Let's put some sounds together and make words. I'm going to say a word very slowly so you can hear each sound. You need to listen carefully and say the sounds. Then we'll put the sounds together and say the word.

My turn. Listen. **/shshsh/ /āāā/ /p/.**
Say the sounds. /shshsh/ /āāā/ /p/.
Again, say the sounds. /shshsh/ /āāā/ /p/.
Let's put it together. What word? *Shape.*

My turn. Listen. **/shshsh/ /aaa/ /d/ /ōōō/.**
Say the sounds. /shshsh/ /aaa/ /d/ /ōōō/.
Again, say the sounds. /shshsh/ /aaa/ /d/ /ōōō/.
Let's put it together. What word? *Shadow.*

(Continue the activity with the following words:
sheet [shshsh-ēēē-t], she [shshsh-ēēē], shell [shshsh-eee-lll], shin [shshsh-iii-nnn], shout [shshsh-ou-t], shut [shshsh-uuu-t], show [shshsh-ōōō], shy [shshsh-īīī].)

Activity 2 Phoneme Segmentation

Show Phonemic Awareness. **Elicit** responses. **Guide** chip placement as needed.
Let's use our chips to show how many sounds there are in a word. For each sound in the word, you'll push one chip up to the arrow on the page. When we finish, we'll read the whole word.

Your turn. Say the sounds you hear in **sock,** and move a chip for each sound. /sss/ /ooo/ /k/.

Move your finger back to the dot. What word? *Sock.*

How many **sounds** are in the word **sock**? *Three.*

Correct. Now move your chips back to the bottom, and let's try another one.

(Continue the activity with the following words: lock, rock, dock, knock, rain, pain, chain, vane, cane.)

Lesson 159 **635**

Part B: Letter Recognition and Formation

6 minutes

Teacher Materials:
Letter Recognition

Student Materials:
Lined paper

Activity 1 — Letter and Name Recognition Cumulative Review—p/P, b/B, y/Y, x/X, j/J, q/Q, z/Z, United States

Display on IWB or **write** letters, capitals and United States on the board in the order shown. **Elicit** responses to questions. **Guide** as needed.

Let's review some of the other letters and capital letters you've learned. Are you ready?

Letter	Question	Student Response
b	What letter?	b.
United States	(Repeat for each letter:) What letter?	U-n-i-t-e-d S-t-a-t-e-s.
Y	What letter?	Capital Y.
j	What letter?	j.
z	What letter?	z.
J	What letter?	Capital J.
P	What letter?	Capital P.
q	What letter?	q.
X	What letter?	Capital X.
y	What letter?	y.
Z	What letter?	Capital Z.
p	What letter?	p.
B	What letter?	Capital B.
x	What letter?	x.
Q	What letter?	Capital Q.

Review as needed.

Activity 2 — Letter Formation Cumulative Review—p/P, b/B, y/Y, x/X, j/J, q/Q, z/Z, United States

Write p, capital P, b, capital B, y, capital Y, x, capital X, j, capital J, q, capital Q, z, capital Z, and United States on the board. **Provide** lined paper to students.

Show me how you can write these letters and capitals.

Guide students as they write the letters and capitals on their paper. **Review** as needed.

 Link letter names to letter sounds as they appear in the program as needed.

9 minutes

Teacher Materials:
Storybook
My Prediction Chart
Story Map

Student Materials:
Storybook
My Prediction Chart
Story Map

Part C: Comprehension Strategies

Activity 1 Confirm Predictions—An After-Reading Strategy

 Direct students to Lessons 158, pages 183–185, in *Storybook*.

Show My Prediction Chart. **Elicit** responses to questions. **Guide** as needed.
In the last lesson, you made a prediction. Let's check that prediction to see whether it is correct. Circle whether or not your prediction was correct.

Discuss accuracy of predictions from Lesson 158.

Remember that it does not matter whether your prediction was correct. Just making and checking predictions as you read keeps you interested in what you are reading.

Activity 2 Identify Story Elements—An After-Reading Strategy

 Direct students to Lessons 157 and 158, pages 180–185, in *Storybook*.

Elicit responses to questions. **Guide** as needed.
Today you'll work by yourself to fill in all the parts of a Story Map for the stories you read in the last lessons. Look at the stories on pages 180–185. Write the title, names of characters, and setting in the correct boxes. Then write a sentence for the beginning, the middle, and the end of the story.

Monitor student as they complete their Story Maps.

Now let's check what you put on your Story Map. What's the title of the story? *"The Fat Eagle."*

Complete your Story Map as students tell you answers.

Who are the main characters in the story? *The fat eagle, the little eagle, and the tiger.*

What's the setting of the story? *Some trees.*

What picture did you draw for what happened first in the story? (Idea: *The little eagle is sitting under a tree.*)

What picture did you draw for what happened next in the story? (Idea: *The tiger is hunting for eagles.*)

What picture did you draw for what happened last in the story? (Idea: *The fat eagle drops on the tiger and scares him away.*)

You'll retell the story in the next lesson.

Lesson 159

Lesson 160

> **Materials**
>
> **Teacher:** *Storybook*; 5-Story Map (from Lesson 159); 1-Phonemic Awareness; 3 manipulatives such as blocks, discs, chips, counters (if not using IWB); Letter Recognition
>
> **Student:** Lined paper; copy of 5-Story Map completed in Lesson 159; *Storybook*; copy of 1-Phonemic Awareness; 3 manipulatives such as blocks, discs, chips, counters

Part A: Phonemic and Phonological Awareness

5 minutes

Teacher Materials:
Phonemic Awareness

3 manipulatives such as blocks, discs, chips, counters

Student Materials:
Phonemic Awareness

3 manipulatives such as blocks, discs, chips, counters

Activity 1 Phoneme Blending

Elicit responses. **Guide** as needed.
Let's put some sounds together and make words. I'm going to say a word very slowly so you can hear each sound. You need to listen carefully and say the sounds. Then we'll put the sounds together and say the word.

My turn. Listen. **/vvv/ /āāā/ /sss/.**
Say the sounds. /vvv/ /āāā/ /sss/.
Again, say the sounds. /vvv/ /āāā/ /sss/.
Let's put it together. What word? *Vase.*

My turn. Listen. **/vvv/ /aaa/ /nnn/.**
Say the sounds. /vvv/ /aaa/ /nnn/.
Again, say the sounds. /vvv/ /aaa/ /nnn/.
Let's put it together. What word? *Van.*

(Continue the activity with the following words:
vein [vvv-āāā-nnn], vent [vvv-eee-nnn-t], vet [vvv-eee-t], vine [vvv-īīī-nnn], voice [vvv-oi-sss], vote [vvv-ōōō-t], valley [vvv-aaa-lll-ēēē], veil [vvv-āāā-lll].)

Activity 2 Phoneme Segmentation

Show Phonemic Awareness. **Elicit** responses. **Guide** chip placement as needed.
Let's use our chips to show how many sounds there are in a word. For each sound in the word, you'll push one chip up to the arrow on the page. When we finish, we'll read the whole word.

Your turn. Say the sounds you hear in **sun,** and move a chip for each sound. /sss/ /uuu/ /nnn/.

Move your finger back to the dot. What word? *Sun.*

How many **sounds** are in the word **sun?** *Three.*

Correct. Now move your chips back to the bottom, and let's try another one.

(Continue the activity with the following words: bun, fun, run, ton, boat, goat, coat, vote, tote.)

638 Lesson 160

Part B: Letter Recognition and Formation

6 minutes

Teacher Materials:
Letter Recognition

Student Materials:
Lined paper

Activity 1 Letter Recognition Cumulative Review—(School Name), (City Name), (State Name), United States

Display on IWB or **write** names on the board in the order shown. **Elicit** responses to questions. **Guide** as needed.

This week you've shown you know the letters and capital letters. Let's review the letters you've learned. Are you ready?

Letter	Question	Student Response
United States	(Repeat for each letter:) What letter?	*U-n-i-t-e-d S-t-a-t-e-s.*
(school's name)	(Repeat for each letter:) What letter?	(Appropriate letters.)
(state's name)	(Repeat for each letter:) What letter?	(Appropriate letters.)
(city's name)	(Repeat for each letter:) What letter?	(Appropriate letters.)

Review as needed.

Activity 2 Letter Formation Cumulative Review—(School Name), (City Name), (State Name), United States

Write (school's name), (city's name), (state's name), and United States on the board. **Provide** lined paper to students.

Show me how you can write these letters and capitals.

Guide students as they write the letters and capitals on their paper. **Review** as needed.

 Link letter names to letter sounds as they appear in the program as needed.

Discuss how the place-names students have learned relate to one another.
Continue the activity by discussing with students the locations of different classroom objects. **Have** students draw a simple map of the classroom.

Lesson 160   **639**

Part C: Comprehension Strategies

9 minutes

Teacher Materials:
Storybook
Story Map

Student Materials:
Storybook
Story Map

Activity 1 Retell the Story—An After-Reading Strategy

Assign student partners. **Elicit** responses to questions. **Guide** as needed.
You filled out your Story Map in the last lesson for "The Fat Eagle." Now it's time to retell the story to your partner from the words and pictures on your Story Map. Then your partner can retell the whole story to you. Decide who will go first, and then retell the whole story. Add suggestions to make your neighbor's writing better if you think it needs it.

Monitor student partners as they retell story using Story Map as a guide.

Activity 2 Comprehension Monitoring: Read with Prosody—A During-Reading Strategy

Elicit responses to questions. **Guide** as needed.
When you read stories, you'll understand the story better if you read the story the right way. You need to look for the end marks of the sentences and take a little breath after each sentence. If you don't stop after each sentence, the story will not make sense.

Listen to me read the first page of the story the right way. Then we'll read the second page of the story together the right way by taking a little breath after each sentence.

Model reading first page of story with prosody.

Read second page of story with students to help them practice reading with prosody.

Remember that reading the story the right way will help you understand the story.

640 Lesson 160

Appendix A

Name _____   Date _____

1: My Prediction Chart

Book Title:

↓

I Predict That:

↓

Was My Prediction Correct?

Yes   No

Name _____ **Date** _____

2: Character Sheet

A4

Copyright © The McGraw-Hill Companies, Inc. Permission is granted to reproduce for classroom use.

Name _____   Date _____

3: Setting Sheet

Setting

**First
Setting**

Another

Name _____   Date _____

4: Story Map

Beginning

Middle

End

A6

Name _____   Date _____

5: Story Map

Title: _____

Characters

Who:

Setting

Where:

Events

Beginning:

Middle:

End:

Copyright © The McGraw-Hill Companies, Inc. Permission is granted to reproduce for classroom use.

A7

Name _____ Date _____

6: KWL Chart

Topic:

What I **K**now	What I **W**onder	What I **L**earned

Copyright © The McGraw-Hill Companies, Inc. Permission is granted to reproduce for classroom use.

A8

Name _____   Date _____

7: Mental Images Chart

Name _____   Date _____

8: My Book Review

Book 1: _____

Book 2: _____

Which book did you like the best?

Why did you like that book the best?

Phonemic Awareness

1-PA

Copyright © The McGraw-Hill Companies, Inc. Permission is granted to reproduce for classroom use.

2-PA

4-PA

5-PA

Copyright © The McGraw-Hill Companies, Inc. Permission is granted to reproduce for classroom use.

6-PA

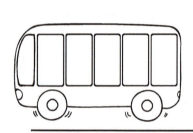  

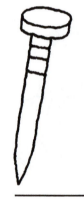  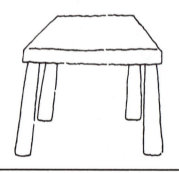

8-PA

10-PA

 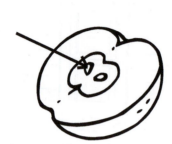 

  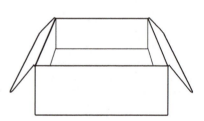

Copyright © The McGraw-Hill Companies, Inc. Permission is granted to reproduce for classroom use.

11-PA

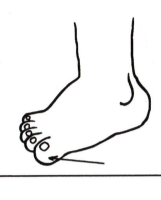  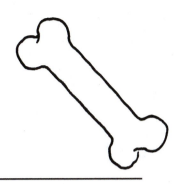

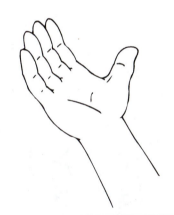  

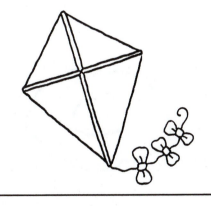  

Copyright © The McGraw-Hill Companies, Inc. Permission is granted to reproduce for classroom use.

12-PA

13-PA

14-PA2

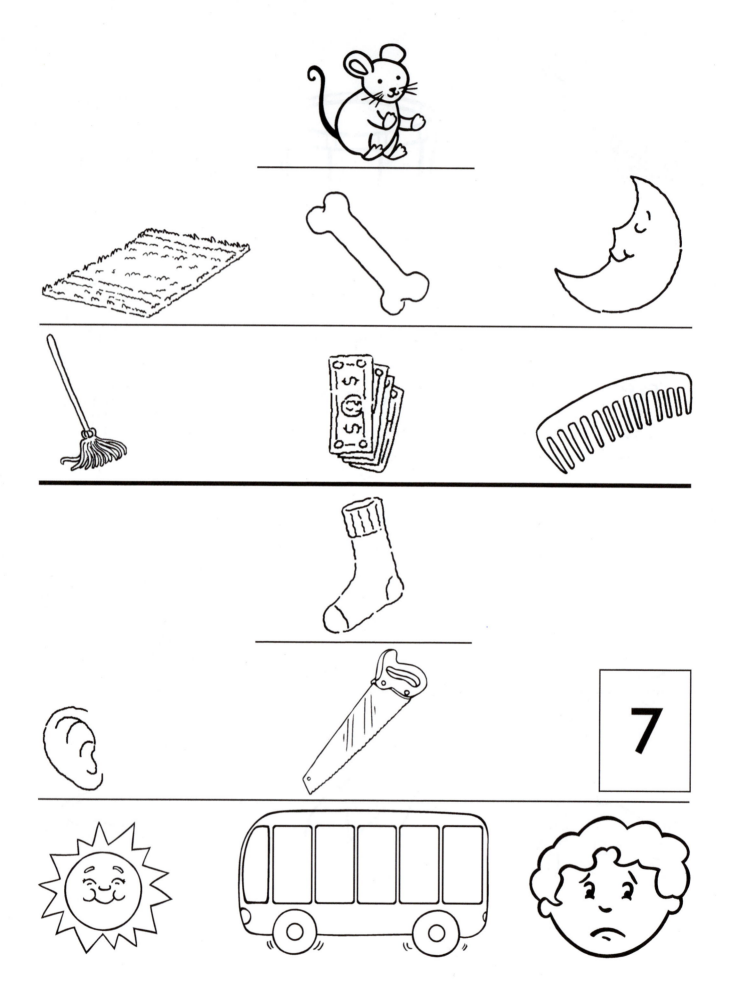

15-PA

16-PA

18-PA

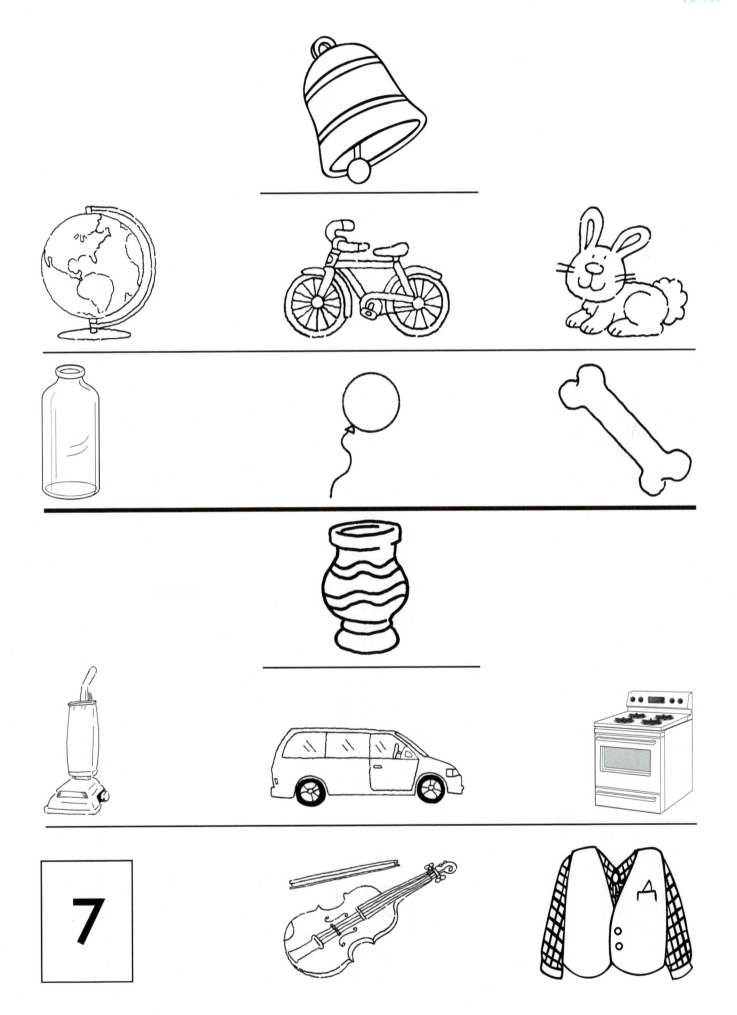

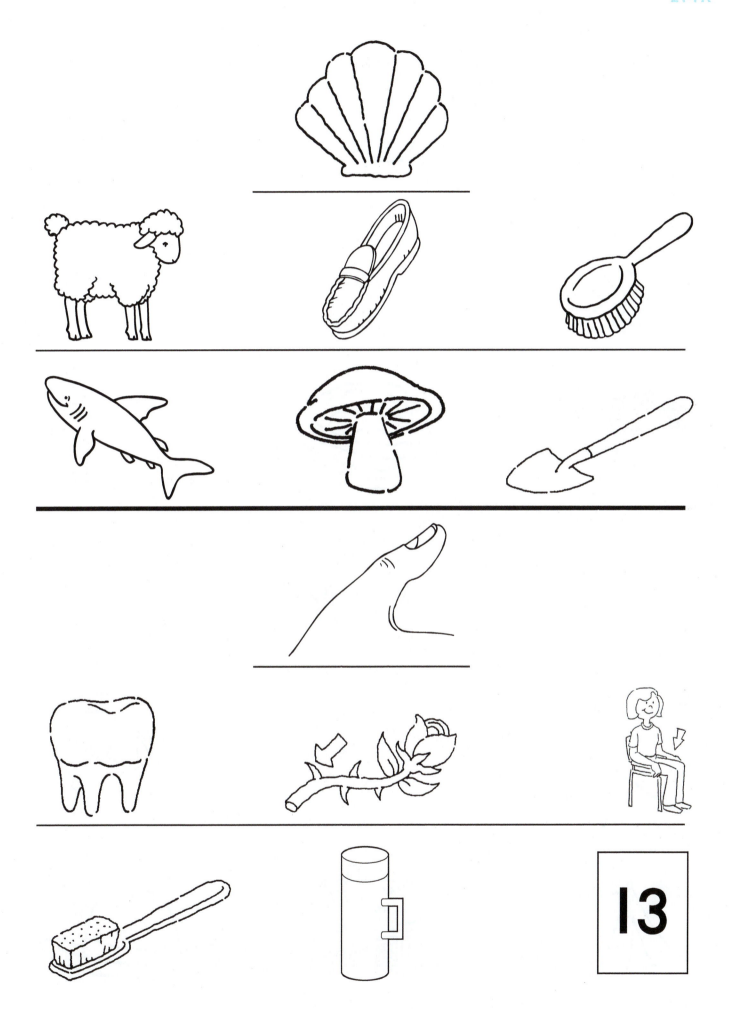

22-PA

23-PA

24-PA

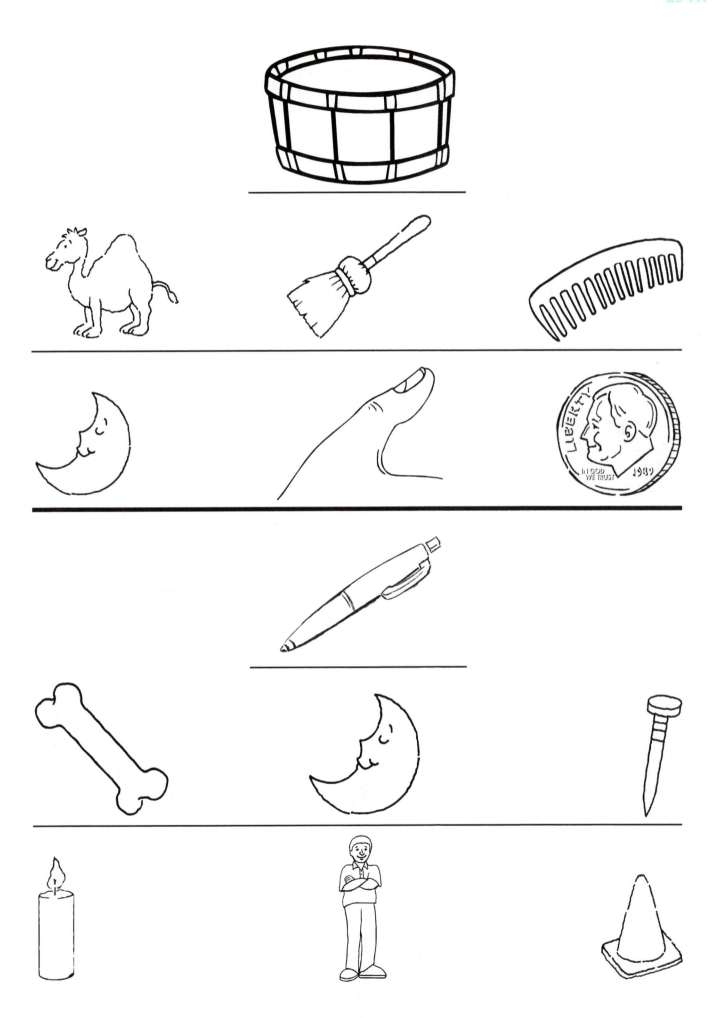

26-PA

27-PA

28-PA

29-PA

30-PA

32-PA

Picture-Sound Cards

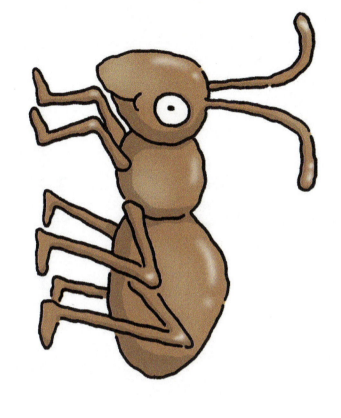

1

/a/

/a/

alligator

SRA Phonemic Awareness Picture-Sound Cards
Copyright © SRA/McGraw-Hill

2

/a/

/a/

ant

SRA Phonemic Awareness Picture-Sound Cards
Copyright © SRA/McGraw-Hill

3

/a/

/a/

apple

SRA Phonemic Awareness Picture-Sound Cards
Copyright © SRA/McGraw-Hill

4

/a/

/a/

axe

SRA Phonemic Awareness Picture-Sound Cards
Copyright © SRA/McGraw-Hill

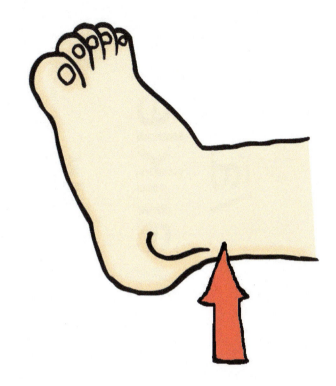

6

/ā/

ankle

SRA Phonemic Awareness Picture-Sound Cards
Copyright © SRA/McGraw-Hill

/ā/

5

/ā/

acorn

SRA Phonemic Awareness Picture-Sound Cards
Copyright © SRA/McGraw-Hill

/ā/

8

/ā/

apron

SRA Phonemic Awareness Picture-Sound Cards
Copyright © SRA/McGraw-Hill

/ā/

7

/ā/

ape

SRA Phonemic Awareness Picture-Sound Cards
Copyright © SRA/McGraw-Hill

/ā/

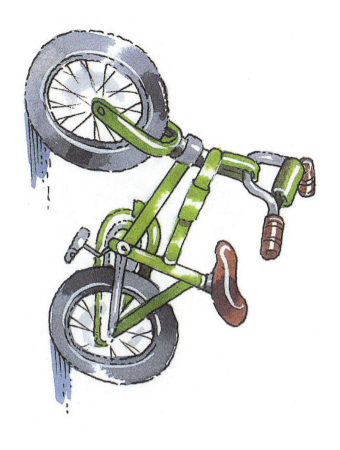

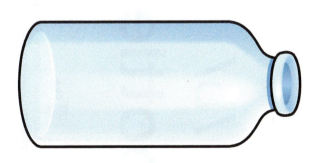

/b/

/b/
bird

/b/
bike

SRA Phonemic Awareness Picture-Sound Cards
Copyright © SRA/McGraw-Hill

/b/
boy

/b/
bottle

SRA Phonemic Awareness Picture-Sound Cards
Copyright © SRA/McGraw-Hill

14

/d/

/d/
dog

SRA
SRA Phonemic Awareness Picture-Sound Cards
Copyright © SRA/McGraw-Hill

13

/d/

/d/
deer

SRA
SRA Phonemic Awareness Picture-Sound Cards
Copyright © SRA/McGraw-Hill

16

/d/

/d/
duck

SRA
SRA Phonemic Awareness Picture-Sound Cards
Copyright © SRA/McGraw-Hill

15

/d/

/d/
door

SRA
SRA Phonemic Awareness Picture-Sound Cards
Copyright © SRA/McGraw-Hill

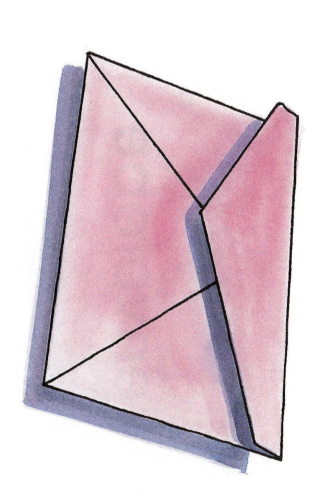

/e/

elephant

SRA Phonemic Awareness Picture-Sound Cards
Copyright © SRA/McGraw-Hill

/e/

egg

SRA Phonemic Awareness Picture-Sound Cards
Copyright © SRA/McGraw-Hill

/e/

envelope

SRA Phonemic Awareness Picture-Sound Cards
Copyright © SRA/McGraw-Hill

/e/

elf

SRA Phonemic Awareness Picture-Sound Cards
Copyright © SRA/McGraw-Hill

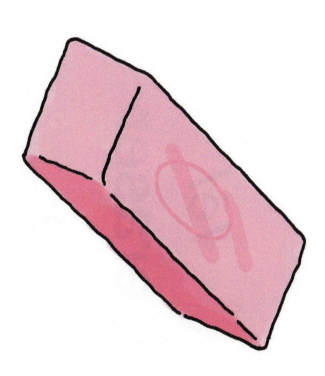

22

/ē/

/ē/

ear

SRA Phonemic Awareness Picture-Sound Cards
Copyright © SRA/McGraw-Hill

21

/ē/

/ē/

eagle

SRA Phonemic Awareness Picture-Sound Cards
Copyright © SRA/McGraw-Hill

24

/ē/

/ē/

eraser

SRA Phonemic Awareness Picture-Sound Cards
Copyright © SRA/McGraw-Hill

23

/ē/

/ē/

eat

SRA Phonemic Awareness Picture-Sound Cards
Copyright © SRA/McGraw-Hill

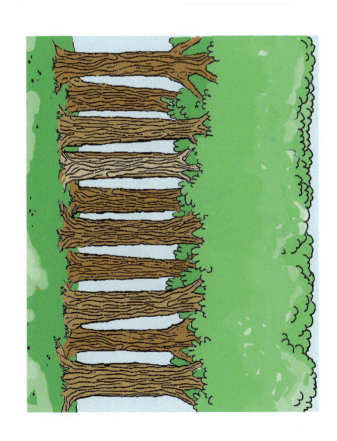

26

/f/

/f/

farm

SRA

SRA Phonemic Awareness Picture-Sound Cards
Copyright © SRA/McGraw-Hill

25

/f/

/f/

fan

SRA

SRA Phonemic Awareness Picture-Sound Cards
Copyright © SRA/McGraw-Hill

28

/f/

/f/

forest

SRA

SRA Phonemic Awareness Picture-Sound Cards
Copyright © SRA/McGraw-Hill

27

/f/

/f/

fish

SRA

SRA Phonemic Awareness Picture-Sound Cards
Copyright © SRA/McGraw-Hill

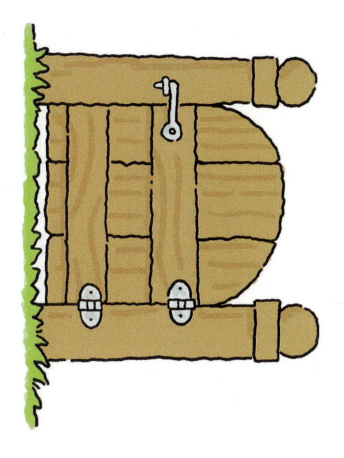

30

/g/

gift

/g/

SRA Phonemic Awareness Picture-Sound Cards
Copyright © SRA/McGraw-Hill

Mc Graw Hill **SRA**

29

/g/

gate

/g/

SRA Phonemic Awareness Picture-Sound Cards
Copyright © SRA/McGraw-Hill

Mc Graw Hill **SRA**

32

/g/

goat

/g/

SRA Phonemic Awareness Picture-Sound Cards
Copyright © SRA/McGraw-Hill

Mc Graw Hill **SRA**

31

/g/

girl

/g/

SRA Phonemic Awareness Picture-Sound Cards
Copyright © SRA/McGraw-Hill

Mc Graw Hill **SRA**

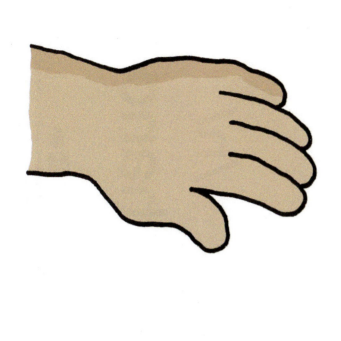
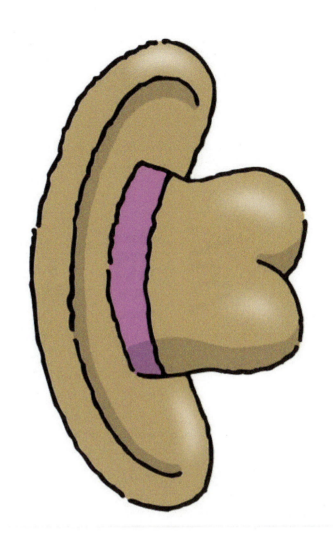

34

/h/

hat

SRA Phonemic Awareness Picture-Sound Cards
Copyright © SRA/McGraw-Hill

/h/

33

/h/

hand

SRA Phonemic Awareness Picture-Sound Cards
Copyright © SRA/McGraw-Hill

/h/

36

/h/

house

SRA Phonemic Awareness Picture-Sound Cards
Copyright © SRA/McGraw-Hill

/h/

35

/h/

horse

SRA Phonemic Awareness Picture-Sound Cards
Copyright © SRA/McGraw-Hill

/h/

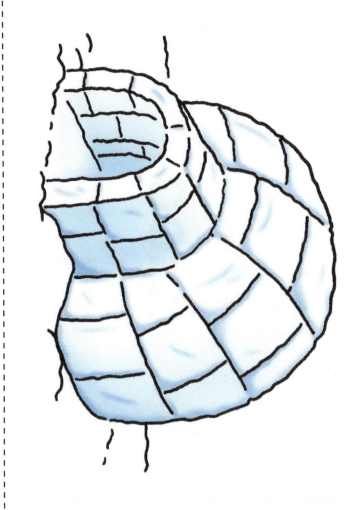

38

/i/

iguana

SRA Phonemic Awareness Picture-Sound Cards
Copyright © SRA/McGraw-Hill

/i/

37

/i/

igloo

SRA Phonemic Awareness Picture-Sound Cards
Copyright © SRA/McGraw-Hill

/i/

40

/i/

instrument

SRA Phonemic Awareness Picture-Sound Cards
Copyright © SRA/McGraw-Hill

/i/

39

/i/

insect

SRA Phonemic Awareness Picture-Sound Cards
Copyright © SRA/McGraw-Hill

/i/

42

/ī/

iron

SRA Phonemic Awareness Picture-Sound Cards
Copyright © SRA/McGraw-Hill

/ī/

41

/ī/

ice cream

SRA Phonemic Awareness Picture-Sound Cards
Copyright © SRA/McGraw-Hill

/ī/

44

/ī/

ivy

SRA Phonemic Awareness Picture-Sound Cards
Copyright © SRA/McGraw-Hill

/ī/

43

/ī/

island

SRA Phonemic Awareness Picture-Sound Cards
Copyright © SRA/McGraw-Hill

/ī/

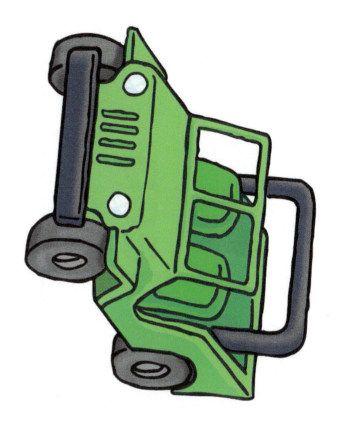

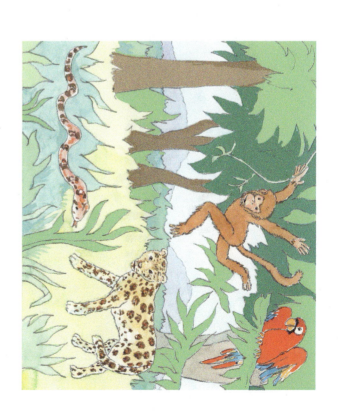

46

/j/

jeep

Mc Graw Hill **SRA**

SRA Phonemic Awareness Picture-Sound Cards
Copyright © SRA/McGraw-Hill

/j/

45

/j/

jar

Mc Graw Hill **SRA**

SRA Phonemic Awareness Picture-Sound Cards
Copyright © SRA/McGraw-Hill

/j/

48

/j/

jungle

Mc Graw Hill **SRA**

SRA Phonemic Awareness Picture-Sound Cards
Copyright © SRA/McGraw-Hill

/j/

47

/j/

jump

Mc Graw Hill **SRA**

SRA Phonemic Awareness Picture-Sound Cards
Copyright © SRA/McGraw-Hill

/j/

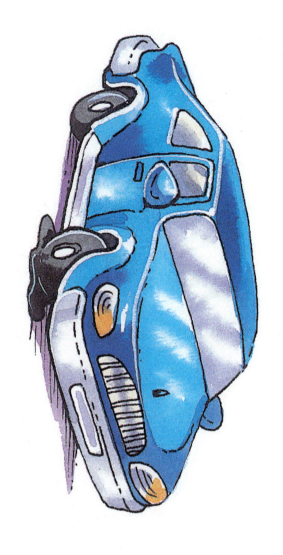

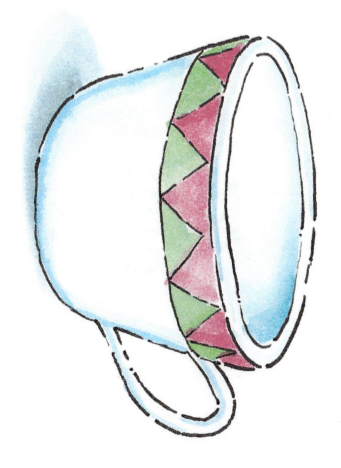

50

/k/

/k/

cat

SRA

SRA Phonemic Awareness Picture-Sound Cards
Copyright © SRA/McGraw-Hill

49

/k/

/k/

car

SRA

SRA Phonemic Awareness Picture-Sound Cards
Copyright © SRA/McGraw-Hill

52

/k/

/k/

kite

SRA

SRA Phonemic Awareness Picture-Sound Cards
Copyright © SRA/McGraw-Hill

51

/k/

/k/

cup

SRA

SRA Phonemic Awareness Picture-Sound Cards
Copyright © SRA/McGraw-Hill

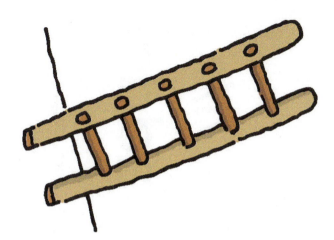

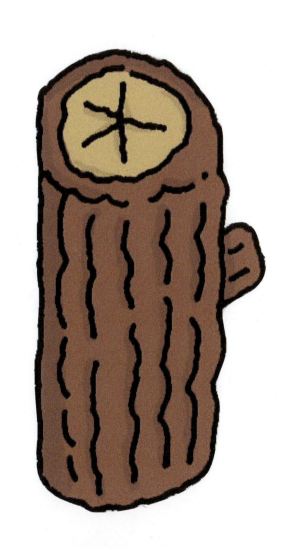

54

/l/

/l/

leaf

SRA Phonemic Awareness Picture-Sound Cards
Copyright © SRA/McGraw-Hill

53

/l/

/l/

ladder

SRA Phonemic Awareness Picture-Sound Cards
Copyright © SRA/McGraw-Hill

56

/l/

/l/

log

SRA Phonemic Awareness Picture-Sound Cards
Copyright © SRA/McGraw-Hill

55

/l/

/l/

lion

SRA Phonemic Awareness Picture-Sound Cards
Copyright © SRA/McGraw-Hill

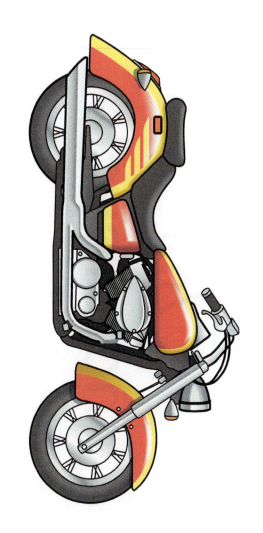

57

/m/

man

SRA Phonemic Awareness Picture-Sound Cards
Copyright © SRA/McGraw-Hill

/m/

58

/m/

monkey

SRA Phonemic Awareness Picture-Sound Cards
Copyright © SRA/McGraw-Hill

/m/

59

/m/

motorcycle

SRA Phonemic Awareness Picture-Sound Cards
Copyright © SRA/McGraw-Hill

/m/

60

/m/

mouse

SRA Phonemic Awareness Picture-Sound Cards
Copyright © SRA/McGraw-Hill

/m/

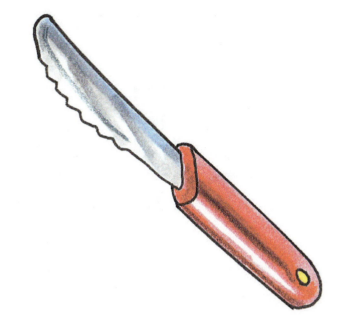
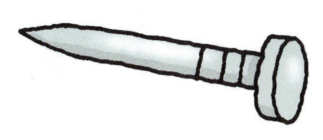

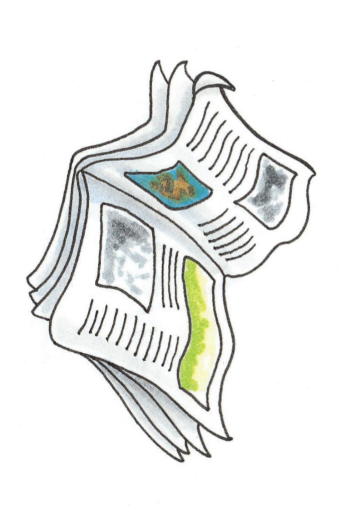

62

/n/

nail

/n/

McGraw-Hill SRA
SRA Phonemic Awareness Picture-Sound Cards
Copyright © SRA/McGraw-Hill

61

/n/

knife

/n/

McGraw-Hill SRA
SRA Phonemic Awareness Picture-Sound Cards
Copyright © SRA/McGraw-Hill

64

/n/

newspaper

/n/

McGraw-Hill SRA
SRA Phonemic Awareness Picture-Sound Cards
Copyright © SRA/McGraw-Hill

63

/n/

nest

/n/

McGraw-Hill SRA
SRA Phonemic Awareness Picture-Sound Cards
Copyright © SRA/McGraw-Hill

/o/

/o/
olive

66

SRA Phonemic Awareness Picture-Sound Cards
Copyright © SRA/McGraw-Hill

/o/

/o/
octopus

65

SRA Phonemic Awareness Picture-Sound Cards
Copyright © SRA/McGraw-Hill

/o/

/o/
ox

68

SRA Phonemic Awareness Picture-Sound Cards
Copyright © SRA/McGraw-Hill

/o/

/o/
ostrich

67

SRA Phonemic Awareness Picture-Sound Cards
Copyright © SRA/McGraw-Hill

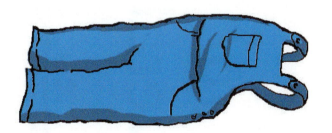

70

/ō/

/ō/
open

SRA

SRA Phonemic Awareness Picture-Sound Cards
Copyright © SRA/McGraw-Hill

69

/ō/

/ō/
ocean

SRA

SRA Phonemic Awareness Picture-Sound Cards
Copyright © SRA/McGraw-Hill

72

/ō/

/ō/
overalls

SRA

SRA Phonemic Awareness Picture-Sound Cards
Copyright © SRA/McGraw-Hill

71

/ō/

/ō/
oval

SRA

SRA Phonemic Awareness Picture-Sound Cards
Copyright © SRA/McGraw-Hill

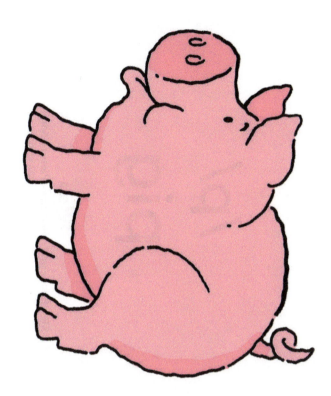

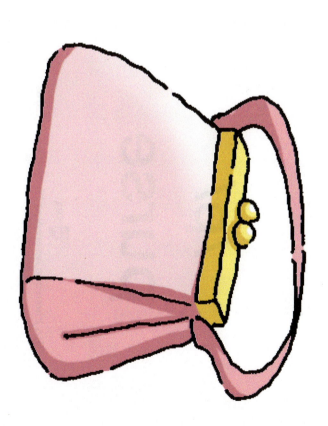

74

/p/

/p/

pig

SRA Phonemic Awareness Picture-Sound Cards
Copyright © SRA/McGraw-Hill

73

/p/

/p/

pencil

SRA Phonemic Awareness Picture-Sound Cards
Copyright © SRA/McGraw-Hill

76

/p/

/p/

purse

SRA Phonemic Awareness Picture-Sound Cards
Copyright © SRA/McGraw-Hill

75

/p/

/p/

pitcher

SRA Phonemic Awareness Picture-Sound Cards
Copyright © SRA/McGraw-Hill

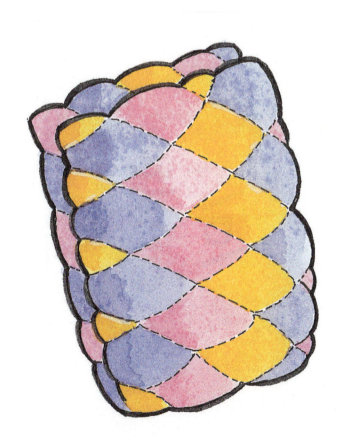

/q/

quarter

SRA Phonemic Awareness Picture-Sound Cards
Copyright © SRA/McGraw-Hill

/q/

queen

SRA Phonemic Awareness Picture-Sound Cards
Copyright © SRA/McGraw-Hill

/q/

question mark

SRA Phonemic Awareness Picture-Sound Cards
Copyright © SRA/McGraw-Hill

/q/

quilt

SRA Phonemic Awareness Picture-Sound Cards
Copyright © SRA/McGraw-Hill

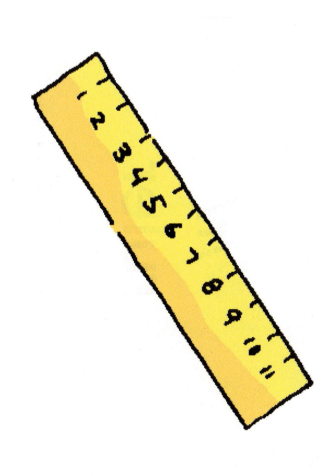

82

/r/

/r/
rake

SRA Phonemic Awareness Picture-Sound Cards
Copyright © SRA/McGraw-Hill

81

/r/

/r/
rabbit

SRA Phonemic Awareness Picture-Sound Cards
Copyright © SRA/McGraw-Hill

84

/r/

/r/
ruler

SRA Phonemic Awareness Picture-Sound Cards
Copyright © SRA/McGraw-Hill

83

/r/

/r/
rock

SRA Phonemic Awareness Picture-Sound Cards
Copyright © SRA/McGraw-Hill

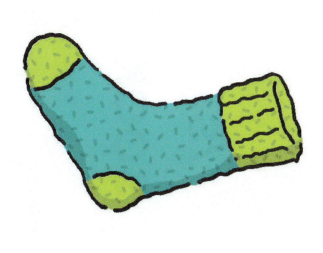

/s/

/s/
saw

SRA Phonemic Awareness Picture-Sound Cards
Copyright © SRA/McGraw-Hill

/s/

/s/
sandwich

SRA Phonemic Awareness Picture-Sound Cards
Copyright © SRA/McGraw-Hill

/s/

/s/
sock

SRA Phonemic Awareness Picture-Sound Cards
Copyright © SRA/McGraw-Hill

/s/

/s/
sink

SRA Phonemic Awareness Picture-Sound Cards
Copyright © SRA/McGraw-Hill

90

/t/

/t/

tiger

SRA Phonemic Awareness Picture-Sound Cards
Copyright © SRA/McGraw-Hill

89

/t/

/t/

table

SRA Phonemic Awareness Picture-Sound Cards
Copyright © SRA/McGraw-Hill

92

/t/

/t/

turtle

SRA Phonemic Awareness Picture-Sound Cards
Copyright © SRA/McGraw-Hill

91

/t/

/t/

toothbrush

SRA Phonemic Awareness Picture-Sound Cards
Copyright © SRA/McGraw-Hill

94

/u/

umpire

Mc Graw Hill · SRA

SRA Phonemic Awareness Picture-Sound Cards
Copyright © SRA/McGraw-Hill

/u/

93

/u/

umbrella

Mc Graw Hill · SRA

SRA Phonemic Awareness Picture-Sound Cards
Copyright © SRA/McGraw-Hill

/u/

96

/u/

up

Mc Graw Hill · SRA

SRA Phonemic Awareness Picture-Sound Cards
Copyright © SRA/McGraw-Hill

/u/

95

/u/

under

Mc Graw Hill · SRA

SRA Phonemic Awareness Picture-Sound Cards
Copyright © SRA/McGraw-Hill

/u/

98

/ū/

/ū/

unicorn

SRA Phonemic Awareness Picture-Sound Cards
Copyright © SRA/McGraw-Hill

97

/ū/

/ū/

ukulele

SRA Phonemic Awareness Picture-Sound Cards
Copyright © SRA/McGraw-Hill

100

/ū/

/ū/

uniform

SRA Phonemic Awareness Picture-Sound Cards
Copyright © SRA/McGraw-Hill

99

/ū/

/ū/

unicycle

SRA Phonemic Awareness Picture-Sound Cards
Copyright © SRA/McGraw-Hill

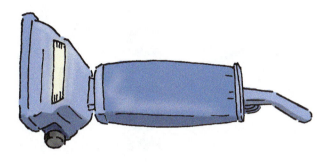
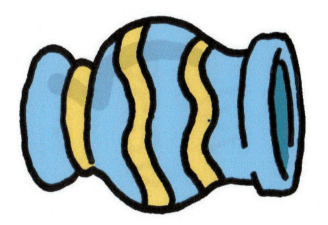
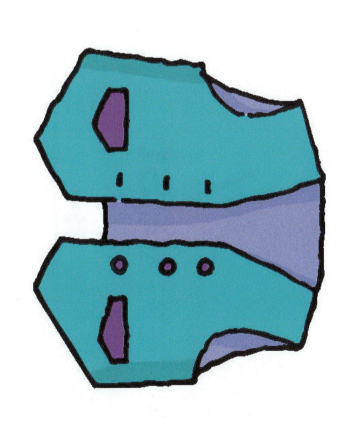

102

/v/

vase

/v/

SRA Phonemic Awareness Picture-Sound Cards
Copyright © SRA/McGraw-Hill

Mc Graw Hill **SRA**

101

/v/

vacuum

/v/

SRA Phonemic Awareness Picture-Sound Cards
Copyright © SRA/McGraw-Hill

Mc Graw Hill **SRA**

104

/v/

violin

/v/

SRA Phonemic Awareness Picture-Sound Cards
Copyright © SRA/McGraw-Hill

Mc Graw Hill **SRA**

103

/v/

vest

/v/

SRA Phonemic Awareness Picture-Sound Cards
Copyright © SRA/McGraw-Hill

Mc Graw Hill **SRA**

/w/

/w/
wagon

SRA Phonemic Awareness Picture-Sound Cards
Copyright © SRA/McGraw-Hill

/w/

/w/
watch

SRA Phonemic Awareness Picture-Sound Cards
Copyright © SRA/McGraw-Hill

/w/

/w/
window

SRA Phonemic Awareness Picture-Sound Cards
Copyright © SRA/McGraw-Hill

/w/

/w/
woman

SRA Phonemic Awareness Picture-Sound Cards
Copyright © SRA/McGraw-Hill

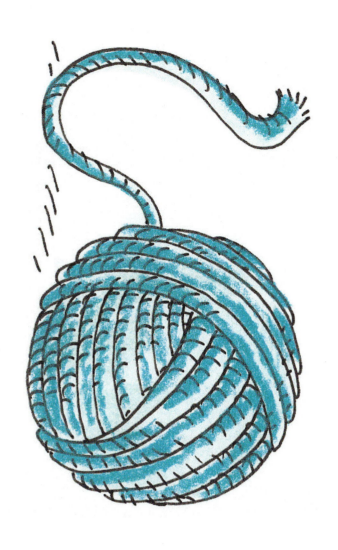

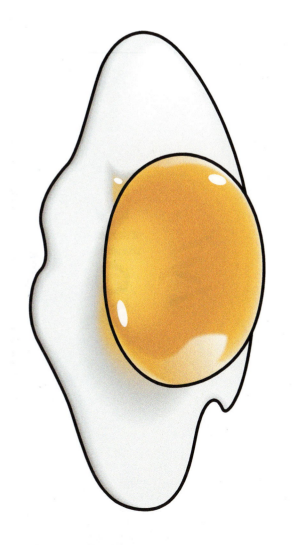

/y/

/y/
yellow

SRA Phonemic Awareness Picture-Sound Cards
Copyright © SRA/McGraw-Hill

/y/

/y/
yarn

SRA Phonemic Awareness Picture-Sound Cards
Copyright © SRA/McGraw-Hill

/y/

/y/
yo-yo

SRA Phonemic Awareness Picture-Sound Cards
Copyright © SRA/McGraw-Hill

/y/

/y/
yolk

SRA Phonemic Awareness Picture-Sound Cards
Copyright © SRA/McGraw-Hill

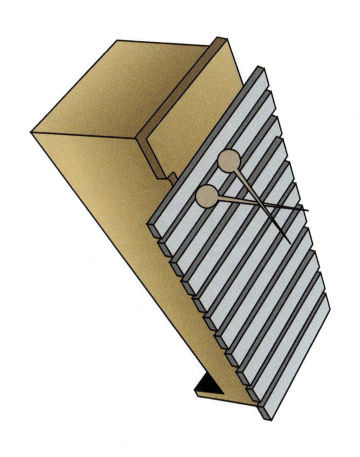

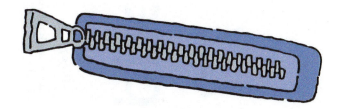

114

/z/
zebra

SRA Phonemic Awareness Picture-Sound Cards
Copyright © SRA/McGraw-Hill

113

/z/
xylophone

SRA Phonemic Awareness Picture-Sound Cards
Copyright © SRA/McGraw-Hill

116

/z/
zoo

SRA Phonemic Awareness Picture-Sound Cards
Copyright © SRA/McGraw-Hill

115

/z/
zipper

SRA Phonemic Awareness Picture-Sound Cards
Copyright © SRA/McGraw-Hill

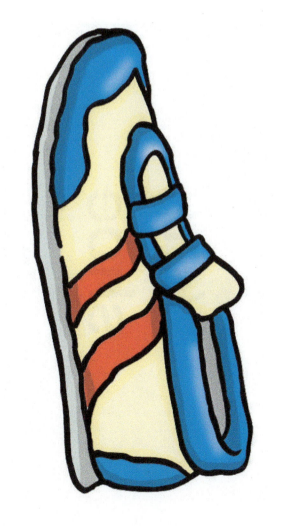

118

/sh/

/sh/
shirt

SRA Phonemic Awareness Picture-Sound Cards
Copyright © SRA/McGraw-Hill

117

/sh/

/sh/
sheep

SRA Phonemic Awareness Picture-Sound Cards
Copyright © SRA/McGraw-Hill

120

/sh/

/sh/
shovel

SRA Phonemic Awareness Picture-Sound Cards
Copyright © SRA/McGraw-Hill

119

/sh/

/sh/
shoe

SRA Phonemic Awareness Picture-Sound Cards
Copyright © SRA/McGraw-Hill

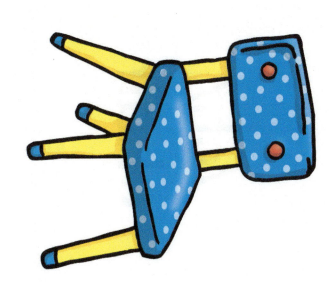

/ch/

/ch/
chair

SRA Phonemic Awareness Picture-Sound Cards
Copyright © SRA/McGraw-Hill

/ch/

/ch/
checkers

SRA Phonemic Awareness Picture-Sound Cards
Copyright © SRA/McGraw-Hill

/ch/

/ch/
cheese

SRA Phonemic Awareness Picture-Sound Cards
Copyright © SRA/McGraw-Hill

/ch/

/ch/
chicken

SRA Phonemic Awareness Picture-Sound Cards
Copyright © SRA/McGraw-Hill

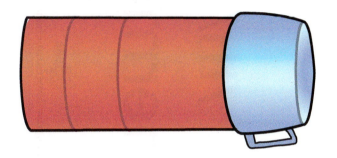

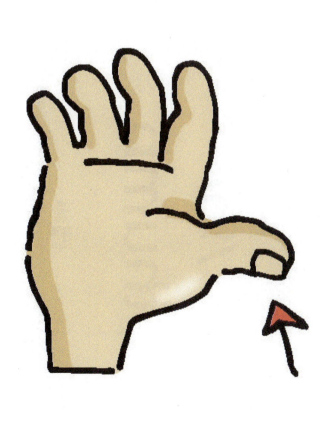

/th/

thigh

SRA Phonemic Awareness Picture-Sound Cards
Copyright © SRA/McGraw-Hill

/th/

thermos

SRA Phonemic Awareness Picture-Sound Cards
Copyright © SRA/McGraw-Hill

/th/

thumb

SRA Phonemic Awareness Picture-Sound Cards
Copyright © SRA/McGraw-Hill

/th/

thorn

SRA Phonemic Awareness Picture-Sound Cards
Copyright © SRA/McGraw-Hill

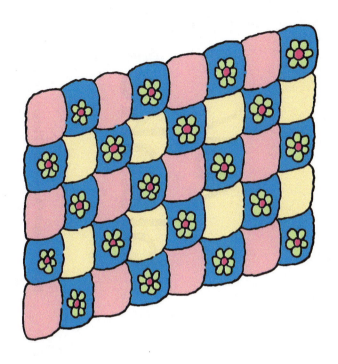

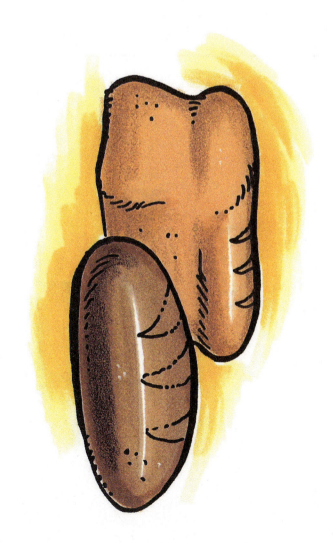

130

/bl/

blue

SRA Phonemic Awareness Picture-Sound Cards
Copyright © SRA/McGraw-Hill

/bl/

129

/bl/

blanket

SRA Phonemic Awareness Picture-Sound Cards
Copyright © SRA/McGraw-Hill

/bl/

132

/br/

broom

SRA Phonemic Awareness Picture-Sound Cards
Copyright © SRA/McGraw-Hill

/br/

131

/br/

bread

SRA Phonemic Awareness Picture-Sound Cards
Copyright © SRA/McGraw-Hill

/br/

134

/cl/

/cl/
cloud

SRA Phonemic Awareness Picture-Sound Cards
Copyright © SRA/McGraw-Hill

Mc Graw Hill SRA

133

/cl/

/cl/
clock

SRA Phonemic Awareness Picture-Sound Cards
Copyright © SRA/McGraw-Hill

Mc Graw Hill SRA

136

/cr/

/cr/
crayon

SRA Phonemic Awareness Picture-Sound Cards
Copyright © SRA/McGraw-Hill

Mc Graw Hill SRA

135

/cr/

/cr/
crab

SRA Phonemic Awareness Picture-Sound Cards
Copyright © SRA/McGraw-Hill

Mc Graw Hill SRA

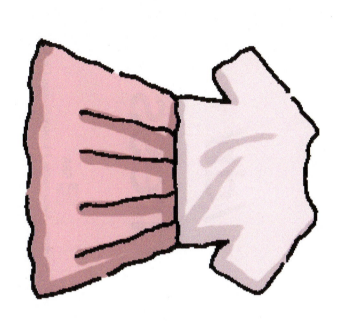

138

/dr/

drill

SRA

SRA Phonemic Awareness Picture-Sound Cards
Copyright © SRA/McGraw-Hill

/dr/

137

/dr/

dress

SRA

SRA Phonemic Awareness Picture-Sound Cards
Copyright © SRA/McGraw-Hill

/dr/

140

/fl/

flower

SRA

SRA Phonemic Awareness Picture-Sound Cards
Copyright © SRA/McGraw-Hill

/fl/

139

/fl/

flag

SRA

SRA Phonemic Awareness Picture-Sound Cards
Copyright © SRA/McGraw-Hill

/fl/

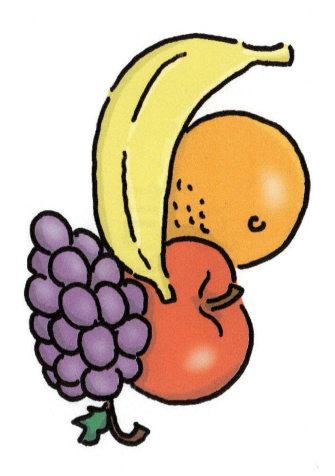
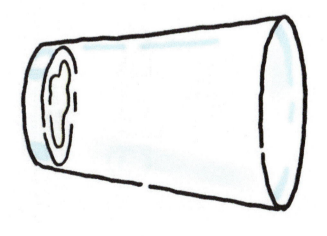
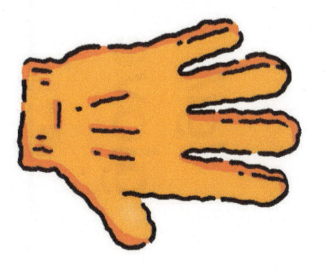

142

/fr/

fruit

Mc Graw Hill **SRA**

SRA Phonemic Awareness Picture-Sound Cards
Copyright © SRA/McGraw-Hill

/fr/

141

/fr/

frog

Mc Graw Hill **SRA**

SRA Phonemic Awareness Picture-Sound Cards
Copyright © SRA/McGraw-Hill

/fr/

144

/gl/

glove

Mc Graw Hill **SRA**

SRA Phonemic Awareness Picture-Sound Cards
Copyright © SRA/McGraw-Hill

/gl/

143

/gl/

glass

Mc Graw Hill **SRA**

SRA Phonemic Awareness Picture-Sound Cards
Copyright © SRA/McGraw-Hill

/gl/

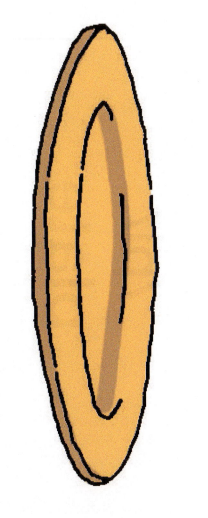

146

/gr/

green

SRA Phonemic Awareness Picture-Sound Cards
Copyright © SRA/McGraw-Hill

/gr/

145

/gr/

grass

SRA Phonemic Awareness Picture-Sound Cards
Copyright © SRA/McGraw-Hill

/gr/

148

/pl/

pliers

SRA Phonemic Awareness Picture-Sound Cards
Copyright © SRA/McGraw-Hill

/pl/

147

/pl/

plate

SRA Phonemic Awareness Picture-Sound Cards
Copyright © SRA/McGraw-Hill

/pl/

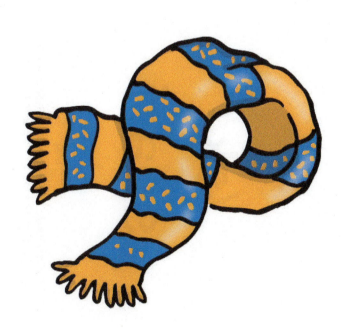

150

/pr/

princess

SRA Phonemic Awareness Picture-Sound Cards
Copyright © SRA/McGraw-Hill

/pr/

149

/pr/

pretzel

SRA Phonemic Awareness Picture-Sound Cards
Copyright © SRA/McGraw-Hill

/pr/

152

/sk/

school

SRA Phonemic Awareness Picture-Sound Cards
Copyright © SRA/McGraw-Hill

/sk/

151

/sk/

scarf

SRA Phonemic Awareness Picture-Sound Cards
Copyright © SRA/McGraw-Hill

/sk/

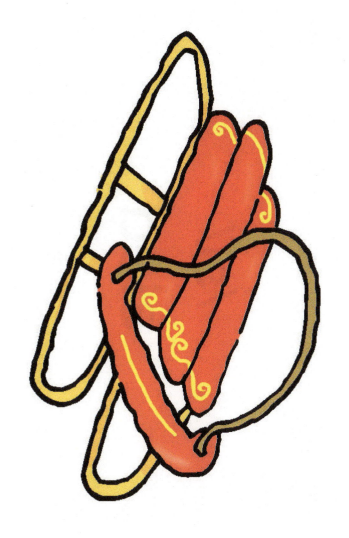

/sl/

sleeping

/sl/

sled

SRA Phonemic Awareness Picture-Sound Cards
Copyright © SRA/McGraw-Hill

SRA Phonemic Awareness Picture-Sound Cards
Copyright © SRA/McGraw-Hill

/sm/

smoke

/sm/

smile

SRA Phonemic Awareness Picture-Sound Cards
Copyright © SRA/McGraw-Hill

SRA Phonemic Awareness Picture-Sound Cards
Copyright © SRA/McGraw-Hill

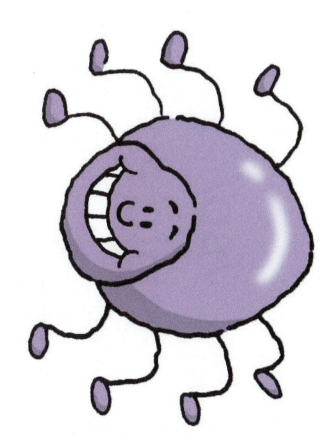

/sn/ **snowman** SRA Phonemic Awareness Picture-Sound Cards Copyright © SRA/McGraw-Hill	/sn/ **snake** SRA Phonemic Awareness Picture-Sound Cards Copyright © SRA/McGraw-Hill
/sp/ **spoon** SRA Phonemic Awareness Picture-Sound Cards Copyright © SRA/McGraw-Hill	/sp/ **spider** SRA Phonemic Awareness Picture-Sound Cards Copyright © SRA/McGraw-Hill

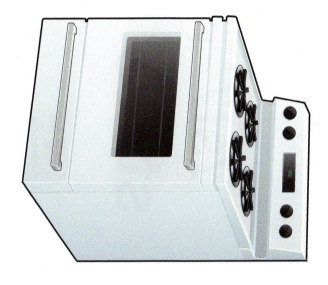

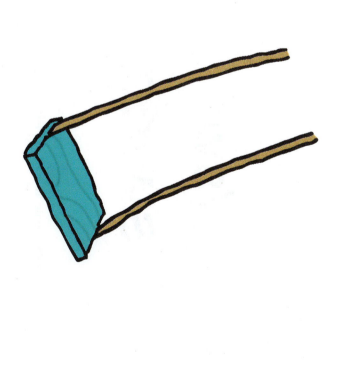

162

/st/

/st/
stove

SRA Phonemic Awareness Picture-Sound Cards
Copyright © SRA/McGraw-Hill

Mc Graw Hill **SRA**

161

/st/

/st/
star

SRA Phonemic Awareness Picture-Sound Cards
Copyright © SRA/McGraw-Hill

Mc Graw Hill **SRA**

164

/sw/

/sw/
swing

SRA Phonemic Awareness Picture-Sound Cards
Copyright © SRA/McGraw-Hill

Mc Graw Hill **SRA**

163

/sw/

/sw/
swimming

SRA Phonemic Awareness Picture-Sound Cards
Copyright © SRA/McGraw-Hill

Mc Graw Hill **SRA**

/tr/

/tr/
train

SRA Phonemic Awareness Picture-Sound Cards
Copyright © SRA/McGraw-Hill

/tr/

/tr/
tree

SRA Phonemic Awareness Picture-Sound Cards
Copyright © SRA/McGraw-Hill

/tw/

/tw/
tweezers

SRA Phonemic Awareness Picture-Sound Cards
Copyright © SRA/McGraw-Hill

/tw/

/tw/
twig

SRA Phonemic Awareness Picture-Sound Cards
Copyright © SRA/McGraw-Hill

Appendix B

Test	Tips for Teachers	Home Connections

Mastery Test 1 (Lessons 1-8) **Approaching Mastery**	• See "What To Do" guidelines for "if the group is weak on Mastery Test 1" on page 52 in *Presentation Book A*.
	• Partner with "at mastery" student and review sounds.
	• Reteach difficult sounds using "good-bye" list: Write difficult sounds on board; place check mark for each day completed correctly; after 3 consecutive days completed correctly, say "good-bye" to sound.
	• Conduct "see-say-write": Student sees sound, says sound, and writes sound until firm.
		• Provide sound flash cards for students to take home for additional practice.
		• Encourage students to share their take-home sheets with their families.
		• Encourage adult at home to conduct "see-say-write" activity for each sound.
		• Have adult at home access SRA's Home Connection Activities listed at *www.sraonline.com*
		  • Direct Instruction
		    • *Reading Mastery Signature Edition*
		      • Activities

At Mastery	• See "What To Do" guidelines for "if the group is firm on Mastery Test 1" on page 52 in *Presentation Book A*. • Have student "be the teacher": Partner with "approaching mastery" student and review sounds. • Direct student to reading and writing center in classroom to reinforce early literacy and writing skills (e.g., audio books, worksheets, picture books, writing paper).	
ELL	• See "Tips for Teachers" for "approaching mastery" and "at mastery" students. • Describe and model mouth formations for sounds, then guide student while practicing with mirror. • Show realia (e.g., an apple) or other visuals (e.g., photograph of apple) of objects with same beginning sounds.	• See "Home Connections" for "approaching mastery" and "at mastery" students. • Provide sounds audiotape to use with sound flash cards at home; encourage students to practice mouth formations with mirror at home. • Encourage adult at home to help students identify realia and other visuals of objects at home with same beginning sounds.
Test		

Mastery Test 2 (Lessons 9-15) **Approaching Mastery**	• See "What To Do" guidelines for "if the group is weak on Mastery Test 2" on page 100 in *Presentation Book A*.
	• Reteach "say it slowly, say it fast."
	• Partner with "at mastery" student and review "say it slowly, say it fast."
		• Encourage adult at home to incorporate "say it slowly, say it fast" activities throughout the day (e.g., stretch out his or her name, food items, leisure activities, or weather terms and have him or her repeat words slowly and say them fast).
		• Have adult at home access SRA's Home Connection Activities listed at *www.sraonline.com*
		  • Direct Instruction
		    • *Reading Mastery Signature Edition*
		      • Activities

B3

Test	Tips for Teachers	Home Connections
At Mastery	• See "What To Do" guidelines for "if the group is firm on Mastery Test 2" on page 100 in *Presentation Book A.* • Have student "be the teacher": Partner with "approaching mastery" student and review "say it slowly, say it fast." • Direct student to reading and writing center in classroom to reinforce early literacy and writing skills.	
ELL	• See "Tips for Teachers" for "approaching mastery" and "at mastery" students. • Describe and model mouth formations for words and sounds in "say it slowly, say it fast," then guide student while practicing with mirror. • Use pantomiming (e.g., act out "going in") and facial expressions (e.g., make a "mad face") to show concepts of words. • Use primary language equivalents when available and then ask student to say words in English.	• See "Home Connections" for "approaching mastery" and "at mastery" students. • Provide audiotape of "say it slowly, say it fast" activity and encourage adult at home to help students practice other "say it slowly, say it fast" activities throughout the day; encourage students to practice with mirror at home, as needed. • Encourage adult at home to help students practice using primary language equivalents and English words when possible.

Mastery Test 3 (Lessons 16-20)
 	
Approaching Mastery
	• See "What To Do" guidelines for "if the group is weak on Mastery Test 3" on page 134 in *Presentation Book A.*
	• Reteach onset and rimes (e.g., first you say "fff" then you say "un").
	• Partner with "at mastery" student and review "first you say _____, then you say _____; now say it fast."
		• Encourage adult at home to incorporate "first you say _____, then you say _____; now say it fast" activities throughout the day (e.g., say beginning sound, rest of word, and say it fast for everyday words—friends' names, things around the house or community).
		• Have adult at home access SRA's Home Connection Activities listed at *www.sraonline.com*
		  • Direct Instruction
		    • *Reading Mastery Signature Edition*
		      • Activities

At Mastery	• See "What To Do" guidelines for "if the group is firm on Mastery Test 3" on page 134 in *Presentation Book A.* • Have student "be the teacher": Partner with "approaching mastery" student and review "first you say _____, then you say _____; now say it fast." • Direct student to reading and writing center in classroom to reinforce early literacy and writing skills.	
ELL	• See "Tips for Teachers" for "approaching mastery" and "at mastery" students. • Describe and model mouth formations for words and sounds in "say it slowly, say it fast," then guide student while practicing with mirror.	• See "Home Connections" for "approaching mastery" and "at mastery" students. • Provide audiotape of "first you say _____, then you say _____; now say it fast" activities and encourage adult at home to help students practice other similar activities throughout the day; encourage students to practice with mirror at home, as needed.

Test	Tips for Teachers	Home Connections
Test	• Show realia or other visuals of objects and concepts, as needed (e.g., show a picture of students having fun). • Use pantomiming, gestures (e.g., show "this is my book") to show concepts of words. • Use primary language equivalents when available and then ask student to say words in English.	• Encourage adult at home to help students identify realia and other visuals of objects and concepts, as needed. • Encourage adult at home to help students practice using primary language equivalents and English words when possible.
Assessment (for Lessons 1–20) **Approaching Mastery**	• See "Remedial Exercises and Retesting the Students" guidelines on pages 34 and 35 in *Curriculum-Based Assessment and Fluency Teacher Handbook*. • Partner with "at mastery" student and review sounds. • Reteach difficult sounds using "good-bye" list. • Conduct "see-say-write" until firm. • Practice circling responses.	• Provide sound flash cards for students to take home for additional practice. • Encourage students to share their take-home sheets with their families. • Encourage adult at home to conduct "see-say-write" activity for each sound. • Have adult at home access SRA's Home Connection Activities listed at *www.sraonline.com* • Direct Instruction • *Reading Mastery Signature Edition* • Activities
At Mastery	• Have student "be the teacher": Partner with "approaching mastery" student and review sounds. • Direct student to reading and writing center in classroom to reinforce early literacy and writing skills.	
ELL **Test**	• See "Tips for Teachers" for "approaching mastery" and "at mastery" students.	• See "Home Connections" for "approaching mastery" and "at mastery" students. • Provide sounds audiotape to use with sound flash cards at home. • Encourage students to practice mouth formations with mirror at home. • Encourage adult at home to help students identify realia and other visuals of objects at home with same beginning sounds.
Mastery Test 4 (Lessons 21-25) **Approaching Mastery**	• See "What To Do" guidelines for "if the group is weak on Mastery Test 4" on page 161 in *Presentation Book A*. • Partner with "at mastery" student and review sounds. • Reteach difficult sounds using "good-bye" list. • Conduct "see-say-write": Student sees sound, says sound, and writes sound three times per sound.	• Provide sound flash cards for students to take home for additional practice. • Encourage students to share their take-home sheets with their families. • Encourage adult at home to conduct "see-say-write" activity for each sound. • Have adult at home access SRA's Home Connection Activities listed at *www.sraonline.com* • Direct Instruction • *Reading Mastery Signature Edition* • Activities

B5

Test	Tips for Teachers	Home Connections
At Mastery	• See "What To Do" guidelines for "if the group is firm on Mastery Test 4" on page 161 in *Presentation Book A*. • Have student "be the teacher": Partner with "approaching mastery" student and review sounds. • Direct student to reading and writing center in classroom to reinforce early literacy and writing skills.	
ELL	• See "Tips for Teachers" for "approaching mastery" and "at mastery" students. • Describe and model mouth formations for sounds, then guide student while practicing with mirror. • Show realia or other visuals of objects with same beginning sounds.	• See "Home Connections" for "approaching mastery" and "at mastery" students. • Provide sounds audiotape to use with sound flash cards at home for additional practice. • Encourage students to practice mouth formations with mirror at home. • Encourage adult at home to help students identify realia and other visuals of objects at home with same beginning sounds.

Mastery Test 5
(Lessons 26-30)
 	
Approaching Mastery
	• See "What To Do" guidelines for "if the group is weak on Mastery Test 5" on page 186 in *Presentation Book A*.
	• Reteach "first you'll say this sound, then you'll say **an**."
	• Partner with "at mastery" student and review "first you'll say this sound, then you'll say **an**."
		• Provide two sound flash cards (**m** and **r**) and directions—"first you'll say this sound, then you'll say **an**"--for students to take home for additional practice.
		• Have adult at home access SRA's Home Connection Activities listed at *www.sraonline.com*
		  • Direct Instruction
		    • *Reading Mastery Signature Edition*
		      • Activities

At Mastery	• See "What To Do" guidelines for "if the group is firm on Mastery Test 5" on page 186 in *Presentation Book A*. • Have student "be the teacher": Partner with "approaching mastery" student and review "first you'll say this sound, then you'll say **an**." • Direct student to reading center in classroom to reinforce early literacy skills.	
ELL	• See "Tips for Teachers" for "approaching mastery" and "at mastery" students. • Describe and model mouth formations for "first you'll say this sound, then you'll say an," then guide student while practicing with mirror. • Show realia or other visuals of objects and concepts, as needed. • Use pantomiming to show concepts. • Use primary language equivalents when available and then ask student to say words in English.	• See "Home Connections" for "approaching mastery" and "at mastery" students. • Provide audiotape and two sound flash cards (m and r) and directions—"first you'll say this sound, then you'll say an" for students to take home for additional practice; encourage students to practice with mirror at home, as needed. • Encourage adult at home to help students identify realia and other visuals of objects and concepts, as needed. • Encourage adult at home to help students practice using primary language equivalents and English words when possible.

Test	Tips for Teachers	Home Connections

Mastery Test 6 (Lessons 31-35)
 	
Approaching Mastery
	• See "What To Do" guidelines for "if the group is weak on Mastery Test 6" on page 217 in *Presentation Book A*.
	• Reteach difficult sounds using "good-bye" list; reteach "what are you going to say first, next, next" and/or "don't stop between the sounds."
	• Partner with "at mastery" student and review difficult sounds and/or "what are you going to say first, next, next" and/or "don't stop between the sounds."
		• Provide sound and word flash cards for students to take home for additional practice.
		• Provide page of words for students to take home to practice "sound it out, say it fast."
		• Have adult at home access SRA's Home Connection Activities listed at *www.sraonline.com*
		  • Direct Instruction
		    • *Reading Mastery Signature Edition*
		      • Activities

At Mastery	• See "What To Do" guidelines for "if the group is firm on Mastery Test 6" on page 217 in *Presentation Book A*. • Have student "be the teacher": Partner with "approaching mastery" student and review difficult sounds and/or "what are you going to say first, next, next" and/or "don't stop between the sounds." • Direct student to reading and writing center in classroom to reinforce early literacy and writing skills.	
ELL	• See "Tips for Teachers" for "approaching mastery" and "at mastery" students. • Describe and model mouth formations for "what are you going to say first, next, next" and/or "don't stop between the sounds," then guide student while practicing with mirror. • Use gestures and facial expressions to show concepts of words. • Use primary language equivalents when available and then ask student to say words in English.	• See "Home Connections" for "approaching mastery" and "at mastery" students. • Provide audiotape for use with sound and word flash cards to take home for additional practice; encourage students to practice with mirror at home, as needed. • Encourage adult at home to help students practice using primary language equivalents and English words when possible.

Test

Test	Tips for Teachers	Home Connections

Mastery Test 7 (Lessons 36-40)
 	
Approaching Mastery
	• See "What To Do" guidelines for "if the group is weak on Mastery Test 7" on page 249 in *Presentation Book A*.
	• Partner with "at mastery" student and review "sound it out, say it fast."
	• Reteach "sound it out, say it fast" as well as any difficult sounds and words using "good-bye" list.
		• Provide sound and word flash cards for students to take home for additional practice.
		• Provide page of words for students to take home to practice "sound it out, say it fast."
		• Encourage students to share their take-home sheets with their families.
		• Have adult at home access SRA's Home Connection Activities listed at *www.sraonline.com*
		  • Direct Instruction
		    • *Reading Mastery Signature Edition*
		      • Activities

B7

Test	Tips for Teachers	Home Connections
At Mastery	• See "What To Do" guidelines for "if the group is firm on Mastery Test 7" on page 249 in *Presentation Book A*. • Have student "be the teacher": Partner with "approaching mastery" student and review "sound it out, say it fast." • Direct student to reading and writing center in classroom to reinforce early literacy and writing skills.	
ELL	• See "Tips for Teachers" for "approaching mastery" and "at mastery" students. • Describe and model mouth formations for "sound it out, say it fast," then guide student while practicing with mirror. • Show realia or other visuals of objects and concepts, as needed. • Use primary language equivalents when available and then ask student to say words in English.	• See "Home Connections" for "approaching mastery" and "at mastery" students. • Provide audiotape for use with sound and word flash cards to take home for additional practice; encourage students to practice with mirror at home, as needed. • Encourage adult at home to help students practice using primary language equivalents and English words when possible.

Assessment (for Lessons 21–40)
 	
Approaching Mastery
	• See "Remedial Exercises and Retesting the Students" guidelines on page 37 in *Curriculum-Based Assessment and Fluency Teacher Handbook*.
	• Partner with "at mastery" student and review sounds and "sound it out, say it fast."
	• Reteach difficult sounds using "good-bye" list.
	• Conduct "see-say-write" until firm.
	• Practice circling responses and "sounding out words to yourself."
		• Provide sound flash cards for students to take home for additional practice.
		• Encourage students to share their take-home sheets with their families.
		• Encourage adult at home to conduct "see-say-write" activity for each sound and word.
		• Provide page of words for students to take home to practice "sound it out, say it fast."
		• Have adult at home access SRA's Home Connection Activities listed at *www.sraonline.com*
		  • Direct Instruction
		    • *Reading Mastery Signature Edition*
		      • Activities

At Mastery	• Have student "be the teacher": Partner with "approaching mastery" student and review sounds and "sound it out, say it fast." • Direct student to reading and writing center in classroom to reinforce early literacy and writing skills.	
ELL	• See "Tips for Teachers" for "approaching mastery" and "at mastery" students. • Describe and model mouth formations for "sound it out, say it fast," then guide student while practicing with mirror. • Show realia or other visuals of objects and concepts, as needed. • Use primary language equivalents when available and then ask student to say words in English.	• See "Home Connections" for "approaching mastery" and "at mastery" students. • Provide audiotape for use with sound and word flash cards to take home for additional practice; encourage students to practice with mirror at home, as needed. • Encourage adult at home to help students identify realia and other visuals of objects and concepts, as needed. • Encourage adult at home to help students practice using primary language equivalents and English words when possible.

Test	Tips for Teachers	Home Connections

Mastery Test 8 (Lessons 41-45)
 	
Approaching Mastery
	• See "What To Do" guidelines for "if the group is weak on Mastery Test 8" on page 278 in *Presentation Book A*.
	• Partner with "at mastery" student and review "sound it out, say it fast."
	• Reteach "sound it out, say it fast" as well as any difficult sounds and words using "good-bye" list.
		• Provide page of words for students to take home to practice "sound it out, say it fast."
		• Encourage students to share their take-home sheets with their families.
		• Provide word flash cards for students to take home for additional practice.
		• Have adult at home access SRA's Home Connection Activities listed at *www.sraonline.com*
		  • Direct Instruction
		    • *Reading Mastery Signature Edition*
		      • Activities

At Mastery	• See "What To Do" guidelines for "if the group is firm on Mastery Test 8" on page 278 in *Presentation Book A*. • Have student "be the teacher": Partner with "approaching mastery" student and review "sound it out, say it fast." • Direct student to reading and writing center in classroom to reinforce early literacy and writing skills.	
ELL **Test**	• See "Tips for Teachers" for "approaching mastery" and "at mastery" students. • Describe and model mouth formations for "sound it out, say it fast," then guide student while practicing with mirror. • Use facial expressions to show concepts of words.	• See "Home Connections" for "approaching mastery" and "at mastery" students. • Provide audiotape for use with sound and word flash cards to take home for additional practice; encourage students to practice with mirror at home, as needed. • Encourage adult at home to help students practice using primary language equivalents and English words when possible.

Mastery Test 9 (Lessons 46-50)
 	
Approaching Mastery
	• See "What To Do" guidelines for "if the group is weak on Mastery Test 9" on page 306 in *Presentation Book A*.
	• Partner with "at mastery" student and review sounds.
	• Reteach difficult sounds using "good-bye" list.
		• Provide sound flash cards for students to take home for additional practice.
		• Encourage students to share their take-home sheets with their families.
		• Encourage adult at home to conduct "see-say-write" activity for each sound.
		• Have adult at home access SRA's Home Connection Activities listed at *www.sraonline.com*
		  • Direct Instruction
		    • *Reading Mastery Signature Edition*
		      • Activities

At Mastery	• See "What To Do" guidelines for "if the group is firm on Mastery Test 9" on page 306 in *Presentation Book A*. • Have student "be the teacher": Partner with "approaching mastery" student and review sounds. • Direct student to reading and writing center in classroom to reinforce early literacy and writing skills.	

B9

Test	Tips for Teachers	Home Connections
ELL	• See "Tips for Teachers" for "approaching mastery" and "at mastery" students. • Describe and model mouth formations for sounds, then guide student while practicing with mirror. • Show realia or other visuals of objects with same beginning sounds.	• See "Home Connections" for "approaching mastery" and "at mastery" students. • Provide audiotape for use with sound and word flash cards to take home for additional practice; encourage students to practice mouth formations with mirror at home. • Encourage adult at home to help students identify realia and other visuals of objects at home with same beginning sounds.

Mastery Test 10 (Lessons 51-55)
 	
Approaching Mastery
	• See "What To Do" guidelines for "if the group is weak on Mastery Test 10" on page 335 in *Presentation Book A.*
	• Partner with "at mastery" student and review "sound it out, say it fast, what word."
	• Reteach "sound it out, say it fast, what word" as well as any difficult sounds and words using "good-bye" list.
		• Provide page of words for students to take home to practice "sound it out, say it fast, what word."
		• Encourage students to share their take-home sheets with their families.
		• Provide "sentence builder" flash cards for students to use for additional practice: Keep word flash cards in envelope and build sentences to read using "sound it out, say it fast, what word."
		• Have adult at home access SRA's Home Connection Activities listed at *www.sraonline.com*
		  • Direct Instruction
		    • *Reading Mastery Signature Edition*
		      • Activities

At Mastery	• See "What To Do" guidelines for "if the group is firm on Mastery Test 10" on page 335 in *Presentation Book A.* • Have student "be the teacher": Partner with "approaching mastery" student and review "sound it out, say it fast, what word." • Direct student to reading and writing center in classroom to reinforce early literacy and writing skills.	
ELL	• See "Tips for Teachers" for "approaching mastery" and "at mastery" students. • Describe and model mouth formations for "sound it out, say it fast, what word," then guide student while practicing with mirror. • Show realia or other visuals illustrating meaning of the sentence. • Use primary language equivalents when available and then ask student to say words and sentence in English.	• See "Home Connections" for "approaching mastery" and "at mastery" students. • Provide audiotape for use with "sentence builder" flash cards and sound and word flashcards to take home for additional practice; encourage students to practice with mirror at home, as needed. • Encourage adult at home to help students practice using primary language equivalents and English words when possible.

Test	Tips for Teachers	Home Connections

Mastery Test 11 (Lessons 56-60)
 	
Approaching Mastery
	• See "What To Do" guidelines for "if the group is weak on Mastery Test 11" on page 22 in *Presentation Book B*.
	• Partner with "at mastery" student and review sounds, "sound it out, what word," and words that rhyme.
	• Reteach "sound it out, what word," rhyming words, as well as any difficult sounds and words using "good-bye" list.
		• Provide sound and word flash cards for students to take home for additional practice.
		• Encourage students to share their take-home sheets with their families.
		• Encourage adult at home to conduct "see-say-write" activity for each sound.
		• Encourage adult at home to review rhyming words with their students.
		• Have adult at home access SRA's Home Connection Activities listed at *www.sraonline.com*
		  • Direct Instruction
		    • *Reading Mastery Signature Edition*
		      • Activities

At Mastery	• See "What To Do" guidelines for "if the group is firm on Mastery Test 11" on page 22 in *Presentation Book B*. • Have student "be the teacher": Partner with "approaching mastery" student and review sounds, "sound it out, what word," and words that rhyme. • Direct student to reading and writing center in classroom to reinforce early literacy and writing skills.	
ELL	• See "Tips for Teachers" for "approaching mastery" and "at mastery" students. • Describe and model mouth formations for individual sounds and "sound it out, what word," then guide student while practicing with mirror. • Show realia or other visuals of objects and concepts, as needed. • Use primary language equivalents when available and then ask student to say words in English.	• See "Home Connections" for "approaching mastery" and "at mastery" students. • Provide audiotape for use with sound and word flash cards to take home for additional practice; encourage students to practice with mirror at home, as needed. • Encourage adult at home to help students identify realia and other visuals of objects and concepts, as needed. • Encourage adult at home to help students practice using primary language equivalents and English words when possible.
Test		

Assessment (for Lessons 41–60)
 	
Approaching Mastery
	• See "Remedial Exercises and Retesting the Students" guidelines on page 39 in *Curriculum-Based Assessment and Fluency Teacher Handbook*.
	• Partner with "at mastery" student and review sounds and "sound it out, say it fast."
	• Reteach difficult sounds and words using "good-bye" list.
	• Conduct "see-say-write" until firm.
	• Practice circling responses "reading words to yourself."
		• Provide sound and word flash cards to take home for additional practice.
		• Send home previously completed take-homes for additional practice.
		• Encourage adult at home to conduct "see-say-write" activity for each sound and word.
		• Provide page of words for students to take home to practice "read each word to yourself."
		• Have adult at home access SRA's Home Connection Activities listed at *www.sraonline.com*
		  • Direct Instruction
		    • *Reading Mastery Signature Edition*
		      • Activities

B11

Test	Tips for Teachers	Home Connections
At Mastery	• Have student "be the teacher": Partner with "approaching mastery" student and review sounds and "sound it out, say it fast." • Direct student to reading and writing center in classroom to reinforce early literacy and writing skills.	
ELL	• See "Tips for Teachers" for "approaching mastery" and "at mastery" students. • Describe and model mouth formations for sounds and "sound it out, say it fast," then guide student while practicing with mirror. • Show realia or other visuals of objects and concepts, as needed. • Use primary language equivalents when available and then ask student to say words in English.	• See "Home Connections" for "approaching mastery" and "at mastery" students. • Provide audiotape for use with sound and word flash cards to take home for additional practice; encourage students to practice with mirror at home, as needed. • Encourage adult at home to help students identify realia and other visuals of objects and concepts, as needed. • Encourage adult at home to help students practice using primary language equivalents and English words when possible.

Mastery Test 12 (Lessons 60-65)
 	
Approaching Mastery
	• See "What To Do" guidelines for "if the group is weak on Mastery Test 12" on page 57 in *Presentation Book B.*
	• Partner with "at mastery" student and review "sound it out, what word."
	• Reteach "sound it out, what word" as well as any difficult sounds and words using "good-bye" list.
	• Review finger placement and tracking for sentence reading.
		• Provide page of words for students to take home to practice "sound it out, what word."
		• Encourage students to share their take-home sheets with their families.
		• Provide "sentence builder" flash cards for students to use for additional practice.
		• Have adult at home access SRA's Home Connection Activities listed at *www.sraonline.com*
		  • Direct Instruction
		    • *Reading Mastery Signature Edition*
		      • Activities

At Mastery	• See "What To Do" guidelines for "if the group is firm on Mastery Test 12" on page 57 in *Presentation Book B.* • Have student "be the teacher": Partner with "approaching mastery" student and review "sound it out, what word." • Direct student to reading and writing center in classroom to reinforce early literacy and writing skills.	
ELL	• See "Tips for Teachers" for "approaching mastery" and "at mastery" students. • Describe and model mouth formations for "sound it out, say it fast," then guide student while practicing with mirror. • Show realia or other visuals illustrating meaning of the sentence. • Use primary language equivalents when available and then ask student to say words and sentence in English.	• See "Home Connections" for "approaching mastery" and "at mastery" students. • Provide audiotape to use with "sentence builder" flash cards and sound and word flashcards to take home for additional practice; encourage students to practice with mirror at home, as needed. • Encourage adult at home to help students identify realia and other visuals illustrating meaning of the sentence. • Encourage adult at home to help students practice using primary language equivalents and English words when possible.

Test	Tips for Teachers	Home Connections

Mastery Test 13 (Lessons 66-70)
 	
Approaching Mastery
	• See "What To Do" guidelines for "if the group is weak on Mastery Test 13" on page 92 in *Presentation Book B*.
	• Partner with "at mastery" student and review sounds.
	• Reteach difficult sounds using "good-bye" list.
		• Provide sound flash cards for students to take home for additional practice.
		• Encourage students to share their take-home sheets with their families.
		• Encourage adult at home to conduct "see-say-write" activity for each sound.
		• Have adult at home access SRA's Home Connection Activities listed at *www.sraonline.com*
		  • Direct Instruction
		    • *Reading Mastery Signature Edition*
		      • Activities

At Mastery	• See "What To Do" guidelines for "if the group is firm on Mastery Test 13" on page 92 in *Presentation Book B*. • Have student "be the teacher": Partner with "approaching mastery" student and review sounds. • Direct student to reading and writing center in classroom to reinforce early literacy and writing skills.	
ELL	• See "Tips for Teachers" for "approaching mastery" and "at mastery" students. • Describe and model mouth formations for sounds, then guide student while practicing with mirror. • Show realia or other visuals of objects with same beginning sounds.	• See "Home Connections" for "approaching mastery" and "at mastery" students. • Provide sounds audiotape to use with sound flash cards at home; encourage students to practice mouth formations with mirror at home. • Encourage adult at home to help students identify realia and other visuals of objects at home with same beginning sounds.

Test

Test	Tips for Teachers	Home Connections

Mastery Test 14 (Lessons 71-75)
 	
Approaching Mastery
	• See "What To Do" guidelines for "if the group is weak on Mastery Test 14" on page 124 in *Presentation Book B*.
	• Partner with "at mastery" student and review "sound it out, what word."
	• Reteach "get ready (with clapping), what word" as well as any difficult sounds and words using "good-bye" list.
	• Review finger placement and tracking for sentence reading.
		• Provide page of words for students to take home to practice "get ready, what word."
		• Encourage students to share their take-home sheets with their families.
		• Provide "sentence builder" flash cards for students to use for additional practice.
		• Have adult at home access SRA's Home Connection Activities listed at *www.sraonline.com*
		  • Direct Instruction
		    • *Reading Mastery Signature Edition*
		      • Activities

B13

Test	Tips for Teachers	Home Connections
At Mastery	• See "What To Do" guidelines for "if the group is firm on Mastery Test 14" on page 124 in *Presentation Book B*. • Have student "be the teacher": Partner with "approaching mastery" student and review "get ready, what word." • Direct student to reading and writing center in classroom to reinforce early literacy and writing skills.	
ELL	• See "Tips for Teachers" for "approaching mastery" and "at mastery" students. • Describe and model mouth formations for "sound it out, say it fast," then guide student while practicing with mirror. • Show realia or other visuals illustrating meaning of the sentence. • Use primary language equivalents when available and then ask student to say words and sentence in English.	• See "Home Connections" for "approaching mastery" and "at mastery" students. • Provide audiotape to use with "sentence builder" flash cards and sound and word flashcards at home; encourage students to practice with mirror at home, as needed. • Encourage adult at home to help students identify realia and other visuals illustrating meaning of the sentence. • Encourage adult at home to help students practice using primary language equivalents and English words when possible.

Mastery Test 15 (Lessons 76–80)
 	
Approaching Mastery
	• See "What To Do" guidelines for "if the group is weak on Mastery Test 15" on page 155 in *Presentation Book B*.
	• Partner with "at mastery" student and review "sound it out, what word" and "read these words the fast way."
	• Reteach "sound it out, what word" and "read these words the fast way" as well as any difficult sounds and words using "good-bye" list.
		• Provide page of words for students to take home to practice "sound it out, what word" and "read these words the fast way."
		• Encourage students to share their take-home sheets with their families.
		• Provide word flash cards for students to take home for additional practice.
		• Have adult at home access SRA's Home Connection Activities listed at *www.sraonline.com*
		  • Direct Instruction
		    • *Reading Mastery Signature Edition*
		      • Activities

At Mastery	• See "What To Do" guidelines for "if the group is firm on Mastery Test 15" on page 155 in *Presentation Book B*. • Have student "be the teacher": Partner with "approaching mastery" student and review "sound it out, what word" and "read these words the fast way." • Direct student to reading and writing center in classroom to reinforce early literacy and writing skills.	

Test

B14

Test	Tips for Teachers	Home Connections
ELL **Test**	• See "Tips for Teachers" for "approaching mastery" and "at mastery" students. • Describe and model mouth formations for sounds and "sound it out, say it fast," then guide student while practicing with mirror. • Show realia or other visuals of objects and concepts, as needed. • Use primary language equivalents when available and then ask student to say words in English.	• See "Home Connections" for "approaching mastery" and "at mastery" students. • Provide audiotape of "sound it out, what word" for use with sound and word flashcards to take home for additional practice; encourage students to practice with mirror at home, as needed. • Encourage adult at home to help students identify realia and other visuals of objects and concepts, as needed. • Encourage adult at home to help students practice using primary language equivalents and English words when possible.

Assessment (for Lessons 61–80)
 	
Approaching Mastery
	• See "Remedial Exercises and Retesting the Students" guidelines on page 41 in *Curriculum-Based Assessment and Fluency Teacher Handbook*.
	• Partner with "at mastery" student and review sounds and "sound it out, say it fast."
	• Reteach difficult sounds and words using "good-bye" list.
	• Conduct "see-say-write" until firm.
	• Practice circling responses "reading words to yourself."
		• Provide sound and word flash cards for students to take home for additional practice.
		• Encourage students to share their take-home sheets with their families.
		• Encourage adult at home to conduct "see-say-write" activity for each sound and word.
		• Provide page of words for students to take home to practice "read each word to yourself."
		• Have adult at home access SRA's Home Connection Activities listed at *www.sraonline.com*
		 • Direct Instruction
		  • *Reading Mastery Signature Edition*
		   • Activities

At Mastery	• Have student "be the teacher": Partner with "approaching mastery" student and review sounds and "sound it out, say it fast." • Direct student to reading and writing center in classroom to reinforce early literacy and writing skills.	
ELL	• See "Tips for Teachers" for "approaching mastery" and "at mastery" students. • Describe and model mouth formations for sounds and "sound it out, say it fast," then guide student while practicing with mirror. • Show realia or other visuals of objects and concepts, as needed. • Use primary language equivalents when available and then ask student to say words in English.	• See "Home Connections" for "approaching mastery" and "at mastery" students. • Provide audiotape for use with sound and word flash cards to take home for additional practice; encourage students to practice with mirror at home, as needed. • Encourage adult at home to help students identify realia and other visuals of objects and concepts, as needed. • Encourage adult at home to help students practice using primary language equivalents and English words when possible.

B15

Test	Tips for Teachers	Home Connections

Mastery Test 16 (Lessons 81-85)
 	
Approaching Mastery
	• See "What To Do" guidelines for "if the group is weak on Mastery Test 16" on page 187 in *Presentation Book B*.
	• Partner with "at mastery" student and review "get ready, what word."
	• Reteach "get ready (with clapping), what word" as well as any difficult sounds and words using "good-bye" list.
	• Review finger placement and tracking for sentence reading.
		• Provide page of words for students to take home to practice "get ready, what word."
		• Encourage students to share their take-home sheets with their families.
		• Provide word flash cards for students to take home for additional practice.
		• Have adult at home access SRA's Home Connection Activities listed at *www.sraonline.com*
		  • Direct Instruction
		    • *Reading Mastery Signature Edition*
		      • Activities

At Mastery	• See "What To Do" guidelines for "if the group is firm on Mastery Test 16" on page 187 in *Presentation Book B*. • Have student "be the teacher": Partner with "approaching mastery" student and review "get ready, what word." Direct student to reading and writing center in classroom to reinforce early literacy and writing skills.	
ELL **Test**	• See "Tips for Teachers" for "approaching mastery" and "at mastery" students. • Describe and model mouth formations for difficult sounds and words, then guide student while practicing with mirror. • Show realia or other visuals illustrating meaning of sentences. • Use primary language equivalents when available and then ask student to say words and sentences in English.	• See "Home Connections" for "approaching mastery" and "at mastery" students. • Provide audiotape to use with sound and word flashcards at home; encourage students to practice with mirror at home, as needed. • Encourage adult at home to help students identify realia and other visuals illustrating meaning of the sentences. • Encourage adult at home to help students practice using primary language equivalents and English words when possible.

Mastery Test 17 (Lessons 86-90)
 	
Approaching Mastery
	• See "What To Do" guidelines for "if the group is weak on Mastery Test 17" on page 218 in *Presentation Book B*.
	• Partner with "at mastery" student and review sounds.
	• Reteach difficult sounds using "good-bye" list.
		• Provide sound flash cards for students to take home for additional practice.
		• Encourage students to share their take-home sheets with their families.
		• Encourage adult at home to conduct "see-say-write" activity for each sound.
		• Have adult at home access SRA's Home Connection Activities listed at *www.sraonline.com*
		  • Direct Instruction
		    • *Reading Mastery Signature Edition*
		      • Activities

Test	Tips for Teachers	Home Connections
At Mastery	• See "What To Do" guidelines for "if the group is firm on Mastery Test 17" on page 218 in *Presentation Book B*. • Have student "be the teacher": Partner with "approaching mastery" student and review sounds. • Direct student to reading and writing center in classroom to reinforce early literacy and writing skills.	
ELL	• See "Tips for Teachers" for "approaching mastery" and "at mastery" students. • Describe and model mouth formations for sounds, then guide student while practicing with mirror. • Show realia or other visuals of objects with same beginning sounds.	• See "Home Connections" for "approaching mastery" and "at mastery" students. • Provide sounds audiotape to use with sound flash cards at home; encourage students to practice mouth formations with mirror at home. • Encourage adult at home to help students identify realia and other visuals of objects at home with same beginning sounds.

Mastery Test 18
(Lessons 91-95)
 	
Approaching Mastery
	• See "What To Do" guidelines for "if the group is weak on Mastery Test 18" on page 253 in *Presentation Book B*.
	• Partner with "at mastery" student and review "get ready, what word."
	• Reteach "get ready (with clapping), what word" as well as any difficult sounds and words using "good-bye" list.
	• Review finger placement and tracking for sentence reading.
		• Provide page of words for students to take home to practice "get ready, what word."
		• Encourage students to share their take-home sheets with their families.
		• Provide word flash cards for students to take home for additional practice.
		• Have adult at home access SRA's Home Connection Activities listed at *www.sraonline.com*
		  • Direct Instruction
		    • *Reading Mastery Signature Edition*
		      • Activities

At Mastery	• See "What To Do" guidelines for "if the group is firm on Mastery Test 18" on page 253 in *Presentation Book B*. • Have student "be the teacher": Partner with "approaching mastery" student and review "get ready, what word." • Direct student to reading and writing center in classroom to reinforce early literacy and writing skills.	
ELL	• See "Tips for Teachers" for "approaching mastery" and "at mastery" students. • Describe and model mouth formations for difficult sounds and words, then guide student while practicing with mirror. • Show realia or other visuals illustrating meaning of sentences. • Use primary language equivalents when available and then ask student to say words and sentences in English.	• See "Home Connections" for "approaching mastery" and "at mastery" students. • Provide audiotape to use with sound and word flashcards at home; encourage students to practice with mirror at home, as needed. • Encourage adult at home to help students identify realia and other visuals illustrating meaning of the sentences. • Encourage adult at home to help students practice using primary language equivalents and English words when possible.

B17

Test	Tips for Teachers	Home Connections

Mastery Test 19 (Lessons 96-100)
 	
 Approaching Mastery
	• See "What To Do" guidelines for "if the group is weak on Mastery Test 19" on page 284 in *Presentation Book B*.
	 • Partner with "at mastery" student and review sounds.
	 • Reteach difficult sounds using "good-bye" list.
		• Provide sound flash cards for students to take home for additional practice.
		 • Encourage students to share their take-home sheets with their families.
		 • Encourage adult at home to conduct "see-say-write" activity for each sound.
		 • Have adult at home access SRA's Home Connection Activities listed at *www.sraonline.com*
		  • Direct Instruction
		   • *Reading Mastery Signature Edition*
		    • Activities

At Mastery	• See "What To Do" guidelines for "if the group is firm on Mastery Test 19" on page 284 in *Presentation Book B*. • Have student "be the teacher": Partner with "approaching mastery" student and review sounds. • Direct student to reading and writing center in classroom to reinforce early literacy and writing skills.	
ELL	• See "Tips for Teachers" for "approaching mastery" and "at mastery" students. • Describe and model mouth formations for sounds, then guide student while practicing with mirror. • Show realia or other visuals of objects and concepts, as needed with same beginning sounds.	• See "Home Connections" for "approaching mastery" and "at mastery" students. • Provide sounds audiotape to use with sound flash cards at home; encourage students to practice mouth formations with mirror at home. • Encourage adult at home to help students identify realia and other visuals of objects and concepts, as needed at home with same beginning sounds.

Test	Tips for Teachers	Home Connections

Assessment (for Lessons 81–100)
 	
 Approaching Mastery
	• See "Remedial Exercises and Retesting the Students" guidelines on pages 43 and 44 in *Curriculum-Based Assessment and Fluency Teacher Handbook*.
	 • Partner with "at mastery" student and review sounds and "sound it out, say it fast."
	 • Reteach difficult sounds and words using "good-bye" list.
	 • Conduct "see-say-write" until firm.
	 • Practice circling responses and "reading words to yourself."
		• Provide sound and word flash cards for students to take home for additional practice.
		 • Encourage students to share their take-home sheets with their families.
		 • Encourage adult at home to conduct "see-say-write" activity for each sound and word.
		 • Provide page of words for students to take home to practice "read each word to yourself."
		 • Have adult at home access SRA's Home Connection Activities listed at *www.sraonline.com*
		  • Direct Instruction
		   • *Reading Mastery Signature Edition*
		    • Activities

Test	Tips for Teachers	Home Connections
At Mastery	• Have student "be the teacher": Partner with "approaching mastery" student and review sounds and "sound it out, say it fast." • Direct student to reading and writing center in classroom to reinforce early literacy and writing skills.	
ELL	• See "Tips for Teachers" for "approaching mastery" and "at mastery" students. • Describe and model mouth formations for sounds and "sound it out, say it fast," then guide student while practicing with mirror. • Show realia or other visuals of objects and concepts, as needed. • Use primary language equivalents when available and then ask student to say words in English.	• See "Home Connections" for "approaching mastery" and "at mastery" students. • Provide audiotape for use with sound and word flash cards to take home for additional practice; encourage students to practice with mirror at home, as needed. • Encourage adult at home to help students identify realia and other visuals of objects and concepts, as needed. • Encourage adult at home to help students practice using primary language equivalents and English words when possible.

Mastery Test 20 (Lessons 101-105)
 	
 Approaching Mastery
	• See "What To Do" guidelines for "if the group is weak on Mastery Test 20" on page 316 in *Presentation Book B*.
	 • Partner with "at mastery" student and review "get ready, what word."
	 • Reteach "get ready (with clapping), what word" as well as any difficult sounds and words using "good-bye" list.
	 • Review finger placement and tracking for sentence reading.
		• Provide page of words for students to take home to practice "get ready, what word."
		 • Encourage students to share their take-home sheets with their families.
		 • Provide word flash cards for students to take home for additional practice.
		 • Have adult at home access SRA's Home Connection Activities listed at *www.sraonline.com*
		   • Direct Instruction
		     • *Reading Mastery Signature Edition*
		       • Activities

At Mastery	• See "What To Do" guidelines for "if the group is firm on Mastery Test 20" on page 316 in *Presentation Book B*. • Have student "be the teacher": Partner with "approaching mastery" student and review "get ready, what word." • Direct student to reading and writing center in classroom to reinforce early literacy and writing skills.	
ELL	• See "Tips for Teachers" for "approaching mastery" and "at mastery" students. • Describe and model mouth formations for difficult sounds and words, then guide student while practicing with mirror. • Show realia or other visuals illustrating meaning of sentences. • Use primary language equivalents when available and then ask student to say words and sentences in English.	• See "Home Connections" for "approaching mastery" and "at mastery" students. • Provide audiotape to use with sound and word flashcards for additional practice; encourage students to practice with mirror at home, as needed. • Encourage adult at home to help students identify realia and other visuals illustrating meaning of sentences. • Encourage adult at home to help students practice using primary language equivalents and English words when possible.

Test	Tips for Teachers	Home Connections
Fluency Checkout (Lesson 108) **Approaching Mastery**	• See guidelines for students who do not read within error or time limit for Lesson 108 on page 5 in *Presentation Book C*. • Partner with "at mastery" student and have him or her model reading story; have student read story. • Reteach difficult words using "good-bye" list. • Review finger placement and tracking for sentence reading. • Have adult model reading story; have student read story until firm. • Use paired reading: Good reader reads until student signals for his or her turn to read. • Develop recording of story read by good reader (e.g., at mastery student, adult); have student listen to recording and whisper read.	• Provide word flash cards for students to take home for additional practice. • Have adult at home model reading story; have students listen and track during story reading; have students then read story; have adult at home review difficult words following story reading.
At Mastery	• See guidelines for students who read within error or time limit for Lesson 108 on page 5 in *Presentation Book C*. • Partner with "approaching mastery" student and model reading story; have student read story. • Have student record self reading story as model for "approaching mastery" student. • Direct student to reading and writing center in classroom to reinforce early literacy and writing skills.	
ELL	• See "Tips for Teachers" for "approaching mastery" and "at mastery" students. • Describe and model mouth formations for difficult sounds and words, then guide student while practicing with mirror. • Use sentence strips to practice reading sentences in story. • Show realia or other visuals illustrating meaning of sentences in story. • Use primary language equivalents when available and then ask student to say words and sentences in English.	• See "Home Connections" for "approaching mastery" and "at mastery" students. • Provide audiotape to use with sentence strips and sound and word flashcards for additional practice; encourage students to practice with mirror at home, as needed. • Provide audiotape of story; have students listen and track during story reading; then students read aloud with tape while tracking; then students read aloud and track independently; have adult at home review difficult words following independent story reading. • Encourage adult at home to help students tell a similar story using primary language equivalents. • Encourage adult at home to help students identify realia and other visuals illustrating meaning of sentences in story.

Test	Tips for Teachers	Home Connections
Fluency Checkout (Lesson 109) **Approaching Mastery**	• See guidelines for students who do not read within error or time limit for Lesson 109 on page 10 in *Presentation Book C.* • Partner with "at mastery" student and have him or her model reading story; have student read story. • Reteach difficult words using "good-bye" list. • Review finger placement and tracking for sentence reading. • Have adult model reading story; have student read story until firm. • Use paired reading. • Develop recording of story read by good reader; have student listen to recording and whisper read.	• Provide word flash cards for students to take home for additional practice. • Have adult at home model reading story; have students listen and track during story reading; have students read story; adult at home review difficult words following story reading.
At Mastery	• See guidelines for students who read within error or time limit for Lesson 109 on page 10 in *Presentation Book C.* • Partner with "approaching mastery" student and model reading story; have student read story. • Have student record self reading story as model for "approaching mastery" student. • Direct student to reading and writing center in classroom to reinforce early literacy and writing skills.	
ELL	• See "Tips for Teachers" for "approaching mastery" and "at mastery" students. • Describe and model mouth formations for difficult sounds and words, then guide student while practicing with mirror. • Use sentence strips to practice reading sentences in story. • Show realia or other visuals illustrating meaning of sentences in story. • Use primary language equivalents when available and then ask student to say words and sentences in English.	• See "Home Connections" for "approaching mastery" and "at mastery" students. • Provide audiotape to use with sentence strips and sound and word flashcards for additional practice; encourage students to practice with mirror at home, as needed. • Provide audiotape of story; have students listen and track during story reading; then students read aloud with tape while tracking; then students read aloud and track independently; have adult at home review difficult words following independent story reading. • Encourage adult at home to help students tell a similar story using primary language equivalents. • Encourage adult at home to help students identify realia and other visuals illustrating meaning of sentences in story.

B21

Test	Tips for Teachers	Home Connections
Fluency Checkout (Lesson 110) **Approaching Mastery**	• See guidelines for students who do not read within error or time limit for Lesson 110 on page 15 in *Presentation Book C*. • Partner with "at mastery" student and have him or her model reading story; have student read story. • Reteach difficult words using "good-bye" list. • Review finger placement and tracking for sentence reading. • Have adult model reading story; have student read story until firm. • Use paired reading. • Develop recording of story read by good reader; have student listen to recording and whisper read.	• Provide word flash cards for students to take home for additional practice. • Have adult at home model reading story; have students listen and track during story reading; have students read story; have adult at home review difficult words following story reading.
At Mastery	• See guidelines for students who read within error or time limit for Lesson 110 on page 15 in *Presentation Book C*. • Partner with "approaching mastery" student and model reading story; have student read story. • Have student record self reading story as model for "approaching mastery" student. • Direct student to reading and writing center in classroom to reinforce early literacy and writing skills.	
ELL	• See "Tips for Teachers" for "approaching mastery" and "at mastery" students. • Describe and model mouth formations for difficult sounds and words, then guide student while practicing with mirror. • Use sentence strips to practice reading sentences in story. • Show realia or other visuals illustrating meaning of sentences in story. • Use primary language equivalents when available and then ask student to say words and sentences in English.	• See "Home Connections" for "approaching mastery" and "at mastery" students. • Provide audiotape to use with sentence strips and sound and word flashcards for additional practice; encourage students to practice with mirror at home, as needed. • Provide audiotape of story; have students listen and track during story reading; then students read aloud with tape while tracking; then students read aloud and track independently; have adult at home review difficult words following independent story reading. • Encourage adult at home to help students tell a similar story using primary language equivalents. • Encourage adult at home to help students identify realia and other visuals illustrating meaning of sentences in story.

Test	Tips for Teachers	Home Connections

Mastery Test 21 (Lessons 106-110) **Approaching Mastery**	• See "What To Do" guidelines for "if the group is weak on Mastery Test 21" on page 16 in *Presentation Book C*.
	• Partner with "at mastery" student and review "read these words the fast way."
	• Reteach "read these words the fast way" as well as any difficult sounds and words using "good-bye" list.
		• Provide page of words for students to take home to practice "read these words the fast way."
		• Encourage students to share their take-home sheets with their families.
		• Provide word flash cards for students to take home for additional practice.
		• Have adult at home access SRA's Home Connection Activities listed at *www.sraonline.com*
		  • Direct Instruction
		    • *Reading Mastery Signature Edition*
		      • Activities

At Mastery	• See "What To Do" guidelines for "if the group is firm on Mastery Test 21" on page 16 in *Presentation Book C*. • Have student "be the teacher": Partner with "approaching mastery" student and review "read these words the fast way." • Direct student to reading and writing center in classroom to reinforce early literacy and writing skills.	
ELL	• See "Tips for Teachers" for "approaching mastery" and "at mastery" students. • Describe and model mouth formations for difficult sounds and words, then guide student while practicing with mirror. • Show realia or other visuals of objects and concepts, as needed. • Use primary language equivalents when available and then ask student to say words in English.	• See "Home Connections" for "approaching mastery" and "at mastery" students. • Provide audiotape for use with sound and word flash cards to take home for additional practice; encourage students to practice with mirror at home, as needed. • Encourage adult at home to help students identify realia and other visuals of objects and concepts, as needed. • Encourage adult at home to help students practice using primary language equivalents and English words when possible.

Test	Tips for Teachers	Home Connections
Fluency Checkout (Lesson 115) **Approaching Mastery**	• See guidelines for students who do not read within error or time limit for Lesson 115 on page 46 in *Presentation Book C*. • Partner with "at mastery" student and have him or her model reading story; have student read story. • Reteach difficult words using "good-bye" list. • Review finger placement and tracking for sentence reading. • Have adult model reading story; have student read story until firm. • Use paired reading. • Develop recording of story read by good reader; have student listen to recording and whisper read.	• Provide word flash cards for students to take home for additional practice. • Have adult at home model reading story; have students listen and track during story reading; have students read story; have adult at home review difficult words following story reading.

B23

Test	Tips for Teachers	Home Connections
At Mastery	• See guidelines for students who read within error or time limit for Lesson 115 on page 46 in *Presentation Book C*. • Partner with "approaching mastery" student and model reading story; have student read story. • Have student record self reading story as model for "approaching mastery" student. • Direct student to reading and writing center in classroom to reinforce early literacy and writing skills.	
ELL	• See "Tips for Teachers" for "approaching mastery" and "at mastery" students. • Describe and model mouth formations for difficult sounds and words, then guide student while practicing with mirror. • Use sentence strips to practice reading sentences in story. • Show realia or other visuals illustrating meaning of sentences in story. • Use primary language equivalents when available and then ask student to say words and sentences in English.	• See "Home Connections" for "approaching mastery" and "at mastery" students. • Provide audiotape to use with sentence strips and sound and word flashcards for additional practice; encourage students to practice with mirror at home, as needed. • Provide audiotape of story; have students listen and track during story reading; then students read aloud with tape while tracking; then students read aloud and track independently; have adult at home review difficult words following independent story reading. • Encourage adult at home to help students tell a similar story using primary language equivalents. • Encourage adult at home to help students identify realia and other visuals illustrating meaning of sentences in story.

Test
 	
Mastery Test 22
(Lessons 111–115)
 	
Approaching Mastery
	• See "What To Do" guidelines for "if the group is weak on Mastery Test 22" on page 47 in *Presentation Book C*.
	• Partner with "at mastery" student and review "read this story the fast way."
	• Reteach "read this story the fast way" as well as any difficult sounds and words using "good-bye" list.
	• Review finger placement and tracking for sentence reading.
		• Provide story for students to take home to practice "read this story the fast way."
		• Encourage students to share their take-home sheets with their families.
		• Provide word flash cards for students to take home for additional practice.
		• Have adult at home access SRA's Home Connection Activities listed at *www.sraonline.com*
		  • Direct Instruction
		    • *Reading Mastery Signature Edition*
		      • Activities

At Mastery	• See "What To Do" guidelines for "if the group is firm on Mastery Test 22" on page 47 in *Presentation Book C*. • Have student "be the teacher": Partner with "approaching mastery" student and review "read this story the fast way." • Direct student to reading and writing center in classroom to reinforce early literacy and writing skills.	

Test	Tips for Teachers	Home Connections
ELL	• See "Tips for Teachers" for "approaching mastery" and "at mastery" students. • Describe and model mouth formations for difficult sounds and words, then guide student while practicing with mirror. • Use sentence strips to practice reading sentences in story. • Show realia or other visuals illustrating meaning of sentences in story. • Use primary language equivalents when available and then ask student to say words and sentences in English.	• See "Home Connections" for "approaching mastery" and "at mastery" students. • Provide audiotape for use with sound and word flashcards, sentence strips, and story to take home for additional practice; encourage students to practice with mirror at home, as needed. • Encourage adult at home to help students identify realia and other visuals illustrating meaning of sentences in story. • Encourage adult at home to help students tell a similar story using primary language equivalents.
Fluency Checkout (Lesson 120) **Approaching Mastery**	• See guidelines for students who do not read within error or time limit for Lesson 120 on page 76 in *Presentation Book C*. • Partner with "at mastery" student and have him or her model reading story; have student read story. • Reteach difficult words using "good-bye" list. • Review finger placement and tracking for sentence reading. • Have adult model reading story; have student read story until firm. • Use paired reading. • Develop recording of story read by good reader; have student listen to recording and whisper read.	• Provide word flash cards for students to take home for additional practice. • Have adult at home model reading story; have students listen and track during story reading; have students read story; have adult at home review difficult words following story reading.
At Mastery	• See guidelines for students who read within error or time limit for Lesson 120 on page 76 in *Presentation Book C*. • Partner with "approaching mastery" student and model reading story; have student read story. • Have student record self reading story as model for "approaching mastery" student. • Direct student to reading and writing center in classroom to reinforce early literacy and writing skills.	
ELL	• See "Tips for Teachers" for "approaching mastery" and "at mastery" students. • Describe and model mouth formations for difficult sounds and words, then guide student while practicing with mirror. • Use sentence strips to practice reading sentences in story. • Show realia or other visuals illustrating meaning of sentences in story. • Use primary language equivalents when available and then ask student to say words and sentences in English.	• See "Home Connections" for "approaching mastery" and "at mastery" students. • Provide audiotape to use with sentence strips and sound and word flashcards for additional practice; encourage students to practice with mirror at home, as needed. • Provide audiotape of story; have students listen and track during story reading; then students read aloud with tape while tracking; then students read aloud and track independently; have adult at home review difficult words following independent story reading.

B25

Test	Tips for Teachers	Home Connections
		• Encourage adult at home to help students tell a similar story using primary language equivalents. • Encourage adult at home to help students identify realia and other visuals illustrating meaning of sentences in story.
Test		
Mastery Test 23 (Lessons 116-120) **Approaching Mastery**	• See "What To Do" guidelines for "if the group is weak on Mastery Test 23" on page 77 in *Presentation Book C.* • Partner with "at mastery" student and review sounds. • Reteach difficult sounds using "good-bye" list.	• Provide sound flash cards for students to take home for additional practice. • Encourage students to share their take-home sheets with their families. • Encourage adult at home to conduct "see-say-write" activity for each sound. • Have adult at home access SRA's Home Connection Activities listed at *www.sraonline.com* • Direct Instruction • *Reading Mastery Signature Edition* • Activities
At Mastery	• See "What To Do" guidelines for "if the group is firm on Mastery Test 23" on page 77 in *Presentation Book C.* • Have student "be the teacher": Partner with "approaching mastery" student and review sounds. • Direct student to reading and writing center in classroom to reinforce early literacy and writing skills.	
ELL	• See "Tips for Teachers" for "approaching mastery" and "at mastery" students. • Describe and model mouth formations for sounds, then guide student while practicing with mirror. • Show realia or other visuals of objects with same beginning sounds.	• See "Home Connections" for "approaching mastery" and "at mastery" students. • Provide sounds audiotape to use with sound flash cards at home; encourage students to practice mouth formations with mirror at home. • Encourage adult at home to help students identify realia and other visuals of objects at home with same beginning sounds.
Test		
Assessment (for Lessons 101–120) **Approaching Mastery**	• See "Remedial Exercises and Retesting the Students" guidelines on pages 46 and 47 in *Curriculum-Based Assessment and Fluency Teacher Handbook.* • Partner with "at mastery" student and review sounds and "what word." • Reteach difficult sounds and words using "good-bye" list. • Conduct "see-say-write" until firm. • Practice circling responses and "reading words to yourself."	• Provide sound and word flash cards to take home for additional practice. • Encourage students to share their take-home sheets with their families. • Encourage adult at home to conduct "see-say-write" activity for each sound and word. • Provide page of words for students to take home to practice "what word." • Have adult at home access SRA's Home Connection Activities listed at *www.sraonline.com* • Direct Instruction • *Reading Mastery Signature Edition* • Activities

Test	Tips for Teachers	Home Connections
At Mastery	• Have student "be the teacher": Partner with "approaching mastery" student and review sounds and "what word." • Direct student to reading and writing center in classroom to reinforce early literacy and writing skills.	
ELL	• See "Tips for Teachers" for "approaching mastery" and "at mastery" students. • Describe and model mouth formations for sounds, then guide student while practicing with mirror. • Show realia or other visuals of objects and concepts, as needed. • Use primary language equivalents when available and then ask student to say words in English.	• See "Home Connections" for "approaching mastery" and "at mastery" students. • Provide audiotape for use with sound and word flash cards to take home for additional practice; encourage students to practice with mirror at home, as needed. • Encourage adult at home to help students identify realia and other visuals of objects and concepts, as needed. • Encourage adult at home to help students practice using primary language equivalents and English words when possible.
Fluency Checkout (Lesson 125) **Approaching Mastery**	• See guidelines for students who do not read within error or time limit for Lesson 125 on page 111 in *Presentation Book C.* • Partner with "at mastery" student and have him or her model reading story; have student read story. • Reteach difficult words using "good-bye" list. • Review finger placement and tracking for sentence reading. • Have adult model reading story; have student read story until firm. • Use paired reading. • Develop recording of story read by good reader; have student listen to recording and whisper read.	• Provide word flash cards to take home for additional practice. • Have adult at home model reading story; have students listen and track during story reading; have students read story; have adult at home review difficult words following story reading.
At Mastery	• See guidelines for students who read within error or time limit for Lesson 125 on page 111 in *Presentation Book C.* • Partner with "approaching mastery" student and model reading story; have student read story. • Have student record self reading story as model for "approaching mastery" student. • Direct student to reading and writing center in classroom to reinforce early literacy and writing skills.	

B27

Test	Tips for Teachers	Home Connections
ELL	• See "Tips for Teachers" for "approaching mastery" and "at mastery" students. • Describe and model mouth formations for difficult sounds and words, then guide student while practicing with mirror. • Use sentence strips to practice reading sentences in story. • Show realia or other visuals illustrating meaning of sentences in story. • Use primary language equivalents when available and then ask student to say words and sentences in English.	• See "Home Connections" for "approaching mastery" and "at mastery" students. • Provide audiotape to use with sentence strips and sound and word flashcards for additional practice. Encourage students to practice with mirror at home, as needed. • Provide audiotape of story; have students listen and track during story reading; then students read aloud with tape while tracking; then students read aloud and track independently; have adult at home review difficult words following independent story reading. • Encourage adult at home to help students tell a similar story using primary language equivalents. • Encourage adult at home to help students identify realia and other visuals illustrating meaning of sentences in story.

Mastery Test 24 (Lessons 121-125)
 	
Approaching Mastery
	• See "What To Do" guidelines for "if the group is weak on Mastery Test 24" on page 112 in *Presentation Book C*.
	• Partner with "at mastery" student and review "read this story the fast way."
	• Reteach "read this story the fast way" as well as any difficult sounds and words using "good-bye" list.
	• Review finger placement and tracking for sentence reading.
		• Provide story for students to take home to practice "read this story the fast way."
		• Encourage students to share their take-home sheets with their families.
		• Provide word flash cards for students to take home for additional practice.
		• Have adult at home access SRA's Home Connection Activities listed at *www.sraonline.com*
		  • Direct Instruction
		    • *Reading Mastery Signature Edition*
		      • Activities

At Mastery	• See "What To Do" guidelines for "if the group is firm on Mastery Test 24" on page 112 in *Presentation Book C*. • Have student "be the teacher": Partner with "approaching mastery" student and review "read this story the fast way." • Direct student to reading and writing center in classroom to reinforce early literacy and writing skills.	
ELL	• See "Tips for Teachers" for "approaching mastery" and "at mastery" students. • Describe and model mouth formations for difficult sounds and words, then guide student while practicing with mirror. • Use sentence strips to practice reading sentences in story. • Show realia or other visuals illustrating meaning of sentences in story. • Use primary language equivalents when available and then ask student to say words and sentences in English.	• See "Home Connections" for "approaching mastery" and "at mastery" students. • Provide audiotape for use with sound and word flashcards, sentence strips, and story to take home for additional practice; encourage students to practice with mirror at home, as needed. • Encourage adult at home to help students identify realia and other visuals illustrating meaning of sentences in story. • Encourage adult at home to help students tell a similar story using primary language equivalents.

Test	Tips for Teachers	Home Connections
Fluency Checkout (Lesson 130) **Approaching Mastery**	• See guidelines for students who do not read within error or time limit for Lesson 130 on page 141 in *Presentation Book C.* • Partner with "at mastery" student and have him or her model reading story; have student read story. • Reteach difficult words using "good-bye" list. • Review finger placement and tracking for sentence reading. • Have adult model reading story; have student read story until firm. • Use paired reading. • Develop recording of story read by good reader; have student listen to recording and whisper read.	• Provide word flash cards for students to take home for additional practice. • Have adult at home model reading story; have students listen and track during story reading; have students read story; have adult at home review difficult words following story reading.
At Mastery	• See guidelines for students who read within error or time limit for Lesson 130 on page 141 in *Presentation Book C.* • Partner with "approaching mastery" student and model reading story; have student read story. • Have student record self reading story as model for "approaching mastery" student. • Direct student to reading and writing center in classroom to reinforce early literacy and writing skills.	
ELL	• See "Tips for Teachers" for "approaching mastery" and "at mastery" students. • Describe and model mouth formations for difficult sounds and words, then guide student while practicing with mirror. • Use sentence strips to practice reading sentences in story. • Show realia or other visuals illustrating meaning of sentences in story. • Use primary language equivalents when available and then ask student to say words and sentences in English.	• See "Home Connections" for "approaching mastery" and "at mastery" students. • Provide audiotape to use with sentence strips and sound and word flashcards for additional practice; encourage students to practice with mirror at home, as needed. • Provide audiotape of story; have students listen and track during story reading; then students read aloud with tape while tracking; then students read aloud and track independently; have adult at home review difficult words following independent story reading. • Encourage adult at home to help students tell a similar story using primary language equivalents. • Encourage adult at home to help students identify realia and other visuals illustrating meaning of sentences in story.

B29

Test	Tips for Teachers	Home Connections

Mastery Test 25 (Lessons 126-130)
 	
Approaching Mastery
	• See "What To Do" guidelines for "if the group is weak on Mastery Test 25" on page 142 in *Presentation Book C*.
	• Partner with "at mastery" student and review "read these words the fast way."
	• Reteach "read these words the fast way" as well as any difficult sounds and words using "good-bye" list.
		• Provide word list for students to take home to practice "read these words the fast way."
		• Encourage students to share their take-home sheets with their families.
		• Provide word flash cards for students to take home for additional practice.
		• Have adult at home access SRA's Home Connection Activities listed at *www.sraonline.com*
		  • Direct Instruction
		    • *Reading Mastery Signature Edition*
		      • Activities

At Mastery	• See "What To Do" guidelines for "if the group is firm on Mastery Test 25" on page 142 in *Presentation Book C*. • Have student "be the teacher": Partner with "approaching mastery" student and review "read these words the fast way." • Direct student to reading and writing center in classroom to reinforce early literacy and writing skills.	
ELL	• See "Tips for Teachers" for "approaching mastery" and "at mastery" students. • Describe and model mouth formations for difficult sounds and words, then guide student while practicing with mirror. • Show realia or other visuals of objects and concepts, as needed. • Use primary language equivalents when available and then ask student to say words in English.	• See "Home Connections" for "approaching mastery" and "at mastery" students. • Provide audiotape for use with sound and word flash cards to take home for additional practice; encourage students to practice with mirror at home, as needed. • Encourage adult at home to help students identify realia and other visuals of objects and concepts, as needed. • Encourage adult at home to help students practice using primary language equivalents and English words when possible.

Test	Tips for Teachers	Home Connections
Fluency Checkout (Lesson 135) **Approaching Mastery**	• See guidelines for students who do not read within error or time limit for Lesson 135 on page 171 in *Presentation Book C*. • Partner with "at mastery" student and have him or her model reading story; have student read story. • Reteach difficult words using "good-bye" list. • Review finger placement and tracking for sentence reading. • Have adult model reading story; have student read story until firm. • Use paired reading. • Develop recording of story read by good reader; have student listen to recording and whisper read.	• Provide word flash cards for students to take home for additional practice. • Have adult at home model reading story; have students listen and track during story reading; have students read story; have adult at home review difficult words following story reading.

B30

Test	Tips for Teachers	Home Connections
At Mastery	• See guidelines for students who read within error or time limit for Lesson 135 on page 171 in *Presentation Book C*. • Partner with "approaching mastery" student and model reading story; have student read story. • Have student record self reading story as model for "approaching mastery" student. • Direct student to reading and writing center in classroom to reinforce early literacy and writing skills.	
ELL	• See "Tips for Teachers" for "approaching mastery" and "at mastery" students. • Describe and model mouth formations for difficult sounds and words, then guide student while practicing with mirror. • Use sentence strips to practice reading sentences in story. • Show realia or other visuals illustrating meaning of sentences in story. • Use primary language equivalents when available and then ask student to say words and sentences in English.	• See "Home Connections" for "approaching mastery" and "at mastery" students. • Provide audiotape to use with sentence strips and sound and word flashcards for additional practice; encourage students to practice with mirror at home, as needed. • Provide audiotape of story; have students listen and track during story reading; then students read aloud with tape while tracking; then students read aloud and track independently; have adult at home review difficult words following independent story reading. • Encourage adult at home to help students tell a similar story using primary language equivalents. • Encourage adult at home to help students identify realia and other visuals illustrating meaning of sentences in story.

Test
 	
Mastery Test 26
(Lessons 131-135)
 	
Approaching Mastery
	• See "What To Do" guidelines for "if the group is weak on Mastery Test 26" on page 172 in *Presentation Book C*.
	• Partner with "at mastery" student and review "read this story the fast way."
	• Reteach "read this story the fast way" as well as any difficult sounds and words using "good-bye" list.
	• Review finger placement and tracking for sentence reading.
		• Provide story for students to take home to practice "read this story the fast way."
		• Encourage students to share their take-home sheets with their families.
		• Provide word flash cards for students to take home for additional practice.
		• Have adult at home access SRA's Home Connection Activities listed at *www.sraonline.com*
		  • Direct Instruction
		    • *Reading Mastery Signature Edition*
		      • Activities

At Mastery	• See "What To Do" guidelines for "if the group is firm on Mastery Test 26" on page 172 in *Presentation Book C*. • Have student "be the teacher": Partner with "approaching mastery" student and review "read this story the fast way." • Direct student to reading and writing center in classroom to reinforce early literacy and writing skills.	

B31

Test	Tips for Teachers	Home Connections
ELL	• See "Tips for Teachers" for "approaching mastery" and "at mastery" students. • Describe and model mouth formations for difficult sounds and words, then guide student while practicing with mirror. • Use sentence strips to practice reading sentences in story. • Show realia or other visuals illustrating meaning of sentences in story. • Use primary language equivalents when available and then ask student to say words and sentences in English.	• See "Home Connections" for "approaching mastery" and "at mastery" students. • Provide audiotape for use with sound and word flashcards, sentence strips, and story to take home for additional practice; encourage students to practice with mirror at home, as needed. • Encourage adult at home to help students identify realia and other visuals illustrating meaning of sentences in story. • Encourage adult at home to help students tell a similar story using primary language equivalents.
Fluency Checkout (Lesson 140) **Approaching Mastery**	• See guidelines for students who do not read within error or time limit for Lesson 140 on page 202 in *Presentation Book C.* • Partner with "at mastery" student and have him or her model reading story; have student read story. • Reteach difficult words using "good-bye" list. • Review finger placement and tracking for sentence reading. • Have adult model reading story; have student read story until firm. • Use paired reading. • Develop recording of story read by good reader; have student listen to recording and whisper read.	• Provide word flash cards for students to take home for additional practice. • Have adult at home model reading story; have students listen and track during story reading; have students read story; have adult at home review difficult words following story reading.
At Mastery	• See guidelines for students who read within error or time limit for Lesson 140 on page 202 in *Presentation Book C.* • Partner with "approaching mastery" student and model reading story; have student read story. • Have student record self reading story as model for "approaching mastery" student. • Direct student to reading and writing center in classroom to reinforce early literacy and writing skills.	
ELL	• See "Tips for Teachers" for "approaching mastery" and "at mastery" students. • Describe and model mouth formations for difficult sounds and words, then guide student while practicing with mirror. • Use sentence strips to practice reading sentences in story. • Show realia or other visuals illustrating meaning of sentences in story. • Use primary language equivalents when available and then ask student to say words and sentences in English.	• See "Home Connections" for "approaching mastery" and "at mastery" students. • Provide audiotape to use with sentence strips and sound and word flashcards for additional practice; encourage students to practice with mirror at home, as needed.

Test	Tips for Teachers	Home Connections
Test		• Provide audiotape of story; have students listen and track during story reading; then students read aloud with tape while tracking; then students read aloud and track independently; have adult at home review difficult words following independent story reading. • Encourage adult at home to help students tell a similar story using primary language equivalents. • Encourage adult at home to help students identify realia and other visuals illustrating meaning of sentences in story.
Mastery Test 27 (Lessons 136-140) **Approaching Mastery**	• See "What To Do" guidelines for "if the group is weak on Mastery Test 27" on page 203 in *Presentation Book C.* • Partner with "at mastery" student and review "read these words the fast way." • Reteach "read these words the fast way" as well as any difficult sounds and words using "good-bye" list.	• Provide word list for students to take home to practice "read these words the fast way." • Encourage students to share their take-home sheets with their families. • Provide word flash cards for students to take home for additional practice. • Have adult at home access SRA's Home Connection Activities listed at *www.sraonline.com* • Direct Instruction • *Reading Mastery Signature Edition* • Activities
At Mastery	• See "What To Do" guidelines for "if the group is firm on Mastery Test 27" on page 203 in *Presentation Book C.* • Have student "be the teacher": Partner with "approaching mastery" student and review "read these words the fast way." • Direct student to reading and writing center in classroom to reinforce early literacy and writing skills.	
ELL	• See "Tips for Teachers" for "approaching mastery" and "at mastery" students. • Describe and model mouth formations for difficult sounds and words, then guide student while practicing with mirror. • Show realia or other visuals of objects and concepts, as needed. • Use primary language equivalents when available and then ask student to say words in English.	• See "Home Connections" for "approaching mastery" and "at mastery" students. • Provide audiotape for use with sound and word flash cards to take home for additional practice; encourage students to practice with mirror at home, as needed. • Encourage adult at home to help students identify realia and other visuals of objects and concepts, as needed. • Encourage adult at home to help students practice using primary language equivalents and English words when possible.

B33

Test	Tips for Teachers	Home Connections

Assessment (for Lessons 121–140)
 	
Approaching Mastery
	• See "Remedial Exercises and Retesting the Students" guidelines on pages 49 and 50 in *Curriculum-Based Assessment and Fluency Teacher Handbook*.
	• Partner with "at mastery" student and review sounds and "read words and story to yourself."
	• Reteach difficult sounds and words using "good-bye" list.
	• Conduct "see-say-write" until firm.
	• Practice circling responses and "reading words and story to yourself."
		• Provide sound and word flash cards for students to take home for additional practice.
		• Encourage students to share their take-home sheets with their families.
		• Encourage adult at home to conduct "see-say-write" activity for each sound and word.
		• Have adult at home access SRA's Home Connection Activities listed at *www.sraonline.com*
		  • Direct Instruction
		    • *Reading Mastery Signature Edition*
		      • Activities

At Mastery	• Have student "be the teacher": Partner with "approaching mastery" student and review sounds and "what word." • Direct student to reading and writing center in classroom to reinforce early literacy and writing skills.	
ELL	• See "Tips for Teachers" for "approaching mastery" and "at mastery" students. • Describe and model mouth formations for sounds, then guide student while practicing with mirror. • Show realia or other visuals of objects and concepts, as needed and to illustrate meaning of sentences. • Use primary language equivalents when available and then ask student to say words and sentences in English.	• See "Home Connections" for "approaching mastery" and "at mastery" students. • Provide audiotape for use with sound and word flash cards and sentence strips to take home for additional practice; encourage students to practice with mirror at home, as needed. • Encourage adult at home to help students identify realia and other visuals of objects and concepts, as needed and to illustrate meaning of sentences at home. • Encourage adult at home to help students practice using primary language equivalents and English words and sentences when possible.
Test **Fluency Checkout** (Lesson 145) **Approaching Mastery**	• See guidelines for students who do not read within error or time limit for Lesson 145 on page 233 in *Presentation Book C*. • Partner with "at mastery" student and have him or her model reading story; have student read story. • Reteach difficult words using "good-bye" list. • Review finger placement and tracking for sentence reading. • Have adult model reading story; have student read story until firm. • Use paired reading. • Develop recording of story read by good reader; have student listen to recording and whisper read.	• Provide word flash cards for students to take home for additional practice. • Have adult at home model reading story; have students listen and track during story reading; have students read story; have adult at home review difficult words following story reading.

B34

Test	Tips for Teachers	Home Connections
At Mastery	• See guidelines for students who read within error or time limit for Lesson 145 on page 233 in *Presentation Book C.* • Partner with "approaching mastery" student and model reading story; have student read story. • Have student record self reading story as model for "approaching mastery" student. • Direct student to reading and writing center in classroom to reinforce early literacy and writing skills.	
ELL	• See "Tips for Teachers" for "approaching mastery" and "at mastery" students. • Describe and model mouth formations for difficult sounds and words, then guide student while practicing with mirror. • Use sentence strips to practice reading sentences in story. • Show realia or other visuals illustrating meaning of sentences in story. • Use primary language equivalents when available and then ask student to say words and sentences in English.	• See "Home Connections" for "approaching mastery" and "at mastery" students. • Provide audiotape to use with sentence strips and sound and word flashcards for additional practice; encourage students to practice with mirror at home, as needed. • Provide audiotape of story; have students listen and track during story reading; then students read aloud with tape while tracking; then students read aloud and track independently; have adult at home review difficult words following independent story reading. • Encourage adult at home to help students tell a similar story using primary language equivalents. • Encourage adult at home to help students identify realia and other visuals illustrating meaning of sentences in story.

Test
 	
Mastery Test 28 (Lessons 141-145)
 	
Approaching Mastery
	• See "What To Do" guidelines for "if the group is weak on Mastery Test 28" on page 234 in *Presentation Book C.*
	• Partner with "at mastery" student and review "read this story the fast way."
	• Reteach "read this story the fast way" as well as any difficult sounds and words using "good-bye" list.
	• Review finger placement and tracking for sentence reading.
		• Provide story for students to take home to practice "read this story the fast way."
		• Encourage students to share their take-home sheets with their families.
		• Provide word flash cards for students to take home for additional practice.
		• Have adult at home access SRA's Home Connection Activities listed at *www.sraonline.com*
		  • Direct Instruction
		    • *Reading Mastery Signature Edition*
		      • Activities

At Mastery	• See "What To Do" guidelines for "if the group is firm on Mastery Test 28" on page 234 in *Presentation Book C.* • Have student "be the teacher": Partner with "approaching mastery" student and review "read this story the fast way." • Direct student to reading and writing center in classroom to reinforce early literacy and writing skills.	

B35

Test	Tips for Teachers	Home Connections
ELL	• See "Tips for Teachers" for "approaching mastery" and "at mastery" students. • Describe and model mouth formations for difficult sounds and words, then guide student while practicing with mirror. • Use sentence strips to practice reading sentences in story. • Show realia or other visuals illustrating meaning of sentences in story. • Use primary language equivalents when available and then ask student to say words and sentences in English.	• See "Home Connections" for "approaching mastery" and "at mastery" students. • Provide audiotape for use with sound and word flashcards, sentence strips, and story to take home for additional practice; encourage students to practice with mirror at home, as needed. • Encourage adult at home to help students identify realia and other visuals illustrating meaning of sentences in story. • Encourage adult at home to help students tell a similar story using primary language equivalents.
Fluency Checkout (Lesson 150) **Approaching Mastery**	• See guidelines for students who do not read within error or time limit for Lesson 150 on page 266 in *Presentation Book C.* • Partner with "at mastery" student and have him or her model reading story; have student read story. • Reteach difficult words using "good-bye" list. • Review finger placement and tracking for sentence reading. • Have adult model reading story; have student read story until firm. • Use paired reading. • Develop recording of story read by good reader; have student listen to recording and whisper read.	• Provide word flash cards for students to take home for additional practice. • Have adult at home model reading story; have students listen and track during story reading; have students read story; have adult at home review difficult words following story reading.
At Mastery	• See guidelines for students who read within error or time limit for Lesson 150 on page 266 in *Presentation Book C.* • Partner with "approaching mastery" student and model reading story; have student read story. • Have student record self reading story as model for "approaching mastery" student. • Direct student to reading and writing center in classroom to reinforce early literacy and writing skills.	
ELL	• See "Tips for Teachers" for "approaching mastery" and "at mastery" students. • Describe and model mouth formations for difficult sounds and words, then guide student while practicing with mirror. • Use sentence strips to practice reading sentences in story. • Show realia or other visuals illustrating meaning of sentences in story. • Use primary language equivalents when available and then ask student to say words and sentences in English.	• See "Home Connections" for "approaching mastery" and "at mastery" students. • Provide audiotape to use with sentence strips and sound and word flashcards for additional practice; encourage students to practice with mirror at home, as needed.

B36

Test	Tips for Teachers	Home Connections
		• Provide audiotape of story; have students listen and track during story reading; then students read aloud with tape while tracking; then students read aloud and track independently; have adult at home review difficult words following independent story reading. • Encourage adult at home to help students tell a similar story using primary language equivalents. • Encourage adult at home to help students identify realia and other visuals illustrating meaning of sentences in story.

Test
 	
Mastery Test 29
(Lessons 146-150)
 	
Approaching Mastery
	• See "What To Do" guidelines for "if the group is weak on Mastery Test 29" on page 267 in *Presentation Book C.*
	• Partner with "at mastery" student and review "read these words the fast way."
	• Reteach "read these words the fast way" as well as any difficult sounds and words using "good-bye" list.
		• Provide word list for students to take home to practice "read these words the fast way."
		• Encourage students to share their take-home sheets with their families.
		• Provide word flash cards for students to take home for additional practice.
		• Have adult at home access SRA's Home Connection Activities listed at
		www.sraonline.com
		  • Direct Instruction
		    • *Reading Mastery Signature Edition*
		    • Activities

At Mastery	• See "What To Do" guidelines for "if the group is firm on Mastery Test 29" on page 267 in *Presentation Book C.* • Have student "be the teacher": Partner with "approaching mastery" student and review "read these words the fast way." • Direct student to reading and writing center in classroom to reinforce early literacy and writing skills.	
ELL	• See "Tips for Teachers" for "approaching mastery" and "at mastery" students. • Describe and model mouth formations for difficult sounds and words, then guide student while practicing with mirror. • Show realia or other visuals of objects and concepts, as needed. • Use primary language equivalents when available and then ask student to say words in English.	• See "Home Connections" for "approaching mastery" and "at mastery" students. • Provide audiotape for use with sound and word flash cards to take home for additional practice; encourage students to practice with mirror at home, as needed. • Encourage adult at home to help students identify realia and other visuals of objects and concepts, as needed. • Encourage adult at home to help students practice using primary language equivalents and English words when possible.

B37

Test	Tips for Teachers	Home Connections
Fluency Checkout (Lesson 155) **Approaching Mastery**	• See guidelines for students who do not read within error or time limit for Lesson 155 on page 305 in *Presentation Book C.* • Partner with "at mastery" student and have him or her model reading story; have student read story. • Reteach difficult words using "good-bye" list. • Review finger placement and tracking for sentence reading. • Have adult model reading story; have student read story until firm. • Use paired reading. • Develop recording of story read by good reader; have student listen to recording and whisper read.	• Provide word flash cards for students to take home for additional practice. • Have adult at home model reading story; have students listen and track during story reading; have students read story; have adult at home review difficult words following story reading.
At Mastery	• See guidelines for students who read within error or time limit for Lesson 155 on page 305 in *Presentation Book C.* • Partner with "approaching mastery" student and model reading story; have student read story. • Have student record self reading story as model for "approaching mastery" student. • Direct student to reading and writing center in classroom to reinforce early literacy and writing skills.	
ELL	• See "Tips for Teachers" for "approaching mastery" and "at mastery" students. • Describe and model mouth formations for difficult sounds and words, then guide student while practicing with mirror. • Use sentence strips to practice reading sentences in story. • Show realia or other visuals illustrating meaning of sentences in story. • Use primary language equivalents when available and then ask student to say words and sentences in English.	• See "Home Connections" for "approaching mastery" and "at mastery" students. • Provide audiotape to use with sentence strips and sound and word flashcards for additional practice; encourage students to practice with mirror at home, as needed. • Provide audiotape of story; have students listen and track during story reading; then students read aloud with tape while tracking; then students read aloud and track independently; have adult at home review difficult words following independent story reading. • Encourage adult at home to help students tell a similar story using primary language equivalents. • Encourage adult at home to help students identify realia and other visuals illustrating meaning of sentences in story.

Test	Tips for Teachers	Home Connections

Mastery Test 30 (Lessons 151-155)
 	
Approaching Mastery
	• See "What To Do" guidelines for "if the group is weak on Mastery Test 30" on page 306 in *Presentation Book C*.
	• Partner with "at mastery" student and review "read this story the fast way."
	• Reteach "read this story the fast way" as well as any difficult sounds and words using "good-bye" list.
	• Review finger placement and tracking for sentence reading.
		• Provide story for students to take home to practice "read this story the fast way."
		• Encourage students to share their take-home sheets with their families.
		• Provide word flash cards for students to take home for additional practice.
		• Have adult at home access SRA's Home Connection Activities listed at *www.sraonline.com*
		  • Direct Instruction
		    • *Reading Mastery Signature Edition*
		      • Activities

At Mastery	• See "What To Do" guidelines for "if the group is firm on Mastery Test 30" on page 306 in *Presentation Book C*. • Have student "be the teacher": Partner with "approaching mastery" student and review "read this story the fast way." • Direct student to reading and writing center in classroom to reinforce early literacy and writing skills.	
ELL	• See "Tips for Teachers" for "approaching mastery" and "at mastery" students. • Describe and model mouth formations for difficult sounds and words, then guide student while practicing with mirror. • Use sentence strips to practice reading sentences in story. • Show realia or other visuals illustrating meaning of sentences in story. • Use primary language equivalents when available and then ask student to say words and sentences in English.	• See "Home Connections" for "approaching mastery" and "at mastery" students. • Provide audiotape for use with sound and word flashcards, sentence strips, and story to take home for additional practice; encourage students to practice with mirror at home, as needed. • Encourage adult at home to help students identify realia and other visuals illustrating meaning of sentences in story. • Encourage adult at home to help students tell a similar story using primary language equivalents.
Test		
Fleuncy Checkout (Lesson 160) **Approaching Mastery**	• See guidelines for students who do not read within error or time limit for Lesson 160 on page 344 in *Presentation Book C*. • Partner with "at mastery" student and have him or her model reading story; have student read story. • Reteach difficult words using "good-bye" list. • Review finger placement and tracking for sentence reading. • Have adult model reading story; have student read story until firm. • Use paired reading. • Develop recording of story read by good reader; have student listen to recording and whisper read.	• Provide word flash cards for students to take home for additional practice. • Have adult at home model reading story; have students listen and track during story reading; have students read story; have adult at home review difficult words following story reading.

B39

Test	Tips for Teachers	Home Connections
At Mastery	• See guidelines for students who read within error or time limit for Lesson 160 on page 344 in *Presentation Book C*. • Partner with "approaching mastery" student and model reading story; have student read story. • Have student record self reading story as model for "approaching mastery" student. • Direct student to reading and writing center in classroom to reinforce early literacy and writing skills.	
ELL	• See "Tips for Teachers" for "approaching mastery" and "at mastery" students. • Describe and model mouth formations for difficult sounds and words, then guide student while practicing with mirror. • Use sentence strips to practice reading sentences in story. • Show realia or other visuals illustrating meaning of sentences in story. • Use primary language equivalents when available and then ask student to say words and sentences in English.	• See "Home Connections" for "approaching mastery" and "at mastery" students. • Provide audiotape to use with sentence strips and sound and word flashcards for additional practice; encourage students to practice with mirror at home, as needed. • Provide audiotape of story; have students listen and track during story reading; then students read aloud with tape while tracking; then students read aloud and track independently; have adult at home review difficult words following independent story reading. • Encourage adult at home to help students tell a similar story using primary language equivalents. • Encourage adult at home to help students identify realia and other visuals illustrating meaning of sentences in story.

Test
 	
Assessment (for Lessons 141–160)
 	
Approaching Mastery
	• See "Remedial Exercises and Retesting the Students" guidelines on pages 52 and 53 in *Curriculum-Based Assessment and Fluency Teacher Handbook*.
	• Partner with "at mastery" student and review sounds and "what word."
	• Reteach difficult sounds and words using "good-bye" list.
	• Conduct "see-say-write" until firm.
	• Practice circling responses and "reading words to yourself."
	• Review vocabulary and comprehension activities.
		• Provide sound and word flash cards for students to take home for additional practice.
		• Encourage students to share their take-home sheets with their families.
		• Encourage adult at home to conduct "see-say-write" activity for each sound and word.
		• Have adult at home review vocabulary and comprehension activities.
		• Have adult at home access SRA's Home Connection Activities listed at *www.sraonline.com*
		  • Direct Instruction
		    • *Reading Mastery Signature Edition*
		      • Activities

At Mastery	• Have student "be the teacher": Partner with "approaching mastery" student and review sounds and "what word." • Direct student to reading and writing center in classroom to reinforce early literacy and writing skills.	

Test	Tips for Teachers	Home Connections
ELL	• See "Tips for Teachers" for "approaching mastery" and "at mastery" students. • Describe and model mouth formations for sounds, then guide student while practicing with mirror. • Show realia or other visuals of objects and concepts, as needed and to illustrate meaning of sentences. • Use primary language equivalents when available and then ask student to say words and sentences in English.	• See "Home Connections" for "approaching mastery" and "at mastery" students. • Provide audiotape for use with sound and word flash cards and sentence strips to take home for additional practice; encourage students to practice with mirror at home, as needed. • Encourage adult at home to help students identify realia and other visuals of objects and concepts, as needed and to illustrate meaning of sentences at home. • Encourage adult at home to help students practice using primary language equivalents and English words and sentences when possible.

B41

Appendix C

Levels of Support for Students with Intellectual Disabilities

The following table presents helpful tips to help ensure maximum access for students with intellectual disabilities. These suggestions use foundational skills that are clearly linked to the **Reading Mastery** content to aid such students in achieving academic success. These suggestions are provided at three levels of support (from least to most) to allow all learners the opportunity to access learning at the highest possible in program materials.

Levels of Support for Students with Intellectual Disabilities
Reading Mastery Signature Edition
Grade K

Level 1 (less support needed): The student will

- locate printed words on a page.
- hold a book correctly, turning pages one at a time, front to back.
- name ten or more letters.
- recognize that sentences are made of words.
- identify words that rhyme.
- segment auditory sentences into individual words.
- match familiar words that start with the same sounds.
- identify own first and last name in print.
- use new vocabulary that is taught directly.
- listen to and talk about stories.
- identify and describe persons, objects, and actions in read-aloud stories and everyday life.
- determine if pictures are real or make believe.
- answer literal yes/no questions based on read-aloud stories.
- identify characters in read-aloud stories.
- select fiction/nonfiction materials to view or listen to for pleasure.
- select materials to view or read for pleasure.

Level 2 (more support needed): The student will

- hold books correctly, turning pages one at a time.
- locate print on a page or in the classroom.
- identify one or more letters in own name.
- identify sounds that are the same.
- imitate rhyming words.
- distinguish whether sounds are the same or different.
- match own first name in print.
- use new vocabulary that is taught directly.
- listen to and interact with familiar stories.
- identify pictures in familiar read-aloud stories.
- identify familiar characters or objects pictured in read-aloud stories.
- select fiction/nonfiction materials to view or listen to for pleasure.
- recognize familiar read-aloud informational text.

Level 3 (most support needed): The student will

- respond to a familiar person reading a book aloud.
- identify a picture of self.
- respond to rhythm.
- respond to sounds in the classroom.
- respond to own name or other familiar spoken words.
- respond to spoken words used as prompts or cues.
- respond to spoken words/gestures/signs in familiar stories.
- respond to new vocabulary that is taught directly.
- identify persons and objects in familiar activities.
- respond to familiar read-aloud stories.
- attend to pictures or symbols used in routines.
- indicate a preference for familiar fiction/nonfiction materials to view or listen to for pleasure.

C3

Appendix D

Strand Component	Lessons 1-5	Lessons 6-10	Lessons 11-15	Lessons 16-20
Core Lesson Connections	**Phonemic and Phonological Awareness** *Word Segmentation –* 1:a1; 2:a1; 3:a1; 4:a1; 5:a1 *Rhyme Recognition –* 1:a2; 2:a2; 3:a2; 4:a2; 5:a2 *Letter Recognition and Formation* **Comprehension Strategies** *Listening* **Comprehension** – 1:c1; 2:c1; 3:c1; 4:c1; 5:c1 *Story Recall* – 1:c2; 2:c2; 3:c2; 4:c2; 5:c2 **Vocabulary** – 5:d1	**Phonemic and Phonological Awareness** *Word Segmentation –* 6:a1; 7:a1; 8:a1; 9:a1; 10:a1 *Rhyme Recognition* – 6:a2; 7:a2; 8:a2; 9:a2; 10:a2 *Syllable Blending* – 6:a3; 7:a3; 8:a3; 9:a3; 10:a3; 10:a4 *Letter Recognition and Formation* **Comprehension Strategies** *Listening* **Comprehension** – 6:c1; 7:c1; 8:c1; 9:c1; 10:c1 *Story Recall* – 6:c2; 7:c2; 8:c2; 9:c2; 10:c2 **Vocabulary** – 10:d1	**Phonemic and Phonological Awareness** *Word Segmentation –* 11:a1; 13:a1; 13:a2; 15:a1 *Rhyme Recognition* – 11:a2; 13:a3 *Syllable Blending* – 12:a2; 12:a3; 14:a2; 14:a3; 15:a3 *Syllable Segmentation* – 12:a4; 14:a4 *Rhyme Production* – 12:a1; 14:a1; 15:a2 *Letter Recognition and Formation* – 11:b; 12:b; 13:b; 14:b; 15:b **Comprehension Strategies** *Listening* **Comprehension** – 11:c1; 12:c1; 13:c1; 14:c1; 15:c1 *Story Recall* – 11:c2; 12:c2; 13:c2; 14:c2; 15:c2 **Vocabulary** – 15:d1	**Phonemic and Phonological Awareness** *Word Segmentation –* 17:a1; 19:a1 *Rhyme Recognition –* 16:a1; 17:a2; 19:a2 *Syllable Blending* – 17:a3; 19:a3 *Syllable Segmentation* – 16:a2; 18:a2; 18:a3; 20:a2; 20:a3 *Rhyme Production* – 18:a1; 20:a1 *Letter Recognition and Formation* – 16:b; 17:b; 18:b; 19:b; 20:b **Comprehension Strategies** *Listening* **Comprehension** – 16:c1; 17:c1; 18:c1; 19:c1; 20:c1 *Story Recall* – 16:c2; 17:c2; 18:c2; 19:c2; 20:c2 **Vocabulary** – 20:d1
Reading Strand *Reading Mastery*	**Presentation Book A** **Phonemic Awareness** – 1:1; 1:2; 1:3; 1:8; 1:9; 1:10; 1:12; 1:13; 1:14; 2:1; 2:6; 2:7; 2:8; 2:10; 2:11; 2:12; 3:1; 3:6; 3:7; 3:8; 3:10; 3:11; 3:12; 4:1; 4:6; 4:7; 4:8; 4:10; 4:11; 4:12; 4:13; 5:1; 5:6; 5:7; 5:8; 5:10; 5:11; 5:12; 5:13 **Print Awareness** – 1:17; 1:18; 1:19; 1:20; 1:23; 1:24; 1:25; 2:13; 2:14; 2:15; 2:16; 2:17; 2:19; 2:20; 2:21; 2:22; 2:23; 3:13; 3:14; 3:15; 3:16; 3:17; 3:19; 3:20; 3:21; 3:22; 3:23; 4:14; 4:15; 4:16; 4:17; 4:18; 4:19; 4:20; 5:14; 5:15; 5:16; 5:17; 5:19; 5:20 **Letter Sound Correspondence** – 1:4; 1:7; 1:11; 1:15; 1:16; 1:21; 2:2; 2:5; 2:9; 2:18; 3:2; 3:5; 3:9; 3:18; 4:2; 4:5; 4:9; 5:2; 5:5; 5:9 **Phonics and Word Recognition** **Fluency** – 1:8; 1:10; 1:12	**Presentation Book A** **Phonemic Awareness** – 6:1; 6:6; 6:7; 6:8; 6:11; 6:12; 6:13; 6:14; 7:1; 7:6; 7:7; 7:8; 7:11; 7:12; 7:13; 7:14; 8:1; 8:6; 8:7; 8:8; 8:10; 8:11; 8:12; 8:13; 8:14; 9:1; 9:6; 9:7 ; 9:8; 9:10; 9:11; 9:12; 10:1; 10:6; 10:7; 10:8; 10:10; 10:11; 10:12; 10:13; 10:14 **Print Awareness** – 6:15; 6:16; 6:17; 6:18; 6:19; 6:20; 6:21; 7:15; 7:16; 7:17; 7:18; 7:19; 7:20; 7:21; 8:15; 8:16; 8:17; 8:18; 8:19; 8:20; 8:21; 9:15; 9:16; 9:17; 9:18; 9:19; 9:20; 9:21; 10:15; 10:16; 10:17; 10:18; 10:19; 10:20; 10:21 **Letter Sound Correspondence** – 6:2; 6:5; 6:9; 6:10; 7:2; 7:5; 7:9; 7:10; 8:2; 8:5; 8:9; 9:2; 9:5; 9:9 **Phonics and Word Recognition** **Fluency**	**Presentation Book A** **Phonemic Awareness** – 11:1; 11:6; 11:7; 11:9; 11:10; 11:11; 11:12; 11:13; 12:1; 12:6; 12:7; 12:10; 12:11; 12:12; 12:13; 13:1; 13:5; 13:6; 13:7; 13:8; 13:9; 13:10; 13:11; 14:1; 14:5; 14:6; 14:9; 14:10: 14:11; 14:12; 15:1; 15:5; 15:6; 15:8; 15:11 **Print Awareness** – 11:14; 11:15; 11:16; 11:17; 11:18; 11:19; 11:20; 11:21; 11:22; 11:23; 11:24; 12:14; 12:15; 12:16; 12:17; 12:18; 12:19; 12:20; 12:21; 12:22; 12:23; 13:12; 13:13; 13:14; 13:15; 13:16; 13:17; 13:18; 14:13; 14:14; 14:15; 14:16; 14:17; 14:18; 14:19; 15:12; 15:13; 15:14; 15:15; 15:16; 15:17; 15:18 **Letter Sound Correspondence** – 11:2; 11:5; 11:8; 12:2; 12:5; 12:8; 12:9; 13:2; 13:4; 13:7; 14:2; 14:4; 14:7; 14:8; 15:2; 15:4; 15:7; 15:9	**Presentation Book A** **Phonemic Awareness** – 16:1; 16:5; 16:6; 16:10; 16:11; 16:12; 16:13; 16:14; 16:15; 16:16; 16:17; 17:4; 17:5; 17:8; 17:9; 17:10; 17:11; 17:12; 17:13; 17:14; 17:15; 18:2; 18:3; 18:9; 18:10; 18:11; 19:1; 19:3; 19:4; 19:9; 19:10; 19:11; 20:2; 20:3; 20:8 20:9; 20:10 **Print Awareness** – 16:18; 16:19; 16:20; 16:21; 16:22; 16:23; 16:24; 17:16; 17:17; 17:18; 17:19; 17:20; 17:21; 17:22; 18:12; 18:13; 18:14; 18:15; 18:16; 18:17; 19:12; 19:13; 19:16; 19:17; 19:18; 19:19; 19:20; 20:11; 20:12; 20:15; 20:16; 20:17; 20:18; 20:19 **Letter Sound Correspondence** – 16:2; 16:4; 16:7; 16:8; 16:9; 17:1; 17:3; 17:6; 17:7; 18:1; 18:4; 18:5; 18:6; 18:7; 18:8; 19:2; 19:5; 19:6; 19:7; 19:8; 19:14; 19:15; 20:4; 20:6; 20:7; 20:13; 20:14

D3

Strand Component	Lessons 1-5	Lessons 6-10	Lessons 11-15	Lessons 16-20
Reading Strand *Reading Mastery* (continued)	**Comprehension** – 1:5; 1:6; 1:10; 2:3; 2:4; 2:8; 2:19; 3:3; 3:4; 3:8; 4:3; 4:4; 4:8 **Informal Assessment** – 1:3; 1:5; 1:6: 1:7; 1:11; 1:16; 1:18; 1:23; 1:24; 1:25; 1:26; 2: 1; 2:2; 2:3; 2:4; 2:5; 2:6; 2:7; 2:8; 2:9; 2:10; 2:11; 2:12; 2:14; 2:16; 2:18; 2:20; 2:21; 2:22; 2:23; 3:1; 3:2; 3:3; 3:4; 3:5; 3:7; 3:9; 3:11; 3:12; 3:14; 3:16; 3:18; 3:20; 3:21; 3:22; 3:23; 4:1; 4:2; 4:3; 4:4; 4:5; 4:7; 4:9; 4:12: 4:13; 4:14; 4:15; 4:16; 4:17; 4:18; 4:19; 4:20; 4:20; 4:21; 5:1; 5:2; 5:3; 5:4; 5:5; 5:7; 5:9; 5:12; 5:13; 5:14; 5:15; 5:16; 5:17; 5:18; 5:19; 5:20; 5:21	**Comprehension** – 6:3; 6:4; 7:3; 7:4; 8:3; 8:4; 9:3; 9:4; 10:3; 10:4 **Informal Assessment** – 6:1; 6:2; 6:3; 6:4; 6:5; 6:6; 6:7; 6:8; 6:9; 6:10; 6:12; 6:14; 6:16; 6:17; 6:18; 6:19; 6:20; 6:21; 6:22; 7:1; 7:2; 7:3; 7:4; 7:5; 7:6; 7:7; 7:8; 7:9; 7:10; 7:12; 7:14; 7:16; 7:17; 7:18; 7:19; 7:20; 7:21; 7:22; 8:1; 8:2; 8:3; 8:4; 8:5; 8:6; 8:7; 8:8; 8:9; 8:10; 8:11; 8:12; 8:14; 8:15; 8:16; 8:17; 8:18; 8:19; 8:20; 8:21; 8:22; 9:1; 9:2; 9:3; 9:4; 9:6; 9:7; 9:8; 9:9; 9:10; 9:11; 9:12; 9:14; 9:15; 9:16; 9:17; 9:18; 9:19; 9:20; 9:21; 9:22; 10:1; 10:2; 10:3; 10:4; 10:5; 10:6; 10:7; 10:8; 10:9; 10:10; 10:11; 10:12; 10:14; 10:15; 10:16; 10:17; 10:18; 10:19; 10:20; 10:21; 10:22	**Phonics and Word Recognition** **Fluency Comprehension** – 11:3; 11:4; 12:3; 12:4; 13:3; 14:3; 15:3 **Informal Assessment** – 11:1; 11:2; 11:3; 11:4; 11:5; 11:6; 11:7; 11:8; 11:9; 11:10; 11:11; 11:13; 11:14; 11:15; 11:16; 11:17; 11:18; 11:19; 11:20; 11:21; 11:22; 11:23; 11:24; 11:25; 12:1; 12:2; 12:3; 12:4; 12:5; 12:6; 12:7; 12:8; 12:9; 12:10; 12:11; 12:13; 12:14; 12:15; 12:16; 12:17; 12:18; 12:19; 12:20; 12:21; 12:22; 12:23; 12:24; 13:1; 13:2; 13:3; 13:4; 13:5; 13:6; 13:7; 13:8; 13:9; 13:12; 13:13; 13:14; 13:15; 13:16; 13:17; 13:18; 13:19; 14:1; 14:2; 14:3; 14:4; 14:5; 14:6; 14:7; 14:8; 14:9; 14:10; 14:12; 14:13; 14:14; 14:15; 14:16; 14:17; 14:18; 14:19; 14:20; 15:1; 15:2; 15:3; 15:4; 15:5; 15:6; 15:7; 15:8; 15:9; 15:11; 15:12; 15:13; 15:14; 15:15; 15:16; 15:17; 15:18; 15:19	**Phonics and Word Recognition** **Fluency** **Comprehension** – 16:3; 17:2 **Informal Assessment** – 16:2; 16:3; 16:5; 16:6; 16:7; 16:8; 16:9; 16:11; 16:12; 16:13; 16:14; 16:15; 16:16; 16:17; 16:18; 16:19; 16:20; 16:21; 16:22; 16:23; 16:24; 17:1; 17:2; 17:3; 17:4; 17:5; 17:6; 17:7; 17:8; 17:9; 17:10; 17:11; 17:12; 17:13; 17:16; 17:17; 17:18; 17:19; 17:20; 17:21; 17:22; 18:1; 18:2; 18:3; 18:5; 18:7; 18:8; 18:11; 18:12; 18:13; 18:14; 18:15; 18:16; 18:17; 18:18; 19:1; 19:2; 19:3; 19:4; 19:5; 19:7; 19:8; 19:9; 19:10; 19:11; 19:12; 19:13; 19:15; 19:16; 19:17; 19:18; 19:19; 19:20; 20:1; 20:2; 20:3; 20:4; 20:6; 20:7; 20:7; 20:8; 20:9; 20:10; 20:11; 20:12; 20:15; 20:16; 20:17; 20:18; 20:19
Language Strand	(See Language Arts Presentation Book A.)	(See Language Arts Presentation Book A.)	(See Language Arts Presentation Book A.)	(See Language Arts Presentation Book A.)
Literature Strand	Literature Collection			Literature Collection – *What Are You Called?*
Formal Assessment *Reading Mastery*		In Program Mastery Test – 8	In Program Mastery Test – 15	In Program Mastery Test – 20

Strand Component	Lessons 21-25	Lessons 26-30	Lessons 31-35	Lessons 36-40
Core Lesson Connections	**Phonemic and Phonological Awareness** *Syllable Blending* – 21:a2; 23:a2 *Syllable Segmentation* – 21:a3; 22:a1; 23:a3; 24:a1 *Syllable Deletion* – 22:a2; 24:a2; 25:a2 *Rhyme Production* – 21:a1; 23:a1; 25:a1 *Onset-rime Blending* – 22:a3; 24:a3; 25:a3 *Letter Recognition and Formation* – 21:b; 22:b; 23:b; 24:b; 25:b	**Phonemic and Phonological Awareness** *Syllable Blending* – 26:a1; 28:a1; 29:a2 *Syllable Segmentation* – 26:a2; 28:a2; 30:a1 *Syllable Deletion* – 27:a2; 30:a2 *Rhyme Production* – 27:a1; 29:a1 *Onset-rime Blending* – 27:a3; 30:a3 *Letter Recognition and Formation* – 26:b; 27:b; 28:b; 29:b; 30:b	**Phonemic and Phonological Awareness** *Syllable Segmentation* – 31:a2; 33:a2; 35:a2 *Syllable Deletion* – 32:a1; 34:a1 *Rhyme Production* – 31:a1; 33:a1; 35:a1 *Onset-rime Blending* – 31:a3; 32:a2; 34:a2 *Onset-rime Segmentation* – 33:a3; 35:a3 *Phoneme Isolation* – 32:a3; 34:a3 *Letter Recognition and Formation* – 31:b; 32:b; 33:b; 34:b: 35:b	**Phonemic and Phonological Awareness** *Syllable Segmentation* – 37:a2; 39:a2 *Syllable Deletion* – 36:a1; 38:a1; 40:a1 *Rhyme Production* – 37:a1; 39:a1 *Onset-rime Blending* – 36:a2; 38:a2; 40:a2 *Onset-rime Segmentation* – 37:a3; 39:a3 *Phoneme Isolation* – 36:a3; 38:a3; 40:a3 *Letter Recognition and Formation* – 36:b; 37:b; 38:b; 39:b: 40:b

Strand Component	Lessons 21-25	Lessons 26-30	Lessons 31-35	Lessons 36-40
Core Lesson Connections *(continued)*	**Comprehension Strategies** *Listening* **Comprehension** – 21:c1; 22:c1; 23:c1; 24:c1; 25:c1 *Story Recall* – 21:c2; 22:c2; 23:c2; 24:c2 *Make a Connection* – 25:c2 *Writing* – 25:c2 **Vocabulary** – 25:d130:c2	**Comprehension Strategies** *Listening* **Comprehension** – 26:c1; 27:c1; 28:c1; 29:c1; 30:c1 *Make a Connection* – 26:c2; 27:c2; 28:c2; 29:c2; 30:c2 *Writing* – 26:c2; 27:c2; 28:c2; 29:c2; 30:c2 **Vocabulary** – 30:d1	**Comprehension Strategies** *Listening* **Comprehension** – 31:c3; 32:c3; 33:c2; 34:c2; 35:c2 *Title Identification* – 31:c1 *Title and Author Identification* – 32:c1; 33:c1; 35:c1 *Title, Author, and Illustrator Identification* – 34:c1 *Make Predictions* – 31:c2 *Confirm Predictions* – 32:c2 *Make and Confirm Predictions* – 33:c3; 34:c3; 35:c3 *Writing* – 40:c4	**Comprehension Strategies** *Listening* **Comprehension** – 36:c3; 37:c2; 38:c2; 39:c2 *Title, Author, and Illustrator Identification* – 36:c1; 37:c1; 38:c1; 39:c1; 40:c1 *Make Predictions* – 36:c2 *Confirm Predictions* – 37:c4 *Make and Confirm Predictions* – 38:c3; 39:c3; 40:c2 *Establish Purpose for Reading* – 37:c3 *Story Retell* – 40:c3 *Writing* – 45:c3
Reading Strand *Reading Mastery*	**Presentation Book A** **Phonemic Awareness** – 21:2; 21:3; 21:6; 22:2; 22:3; 22:6; 23:1; 23:3; 23:4; 23:6; 24:2; 24:3; 24:6; 25:2; 25:4 **Print Awareness** – 21:11; 21:12; 21:13; 21:14; 21:15; 22:10; 22:11; 22:12; 22:13; 22:14; 22:15; 23:9; 23:`0; 23:11; 23:12; 23:13; 23:14; 24:9; 24:10; 24:11; 24:12; 24:13; 24:14; 25:7; 25:8; 25:9; 25:10; 25:11; 25:12 **Letter Sound Correspondence** – 21:1; 21:4; 21:5; 21:7; 21:8; 21:9; 21:10; 22:1; 22:4; 22:5; 22:7; 22:8; 22:9; 23:2; 23:5; 23:7; 23:8; 24:1; 24:4; 24:5; 24:7; 24:8; 25:1; 25:3; 25:5; 25:6 **Phonics and Word Recognition** – 24:9 **Fluency** **Comprehension**	**Presentation Book A** **Phonemic Awareness** – 26:3; 26:7; 27:1; 27:4; 28:3; 29:2; 30:3 **Print Awareness** – 26:10; 26:11; 26:12; 26:13; 26:14; 27:9; 27:10; 27:11; 27:12; 27:13; 27:14; 28:8; 28:9; 28:10; 28:11; 28:12; 28:13; 29:9; 29:10; 29:11; 29:12; 29:13; 29:14; 29:15; 29:16; 30:12; 30:13; 30:14; 30:15; 30:16; 30:17; 30:18; 30:19; 30:20 **Letter Sound Correspondence** – 26:1; 26:2; 26:4; 26:5; 26:6; 26:8; 26:9; 27:2; 27:3; 27:5; 27:6; 27:7; 27:8; 28:1; 28:2; 28:4; 28:5; 28:6; 28:7; 28:8; 29:1; 29:3; 29:4; 29:5; 29:6; 29:7; 29:8; 30:1; 30:2; 30:4; 30:5; 30:6; 30:7; 30:8; 30:9; 30:10; 30:11; 30:12 **Phonics and Word Recognition** – 28:6 **Fluency** **Comprehension**	**Presentation Book A** **Phonemic Awareness** – 31:1; 31:4; 31:5; 31:6; 31:8; 32:3; 32:4; 32:5; 32:6; 32:7; 33:2; 33:3; 33:4; 33:5; 33:6; 33:7; 34:1; 34:4; 34:5; 34:6; 34:7; 34:8; 34:10; 35:3; 35:4; 35:5; 35:6; 35:7; 35:10 **Print Awareness** – 31:15; 31:19; 32:18; 33:17; 34:20; 35:20 **Letter Sound Correspondence** – 31:2; 31:3; 31:7; 31:13; 31:14; 31:17; 31:18; 32:1; 32:2; 32:8; 32:9; 32:15; 32:16; 32:17; 33:1; 33:8; 33:14; 33:15; 33:16; 34:2; 34:3; 34:9; 34:17; 34:18; 34:19; 35:1; 35:2; 35:8; 35:9; 35:17; 35:18; 35:19 **Phonics and Word Recognition** – 31:9; 31:10; 31:11; 31:12; 32:10; 32:11; 32:12; 32:13; 33:9; 33:10; 33:11; 33:12; 34:11; 34:12; 34:13: 34:14 35:11; 35:12; 35:13; 35:14 **Fluency** **Comprehension**	**Presentation Book A** **Phonemic Awareness** – 36:2; 36:3; 37:2; 37:3; 37:11; 38:1; 38:4; 38:5; 38:11; 39:3; 39:6; 40:2; 40:8 **Print Awareness** – 36:14; 36:15; 37:19; 38:19; 39:19; 40:14; 40:20 **Letter Sound Correspondence** – 36:1; 36:4; 36:10; 36:11; 36:12; 36:13; 37:1; 37:4; 37:5; 37:14; 37:15; 37:16; 37:17; 37:18; 38:2; 38:3; 38:6; 38:14; 38:15; 38:16; 38:17; 38:18; 39:1; 39:2; 39:4; 39:5; 39:14; 39:15; 39:16; 39:17; 39:18; 40:1; 40:3; 40:4; 40:15; 40:16; 40:17; 40:18; 40:19 **Phonics and Word Recognition** – 36:6; 36:7; 36:8; 37:6; 37:7; 37:9; 37:12; 38:7; 38:8; 38:9; 38:12; 39:7; 39:9; 39:10; 39:11; 39:12; 40:5; 40:6; 40:7; 40:9; 40:10 **Fluency** – 40:12 **Comprehension** – 37:10; 38:10; 39:8; 40:13

D5

Strand Component	Lessons 21-25	Lessons 26-30	Lessons 31-35	Lessons 36-40
Reading Strand *Reading Mastery* (continued)	**Informal Assessment** – 21:1; 21:2; 21:3; 12:4; 211d:5; 21:6; 21:7; 21:8; 21:9; 21:10; 21:11; 21:12; 21:13; 21:14; 21:15; 22:1; 22:2; 22:3; 22:4; 22:5; 22:6; 22:7; 22:8; 22:9; 22:10; 22:11; 22:12; 22:13; 22:14; 22:15; 23:1; 23:2; 23:3; 23:4; 23:5; 23:6; 23:7; 23:8; 23:9; 23:10; 23:11; 23:12; 23:13; 23:14; 24:1; 24:2; 24:3; 24:4; 24:5; 24:6; 24:7; 24:8; 24:9; 24:10; 24:11; 24:12; 24:13; 24:14; 25:1; 25:2; 25:3; 25:4; 25:5; 25:6; 25:7; 25:8; 25:9; 25:10: 25:11; 25:12	**Informal Assessment** – 26:1; 26:2; 26:3; 26:4; 26:5; 26:6; 26:7; 26:8; 26:9; 26:10; 26:11; 26:12; 26:13; 26:14; 27:1; 27:2; 27:3; 27:4; 27:5; 27:6; 27:7; 27:8; 27:9; 27:10; 27:11; 27:12; 27:13; 27:14; 28:1; 28:2; 28:3; 28:4; 28:5; 28:6; 28:7; 28:8; 28:9; 28:9; 28:10; 28:11; 28:12; 28:13; 29:1; 29:2; 29:3; 29:4; 29:5; 29:6; 29:7; 29:8; 29:9; 29:10; 29:11; 29:12; 29:13; 29:14; 29:15; 29:16; 30:1; 30:2; 30:3; 30:4; 30:5; 30:6; 30:7; 30:8 ;30:9; 30:10; 30:11; 30:12; 30:13; 30:14; 30:15; 30:16; 30:17; 30:18; 30:19; 30:20	**Informal Assessment** – 31:1; 31:2; 31:3; 31:4; 31:5; 31:6; 31:7; 31:8; 31:9; 31:10; 31:11; 31:12 32:1; 32:2; 32:3; 32:4; 32:5; 32:6; 32:7; 32:8; 32:10; 32:11; 32:12: 32:13 33:1; 33:2; 33:3; 33:4; 33:5; 33:6; 33:7; 33:9; 33:10; 33:11; 33:12 34:1; 34:2; 34:3; 34:4; 34:5; 34:6; 34:7; 34:8; 34:9; 34:10; 34:11; 34:12; 34:13; 34:15 35:1; 35:2; 35:3; 35:4; 35:5; 35:6; 35:7; 35:8; 35:10; 35:11; 35:12; 35:13; 35:15	**Informal Assessment** – 36:1; 36:2; 36:3; 26:4; 26:5; 26:6; 36:7; 36:9; 37:1; 37:2; 37:3; 37:4; 37:5; 37:10; 37:11; 37:12; 37:13; 38:1; 38:2; 38:3; 38:4; 38:5; 38:6; 38:7; 38:8; 38:9; 38:12; 39:1; 39:2; 39:3; 39:4; 39:5; 39:6; 39:7; 39:9; 39:10; 39:11; 39:13; 40:1; 40:2; 40:3; 40:4; 40:5; 40:6; 40:7; 40:8; 40:11
Language Strand	(See Language Presentation Book A.)	(See Language Presentation Book A.)	(See Language Presentation Book A.)	(See Language Presentation Book A.)
Literature Strand	**Literature Collection** – *What Are You Called?*	**Literature Collection** – *What Are You Called?*	**Literature Collection** – *Dog Went for a Walk*	**Literature Collection** – *Dog Went for a Walk*
Formal Assessment *Reading Mastery*	**In Program Mastery Test** – 25	**In Program Mastery Test** – 30	**In Program Mastery Test** – 35	**In Program Mastery Test** – 40

Strand Component	Lessons 41-45	Lessons 46-50	Lessons 51-55	Lessons 56-60
Core Lesson Connections	**Phonemic and Phonological Awareness** *Syllable Deletion* – 41:a1; 43:a1; 45:a1 *Onset-rime Blending* – 42:a1; 44:a1 *Onset-rime Segmentation* – 41:a2; 43:a2; 45:a2 *Phoneme Isolation* – 41:a3; 42:a2; 43:a3; 44:a2; 45:a3 *Letter Recognition and Formation* – 41:b; 42:b; 43:b; 44:b: 45:b **Comprehension Strategies** *Listening Comprehension* – 41:c3; 42:c1; 43:c1; 44:c1; 45:c1 *Title, Author, and Illustrator Identification* – 41:c1 *Confirm Predictions* – 47:c5 *Make and Confirm Predictions* – 41:c2 *Story Elements* – 41:c4; 42:c2; 43:c2; 44:c2; 45:c2 *Writing* – 50:c3	**Phonemic and Phonological Awareness** *Syllable Blending* *Syllable Segmentation* *Syllable Deletion* – 47:a1; 49:a1 *Rhyme Production* *Onset-rime Blending* – 46:a1; 48:a1; 50:a1 *Onset-rime Segmentation* – 47:a2; 49:a2 *Phoneme Isolation* – 46:a2; 47:a3; 48:a2; 49:a3; 50:a2 *Letter Recognition and Formation* – 46:b; 47:b; 48:b; 49:b: 50:b **Comprehension Strategies** *Listening Comprehension* – 46:c3; 47:c1; 48:c1; 49:c1; 50:c1 *Title, Author, and Illustrator Identification* – 46:c1 *Make Predictions* – 46:c2 *Confirm Predictions* – 46:c5 *Story Retell* – 50:c2 *Story Elements* – 46:c4; 47:c2; 48:c2; 49:c2 *Writing* – 50:c3	**Phonemic and Phonological Awareness** *Onset-rime Segmentation* – 52:a2; 54:a1 *Phoneme Isolation* – 51:a1; 51:a2; 52:a2; 53:a1; 53:a2; 54:a2; 55:a1; 55:a2 *Letter Recognition and Formation* – 51:b; 52:b; 53:b; 54:b: 55:b **Comprehension Strategies** *Listening Comprehension* – 51:c2; 52:c1; 53:c1; 54:c1; 55:c1 *Title, Author, and Illustrator Identification* – 51:c1 *Story Elements* – 51:c3; 52:c2; 53:c2; 54:c2; 55:c2 *Writing* – 55:c2	**Phonemic and Phonological Awareness** *Syllable Blending* *Syllable Segmentation* *Syllable Deletion* *Rhyme Production* *Onset-rime Blending* *Onset-rime Segmentation* – 56:a1; 58:a1; 60:a1 *Phoneme Isolation* – 56:a2; 57:a1; 57;a2; 58:a2; 59:a1; 59:a2; 60:a2 *Letter Recognition and Formation* – 56:b; 57:b; 58:b; 59:b: 60:b **Comprehension Strategies** *Listening Comprehension* – 57:c1; 58:c1; 59:c1; 60:c1 *Title, Author, and Illustrator Identification* – 56:c1 *Make Predictions* – 56:c2 *Confirm Predictions* – 56:c3 *Story Retell* – 60:c2 *Story Elements* – 57:c2; 58:c2; 59:c2 *Writing* – 59:c2; 59:c3; 60:c3

D6

Strand Component	Lessons 41-45	Lessons 46-50	Lessons 51-55	Lessons 56-60
Reading Strand *Reading Mastery*	**Presentation Book A** **Phonemic Awareness** – 41:1; 41:14; 42:12: 42:13; 43:11; 43:12; 44:12; 44:13; 45:12; 45:13 **Print Awareness** – 41:20; 41:26; 42:22; 42:29; 43:20; 43:25; 44:21; 44:26; 45:20; 45:25 **Letter Sound Correspondence** – 41:2; 41:4; 41:6; 41:21; 41:22; 41:23; 41:24; 41:25; 42:1; 42:2; 42:4; 42:6; 42:23; 42:24; 42:25; 42:26; 42:27; 42:28; 43:1; 43:3; 43:5; 43:18; 43:19; 43:21; 43:22; 43:23: 43:24; 44:1; 44:2; 44:3; 44:5; 44:19; 44:20; 44:22; 44:23; 44:24; 44:25; 45:1; 45:2; 45:4; 45:19; 45:21; 45:22; 45:23; 45:24 **Phonics and Word Recognition** – 41:8; 41:9; 41:10; 41:11; 41:12; 41:15; 41:16; 42:7; 42:8; 42:9; 42:10; 42:14; 42:17; 42:18; 43:6; 43:7; 43:8; 43:9; 43:13; 43:14; 44:7; 44:8; 44:9; 44:10; 44:14; 44:15; 45:7; 45:8; 45:9; 45:10; 45:14; 45:15 **Fluency** – 41:18; 42:20; 43:16; 44:17; 45:17 **Comprehension** – 41:19; 42:21; 43:17; 44:18; 45:18 **Informal Assessment** – 41:1; 41:3; 41:5; 41:7; 41:9; 41:10; 41:11; 41:12; 41:13; 41:14; 41:1742:2; 42:3; 42:5; 42:6; 42:11; 42:15; 42:1943:2; 43:4; 43:10; 43:11; 43:12; 43:15; 44:2; 44:4; 44:6; 44:11; 44:12; 44:13; 44:16; 45:3; 45:5; 45:11; 45:12; 45:13	**Presentation Book A** **Phonemic Awareness** – 46:12; 46:13; 47:11; 47:12; 48:1; 48:14; 48:15; 49:12; 49:13; 50:13; 50:14 **Print Awareness** – 46:20; 46:25; 47:19; 47:24; 48:21; 48:23; 43:28; ;49:19; 49:20; 49:26; 50:22; 50:26 **Letter Sound Correspondence** – 46:1; 46:2; 46:4; 46:19; 46:21; 46:22; 46:23; 46:24; 47:1; 47:2; 47:4; 47:6; 48:2; 48:4; 48:6; 48:22; 48:24; 48:25; 48:26; 48:27; 49:1; 49:2; 49:4; 49:20; 49:22; 49:23; 49:24; 49:25; 50:1; 50:2; 50:4; 50:20; 50:21; 50:23; 50:24; 50:25 **Phonics and Word Recognition** – 46:6; 46:7; 46:8; 46:9; 46:10; 46:14; 46:15; 47:5; 47:6; 47:7; 47:8; 47:9; 47:11; 48:8; 48:9; 48:10; 48:11; 48:12; 48:14; 48:15; 48:16; 48:17; 49:6; 49:7; 49:8; 49:9; 49:10; 49:12; 49:13; 49:14; 49:15; 50: 6; 50:7; 50:8; 50:9; 50:10; 50:11; 50:14; 50:15; 50:16 **Fluency** – 46:17; 47:16; 48:19; 49:17; 50:18 **Comprehension** – 46:18; 47:17; 48:20; 49:18; 50:19 **Informal Assessment** – 46:3; 46:5; 46:11; 46:12; 46:13; 46:16; 47:3; 47:10; 47:11; 47:12; 47:15; 48:3; 48:5; 48:7; 48:11; 48:12; 48:13; 48:18; 49:3; 49:5; 49:11; 49:12; 49:13; 49:16; 50:3; 50:5; 50:12; 50:13; 50:14; 50:17	**Presentation Book A** **Phonemic Awareness** **Print Awareness** – 51:23; 51:25; 51:28; 52:19; 52:21; 52:24; 53:20; 53:22; 53:25; ;54:18; 54:19; 54:22; 55:22; 55:23; 55:26 **Letter Sound Correspondence** – 51:1; 51:2; 51:3; 51:4; 51:7; 52:1; 52:2; 52:4; 52:6; 53:1; 53:2; 53:6; 54:1; 54:2; 55:1; 55:3; 55:4 **Phonics and Word Recognition** – 51:8; 51:9; 51:10; 51:11; 51:12; 51:14; 51:15; 51:17; 51:18; 51:19; 52:7; 52:8; 52:9; 52:10; 52:12; 52:13; 52:14; 52:15; 53:6; 53:7; 53:8; 53:9; 53:11; 53:12; 53:14; 53:15; 53:16; 54:4; 54:5; 54:6; 54:7; 54:8; 54:10; 54:11; 54:12; 54:13 55:5; 55:6; 55:7; 55:8; 55:9; 55:11; 55:12; 55:13; 55:15; 55:16; 55:17 **Fluency** – 51:21; 51:26; 51:27; 52:17; 52:22; 52:23; 53:18; 53:23; 53:24; 54:15; 54:20; 54:21; 55:19; 55:24; 55:25 **Comprehension** – 51:22; 52:18; 53:19; 54:16; 55:20 **Informal Assessment** – 51:2; 51:6; 51:13; 51:16; 51:20; 52:3; 52:5; 52:11; 52:16; 53:3; 53:5; 53:10; 53:13; 53:17; 54:3; 54:9; 54:14; 55:10; 55:14; 55:18 **SPELLING** **Phonemic Awareness** – 5:3 **Letter Sound Correspondence** – 1:1; 2:1; 3:1; 3:2; 4:1; 4:2; 5:1; 5:2 **Decoding and Word Recognition**	**Presentation Book A/ Presentation Book B** **Phonemic Awareness** – 56:14; 56:15; 57:12; 60:16 **Print Awareness** – 56:22; 56:23; 56:26; 57:20; 57:21; 57:24; 58:21; 58:22; 58:25; 59:22; 59:23; 59:26; 60:24; 60:25; 60:28 **Letter Sound Correspondence** – 56:1; 56:3; 56:5; 57:1; 57:2; 58:1; 58:2; 58:3; 59:1; 59:4; 60:1; 60:2; 60:4 **Phonics and Word Recognition** – 56:6; 56:7; 56:8; 56:9; 56:11; 56:12; 56:14; 56:15; 56:16; 56:17; 57:4; 5&5; 57:6; 57:7; 57:9; 57:10; 57:11; 57:12; 57:13; 57:14; 58:5; 58:6; 58:7; 58:8; 58:9; 58:10; 58:11; 58:12; 58:13; 58:14; 58:15; 59:6; 59:7; 59:8; 59:9; 59:11: 59:12; 59:13; 59:14; 59:15; 59:16; 60:7; 60:8; 60:10; 60:11; 60:13; 60:14; 60:15; 60:16; 60:17; 60:18 **Fluency** – 56:14; 56:15; 56:19; 56:24; 56:25; 57:12; 57:16; 57:18; 57:22; 57:23; 58:17; 58:19; 58:23; 58:24; 59:18; 59:20; 59:24; 59:25; 60:15; 60:20; 60:22; 60:26; 60:27 **Comprehension** – 56:20; 57:17; 58:18; 59:19; 60:21 **Informal Assessment** – 56:2; 56:4; 56:10; 56:13; 56:13; 56:14; 56:15; 56:18; 57:3; 57:8; 57:15; 58:4; 58:9; 58:16;;59:3; 59:5; 59:10: 59:17; 60:3; 60:5; 60:9; 60:12; 60:16; 60:19 **SPELLING** **Phonemic Awareness** – 6:3; 7:3; 8:3; 9:2; 9:3; 10:4 **Letter Sound Correspondence** – 6:1; 6:2; 7:1; 7:2; 8:1; 8:2; 9:1; 10:1; 10:3 **Decoding and Word Recognition** – 9:3; 10:5; 10:6
Language Strand	(See Language Arts Presentation Book A.)	(See Language Arts Presentation Book A.)	(See Language Arts Presentation Book B.)	(See Language Arts Presentation Book B.)
Literature Strand	Literature Collection – *Dog Went for a Walk*	Literature Collection – *Goodnight*	Literature Collection – *Goodnight*	Literature Collection – *Goodnight*

D7

Strand Component	Lessons 41-45	Lessons 46-50	Lessons 51-55	Lessons 56-60
Formal Assessment *Reading Mastery*	In Program Mastery Test – 45	In Program Mastery Test – 50	In Program Mastery Test – 55	In Program Mastery Test – 60

Strand Component	Lessons 61-65	Lessons 66-70	Lessons 71-75	Lessons 76-80
Core Lesson Connections	**Phonemic and Phonological Awareness** *Phoneme Isolation* – 61:a1; 61:a2; 62:a1; 62:a2; 63:a1; 63:a2; 64:a1; 64:a2; 65:a1; 65:a2 *Letter Recognition and Formation* – 61:b; 62:b; 63:b; 64:b: 65:b **Comprehension Strategies** *Listening Comprehension* – 61:c3; 63:c1; 64:c1; 65:c1 *Title, Author, and Illustrator Identification* – 61:c1; 62:c2 *Story Elements* – 61:c4; 62:c3; 62:c4; 63:c2; 64:c2; 65:c2 *Activate Background Knowledge* – 61:c2; 62:c1 *Writing* – 62:c1	**Phonemic and Phonological Awareness** *Phoneme Isolation* – 66:a1; 66:a2; 67:a1; 67:a2; 68:a1; 68:a2; 69:a1; 69:a2; 70:a1; 70:a2 *Letter Recognition and Formation* – 66:b; 67:b; 68:b; 69:b: 70:b **Comprehension Strategies** *Listening Comprehension* – 67:c1; 68:c1; 69:c1; 70:c1 *Title, Author, and Illustrator Identification* – 66:c1 *Make Predictions* – 66:c3 *Confirm Predictions* – 66:c4 *Story Retell* – 70:c2 *Story Elements* – 67:c2; 67:c3; 68:c2; 69:c2 *Activate Background Knowledge* – 66:c2 *Writing* – 66:c2; 70:c3	**Phonemic and Phonological Awareness** *Phoneme Isolation* – 71:a1; 71:a2; 72:a1; 72:a2; 73:a1; 73:a2; 74:a1; 74:a2; 75:a1; 75:a2 *Phoneme Identity* – 71:a3; 73:a3; 75:a3 *Letter Recognition and Formation* – 71:b; 72:b; 73:b; 74:b: 75:b **Comprehension Strategies** *Listening Comprehension* – 71:c3; 72:c1; 73:c1; 74:c1; 75:c1 *Title, Author, and Illustrator Identification* – 71:c1 *Story Elements* – 71:c4; 72:c2; 73:c2; 74:c2; 75:c2 *Activate Background Knowledge* – 71:c2 *Writing* – 71:c2	**Phonemic and Phonological Awareness** *Phoneme Isolation* – 76:a1; 76:a2; 77:a1; 77:a2; 78:a1; 78:a2; 79:a1; 79:a2; 80:a1; 80:a2 *Phoneme Identity* – 77:a3; 79:a3 *Letter Recognition and Formation* – 76:b; 77:b; 78:b; 79:b: 80:b **Comprehension Strategies** *Listening Comprehension* – 77:c1; 78:c1; 79:c1; 80:c1 *Title, Author, and Illustrator Identification* – 76:c1 *Make Predictions* – 76:c3 *Confirm Predictions* – 76:c4 *Story Retell* – 80:c2 *Story Elements* – 77:c2; 77:c3; 78:c2; 79:c2 *Activate Background Knowledge* – 76:c2 *Writing* – 76:c2; 80:c3
Reading Strand *Reading Mastery*	**Presentation Book B** **Phonemic Awareness** – 61:16; 62:11; 63:13; 63:15; 63:17; 63:19; 65:12 **Print Awareness** – 61:18; 61:25; 61:29; 62:26; 62:27; 62:30; 63:21; 63:30; 63:34; 64:28; 64:32; 65:31; 65:34 **Letter Sound Correspondence** – 61:1; 61:2; 61:5; 62:1; 62:2; 62:4; 62:6; 63:1; 63:2; 63:3; 64:1; 64:2; 64:5; 64:7; 65:1; 65:2; 65:3 **Phonics and Word Recognition** – 61:7; 61:8; 61:9; 61:12; 61:13; 61:14; 61:17; 61:19; 61:20; 62:7; 62:8; 62:9; 62:11; 62:12; 62:13; 62:14; 62:15; 62:19; 62:20; 63:6; 63:7; 63:8; 63:10; 63:13; 63:14; 63:15; 63:17; 63:19; 63:22; 63:23; 64:8; 64:9; 64:11; 64:13: 64:15; 64:18; 64:19; 64:20; 64:21; 65:6; 65:8; 65:10; 65:12; 65:13; 65:15; 65:22; 65:23; 65:24	**Presentation Book B** **Phonemic Awareness** – 66:11; 66:16; 67:10; 68:12; 68:23; 68:25; 70:6; 70:16 **Print Awareness** – 66:31; 66:34; 67:28; 67:32; 68:34; 68:38; 69:34; 69:38; 70:32; 70:35 **Letter Sound Correspondence** – 66:1; 66:2; 66:4; 67:1; 67:2; 68:1; 68:3; 68:5; 69:1; 69:2; 69:4; 69:6; 70:1; 70:2; 70:4 **Phonics and Word Recognition** – 66:6; 66:7; 66:8; 66:11; 66:12; 66:14; 66:16; 66:18; 66:20; 66:23; 66:24; 67:5; 67:6; 67:7; 67:9; 67:10; 67:11; 67:13; 67:14; 67:16; 67:18; 67:19; 67:21; 67:22; 68:7; 68:9; 68:11; 68:12; 68:13; 68:14; 68:16; 68:18; 68:20; 68:22; 68:23; 68:25; 68:27; 68:28; 69:7; 69:9; 69:11; 69:12; 69:14; 69:16; 69:17; 69:19; 69:21; 69:23; 69:24; 69:25; y70:6; 70:8; 70:10; 70:12; 70:14; 70:16; 70:17; 70:19; 70:21; 70:23	**Presentation Book B** **Phonemic Awareness** – 71:7; 71:12; 72:17; 73:10; 73:14; 74:7; 74:9; 74:20; 75:15; 75:16; 75:17 **Print Awareness** – 71:26; 71:29; 72:32; 72:35; 73:27; 73:30; 74:29; 74:32; 75:27; 75:30 **Letter Sound Correspondence** – 71:1; 71:2; 72:3; 72:5; 73:1; 73:2; 73:4; 74:1; 74:2; 74:4; 74:6; 75:1; 75:2 **Phonics and Word Recognition** – 71:4; 71:5; 71:6; 71:7; 71:8; 71:10; 71:13; 71:14; 71:15; 71:18; 71:19; 72:7; 72:9; 72:11; 72:13; 72:15; 72:17; 72:19; 72:20; 72:21; 72:24; 72:25; 73:6; 73:8; 73:10; 73:12; 73:14; 73:15; 73:16; 73:17; 73:20; 73:21; 74:7; 74:9; 74:11; 74:12; 74:13; 74:16; 74:17; 74:18; 74:20; 74:21; 74:22; 74:23; 75:4; 75:6; 75:8; 75:10; 75:11; 75:12; 75:15; 75:16; 75:17; 75:20; 75:21; 75:24	**Presentation Book B** **Phonemic Awareness** – 76:7; 76:10; 76:15; 77:13; 77:14; 78:6; 79:12; 80:15 **Print Awareness** – 76:28; 76:31; 77:30; 77:33; 78:29; 78:32; 79:27; 79:30; 80:29; 80:32 **Letter Sound Correspondence** – 76:1; 76:3; 76:5; 77:1; 77:2; 77:4; 77:6; 78:1; 78:2; 78:4; 79:1; 79:3; 79:5; 80:1; 80:3; 80:5 **Phonics and Word Recognition** – 76:7; 76:9; 76:10; 76:11; 76:13; 76:15; 76:16; 76:17; 76:18; 76:21; 76:22; 76:25; 77:7; 77:9; 77:11; 77:13; 77:14; 77:16; 77:18; 77:19; 77:20; 77:23; 77:24; 77:27; 78:6; 78:7; 78:11; 78:13; 78:15' 78:17; 78:18; 78:19; 78:22; 78:23; 78:26; 79:6; 79:8; 79:9; 79:10; 79:12; 79:13; 79:15; 79:16; 79:17; 79:20; 79:21; 79:24; 80:7; 80:9; 80:11; 80:13; 80:15; 80:16; 80:17; 80:18; 80:19; 80:22; 80:23; 80:26

Strand Component	Lessons 61-65	Lessons 66-70	Lessons 71-75	Lessons 76-80
Reading Strand *Reading Mastery* (continued)	**Fluency –** 61:16; 61:21; 61:23; 61:27; 61:28; 62:11; 62:22; 62:24; 62:28; 62:29; 63:13; 63:15; 63:17; 63:19; 63:25; 63:27; 63:28; 63:31; 63:32:63:33; 64:9; 64:11; 64:13; 64:15; 64:18' 64:23; 64:25; 64:26; 64:29; 64:30; 64:31; 65:6; 65:8; 65:10; 65:12; 65:13; 65:15; 65:17; 65:19; 65:21; 65:26; 65:28; 65:29; 65:32; 65:33 **Comprehension –** 61:22; 62:23; 63:26; 64:24; 65:27 **Informal Assessment** – 61:3; 61:5; 61:9; 61:12; 61:16; 61:19; 62:3; 62:5; 62:10; 62:16; 62:17; 62:21; 63:3; 63:5; 63:9; 63:11; 63:12; 63:16; 63:18; 63:20; 63:24; ;64:2; 64:4; 64:6; 64:10; 64:12; 64:14; 64:16; 64:17; 64:22; 65:3; 65:5; 65:7; 65:9; 65:11; 65:14; 65:16; 65:18; 65:20; 65:25 **SPELLING** **Phonemic Awareness** – 11:3 **Letter Sound Correspondence –** 11:1; 11:2; 12:1; 12:2; 13:1; 13:2; 14:1; 15:1 **Decoding and Word Recognition –** 11:4; 11:5; 12:3; 12:4; 12:5; 13:3; 14:2; 15:2; 15:3	**Fluency –** 66:7; 66:9; 66:11; 66:12; 66:14; 66:16; 66:18; 66:20; 66:22; 66:26; 66:28; 66:29; 66:32; 66:33; 67:7; 67:9; 67:10; 67:14; 67:16; 67:18; 67:19; 67:24; 67:26; 67:29; 67:30; 67:31; 68:7; 68:9; 68:12; 68:14; 68:16; 68:18; 68:20; 68:22; 68:23 68:25; 68:30; 68:32; 68:35; 68:36; 68:37; 69:7; 69:9; 69:12; 69:15; 69:18; 69:20; 69:22; 69:23; 69:25; 69:30; 69:32; 69:35; 69:36; 69:37; 70:8; 70:10; 70:12; 70:14; 70:17; 70:19; 70:21; 70:23; 70:27; 70:29; 70:30; 70:33; 70:34; 70:36 **Comprehension –** 66:27; 67:25; 68:31; 69:31; 70:28 **Informal Assessment** – 66:3; 66:5; 66:13; 66:15; 66:17; 66:19; 66:21; 66:22; 66:25; 67:3; 67:8; 67:12; 67:15; 67:17/ 67:20; 67:23; 68:2; 68:4; 68:6; 68:8; 68:10; 68:15; 68:17; 68:190; 68:21; 68:24; 68:26; 68:29; 69:3; 69:5; 69:8; 69:10; 69:13; 69:16; 69:19; 69:21; 69:24; 69:26; 69:29; 70:3; 70:5; 70:7; 70:9; 70:11; 70:123; 70;15; 70:18; 70:20; 70:22; 70:26 **SPELLING** **Phonemic Awareness** **Letter Sound Correspondence –** 16:1; 16:2; 17:1; 18:1; 19:1; 20:1; 20:2 **Decoding and Word Recognition –** 16:3; 17:2; 18:2; 19:2; 20:3	**Fluency –** 71:7; 71;12; 71:16; 71:21; 71:23; 71:27; 71:28; 72:17; 72:22; 72:27; 72:29; 72:33; 72:34; 73:10; 73:14; 73:18; 73:23; 73:25; 73:28; 73:29; 74:7; 74:9; 74:14; 74:20; 74:23; 74:25; 74:27; 74:30; 74:31; 75:13; 75:15; 75:16; 75:17; 75:24; 75:28; 75:29 **Comprehension –** 71:22; 71:24; 71:30; 72:28; 72:30; 72:36; 73:24; 73:31; 74:26; 74:33; 75:21; 75:22; 75:31 **Informal Assessment** – 71:3; 71:9; 71:11; 71:17; 71:20; 72:2; 72:4; 72:6; 72:8; 72:10; 72:12; 72:14; 72:16; 72:18; 72:23; 72:26; 73:3; 73:5; 73:7; 73:9; 73:11; 73:13; 73:19; 73:22; 74:3; 74:5; 74:8; 74:10; 74:15; 74:19; 74:24; ;75:3; 75:5; 75:7; 75:9; 75:14; 75:19; 75:25 **SPELLING** **Phonemic Awareness** **Letter Sound Correspondence –** 21:1; 22:1; 23:1; 24:1; 25:1 **Decoding and Word Recognition –** 21:2; 21:3; 21:4; 21:5; 22:2; 22:3; 22:4; 22:5; 23:2; 23:3; 24:2; 24:3; 24:4; 24:5; 24:6; 25:2; 25:3; 25:4; 25:5	**Fluency –** 76:7; 76:10; 76:15; 76:19; 76:24; 76:25; 76:29; 76:31; 77:13; 77:14; 77:16; 77:21; 77:26; 77:27; 77:31; 77:32; 78:6; 78;9; 78:20; 78:24; 78:26; 78:30; 78:31; 79:12; 79:18; 79:23; 79:24; 79:28; 79:29; 80:15; 80:20; 80:25; 80:26; 80:30; 80:31 **Comprehension –** 76:22; 76:23; 76:32; 77:24; 77:25; 77:34; 78:23; 78:24; 78:33; 79:21; 79:22; 79:31; 80:23; 80:24; 80:33 **Informal Assessment** – 76:4; 76:6; 76:8; 76:9; 76:10; 76:12; 76:14; 76:20; 76:26; 77:3; 77:5; 77:8; 77:10; 77:12; 77:15; 77:17; 77:22; 77:28; 78:3; 78:5; 78:8; 78:10; 78:12; 78:14; 78:16; 78;21; 78:27; 79:2; 79:4; 79:7; 79:11; 79:14; 79:19; 79:25; 80:2; 80:4; 80:6; 80:8; 80:10; 80:12; 80:14; 80:21; 80:27 **SPELLING** **Phonemic Awareness** **Letter Sound Correspondence** **Decoding and Word Recognition –** 26:1; 26:2; 26:3; 26:4; 27:1; 27:2; 28:1; 28:2; 28:3; 29:1; 30:1
Language Strand	**(See Language Presentation Book B.)**	**(See Language Presentation Book B.)**	**(See Language Presentation Book B.)**	**(See Language Presentation Book B.)**
Literature Strand	**Literature Collection –** *Farmer Schnuck*	**Literature Collection –** *Farmer Schnuck*	**Literature Collection –** *Farmer Schnuck*	**Literature Collection –** *This and That*
Formal Assessment *Reading Mastery*	**In Program Mastery Test –** 65	**In Program Mastery Test –** 70	**In Program Mastery Test –** 75	**In Program Mastery Test –** 80

D9

Strand Component	Lessons 81-85	Lessons 86-90	Lessons 91-95	Lessons 96-100
Core Lesson Connections	**Phonemic and Phonological Awareness** *Phoneme Isolation* – 81:a1; 81:a2; 82:a1; 82:a2; 83:a1; 83:a2; 84:a1; 84:a2; 85:a1; 85:a2 *Phoneme Identity* – 81:a3; 83:a3; 85:a3 *Phoneme Categorization* – 82:a3; 84:a3 *Letter Recognition and Formation* – 81:b; 82:b; 83:b; 84:b: 85:b **Comprehension Strategies** *Listening Comprehension* – 81:c3; 82:c1; 83:c1; 84:c1; 85:c1 *Title, Author, and Illustrator Identification* – 81:c1 *Story Elements* – 81:c4; 82:c2; 83:c2; 84:c2; 85:c2 *Activate Background Knowledge* – 81:c2 *Writing* – 81:c2; 85c2	**Phonemic and Phonological Awareness** *Phoneme Isolation* – 86:a1; 86:a2; 87:a1; 87:a2; 88:a1; 88:a2; 89:a1; 89:a2; 90:a1; 90:a2 *Phoneme Identity* – 87:a3; 89:a3 *Phoneme Categorization* – 86:a3; 88:a3; 90:a3 *Letter Recognition and Formation* – 86:b; 87:b; 88:b; 89:b: 90:b **Comprehension Strategies** *Listening Comprehension* – 87:c1; 88:c1; 88:c1; 89:c1; 90:c1 *Title, Author, and Illustrator Identification* – 86:c1 *Make Predictions* – 86:c3 *Confirm Predictions* – 86:c4 *Story Retell* – 90:c2 *Story Elements* – 87:c2; 87:c3; 88:c2 *Activate Background Knowledge* – 86:c2 *Story Grammar* – 89:c2 *Writing* – 86:c2; 89:c2; 90:c3	**Phonemic and Phonological Awareness** *Phoneme Isolation* – 91:a1; 91:a2; 92:a1; 92:a2; 93:a1; 93:a2; 94:a1; 94:a2; 95:a1; 95:a2 *Phoneme Identity* – 91:a3; 93:a3; 95:a3 *Phoneme Categorization* – 92:a3; 94;a3 *Phoneme Blending* – 92:a4; 94:a4 *Letter Recognition and Formation* – 91:b; 92:b; 93:b; 94:b: 95:b **Comprehension Strategies** *Listening Comprehension* – 92:c1; 93:c1; 94:c1; 95:c1 *Title, Author, and Illustrator Identification* – 91:c1 *Make Predictions* – 91:c3 *Confirm Predictions* – 91:c4 *Story Elements* – 92:c2; 95:c2 *Activate Background Knowledge* – 91:c2 *Make Connections* – 93:c2; 94:c2 *Writing* – 91:c2; 95:c2	**Phonemic and Phonological Awareness** *Phoneme Isolation* – 96:a1; 96:a2; 97:a1; 97:a2; 98:a1; 98:a2; 99:a1; 99:a2; 100:a1; 100:a2 *Phoneme Identity* – 97:a3; 99:a3 *Phoneme Categorization* – 96:a3; 98:a3; 100:a3 *Phoneme Blending* – 96:a4; 98:a4; 100:a4 *Letter Recognition and Formation* – 96:b; 97:b; 98:b; 99:b: 100:b **Comprehension Strategies** *Listening Comprehension* – 97:c1; 98:c1; 99:c1; 100:c1 *Title, Author, and Illustrator Identification* – 96:c1 *Make Predictions* – 96:c3 *Confirm Predictions* – 96:c4 *Story Retell* – 100:c2 *Story Elements* – 97:c3 *Activate Background Knowledge* – 96:c2 *Story Grammar* – 99:c2 *Make Connections* – 97:c2; 98:c2 *Writing* – 96:c2; 97:c2; 98:c2; 99:c2; 100:c3
Reading Strand *Reading Mastery*	**Presentation Book B** **Phonemic Awareness** – 81:18; 81:20; 82:7; 82:18; 83:7; 84:16; 84:18; 85:14; 85:16 **Print Awareness** – 81:31; 81:34; 82:27; ;83:24; ;84:29; 85:26 **Letter Sound Correspondence** – 81:1; 81:2; 81:4; 81:6; 82:1; 82:2; 82:4; 82:6; 82:31; 83:1; 83:2; 83:27; 84:1; 84:2; 84:4; 85:1; 85:3 **Phonics and Word Recognition** – 81:7; 81:8; 81:9; 81:12; 81:13; 81:14; 81:15; 81:18; 81:20; 81:24; 81:25; 81:28; 82:7; 82:8; 82:9; 82:12; 82:13; 82:14; 82:15; 82:18; 82:20; 82:21; 82:24; 83:4; 83:5; 83:6; 83:7; 83:10; 83:11; 83:12; 83:13; 83:16; 83:17; 83:20; 84:5; 84:6; 84:7; 84:8; 84:11; 84:12; 84:13; 84:16; 84:18; 84:22; 84:23; 84:26; 85:4; 85:5; 85:6; 85:9; 85:10; 85:11; 85:14; 85:16; 85:19; 85:20; 85:23	**Presentation Book B** **Phonemic Awareness** – 86:16; 86:18; 87:7; 87:11; 87:13; 88:10; 88:14; 88:16; 89:14 **Print Awareness** – 86:28; 87:20; 87:27; 88:22; 88:28; 89:20; 89:26; 90:21; 90:27 **Letter Sound Correspondence** – 86:1; 86:3; 86:5; 86:30; 87:1; 87:3; 87:29; 88:1; 88:3; 88:5; 88:31; 89:1; 89:2; 89:4; 89:29; 90:1; 90:2; 90:4; 90:6; 90:30 **Phonics and Word Recognition** – 86:6; 86:7; 86:8; 86:11; 86:12; 86:13; 86:16; 86:18; 86:20; 86:21; 86:24; 87:4; 87:5; 87:6; 87:7; 87:11; 87:13; 87:17; 87:18; 87:21; 87:22; 88:7; 88:8; 88:9; 88:10; 88:14; 88:16; 88:19; 88:20; 88:23; 88:24; 89:6; 89:7; 89:12; 89:13; 89:14; 89:17; 89:18; 89:21; 89:22; 90:7; 90:8; 90:9; 90:12; 90:13; 90:14; 90:18; 90:19; 90:22; 90:23	**Presentation Book B** **Phonemic Awareness** – 91:4; 92:18; 95:11 **Print Awareness** – 91:23; 91:26; 92:28; 92:31; 93:29; 93:31; 94:24; 94:31; 95:21; 95:28 **Letter Sound Correspondence** – 91:1; 91:2; 91:27; 92:1; 92:3; 92:5; 92:32; 93:1; 93:2; 93:4; 93:6; 93:32; 94:1; 94:2; 94:4; 94:6; 94:32; 95:1; 95:3; 95:29 **Phonics and Word Recognition** – 91:4; 91:5; 91:6; 91:9; 91:10; 91:11; 91:12; 91:13; 91:17; 91:18; 91:20; 91:23; 92:7; 92:9; 92:10; 92:13; 92:14; 92:15; 92:18; 92:19; 92:22; 92:23; 92:25; 93:7; 93:8; 93:9; 93:10; 93:13; 93:14; 93:15; 93:16; 93:19; 93:23; 93:24; 93:26; 94:7; 94:8; 94:9; 94:10; 94:13; 94:14; 94:15; 94:18; 94:19; 94:20; 94:25; 94;26; 95:5; 95:6; 95:7; 95:8; 95:11; 95:12; 95:16; 95:17; 95:22; 95:23	**Presentation Book B** **Phonemic Awareness** – 99:8 **Print Awareness** – 96:18; 96:25; 97:18; 97:25; 98:18; 98:23; 99:15; 99:21; 100:14; 100:20 **Letter Sound Correspondence** – 96:1; 96:3; 96:26; 97:1; 97:3; 97:4; 97:26; 98:1; 98:2; 98:3; 98:25; 99:1; 99:2; 99:4; 99:23; 100:1; 100:2; 100:4; 100:21 **Phonics and Word Recognition** – 96:4; 96:7; 96:9; 96:10; 96:13; 96:16; 96:19; 96:2097.5; 97:8; 97:9; 97:10; 97:11; 97:19; 97:20; 98:5; 98:9; 98:11; 98:14; 98:15; 98:18; 98:19; 99:6; 99:7; 99:8; 99:9; 99:12; 99:16; 99:17; 100:7; 100:10; 100:13; 100:14; 100:15

Strand Component	Lessons 81-85	Lessons 86-90	Lessons 91-95	Lessons 96-100
Reading Strand *Reading Mastery* (continued)	**Fluency** – 81:10; 81:16; 81:18; 81:20; 81:22; 81:27; 81:28; 81:32; 81:33; 82:7; 82:10; 82:16; 82:18; 82:23; 82:24; 83:7; 83:8; 83:14; 83:19; 83:20; 83:25; 83:26; 84:9; 84:14; 84:16; 84:18; 84;20; 84:25; 84:26; 84:30; 84:31; 85:7; 85:12; 85:14; 85:16; 85:17; 85:22; 85:23; 85:27; 85:28	**Fluency** – 86:9; 86:14; 86:16; 86:18; 86:23; 86:24; 86:26; 86:29; 87:7; 87:11; 87:13; 87:15; 87:21; 87:22; 87:24; 87:2588:10; 88:12; 88:14; 88:16; 88:17; 88:23; 88:24; 88:26; 88:29; 88:30; 89:10; 89:14; 89:15; 89:21; 89:22; 89:27; 89:28; 90:10; 90:16; 90:22; 90:23; 90:25; 90:28; 90:29	**Fluency** – 91:4; 91:7; 91:15; 91:20; 91:22; 91;24; 91:28; 91:29; 92:11; 92:16; 92:18; 92:20; 92:25; 92:27; 923:29; 92:33; 92:34; 93:11; 93:17; 93:21; 93:26; 93:28; 93:33; 93:34; 94:11; 94:16; 94:22; 94:26; 94:29; 94:33; 94;34; 95:9; 95:11; 95:14; 95:19; 95:23; 95:26; 95:30; 95:31	**Fluency** – 96:5; 96:11; 96:14; 96:20; 96:23; 96:27; 96:28; 97:6; 97:13; 97:16; 97:20; 97:23; 97:26; 97:27; 97:28; 98:6; 98:11; 98:12; 98:16; 98:19; 98:22; 98:26; 98:27; 99:10; 99:13; 99:17; 99:20; 99:24; 99:25; 100:8; 100:11; 100:15; 100:18; 100:22; 100:23
	Comprehension – 81:25; 81:35; 82:21; 82:22; 82:26; 82:32; 83:17; 83:18; 83:22; 82:28; 84:23; 84:24; 84:33; 85:20; 85:21; 85:30	**Comprehension** – 86:21; 86:22; 86:31; 87:"18; 87:19; 87:30; 88:20; 88:21; 88:32; 89:18; 89:19; 89:30; 90:19; 90:20; 90:31	**Comprehension** – 91:18; 91:19; 91:30; 92:23; 92:24; 92:35; 93:24; 93:25; 93:35; 94:26; 94:27; 94:35; 95:23; 95:24; 95:32	**Comprehension** – 96:20; 96:21; 96:29; 97:20; 97:21; 97:29; 98:19; 98:20; 98:28; 99:16; 99:17; 99:18; 99:26; 100:14; 100:15; 100:16; 100:24
	Informal Assessment – 81:3; 81:5; 81:11; 81:17 81:19; 81:21; 81:23; 81:29; 82:3; 82:5; 82:11; 82:17; 82:19; 82:25; 83:3; 83:9; 83:15; 83:21; 84:3; 84:10; 84:15; 84:17; 84:19; 84:21; 84:27; 85;2; 85:8; 85:13; 85:15; 85:18; 85:24	**Informal Assessment** – 86:2; 86:4; 86:10; 86:15; 86:17; 86:19; 86:25; 87:2; 87:8; 87:10; 87:14; 87:16; 87:23; 88:2; 88:4; 88:6; 88:11; 88:12; 88:15; 88:17; 88:25; 89:3; 89:5; 89:11; 89:16; 89:23; 90:3; 90:5; 90:11; 90:15; 90:17; 90:24	**Informal Assessment** – 91:3; 91:8; 91:14; 91:16; 91:21; 92:2; 92:4; 92:6; 92:8; 92:12; 92:17; 92:21; 92:26; 93:3; 93:5; 93:12; 93:17; 93:20; 93:22; 93:27; 94:3; 94:5; 94:12; 94:17; 94:21; 94:23; 94:28; 95:2; 95:4; 95:10; 95:13; 95:15; 95:18; 95:20; 95:25	**Informal Assessment** – 96:2; 96:6; 96:8; 96:12; 96:15; 96:17; 96:22; 97:2; 97:7; 97:12; 97:14; 97:17; 97:22; 98:4; 98:7; 98:10; 98:13; 98:17; 98:21; 99:3; 99:5; 99:11; 99:14; 99:16; 99:19; 100:3; 100:9; 100:12; 100:17
	SPELLING **Phonemic Awareness** **Letter Sound Correspondence** – 31:1; 32:1; 34:1; 35:1 **Decoding and Word Recognition** – 31:2; 32:2; 33:1; 34:2; 34:3; 34:4; 35:2; 35:3	**SPELLING** **Phonemic Awareness** **Letter Sound Correspondence** **Decoding and Word Recognition** – 36:1; 36:2; 36:3; 36:4; 36:5; 37:1; 37:2; 37:3; 37:4; 37:5; 37:6; 37:7; 38:1; 38:2; 38:3; 38:4; 38:5; 38:6; 38:7; 39:1; 39:2; 39:3; 39:4; 39:5; 39:6; 39:7; 40:1; 40:2; 40:3; 40:4; 40:5	**SPELLING** **Phonemic Awareness** **Letter Sound Correspondence** – 43:1; 44:1 **Decoding and Word Recognition** – 41:1; 41:2; 41:3; 41:4; 42:1; 42:2; 42:3; 42:4; 43:2; 43:3; 43:4; 44:2; 44:3; 44:4; 44:5; 44:6; 44:7; 45:1; 45:2; 45:3; 45:4; 45;5	**SPELLING** **Phonemic Awareness** **Letter Sound Correspondence** **Decoding and Word Recognition** – 46:1; 46:2; 46:3; 46:4; 46:5; 47:1; 47:2; 47:3; 47:4; 48:1; 49:1; 50:1
Language Strand	(See Language Presentation Book B.)	(See Language Presentation Book C.)	(See Language Presentation Book C.)	(See Language Presentation Book C.)
Literature Strand	Literature Collection – *This and That*	Literature Collection – *This and That*	Literature Collection – *Henrietta's First Winter*	Literature Collection – *Henrietta's First Winter*
Formal Assessment *Reading Mastery*	In Program Mastery Test – 85	In Program Mastery Test – 90	In Program Mastery Test – 95	In Program Mastery Test – 100

D11

Strand Component	Lessons 101-105	Lessons 106-110	Lessons 111-115	Lessons 116-120
Core Lesson Connections	**Phonemic and Phonological Awareness** *Phoneme Isolation* – 101:a1; 102:a1; 102:a2; 103:a1; 104:a1; 104:a2; 105:a1 *Phoneme Identity* – 102:a3; 104:a3 *Phoneme Categorization* – 101:a2; 103:a2; 105:a2 *Phoneme Blending* – 102:a4; 104:a4 *Letter Recognition and Formation* – 101:b; 102:b; 103:b; 104:b: 105:b **Comprehension Strategies** *Listening Comprehension* – 102:c1; 103:c1; 104:c1; 105:c1 *Title, Author, and Illustrator Identification* – 101:c1 *Make Predictions* – 101:c3 *Confirm Predictions* – 101:c4 *Story Retell* – 103:c3 *Story Elements* – 102:c2; 105:c2 *Activate Background Knowledge* – 101:c2 *Make Connections* – 103:c2; 104:c2 *Writing* – 105:c2	**Phonemic and Phonological Awareness** *Phoneme Isolation* – 106:a1; 106:a2; 106:a3; 107:a1; 108:a1; 108:a2; 109:a1; 110:a1; 110:a2 *Phoneme Identity* – 108:a3; 110:a3 *Phoneme Categorization* – 107:a2; 109:a2 *Phoneme Blending* – 106:a4; 108:a4; 110:a4 *Letter Recognition and Formation* – 106:b; 107:b; 108:b; 109:b: 110:b **Comprehension Strategies** *Listening Comprehension* – 107:c1; 108:c1; 109:c1; 110:c1 *Title, Author, and Illustrator Identification* – 106:c1 *Make Predictions* – 106:c3 *Confirm Predictions* – 106:c4 *Story Retell* – 110:c2 *Story Elements* – 109:c3 *Activate Background Knowledge* – 106:c2 *Make Connections* – 107:c2; 108:c2 *Identify Main Idea* – 107:c3; 108:c3; 109:c2 *Writing* – 106:c2; 107:c2; 110:c3	**Phonemic and Phonological Awareness** *Phoneme Isolation* – 111:a1; 112:a1; 113:a1; 114:a1; 115:a1 *Phoneme Identity* – 112:a2; 114:a2 *Phoneme Categorization* – 112:a3; 114:a3 *Phoneme Blending* – 111:a2; 113:a2 *Phoneme Segmentation* – 112:a4; 114:a4; 115:a2 *Letter Recognition and Formation* – 111:b; 112:b; 113:b; 114:b: 115:b **Comprehension Strategies** *Listening Comprehension* – 112:c1; 113:c1; 114:c1; 115:c1 *Title, Author, and Illustrator Identification* – 111:c1 *Make Predictions* – 111:c3 *Confirm Predictions* – 111:c4 *Story Retell* – 115:c2 *Story Elements* – 112:c2 *Activate Background Knowledge* – 111:c2 *Make Connections* – 113:c2; 114:c2 *Identify Main Idea* – 112:c3; 113:c3 *Writing* – 113:c2	**Phonemic and Phonological Awareness** *Phoneme Isolation* – 117:a1; 119:a1 *Phoneme Identity* – 116:a1; 117:a2; 119:a2 *Phoneme Categorization* – 116:a2; 118:a1; 120:a1 *Phoneme Blending* – 116:a3; 117:a3; 119:a3 *Phoneme Segmentation* – 118:a2; 120:a2 *Letter Recognition and Formation* – 116:b; 117:b; 118:b; 119:b: 120:b **Comprehension Strategies** *Listening Comprehension* – 117:c1; 118:c1; 119:c1; 120:c1 *Title, Author, and Illustrator Identification* – 116:c1 *Make Predictions* – 116:c3 *Confirm Predictions* – 116:c4 *Story Retell* – 120:c2 *Story Elements* – 119:c2 *Activate Background Knowledge* – 116:c2 *Make Connections* – 117:c2; 118:c2 *Identify Main Idea* – 117:c3; 118:c3 *Writing* – 116:c2; 119:c2; 120:c3
Reading Strand *Reading Mastery*	**Presentation Book B** **Phonemic Awareness** **Print Awareness** – 101:16; 101:22; 102:16; 102:22; 103:20; 103:26; 104:21; 105:18; 105:2 **Letter Sound Correspondence** – 101:1; 101:3; 101:23; 102:1; 102:3; 102:5; 102:23; 103:1; 103:2; 103:4; 103:27; 104:1; 104:2; 104:4; 104:6; 104:22; 105:1; 105:3; 105:26 **Phonics and Word Recognition** – 101:4; 101:7; 101:9; 101:11; 101:12; 101:13; 101:16; 101:17; 102:7; 102:10; 102:13; 102:14; 102:16; 102:17; 103:6; 103:9; 103:11; 103:12; 103:15; 103:17; 103:20; 103:21; 104:7; 104:10; 104:13; 104:14; 104:15; 104:16; 105:4; 105:6; 105:7; 105:10; 105:12; 105:15; 105:19; 105:20	**Presentation Book B / Presentation Book C** **Phonemic Awareness** – 107:6 **Print Awareness** – 106:13; 106:20; 107:25; 108:25; 109:21; 110:19 **Letter Sound Correspondence** – 106:1; 106:3; 106:21; 107:1; 107:3; 107:4; 107:26; 108:1; 108:3; 108:5; 108:26; 109:1; 109:2; 109:4; 109:6; 109:22; 110:1; 110:3; 110:20 **Phonics and Word Recognition** – 106:4; 106:7; 106:8; 106:10; 107:6; 107:7; 107:9; 107:11; 107:13; 107:14; 107:17; 107:19; 107:20; 108:7; 108:8; 108:10; 108:13; 108:14; 108:15; 108:16; 108:17; 108:20; 109:7; 109:10; 109:11; 109:12; 109:13; 109:14; 109:16; 110:5; 110:8;	**Presentation Book C** **Phonemic Awareness** – 113:19; 115:12 **Print Awareness** – 111:18; 112:23; 113:26; 114:28; 115:28 **Letter Sound Correspondence** – 111:1; 111:2; 111:4; 111:19; 112:1; 112:2; 112:24; 113:1; 113:3; 113:5; 113:27114:1; 114:2; 114:4; 114:29; 115:1; 115:3; 115:5; 115:29 **Phonics and Word Recognition** – 111:5; 111:8; 111:9; 111:13; 112:4; 112:5; 112:6; 112:7; 112:9; 112:10; 112:13; 112:14; 112:16; 112:18; 113:7; 113:9; 113:10; 113:13; 113:15; 113:18; 113:19; 113:21; 114:6; 114:8; 114:9; 114:13; 114:16; 114:18; 114:22; 115:6; 115:8; 115:11; 115:12; 115:13; 115:14; 115:17; 115:19; 115:22	**Presentation Book C** **Phonemic Awareness** **Print Awareness** – 116:24; 117:23; 118:19; 119:24; 120:27 **Letter Sound Correspondence** – 116:1; 116:2; 116:25; 117:1; 117:2; 117:24; 118:1; 118:2; 118:3; 118:20; 119:1; 119:2; 119:4; 119:25; 120:1; 120:2; 120:4; 120:6; 120:29 **Phonics and Word Recognition** – 116:4; 116:7; 116:9; 116:11; 116:13; 116:14; 116:18; 117:4; 117:7; 117:9;; 117:11; 117:13; 117:14; 117:18; 118:5; 118:8; 118:9; 118:10; 118:11; 118:14; 119:6; 119:10; 119:14; 119:16; 119:19; 120:7; 120:8; 120:11; 120:12; 120:13; 120:14; 120:17

D12

Strand Component	Lessons 101-105	Lessons 106-110	Lessons 111-115	Lessons 116-120
Reading Strand *Reading Mastery* (continued)	**Fluency –** 101:5; 101:10; 101:14; 101;17; 101:20; 101:24; 101:25; 102:8; 102:11; 102:17; 102:20; 102:24; 102:25; 103:7; 103:13; 103:18; 103:21; 103:24; 103:28; 103:29; 104:8; 104:11; 104:14; 104:16; 104:19; 104:23; 104:24; 105:8; 105:13; 105:16; 105:20; 105:23; 105:27; 105:28 **Comprehension –** 101:16; 101:17; 101:18; 101:26; 102:17; 102:18; 102:26; 103:21; 103:30; 104:16; 104:17; 104:25; 105:19; 105:20; 105:21; 105:29 **Informal Assessment** – 101:2; 101:6; 101:8; 101:15; 101:19; 102:2; 102:4; 102:6; 102:9; 102:12; 102:15; 102:19; 104:3; 104:5; 104:9; 104:12; 104:18; 105:2; 105:5; 105:9; 105:11; 105:14; 105:17; 105:19; 105:22 **SPELLING** **Phonemic Awareness** **Letter Sound Correspondence –** 54:1; 55:1 **Decoding and Word Recognition –** 51:1; 52:1; 53:1; 54:2; 55:2; 55:3; 55:4; 55:5; 55:6; 55:7	110:9; 110:10; 110:11; 110:14 **Fluency –** 106:5; 106:10; 106:11; 106:15; 106:18; 106:22; 106:23; 107:6; 107:15; 107:22; 107:27; 107:28; 108:7; 108:11; 108:18; 108:22; 108:27; 108:28; 109:8; 109:15; 109:18; 109:23; 109:24; 110:6; 110:12; 110:16; 110:21; 110:22 **Comprehension –** 106:14; 106:24; 107:22; 107:23; 107:29; 108:22; 108:23; 108:29; 109:18; 109:19; 109:25; 110:16; 110:17; 110:23 **Informal Assessment** – 106:2; 106:6; 106:9; 106:14; 106:17; 107:2; 107:5; 1076:8; 107:10; 107:12; 107:16; 107:18; 107:21; 108:2; 108:4; 108:6; 108:9; 108:12; 108:19; 108:21; 109:3; 109:5; 109:9; 109:17; 110:2; 110:4; 110:7; 110:9; 110:13; 110:15 **SPELLING** **Phonemic Awareness** **Letter Sound Correspondence** **Decoding and Word Recognition –** 56:1; 56:2; 56:3; 56:4; 57:1; 57:2; 57:3; 58:1; 58:2; 58:3; 59:1; 59:2; 59:3; 60:1; 60:2; 60:3	**Fluency –** 111:6; 111:8; 111:11; 111:15; 111:20; 111:21; 112:11; 112:20; 112:25; 112:26; 113:11; 113:16; 113:19; 113:23; 113:28; 113:29; 114:11; 114:14; 114:20; 114:24; 114:30; 114:31; 115:9; 115:12; 115:15; 115:24; 115:30; 115:31 **Comprehension –** 111:15; 111:16; 111:22; 112:20; 112:27; 113:23; 113:24; 113:30; 114:24; 114:25; 114:26; 114:32; 115:21; 115:24; 115:25; 115:26; 115:32 **Informal Assessment** – 111:3; 111:7; 111:10; 111:12; 111:14; 112:3; 112:8; 112:12; 112:15; 112:17; 112:19; 113:2; 113:4; 113:6; 113:8; 113:12; 113:14; 113:17; 113:22; 114:3; 114:5; 114:7; 114:10; 114:12; 114:15; 114:17; 114:19; 114:21; 114:23; 115:2; 115:4; 115:7; 115:10; 115:16; 115:18; 115:20; 115:23 **SPELLING** **Phonemic Awareness** **Letter Sound Correspondence –** 61:1; 62:1; 64:1; 65:1 **Decoding and Word Recognition –** 61:2; 61:3; 61:4; 61:5; 61:6; 62:2; 62:3; 62:4; 62:5; 62:6; 62:7; 63:1; 63:2; 63:3; 63;4; 63;5; 63:6; 64:2; 64:3; 64:4; 64:5; 64;6; 64:7; 65:2; 65:3; 65:4; 65:5	**Fluency –** 116:5; 116:15; 116:20; 116:25; 116:26; 117:5; 117:15; 117:20; 117:25; 117:26; 118:6; 118:12; 118:16; 118:21; 118:22; 119:12; 119:17; 119:21; 119:26; 119:27; ;120:9; 120:14; 120:15; 120:18; 120:22; 120:28 **Comprehension –** 116:17; 116:20; 116:21; 116:27; 117:17; 117:20; 117:21; 117:27; 118:13; 118:16; 118:17; 118:23; 119:21; 119:22; 119:28; 120:22; 120:23; 120:24; 120:25; 120:30 **Informal Assessment** – 116:3; 116:6; 116:8; 116:10; 116:12; 116:14; 116:17; 116:20; 117:3; 117: 6; 117:8; 117:10; 117:12; 117:16; 117:19; 118:4; 118:7; 118:15; 119:3; 119:5; 119:11; 119:13; 119:15; 119:18; 119:20; 120:3; 120:5; 120:10; 120:16; 120:19; 120:21 **SPELLING** **Phonemic Awareness** **Letter Sound Correspondence –** 68:1; 69:1 **Decoding and Word Recognition –** 66:1; 66:2; 66:3; 67:1; 68:2; 68:3; 68:4; 69:2; 69:3; 69:4; 69:5; 70:1; 70:2; 70:3
Language Strand	**(See Language Presentation Book C.)**	**(See Language Presentation Book C.)**	**(See Language Presentation Book C.)**	**(See Language Presentation Book C.)**
Literature Strand	**Literature Collection –** *Henrietta's First Winter*	**Literature Collection –** *Maxie's Cat*	**Literature Collection –** *Maxie's Cat*	**Literature Collection –** *Maxie's Cat*
Formal Assessment *Reading Mastery*	**In Program Mastery Test –** 105	**In Program Mastery Test –** 110	**In Program Mastery Test –** 115	**In Program Mastery Test –** 120 **Individual Reading Checkout –** 120:30

D13

Strand Component	Lessons 121-125	Lessons 126-130	Lessons 131-135	Lessons 136-140
Core Lesson Connections	**Phonemic and Phonological Awareness** *Phoneme Identity* – 121:a1; 123:a1; 125:a1 *Phoneme Categorization* – 122:a1; 124:a1 *Phoneme Blending* – 121:a2; 123:a2; 125:a2 Phoneme Segmentation – 122:a2; 124:a2 *Letter Recognition and Formation* – 121:b; 122:b; 123:b; 124:b: 125:b **Comprehension Strategies** *Listening Comprehension* – 122:c1; 123:c1; 124: c1; 125:c1 *Title, Author, and Illustrator Identification* – 121:c1 *Make Predictions* – 121:c3 *Confirm Predictions* – 121:c4 *Establish a Purpose for Reading* – 121: c2 *Story Retell* – 125:c2 *Story Elements* – 122:c2 *Make Connections* – 123:c2; 124:c2 *Identify Main Idea* – 122:c3; 123:c3 *Writing* – 123:c2	**Phonemic and Phonological Awareness** *Phoneme Identity* – 127:a1; 129:a1 *Phoneme Categorization* – 126:a1; 128:a1; 130:a1 *Phoneme Blending* – 127:a2; 129:a2 *Phoneme Segmentation* – 126:a2; 128:a2; 130:a2 *Letter Recognition and Formation* – 126:b; 127:b; 128:b; 129:b: 130:b **Comprehension Strategies** *Listening Comprehension* – 127:c1; 128:c1; 129:c1; 130:c1 *Title, Author, and Illustrator Identification* – 126:c2 *Establish a Purpose for Reading* – 126:c1 *Identify Main Idea* – 127:c3 *K.W.L* – 126:c3; 126:c4; 127:c2; 128:c2 *Summarize Expository Text* – 129:c2; 130:c2 *Illustrate Expository Text* – 129:c3; 130:c3 *Writing* – 130:c4	**Phonemic and Phonological Awareness** *Phoneme Identity* – 131:a1; 133:a1; 135:a1 *Phoneme Categorization* – 132:a1; 134:a1 *Phoneme Blending* – 131:a2; 133:a2; 135:a2 *Phoneme Segmentation* – 132:a2; 134:a2 *Letter Recognition and Formation* – 131:b; 132:b; 133:b; 134:b: 135:b **Comprehension Strategies** *Listening Comprehension* – 132:c1; 133:c1; 134:c1; 135:c1 *Title, Author, and Illustrator Identification* – 131:c2 *Establish a Purpose for Reading* – 131:c1 *Identify Main Idea* – 132:c3 *K.W.L* – 131:c3; 131:c4; 132:c2; 133:c2 *Summarize Expository Text* – 134:c2; 135:c2 *Illustrate Expository Text* *Illustrate and Retell Expository Text* – 134:c3; 135:c3	**Phonemic and Phonological Awareness** *Phoneme Identity* – 137:a1; 139:a1 *Phoneme Categorization* – 136:a1; 138:a1; 140:a1 *Phoneme Blending* – 137:a2; 139:a2 *Phoneme Segmentation* – 136:a2; 138:a2; 140:a2 *Letter Recognition and Formation* – 136:b; 137:b; 138:b; 139:b: 140:b **Comprehension Strategies** *Listening Comprehension* – 137:c1; 138:c1; 139:c1; 140:c1 *Title, Author, and Illustrator Identification* – 136:c2 *Establish a Purpose for Reading* – 136:c1 *Identify Main Idea* – 137:c3 *K.W.L* – 136:c3; 136:c4; 137:c2; 138:c2 *Summarize Expository Text* – 139:c2; 140:c2 *Illustrate and Retell Expository Text* – 139:c3; 140:c3 *Writing* – 136:c2; 137:c2; 140:c4
Reading Strand *Reading Mastery*	**Presentation Book C** **Phonemic Awareness** – 125:10 **Print Awareness** – 121:28; 122:25; 123:24; 124:25; 125:22 **Letter Sound Correspondence** – 121:1; 121:3; 121:5; 121:30; 122:1; 122:2; 122:4; 122:6; 122:27; 123:1; 123:4; 123:26; 124:1; 124:3; 124:5; 125:27; 125:1; 125:2; 125:4; 125:24 **Phonics and Word Recognition** – 121:7; 121:10; 121:11; 121:13; 121:14; 121:17; 121:18; 121:21; 122:7; 122:8; 122:11; 122:14; 122:16; 122:19; 123:6; 123:9; 123:10; 123:13; 123:14; 123:15; 123:16; 123:17; 123:18; 124:7; 124:10; 124:12; 124:15; 124:16; 124:19; 125:7; 125:10; 125:11; 125:14; 125:17	**Presentation Book C** **Phonemic Awareness** – 127:10; 129:14 **Print Awareness** – 126:21; 127:26; 128:25; 129:23; 130:23 **Letter Sound Correspondence** – 126:1; 126:3; 126:4; 126:24; 127:1; 127:3; 127:5; 127:29; 128:1; 128:2; 128:4; 128:28; 129:1; 129:3; 129:26; 130:1; 130:2 **Phonics and Word Recognition** – 126:5; 126:6; 126:7; 126:8; 126:9; 126:12; 126:15; 127:7; 127:8; 127:10; 127:11; 127:12; 127:15; 127:16; 127:20; 128:6; 128:7; 128:8; 128:9; 128:10 128:12; 128:13; 128:14; 128:15; 128:20; 129:5; 129:8; 129:9; 129:10; 129:14; 129:15; 129:18; 130:4; 130:7; 130:9; 130:13; 130:14; 130:15; 130:18	**Presentation Book C** **Phonemic Awareness** **Print Awareness** – 131:22; 132:26; 133:33; 134:26; 135:23 **Letter Sound Correspondence** – 131:1; 131:3; 131:5; 131:20; 132:1; 132:2; 132:4; 132:24; 133:1; 133:2; 133:4; 133:6; 133:31; 134:1; 134:2; 134:24; 135:1; 135:3; 135:5; 135:24 **Phonics and Word Recognition** – 131:7; 131:8; 131:11; 131:14; 132:6; 132:9; 132:10; 132:12; 132:13; 132:14; 132:15; 132:18; 133:7; 133:9; 133:12; 133:13; 133:15; 133:16; 133:19; 133:21; 133:25; 134:4; 134:5; 134:6; 134:7; 134:11; 134:13; 134:16; 134:18; 135:7; 135:8; 135:9; 135:11; 135:13; 135:16	**Presentation Book C** **Phonemic Awareness** **Print Awareness** – 136:30; 137:28; 138:26; 139:31; 140:27 **Letter Sound Correspondence** – 136:1; 136:2; 136:4; 136:28; 137:1; 137:2; 137:26; 138:1; 138:2; 138:24; 139:1; 139:3; 139:5; 139:29 140:1; 140:2; 140:4; 140:28 **Phonics and Word Recognition** – 136:7; 136:8; 136:11; 136:12; 136:16; 136:18; 136:22; 137:4; 137:6; 137:9; 137:11; 137:12; 137:15; 137:17; 137:20; 138:4; 138:6; 138:9; 138:10; 138:11; 138:14; 138:15; 138:16; 138:18; 139:7; 139:8; 139:11; 139:13; 139:17; 139:19; 139:23; 140:6; 140:7; 140:8; 140:9; 140:12; 140:14; 140:17; 140:18; 140:20; 140:21

Strand Component	Lessons 121-125	Lessons 126-130	Lessons 131-135	Lessons 136-140
Reading Strand *Reading Mastery* (continued)	**Fluency –** 121:8; 121:15; 121:19; 121:23; 121:29; 122:9; 122:12; 122:17; 122:21; 122:26; 123:7; 123:11; 123:20; 123:25; 124:8; 124:13; 124:17; 124:21; 124:23; 125:8; 125:12; 125:15; 125:19; 125:21 **Comprehension –** 121:23; 121:24; 121:25; 121:26; 121:31; 122:21; 122:22; 122:23; 122:28; 123:20; 123:21; 123:21; 123:27; 124:21; 124:22; 124:26; 124:28; 125:19; 125:20; 125:23 **Informal Assessment** – 121:2; 121:4; 121:6; 121:9; 121:12; 121:16; 121:20; 121:22; 122:3; 122:5; 122:10; 122:13; 122:18; 122:20; 123:2; 123:5; 123:8; 123:12; 123:17; 123:19; 124:2; 124:4; 124:6; 124:9; 124:11; 124:13; 124:18; 124:20; 125:3; 125:5; 125:9; 125:13; 125:16; 125:18 **SPELLING** **Phonemic Awareness** **Letter Sound Correspondence** **Decoding and Word Recognition –** 71:1; 72:1; 73:1; 73:2; 73:3; 74:1; 74:2; 74:3; 74:4; 75:1; 75:2; 75:3	**Fluency –** 126:10; 126:13; 126:17; 126:22; 127:8; 127:13; 127:18; 127:22; 127:27; 128:8; 128:13; 128:18; 128:22; 128:27; 129:6; 129:12; 129:16; 129:20; 129:24; 130:5; 130:11; 130:16; 130:20; 130:25 **Comprehension –** 126:17; 126:18; 126:19; 126:23; 126:25; 127:22; 127:23; 127:24; 127:28; 127:30; 128:22; 128:23; 128:37; 128:29; 129:20; 129:21; 129:25; 129:27; 130:20; 130:21; 130:24; 130:25 **Informal Assessment** – 126:2; 126:11; 126:14; 126:16; 127:2; 127:4; 127:6; 127:9; 127:14; 127:17; 127:19; 127:21; 128:3; 128:5; 128:11; 128:16; 128:19; 128:21; 129:2; 129:4; 129:7; 129:11; 129:13; 129:17; 129:19; 130:3; 130:6; 130:8; 130:10; 130:12; 130:17; 130:19 **SPELLING** **Phonemic Awareness** **Letter Sound Correspondence** **Decoding and Word Recognition –** 76:1; 76:2; 76:3; 76:4; 77:1; 78:1; 78:2; 78:3; 78:4; 79:1; 79:2; 79:3; 79:4; 79:5; 80:1; 80:2; 80:3	**Fluency –** 131:9; 131:12; 131:16; 132:7; 132:16; 132:20; 133:27; 133:28; 133:29; 133:32; 133:34; 134:9; 134:14; 134:20; 135:10; 135:14; 135:18 **Comprehension –** 131:16; 131:17; 131:18; 131:21; 131:23; 132:20; 132:21; 132:22; 132:25; 132:27; 133:27; 133:28; 133:29; 133:32; 133:34; 134:20; 134:21; 134:23; 134:24; 134:27; 135:18; 135:19; 135:21; 135:22; 135:24 **Informal Assessment** – 131:2; 131:4; 131:6; 131:10; 131:13; 131:15; 132:3; 132:5; 132:8; 132:11; 132:17; 132:19; 133:3; 133:5; 133:8; 133:11; 133:18; 133:20; 133:22; 133:24; 133:26; 134:3; 134:8; 134:10; 134:12; 134:17; 134:19; 135:2; 135:4; 135:6; 135:10; 135:12; 135:15; 135:17 **SPELLING** **Phonemic Awareness** **Letter Sound Correspondence –** 83:1; 84:1 **Decoding and Word Recognition –** 81:1; 81:2; 82:1; 82:2; 82:3; 83:2; 83:3; 83:4; 84:2; 84:3; 84:4; 84:5; 84:6; 85:1; 85:2; 85:3; 85:4	**Fluency –** 136:9; 136:14; 136:20; 136:24; 137:7; 137:12; 137:18; 137:22; 138:7; 138:12; 138:17; 138:20; 139:9; 139:15; 139:21; 139:25; 140:7; 140:10; 140:15; 140:19; 140:22 **Comprehension –** 136:24; 136:25; 136:27; 136:29; 136:31; 137:22; 137:23; 137:25; 137:27; 137:29; 138:20; 138:21; 138:23; 138:25; 138:27; 139:25; 139:26; 139:28; 139:30; 139:32; 140:22; 140:23; 140:25; 140:26; 140:28 **Informal Assessment** – 136:3; 136:5; 136:10; 136:13; 136:15; 136:17; 136:19; 136:21; 136:23; 137:3; 137:5; 137:8; 137:10; 137:14; 137:16; 137:19; 137:21; 138:3; 138:5; 138:8; 138:13; 138:19; 139:2; 139:4; 139:; 139:10; 139:12; 139:14; 139:16; 139:18; 139:20; 139:22; 139:24; 140:3; 140:5; 140:11; 140:13; 140:16; 140:21 **SPELLING** **Phonemic Awareness** **Letter Sound Correspondence** **Decoding and Word Recognition –** 86:1; 86:2; 86:3; 86:4; 87:1; 87:2; 87:3; 87:4; 88:1; 88:2; 88:3; 88:4; 88:5; 89:1; 89:2; 89:3; 89:4; 89:5; 90:1; 90:2; 90:3; 90:4; 90:5
Language Strand	**(See Language Presentation Book D.)**	**(See Language Presentation Book D.)**	**(See Language Presentation Book D.)**	**(See Language Presentation Book D.)**
Literature Strand	**Literature Collection –** *The Perfects*	**Literature Collection –** *The Perfects*	**Literature Collection –** *The Perfects*	**Literature Collection – *Nibbly Mouse***
Formal Assessment *Reading Mastery*	**In Program Mastery Test –** 125 **Individual Reading Checkout –** 125:25	**In Program Mastery Test –** 130 **Individual Reading Checkout –** 130:26	**In Program Mastery Test –** 135 **Individual Reading Checkout –** 135:25	**In Program Mastery Test –** 140 **Individual Reading Checkout –** 140:29

D15

Strand Component	Lessons 141-145	Lessons 146-150	Lessons 151-155	Lessons 156-160
Core Lesson Connections	**Phonemic and Phonological Awareness** *Phoneme Categorization –* 141:a1; 142:a1; 143:a1; 144:a1; 145:a1 *Phoneme Blending –* 141:a2; 142:a2; 143:a2; 144:a2; 145:a2 *Phoneme Segmentation –* 141:a3; 142:a3; 143:a3; 144:a3; 145:a3 *Letter Recognition and Formation –* 141:b; 142:b; 143:b; 144:b: 145:b **Comprehension Strategies** *Listening Comprehension –* 142:c1; 143:c1; 144:c1; 145:c1 *Title, Author, and Illustrator Identification –* 141:c2 *Establish a Purpose for Reading –* 141:c1 *Identify Main Idea –* 142:c3 *K.W.L –* 141:c3; 141:c4; 142:c2; 143:c2 *Summarize Expository Text –* 144:c2; 145:c2 *Illustrate and Retell Expository Text –* 144:c3; 145:c3 *Writing –* 141:c2; 142:c2	**Phonemic and Phonological Awareness** *Phoneme Blending –* 146:a1; 147:a1; 148:a1; 149:a1; 150:a1 *Phoneme Segmentation –* 146:a2; 147:a2; 148:a2; 149:a2; 150:a2 *Letter Recognition and Formation –* 146:b; 147:b; 148:b; 149:b: 150:b **Comprehension Strategies** *Establish a Purpose for Reading –* 146:c1; 147:c3; 148:c3; 149:c3; 150:c3 *Sequence and Retell Story –* 146: c2; 147:c1; 148:c1; 149:c1; 150:c1 *Mental Imaging –* 146:c3; 147:c2; 148:c2149:c2; 150:c2 *Writing –* 150:c2	**Phonemic Awareness –** 151:a; 152:a; 153:a; 154:a; 155:a **Vocabulary Development –** 151:b; 152:b; 153:b; 154:b; 155:b **Comprehension –** 151:c; 152:c; 153:c; 154:c; 155:c **Fluency –** 151:d; 152:d; 153:d; 154:d; 155:d *Writing –* 151:c3; 152:c2; 153:c2; 154:c2; 155:c3	**Phonemic Awareness –** 156:a; 157:a; 158:a; 159:a; 160:a **Vocabulary Development –** 156:b; 157:b; 158:b; 159:b; 160:b **Comprehension –** 156:c; 157:c; 158:c; 159:c; 160:c **Fluency –** 156:d; 157:d; 158:d; 159:d; 160:d *Writing –* 159:c2; 160:c2
Reading Strand *Reading Mastery*	**Presentation Book C** **Phonemic Awareness** – 144:9 **Print Awareness –** 141:30; 142:26; 143:26; 144:25; 145:30 **Letter Sound Correspondence –** 141:1; 141:2; 141:4; 141:6; 141:28; 142:1; 142:3; 142:5; 142:24; 143:1; 143:2; 143:4; 143:24144:1; 144:3; 144:5; 144:21; 144:23; 145:1; 145:3; 145:5; 145:26; 145:29 **Phonics and Word Recognition –** 141:8; 141:9; 141:10; 141:13; 141:14; 141:17; 141:19; 141:22; 141:23; 142:7; 142:8; 142:9; 142:12; 142:13; 142:14; 142:15; 142:18; 142:19; 143:6; 143:7; 143:9; 143:10; 143:12; 143:14; 143:16; 143:18; 143:19; 144:6; 144;9; 144:10; 144:11; 144:12; 144:16; 144:17; 145:7; 145:8; 145:9; 145:13; 145:14; 145:15; 145:18; 145:21; 145:22	**Presentation Book C** **Phonemic Awareness** – 147:16; 148:4; 150:15 **Print Awareness –** 146:28; 147:30; 148:26; 149:27; 150:32 **Letter Sound Correspondence –** 146:1; 146:2; 146:4; 146:6; 146:24; 146:27; 147:1; 147:2; 147:4; 147:27; 147:29; 148:1; 148:2; 148:23; 148:24; 149:1; 149:2; 149:3; 149:24; 149:26; 150:1; 150:2; 150:4; 150:32 **Phonics and Word Recognition –** 146:7; 146:10; 146:12; 146:14; 146:16; 146:17; 146:19; 146:20; 147:6; 147:9; 147:11; 147:12; 147:13; 147:16; 147:17; 147:21; 147:22; 148:4; 148:5; 148:8; 148:9; 148:12; 148:14; 148:17; 148:18;; 149:5; 149:7; 149:10; 149:11; 149:12; 149:14; 149:18; 149:19; 150:6; 150:9; 150:11; 150:13; 150; 15; 150:16; 150:19; 150:21; 150:25; 150:26	**Presentation Book C** **Letter / Sound Correspondence –** 151:2; 154:3; 155:2 **Phonics and Word Recognition –** 151:1-4; 151:6; 152:1-4; 152:6; 153:1-4; 153:6; 154:1-3; 154:5; 155:1-4; 155:6 **Fluency –** 151:1-4; 152:1-4; 153:1-4; 154:1-3; 155:1-4 **Comprehension –** 151:5-7; 151:9; 152:5-7; 152:9; 153:5-7; 153:9; 154:4-5; 154:8; 155:5-8 **Spelling –** 151:1-3; 152:1-3; 153:1-3; 154:1-3; 155:1-3	**Presentation Book C** **Letter / Sound Correspondence –** 157:4; 159:2; 160:2 **Phonics and Word Recognition –** 156:1-4; 156:6; 157:1-4; 157:6; 158:1-4; 158:6; 159:1-3; 159:5; 160:1-4; 160:6 **Fluency –** 156:1-4; 157:1-4; 158:1-4; 159:1-3; 160:1-4 **Comprehension –** 156:5-7; 156:9; 157:5-7; 157:9; 158:5-7; 158:9; 159:4-6; 159:8; 160:5-7; 160:9 **Spelling –** 156:1-3; 157:1-3; 158:1-3; 159:1-3; 160:1; 160:2

Strand Component	Lessons 141-145	Lessons 146-150	Lessons 151-155	Lessons 156-160
Reading Strand *Reading Mastery* (continued)	**Fluency –** 141:11; 141:15; 141:20; 141:24; 142:10; 142:16; 142:20; 143:8; 143:20; 144:7; 144:14; 145:10; 145:16; 145:19; 145:23 **Comprehension –** 141:24; 141:25; 141:27; 141:29; 141:31; 142:20; 142:21; 142:23; 142:25; 142:27; 143:20; 143:21; 143:23; 143:25; 143:27; 144:18; 144:19; 144:20; 144:21; 144:22; 145:23; 145:24; 145:25; 145:26; 145:27 **Informal Assessment –** 141:3; 141:5; 141:12; 141:16; 141:18; 141:21; 141:23; 142:2; 142:4; 142:6; 142:11; 142:17; 142:19; 143:3; 143:5; 143:9; 143:11; 143:13; 143:15; 143:17; 143:19; 144:2; 144:4; 144:8; 144:13; 144:15; 144:17; 145:2; 145:4; 145:6; 145:11; 145:17; 145:20; 145:22 **SPELLING** **Phonemic Awareness –** 95:1 **Letter Sound Correspondence** **Decoding and Word Recognition –** 91:1; 91:2; 91:3; 92:1; 92:2; 92:3; 92:4; 93:1; 93:2; 93:3; 93:4; 93:5; 93:6; 94:1; 94:2; 94:3; 94:4; 94:5; 94;6; 95:2; 95:3; 95:4; 95:5	**Fluency –** 146:8; 146:15; 146:18; 146:21; 147:7; 147:14; 147:19; 147:23; 148:6; 148:8; 148:10; 148:15; 148:19; 149:8; 149:16; 149:20; 150:7; 150:14; 150; 18; 150:23; 150:27 **Comprehension –** 146:21; 146:22; 146:23; 146:24; 146:25; 147:23; 147:25; 147:27; 147:28; 148:19; 148:20; 148:22; 148:23; 148:24; 149:20; 149:21; 149:23; 149:24; 149:25; 150:27; 150:28; 150:30; 150:32 **Informal Assessment –** 146:3; 146:5; 146:9; 146:11; 146:13; 146:20; 147:3; 147:5; 147:8; 147:10; 147:15; 147:18; 147:20; 147:22; 148:3; 148:7; 148:11; 148:13; 148:16; 149:4; 149:6; 149:9; 149:13; 149:15; 149:17; 149:19; 150:3; 150:5; 150:8; 150:10; 150:12; 150; 17; 150:20; 150:22; 150:26 **SPELLING** **Phonemic Awareness** **Letter Sound Correspondence –** 96:1 **Decoding and Word Recognition –** 96:2; 96:3; 96:4; 96:5; 96:6; 97:1; 97:2; 97:3; 98:1; 98:2; 98:3; 98:4; 98:5; 99:1; 99:2; 99:3; 99:4; 99:5; 99:6; 100:1; 100:2; 100:3; 100:4; 100:5		
Language Strand	(See Language Presentation Book D.)	(See Language Presentation Book D.)	(See Language Presentation Book D.)	(See Language Presentation Book D.)
Literature Strand	**Literature Collection** – *Nibbly Mouse*	**Literature Collection** – *Nibbly Mouse*	**Literature Collection** – *Henrietta's First Winter*	**Literature Collection** – *Henrietta's First Winter*
Formal Assessment *Reading Mastery*	**In Program Mastery Test –** 145 **Individual Reading Checkout –** 145:31	**In Program Mastery Test –** 150 **Individual Reading Checkout –** 150:33	**Individual Reading Checkout –** 155:9	**Individual Reading Checkout –** 160:10 **Reading Benchmark Test –** 160

D17

Appendix E

English Language Arts Standards

GRADE K

GRADE K STANDARDS		PAGE REFERENCES
Reading Standards for Literature: Key Ideas and Details		
RL.K.1	With prompting and support, ask and answer questions about key details in a text.	This Common Core State Standard is covered whenever students participate in classroom discussions about stories. **Reading Presentation Book B:** (Lesson.Exercise) 75.21, 76.22, 77.24, 78.23, 79.21, 80.23, 81.25, 82.21, 83.17, 84.23, 85.20, 86.21, 87.18, 88.20, 89.18, 90.19, 91.18, 92.23, 93.24, 94.25, 94.26, 95.22, 95.23, 96.19, 96.20, 97.19, 97.20, 98.19, 99.16, 99.17, 100.15, 101.17, 102.17, 103.21, 104.16, 105.19, 105.20, 106.14, 106.15, 107.22 **Reading Presentation Book C:** (Lesson.Exercise) 108.22, 109.18, 110.16, 111.15, 112.20, 113.23, 114.24, 115.24, 116.21, 117,.20, 118.16, 119.21, 1120.22, 121.23, 122.21, 123.20, 124.21, 125.19, 126.17, 127.22, 128.22, 129.20, 130.20, 131.16, 131.18, 132.20, 132.22, 133.27, 133.29, 134.20, 135.18, 136.24, 137.22, 138.20, 139.25, 140.22, 141.24, 142.20, 143.20, 144.18, 144.20, 145.23, 145.25, 146.21, 146.23, 147.23, 147.25, 148.19, 149.20, 150.27, 151.25, 152.28, 153.28, 154.26, 155.29, 156.28, 157.27, 158.29, 159.21, 160.17 **Language Presentation Book A:** Storybook 1: pages 1–39 **Language Presentation Book B:** Storybook 2: pages 1–48 **Language Presentation Book C:** Storybook 3: pages 1–42 **Language Presentation Book D:** Storybook 4: pages 1–41 **Core Lesson Connections:** (Lesson.Part.Activity) 1.C.1, 1.C.2, 2.C.1, 2.C.3, 3.C.1, 3.C.3, 4.C.1, 4.C.3, 5.C.1, 5.C.3, 6.C.1, 6.C.2, 7.C.1, 7.C.3, 8.C.1, 8.C.3, 9.C.1, 9.C.3, 10.C.1, 10.C.3, 11.C.1, 11.C.2, 12.C.1, 12.C.2, 13.C.1, 13.C.2, 14.C.1, 14.C.2, 15.C.1, 15.C.2, 16.C.1, 16.C.2, 17.C.1, 17.C.2, 18.C.1, 18.C.2, 19.C.1, 19.C.2, 20.C.1, 20.C.2, 21.C.1, 21.C.2, 22.C.1, 22.C.2, 23.C.1, 23.C.2, 24.C.1, 24.C.2, 25.C.1, 26.C.1, 27.C.1, 28.C.1, 29.C.1, 30.C.1, 42.C.2, 43.C.2, 46.C.3, 52.C.2, 57.C.2, 67.C.3, 77.C.3, 87.C.3, 92.C.2, 97.C.3, 102.C.2, 112.C.2, 117.C.3, 118.C.3, 122.C.2, 122.C.3, 123.C.3, 126.C.4, 131.C.4, 136.C.4, 141.C.4, 151.C.1, 152.C.1, 153.C.1, 154.C.1, 155.C.1, 157.C.2, 158.C.1, 159.C.2 **Literature Guide:** Lessons 35, 50, 65, 80, 95, 110, 125, 140, 155 **Read Aloud Library:** (Week.Day) 1.2, 2.2, 3.2, 4.2, 5.2, 6.2, 7.2, 8.2, 9.2, 10.2, 11.2, 12.2, 13.2, 14.2, 15.2, 16.2, 17.2, 18.2, 19.2, 20.2
RL.K.2	With prompting and support, retell familiar stories, including key details.	**Reading Presentation Book B:** Planning page 284b **Reading Presentation Book C:** Planning pages 77b **Core Lesson Connections:** (Lesson.Part.Activity) 40.C.3, 50.C.2, 60.C.2, 70.C.2, 80.C.2, 87.C.2, 90.C.2, 100.C.2, 103.C.3, 105.C.2, 110.C.2, 115.C.2, 120.C.2, 125.C.2, 129.C.2, 130.C.2, 134.C.2, 135.C.2, 139.C.2, 140.C.2, 144.C.2, 145.C.2, 146.C.2, 147.C.1, 148.C.1, 149.C.1, 150.C.1, 151.C.1, 152.C.1, 153.C.1, 1564.C.1, 155.C.1, 156.C.1, 157.C.2, 158.C.1, 160.C.1 **Read Aloud Library:** (Week.Day) 1.3, 2.3, 3.3, 4.3, 5.3, 6.3, 7.3, 8.3, 9.3, 10.3, 11.3, 12.3, 13.3, 14.3, 15.3, 16.3, 16.5, 17.3, 17.5, 18.3, 18.5, 19.3, 19.5, 20.3, 20.5

E3

GRADE K STANDARDS		PAGE REFERENCES
RL.K.3	With prompting and support, identify characters, settings, and major events in a story.	**Reading Presentation Book C:** Planning pages 77b, 203b **Core Lesson Connections:** (Lesson.Part.Activity) 41.C.3, 41.C.4, 42.C.2, 43.C.1, 43.C.2, 44.C.2, 45.C.2, 46.C.3, 46.C.4, 47.C.1, 47.C.2, 48.C.1, 48.C.2, 49.C.2, 50..1, 50.C.2, 52.C.2, 57.C.1, 57.C.2, 58.C.1, 58.C.2, 59.C.2, 60.C.1, 60.C.2, 61.C.3, 62.C.4, 67.C.1, 67.C.3, 68.C.1, 70.C.1, 70.C.2, 77.C.1, 77.C.3, 79.C.2, 87.C.1, 87.C.3, 89.C.2, 92.C.2, 95.C.2, 97.C.3, 99.C.2, 102.C.1, 102.C.2, 109.C.2, 110.C.1, 112.C.1, 112.C.2, 122.C.1, 122.C.2, 151.C.1, 152.C.1, 153.C.1, 154.C.1, 155.C.1, 159.C.2 **Read Aloud Library:** (Week.Day) 3.4, 4.4, 5.3, 5.4, 6.3, 6.4, 7.3, 7.4, 8.3, 8.4, 8.5, 9.4, 11.3
Reading Standards for Literature: Craft and Structure		
RL.K.4	Ask and answer questions about unknown words in a text.	**This Common Core State Standard is covered whenever students participate in classroom discussions about word meanings.** **Core Lesson Connections:** (Lesson.Part.Activity) 1.C.1, 1.C.2, 2.C.1, 2.C.2, 3.C.1, 3.C.2, 4.C.1, 4.C.2, 5.C.1, 5.C.2, 6.C.1, 7.C.1, 7.C.2, 8.C.1, 8.C.2, 9.C.1, 9.C.2, 10.C.1, 10.C.2, 11.C.1, 12.C.1, 13.C.1, 14.C.1, 15.C.1, 16.C.1, 17.C.1, 18.C.1, 19.C.1, 20.C.1, 21.C.1, 22.C.1, 23.C.1, 24.C.1, 25.C.1, 26.C.1, 27.C.1, 28.C.1, 29.C.1, 30.C.1 **Literature Guide (pgs 8–9):** Lessons 20, 80, 140 **Read Aloud Library:** (Week.Day) 1.1–5, 2.1–5, 3.1–5, 4.1–5, 5.1–5, 6.1–5, 7.1–5, 8.1–5, 9.1–5, 10.1–5, 11.1–5, 12.1–5, 13.1–5, 14.1–5, 15.1–5, 16.1–15, 17.1–5, 18.1–5, 19.1–5, 20.1–5
RL.K.5	Recognize common types of texts (e.g., storybooks, poems).	**Read Aloud Library:** (Week.Day) 1.5, 2.5, 3.5, 4.5, 5.5, 6.5, 7.5, 8.5, 9.5, 10.5, 11.5, 12.5, 13.5, 14.5, 15.5, 16.15, 17.5, 18.5, 19.5, 20.5
RL.K.6	With prompting and support, name the author and illustrator of a story and define the role of each in telling the story.	**Core Lesson Connections:** (Lesson.Part.Activity) 32.C.1, 33.C.1, 34.C.1, 35.C.1, 36.C.1, 37.C.1, 38.C.1, 39.C.1, 40.C.1, 41.C.1, 45.C.1, 46.C.1, 51.C.1, 55.C.1, 56.C.1, 61.C.1, 66.C.1, 71.C.1, 76.C.1, 81.C.1, 86.C.1, 91.C.1, 96.C.1, 101.C.1, 106.C.1, 111.C.1, 116.C.1, 121.C.1, 126.C.2, 131.C.2, 136.C.2, 141.C.2 **Read Aloud Library:** 1.1, 2.1, 3.1, 4.1, 5.1, 6.1, 7.1, 8.1, 9.1, 10.1, 11.1, 12.1, 13.1, 14.1, 15.1, 16.1, 17.1, 18.1, 19.1, 20.1
Reading Standards for Literature: Integration of Knowledge and Ideas		
RL.K.7	With prompting and support, describe the relationship between illustrations and the story in which they appear (e.g., what moment in a story an illustration depicts).	**Core Lesson Connections:** (Lesson.Part.Activity) 49.C.1, 49.C.2, 55.C.1, 55.C.2, 59.C.1, 59.C.2, 65.C.1, 65.C.2, 69.C.1, 69.C.2, 75.C.1, 75.C.2, 85.C.1, 85.C.2, 89.C.1, 89.C.2, 95.C.1, 95.C.2, 99.C.1, 99.C.2, 105.C.1, 105.C.2, 109.C.1, 109.C.3, 119.C.1. 119.C.2 **Read Aloud Library:** (Week.Day) 1.1, 2.1, 3.1, 4.1, 5.1, 6.1, 7.1, 8.1, 9.1, 10.1, 11.1, 12.1, 13.1, 14.1, 15.1, 16.1, 17.1, 18.1, 19.1, 20.1
RL.K.8	*(Not applicable to literature)*	
RL.K.9	With prompting and support, compare and contrast the adventures and experiences of characters in familiar stories.	**Core Lesson Connections:** (Lesson.Part.Activity) 62.C.3, 94.C.1, 94.C.2, 98.C.1, 98.C,2, 104.C.1, 104.C.2, 108.C.1, 108.C.2, 114.C.1, 114.C.2, 118.C.2, 118.C.3, 124.C.1, 124.C.2

GRADE K STANDARDS		PAGE REFERENCES
Reading Standards for Literature: Range of Reading and Level of Text Complexity		
RL.K.10	Actively engage in group reading activities with purpose and understanding.	**This Common Core State Standard is covered whenever students participate in classroom discussions about stories.** **Reading Presentation Book B:** (Lesson.Exercise) 91.17–21, 92.22–26, 93.23–27, 94.25–28, 95.22–25, 96.19–22, 97.19–22, 98.18–21, 99.16–19, 100.14–17, 101.16–18, 102.16–19, 103.20–21, 104.15–18, 105.19–22, 106.14–17, 107.20–23 **Reading Presentation Book C:** (Lesson.Exercise) 108.20–23, 109.16–19, 110.–14–17, 111.13–16, 112.18–21, 113.21–24, 114.22–25, 115.22–25, 116.19–22, 117.18–21, 118.14–17, 119.19–22, 120.20–23, 121.21–24, 122.19–22, 123.18–21, 124.19–22, 125.17–20, 126.15–18, 127.20–23, 128.20–23, 129.18–21, 130.18–21, 131.14–17, 132.18–21, 133.25–28, 134.18–21, 135.16–19, 136.22–25, 137.20–23, 138.18–21, 139.23–26, 140.20–23, 141.22–25, 142.18–21, 143.18–21, 144.16–19, 145.21–24, 146.19–22, 147.21–24, 148.17–20, 149.18–21, 150.25–28, 151.23–26, 152.26–29, 153.26–29, 154.24–27, 155.27–30, 156.26–29, 157.25–28, 158.27–30, 159.19–22, 160.15–18 **Storybook:** Lessons 91–160 **Core Lesson Connections:** (Lesson.Part.Activity) 1.C.1, 1.C.2, 2.C.1, 2.C.3, 3.C.1, 3.C.3, 4.C.1, 4.C.3, 5.C.1, 5.C.3, 6.C.1, 6.C.2, 7.C.1, 7.C.3, 8.C.1, 8.C.3, 9.C.1, 9.C.3, 10.C.1, 10.C.3, 11.C.1, 11.C.2, 12.C.1, 12.C.2, 13.C.1, 13.C.2, 14.C.1, 14.C.2, 15.C.1, 15.C.2, 16.C.1, 16.C.2, 17.C.1, 17.C.2, 18.C.1, 18.C.2, 19.C.1, 19.C.2, 20.C.1, 20.C.2, 21.C.1, 21.C.2, 22.C.1, 22.C.2, 23.C.1, 23.C.2, 24.C.1, 24.C.2, 25.C.1, 26.C.1, 27.C.1, 28.C.1, 29.C.1, 30.C.1, 31.C.3, 32.C.3, 33.C.2, 34.C.3, 35.C.3, 36.C.3, 37.C.3, 38.C.3, 39.C.3, 40.C.2, 41.C.3, 42.C.1, 44.C.1, 45.C.1, 46.C.3, 47.C.1, 48.C.1, 49.C.1, 50.C.1, 51.C.2, 52.C.1, 53.C.1, 54.C.1, 55.C.1, 56.C.2, 57.C.1, 58.C.1, 59.C.1, 60.C.1, 61.C.1, 62.C.2, 63.C.1, 64.C.1, 65.C.1, 66.C.3, 67.C.1, 68.C.1, 69.C.1, 70.C.1, 71.C.3, 72.C.1, 73.C.1, 74.C.1, 75.C.1, 76.C.3, 77.C.1, 78.C.1, 79.C.1, 80.C.1, 81.C.3, 82.C.1, 83.C.1, 84.C.1, 85.C.1, 86.C.3, 87.C.1, 88.C.1, 89.C.1, 90.C.1, 91.C.3, 92.C.1, 93.C.1, 94.C.1, 95.C.1, 96.C.3, 97.C.1, 98.C.2, 99.C.1, 100.C.1, 101.C.2, 102.C.1, 103.C.1, 104.C.1, 105.C.1, 106.C.3, 107.C.1, 108.C.1, 109.C.1, 110.C.1, 111.C.3, 112.C.1, 113.C.1, 114.C.1, 115.C.1, 116.C.3, 117.C.1, 118.C.1, 119.C.1, 120.C.1, 121.C.1, 122.C.3, 123.C.1, 124.C.1, 125.C.1, 151.C.2, 152.C.2, 153.C.2, 154.C.2, 155.C.2, 157.C.3, 158.C.2, 160.C.2 **Literature Guide (pgs 8–9):** Lessons 35, 50, 65, 80, 95, 110, 125, 140, 155 **Read Aloud Library:** (Week.Day) 1.1, 1.2, 1.5, 2.1, 2.2, 2.5, 3.1, 3.2, 3.5, 4.1, 4.2, 4.5, 5.1, 5.2, 5.5, 6.1, 6.2, 6.5, 7.1, 7.2, 7.5, 8.1, 8.2, 8.5, 9.1, 9.2, 9.5, 10.1, 10.2, 10.5, 11.1, 11.2, 11.5, 12.1, 12.2, 12.5, 13.1, 13.2, 13.5, 14.1, 14.2, 14.5, 15.1, 15.2, 15.5, 16.1, 16.2, 16.5, 17.1, 17.2, 17.5, 18.1, 18.2, 18.5, 19.1, 19.2, 19.5, 20.1, 20.2, 20.5
Reading Standards for Informational Text: Key Ideas and Details		
RI.K.1	With prompting and support, ask and answer questions about key details in a text.	**This Common Core State Standard is covered whenever students participate in classroom discussions about informational text.** **Core Lesson Connections:** (Lesson.Part.Activity) 126.C.3, 126.C.4, 127.C.1, 127.C.2, 127.C.3, 128.C.1, 128.C.2, 129.C.2, 130.C.2, 131.C.3, 131.C.4, 132.C.2, 132.C.3, 133.C.2, 134.C.2, 134.C.3, 135.C.2, 135.C.3, 137.C.2, 137.C.3, 138.C.2, 139.C.2, 139.C.3, 140.C.2, 140.C.3, 142.C.2, 142.C.3, 143.C.2, 144.C.2, 144.C.3, 145.C.2, 145.C.3 **Literature Guide (pgs 8–9):** Lesson 20 **Read Aloud Library:** (Week.Day) 21.2–5, 22.2–5, 23.2–5, 24.2–5, 25.2–5, 26.2–5, 27.2–5, 28.2–5, 29.2–5, 30.2–5

E5

GRADE K STANDARDS		PAGE REFERENCES
RI.K.2	With prompting and support, identify the main topic and retell key details of a text.	**Core Lesson Connections:** (Lesson.Part.Activity) 126.C.3, 126.C.4, 127.C.1, 127.C.3, 128.C.1, 128.C.2, 129.C.2, 130.C.2, 131.C.3, 131.C.4, 132.C.2, 132.C.3, 133.C.2, 134.C.2, 134.C.3, 135.C.2, 135.C.3, 137.C.2, 137.C.3, 138.C.2, 139.C.2, 139.C.3, 140.C.2, 140.C.3, 142.C.2, 142.C.3, 143.C.2, 144.C.2, 144.C.3, 145.C.2, 145.C.3 **Read Aloud Library:** (Week.Day) 21.2–3, 22.2–3, 23.2–5, 24.2–3, 25.2–3, 26.2–3, 27.2–3, 28.2–3, 29.2–3, 30.2–3
RI.K.3	With prompting and support, describe the connection between two individuals, events, ideas, or pieces of information in a text.	**Core Lesson Connections:** (Lesson.Part.Activity) 128.C.1, 128.C.2, 133.C.2, 138.C.2, 143.C.2

Reading Standards for Informational Text: Craft and Structure

GRADE K STANDARDS		PAGE REFERENCES
RI.K.4	With prompting and support, ask and answer questions about unknown words in a text.	**Literature Guide (pgs 8–9):** Lesson 20 **Read Aloud Library:** (Week.Day) 21.2–5, 22.2–5, 23.2–5, 24.2–5, 25.2–5, 26.2–5, 27.2–5, 28.2–5, 29.2–5, 30.2–5
RI.K.5	Identify the front cover, back cover, and title page of a book.	**Core Lesson Connections:** (Lesson.Part.Activity) 126.C.2, 131.C.1, 136.C.1, 141.C.1 **Read Aloud Library:** (Week.Day) 21.1, 22.1, 23.1, 24.1, 25.1, 26.1, 27.1, 28.1, 29.1, 30.1
RI.K.6	Name the author and illustrator of a text and define the role of each in presenting the ideas or information in a text.	**Core Lesson Connections:** (Lesson.Part.Activity) 126.C.2, 131.C.2, 136.C.2, 141.C.1 **Read Aloud Library:** (Week.Day) 21.1, 22.1, 23.1, 24.1, 25.1, 26.1, 27.1, 28.1, 29.1, 30.1

Reading Standards for Informational Text: Integration of Knowledge and Ideas

GRADE K STANDARDS		PAGE REFERENCES
RI.K.7	With prompting and support, describe the relationship between illustrations and the text in which they appear (e.g., what person, place, thing, or idea in the text an illustration depicts).	**Core Lesson Connections:** (Lesson.Part.Activity) 129.C.1, 129.C.3, 130.C.1, 130.C.3, 134.C.1, 134.C.3, 135.C.1, 135.C.3, 139.C.1, 139.C.3, 140.C.1, 140.C.3, 144.C.1, 144.C.3, 145.C.1, 145.C.3 **Read Aloud Library:** (Week.Day) 21.1, 22.1, 23.1, 24.1, 25.1, 26.1, 27.1, 28.1, 29.1, 30.1
RI.K.8	With prompting and support, identify the reasons an author gives to support points in a text.	**Core Lesson Connections:** (Lesson.Part.Activity) 126.C.5, 127.C.4, 128.C.3, 132.C.4, 139.C.3
RI.K.9	With prompting and support, identify basic similarities in and differences between two texts on the same topic (e.g., in illustrations, descriptions, or procedures).	**Core Lesson Connections:** (Lesson.Part.Activity) 126.C.3, 128.C.2, 133.C.2, 138.C.2, 143.C.2 **Read Aloud Library:** (Week.Day) 21.5, 22.5, 23.5, 24.5, 25.5, 26.5, 27.5, 28.5, 29.5, 30.5

Reading Standards for Informational Text: Range of Reading and Level of Text Complexity

GRADE K STANDARDS		PAGE REFERENCES
RI.K.10	Actively engage in group reading activities with purpose and understanding.	**Core Lesson Connections:** (Lesson.Part.Activity) 126.C.4, 127.C.1, 128.C.1, 129.C.1, 130.C.1, 131.C.4, 132.C.1, 133.C.1, 134.C.1, 135.C.1, 136.C.4, 137.C.1, 138.C.1, 129.C.1, 140.C.1, 141.C.4, 141.C.1, 142.C.1, 143.C.1, 144.C.1, 145.C.1 **Read Aloud Library:** (Week.Day) 21.1–2, 22.1–2, 23.1–2, 24.1–2, 25.1–2, 26.1–2, 27.1–2, 28.1–2, 29.1–2, 30.1–2

E6

GRADE K STANDARDS		PAGE REFERENCES
Reading Standards for Foundational Skills: Print Concepts		
RF.K.1	Demonstrate understanding of the organization and basic features of print.	
RF.K.1a	Follow words from left to right, top to bottom, and page by page.	**In Reading Mastery, students are expected to point to words from left to right, top to bottom as they read. The following examples illustrate how concepts are introduced.** **Reading Presentation Book A:** (Lesson.Exercise) 48.16–18, 49.14–16, 50.15–17, 51.18–20, 52.14–16, 53.15–17, 54.12–14, 55.16–18, 56.16–18 **Reading Presentation Book B:** (Lesson.Exercise) 57.13, 58.14, 59.15, 60.17, 61.18–19, 62.18–19, 63.21–22
RF.K.1b	Recognize that spoken words are represented in written language by specific sequences of letters.	**In Reading Vocabulary exercises, students regularly sound out words.** **To ensure that students understand that they are reading real words, the program specifies "meaning" sentences to be presented after students read certain words.** **Reading Presentation Book A:** (Lesson.Exercise) 28.6–8, 29.7–8, 30.9–11, 31.9–11, 32.10–12, 33.9–11, 34.11–14, 35.11–14, 36.5–8, 37.6–9, 37.11, 37.12, 38.7–9, 38.11, 38.12, 39.6, 39.7, 39.9–12, 40.5–10, 41.8–16, 42.7–15, 42.17, 42.18, 43.6–15, 44.7–16, 45.7–16, 46.6–16, 47.5–15, 48.8–18, 49.6–16, 50.6–17, 52.8–20, 53.7–16, 54.4–15, 55.5–19, 56.6–19 **Reading Presentation Book B:** (Lesson.Exercise) 57.4–12, 58.5–13, 59.6–14, 60.7–16, 61.7–17, 62.7–17, 63.6–19, 64.8–19, 65.6–22, 66.6–22, 67.5–20, 68.7–26, 69.7–26, 70.6–23, 71.4–17, 72.7–23, 73.6–19, 74.7–21, 75.4–19, 76.7–20, 77.7–22, 78.6–21, 79.6–19, 80.7–21, 81.7–23, 82.7–19, 83.4–15, 84.5–21, 85.4–18, 86.6–19, 87.4–16, 88.7–18, 89.6–16, 90.7–17, 91.4–16, 92.7–21, 93.7–22, 94.7–23, 95.5–20, 96.4–17, 97.5–17, 98.5–17, 99.6–14, 100.7–13, 101.4–15, 102.7–15, 103.6–19, 104.7–14, 105.4–17, 106.4–12, 107.6–19 **Reading Presentation Book C:** (Lesson.Exercise) 108.7–19, 109.7–15, 110.5–13, 111.5–12, 112.4–17, 113.7–20, 114.6–21, 115.6–20, 116.4–17, 117.4–16, 118.5–12, 119.6–18, 120.7–19, 121.7–20, 122.7–18, 123.6–17, 124.7–18, 125.7–16, 126.5–14, 127.7–19, 128.6–19, 129.5–17, 130.4–17, 131.7–13, 132.6–17, 133.7–24, 134.4–17, 135.7–15, 136.7–21, 137.4–19, 138.4–17, 139.7–22, 140.6–19, 141.7–21, 142.7–17, 143.6–17, 144.6–15, 145.7–20, 146.7–18, 147.6–20, 148.4–16, 149.5–17, 150.6–14, 151.7–19, 152.7–22, 153.6–22, 154.7–20, 155.7–23, 156.7–22, 157.6–21, 158.5–23, 159.6–15, 160.1–11
RF.K.1c	Understand that words are separated by spaces in print.	**Three- and four-word stories begin in lesson 48. Boxes on the line between the words prompt the separation. The boxes become gradually smaller in size and word–finding activities are introduced at lesson 57 to facilitate the transition to normal spacing at lesson 87.** **Workbook A:** Worksheets 48–56 **Reading Presentation Book B:** (Lesson.Exercise) 57.18, 58.19, 59.20, 60.22, 61.23, 62.24, 63.27, 64.25, 65.28, 66.28, 67.26, 68.32, 69.32, 70.29, 71.23, 72.29, 73.25, 74.27, 75.23, 76.24, 77.26, 78.25, 79.23, 80.25, 81.27, 82.23, 83.19, 24.25, 85.22, 86.23 **Workbook B:** Worksheets 57–86

E7

GRADE K STANDARDS		PAGE REFERENCES
RF.K.1d	Recognize and name all upper- and lowercase letters of the alphabet.	**Core Lesson Connections:** (Lesson.Part.Activity) 11.B.1, 11.B.2, 12.B.1, 12.B.2, 13.B.1, 13.B.2, 14.B.1, 14.B.2, 15.B.1, 15.B.2, 16.B.1, 16.B.2, 17.B.1, 17.B.2, 18.B.1, 18.B.2, 19.B.1, 19.B.2, 20.B.1, 20.B.2, 21.B.1, 21.B.2, 22.B.1, 22.B.2, 23.B.1, 23.B.2, 24.B.1, 24.B.2, 25.B.1, 25.B.2, 26.B.1, 26.B.2, 27.B.1, 27.B.2, 28.B.1, 28.B.2, 29.B.1, 29.B.2, 30.B.1, 30.B.2, 31.B.1, 31.B.2, 32.B.1, 32.B.2, 33.B.1, 33.B.2, 34.B.1, 34.B.2, 35.B.1, 35.B.2, 36.B.1, 36.B.2, 37.B.1, 37.B.2, 38.B.1, 38.B.2, 39.B.1, 39.B.2, 40.B.1, 40.B.2, 41.B.1, 41.B.2, 42.B.1, 42.B.2, 43.B.1, 43.B.2, 44.B.1, 44.B.2, 45.B.1, 45.B.2, 46.B.1, 46.B.2, 47.B.1, 47.B.2, 48.B.1, 48.B.2, 49.B.1, 49.B.2, 50.B.1, 50.B.2, 51.B.1, 51.B.2, 52.B.1, 52.B.2, 53.B.1, 53.B.2, 54.B.1, 54.B.2, 55.B.1, 55.B.2, 56.B.1, 56.B.2, 57.B.1, 57.B.2, 58.B.1, 58.B.2, 59.B.1, 59.B.2, 60.B.1, 60.B.2, 61.B.1, 61.B.2, 62.B.1, 62.B.2, 63.B.1, 63.B.2, 64.B.1, 64.B.2, 65.B.1, 65.B.2, 66.B.1, 66.B.2, 67.B.1, 67.B.2, 68.B.1, 68.B.2, 69.B.1, 69.B.2, 70.B.1, 70.B.2, 71.B.1, 71.B.2, 72.B.1, 72.B.2, 73.B.1, 73.B.2, 74.B.1, 74.B.2, 75.B.1, 75.B.2, 76.B.1, 76.B.2, 77.B.1, 77.B.2, 78.B.1, 78.B.2, 79.B.1, 79.B.2, 80.B.1, 80.B.2, 81.B.1, 81.B.2, 82.B.1, 82.B.2, 83.B.1, 83.B.2, 84.B.1, 84.B.2, 85.B.1, 85.B.2, 86.B.1, 86.B.2, 87.B.1, 87.B.2, 88.B.1, 88.B.2, 89.B.1, 89.B.2, 90.B.1, 90.B.2, 91.B.1, 91.B.2, 92.B.1, 92.B.2, 93.B.1, 93.B.2, 94.B.1, 94.B.2, 95.B.1, 95.B.2, 96.B.1, 96.B.2, 97.B.1, 97.B.2, 98.B.1, 98.B.2, 99.B.1, 99.B.2, 100.B.1, 100.B.2, 101.B.1, 101.B.2, 102.B.1, 102.B.2, 103.B.1, 103.B.2, 104.B.1, 104.B.2, 105.B.1, 105.B.2, 106.B.1, 106.B.2, 107.B.1, 107.B.2, 108.B.1, 108.B.2, 109.B.1, 109.B.2, 110.B.1, 110.B.2, 111.B.1, 111.B.2, 112.B.1, 112.B.2, 113.B.1, 113.B.2, 114.B.1, 114.B.2, 115.B.1, 115.B.2, 116.B.1, 116.B.2, 117.B.1, 117.B.2, 118.B.1, 118.B.2, 119.B.1, 119.B.2, 120.B.1, 120.B.2, 121.B.1, 121.B.1, 122.B.1, 122.B.2, 123.B.1, 123.B.2, 124.B.1, 124.B.2, 125.B.1, 125.B.2, 126.B.1, 126.B.2, 127.B.1, 127.B.2, 128.B.1, 128.B.2, 129.B.1, 129.B.2, 130.B.1, 130.B.2, 131.B.1, 131.B.2, 132.B.1, 132.B.2, 133.B.1, 133.B.2, 134.B.1, 134.B.2, 135.B.1, 135.B.2, 136.B.1, 136.B.2, 137.B.1, 137.B.2, 138.B.1, 138.B.2, 139.B.1, 139.B.2, 140.B.1, 140.B.2, 141.B.1, 141.B.2, 142.B.1, 132.B.2, 143.B.1, 143.B.2, 144.B.1, 144.B.2, 145.B.1, 145.B.2, 146.B.1, 146.B.2, 147.B.1, 147.B.2, 148.B.1, 148.B.2, 149.B.1, 149.B.2, 150.A.1, 150.B.2, 151.B.1, 151.B.2, 152.B.1, 152.B.2, 153.B.1, 153.B.2, 154.B.1, 154.B.2, 155.B.1, 155.B.2, 156.B.1, 156.B.2, 157.B.1, 157.B.2, 158.B.1, 158.B.2, 159.B.1, 159.B.2, 160.B.1, 160.B.2
Reading Standards for Foundational Skills: Phonological Awareness		
RF.K.2	Demonstrate understanding of spoken words, syllables, and sounds (phonemes).	
RF.K.2a	Recognize and produce rhyming words.	**Reading Presentation Book A:** (Lesson.Exercise) 16.10, 19.9, 21.6, 26.6, 27.5, 27.6, 28.4, 29.3, 29.4, 30.4–6, 31.4–6, 32.5, 32.6, 33.2–6, 34.4–8, 35.3–7, 36.3, 37.3, 37.11, 38.5, 38.11 **Core Lesson Connections:** (Lesson.Part.Activity) 1.A.2, 2.A.2, 3.A.2, 4.A.2, 5.A.2, 6.A.2, 7.A.2, 8.A.2, 9.A.2, 10.A.1, 11.A.2, 12.A.1, 13.A.3, 14.A.1, 15.A.2, 16.A.1, 17.A.2, 18.A.1, 19.A.2, 20.A.1, 21.A.1, 23.A.1, 25.A.1, 27.A.1, 29.A.1, 31.A.1, 33.A.1, 35.A.1, 37.A.1, 39.A.1

E8

GRADE K STANDARDS		PAGE REFERENCES
RF.K.2b	Count, pronounce, blend, and segment syllables in spoken words.	**Reading Mastery Signature Edition emphasizes blending (Say–It–Fast Exercises) and Segmenting (Say–the–Sounds Exercises) in preparation for sounding out words.** **Reading Presentation Book A:** (Lesson.Exercise) 1.8–10, 2.6–8, 3.6–8, 3.10–12, 4.6–8, 4.11–13, 5.6–8, 5.11, 5.12, 6.6–8, 6.13, 6.14, 7.6–8, 7.13, 7.14, 8.6–8, 8.13, 8.14, 9.6–8, 9.13, 9.14, 10.6–8, 10.13, 10.14, 11.7, 11.12, 11.13, 12.7, 12.12, 12.13, 13.6, 13.10, 13.11, 14.11, 14.12, 15.6, 15.10, 15.11, 16.6, 19.4, 22.3 **Core Lesson Connections:** (Lesson.Part.Activity) 6.A.3, 7.A.3, 8.A.3, 9.A.3, 10.A.3, 12.A.2–4, 14.A.2–4, 15.A.3, 16.A.2, 17.A.3, 18.A.2, 18.A.3,, 19.A.3, 20.A.2, 20.A.3, 21.A.2, 21.A.3, 22.A.1–3, 23.A.2, 23.A.3, 24.A.1–3, 25.A.2, 25.A.3, 26.A.1, 26.A.2, 27.A.2, 27.A.3, 28.A.1, 28.A., 29.A.2, 30.A.1–3, 31.A.2, 31.A.2, 32.A.2, 33.A.2, 33.A.3, 34.A.2, 35.A.2, 35.A.3, 36.A.2, 37.A.2, 37.A.3, 38.A.2, 39.A.2, 29.A.3, 40.A.2, 41.A.2, 42.A.1, 43.A.2, 44.A.1, 45.A.2, 46.A.1, 47.A.2, 48.A.1, 49.A.2, 50.A.1, 52.A.1, 54.A.1, 56.A.1, 58.A.1, 60.A.1
RF.K.2c	Blend and segment onsets and rimes of single-syllable spoken words.	**Reading Presentation Book A:** (Lesson.Exercise) 16.10, 19.9, 21.6, 26.6, 27.5, 27.6, 28.4, 29.3, 29.4, 30.4–6, 31.4–6, 32.5, 32.6, 33.2–6, 34.4–8, 35.3–7, 36.3, 37.3, 37.11, 38.5, 38.11 **Core Lesson Connections:** (Lesson.Part.Activity) 22.A.3, 24.A.3, 30.A.3, 31.A.3, 32.A.2, 33.A.3, 34.A.2, 35.A.3, 36.A.2, 37.A.3, 38.A.2, 39.A.3, 40.A.2, 41.A.2, 42.A.1, 43.A.2, 44.A.1, 44.A.2, 45.A.2, 46.A.2, 47.A.2, 48.A.1, 49.A.2, 50.A.1, 52.A.1, 54.A.1, 56.A.1, 58.A.1, 60.A.1
RF.K.2d	Isolate and pronounce the initial, medial vowel, and final sounds (phonemes) in three-phoneme (consonant-vowel-consonant, or CVC) words.[1] (This does not include CVCs ending with /l/, /r/, or /x/.)	**Core Lesson Connections:** (Lesson.Part.Activity) 32.A.3, 34.A.3, 36.A.3, 38.A.3, 40.A.3, 41.A.3, 42.A.2, 43.A.3, 44.A.2, 45.A.3, 46.A.2, 47.A.3, 48.A.2, 49.A.3, 50.A.2, 51.A.1, 51.A.2, 52.A.2, 53.A.1, 53.A.2, 54.A.2, 55.A.1, 55.A.2, 56.A.2, 57.A.1, 57.A.2, 58.A.2, 59.A.1, 59.A.2, 60.A.2, 61.A.1, 61.A.2, 62.A.1, 62.A.2, 63.A.1, 63.A.2, 64.A.1, 64.A.2, 65.A.1, 65.A.2, 66.A.1, 66.A.2, 67.A.1, 67.A.2, 68.A.1, 68.A.2, 69.A.1, 69.A.2, 70.A.1, 70.A.2, 71.A.1, 71.A.2, 73.A.1, 73.A.2, 74.A.1, 74.A.2, 75.A.1, 75.A.2, 76.A.1, 76.A.2, 77.A.1, 77.A.2, 78.A.1, 78.A.2, 79.A.1, 79.A.2, 80.A.1, 80.A.2, 81.A.1, 81.A.2, 82.A.1, 82.A.2, 83.A.1, 83.A.2, 84.A.1, 84.A.2, 85.A.1, 85.A.2, 86.A.1, 86.A.2, 87.A.1, 87.A.2, 88.A.1, 88.A.2, 89.A.1, 89.A.2, 90.A.1, 90.A.2, 91.A.1, 91.A.2, 92.A.1, 92.A.2, 93.A.1, 93.A.2, 94.A.1, 94.A.2, 95.A.1, 95.A.2, 96.A.1, 96.A.2, 97.A.1, 97.A.2, 98.A.1, 98.A.2, 99.A.1, 99.A.2, 100.A.1, 100.A.2, 101.A.1, 102.A.1, 102.A.2, 103.A.1, 104.A.1, 104.A.2, 105.A.1, 106.A.1, 106.A.2, 107.A.1, 108.A.1, 108.A.2, 109.A.1, 110.A.1, 110.A.2, 111.A.1, 112.A.1, 113.Z.1, 114.A.1, 115.A.1, 116.A.1, 117.A.1, 119.A.1, 121.A.1, 123.A.1
	[1] Words, syllables, or phonemes written in /slashes/ refer to their pronunciation or phonology. Thus, /CVC/ is a word with three phonemes regardless of the number of letters in the spelling of the word.	
RF.K.2e	Add or substitute individual sounds (phonemes) in simple, one-syllable words to make new words.	**Reading Presentation Book A:** (Lesson.Exercise) 16.10, 19.9, 21.6, 26.6, 27.5, 27.6, 28.4, 29.3, 29.4, 30.4–6, 31.4–6, 32.5, 32.6, 33.2–6, 34.4–8, 35.3–7, 36.3, 37.3, 37.11, 38.5, 38.11 39.6, 40.8, 41.14, 42.12, 42.13, 43.11, 43.12, 44.12, 44.13, 45.12, 45.13, 46.12, 46.13, 47.11, 47.12, 48.14, 48.15, 49.12, 49.13, 50.13, 50.14, 51.17, 52.12, 52.13, 53.14, 54.10, 54.11, 55.15, 56.14, 56.15
Reading Standards for Foundational Skills: Phonics and Word Recognition		
RF.K.3	Know and apply grade-level phonics and word analysis skills in decoding words.	

E9

GRADE K STANDARDS		PAGE REFERENCES
RF.K.3a	Demonstrate basic knowledge of letter-sound correspondences by producing the primary or most frequent sound for each consonant.	**Reading Presentation Book A:** (Lesson.Exercise) 4.5, 5.2, 5.5, 5.9. 6,2, 6.5, 6.9, 7.2, 7.5, 7.9, 8.2, 8.5, 8.9, 9.2, 9.5, 9.9, 0.2, 10.5, 10;9, 11.2, 11.5, 11.8, 12.2, 12.8, 13.4, 13.7, 13.9, 14.2, 14.4, 14.7, 14.10, 15.2, 15.4, 15.7–9, 16.2, 16.4, 16.7–9, 17.1, 17.3, 17.6, 17.7, 18.1, 18.4, 18.5, 18.7, 19.1, 19.5, 19.8, 20.4, 20.5, 20.7, 21.1, 21.4, 21.7, 21.8, 22.1, 22.5, 22.8, 23.1, 23.5, 23.7, 23.8, 24.1, 24.4, 24.5, 24.7, 24.8, 25.1–3, 25.5, 26.1, 26.2, 26.5, 26.6, 26.8, 27.1, 27.2, 27.5–7, 28.1, 28.2, 28.4, 28.5, 29.1, 29.3–6, 30.1, 30.2, 30.4–38, 31.2–7, 32.1, 32.6–9, 33.1–6, 33.8, 34.3–10, 35.1–9, 36.1, 36.3, 36.4, 37.1, 37.3–5, 38.2, 38.3, 38.5, 38.6, 39.1, 39.4, 39.5, 40.1, 40.3, 40.4, 41.2–7, 42.1–6, 43.1–5, 44.1–6, 45.1–6, 46.1–6, 47.1–4, 48.2–7, 49.1–5, 50.1–5, 51.3–7, 52.2–6, 53.2–5, 54.1–3, 55.1–4, 56.1–5 **Reading Presentation Book B:** (Lesson.Exercise) 57.1–3, 58.3–4, 59.4–5, 60.2–6, 61.1–6, 62.1–6, 63.1–5, 64.5–7, 65.4–5, 66.4–5, 67.1–4, 68.1–6, 69.1–6, 70.1–5, 71.1–3, 72.1–6, 73.1–5, 74.1–6, 75.1–3, 76.1–6, 77.1–6, 78.1–5, 79.1–5, 80.1–6, 81.1–6, 82.1–6, 83.1–3, 84.1–4, 85.1–3, 86.1–5, 87.1–3, 88.3–6, 89.2–5, 90.2–6, 91.1–3, 92.1–6, 93.1–6, 94.1–6, 95.1–4, 96.1–3, 97.1–3, 98.4, 99.4–5, 100.4–6, 101.1–3, 102.1–6, 103.1–5, 104.1–6, 105.1–3, 106.1–3, 107.1–5 **Reading Presentation Book C:** (Lesson.Exercise) 108.1–6, 109.1–6, 110.1–4, 111.1–4, 112.1–3, 113.1–6, 114.1–5, 115.1–5, 116.1–3, 117.2–3, 118.3–4, 119.4–5, 120.4–6, 121.1–6, 122.1–6, 123.1–5, 124.1–6, 125.1–6, 126.1–4, 127.5–6, 128.4–5, 129.1–4, 130.1–3, 131.1–6, 132.1–5, 133.1–6, 134.1–3, 135.1–6, 136.1–6, 137.1–3, 138.1–3, 139.1–6, 140.1–5, 141.1–6, 142.3–6, 143.2–5, 144.2–5, 145.1–6, 146.1–6, 147.1–5, 148.1–3, 149.1–4, 150.1–5, 151.2–6, 152.1–6, 153.1–5, 154.1–6, 155.1–6, 156.1–6, 157.1–5, 158.3–5, 159.2–5
RF.K.3b	Associate the long and short sounds with the common spellings (graphemes) for the five major vowels.	**In Reading Mastery Signature Edition, macrons (long lines over vowels) differentiate long vowel sounds from short vowel sounds. When the vowels appear in words, words are spelled correctly but letters that are not pronounced appear in small letters. By the middle of Grade 1, all letters are presented in traditional orthography.** **Reading Presentation Book A:** (Lesson.Exercise) 1.4, 1.7, 1.11, 2.2, 2.5, 2.9, 3.2, 3.5, 3.9, 4.2, 4.9, 5.5, 59. 6,2, 6.5, 6.9, 7.2, 7.5, 7.9, 8.2, 8.5, 8.9, 9.2, 9.9, 10.5, 10.9, 12.5, 12.8, 13.2, 13.4, 13.7, 13.9, 14.2, 14.4, 14.7, 14.10, 15.2, 15.4, 15.7–9, 16.2, 16.7–9, 17.3, 17.6, 17.7, 18.1, 18.5, 18.7, 19.1, 19.5, 19.6, 19.8, 20.1, 20.5, 20.7, 21.1, 21.4, 21.7, 21.8, 22.1, 22.5, 22.8, 23.1, 23.7, 23.8, 24.4, 24.5, 24.7, 24.8, 25.1–3, 25.5, 26.1, 26.2, 26.5, 26.6, 26.8, 27.1, 27.5–7, 28.2, 28.4, 28.5, 29.1, 29.3–6, 30.2, 30.4–38, 31.2, 31.3, 32.1, 32.2, 33.1, 33.8, 34.2, 34.3, 34.9, 35.1, 35.2, 35.8, 35.9, 36.1, 36.4, 37.1, 37.4–5, 38.3, 38.38.6, 39.2, 39.4, 39.5, 40.1, 40.3, 40.4, 41.2–6, 42.1–6, 43.3–5, 44.5–6, 45.2–6, 46.4–5, 47.1–4, 48.6–7, 49.4–5, 50.4–5, 51.1–6, 52.1–6, 53.1–5, 54.1–3, 55.1–4, 56.1–5; **Reading Presentation Book B:** (Lesson.Exercise) 57.1–3, 58.1–4, 59.1–5, 60.1–6, 61.3–6, 62.4–6, 63.1–5, 64.1–7, 65.1–5, 66.1–5, 67.1–4, 68.5–6, 69.4–6, 70.1–5, 71.1–3, 72.3–6, 73.1–5, 74.2–6, 75.1–3, 76.3–6, 77.2–6, 78.4–5, 79.1–5, 80.5–6, 81.4–6, 82.4–6, 83.1–3, 84.1–4, 85.1–3, 86.1–5, 87.1–3, 88.1–6, 89.1–5, 90.1–6, 91.1–3, 92.1–6, 93.4–6, 94.4–6, 95.1–4, 96.1–2, 97.1–4, 98.1–4, 99.1–5, 100.1–6, 101.1–2, 102.5–6, 103.4–5, 104.4–6, 105.1–3, 106.1–3, 107.1–5 **Reading Presentation Book C:** (Lesson.Exercise) 108.5–6, 109.4–6, 110.3–4, 111.2–4, 112.1–3, 113.5–6, 114.4–5, 115..3–5, 116.2–3, 117.1–3, 118.1–4, 119.1–5, 120.1–6, 121.5–6, 122.4–6, 123.4–5, 124.3–6, 125.1–6, 126.1–4, 127.1–6, 128.1–5, 129.1–4, 130.1–3, 131.5–6, 132.2–5, 133.2–6, 134.1–3, 135.1–6, 136.1–6, 137.2–3, 138.1–3, 139.5–6, 140.5–5, 141.4–6, 142.1–6, 143.1–5, 144.1–5, 145.5–6, 146.4–6, 147.4–5, 148.1–3, 149.1–4, 150.1–5, 151.1–6, 152.3–6, 153.1–5, 154.5–6, 155.4–6, 156.5–6, 157.4–5, 158.1–, 159.1–5

E10

GRADE K STANDARDS		PAGE REFERENCES
RF.K.3c	Read common high-frequency words by sight (e.g., the, of, to, you, she, my, is, are, do, does).	**In Reading Mastery Signature Edition, students reread words "the fast way" on reading–vocabulary pages. The rereading step is designed to help students with whole–word reading and with remembering words.** **Reading Presentation Book B:** (Lesson.Exercise) 96.4–17, 97.5–17, 98.5–17, 99.12–14, 100.7–12, 101.4–6, 101.9–10, 101.13–15, 102.7–12, 103.6–8, 103.12–14, 103.17–19, 104.7–12, 105.6–9, 105.12–17, 106.4–6, 106.10–12,107.8–9, 107.14–16 **Reading Presentation Book C:** (Lesson.Exercise) 108.10–12, 108.15, 109.7–9, 109.15, 110.5–7, 110.12–13, 111.5–7, 111.11–12, 112.11–15, 112.20–21, 113.11–12, 113.15–17, 114.11–15, 114.20–21, 115.8–10, 115.15–16, 116.8–10, 117.4–6, 117.15–16, 118.5–7, 118.11–12,119.12–13, 119.16–18, 120.8–10, 120.15–19, 121.7–9, 121.14–16, 121.18–20, 122.8–13, 122.16–18,123.6–8, 123.10–12, 128.17, 124.7–9, 124.12–14, 124.16–18, 125.7–9, 125.11–16, 126.7–14, 127.7–9, 127.13–14, 127.18, 128.10, 128.15–19, 129.5–7, 129.12–13, 129.17, 130.4–6, 130.11–12, 130.16–17, 131.8–13, 132.6–8, 132.11, 132.16–17,133.9–11, 133.17–18, 133.23–24, 134.9–10, 134.13–15, 134.17,135.9–10, 135.13–15, 136.8–10, 136.15–15, 136.20–21, 137.6–8, 137.14, 137.18–19, 138.6–8, 138.12–13, 138.17, 139.10, 139.15–16, 139.21–22, 140.10–11, 140.14–16, 140.18–19, 141.11, 141.15–16, 141.19–21, 142.9–12, 142.16–17, 143.7–8, 144.6–8, 144.14–15, 145.10–11, 145.17–20, 146.7–9, 146.15, 146.18, 147.6–8, 147.14–15, 147.19–20, 148.5–7, 148.10–11, 148.15–16, 149.7–9, 149.16–17, 150.6–8, 150.14, 150.18, 150.23–24, 151.7–9, 151.13–14, 151.18–19, 152.7–9, 152.16–17, 152.21–22, 153.8–10, 153.16–17, 153.21–22, 154.10–11, 154.13–15, 154.19–20, 155.9–11, 155.14–15, 155.19–20, 155.22–23, 156.7–9, 156.13–14, 156.17–18, 156. 21–22, 157.7–8, 157.11–16, 157.19–20, 158.6–8, 158.13–17, 158.21–23, 159.6–11, 159.15, 160.1–6, 160.10–11
RF.K.3d	Distinguish between similarly spelled words by identifying the sounds of the letters that differ.	**In Reading Mastery Signature Edition, students sound out words in every lesson, starting at lesson 28. Beginning at lesson 37, students read some words by applying rhyming skills. Sounding–out and rhyming prepare students to read words that are very similar. When reading words "the fast way," errors are corrected by having students sound out the word to focus on sounds of letters. The following examples are representative of exercises that meet this standard:** **Reading Presentation Book A:** (Lesson.Exercise) 38.11, 39.6, 41.14, 44.8, 44.10, 46.6, 46.8, 50.13–15 **Reading Presentation Book B:** (Lesson.Exercise) 60.13–14, 63.17–20, 67.7–9, 68.7–11, 74.16–17; **Reading Presentation Book C:** (Lesson.Exercise) 108.7, 118.5–7, 120.11–19, 121.18–20, 122.15–18

E11

GRADE K STANDARDS		PAGE REFERENCES
Reading Standards for Foundational Skills: Fluency		
RF.K.4	Read emergent-reader texts with purpose and understanding.	**Reading Presentation Book B:** (Lesson.Exercise) 91.17–21, 92.22–26, 93.23–27, 94.25–28, 95.22–25, 96.19–22, 97.19–22, 98.18–21, 99.16–19, 100.14–17, 101.16–18, 102.16–19, 103.20–21, 104.15–18, 105.19–22, 106.14–17, 107.20–23 **Reading Presentation Book C:** (Lesson.Exercise) 108.20–23, 109.16–19, 110.–14–17, 111.13–16, 112.18–21, 113.21–24, 114.22–25, 115.22–25, 116.19–22, 117.18–21, 118.14–17, 119.19–22, 120.20–23, 121.21–24, 122.19–22, 123.18–21, 124.19–22, 125.17–20, 126.15–18, 127.20–23, 128.20–23, 129.18–21, 130.18–21, 131.14–17, 132.18–21, 133.25–28, 134.18–21, 135.16–19, 136.22–25, 137.20–23, 138.18–21, 139.23–26, 140.20–23, 141.22–25, 142.18–21, 143.18–21, 144.16–19, 145.21–24, 146.19–22, 147.21–24, 148.17–20, 149.18–21, 150.25–28, 151.23–26, 152.26–29, 153.26–29, 154.24–27, 155.27–30, 156.26–29, 157.25–28, 158.27–30, 159.19–22, 160.15–18 **Storybook:** Lessons 91–160 **Core Lesson Connections:** (Lesson.Part.Activity) 146.C.2–3, 147.C.1–3. 148.C.1–3, 149.C.1–3, 150.C.1–3, 151.C.1–3, 152.C.1–3, 153.C.1–3, 154.C.1–3, 155.C.1–3, 156.C.1–3, 157.C.1–3, 158.C.1–3, 159.C.1–3, 160.C.1 **Literature Guide (pages 8–9):** Lessons 20, 35, 50, 65, 80, 95, 110, 125, 140, 155
Writing Standards: Text Types and Purposes		
W.K.1	Use a combination of drawing, dictating, and writing to compose opinion pieces in which they tell a reader the topic or the name of the book they are writing about and state an opinion or preference about the topic or book (e.g., *My favorite book is...*).	**Read Aloud Library:** (Week.Day) 13.3, 15.3, 16.3
W.K.2	Use a combination of drawing, dictating, and writing to compose informative/explanatory texts in which they name what they are writing about and supply some information about the topic.	**Reading Presentation Book A:** Planning page 134b **Core Lesson Connections:** (Lesson.Part.Activity) 129.C.3, 130.C.3, 134.C.3, 135.C.3, 139.C.3, 140.C.3, 144.C.3, 145.C.3 **Read Aloud Library:** (Week.Day) 21.3, 22.3, 23.3, 24.3, 25.3, 26.3, 27.3, 28.3, 29.3, 30.3
W.K.3	Use a combination of drawing, dictating, and writing to narrate a single event or several loosely linked events, tell about the events in the order in which they occurred, and provide a reaction to what happened.	**Core Lesson Connections:** (Lesson.Part.Activity) 40.C.2, 50.C.2, 60.C.2, 70.C.2, 75.C.2, 79.C.2, 80.C.2, 85.C.2, 87.C.2, 90.C.2, 95.C.2, 99.C.2, 100.C.2, 105.C.2, 109.C.3, 110.C.2, 120.C.2, 147.C.1, 148.C.1, 149.C.1, 150.C.1, 151.C.1, 152.C.1, 153.C.1, 154.C.1, 155.C.1, 159.C.2 **Read Aloud Library:** (Week.Day) 1.3, 2.3, 3.3, 4.3, 19.3
Writing Standards: Production and Distribution of Writing		
W.K.4	*(Begins in Grade 3)*	
W.K.5	With guidance and support from adults, respond to questions and suggestions from peers and add details to strengthen writing as needed.	**Core Lesson Connections:** (Lesson.Part.Activity) 45.C.3, 55.C.2, 59.C.2, 59.C.3, 85.C.2, 89.C.2, 95.C.2, 99.C.2, 105.C.2, 119.C.2, 136.C.2, 137.C.2, 141.C.2, 142.C.2, 150.C.2, 153.C.2, 154.C.2, 159.C.2, 160.C.2

	GRADE K STANDARDS	PAGE REFERENCES
W.K.6	With guidance and support from adults, explore a variety of digital tools to produce and publish writing, including in collaboration with peers.	**Core Lesson Connections:** (Lesson.Part.Activity) 45.C.3, 55.C.2, 59.C.2, 59.C.3, 85.C.2, 89.C.2, 95.C.2, 99.C.2, 105.C.2, 119.C.2, 136.C.2, 137.C.2, 141.C.2, 142.C.2, 150.C.2, 153.C.2, 154.C.2, 159.C.2, 160.C.2
Writing Standards: Research to Build and Present Knowledge		
W.K.7	Participate in shared research and writing projects (e.g., explore a number of books by a favorite author and express opinions about them).	**Core Lesson Connections:** (Lesson.Part.Activity) 40.C.4, 50.C.3, 60.C.3, 70.C.3, 80.C.3, 90.C.3, 100.C.3, 110.C.3, 120.C.3, 130.C.4, 140.C.4
W.K.8	With guidance and support from adults, recall information from experiences or gather information from provided sources to answer a question.	**Core Lesson Connections:** (Lesson.Part.Activity) 25.C.2, 26.C.2, 27.C.2, 28.C.2, 29.C.2, 30.C.2, 61.C.1, 66.C.2, 71.C.2, 76.C.2, 81.C.2, 86.C.2, 91.C.2, 93.C.2, 96.C.2, 97.C.2, 106.C.2, 107.C.2, 113.C.2, 116.C.2, 123.C.2, 151.C.3, 151.C.3
W.K.9	*(Begins in Grade 4)*	
Writing Standards: Range of Writing		
W.K.10	*(Begins in Grade 3)*	
Speaking & Listening Standards: Comprehension and Collaboration		
SL.K.1	Participate in collaborative conversations with diverse partners about *kindergarten topics and texts* with peers and adults in small and larger groups.	
SL.K.1a	Follow agreed-upon rules for discussions (e.g., listening to others and taking turns speaking about the topics and texts under discussion).	**Core Lesson Connections:** (Lesson.Part.Activity) 33.C.2, 34.C.2, 35.C.2, 36.C.3, 37.C.2, 38.C.2, 40.C.3, 50.C.2, 58.C.2, 60.C.2 **Read Aloud Library:** (Week.Day) 1.1, 2.1, 3.1, 4.1, 5.1, 6.1, 7.1, 8.1, 9.1, 10.1, 11.1, 12.1, 13.1, 14.1, 15.1, 16.1, 17.1, 18.1, 19.1, 20.1, 21.1, 22.1, 23.1, 24.1, 25.1, 26.1, 27.1, 28.1, 29.1, 30.1
SL.K.1b	Continue a conversation through multiple exchanges.	**Read Aloud Library:** (Week.Day) 1.1–5, 2.1–5, 3.1–5, 4.1–5, 5.1–5, 6.1–5, 7.1–5, 8.1–5, 9.1–5, 10.1–5, 11.1–5, 12.1–5, 13.1–5, 14.1–5, 15.1–5, 16.1–15, 17.1–5, 18.1–5, 19.1–5, 20.1–5, 21.1–5, 22.1–5, 23.1–5, 24.1–5, 25.1–5, 26.1–5, 27.1–25, 28.1–5, 29.1–5, 30.1–5
SL.K.2	Confirm understanding of a text read aloud or information presented orally or through other media by asking and answering questions about key details and requesting clarification if something is not understood.	**Language Presentation Book A:** Storybook 1: pages 1–39 **Language Presentation Book B:** Storybook 2: pages 1–48 **Language Presentation Book C:** Storybook 3: pages 1–42 **Language Presentation Book D:** Storybook 4: pages 1–41 **Literature Guide (pages 8–9):** Lessons 20, 35, 50, 65, 80, 95, 110, 125, 140, 155 **Read Aloud Library:** (Week.Day) 1.1–5, 2.1–5, 3.1–5, 4.1–5, 5.1–5, 6.1–5, 7.1–5, 8.1–5, 9.1–5, 10.1–5, 11.1–5, 12.1–5, 13.1–5, 14.1–5, 15.1–5, 16.1–15, 17.1–5, 18.1–5, 19.1–5, 20.1–5, 21.1–5, 22.1–5, 23.1–5, 24.1–5, 25.1–5, 26.1–5, 27.1–25, 28.1–5, 29.1–5, 30.1–5

	GRADE K STANDARDS	PAGE REFERENCES
SL.K.3	Ask and answer questions in order to seek help, get information, or clarify something that is not understood.	**Language Presentation Book C:** Extended Language Activities: page v (Lessons 116–120) **Core Lesson Connections:** (Lesson.Part.Activity) 126.C.4, 131.C.4, 136.C.4, 141.C.4
	**Speaking & Listening Standards: Presentation of Knowledge and Ideas**	
SL.K.4	Describe familiar people, places, things, and events and, with prompting and support, provide additional detail.	The Reading Mastery Language Strand is a comprehensive oral language program that prepares students to understand commonly used vocabulary, sentence forms, and instructions used in school settings. The following examples are representative of varied types of exercises that prepare them to describe actions, objects, and events: **Language Presentation Book A:** (Lesson.Exercise) 17.6, 24.6, 31.5, 32.4, 32.5, 38.6–7, 41.4, 41.7, 42.7, 47.9 **Language Presentation Book B:** (Lesson.Exercise) 51.6, 56.4, 59.4, 60.6, 65.11, 70.6, 71.3, 76.10, 84.7 **Language Presentation Book C:** (Lesson.Exercise) 90.3, 90.8, 91.3, 92.5–6, 98.7, 100.6, 106.7, 110.11 **Language Presentation Book D:** (Lesson.Exercise) 121.9, 122.4, 125.5, 127.6, 131.4, 137.6, 141.11
SL.K.5	Add drawings or other visual displays to descriptions as desired to provide additional detail.	**Reading Presentation Book B:** Planning page 155b **Reading Presentation Book C:** Planning page 77b **Language Presentation Book A:** Expanded Language Activities: page v (11–15) **Language Presentation Book B:** Extended Language Activities: page v (61–65) **Language Presentation Book C:** Extended Language Activities: page v (106–110) **Language Presentation Book D:** Extended Language Activities: page v (121–125, 131–135, 136–140, 141–145, 146–150) **Core Lesson Connections:** (Lesson.Part.Activity) 45.C.2, 49.C.2, 55.C.2, 59.C.2, 65.C.2, 69.C.2, 75.C.2, 79.C.2, 85.C.2, 89.C.2, 95.C.2, 99.C.2, 100.C.2, 105.C.2, 109.C.2, 119.C.2, 129.C.3, 130.C.3, 134.C.3, 135.C.3, 139.C.3, 140.C.3, 144.C.3, 145.C.3, 159.C.2 **Read Aloud Library:** (Week.Day) 14.3, 15.3, 19.4, 21.3, 22.3, 23.3, 24.3
SL.K.6	Speak audibly and express thoughts, feelings, and ideas clearly.	**Language Presentation Book D:** (Lesson, Exercise) 121.7–8, 122.7, 125.2, 126.6, 127.5, 128.9, 131.9,131.11, 132.7, 138.9, 139.3, 140.4, 141.4–6, 142.8, 144.6, 145.6, 146.7, 146.12, 148.13, 150.4 **Literature Guide (pages 8–9):** Lessons 20, 35, 50, 65, 80, 95, 110, 125, 140, 155 **Read Aloud Library:** (Week.Day) 1.1, 2.1, 3.1, 4.1, 5.1, 6.1, 7.1, 8.1, 9.1, 10.1, 11.1 12.1, 13.1, 14.1, 15.1, 16.1, 17.1, 18.1, 19.1, 20.1, 21.1, 22.1, 23.1, 24.1, 25.1, 26.1, 27.1, 28.1, 29.1, 30.1
	**Language Standards: Conventions of Standard English**	
L.K.1	Demonstrate command of the conventions of standard English grammar and usage when writing or speaking.	

E14

GRADE K STANDARDS		PAGE REFERENCES
L.K.1a	Print many upper- and lowercase letters.	**Reading Presentation Book A:** (Lesson.Exercise) 1.19, 1.20, 1.23, 2.17, 2.20, 3.17, 3.20, 4.16, 4.17, 5.16, 5.17, 6.17, 6.18, 7.17, 7.18, 8.17, 8.18, 9.17, 9.18, 10,17, 10.18, 11.18, 11.19, 11.22, 12.18, 12.18, 13.14, 13.15, 14.15, 14.16, 15.14, 15.15, 16.19, 16.20, 17.17, 17.18, 18.14, 18.15, 19.16, 19.17, 20.15, 20.16, 21.11, 21.12, 22.11, 22.12, 23.10, 23.11, 24.10, 24.11, 25.8, 26.10, 27.10, 28.9, 29.12, 30.16, 31.16, 32.14, 33.13, 34.15, 35.16, 36.10, 37.14, 38.14, 39.14, 40.15, 41.20, 41.21, 42.22, 42.24, 43.19, 44.20, 45.29, 46.19, 47.18, 48.21, 48.22, 49.19, 49.20, 50.21, 51.24, 52.20, 53.21, 54.17, 55.21, 56.21 **Reading Presentation Book B:** (Lesson.Exercise) 57.19, 58.20, 59.21, 60.23, 61.24, 62.25, 63.29, 64.26, 65.30, 66.30, 67.27, 68.33, 69.33, 70.31, 71.25, 72.31, 73.26, 74.28, 75.26, 76.27, 77.29, 78.28, 79.26, 80.28, 81.30, 82.27, 83.23, 84.28, 85.25, 86.27, 87.26, 88.27, 89.25, 90.26, 91.25, 92.30, 93.30, 94.40, 95.27, 96.24, 97.24, 98.23, 99.21, 100.19, 101.21, 102.21, 103.25, 104.20, 105.24, 10–6.19, 107.24 **Reading Presentation Book C:** (Lesson.Exercise) 108.24, 109.20, 110.18, 111.17, 112.22, 113.25, 114.27, 115.27, 115.23, 117.22, 118.18, 119.23, 120.26, 121.27, 122.24, 123.23, 124.24, 125.22, 126.20, 127.25, 128.24, 129.22, 130.22, 131.19, 132.23, 133.30, 134.22, 135.20, 136.26, 137.24, 138.22, 139.27, 140.24, 141.26, 142.22, 143.22, 144.23, 145.28, 146.26, 147.27, 148.21, 149.22, 150.29, 151.27, 152.30, 153.30, 154.28, 155.31, 156.30, 157.29, 158.31, 159.23, 160.23 **Workbook A:** Lessons 1–56 **Workbook B:** Lessons 57–107 **Workbook C:** Lessons 108–160 **Core Lesson Connections:** (Lesson.Part.Activity) 11.B.2, 12.B.2, 13.B.2, 14.B.2, 15.B.2, 16.B.2, 17.B.2, 18.B.2, 19.B.2, 20.B.2, 21.B.2, 22.B.2, 23.B.2, 24.B.2, 25.B.2, 26.B.2, 27.B.2, 28.B.2, 29.B.2, 30.B.2, 31.B.2, 32.B.2, 33.B.2, 34.B.2, 35.B.2, 36.B.2, 37.B.2, 38.B.2, 39.B.2, 40.B.2, 41.B.2, 42.B.2, 43.B.2, 44.B.2, 45.B.2, 46.B.2, 47.B.2, 48.B.2, 49.B.2, 50.B.2, 51.B.2, 52.B.2, 53.B.2, 54.B.2, 55.B.2, 56.B.2, 57.B.2, 58.B.2, 59.B.2, 60.B.2, 61.B.2, 62.B.2, 63.B.2, 64.B.2, 65.B.2, 66.B.2, 67.B.2, 68.B.2, 69.B.2, 70.B.2, 71.B.2, 72.B.2, 73.B.2, 74.B.2, 75.B.2, 76.B.2, 77.B.2, 78.B.2, 79.B.2, 80.B.2, 81.B.2, 82.B.2, 83.B.2, 84.B.2, 85.B.2, 86.B.2, 87.B.2, 88.B.2, 89.B.2, 90.B.2, 91.B.2, 92.B.2, 93.B.2, 94.B.2, 95.B.2, 96.B.2, 97.B.2, 98.B.2, 99.B.2, 100.B.2, 101.B.2, 102.B.2, 103.B.2, 104.B.2, 105.B.2, 106.B.2, 107.B.2, 108.B.2, 109.B.2, 110.B.2, 111.B.2, 112.B.2, 113.B.2, 114.B.2, 115.B.2, 116.B.2, 117.B.2, 118.B.2, 119.B.2, 120.B.2, 121.B.2, 122.B.2, 123.B.2, 124.B.2, 125.B.2, 126.B.2, 127.B.2, 128.B.2, 129.B.2, 130.B.2, 131.B.2, 132.B.2, 133.B.2, 134.B.2, 135.B.2, 136.B.2, 137.B.2, 138.B.2, 139.B.2, 140.B.2, 141.B.2, 142.B.2, 143.B.2, 144.B.2, 145.B.2, 146.B.2, 147.B.2, 148.B.2, 149.B.2, 150.B.2, 151.B.2, 152.B.2, 153.B.2, 154.B.2, 155.B.2, 156.B.2, 157.B.2, 158.B.2, 159.B.2, 160.B.2 **Spelling Presentation Book:** Lessons 1–111
L.K.1b	Use frequently occurring nouns and verbs.	**In the Language Strand, Object Identification exercises require students to identify common objects; Actions exercises help students learn concepts by doing actions and by describing actions. The following examples are representative of the activities that help them use nouns and verbs:** **Language Presentation Book A:** (Lesson.Exercise) 1.1, 1.4, 10.1, 10.4, 14.3–5, 19.7, 21.8, 24.4, 24.6, 31.1, 34.1, 34.11, 37.8, 38.6, 42.6, 42.8, 45.1, 45.7, 49.8 **In Locations exercises, students learn the names of things that are observed in each location.** **Language Presentation Book D:** (Lesson, Exercise) 128.9, 129.7, 132.6, 133.8, 136.8, 138.8–10, 141.11, 143.9, 145.11, 147.9, 148.13, 149.10
L.K.1c	Form regular plural nouns orally by adding /s/ or /es/ (e.g., *dog, dogs; wish, wishes*).	**Language Presentation Book B:** (Lesson.Exercise) 51.2, 52.2, 53.3, 54.2, 54.6, 55.3, 55.7, 56.2, 56.10, 57.3, 57.7, 58.8, 59.2, 59.7, 60.2, 60.7, 61.4, 61.7, 62.7, 63.2, 67.7, 68.7, 70.4, 73.6, 79.9; **Reading Presentation Book B:** Planning page 284b

E15

GRADE K STANDARDS		PAGE REFERENCES
L.K.1d	Understand and use question words (interrogatives) (e.g., *who, what, where, when, why, how*).	**Language Presentation Book D:** (Lesson, Exercise) 121.9, 122.10, 123.6, 124.7, 125.6, 126.10, 127.9, 128.11, 130.9, 131.8, 133.12, 137.7, 138.7, 139.11, 140.6, 147.8, **Language Presentation Book A:** Storybook 1: pages 1–39 **Language Presentation Book B:** Storybook 2: pages 1–48 **Language Presentation Book C:** Storybook 3: pages 1–42 **Language Presentation Book D:** Storybook 4: pages 1–41 **Reading Presentation Book B:** (Lesson.Exercise) 75.21, 76.22, 77.24, 78.23, 79.21, 80.23, 81.25, 82.21, 83.17, 84.23, 85.20, 86.21, 87.18, 88.20, 89.18, 90.19, 91.18, 92.23, 93.24, 94.25, 94.26, 95.22, 95.23, 96.19, 96.20, 97.19, 97.20, 98.19, 99.16, 99.17, 100.15, 101.17, 102.17, 103.21, 104.16, 105.19, 105.20, 106.14, 106.15, 107.22 **Reading Presentation Book C:** (Lesson.Exercise) 108.22, 109.18, 110.16, 111.15, 112.20, 113.23, 114.24, 115.24, 116.21, 117,.20, 118.16, 119.21, 1120.22, 121.23, 122.21, 123.20, 124.21, 125.19, 126.17, 127.22, 128.22, 129.20, 130.20, 131.16, 131.18, 132.20, 132.22, 133.27, 133.29, 134.20, 135.18, 136.24, 137.22, 138.20, 139.25, 140.22, 141.24, 142.20, 143.20, 144.18, 144.20, 145.23, 145.25, 146.21, 146.23, 147.23, 147.25, 148.19, 149.20, 150.27, 151.25, 152.28, 153.28, 154.26, 155.29, 156.28, 157.27, 158.29, 159.21, 160.17 **Literature Guide (pages 8–9):** Lessons 20, 35, 50, 65, 80, 95, 110, 125, 140, 155 **Read Aloud Library:** (Week.Day) 1.2, 2.2, 3.2, 4.2, 5.2, 6.2, 7.2, 8.2, 9.2, 10.2, 11.2, 12.2, 13.2, 14.2, 15.2, 16.2, 17.2, 18.2, 19.2, 20.2, 21.2, 22.2, 23.2, 24.C, 25.2, 26.2, 26.3, 27.2, 27.3, 28.2, 28.3, 29.2, 29.3, 30.2, 30.3
L.K.1e	Use the most frequently occurring prepositions (e.g., *to, from, in, out, on, off, for, of, by, with*).	**Language Presentation Book A:** (Lesson.Exercise) 27.3, 28.2, 29.4, 30.3, 31.3, 31.5, 32.1, 32.5, 34.4, 34.6, 35.4, 36.3, 36.5, 37.4, 37.6, 38.4, 39.4, 40.5, 41.4, 42.1, 44.6, 46.2, 46.7, 47.2, 47.6, 48.1, 48.7, 49.7, 50.7 **Language Presentation Book B:** (Lesson.Exercise) 51.5, 52.5, 53.5, 54.4, 54.7, 55.8, 56.4, 56.7, 57.4, 57.7, 58.2, 58.10, 59.9, 60.9, 61.10, 63.8, 64.11, 65.10, 66.8, 66.10, 67.1, 67.3, 68.1, 68.5, 69.2, 69.7, 69.10, 70.1, 70.7, 73.1, 76.2, 76.8, 77.1, 79.9, 81.1, 82.1, 85.1 **Language Presentation Book C:** (Lesson.Exercise) 86.1, 87.1, 107.1

GRADE K STANDARDS		PAGE REFERENCES
L.K.1f	Produce and expand complete sentences in shared language activities.	**Reading Presentation Book B:** Planning pages 155b, 284b **Reading Presentation Book C:** Planning pages 203b **In the Language Strand, students learn to "Say the whole thing"—that is, make a statement about what they are doing or observing.** **Language Presentation Book A:** (Lesson.Exercise) 3.2, 4.4, 5.2, 5.7, 6.4, 6.7, 7.1, 7.4, 7.5, 7.7, 8.1, 8.4, 8.5, 8.7, 9.1, 9.4–6, 10.1, 10.4–6, 11.1, 11.4–6, 12.1, 12.4–7, 13.1, 13.4–7, 14.1, 14.3–5, 15.1, 15.3–7, 16.1, 1.3–6, 17.1, 17.4–6, 18.1, 18.4–7, 19.1, 19.3, 19.5–7, 20.1, 20.2, 20.4–6, 21.1, 21.3, 21.5–8, 22.1, 22.5–7, 23.1, 22.5–7, 24.1, 24.3, 24.5, 24.6, 25.1–3, 25.6–9,, 16.1–6, 26.8, 27.1, 27.3–5, 27.7, 28.1–5, 28.7, 28.8, 29.1, 29.2, 29.4–8, 30.1–5, 30.7, 30.8, 31.1–5, 31.7, 31.8, 32.1, 32.3, 32.5–8, 33.1, 33.3–8, 34.1, 3.2, 34.4, 34.6–11, 35.1, 35.3–9, 36.1, 36.4–7, 37.1, 37.4, 37.5, 37.7, 37.8, 39.1, 39.4–7, 40.1, 40.4–8, 41.1, 42.3–8, 42.1, 42.3–8, 43.1, 43.3–7, 44.1, 44.3–7, 45.1–7, 46.1–7, 47.1, 47.2, 47.5–8, 48.1–3, 48.5–8, 49.1, 49.2, 49.4–7, 50.1, 50.3–7; **Language Presentation Book B:** (Lesson.Exercise) 51.1, 51.3–7, 52.1, 52.5–8, 53.1, 53–49., 54.1, 54.4, 54.5, 54.7–9, 55.1, 55.4–10, 56.1, 56.4–10, 57.1, 57.4–9, 58.1, 58.2, 58.4–10, 59.1, 59.4–11, 60.1–3, 60.5–7, 60.9, 60.10, 61.1, 61.3–10, 62.1, 62.2, 62.6–9, 63.1, 63.2, 63.6–12, 64.1, 64.44, 64.7–11, 65.1, 65.2, 65.5–8, 65.10, 65.11, 66.1, 66.4–10, 67.1, 67.3, 67.4, 67.6–13, 68.1, 68.3, 68.5–11, 69.1, 69.2, 69.4, 69.7–10, 70.1–5, 70.7, 70.8, 71.1, 71.3, 71.5–8, 72.1–5, 72.7, 73.1–8, 74.1, 74.3–7, 75.1, 75.3, 75.4, 75.6–8, 76.1, 76.2, 76.4, 76.5, 76.7–10, 77.1, 77.4–10, 78.1, 78.3–8, 79.1, 79.3–9, 80.1, 80.3–8, 81.1, 81.3, 81.5–10, 82.1, 82.2, 824–10, 83.1, 83.3, 83.4–7, 84.1–3, 84.6–9, 85.1, 85.3–6, 85.8, 85.9; **Language Presentation Book C:** (Lesson.Exercise) 86.1, 86.2, 86.4, 86.7–9, 87.1, 87.3–5, 88.1, 88.3, 88.6–8, 89.2, 89.5–9, 90.2–5, 90.7, 90.8, 91.1–7, 92.1–9, 93.1–8, 93.10, 94.1–9, 95.1–7, 95.9, 95.10, 96.1–4, 96.6–8, 96.10, 97.1–9, 98.1–5, 98.7–10, 99.1–4, 99.6–10, 100.2, 100.4–8, 101.1–5, 101.7–10, 102.1–4, 102.7, 102.9, 103.1, 103.3, 1003.4, 103.6–9, 104.2, 104.4, 104.6–9, 105.1–6, 105.8–11, 106.1, 106.2–6, 106.8, 107.1–3, 107.5, 107.8–10, 108.1–3, 108.7, 108.9, 108.10, 109.1, 109.2, 109.4, 109.7–9, 110.1, 110.2, 110.4–8, 110.10, 110.12, 111.1, 111.2, 111.4, 111.5, 111.7–10, 112.1–4, 112.6, 112.7, 112.9–12, 113.1–3, 113.5–8, 114.10, 114.1, 114.2, 114.4–6, 114.8, 114.9, 115.1–5, 115.7, 115.9, 115.10, 115.12, 116.1–3, 116.5–8, 117.1, 117.3, 117.5–9, 118.1, 118.2, 118.4, 118.6–10, 119.1–5, 119.7–9, 120.1–8; **Language Presentation Book D:** (Lesson.Exercise) 121.1–8, 122.1–8, 122.11, 123.1–5, 122.7–9, 124.1–11, 125.3–11, 126.3–10, 127.3–5, 127.7, 127.8, 128.2–11, 129.2–8, 130.2–8, 131.1, 131.3–11, 132.1, 132.3–10, 133.1–4, 133.6–12, 124.1, 134.3, 134.4, 134.6–13, 135.1, 135.4–8, 136.1, 136.3–11, 137.1, 137.3–6, 137.8, 138.1, 138.3–6, 138.9–12, 139.1, 139.2, 139.4–10, 140.1, 140.2, 140.4, 140.5, 140.7–10, 141.1–3, 141.6–8, 141.10, 141.11, 142.1, 142.4–12, 143.1, 143.2, 143.4, 143.6, 143.7, 144.1–4, 144.6–10, 145.1–3, 145.6–9, 146.1–4, 146.9–12, 147.1, 147.2, 147.4, 147.6, 147.7, 148.2–4, 148.6–13, 149.1–3, 149.5–8, 150.1–3, 150.6–11; **Read Aloud Library:** (Week.Day) 22.5, 23.5, 24.5, 25.5
L.K.2	Demonstrate command of the conventions of standard English capitalization, punctuation, and spelling when writing.	
L.K.2a	Capitalize the first word in a sentence and the pronoun *I*.	**Spelling Teacher Presentation Book:** (Lesson.Exercise) 82.3, 83.4, 84.6, 85.4, 86.5, 87.4, 88.5, 89.5, 90.5, 91.3, 92.4, 93.6, 94.6, 95.5, 96.7, 97.4, 98.5, 99.6, 100.5, 101.6, 102.5, 103.5, 104.6, 105.6, 106.6, 107.5, 108.5, 109.5, 110.3, 111.4

E17

GRADE K STANDARDS		PAGE REFERENCES
L.K.2b	Recognize and name end punctuation.	**Reading Presentation Book B:** (Lesson.Exercise) 87.20, 88.22, 89.20, 90.21, 91.20, 92.25, 93.26, 94.24, 94.26, 95.21, 95.23, 96.18, 96.20, 97.18, 97.20, 98.18, 98.19, 99.15. 99.17, 100.14, 100.15, 101.16, 101.17, 102.16, 102.17, 103.20, 103.21, 104.16, 105.18, 105.20, 106.13, 106.15 **Reading Presentation Book C:** (Lesson.Exercise) 108.25, 109.21, 110.19, 111.18, 112.23, 113.26, 114.28, 115.28, 116.24, 117.23, 118.19, 119.24. 120.27, 121.28, 122.25, 123.24, 124.25, 125.22, 126.21, 127.26, 128.25, 129.23, 130.23, 131.22, 132.26, 133.33, 134.26, 135.23, 136.30, 137.28, 138.26, 139.31, 140.27, 141.30, 142.26, 143.26, 144.24, 145.30, 146.28, 147.30, 148.26, 149.27, 150.31, 151.32, 152.35, 153.35, 154.33, 155.33, 156.25, 157.34, 158.36, 159.28, 160.24 **Spelling Presentation Book:** Lessons 82.3, 83.4, 84.6, 85.4, 86.5, 87.4, 88.5, 89.5, 90.5, 91.3, 92.4, 93.6, 94.6, 95.5, 96.7, 97.4, 98.5, 99.6, 100.5, 101.6, 102.5, 103.5, 104.6, 105.6, 106.6, 107.5, 108.5, 109.5, 110.3, 111.4
L.K.2c	Write a letter or letters for most consonant and short-vowel sounds (phonemes).	**Spelling Teacher Presentation Book:** Lessons 1–111
L.K.2d	Spell simple words phonetically, drawing on knowledge of sound-letter relationships.	**Spelling Teacher Presentation Book:** Lessons 1–111
Language Standards: Knowledge of Language		
L.K.3	*(Begins in Grade 2)*	
Language Standards: Vocabulary Acquisition and Use		
L.K.4	Determine or clarify the meaning of unknown and multiple-meaning words and phrases based on kindergarten reading and content.	
L.K.4a	Identify new meanings for familiar words and apply them accurately (e.g., knowing *duck* is a bird and learning the verb to *duck*).	**Reading Presentation Book:** Planning page 22b **Literature Guide (pages 8–9):** Lessons 20, 25, 30, 80, 85, 90 **Read Aloud Library:** (Week.Day) 1.1–5, 2.1–5, 3.1–5, 4.1–5, 5.1–5, 6.1–5, 7.1–5, 8.1–5, 9.1–5, 10.1–5, 11.1–5, 12.1–5, 13.1–5, 14.1–5, 15.1–5, 16.1–15, 17.1–5, 18.1–5, 19.1–5, 20.1–5, 21.1–5, 22.1–5, 23.1–5, 24.1–5, 25.1–5, 26.1–5, 27.1–25, 28.1–5, 29.1–5, 30.1–5
L.K.4b	Use the most frequently occurring inflections and affixes (e.g., *-ed*, *-s*, *re-*, *un-*, *pre-*, *-ful*, *-less*) as a clue to the meaning of an unknown word.	**The Language Strand introduces Comparatives to prepare students to meet this standard.** **Language Presentation Book D:** (Lesson.Exercise) 131.7, 132.9, 133.11, 134.13, 135.8, 136.10, 137.8, 139.10, 142.11, 146.11
L.K.5	With guidance and support from adults, explore word relationships and nuances in word meanings.	

E18

GRADE K STANDARDS		PAGE REFERENCES
L.K.5a	Sort common objects into categories (e.g., shapes, foods) to gain a sense of the concepts the categories represent.	**Reading Presentation Book B:** Planning page 22b **Language Presentation Book B:** (Lesson.Exercise) 51.6, 52.7, 53.8, 53.9, 54.8, 54.9, 55.10, 56.9, 57.8, 58.9, 59.9, 60.11, 61.5, 61.6, 62.6, 63.9, 63.10, 64.3, 64.7, 65.6, 65.8, 66.4, 66.7, 67.9, 67.10, 68.9, 69.4, 70.2, 71.6, 71.7, 72.3, 73.3, 73.4, 74.5, 74.6, 75.4, 75.7, 76.9, 77.5, 77.6, 77.9, 77.10, 78.5, 78.8, 79.3, 79.7, 79.8, 80.4, 80.7, 81.5, 81.9, 82.6, 82.9, 83.5, 94.8, 85.3, 85.8 **Language Presentation Book C:** (Lesson.Exercise) 86.9, 87.8, 88.2, 88.8, 89.8, 90.7, 91.7, 93.8, 95.10, 96.10, 97.9, 98.9, 99.5, 99.10, 101.9, 102.6, 102.7, 103.9, 104.7, 105.11, 107.10, 108.2, 111.3, 111.7, 112.7, 113.6, 113.7, 114.3, 114.6, 114.9, 115.7, 115.8, 115.10, 116.8, 117.2, 117.6, 118.3, 118.10, 119.3, 119.4, 119.8, 120.8 **Language Presentation Book D:** (Lesson.Exercise) 121.4, 121.5, 122.4, 122.8, 123.2, 123.8, 124.9, 124.10, 125.2, 125.10, 126.2, 127.2, 127.8, 128.10, 130.6, 131.2, 132.2, 133.9, 134.2, 134.12, 135.2, 135.3, 135.7, 136.2, 136.6, 137.2, 138.2, 139.3, 140.4, 141.4, 141.5, 142.2, 142.3, 142.10, 143.3, 143.5, 145.4, 146.5, 146.6, 146.8, 147.5, 148.4, 148.5, 148.8, 149.4, 150.4, 150.5
L.K.5b	Demonstrate understanding of frequently occurring verbs and adjectives by relating them to their opposites (antonyms).	**Reading Presentation Book C:** Planning page 77b **Language Presentation Book A:** (Lesson.Exercise) 24.2, 25.5, 25.6, 26.4, 27.5, 29.6, 30.6, 30.7, 31.6, 32.8, 33.8, 34.7, 34.9, 35.5, 37.7, 38.3, 39.5, 40.8, 41.5, 41.6, 42.4, 42.5, 43.4, 43.5, 44.4, 45.3, 45.4, 45.6, 46.5, 46.6, 47.7, 47.8, 48.6, 49.5, 49.6, 50.6 **Language Presentation Book B:** (Lesson.Exercise) 51.7, 52.8, 53.6, 54.4, 55.9, 57.9, 58.7, 59.10, 60.8, 61.8, 63.12, 64.10, 65.9, 67.12, 68.12, 77.8, 80.2, 81.6, 82.4, 84.3 **Language Presentation Book C:** (Lesson.Exercise) 86.2, 87.2, 88.4, 89.3, 91.3, 94.5, 95.7, 100.6, 101.5, 103.6, 104.4, 105.3, 106.8, 107.3, 107.8, 108.3, 109.4, 110.10, 111.9, 112.9, 112.12, 114.5, 115.12, 117.8, 118.6, 120.4 **Language Presentation Book D:** (Lesson.Exercise) 121.3, 122.5, 123.5, 124.4, 124.5, 125.3, 125.4, 126.3, 126.4, 127.3, 128.3, 128.4, 129.3, 129.4, 130.2, 130.3, 131.3, 132.3, 132.4, 133.3, 134.7, 134.8, 135.4, 136.3, 136.4, 137.3, 138.3, 139.4, 140.2, 141.3, 142.5, 142.6, 143.4, 144.3, 14.4, 145.3, 146.3, 146.4, 147.2, 148.2, 148.3, 149.2, 150.2

E19

GRADE K STANDARDS		PAGE REFERENCES
L.K.5c	Identify real-life connections between words and their use (e.g., note places at school that are colorful).	**Language Presentation Book A:** (Lesson.Exercise) 7.5, 8.5, 9.4, 10.4, 11.4, 12.4, 13.4, 14.3, 15.3, 16.3, 17.4, 18.4, 19.3, 20.2, 21.3, 25.2, 26.2, 27.3, 28.2, 28.4, 29.4, 30.3, 31.3, 31.5, 32.5, 33.3, 34.4, 34.6, 35.4, 36.3, 36.5, 37.3, 37.4, 37.6, 38.4, 39.4, 40.5, 41.4, 44.6, 45.2, 46.2, 46.3, 46.7, 46.8, 47.2, 47.5, 47.6, 47.9, 48.2, 48.7, 48.9, 49.7, 50.7 **Language Presentation Book B:** (Lesson.Exercise) 51.5, 52.5, 53.5, 54.7, 55.8, 56.4, 56.7, 57.4, 57.6, 58.2, 58.10, 59.8, 60.9, 61.10, 63.8, 64.1, 64.11, 66.8, 66.10, 67.3, 67.13, 68.1, 68.3, 68.5, 69.2, 69.7, 70.1, 70.7, 71.3, 72.2, 73.12, 74.3, 75.3, 75.5, 76.2, 76.6, 76.8, 77.1, 77.4, 78.3, 79.4, 79.9, 80.3, 81.1, 81.2, 82.1, 82.2, 83.3, 84.3, 85.1, 85.4 **Language Presentation Book C:** (Lesson.Exercise) 86.1, 86.4, 87.1, 87.3, 88.1, 88.3, 89.2, 90.2, 91.2, 92.3, 94.4, 95.2, 96.1, 97.2, 99.4, 101.4, 102.3, 104.6, 105.6, 107.5, 108.7, 109.5, 110.4, 112.4, 113.3, 113.5, 114.4, 115.5, 116.3, 117.1, 118.7, 119.5, 120.5 **Language Presentation Book D:** (Lesson.Exercise) 121.7, 122.6, 123.4, 124.3, 125.7, 126.5, 127.4, 127.6, 128.5, 128.7, 128.9, 129.2, 129.5, 129.7, 130.5, 130.7, 131.9–11, 132.6, 132.7, 132.10, 133.4, 133.8, 133.10, 134.3, 134.10, 135.5, 136.8, 136.9, 137.4, 138.8–11, 139.8, 139.9, 140.9, 140.10, 141.2, 141.10, 141.11, 142.7, 142.12, 143.9, 144.2, 145.2, 145.11, 146.2, 146.12, 147.9, 147.10, 148.6, 148.13, 149.10, 150.3, 150.11 **Read Aloud Library:** (Week.Day) 1.1–5, 2.1–5, 3.1–5, 4.1–5, 5.1–5, 6.1–5, 7.1–5, 8.1–5, 9.1–5, 10.1–5, 11.1–5, 12.1–5, 13.1–5, 14.1–5, 15.1–5, 16.1–15, 17.1–5, 18.1–5, 19.1–5, 20.1–5, 21.1–5, 22.1–5, 23.1–5, 24.1–5, 25.1–5, 26.1–5, 27.1–25, 28.1–5, 29.1–5, 30.1–5
L.K.5d	Distinguish shades of meaning among verbs describing the same general action (e.g., *walk, march, strut, prance*) by acting out the meanings.	**Core Lesson Connections:** (Lesson.Part.Activity) 5.D.1, 10.D.1, 15.D.1, 20.D.1, 25.D.1, 30.D.1
L.K.6	Use words and phrases acquired through conversations, reading and being read to, and responding to texts.	**Read Aloud Library:** (Week.Day) 1.1–5, 2.1–5, 3.1–5, 4.1–5, 5.1–5, 6.1–5, 7.1–5, 8.1–5, 9.1–5, 10.1–5, 11.1–5, 12.1–5, 13.1–5, 14.1–5, 15.1–5, 16.1–15, 17.1–5, 18.1–5, 19.1–5, 20.1–5, 21.1–5, 22.1–5, 23.1–5, 24.1–5, 25.1–5, 26.1–5, 27.1–25, 28.1–5, 29.1–5, 30.1–5